THE BRIDGE TO THE THREE HOLY CITIES

The Sāmānya-praghaṭṭaka of Nārāyaṇa Bhaṭṭa's *Tristhalīsetu*

THE BRIDGE
TO
THE THREE HOLY CITIES

The Sāmānya-praghaṭṭaka of Nārāyaṇa Bhaṭṭa's
Tristhalīsetu

Critically Edited and Translated
by
RICHARD SALOMON

MOTILAL BANARSIDASS
DELHI VARANASI PATNA MADRAS

Head Office: Bungalow Road, Delhi 110 007
Branches: Chowk, Varanasi 221 001
Ashok Rajpath, Patna 800 004
6 Appar Swamy Koil Street, Mylapore,
Madras 600 004

First Edition : Delhi, 1985

ISBN : 0–89581–647–4

Printed in India by Shantilal Jain at Shri Jainendra Press, A-45 Naraina, Phase I, New Delhi 110 028 and published by Narendra Prakash Jain for Motilal Banarsidass, Delhi 110 007.

PREFACE

This book is based on the author's Doctoral Dissertation in the Department of Oriental Studies, University of Pennsylvania, which was begun in June 1973 and completed in August 1975. In the course of this work I received help and encouragement from many people; but I wish to express special thanks to two of them.

First, to my father, George Salomon, who was, as always, my editor and general advisor.

Second, my deepest gratitude goes to my teacher and guide, Dr. Ludo Rocher, of whom I can only say:

> स्वं हितमपि विस्मृत्य परेषां तु हिते रतः ।
> छात्राणामुपकाराय प्रयतते दिवानिशम् ॥
> लूडो रोशे इति ख्यातोऽखिलविद्यापयोनिधिः ।
> गुरुश्च शिष्यसंसेव्यस्तस्मै सर्वं समर्पये ॥

TABLE OF CONTENTS

	Page
PREFACE	v
ABBREVIATIONS	xi
INTRODUCTION	xiii
I. Nārāyaṇa Bhaṭṭa's Tristhalīsetu	xiii
II. The Main Themes of the General Section of the TSS	xiv
III. Relation of the TSS to Other Texts on Tīrtha	xvii
IV. The Influence of Mīmāṃsā in Nārāyaṇa Bhaṭṭa's Work	xxi
V. Nārāyaṇa Bhaṭṭa : His Family, Life, and Work	xxiv
VI. Explanations of Some Basic Terms	xxvii
VII. Synopsis of the Text	xxxi
Critical Apparatus	xxxvii
Note on the Arrangement of the Text	lv

TEXT	*Text Number*	*Page*
मङ्गलश्लोकाः	1	2
पुरुषार्थप्रशंसा	9.1	3
सामान्यतस्तीर्थप्रशंसा	40	9
तीर्थस्वरूपम्	51	12
गौणतीर्थानि	67	15
तीर्थयात्राधिकारिणः	77	18
तीर्थफलतारतम्यकारणानि	106	25
यानविशेषकृतं फलतारतम्यम्	110	26
तीर्थप्रत्याम्नायाः	125.2	31
यात्रायां कालशुद्धिः	133	36
तीर्थगमनविधिः	1.52	40

	Text Number	Page
तीर्थयात्रायां नियमाः	172	48
तीर्थप्राप्तिदिनकृत्यम्	203.4	55
तीर्थोपवासः	211.2	58
तीर्थे मुण्डनम्	226	63
तीर्थस्नानम्	300	86
तर्पणम्	322.2	91
नदीनां रजोदोषः	346	97
तीर्थश्राद्धम्	368	101
तीर्थश्राद्धे निषिद्धानि	406	110
अन्नहेमश्राद्धादिविचारः	507	130
श्राद्धान्तरसमवाये निर्णयः	546.9	140
तीर्थश्राद्धाधिकारिणः	552	142
अधिकारापवादः	570.3	147
तीर्थश्राद्धे सम्प्रदाननिर्णयः	573	148
तीर्थेऽस्थिप्रक्षेपविधिः	624.2	162
(अस्थिप्रक्षेपणस्य) प्रकारः	635	164
(अस्थिप्रक्षेपणस्य) प्रयोगपद्धतिः	639.2	166
प्रकीर्णकास्तीर्थधर्माः	640	168
Interpolated Passages		179
अनुक्रमणिके		180
TRANSLATION		
Introductory verses	1	189
Praise of the Purposes of Men	9.1	191
Praise of Tīrthas in General	40	199
The Nature of Tīrthas	51	202
Secondary Tīrthas	67	206
Those Who are Authorized to Make Pilgrimages	77	210
The Causes of Varying Degrees of Benefit from Tīrthas	106	218
Varying Degrees of Benefit Caused by Particular Vehicles	110	219
Tīrthas as Equivalent Substitutes	125.2	228
Purity of Times for a Pilgrimage	133	235

	Text Number	Page
The Way of Going to Tīrthas	152	239
Observances on a Pilgrimage	172	252
Duties on the Day of Arrival at a Tīrtha	203.4	262
Fasting at a Tīrtha	211.2	265
Shaving at a Tīrtha	226	274
Bathing at a Tīrtha	300	310
Tarpaṇa	322.2	315
Defilement of Rivers	346	323
Śrāddha at a Tīrtha	368	328
Prohibited Elements in Tīrtha-Śrāddha	406	341
Discussion of Śrāddhas	507	378
Determination in the Case of the Coincidence of Śrāddhas	546.9	394
Those Who are Authorized to Perform Tīrtha-Śrāddha	552	397
Exception to Those Who are Authorized to Perform Tīrtha-Śrāddha	570.3	403
Determination of the Beneficiaries in the Tīrtha-Śrāddha	573	404
The Rule of Throwing Bones in a Tīrtha	624.2	426
The Manner (of Throwing Bones in a Tīrtha)	635	429
The Guide for this Procedure	639.2	432
Miscellaneous Laws of Tīrthas	640	435

BIBLIOGRAPHY 448

APPENDICES

A. Index of Tīrthas and Other Geographical Names 458
B. Index of Quotations 467
C. Index of Ślokas and Mantras 473
D. Glossary of Sanskrit Terms in the Translation 496
E. Glossary of Mīmāṃsā and Other Technical Terms 509
F. Index of Mīmāṃsā Texts 519
G. Index of Nyāyas 521

ABBREVIATIONS

AgPu	Agni Purāṇa
ĀśGṛSū	Āśvalāyana Gṛhya Sūtra
ĀśŚrSū	Āśvalāyana Śrauta Sūtra
AitBr	Aitareya Brāhmaṇa
KāKh	Kāśī Khaṇḍa (of the Skanda Purāṇa)
Kāt	Kātyāyana
KātŚrSū	Kātyāyana Śrauta Sūtra
KūPu	Kūrma Purāṇa
KKT	Kṛtyakalpataru
Kh	Khaṇḍa (of a Purāṇa)
GaPu	Garuḍa Purāṇa
GṛSū	Gṛhya Sūtra
GobhGṛSū	Gobhila Gṛhya Sūtra
GauMā	Gautama Māhātmya (of the Brahma Purāṇa)
GVA	Gādhivaṃśānucarita
JNMV	Jaiminīyanyāyamālāvistara
TīCi	Tīrthacintāmaṇi
TīPra	Tīrthaprakāśa (of the Vīramitrodaya)
TaiBr	Taittirīya Brāhmaṇa
TS	Taittirīya Saṃhitā
TSS	Tristhalīsetu
TSS-SS	Tristhalīsetusārasaṃgraha
TV	Tantravārtika
TVK	Tīrthavivecanakāṇḍa (of the Kṛtyakalpataru)
NB	Nārāyaṇa Bhaṭṭa
NS	Nyāyasudhā
PadPu	Padma Purāṇa
Pu	Purāṇa
Pra	Prakaraṇa or Praghaṭṭaka (of the TSS)
PraKh	Prabhāsa Khaṇḍa (of the Skanda Purāṇa)
Bṛh (Śrā)	Bṛhaspati Smṛti (Śrāddha Kāṇḍa)
Bṛh (Saṃ)	,, ,, (Saṃskāra Kāṇḍa)
BrPu	Brahma Purāṇa
BrPu (V)	,, ,, (Veṅkaṭeśvara Press ed.)

BhKh	Bhauma Khaṇḍa (of the Padma Purāṇa)
MaPu	Matsya Purāṇa
MuCi	Muhūrtacintāmaṇi
MaitPari	Maitrāyaṇīya Pariśiṣṭa
MK	Mīmāṃsākośa
MNP	Mīmāṃsānyāyaprakāśa
MP	Madanapārijāta
MBh	Mahābhārata
MS	Mīmāṃsā Sūtra
Yāj	Yājñavalkya
RV	Ṛg Veda
RVKh	Ṛg Veda Khila
VāPu	Vāyu Purāṇa
VāmPu	Vāmana Purāṇa
ViPu	Viṣṇu Purāṇa
ViSm	Viṣṇu Smṛti
VM	Vīramitrodaya
VS	Vājasaneyī Saṃhitā
Śaṅkha (K)	Śaṅkha Smṛti, Kane's ed.
Śab	Śabara
ŚBr	Śatapatha Brāhmaṇa
ŚrāVi	Śrāddhavivekasaṃgraha
SAS	Smṛtyarthasāra
SkPu	Skanda Purāṇa
SP	Sāmānya Praghaṭṭaka (of the TSS)
SṛKh	Sṛṣṭi Khaṇḍa (of the Padma Purāṇa)
HirGṛSū	Hiraṇyakeśin Gṛhya Sūtra

INTRODUCTION

I. Nārāyaṇa Bhaṭṭa's Tristhalīsetu

The *Tristhalīsetu* or 'Bridge to the Three Holy Cities' by Nārāyaṇa Bhaṭṭa (NB), son of Bhaṭṭa Rāmeśvara Sūri, is traditionally considered to be the most authoritative of the many Sanskrit texts on the subjects of tīrtha and pilgrimage. The text consists of four sections (Praghaṭṭaka or Prakaraṇa), called Sāmānya (General)[1], Prayāga, Kāśī, and Gayā. Its date of composition may be fairly definitely fixed at about the middle of the 16th century A.D.[2]

The text has appeared in two printed editions. The first, published in Kāśī (Benares) in 1908 by Vāpu Ācārya and Bhāvu Ācārya, is entitled *Tristhalīsetupraghaṭṭake Sarvatīrthavidhipraghaṭṭākhyaḥ Prathamo Bhāgaḥ*. As the title indicates, this text contains only the first section, or Sāmānya-praghaṭṭaka, of the TSS.[3] This text is nowadays rare and is to be found only with great difficulty both in India and in the west.

The second publication of the TSS was the Ānandāśrama Press edition of 1915 (Ānandāśrama Sanskrit Series no. 78). This edition contains the latter three sections (the Prayāga-, Kāśī- and Gayā-prakaraṇas), but omits the Sāmānya-praghaṭṭaka. No explanation is given for this omission, but it may be that the editor felt it was not necessary to re-publish that part which at that time must have still been available in the Benares edition.

While examining the contents of the collection of Sanskrit manuscripts of the University of Pennsylvania, I came upon three complete manuscripts of the General Section of the TSS,[4] all in an excellent state of preservation. It was upon

1. Henceforth to be referred to as TSS-SP or simply SP.
2. For further details on this point see Part V of this introduction.
3. For a full description of this text see the description of the manuscripts in the Critical Apparatus.
4. The University of Pennsylvania library also possesses severa manuscripts of the other sections of the TSS. See Poleman *A Census*... nos. 2856-2866.

making this discovery that I undertook the present task of editing and translating the General Section.

The three sections of the TSS printed in the Ānandāśrama edition describe in detail the tīrthas and rituals of the three great holy cities of North India—Kāśī (Benares), Prayāga (Allahabad), and Gayā. The General Section explains the basic theory and rules of pilgrimages and tīrtha rituals, as well as special rules applying to the various tīrthas of India. Thus this section may be of broader interest to the student of Indian and comparative religion than the other sections.

It should be noted that there is some variation in the title of the whole text and of its individual sections. The text is sometimes referred to as the 'Śrītīrthasetu,' while the individual sections are called indifferently either 'Praghaṭṭaka' or 'Prakaraṇa.' (Such variation, of course, is not at all unusual in Sanskrit text.)

II. THE MAIN THEMES OF THE GENERAL SECTION OF THE TSS

The bulk of the General Section is taken up by discussions of the procedure and rituals for tīrthas and pilgrimages. Such questions as the nature and theological significance of tīrthas are secondary, at least in terms of the amount of space allotted to them. In keeping with its title, the General Section usually mentions specific tīrthas only in connection with special procedural rules applying to them; unlike other tīrtha texts, such as the *Tīrthaprakāśa* of the *Vīramitrodaya*, it contains no section whose sole purpose is to present lists of tīrthas.

After the brief introductory chapters (III-V) which discuss tīrthas in general, the following chapters (VI-XIII) describe the proper procedure for a pilgrimage up to the time of arrival at the tīrtha. The rest of the General Section (comprising more than two-thirds of the whole Section) consists of detailed descriptions of the various tīrtha rituals, including a number of long and complex considerations of relatively minor points of ritual.

Among these rituals (which are described in their order of performance) the śrāddha rites clearly predominate; over one-third of the entire General Section (chapters XIX-XXV) is taken up by the discussion of tīrtha-śrāddha and its details. The other main rituals discussed at some length are the fast, tonsure, bathing, and tarpaṇa. At the end of the section is found the description of the rite of throwing one's parents' bones into the waters of a tīrtha (Chapters XXVI-XXVIII). (Unlike the others, this ritual can be done only at a tīrtha.)

It should not, however, be concluded from the above summary that NB's concern with tīrthas is entirely legalistic. On the contrary, the spiritual values of tīrthas, though treated relatively briefly, are taken to ultimately outweigh all the various rituals. Thus it is stated over and over in verses quoted from various purāṇas and smṛtis that a tīrtha is worthless for one who is not pure of mind, that bathing at a tīrtha cannot wash away impurities of the spirit, and so on (see 69, 173, 177, 184, etc.). No doubt NB intended to emphasize the ultimate dominance of spiritual values over physical ones when he concluded the General Section with a verse (691) which says that God is known through love and devotion only, and does not really dwell 'on the peaks of mountains' (i.e. at tīrthas or other holy places).

The Concept of 'Tīrtha' in the TSS

Two sorts of definitions of 'tīrtha' are given in the smṛti texts quoted in the TSS. An example of the first type is

> 75. Prabhāvād adbhutād bhūmeḥ salilasya ca tejasā /
> Parigrahān munīnāṃ ca tīrthānāṃ puṇyatā smṛtā //
> "Tīrthas are said to be auspicious because of the extraordinary power of their earth, and the efficacy of their water, and because they were frequented by the sages."

This sort of definition is not particularly enlightening; essentially, it tells us only that tīrthas are special places, or places which are sanctified by tradition. Much more revealing is the second description :

> 41. Sarve prasravaṇāḥ puṇyāḥ sarve puṇyāḥ śiloccayāḥ /
> Nadyaḥ puṇyāḥ sadā sarvā Jāhnavī tu viśeṣataḥ //
> "All springs are auspicious; all mountains are auspicious; all rivers are always auspicious, but especially the Jāhnavī (Gaṅgā)."

This verse is not, as it might seem, mere hyperbole; for it is almost literally true that all major rivers and bodies of water[1] in India are indeed tīrthas, and the difference between them is only a matter of degree. Thus rivers like the Gaṅgā are particularly famed as tīrthas throughout India, by reason of their size, physical beauty, or ancient traditions. But a glance at the list of tīrthas mentioned in the General Section (pp. 458 ff.) will show that it includes virtually all the main rivers of India; other tīrtha texts which are concerned with particular parts of India may present long lists of tīrthas within a small area. Thus the purāṇa verse (not quoted in the TSS):

> Tasmāc chṛṇudhvaṃ vakṣyāmi tīrthāny āyatanāni ca/
> Saṃkṣepeṇa muniśreṣṭhāḥ pṛthivyāṃ yāni kāni ca //
> Vistareṇa na śakyante vaktuṃ varṣaśatair api /
>
> (Brahma Purāṇa 33.7-8b)
>
> "Therefore, O Greatest of Sages, listen as I tell you briefly those tīrthas and shrines which are on the earth; but they cannot be told in detail, even in hundreds of years,"

also is not entirely hyperbole. To compile a complete list of tīrthas in India would in fact be the work of a lifetime.

As verse 41 quoted above indicates, the qualities of a tīrtha are not restricted to bodies of water alone. Many mountains and hills, and certain forests and groves as well rank as tīrthas. But the fact remains that it is the purifying power of water which is the primary virtue of a tīrtha, and these other types of tīrtha are more or less exceptions to the rule.

The Importance of Pilgrimage

Pilgrimage, along with fasts, vows and other such practices, is considered in works on tīrtha as an alternative to religious practice by means of Vedic sacrifice. It is held, moreover, that pilgrimage is even more excellent than sacrifice because it may be performed by anyone at all, be he rich or poor, brāhmaṇa or śūdra

---

1. Except for a few accursed rivers such as the Karmanāśā (see 199. 3ff).

(37.1-39).[1] The dharma of pilgrimage even transcends rules of caste and untouchability; one is not polluted by contact with an untouchable while on a pilgrimage (190-191)[2]. In this respect at least, NB's work shows a democratic outlook which is quite untypical of orthodox brāhmaṇical law.

III. RELATION OF THE TSS TO OTHER TEXTS ON TĪRTHA

The General Section of the TSS is by no means an entirely original work. The general arrangement of the text, and in many cases the specific wording, are derived from a tradition developed in the earlier texts on the subject of tīrtha. In a number of cases, NB borrows passages virtually verbatim from earlier tīrtha and dharmaśāstra texts such as the *Tīrthacintāmaṇi*, *Smṛtyarthasāra*, and *Madanapārijāta*, without acknowledging the source. (The sources of such passages will be given in the notes to the translation.) The originality of the TSS lies in its expanded discussion and comment on various smṛti texts and resolutions of long-standing points of controversy, rather than in its general formation.

The Sources of the TSS : Earlier Texts on Tīrtha

Tīrthas and pilgrimages are extensively described in the epics and purāṇas (particularly in the Tīrthayātrāparvan, comprising chapters 78-148 of the Vanaparvan of the Mahābhārata, and in the Brahma, Skanda,[3] and Vāyu Purāṇas), as well as in some of the earlier dharmāśāstra nibandhas. But it is not until the time of Lakṣmīdhara (early 12th century A.D.) that we know of any independent dharmaśāstra text devoted entirely to

1. NB emphasizes this point in his introductory verses to the other sections of the TSS. Thus in verse 1 of the Prayāga Section (p. 1 of the Ānandāśrama edition) he refers to '...vijitayāgaḥ...Prayāgaḥ'; and in verse 3 of the Gayā Section (p. 316). '...Gayā yāgato' dhikā.'

2. Though it must be admitted that NB and other late authors try to restrict the application of this rule to special circumstances.

3. It is interesting to note that the Kāśī Khaṇḍa of the Skanda Purāṇa, which NB quotes 17 times in the SP alone (and many more times in the Kāśī Prakaraṇa), is not quoted at all by Lakṣmīdhara, and only twice in the *Vīramitrodaya*. See Rangaswami Aiyyangar's Introduction (cited below), p. xli.

these subjects. Lakṣmīdhara's encyclopedic work *Kṛtyakalpataru* includes a book on tīrtha called the *Tīrthavivecanakāṇḍa* (TVK)[1]. Although this text consists mainly of quotations from the smṛti with little or no commentary, it nevertheless forms a framework upon which the later, more detailed tīrtha texts are built, and contains in its brief comments the germs of many a later controversy.

The next important tīrtha text which is now available is the *Tīrthacintāmaṇi* (TīCi) of Vācaspati Miśra of Mithilā, who wrote in the 15th century A.D. The text has been printed in the Bibliotheca Indica, work no. 95, 1912.[2] This text is quite advanced in comparison with that of Lakṣmīdhara, and since it refers to points of controversy not yet raised in the TVK there must have been at least one, if not several texts written on the subject between the time of Lakṣmīdhara and that of Vācaspati. One of these texts must have been by Gaṇeśvara Miśra, whom Vācaspati cites occasionally (for example see TīCi pp. 7, 10); but unfortunately the works of Gaṇeśvara are not extant.

The TīCi contains extensive commentary on some smṛti passages and detailed discussions of controversial points; in this and other respects it is quite closely related to the TSS. Thus it is somewhat surprising that NB never once mentions Vācaspati by name, though he often cites his views and even borrows his exact words on occasion. In giving the opinions of Vācaspati (with which he most often disagrees), NB usually attributes them to 'the easterners' (prācyāḥ). It seems therefore that there was a rather strong rivalry between NB and his followers in Benares on the one hand, and Vācaspati and his colleagues (including Gaṇeśvara Miśra) in Mithilā on the other.

---

1. Published in 1942 in the Gaekwad's Oriental Series, vol. 98, by K. V. Rangaswami Aiyyangar with an extensive introduction, to which I am indebted for much of the information presented in this section of my introduction.

2. Unfortunately this edition seems to have been based on a poor manuscript, containing many omissions and misplaced passages which render the text nearly unintelligible in some places.

The Influence of the TSS : Later Texts on Tīrtha

The most authoritative of the late texts on tīrtha is the *Tīrthaprakāśa* section of the *Vīramitrodaya* by Mitra Miśra (17th century A.D.), published in the Chowkhamba Sanskrit Series, vol. 30 part 10, 1917. Even a brief glance at this text will show how deeply indebted it is to the TSS; its section on the General Laws of Tīrthas (pp. 7-135) is almost entirely based on the General Section of the TSS.[1]

A measure of the importance and popularity of the TSS may be discerned in the fact that as great a scholar as Bhaṭṭoji Dīkṣita found it worth his while to compile a summary of it; this is the *Tristhalīsetusārasaṃgraha* (TSS-SS), published in the Princess of Wales Saraswati Bhavana Texts, no.65 (1936). With occasional minor exceptions this text reproduces the exact words of the original TSS, with most of the intricacies of the arguments omitted. It is important in connection with this work that Bhaṭṭoji's text is mainly concerned with the General Section of the TSS; thirty pages of the printed text are devoted to this section, while the other three sections of the TSS are briefly summarized in ten pages. Thus the text of the TSS-SS, which fortunately is easily obtainable, will prove to be of considerable aid for anyone who may wish to study the TSS-SP in detail.

NB's grandson Kamalākara Bhaṭṭa also wrote a digest of the TSS, which is usually referred to as *Tīrthakamalākara*. It has been published in Benares in 1895.[2]

Likewise other texts such as the *Tīrthenduśekhara* of Nāgeśa Bhaṭṭa, also published in the Saraswati Bhavana Texts, no. 66 (bound together with the TSS-SS) are also closely based on the TSS. Nāgeśa's work is devoted more to the discussion of particular points in the TSS, than to a general summary.[3]

---

1. With the exception of the lists of tīrthas (tīrthānām uddeśāḥ), to which no corresponding section is found in the TSS.

2. There is also another abridgement of the TSS-SP by Gaṅgādhara, called *Tristhalīsetusāmānyapraghaṭṭakasiddhāntasaṃkṣepa*, or *Tīrthayātrā-saṃgraha*. See *Catalogue of Manuscripts in the Akhila Bhāratīya Sanskrit Parishad, Lucknow*, 2nd series, vol. II, serial no. 109.

3. P.V. Kane (*History of Dharmaśāstra* Vol. IV p. 582) also mentions a *Tristhalīsetu-sārasaṃgraha* by Nāgeśa; but I have not been able to locate this work.

Other Texts on Tīrtha

While the number of extant[1] texts which treat of tīrtha as a general subject is relatively small, the 'māhātmyas' and other works on one or several specific tīrthas are almost beyond counting. As these do not bear directly on the present text, they will not be discussed here; the interested reader may consult Kane, *History of Dharmaśāstra* vol. IV p. 582.

One other text is of interest here: the *Tīrthatattva*, or *Tīrthayātrātattva* of Raghunandana, published in the Sanskrit Sahitya Parishad Series, no. 12, Calcutta (in Bengali script). It contains a brief general chapter on the rules of pilgrimage (pp. 1-2) which is rather similar to the "Tīrthagamanavidhiḥ" of the TSS-SP, followed by longer sections on Gayā, Prayāga, and Vārāṇasī (= Kāśī), as in the TSS. Raghunandana was roughly contemporary with NB, and it is not certain which text is the earlier. However, despite the similarities between these two texts in respect to arrangement and date of compilation, there is no other close connection between them.

General Patterns in the Development of the Tīrtha Literature

As has been noted by Rangaswami Aiyyangar,[2] the general pattern in the development of tīrtha texts is a gradual increase in the number of practices prescribed as mandatory and an increasing strictness in the interpretation of smṛti rules. The clearest example is the ritual of tonsure at a tīrtha ('vapana' or 'kṣaura'); this is not prescribed at all by Lakṣmīdhara, is prescribed by early writers such as Vācaspati Miśra at Prayāga only, and finally is prescribed by NB as mandatory at all tīrthas. Typically, NB presents a long and intricate justification of his position on this issue (231.1-277.11) in which he refutes point for point the arguments given by Vācaspati for his interpretation.[3] It is often the case in the SP that extensive arguments are offered in

1. The names of several other texts on tīrtha are known, notably a section of Hemādri's *Caturvargacintāmaṇi* on tīrtha, but these texts are not extant or available only in manuscripts.

2. In his introduction to the TVK, p. liii.

3. See TīCi, pp. 14-17. As mentioned above, NB never acknowledges Vācaspati by name, referring only to "the easterners."

support of a strict interpretation of the laws of the smṛti. Another example may be found in 118-118.8 of the SP, in which NB argues that the prohibition of the use of vehicles applies to all pilgrimages, and not only to pilgrimages to Prayāga as was maintained by Lakṣmīdhara.

IV. THE INFLUENCE OF MĪMĀṂSĀ IN NĀRĀYAṆA BHAṬṬA'S WORK

It is both well-known from tradition and clear from his writings that Nārāyaṇa Bhaṭṭa was highly expert in Pūrvamīmāṃsā. In the TSS, he makes use of Mīmāṃsā rules and techniques to a greater extent than is typical in dharmaśāstra texts, so that some knowledge of Mīmāṃsā is essential for the understanding of large parts of the TSS.

NB was a follower of the dominant Bhāṭṭa school of Mīmāṃsā; he quotes its founder, Kumārila Bhaṭṭa ("Bhaṭṭapādāḥ") nine times in the General Section alone. In the same section he cites seven of Jaimini's Mīmāṃsā sūtras and quotes the commentator ("Bhāṣyakṛt") Śabara four times. Among later Mīmāṃsā texts, he quotes the *Nyāyasudhā* of Bhaṭṭasomeśvara thrice, and also makes reference to the works of Pārthasārathimiśra and Bhavadeva.

Perhaps we can best describe NB's distinctive style by presenting a detailed summary of one of his complex discussions, in the course of which he makes extensive use of Mīmāṃsā rules of interpretation. In 231.1-277.11, NB discusses with an unnamed opponent (who seems to represent Vācaspati Miśra; see above, pp. xviii and xx) the proper interpretation of the compound word 'at all tīrthas' in the smṛti verse 'Shaving... is the rule at all tīrthas' (226), as follows:

The opponent says that 'at all tīrthas' refers to Prayāga, since the compound should be taken as a bahuvrīhi ('all-tīrthas'), as denoting 'that tīrtha (namely Prayāga) in which are all (other) tīrthas.' To explain the plural number in 'all-tīrthas' he invokes the rule of 'unintended plurality' (231.1-3). But NB shows that this rule does not apply in this case (231.3-5).

The opponent then asserts that there is a plurality of Prayāgas (231.8), or of 'all-tīrthas' (232-233.1); but then, according to NB, there is nothing to prove that shaving is to be done only at

Prayāga (233.2-3). The opponent quotes another rule which prescribes shaving at Prayāga (234), saying that this rule particularizes the other, general rule (234.1). But NB disproves this through anaysis of the Mimāṃsā rules of particularization and supersession (234.2-235.7).

NB then presents another possible refutation of the opponent's interpretation of the verse (234) which prescribes shaving at Prayāga. According to this refutation, that verse is merely a 'partial supplementary passage' (avayutyānuvāda), and not an 'absolute prescription' (apūrvavidhi) (235.8-13). Although this argument supports his view (that shaving is done at all tīrthas, not only Prayāga), NB refutes it, because he considers it the wrong way to prove the point (235.15-24). (This practice, which NB calls 'arguing with someone who is on one's own side' (svayūthyavivāda) is characteristic of his style).

NB then gives other arguments against shaving at Prayāga only, even if 'all-tīrthas' *is* taken as a bahuvrīhi (235.25-248.1). Moreover, there are numerous authoritative prescriptions of shaving at tīrthas other than Prayāga (248.2-259.1). NB disposes of the opponent's efforts to question the validity and meaning of these prescriptions (259.2-260).

Returning to the question of the plural number in 'all tīrthas,' NB explains that even if the plurality *were* 'non-intended,' as his opponent maintains, that would lend support to his own (NB's) position, not the opponent's (260.1-7). Both of the Mīmāṃsā rules concerning 'non-intended' grammatical number (the Rule of the Cups and the Rule of the Ruining of Both Offerings) can apply to this case (260.8-262.2). Also if the compound 'all tīrthas' is taken as a karmadhāraya compound rather than as a bahuvrīhi, the non-intended plural would still support the position of shaving at all tīrthas (262.3-7).[1]

NB then shows that 'all tīrthas' should in fact be taken as a karmadhāraya compound rather than as a bahuvrīhi, and that such a plural karmadhāraya could not refer to Prayāga only (262.8-16). Neither can 'all-tīrthas,' taken as a bahuvrīhi, refer

1. This section (260.4-262.7) is another example of 'arguing with one's own position' (svapakṣavivāda); see notes on the translation, 262.7.

to a singular (Prayāga) as occurs in certain Vedic usages (262.17-23); nor can the rule 'at all tīrthas' be taken as a prescription of exclusion (parisaṃkhyā) (262.24-34). There is no obstacle to taking the word 'all' literally (262.36-264). The prescription of shaving at Bhāskarakṣetra cannot be taken as referring to Prayāga (264.3-265.3).

If, asks NB, shaving is to be done only at Prayāga, why is a specific prohibition of shaving at certain tīrthas given? (265.4). The opponent says that this is intended to denote those tīrthas as *especially* unfit for shaving (265.5-6). NB presents a possible refutation of this interpretation (265.7-269.1), but rejects this refutation (269.2-274.3). Then he presents a simpler refutation of the opponent's interpretation (274.4-275.2). Nor can these specific prohibitions be taken as 'amplifications of a prescription of exclusion' (parisaṃkhyāvivaraṇa), or as 'supplementary references to a known fact' (nityānuvāda) (275.3-277.8).

Thus it is established that the prescription 'Shaving...is the rule at all tīrthas' does in fact mean what it says literally, and cannot mean that shaving is done only at Prayāga (277.9-11).

So runs a typical argument by NB. In another part of the General Section an even more complex discussion is found. There, in connection with his discussion of the omission of the invitation of the ancestors in a tīrtha-śrāddha (412.1-502.3), NB eventually leads into a detailed discourse on the modification (ūha) of mantras in the tīrtha-śrāddha—a discourse which NB himself describes as 'digressions and sub-digressions' (502.3).

This discussion of the question of the invitation in tīrtha-śrāddha (which I will not describe here in detail) is especially interesting in that it reveals the influence of Mīmāṃsā ideas not only on NB's techniques of logic and argument, but also on his fundamental notions of the purpose and function of ritual. The main point of this argument is that the invitation of the ancestors is to be omitted only in a śrāddha which is occasioned by one's arrival at a tīrtha, not in any śrāddha which happens to be done at a tīrtha. Common sense would lead one to the opposite conclusion; since it is said in the sacred texts that the ancestors are always present at every tīrtha, it would seem unnecessary to *ever* invite them to a tīrtha. But NB takes his position on the grounds that the ancestors are not really present at a śrāddha (414.5-6), nor is the śrāddha really done for their sake. The act of invitation in a regular śrāddha has an 'invisible purpose'; it must be done simply because it is prescribed in the sacred texts, even though it does not produce any humanly comprehensible result, such as the presence of the ancestors.

This attitude of NB toward the śrāddha is typical of the formalistic thinking of Pūrva-mīmāṃsā. In Mīmāṃsā it is the ritual act itself which is primary; the deities invoked in it are secondary, serving as mere functionaries. NB considers the position of the ancestors in śrāddha to be parallel to that of the gods in sacrifice—they are assistants to the act and its result (the apūrva; see note on the translation, 414.6), rather than its beneficiaries or recipients.

Thus NB's interpretation of the tīrtha rites is deeply colored by Mīmāṃsā thought. Unlike many authors of works on dharma-śāstra who utilize Mīmāṃsā only as a system of logic and interpretation, NB reveals himself to be a true Mīmāṃsaka.

V. NĀRĀYAṆA BHAṬṬA : HIS FAMILY, LIFE, AND WORKS

Nārāyaṇa Bhaṭṭa was the founder and one of the greatest members of the renowned Bhaṭṭa family of "southern" (i.e., Maharashtrian) pandits at Benares. We are fortunate in that there is a relative wealth of biographical information available concerning NB and his line; not only from the living Benares tradition and from clues provided in his own works, but above all from a rare biography of the early Bhaṭṭas, the *Gādhivaṃśānucarita* (GVA) by NB's second son Śaṅkara Bhaṭṭa.[1]

1. This work was described by Haraprasad Shastri in "Dakshini Pandits at Benares" in *Indian Antiquary* 41, 1912, pp. 7-13. Only one ms. of the text is known, and it has not to the best of my knowledge been published.

Other biographical information on NB and his relatives can be found in Kane's *History of Dharmaśāstra* Vol. I, pp. 419-21, and in the introduction of his edition of the *Vyavahāramayūkha* of Nīlakaṇṭha Bhaṭṭa (NB's grandson) (Bombay Sanskrit Series 80, 1926); also see the introduction to Raosaheb V. N. Mandlik's edition of the same text (1879), and the 'prāstāvikam' (at the end of the volume) to the *Nirṇayasindhu* of NB's grandson Kamalākara Bhaṭṭa (Chowkhamba Sanskrit Series 52). Mandlik's edition of the *Vyavahāramayūkha* contains a genealogical table of the Bhaṭṭas which continues down to the 19th century A.D., but Kane considers the information provided therein to be subject to doubt.

From the introductory verses and colophons of the TSS we learn only of NB's father and grandfather, Bhaṭṭa Rāmeśvara and Bhaṭṭa Govinda. But in the concluding verses of NB's commentary on Kedāra's *Vṛttaratnākara* (see *Catalogue of Sanskrit Manuscripts in the India Office Library*, Vol. I, pp. 303-4), we find the names of Bhaṭṭa Govinda's father and grandfather, Cāṅgadeva (or Aṅgadeva) and Nāgapāśa (or Nāganātha).[1]

NB himself, we are told in the GVA, was born during the course of Rāmeśvara's pilgrimage to Dvārakā (at the tip of the Kathiawar peninsula) in the month of Caitra of the Śaka year 1435, that is, in March-April of 1514 A.D. He was the eldest of three sons, his brothers being Śrīdhara and Mādhava. NB belonged to the Viśvāmitra or Gādhi gotra, and was a Ṛg Veda brāhmaṇa and a follower of the Āśvalāyana sūtras.

NB must have still been a child when he went with his father to Benares, where he spent the rest of his life. All his religious and secular education came from his father, as he tells us in the sixth introductory verse of the TSS (...pitur eva yaḥ śrutīḥ smṛtīḥ samālocya ca deśarītīḥ...). At Benares he won renown as a great scholar and collector of manuscripts, and he established the status of the southern pandits there. He is also said to have defeated the Mithilā and Gauḍa pandits in debate at the court of Ṭoḍar Mal in Delhi.[2] A well-known legend in the Benares tradition tells how NB persuaded the Muslim king to rebuild the temple of Viśveśvara by miraculously bringing rain in the midst of a drought caused by the anger of the gods at the king's destruction of the temple.[3]

Among NB's many works, the TSS is by far the most important. We do not know its precise date of composition,

---

1. This information presumably was given also in the first folio of the GVA, which unfortunately is lost. For the variant readings of these names, see Kane's *Vyavahāramayūkha*, p. v.

2. This incident recounted in the GVA is very much in keeping with what we know of NB's rivalry with the "easterners" from his own works; see above, p. xviii.

3. As recounted in the prāstāvikam to the *Prayogaratna* (Nirnaya Sagara ed.) under the heading 'Nārāyaṇabhaṭṭaihyam' (folio 2). The incident is not mentioned in the GVA.

but since NB's *Vṛttaratnākaravyākhyā* is dated in Vikrama 1602 = A.D. 1545,[1] we may assume that the TSS was also written about the middle of the sixteenth century A.D.

His other two best-known works, the *Prayogaratna* and the *Antyeṣṭipaddhati*, or *Nārāyaṇabhaṭṭī* and *Uttaranārāyaṇabhaṭṭī*, were published together in loose folios by the Nirnaya Sagara Press (2nd ed., Bombay 1937). These two texts, as well as the TSS, are still in use among orthodox brāhmaṇas in northern India.

Among the numerous other works attributed to NB, none of which are available in printed editions, are the *Rudrapaddhati*, the commentary on the *Vṛttaratnākara* mentioned above, the *Vṛttaratnāvalī*, and a *Prākṛtavivṛti* on *Abhijñāna-śākuntala*. He also is the author of such works on Mīmāṃsā as a commentary on Pārthasārathimiśra's *Śāstradīpikā*, and he commented on the kārikās of Mādhavācārya's *Kālanirṇaya*. The well-known text *Dharmapravṛtti* is often attributed to our Nārāyaṇa, though according to Kane that author is not the same Nārāyaṇa.[2]

Aufrecht's *Catalogus Catalogorum* lists, besides those mentioned above, some twenty-one other minor works by our NB. At least some of these, as Kane notes, are probably sections or alternate titles of his other works. For example the *Antyeṣṭiprayoga* is probably the same as the *Antyeṣṭipaddhati*, the *Prayāgasetu* is probably the *Prayāga-prakaraṇa* of the TSS, and so on. The rest of the works are mostly handbooks for various rituals like the establishment of liṅgas, tanks, etc., and texts on astrological topics.

Nārāyaṇa Bhaṭṭa's Descendants

Several famous pandits are to be found among the descendants of NB. His eldest son Rāmakṛṣṇa Bhaṭṭa was, like his father, a follower of Bhāṭṭa Mīmāṃsā, and wrote a commentary on the *Tantravārtika* as well as several other works.

1. *India Office Catalogue*, Vol. I., p. 304.

2. *History of Dharmaśāstra* I. 421. "Nārāyaṇa Bhaṭṭa" as the name of a pandit is roughly the equivalent of "John Smith" among Englishmen. There is a large number of authors with this name, and they must be kept apart carefully. The two other most famous Nārāyaṇa Bhaṭṭas are the author of the drama *Veṇīsaṃhāra*, and Nārāyaṇa Bhaṭṭa of Kerala, a well-known grammarian.

NB's second son Śaṅkara Bhaṭṭa wrote, in addition to the *Gādhivaṃśānucarita* described above, such well-known works as the *Dvaitanirṇaya* and the *Mīmāṃsābālaprakāśa*, and many other lesser texts as well. Śaṅkara is said to have been the guru of the great Bhaṭṭoji Dīkṣita, which is credible in view of Bhaṭṭoji's close acquaintance with his father's work (see above, p. xix). NB's third son Govinda is not known as an author.

Through Rāmakṛṣṇa and his wife Umā, NB had three grandsons, all of them prominent writers on dharmaśāstra and related subjects. The second born, Kamalākara Bhaṭṭa, is the greatest of them, being the author of the *Nirṇayasindhu* and twenty-one other books, including an abridgement of the TSS (see above, p. xix). Rāmakṛṣṇa's eldest son Dinakara or Divākara Bhaṭṭa wrote the *Bhāṭṭadinākara*, *Śāntisāra* and *Dinākaroddyota*. The third son was Lakṣmaṇa Bhaṭṭa, author of the *Ācāraratna*, *Gotrapravaranirṇaya*, and others. Through Dinākara NB had a very famous great-grandson in Viśveśvara Bhaṭṭa, known as Gāgābhaṭṭa, who, besides writing a Mīmāṃsā text called *Bhāṭṭacintāmaṇi* and other works, is famed for having presided at the abhiṣeka of the great Maratha warrior Śivājī.[1]

Through his second son Śaṅkara too NB had descendants of note, the greatest of whom was Śaṅkara's fourth and last son Nīlakaṇṭha Bhaṭṭa, author of an important encyclopedia of dharmaśāstra entitled *Bhāgavantabhāskara*, consisting of '*mayūkhas*' on various subjects (*Vyavahāramayūkha*, *Prāyaścittamayūkha*, *Śrāddhamayūkha*, etc.).

VI. EXPLANATIONS OF SOME BASIC TERMS

A few basic terms which appear especially frequently in the SP will be briefly explained here; as these and other words imply far more than can possibly be expressed in a simple English word or phrase, they are left in Sanskrit in the translation. More detailed information concerning these subjects will be found in the text itself, in the footnotes to the translation, and in the Glossary of Sanskrit Terms in the Translation (Appendix D) under the headings of more specific terms.

1. From this fact we may suppose that the Bhaṭṭa family, despite its long residence in Benares, did not cut off its ties with its native Maratha country.

GENEALOGICAL CHART OF NĀRĀYAṆA BHAṬṬA'S FAMILY

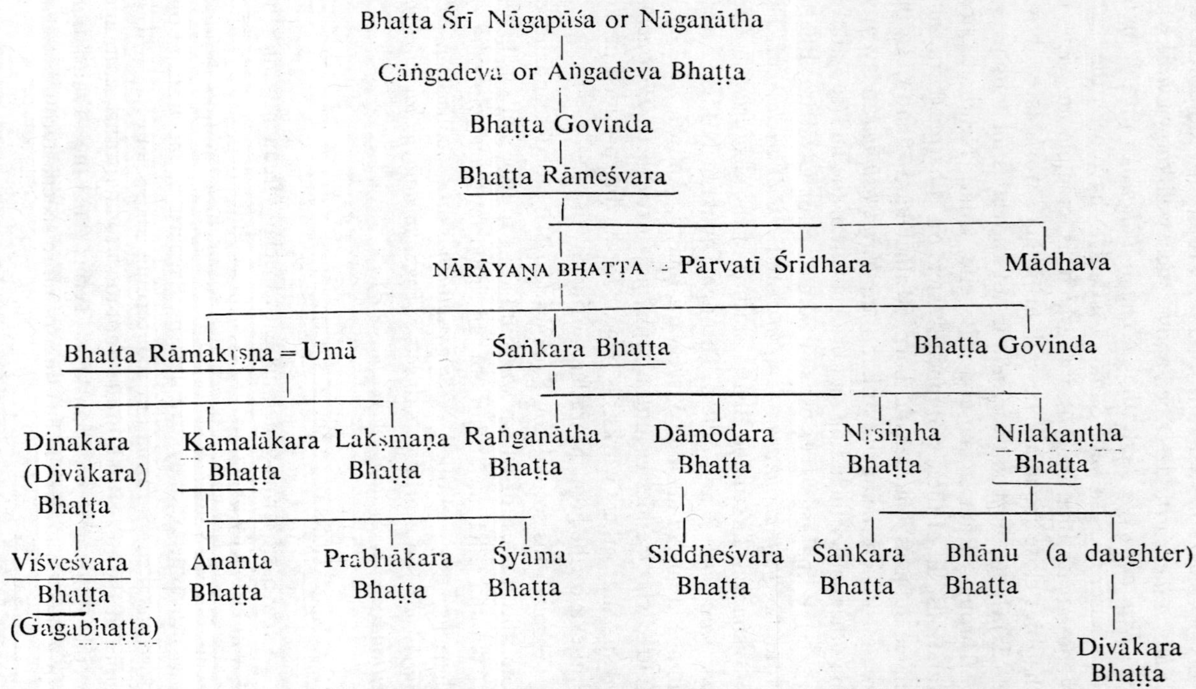

(Note : The names of the most prominent members of the family are underlined.)

a. *Tīrtha.*

NB's specific definitions and concept of tīrtha have been discussed above (pp. xv-xvi). More generally, a tīrtha is any holy or sanctified place in India which is considered especially appropriate for pilgrimages and the performance of such religious rites as śrāddha, fasts, vows, etc. (but not for Vedic sacrifices). A preoccupation with such shrines is characteristic, not only of Hinduism, but of Indian religions in general. Although tīrthas were not prominent in early Vedic religion as we know it, this practice of veneration of holy places is undoubtedly very ancient.

The word 'tīrtha'[1] is derived from the verb root tṛ, 'to cross, ford,' and its original meaning was 'a crossing point or place of entry into a body of water.' Thus the etymology of the word itself shows that a tīrtha proper is a body of water, although cetain forests, hills, caves, etc. are also ranked as tīrthas (above, p. xvi).

Tīrthas vary widely not only in degree of spiritual efficacy, but also in the rites considered especially appropriate to them. Thus for instance Gayā is considered an especially auspicious place for the performance of śrāddha, but the tonsure ritual is prohibited there (see text, 370, 372 etc., and 226). In many but not all cases, a particular deity is associated with a particular tīrtha.

The various types and classification of tīrthas are discussed in the text; see especially chapters IV and V.

b. *Śrāddha*

The śrāddha rites of various sorts are the principal Hindu ceremonies for the veneration of the ancestors. As in the case of tīrtha, śrāddha does not appear to be very prominent in the early Vedic texts, but becomes one of the most important rites in classical and modern Hinduism. Performance of śrāddha is theoretically mandatory for Hindus of all castes, as the food offered to the ancestors by their offspring is believed to be their only sustenance after death. The first duty of every son is to offer

1. Normally neuter, but occasionally masculine, for instance in the text, 76.

śrāddha to his father and paternal grandfather and great-grandfather, and to other ancestors as well. (Śrāddha means literally 'an act of devotion,' from śraddhā, 'faith, devotion.')

The predominance of śrāddha is especially striking in the tīrtha ritual. Although śrāddha is performed last among the mandatory tīrtha rites, it is clearly the most important of them. Thus more than one-third of the entire SP is devoted to discussion of the theory and practice of tīrtha-śrāddha.

A complete śrāddha is a lengthy and complex ritual. Its main elements are three : the offering of balls of rice or other food (piṇḍa) to the ancestors; the pouring of oblations into the fire (agnaukaraṇa); and the feeding of brāhmaṇas who symbolically represent the ancestors (brāhmaṇabhojana). The various other minor procedures which are mentioned in the SP will be explained in the footnotes and in the Glossary of Sanskrit Terms.

There is a great number of different types of śrāddha and various classifications of them. The most important classification is into regular or mandatory (nitya), specially occasioned (naimittika), and optional (kāmya). Tīrtha-śrāddha, with which we are mainly concerned, is generally 'specially occasioned,' that is, occasioned by the special event of arrival at a tīrtha. Other classes of śrāddha, such as pārvaṇa vs. ekoddiṣṭa, and other occasions, such as aṣṭakā days, manvādi days etc., will be explained in the Glossary.

c. *Tarpaṇa*

The rite of tarpaṇa, or 'satiation' (from √tṛp 'to be satisfied') is theoretically to be performed separately for gods, seers, and ancestors. Unlike śrāddha, in which solid food is given, tarpaṇa consists of offerings of handfuls of water, or of water mixed with sesamum (tilatarpaṇa). Tarpaṇa is performed both as a separate ritual, and as an auxiliary of the bathing ritual (see text 322.2).

The separate tarpaṇa ritual, when performed at a tīrtha, is primarily directed to the ancestors. Thus NB prescribes first separate tarpaṇa offerings for one's various relatives, and then a single offering for all of the gods and other beings (326.1). He also permits a single, abbreviated tarpaṇa for all beings, including the ancestors (334.14ff.).

VII. SYNOPSIS OF THE TEXT

I. Introductory Verses (1-9)

NB invokes the deities Sarasvatī, Gaṇeśa, and Rāma (1-3), eulogizes his father (4-5), introduces himself and his work (6), begs his readers' tolerance (7-8), and describes the scheme of the text (9).

II. Praise of the Purposes of Men (9.1-39.1)

Descriptions of the four purposes of men. Of them, two—Dharma and Artha—are not literally 'purposes' of men, but really means to the purposes, namely happiness and the absence of suffering (9.1-26.6). Of the four purposes, Dharma is the most important (27.7-37). Within Dharma, such practices as pilgrimage are especially excellent, because anyone may perform them regardless of caste, wealth, etc. (37.1-39.1).

III. Praise of Tīrthas in General (40-50.1)

Well-known quotations from the epics and purāṇas stating the excellence of tīrthas.

IV. The Nature of Tīrthas (51-66).

Description and definition of tīrthas (51-52) and the various classifications of tīrthas (53-61). A few lists of tīrthas (62-66).

V. Secondary Tīrthas (67-76)

Not only earthly places, but also various virtues are tīrthas. The former are worthless without the latter.

VI. Those Who are Authorized to Make Pilgrimages (77-105.1)

Brāhmaṇas of various sorts (77-89), kṣatriyas (89.1-90.2), vaiśyas (90.3), śūdras (90.4-96.1), mixed castes (96.2-97.1) women (97.2-102.2), and anyone who wants to throw his parents,' bones in a tīrtha (102.3), or who is a penitent (102.4-105.1) are all authorized to make pilgrimages.

VII. The Causes of Varying Degrees of Benefit from Tīrthas (106-109)

The special circumstances which cause an increase or decrease in the benefit derived from a tīrtha.

VIII. Varying Degrees of Benefit Caused by Particular Vehicles (110-125.1)

One must not go by ox-cart on a pilgrimage (110-112, 117-117.2). Use of shoes or umbrellas lessens the benefit (112.1-116. 12). These prohibitions apply to all tīrthas, not only to Prayāga (118-118.8). Boat travel is also prohibited except when unavoidable (121-124.1). One may go for the sake of a pilgrimage to places which are normally forbidden (124.2-125.1).

IX. Tīrthas as Equivalent Substitutes (125.2-132)

Pilgrimage may be made for the sake of penance (125.2-129). Different pilgrimages are equivalent to different amounts of penances (129.1-132).

X. Purity of Times for Pilgrimage (133-151.1)

The auspicious and inauspicious astrological times for pilgrimage.

XI. The Way of Going to Tirthas (152-171.5)

The general procedure for going to the tīrtha, including the preliminary śrāddha, fast, etc. (152-162.10). Benefit accrues not only from the tīrtha itself but also from the journey (162.11-166.5). This benefit from the journey varies according to the tīrtha to which one goes (166.6-171.5).

XII. Observances on a Pilgrimage (172-203.3)

One must maintain self-discipline, faith, purity, etc. on pilgrimage; otherwise, it is done in vain (172-197.1). Procedure in case of death or inability to complete the pilgrimage, and in other special cases (197.2-203.3).

XIII. Duties on the Day of Arrival at a Tīrtha (203.4-211.1)

Paying homage to and bathing in the tīrtha upon arrival (203.4-207.1), and the second bath in the tīrtha (207.2-211.1).

XIV. Fasting at a Tirtha (211.2-225.6)

Discussion of the proper time for the tīrtha fast; there is an optional choice between the day of arrival and the day before arrival, since both procedures are prescribed by authoritative texts (211.2-220.1). An act such as fasting can be occasioned by a circumstance which is to arise in the future, such as the arrival at the tīrtha (220.2-224.3). The fast is mandatory (224.4-225.6).

XV. Shaving at a Tīrtha (226-299.3)

Shaving is to be done 'at all tīrthas' with a few specified exceptions (226-231). 'All tīrthas' does *not* refer to Prayāga in the sense that it 'contains all tīrthas'; this point is discussed at length with all possible interpretations of the compound word 'at all tīrthas' (231.1-277.11).

Consideration of the proper declaration for shaving (278.4-281.19). The proper order of shaving the different parts of the body (281.20-286.3). Special rules for ascetics, etc. (286.4-289.3). Shaving is to be done at a tīrtha even in a forbidden time (289.6-296.1). Disposition of the shaven hair (297-299.2).

XVI. Bathing at a Tīrtha (300-322.1)

The virtues of bathing at a tīrtha (300-304). Restrictions and special rules concerning bathing (304.1-315.2). Bathing for another's sake (315.3-320.4). Other special rules (320.5-322.1).

XVII. Tarpaṇa (322.2-345).

The requirement of performing tarpaṇa at a tīrtha for the ancestors (322.2-326). Tarpaṇa for others also (326.1-329). Some special rules (330-332). The order of relatives receiving tarpaṇa (332.1-334.13). The abbreviated tarpaṇa (334.14-338.6). Restrictions on tarpaṇa do not apply at a tīrtha (338.7-343). Special rules on who may perform tarpaṇa at a tīrtha (343.2-345).

XVIII. Defilement of Rivers (346-367)

Various kinds of rivers are impure at certain times (346-353). Certain rivers are exempt from this impurity (353.1-357.1) Other special rules and exceptions (358-367).

XIX. Śraddha at a Tīrtha (368-405)

Śrāddha should be done at all tīrthas (368-380.1). Śrāddha to be done immediately after tarpaṇa, regardless of the time and other circumstances (380.2-388.1). If śrāddha cannot be done immediately, it should be done on the following day (388.2-389.10); exceptions to this (389.11-13). Restrictions as to the time of śrāddha do not apply to tīrtha-śraddha (389.14-393.4); neither do restrictions on the giving of piṇḍas (393.5-400). But this is so only when one arrives unexpectedly at a tīrtha (400.1-4). More special rules concerning the time for śrāddha (400.5-401.2). Brāhmaṇas for tīrtha-śrāddha are not to be examined (401.3-405)

XX. Prohibited Elements in Tīrtha-śrāddha (406-506.4)

The water-offering and the invitation are to be left out of a tīrtha-śrāddha (406-412). This applies only to a tīrtha-śrāddha occasioned by arrival at the tīrtha, not to any śrāddha done at a tīrtha; a long discussion on this point; and in connection with it, a discussion of the function of the ancestors in a śrāddha as compared to that of the gods in a sacrifice (412.1-463.2). Also in connection with this point, a discussion of the modification of the mantras in tīrtha-śrāddha (463.3-495.12), and of mantra-less śrāddhas (495.13-502.3).

Consideration of the appropriate Viśvedeva deities for different kinds of tīrtha-śrāddhas (502.4-506.4).

XXI. Discussion of Śrāddhas with Cooked Food, Raw Food, and Gold, and Other Matters (507-546.8)

The appropriate circumstances for different materials in śrāddha (507-513). Special rules for these materials (513.1-525), including discussion of modification of mantras (523.2-524.6). Procedure when brāhmaṇas are not available, and other special rules (525.1-531.2). Description and use of piṇḍas (531.3-539.1). Substitutes when complete rites are not possible (539.2-540.4).

Procedure for śrāddhas when several are occasioned on the same day (540.5-544.1). Combined performance etc. of such śrāddhas (544.2-546.8).

XXII. Determination in the Case of the Coincidence (of the Tīrtha-śrāddha) with Other Śrāddhas (546.9-551.3)

Conditions determining whether or not the tīrtha-śrāddha and other śrāddhas to be done on the same day must be done separately (546.9-550.1). Repetition of tīrtha-śrāddha (550.2-551.3).

XXIII. Those Who are Authorized to Perform Tīrtha-śrāddha (552-570.2)

Sons etc. can perform śrāddha for their fathers etc. at a tīrtha (552-553.2), even if the father is alive, except in certain cases (553.3-561.3). Śrāddha by brothers (561.4-563), widows (563.1-566.2), the uninitiated (566.3-568), and others (568.1-570.2).

XXIV. Exception to Those who are Authorized to Perform Tīrtha-śrāddha (570.3-572.1)

Ascetics and outcastes may not perform tīrtha-śrāddha.

XXV. Determination of the Beneficiaries in the Tīrtha-śrāddha (573-624.1)

Śrāddha may be done for the father etc. (573-574.1), the maternal grandfather etc. (574.2-576), the mother etc. in some cases (576.1-579.1), and the maternal grandmother etc. optionally (579.2-581.3). Rules concerning separate śrāddha for the mother, etc. (581.4-585.3), and the father's other wives (585.4-587.8). Śrāddha for paternal uncles, sons, teachers etc. (587.9-594.2). The order of these śrāddhas (594.3-599.3). Which are regular and which are optional (599.4-6). Rules for separate and combined performance in these śrāddhas (599.7-604.2). Śrāddha performed on behalf of others (604.3-607). Beneficiaries in a śrāddha by a widow (607.1-610.16). Beneficiaries in a śrāddha by one whose father is alive (610.17-615.1), and by one whose mother is alive (615.2-13). One whose father is alive may perform śrāddha for another's sake, or for his own (617.4-8) Special rules at Gayā (617.9-618.5). More rules for śrāddha by one whose father is alive (618.6-16), and by one whose mother etc. is alive (618.17-619.2).

Offering of a piṇḍa common to all relatives, friends, etc. (619.3-623.3). Abbreviated śrāddha (623.4-624.1).

XXVI. The Rule of Throwing Bones in a Tīrtha (624.2-634)

The benefit of throwing one's parents' bones into a tīrtha (624.2-628.1). The proper times for this ritual (628.2-632). Other special rules (632.1-634).

XXVII. The Manner (of Throwing Bones in a Tīrtha) (635-639.1)

The appropriate materials etc. for this ritual.

XXVIII. The Guide for this Procedure (639.2-22)

Summary of the procedure of the bone-throwing ritual (639.2-16). The proper time for this in relation to the other tīrtha rites (639.17-22).

XXIX. Miscellaneous Laws of Tīrthas (640-691).

Various tīrtha rituals and special rites for Śiva (640-650.1). Accepting gifts at tīrthas forbidden (650.2-653.4). More rules concerning sins done at a tīrtha and other matters (654-660). One should not think of other places when at a tīrtha (661-664). Dedication of pilgrimage, etc. to Viṣṇu; period of stay at a tīrtha, etc. (664.1-668.1). Procedure at rivers crossed while on a pilgrimage (668.2-671.6). Limits of the tīrtha (671.7-678.2). Rules for worship of liṅgas (678.3-682). More prohibited and recommended times for pilgrimage (682.1-685.4). Other miscellaneous rules (686-691).

CRITICAL APPARATUS

I. DESCRIPTION OF THE MANUSCRIPTS

1. Siglum Pl. Poleman no.2865, University of Pennsylvania (UP) no. 279.82 folios, 14.4 x 5.5 in., 9 lines per side, c. 50 akṣaras per line.

Part of a complete manuscript of all four sections of the TSS, the other parts being catalogued as separate mss. in the UP collection, nos. 281, 280, and 278.

Title page (in a later hand) : Tristhalasetau sāmānyapraghaṭṭakaprārambhaḥ 1.

Begins : Śrīgaṇeśāya namaḥ mātāpitṛbhyāṃ namaḥ Sarasvatīṃ namasyāmaḥ...

Ends: ...Prakīrṇakatīrthadharmaprakaraṇaṃ samāptaṃ. Samāptaś ca praghaṭṭakaḥ. Itaḥ paraṃ Prayāgaprakaraṇaṃ bhaviṣyati.

Folio numbers written on both left and right margins of verso. Above left hand number appear various abbreviations of the title such as 'TraSePra' and 'TraSā.' Above the right hand number on most of the folios is a scribe's signature 'Rāma.'

The ms. is uniformly clear and well-written in large Devanāgarī characters in black ink on yellow or white paper. Contains fairly numerous marginal corrections and additions in a later hand. The text itself has minor corrections in yellow ink and certain longer errors are crossed over with black ink.

Generally a reliable ms.

2. Siglum P2. Poleman no. 2856, UP no. 1661. 130 + 4 folios, 7.9 x 4.1 in., 9 lines per side, c.30 akṣaras per line. Dated Śaka 1754 = A.D. 1832.

The Sāmānya-praghaṭṭaka of the TSS with a detailed anukramaṇikā at the end on four folios separately numbered 1-4.

Title page : Atha Tristhalisetūprārambhoyaṃ. Śrīkṛṣṇāyeti.

Begins : Śrīgaṇeśāya namaḥ. Sarasvatīm namasyāmaḥ...

Text proper ends (f.130a) : ...Prakīrṇatīrthadharmaprakaraṇaṃ samāptaṃ Śrīkṛṣṇārpaṇam astu Śake 1754 nandananāmasaṃvatsare māsottamamāse Āśvinamāse śuklapakṣe trayodaśyāṃ tithau Ravivāsare taddine Devopanāmakarāmacandrasūnupuruṣottamena likhitaṃ (.) Visargabindumātrāṇī padapādākṣarāṇi ca nyūnāni cātiriktāni kṣamasva parameśvara (.) Bhagnapṛṣṭikaṭigrīvastabdhadṛṣṭir adhomukhaṃ kaṣṭena likhitaṃ granthaṃ yatnena pratipālayet. Evaṃ granthasaṃkhyā 2322.

On f.130b: Iti Tristhalīsetū samāptoyam. Śrīkṛṣṇa.

The anukramaṇikā ends (f.4a) : Iti Tristhalī anukramaṇikā samāptaḥ [sic !]. Śrīkṛṣṇārpaṇam astu. Evaṃ grathasaṃkhyā 52. [In Marathi, in a different hand :] Akṣare patrācī ekuṇa 1675, etc. (f.4b): Iti Triḥsthalī avatarṇikā samāptaḥ [sic!].

Folio numbers written in left and right margins of each verso. Above left number on most folios is written 'TriPra.'

The ms. is well-written in a fairly neat, legible Devanāgarī. Contains some marginal corrections and additions in a later hand, and frequent minor corrections in the text itself in yellow ink.

A highly reliable ms.

From the note added at the end of the anukramaṇikā in Marathi, it appears that the ms. was written in Maharashtra or by a Maharashtrian.

3. Siglum P3. Poleman no. 2865. UP no. 282. 77 folios, 11.25x 5 in., 10-14 lines per side, 45-50 akṣaras per line.

The Sāmānya-praghaṭṭaka of the TSS with a brief anukramaṇikā added in a different hand on the last folio.

Title page (f. la, in a different hand) : Tristhalīsetau Tīrthapraghaṭṭākhyaprathamaprakaraṇaprārambhaḥ.

Begins (f.1b) : Śrīgaṇādhipataye namaḥ. Śrībhaṭṭarāmeśvaracaraṇayugalāya namaḥ. Sarasvatīṃ namasyāmaḥ... (In margin :) Tristhalīsetupraghaṭṭaka.

Ends (f.76b):...Prakīrṇakatīrthadharmaprakaraṇaṃ samāptaṃ cha cha cha. (In a different hand :) Granthasaṃkhyā 2300. (Below this appears the anukramaṇikā.)

F.77 : Iti Tristhaḷīsetau tīrthapraghaṭṭakaprakaraṇam idaṃ prathamam.

Folios are numbered on both margins of verso.

The ms. is in three different Devanāgarī hands, as follows :

1st hand : ff. 1-27. Some signed 'Rāma'

2nd hand : ff. 28-47. Unsigned

3rd hand : ff. 48-61. Signed 'Heramba'

1st hand : ff.62-77. Signed 'Rāma'

In all parts, the writing is legible but somewhat sloppy. The ms. has the usual marginal additions and corrections in a later hand, and minor corrections in the text in yellow ink.

A reliable ms. with relatively few errors. The frequent use of the Marathi ḷ (ळ) in place of Sanskrit l indicates the probable provenance of the ms. in Maharashtra.

4. Siglum Cl. Shastri, *Descriptive Catalogue of Sanskrit Manuscripts...*, Vol. III, p.493, no.2430 (ms. no.1770). 90 folios (numbered 88), 8 1/2 x 4 in., 11 lines per side, c. 35 akṣaras per line. Dated Saṃvat 1738 = A.D. 1682.

The Sāmānya-praghaṭṭaka of the TSS. Has only the first two and last of the introductory ślokas.

Title page : Bhaṭṭarāmadevasutaraṅganāthasyedaṃ pustakaṃ

Pustakam idam Daśaputraviṣṇoḥ

Tristhalīsetau Sāmānyapraghaṭṭakaḥ

(Also various marginal notes.)

Begins : Śrīgaṇeśāya namaḥ. Sarasvatīṃ namasyāmaḥ...

Ends... Prakīrṇakatīrthadharmmaprakaraṇaṃ samāptaṃ. Saṃvat 1738 kā Bhādra vā sudi 14.

Folios numbered on both margins of verso.

The ms. is in two Devanāgarī hands: ff. 1-58 in the first, ff.59-88 in the second. There are two consecutive folios both numbered 5, and two numbered 6. The second f.6 is labelled 'śodhapatraṃ.'

The ms. is clearly written but is full of scribal errors and omissions. It is a highly unrealiable ms. It contains the usual marginal and textual additions and corrections in a later hand.

Furthermore, a good number of long passages are either misplaced or omitted in Cl. Comparison of the length of these passages reveals that they are each of approximately equal length, or in multiples of two or three times that length. The conclusion clearly to be drawn from this evidence is that the ms. from which Cl was copied (which we will call here Cl*) had both missing folios and folios placed out of order.

The first occurrence of this is on f.6 of Cl, in which a large section probably corresponding to f.8 of Cl* is omitted, and then added on the second f.6, labelled 'śodhapatraṃ.' Apparently f.8 of Cl* was misplaced, possibly appearing after f.9.

Later on in the ms., in a long section corresponding to the text section 537-600, the text of Cl is completely out of order. By comparing the length and positions of the misplaced passages it is possible to calculate the number and order of the misarranged folios of the proto-ms. Cl* which caused the defects in this part of Cl. The result is that the folios of the corresponding section of Cl* must have been in the following incorrect order when Cl was copied from them (here X = the folio of Cl* immediately preceding the first missing folio):

(X+1 – missing)
X+2 through X+4
X+9
X+5 through X+7
(X+8 – missing)
(X+10 and X+11 – missing)
X+12, X+13, etc. in correct order.

By calculating the length of these misplaced passages and the number of folios of Cl* which they represent, and then comparing these figures to the length of the entire text, we arrive at a probable figure of X = 80. That is to say that the first missing folio of Cl* was probably its folio no.81. Thus the defective arrangement of Cl* in the text section in question was most likely :

80
(81 missing)

82-84

89

85-87

(88 missing)

(90-91 missing)

92, 93 etc.

5. Siglum C2. In Rajendralal Mitra, *Notices of Sanskrit Manuscripts* Vol.II pp. 202-3, no. 797. In collection of Asiatic Society (Calcutta), call no. III. G.45. 103 folios, 11 x 4.75 in., 9 lines per side, c.40 akṣaras per line. Devanāgarī. No date.

The Tristhalīsetu-sāmānya-praghaṭṭakaḥ.

Begins : Śrīgaṇeśāya namaḥ. Śrībhaṭṭarāmeśvaracaraṇa-yugalāya namaḥ. Sarasvatīṃ namasyāmaḥ...

Ends :...Prakīrṇatīrthadharmaprakaraṇaṃ samāptaṃ samāptaś ca praghaṭṭakaḥ. Itaḥ paraṃ Prayāgaprakaraṇaṃ bhaviṣyati.

Folios numbered on verso and signed 'Rāma.' Corrections and additions in later hand in text and margins.

A moderately reliable ms. with an average number of scribal errors.

6. Siglum K. Published edition, Kāśī (Benares), 1908. 85 pages+ 'Viṣayāṇāṃ sūcī' of 5 pages and 'Śuddhipatraṃ' of 3 pages. 27 lines per page. No introductory material or notes.

The *Śrītristhalīsetupraghaṭṭake Sarvatīrthavidhipraghaṭṭākhyaḥ Prathamo Bhāgaḥ.*

Title page :

Śrī

Tristhalīsetupraghaṭṭake

Sarvatīrthavidhipraghaṭṭākhyaḥ

Prathamo Bhāgaḥ

———

Śrīmadbhaṭṭarāmeśvarasūrisūnunārāyaṇabhaṭṭaviracitaḥ

———

Śrī Vāpu-ācārya-Bhāvu-ācāryābhyāṃ sarvajanopakārāya bahutaraprācīnagranthaiḥ saṃśodhya

Kāśyāṃ

Candraprabhāyantrālaye mudrāpitaḥ

———

Asya sarve'py adhikārāḥ svāyattīkṛtāḥ

———

Benares
Printed by Gauri Shanker Lal at Chandraprabha Press
Published by Bapoo Acharya Bhaoo Acharya
1908

———

The text begins : Śrīgaṇādhipataye namaḥ. Śrībhattarāmeśvaracaraṇayugalāya namaḥ. Sarasvatīṃ namasyāmaḥ...

Ends :...Prakīrṇakatīrthadharmaprakaraṇaṃ samāptaṃ

The text is fairly reliable but contains a considerable number of misprints and incorrect readings, some of which are corrected in the Śuddhipatraṃ. It also includes several passages which are evidently interpolations.

Although according to the title page the text is "edited from a large number of old texts," there is no mention of the manuscripts or editing procedures used.

7. Siglum Ll. *Catalogue of Sanskrit Manuscripts in the India Office Library*, Vol.I pt.I, p.552, no.1719 (library no.515). 73 folios, 10 x 3.75 in., 10-11 lines per side, 42-48 akṣaras per line. No date, but according to the catalogue, "in Devanāgarī of c. 1780 A.D."

The 'Tristhalīsetau Sāmānyapraghaṭṭakaḥ.'

Begins : Śrīgaṇeśāya namaḥ. Sarasvatīṃ namasyāmaḥ...

Ends :...Prakīrṇakatīrthadharmaprakaraṇaṃ samāptaṃ. Samāptaś ca praghaṭṭakaḥ. Ataḥ paraṃ Prayāgaprakaraṇaṃ bhaviṣyati. Śrīrāmāya ṇamaḥ [sic]. Śrīkṛṣṇārpaṇaṃ astu. Śrīr astu. Śubham astu. Śubham astu. Śrīkaṇṭhasyedaṃ.

The ms. is in four hands, as follows :

ff.1-36	1st hand
f.37a, first 3 lines	2nd hand
f.37a -63	3rd hand
f.64a-64b, 2nd line	4th hand
f.64b-73	3rd hand.

However, all folios are signed 'Rāma.'

The ms. is generally poor. The first part (ff.1-36) especially is full of errors, mispellings, omissions, and misplaced passages. The remainder is better but still has frequent omissions and spelling errors, such as confusion of short and long vowels. The ms. has the usual corrections and additions in a later hand.

An unreliable ms.

8. Siglum L2. *Catalogue of Sanskrit Manuscripts tn the India Office Library*, Vol.I pt.1, p.552, no. 1720 (library no.683b). 84 folios (numbered 78) 9.5 x 4 in.. 9-12 lines per side, 30-39 akṣaras per line. No date, but according to the catalogue, "Folios 45-76 about 1650 A.D.; the remainder towards the end of last century." Devanāgarī.

No title page. Text begins: Śrīgaṇeśāya namaḥ. Śrībhaṭṭarāmeśvaracaraṇayugalāya namaḥ. Sarasvatiṃ namasyāmaḥ...

Ends :..Prakīrṇakatīrthadharmaprakaraṇaṃ samāptaṃ. Samāptaś ca praghaṭṭakaḥ. Itaḥ paraṃ Prayāgaprakaraṇaṃ bhaviṣyati.

The numbering of the folios is irregular, as follows :

Numbers on folio	*Actual number of folios*
1-11	1-11
10-24	12-26
1-3	27-29
25-43	30-48
44-44	49-50
45-77	51-83
(Last folio unnumbered)	84

The ms. is written by three different hands in alternation, as follows :

Folios	*Hand*
1-10	1st
11-16 (8 folios)	2nd
17-20	3rd
21	2nd

22-24b, line 7	3rd
24b, line 7—folio 3 (sic)	1st
25-42	2nd
43-44	1st
45-50	2nd
51-51b, line 8	3rd
51b, line 8-57a	2nd
(1 line of 52a and 3 lines of 57a are in 3rd hand)	
57b-58	3rd
59-63a	2nd
63b-73	3rd
74	1st
75-76	3rd
77+last f. (unnumbered)	1st.

It appears that the original ms. was written by two scribes, i.e. hands 2 and 3. Hand 1 is a later scribe who recopied certain parts of the ms. at a later time. It is not clear whether these later parts represented original folios which were lost, mutilated, or highly corrupt. That they are later additions is clear from a note in Marathi on the bottom of f. 24b, 'Puḍheṃ śodhapatraṃ tīna āheta' ('Below are three correction-pages'). (These are the folios anomalously numbered 1-3 in the middle of the text. They seem to provide a long section which had been omitted by the original scribes.)

The sections in the original two hands are sloppily written and inaccurate in spelling, etc. The later hand (1st hand) is clear and accurate.

Corrections by a fourth hand appear in the margins of the folios of all three hands.

The consistent use of ḷ (ळ) for l and the marginal note in Marathi on f. 246 indicate that the ms. was written in Maharashtra or by Maharashtrians.

II. RELATIONSHIPS OF THE MANUSCRIPTS

A. *Stemma codicum*

1. The relation between the eight mss. used and their theoretical prototypes is presented in the following stemma codicum:

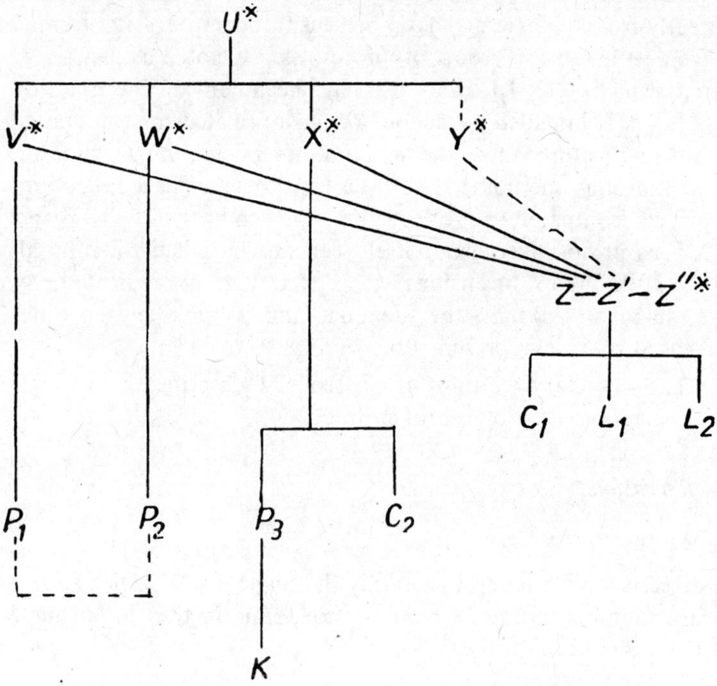

2. Explanation of the stemma:

As will be explained in detail below (II. B), the relationships between the eight mss. used in the edition are complex and not aways entirely clear. We may deduce two main causes for this situation:

a. A great deal of copying and recopying of the text within certain branches of the stemma apparently occurring within a short time after the initial composition of the text.

b. A large measure of mixing and contamination between the mss., resulting in mixed codices whose genealogy is virtually impossible to trace.

These comments apply chiefly to the group Y*-Z-Z'-Z''*-C1-L1-L2. This group has evidently undergone a large amount of mixing and contamination, apparently involving texts from each of the three other recensions. Moreover, it appears likely (see below, II. B. 4) that two if not all three of these mss. have been written by comparing two or more originals, rather than being copied directly from a single ms. To represent this complex situation, I have postulated the group of proto-mss., denoted as Z-Z'-Z''*, from which C1, L1, and L2 have been copied. The notation Z-Z'-Z''* is intended to denote a fund of related mss. (denoted arbitrarily as three mss., the actual number being indeterminate), which must at one point have been kept together in a collection, and been compared to produce the mixed codices C1, L1, and L2. This proto-mixed group itself seems to have had roots in all three of the 'pure' recensions V*, W*, and X* as indicated by the diagonal lines in the stemma, and very likely in other untraced sources, represented as Y*.

The secondary relationship of P1 to P2, described below (II. B. 2) is represented by a broken line.

B. *Recensions*

1. Recension V*.

Recension V* is represented by the single ms. P1 which shows a large number of unique readings not found in the other mss. A few examples :

8	apy astu for apy atra
238.1	tatraiva for tatra
255	brahma- for svarga-
338.3	yo, not in other mss.
357.1	-doṣa-, not in other mss.
438.1	mantravarṇāt for mantraliṅgāt
556	pūrvāsu for sarvāsu
582	tathaiva for svenaiva
604	-pradhānāt for -vidhānāt
686	sampūrṇaṃ for sampannaṃ

Many other examples may be found in the variant readings.

2. Recension W*

Recension W* is represented by a single ms. P2, which carries a number of readings not appearing in the other mss. Examples :

164.19	pāpavato'pāpasya vā, not in other mss.
192.1	yātrādimātrakāryamātra— for yātrādimātrakārya-
211.1	Iti tīrthasnānaṃ, not in other mss.
400.7-401	Tīrthaprāptau...yaugādikaṃ omitted.
427	śruteḥ for śrutiḥ
442.12	Urukarma- for Urukrama-
490.11	Tathā hi, others read Tathā
495.7	-gṛhya-, not in other mss. (except L2)
618.9	bhrātṛtvādinā for pitṛbhrātṛtvādinā

Ms. P2 has been corrected by a later hand by means of comparison with ms. P1 (or another ms. closely related to it; but probably with P1 itself). This is clear from a large number of instances where a reading in P2 is corrected to agree with that of P1. In several instances the corrected reading is actually a less good reading than that of the original in P2; and the corrected reading is often one which is unique to P1. For instance:

	Original reading of P2	*Corrected reading*
8	apy atra	apy astu
56.4	-devamūrti-	-devatāmūrti-
238.1	tatra	tatraiva
255	svarga-	brahma-
389.7	yathā	tathā
416.2	aśabdapūrva-	apūrvaśabdapūrva-
438.1	mantravarṇāt	mantraliṅgāt
510	śraddhayāpi	śrāddhaṃ piṇḍaṃ
618.12	ācāryādivantaṃ	ācāryādivacanaṃ

In all these instances, the corrected reading is one which is unique to ms. P1.

3. Recension X*

On the basis of a number of common readings peculiar to them, mss. P3, C2, and K are taken as representatives of a separate recension X*.

Examples af readings of X*:

130.62	śrutyādi- for śunyādi-
231.4	sarvagrahaṇārtham for sarvagrahagrahaṇārtham
254	Gautamyāṃ for Gomatyāṃ
463.6	-bhūta- for -bhūte
475.1	pravartatteti for pravarteteti (also in P1)
614	pitāmahāt for prapitāmahāt
639.2	tata omitted (in P3 and C2)

From these correspondences it is evident that P3 and C2 are descended from a common ancestor X*. But from a number of points where P3 and C2 diverge it is clear that neither of them can be derived from the other.

K, the printed text of the TSS-SP, can be said to have been "copied " from P3. Although according to the title page the edition is "edited from a large number of old texts," it is evident from a great many instances that the editors not only used P3 (or a ms. very similar to P3) as their prototype, but in fact relied very heavily upon it.

A few examples of K's readings derived from those of P3:

46.1	dāridryābhāvam ity arthaḥ for dāridryābhāvaḥ phalam ity arthaḥ (but corrected in Śuddhipatram)
48	Entire śloka omitted in P3 and K (but added in Śuddhipatram of K)
53	svayaṁbhūta for svayaṃbhūtaṃ
53.1	Brahmāṇḍapurāṇe for Brahmapurāṇe
238.3	mānābhāvāt for tatra pramāṇābhāvāt
387.5	sārthakyādya for sārthakyāya
401.2	vacanaṃ for vaca
412.21	viśeṣaṇa- omitted
545.4	-phala- omitted
617.4	dhṛtatvāt for vṛttatvāt
617.4	kuryāt for kāryaṃ

Many dozens more of such examples could be cited. Such instances as 46.1, 387.5, 617.4 etc., where K reproduces an obviously incorrect reading or a mere scribal error of P3, and such cases as 48, 238.3, 412.21, and 545.4 where K omits a passage lacking in P3, may be taken as virtually certain evidence that K was copied directly from P3 itself.

On the other hand, it can be shown that the editors of K did not rely entirely on P3 alone from such instances as 256.1-257, where the passage 'iti vā pāṭhaḥ...Bhāskarakṣetre' is omitted in P3, but does appear in K. In several cases (e.g. in 46.1 cited above) an incorrect reading in P3 has been reproduced in the text of K but corrected in the Śuddhipatram. Thus it is clear that the editors did consult other manuscripts. But since no information (other than the remark on the title page) is given concerning the procedures used in editing the text, there is no way to determine what other mss. were used.

4. Recension Z-Z'-Z''*

As explained above (II.A.2), the notation Z-Z'-Z''* is intended to denote a fund of mixed codices, influenced by the other recensions V*, W*, and X*, from an undeterminable combination of which derive the highly mixed codices Cl, L1, and L2.

In the case of each of the three mss. Cl, L1, and L2, it has proved impossible to establish any special relationship with any one of the 'pure' recensions (i.e. V*, W*, and X*). Each of these mss. has an approximately equal number of readings which agree with each of the three 'pure' recensions, so that no special relationship can be established. For instance, ms. L2 agrees in some cases with recension V* (ms. P1):

37 dharmaṃ for kāmaṃ
147 bhavacakre for bhacakre
336 tṛptaṃ (others have tṛptiṃ).

In other cases, L2 agrees with recension W* (ms. P2):

234.4 ayam omitted
335 and
336 -stambha- for -stamba-
488.1 -kāryāpaṅktiś for -kāryāpattiś
587.2 sapatnamātāmahībhyo for sapatnamātāmahebhyo.

But elsewhere, L2 agrees with recension X* (mss. P3, C2, K):

85 kṛtvā for gatvā
195.6 parikalpya for parikalayya

235.19,21 anuvādatā for anuvādakatā
254 Gotamyāṃ (X* Gautamyāṃ) for Gomatyāṃ
262.20 -kṛta- (L2 and P3 only) for -bhūta-.

Similar examples can be adduced for mss. C1 and L1. In such a situation we can only conclude that there has been a high degree of mixing and contamination within the recension Z-Z'-Z"*. Since we have in the case of all three representatives of Z-Z'-Z"* readings corresponding with all the other recensions, we may postulate a connection with each of the three prototypes V*, W*, and X*. Furthermore, in the case of ms. C1 frequently, and of mss. L1 and L2 occasionally, we find readings which do not appear in any of the other recensions. Thus in C1 we find such readings as :

90.4 śūdrasyāpi for śūdrāṇām api
91 snātvā for snātās
179 prapannāni for prachannāni
306.1 apavādam āha for apavādaḥ

Although for the most part these readings can be dismissed as capricious changes or scribal errors, it seems advisable to postulate a further source, designated Y* (but unrepresented by any of the mss. used) for the recension Z-Z'-Z"*, in order to accout for the unique readings in C1, and to a lesser extent in L1 and L2.

In all likelihood, a combination of two factors accounts for the extreme degree of mixture in the recension Z-Z'-Z"* :

a. Recopying of corrected mss. : All the mss. used had marginal and linear corrections in a later hand. In certain cases at least it is possible to prove that one ms. was corrected by comparison with another; thus for example P2 was corrected from P1 (see above, II. B.2). If a ms. is copied from such a corrected ms., the new ms. will represent a mixed codex. Thus for instance a ms. copied from corrected P2 would prepresent a mixture of recensions V* and W*.[1] Such correcting of mss. by comparison undoubtedly took place within recension Z-Z'-Z"* and accounts partially for the mixing of recensions therein.

1. None of the mss. concerned could be so derived, however. The case of P2 is cited by way of an example only.

b. It is possible, though it cannot be conclusively proven, that mss. C1 and L1, and possibly L2 also, were actually composed by means of a comparison of two or more mss. of the Z-Z'-Z"* recension. This would further account for the high degree of mixing of readings, and would help to explain the peculiar scribal characteristics of mss. C1, L1 and L2. The frequent omissions, dittographies, and misplaced passages in these mss. (see above, I.4,7,8) become understandable if one supposes that the scribes had before them two or more originals, rather than a single one. Also, the fact that each of these mss. is in two or more different hands may be taken to support the notion of a composite origin.

It may seem somewhat surprising that these highly mixed and generally unreliable mss. seem also to be the oldest among those used. C1, the least reliable of all, is the oldest dated ms., Saṃvat 1738 = A.D. 1682. According to the India Office Catalogue, the earlier portions of L2 are to be dated at about 1650 A.D.

Thus the general history of the mss. must be described as follows :

a. The text of the TSS-SP was recopied frequently within a century after its initial composition (c.1550 A.D.). The manuscripts involved in these early copyings underwent a great deal of correction and conflation, with the result that a body of mixed and generally poor mss. was produced in a relatively short time.

b. Other manuscripts of the text apparently were preserved separately from these, and underwent a more direct and less intensive transmission. These are the representatives of the 'pure' recensions V*, W*, and X*. Altough they are generally later in date, these mss. are far better preserved that those of recension Z-Z'-Z"*.

III. PRINCIPLES FOLLOWED IN CONSTITUTING THE TEXT

A. *General Rules*

1. The mss. have been arranged, according to the stemma given above, into four recensions, of which three— V*, W*, and

X*—are considered 'pure.' Thus the readings of the primary mss. of these recensions—P1, P2, P3, and C2—will be the principal criteria for determining the reading of the original text.

Thus the overall principle will be : The reading of the majority of the three 'pure' recensions is preferred.

a. Reading of P1 and P2 preferred to reading of P3C2. Example : 209 tīrthe snānaṃ, rather than tīrthasnānaṃ.
b. Reading of P1 and P3C2 preferred to reading of P2. Example : 161.3 apararātre rather than aparāhṇe.
c. Reading of P2 and P3C2 preferred to reading of P1. Example : 606 sa mudā rather than sampādya.

2. Because they represent a mixed recension, mss. C1, L1, and L2 cannot be used as primary determinants of the original readings.

Example : 610.9 pañcadaśadaivatyaṃ, the reading of PIP2K, is preferred to pañcadaśadaivatyatāṃ, the reading of P3C2, according to the general principle (a) evoked above, *even though* C1L1L2 support the latter reading. Since the reading -daivatyaṃ is preferable according to the context, and the variant -daivatyatāṃ can be explained as originating from a dittography of the last akṣara, the testimony of the mss. C1L1L2 has been disregarded, even though it seems to confirm the reading of P3C2.

In other cases, however, the testimony of the mixed recension is taken into account as corroborative evidence for a reading in a 'pure' recension.

Example : 369 tīrthe śrāddhaṃ preferred to tīrthaśrāddhaṃ, which would be the reading according to the general principles, because of corroboration of the former reading in the mixed mss. See below, III.B.2.c.

B. *Exceptions to the General Rule*

1. In some cases a reading is chosen because it gives a better sense or is the only grammatically correct reading, even though the general principles would point to another reading.
Examples :

a. 37 kāmaṃ is chosen over dharmaṃ, which is the reading

of P1P2. Here the context demands the reading kāmaṃ, which is also supported by extrinsic testimonia (see below, III.D.1).

b. 526. 1 darbhavaṭor upari in P3C2K is grammatically better than darbhavaṭopari, etc.

c. 541 hanteti, read only in C2 and K, is chosen over hantatiṃ and hantaniṃ, readings in the other mss.

d. 208 saṃnidhātrī, which appears only in P1 (and there apparently as a correction) must be chosen over saṃnidhānī, the reading of all the other mss., which is grammatically unacceptable. (This reading is also supported by external testimonia; see below, III.D.3.)

e. 490.11 Tathā hi, P2, chosen over tathā of other mss. The former gives a better sense in the context, and the absence of 'hi' in other mss. may be explained as a haplography with the first akṣara of the following word (Hiraṇyakeśināṃ).

2. Readings chosen according to the principle of lectio difficilior. Examples :

a. 4 ca sudhā, L1, chosen over vasudhā of other mss.

b. 215.12 vājinavan, read only as a correction in P1 and in corrupted form as janivan in L1, chosen over vājapeyavan of the other mss. The latter is clearly a lectio facilior; and the context of the Mīmāṃsā disussion definitely calls for the reading vājinavan.

c. 369 tīrthe śrāddhaṃ chosen over tīrthaśrāddhaṃ, a lectio facilior. The former reading is unanimously supported by the mixed codices C1L1L2.

3. Emendations : In one case it was necessary to make a minor emendation in the text as it stands in the mss. ;

a. 220.1 After payovratā, all the mss. read 'jalamātrāhāreti vacanaṃ.' 'Jalamātrāhārā' here is clearly an interpolation derived from a marginal or interlinear gloss, based on the text of 251.1, where the same śloka is quoted with the comment 'payovrata jalamātrāhārety arthaḥ.' But here the position of 'jalamātrāhārā' before 'iti vacanaṃ' shows that it does not properly belong in the text.

C. *Miscellaneous*

1. Application of sandhi rules follows the practice of the mss. Where the mss. generally or unanimously do not apply sandhi, the text has been so preserved.

Examples :

a. The mss. do not make sandhi between final -n and initial j-; 292, 393, 412.9. Final d is preserved before j- in 678.

b. Sandhi not applied between final -ṭ and initial v-, 566.

c. External vowel sandhi not applied in pakṣe upapannatvāc, 220.1.

d. Non-standard sandhi in quoted verses : 637 śuciveti (properly śucīva iti); but the meter requires the 'double sandhi.' 349 śuddhā syur in all mss. (instead of śuddhāḥ) is preserved (See Additions and Corrections).

Exception : In a few cases, words written together in sandhi in the mss. have been divided for the sake of clarity or to facilitate the introduction of punctuation in the transliterated text.

Examples :

a. 116.4 ca "Etena for caitena in the mss.

b. 215.2 ca 'Upavāsaṃ for copavāsaṃ.

2. Regularization of orthography.

a. The mss. generally have *ch* for *cch*, even where *cch* is grammatically mandatory. The text has been regularized to read *cch* in all cases.

b. The forms daivatya and devatya sometimes alternate arbitrarily in the mss. In such cases the form daivatya is adopted (e.g. 581).

c. Use of avagraha (') is sporadic in the mss., and has been regularly introduced wherever appropiate in the text.

d. m has been substituted for ṃ in pausa appearing frequently in the mss.

D. *External Testimonia*

Published editions of texts quoted in the TSS-SP are occasionally used to confirm readings.

Examples :

1. 37 kāmaṃ is confirmed by the reading of the critical edition of the MBh.

2. 65 tīrthaṃ liṅgaṃ (rather than tīrthaliṅgaṃ) is confirmed by the reading in the Skanda Purāṇa (Veṅkaṭeśvara Press ed.).

3. 208 saṃnidhātrī is supported by the published TSS-SS, p.13 line 7 (cf. above, II.B.1.d).

However, extrinsic sources are not generally taken to outweigh the evidence of the mss. themselves. Thus for instance in 16, the reading khaṃ is adopted on the basis of the mss., although edited texts and commentaries of Manu Smṛti read kha- or sva- in this passage.

NOTE ON THE ARRANGEMENT OF THE TEXT

The text and translation have been numbered according to the following system: quotations from other works are set in and numbered consecutively. The sentences in the commentary following each quotation are numbered from 1 onward. These sub-numbers are indicated in their proper place in the text in parentheses : (1), (2), etc. When such a passage is referred to elsewhere, its full number is given, that is, the number of the quotation which it follows, plus its own sub-number, with a period in between; e.g. 231.2. At certain points in the translation it has been necessary to rearrange the order of the sentences of the original text in order to give a clear sense in English. In such cases, and wherever else it seems to provide greater clarity, the full numbers rather than sub-numbers are written (see for instance 276.1 and 277.2 in the translation).

As far as possible, quotations have been located and identified in published texts, by chapter and verse when so arranged, otherwise by page number only. Quotations from Mīmāṃsā texts are given by adhyāya, pāda, adhikaraṇa, and sūtra, and also by page number where deemed necessary.

The editions of the texts cited are those which are listed in the bibliography. Where more than one edition of a text is listed in the bibliography, the quotations are identified in the text listed first, unless otherwise noted.

Many quotations have not been identified. Several of the texts cited by NB are not extant or not available in printed editions; for example the *Āditya Purāṇa, Divodāsīya, Smṛtidarpaṇa, Smṛtiratnāvalī,* etc. Quotations attributed by NB to a known text are often not to be found in the extant version of that text. Such quotations, however, are sometimes found in different texts than those to which they are attributed; in such cases, that identification will be noted in the text in parentheses.

Nearly one-third of the quotes in the text are cited by NB without mentioning their source. As far as possible I have attempted to locate these quotations in the various relevant texts.

भग्नपृष्ठकटिग्रीवं स्तब्धदृष्टिरधोमुखम् ।
कष्टेन लिखितं ग्रन्थं यत्नेन प्रतिपालयेत् ।।

Appendix G

INDEX OF NYĀYAS

The following rules and phrases are all cited in the text as 'nyāyas' For their sources and explanations of their significance, see the text, translation, and footnotes.[1]

Asmadāyatte hi śabdaprayoge/

Kim ity avācakaṃ prayokṣyāmahe// 279.1, 281.10

Āgantūnām ante niveśaḥ 639.18

Ānarthakyapratihatānāṃ viparītaṃ balābalam 215.17

Ekatra nirṇītaḥ śāstrārtho'paratrāpi 168

Ekasya tūbhayatve saṃyogapṛthaktvam 166

Aindrānaindrapradāna 486.13

Gṛhamedhīyājyabhāga 493.5

Grahādhikaraṇanyāya, grahaikatvādhikaraṇa-nyāya[2] 261, 262.6

Na hi nindā nindyaṃ ninditum pravartate api tu vidheyaṃ stotum 265.9

Nimitte sati naimittikānuṣṭhānam anantarakāla evāsati pratibandhe kāryam 389.5

Pradhānaphalasyaivāṅge śravaṇa 163.2

Mukhyadravyālābhe tatsadṛśaṃ pratinidheyam 274.5

Sati nimitte naimittikam 220.3

Saṃnidhau tv avibhāgāt 546

Sarvatvam ādhikārikam 264

1. Cf. also the "nyāya-s" given as technical Mīmāṃsā terms in Appendix E. godohananyāya, niṣādasthapatiśabda(nyāya), Pāśanyāya, viśvajin-nyāya.

2. Cf. grahaikatra (adhikaraṇa), Appendix E.

अथ

नारायणभट्टविरचिते

त्रिस्थलीसेतौ

सामान्यप्रघट्टकः

त्रिस्थलीसेतौ तीर्थप्रघट्टाख्यप्रथमप्रकरणप्रारम्भः ।

श्रीगणाधिपतये नमः । श्रीभट्टरामेश्वरचरणयुगलाय नमः ।

1. सरस्वतीं नमस्यामः प्रत्यूहव्यूहहानये ।
यदेकतानचित्तानां चित्ते संवित्तिरुत्तमा ॥

2. विघ्नाधिप नमस्तुभ्यं विघ्नसंघं विघातय ।
प्रचयं रचयात्युच्चं बुद्धिशुद्धिं विधेहि च ॥

3. उन्निद्रपत्रशतपत्रसगोत्रनेत्रं
सुग्रीवमित्रमतिचित्रचरित्रपात्रम् ।
उन्नीलनीलमणिवर्णसवर्णगात्रं
रामं भजे कुलपतिं कमलाकलत्रम् ॥

4. विश्वामित्रकुलोदधौ विधुरिवाखण्डः कलानां निधि-
र्वाग्गुम्फे निखिलेऽपि यस्य च सुधा शिष्यप्रशिष्यैश्चिता ॥
विद्यापद्मविकासनैकतरणिः श्रीभट्टगोविन्दजः
संख्यावद्गणनाग्रणीर्विजयते श्रीभट्टरामेश्वरः ॥

5. श्रिता वाराणसी तेन नगरी न गरीयसी ।
यतोऽन्या नगरी हेमनगरीतिमुपेयुषी ॥

6. शास्त्रेष्वधीती पितुरेव यः श्रुतीः
स्मृतीः समालोच्य च देशरीतीः ।
नारायणस्तत्तनयोऽविमुक्ते
तीर्थत्रयीसेतुमसौ विधत्ते ॥

7. ग्रन्थेऽस्मिन्गुणगणवत्त्वमुच्यते चेत्
स्वं ग्रन्थं गुणगणवन्तमाह को न ।
तत्सन्तः शिरसि कृताञ्जलिस्तु याचे
शोध्यं तत्सदसदिहोच्यते मया यत् ।

---

2. प्रचयम् P2 प्रचरम्, L1 प्रपञ्चम् । 2. उच्चम् K उच्चैर् । 2. विधेहि P1 विधाय । 4. च सुधा all except L1 have वसुधा । 4. शिष्य– P2 शिष्यैः. । 5. तेन । P2 येन । 7. स्वं P2 स्व- ।

8. **खलानां प्रार्थनैषेह खलताखलतास्तु वः ।**
भवतां भूषणेऽप्यत्र दूषणे मास्तु मानसम् ॥

9. **साधारणस्तीर्थविधिः प्रथमं सम्यगुच्यते ।**
प्रयागादित्रयविधिः पश्चादित्यत्र संग्रहः ॥

(1) इह खलु संसारचक्रे परिवर्तमानानां चत्वारः पुरुषार्था धर्मार्थ-काममोक्षाख्याः सकलस्मृतीतिहासपुराणादिषु श्रूयन्ते सेव्यत्वेन । तथा च भारते भीमसेनवचो युधिष्ठिरं प्रति—

10. **धर्मं चार्थञ्च कामञ्च यथावद् वदतां वर ।**
विभज्य काले कालज्ञः सर्वान्सेवेत पण्डितः ॥
मोक्षो वा परमं श्रेय एषां राजन् सुखार्थिनाम् । इति

महाभारत III. 34. 41-42b

(1) तत्र सुखदुःखाभावयोरेव निरुपधीच्छाविषयत्वात् पुरुषेणार्थ्य-मानतया मुख्यं पुरुषार्थत्वम्, तत्साधनस्य तु गौणम् । (2) एवञ्च सति धर्मार्थ-योर्यथायोगं सुखदुःखाभावसाधनत्वाद् औपचारिकी पुरुषार्थता । (3) अत एव प्रवृत्तिनिवृत्त्यात्मकतया द्विविधस्यापि धर्मस्य पुरुषार्थसाधनतोक्ता वृद्धैः—

11. **प्रवृत्तिसंज्ञके धर्मे फलमभ्युदयो मतः ।**
निवृत्तिसंज्ञके धर्मे फलं निःश्रेयसं मतम् ॥ इति ।

स्कान्देऽपि—

12. **धर्मात् सुखञ्च ज्ञानञ्च यस्मादुभयमाप्नुयात् ।**
तस्मात्सर्वं परित्यज्य विद्वान् धर्मं समाचरेत् ॥
लोकद्वयेऽपि यत्सौख्यं तद्धर्मात् प्राप्यते यतः ।
धर्ममेकमतः कुर्यात् सर्वकामार्थसिद्धये ॥

भारते—

13. **धर्म एव प्लवो नान्यः स्वर्गं द्रौपदि गच्छताम् ।**

महाभारत III. 32. 22a-b

---

8. प्रार्थनैषेह P1L1 प्रार्थनैवेह, P2 प्रार्थनेनेह ।8. ऽप्यत्र P1 ऽप्यस्तु । 9.1 पुरुषार्था P1 C1 पुरुषार्थाः । 9.1. पुराणादिषु P1 पुराणेषु । 10. परमं C2 परम–. । 10. राजन् P3 K राम । 11. संज्ञके P1 संज्ञिके (twice) । 12. एकम् P1 एवम् ।

(1) इत्यादि । दुःखाभावसाधनतामपि धर्मस्य

14. **धर्मेण पापमपनुदति**

(1) इति श्रुतिर्दुःखसाधनपापापनोदद्वाराह ।

स्कान्दे च—

15. **दीर्घकालेन तपसा सेवितेन तपोधने ।**
धर्मनिर्धूतपापानां संसिध्यन्ति मनोरथाः ॥

मनुः —

16. **धर्मेण हि सहायेन तमस्तरति दुस्तरम् ।**
धर्मप्रधानं पुरुषं तपसा हतकल्मषम् ॥
परलोकं नयत्याशु भास्वन्तं खं शरीरिणम् ।

मनु IV. 242c-243

(1) प्रायश्चित्तादिधर्मस्य च दुरितक्षयद्वारा दुःखाभावसाधनता सकलश्रुतिस्मृतिपुराणप्रसिद्धा ।

(2) अर्थस्यापि सुखदुःखाभावसाधनतानुभवसिद्धा आगमसिद्धा च,

17. **उच्चा दिवि दक्षिणावन्तो अस्थु–**
र्ये अश्वदाः सह ते सूर्येण ।
हिरण्यदा अमृतत्वं भजन्ते
वासोदाः सोम प्रतिरन्त आयुर् ॥

ऋग्वेद X. 107.2

इति मन्त्रवर्णात्,

18. **सद्यः शुध्यति हेमद**

इति स्मृतेश्च. (1) तुलापुरुषादिदानप्रतिपादकवचनान्यप्यत्र प्रमाणभावं भजन्ते । (2) तेन सिद्धा धर्मार्थयोरौपचारिकी पुरुषार्थता ।

(3) कामस्तु सुखरूपत्वान्मुख्य एव पुरुषार्थः । सुखरूपता च भारते आरण्यके पर्वणि श्रूयते —

19. **द्रव्यार्थस्पर्शसंयोगे या प्रीतिरुपजायते ।**
स कामश्चित्तसंकल्पः शरीरं नास्य दृश्यते ॥

महाभारत III. 34.30

14.1 अपनोद- C1 अपनोदन-। 16. खं P2 C1 C2 स्वं, P3 K स्व–, L1 खे L2 ख– P3 and C1 corrected to खं. 18.2 After धर्मार्थयोर् P1 अपि ।

इति । तथा—

20. **अर्थार्थी पुरुषो राजन् बृहन्तं धर्ममिच्छति ।**
अर्थमिच्छति कामार्थी न कामादन्यमिच्छति ॥
न हि कामेन कामोऽन्यः साध्यते फलमेव तद् । इति ।

महाभारत III. 34.31-32b

21. **इन्द्रियाणाञ्च पञ्चानां मनसो हृदयस्य च ।**
विषये वर्तमानानां या प्रीतिरुपजायते ॥
स काम इति मे बुद्धिः कर्मणां फलमुत्तमम् ।

महाभारत III. 34.37

इति च ।

अत्र हि

22. **मुत् प्रीतिः प्रमदो हर्ष**

अमरकोश 4.24

(1) इत्यादिकोशप्रतिपादितसुखपर्यायप्रीतिशब्देनाभिधानात् फलान्तराभावाभिधानात् फलरूपताभिधानाच्च कामस्य सुखरूपता । अत एव स्मृत्यधिकरणवार्तिके—

23. **यावद् धर्ममोक्षसम्बन्धि तद् वेदप्रभवम् ।**
यत्त्वर्थसुखविषयं तल्लोकव्यवहारपूर्वकम्

TV 1.3.1.2 (p. 166)

(1) इति सुखशब्देनैव काम उपात्तः ।

अर्थवादाधिकरणेऽपि—

24. **धर्मार्थकाममोक्षाधर्मानर्थदुःखसंसारसाध्यसाधन-**
प्रतिपत्तिरुपादानपरित्यागाङ्गभूता फलम्

TV 1.2.1.7 (P. 116)

(1) इत्यत्र कामप्रतियोगित्वेन दुःखं वदतो वार्तिककारस्य सुखमेव कामपुरुषार्थः सम्मतः ।

यत्तु भागवते—

25. **कामस्य नेन्द्रियप्रीतिर्लाभो जीवेत यावते— ।**

---

20. इच्छति C1 ऋच्छति । 21. च C1 हि. । 22.1. कोश-. P3 C1 C2 कोष- । 22.1. प्रीतिशब्देन, L1 प्रतिशब्देन ।

(1) –ति कामस्यापीन्द्रियप्रीत्याख्यसुखफलसाधनतामङ्गीकृत्य तन्निराकरणम्;

यच्चान्यत्र—

26. **धर्मादर्थोऽर्थतः कामः कामात् प्रीतिरनुत्तमे—।**

(1) ति प्रीतिसाधनताभिधानं, तद् विषयोपभोगे कामाख्यसुखसाधनत्वाद् गौणं कामत्वमङ्गीकृत्य व्याख्येयम्। (2) यद्वा तत्रापि कामशब्दः सुखपर एव। (3) इन्द्रियप्रीतिशब्द एव त्विन्द्रियतृप्तिपरः, सुखापरपर्यायायाः प्रीतेरिन्द्रियधर्मत्वाभावात्।

(4) तत्सिद्धमेतत् कामस्य सुखरूपत्वान्मुख्यपुरुषार्थत्वमिति। (5) मोक्षोऽपि मतभेदेन सुखदुःखाभावान्यतररूप इति तस्यापि मुख्यमेव पुरुषार्थत्वम्।

(6) चतुर्षु तु साधारणः पुरुषार्थत्वव्यवहारश्छत्र्यछत्रिसमुदाये छत्रिशब्दवत् सृष्ट्यसृष्टिप्राणभृदप्राणभृत्समुदाययोः सृष्टिप्राणभृच्छब्दवच्चौपचारिकः।

(7) तदेतेषु चतुर्षु पुरुषार्थेषु धर्मो मुख्यः, पुरुषार्थान्तरहेतुत्वाद् विद्यादिहेतुत्वाच्च। तदुक्तं कौर्म्ये—

27. **धर्मात् सञ्जायते ह्यर्थो धर्मात् कामोऽभिजायते।**
धर्मादेव परं ब्रह्म तस्माद् धर्मं समाचरेद्॥

कूर्मपुराण 1.2.52

इति। (1) 'परं ब्रह्म' मोक्षः।

तथा—

28. **ऊर्ध्वबाहुर्विरौम्येष न च कश्चिच्छृणोति मे।**
धर्मादर्थश्च कामश्च स किमर्थं न सेव्यते॥

महाभारत 18.5.49

तथा—

29. **निवृत्तिसंज्ञके धर्मे फलं निःश्रेयसं मतम्।** (=11)

भारते—

30. **विद्या वित्तं वपुः शौर्यं कुले जन्म नीरोगता।**
संसारोच्छित्तिहेतुश्च धर्मादेव प्रकीर्तितः॥

स्कान्दे—

31. **धर्माद् राज्यं धनं सौख्यमधर्माद् दुःखसम्भवः।**
तस्माद् धर्मं सुखार्थाय कुर्यात् पापं विवर्जयेत्॥

25.1 निराकरणं C1 निराकृतं। 27. ऽभिजायते L1 ऽपि जायते। 29. संज्ञके P1 संज्ञिके। 30. कुले P3 K कुलम्।

याज्ञवल्क्यः—

32. **कर्मणा मनसा वाचा यत्नाद् धर्मं समाचरेत् ।**

याज्ञ० 1.156 a-b

मनुः—

33. **धर्म एव हतो हन्ति धर्मो रक्षति रक्षितः ।**
तस्माद् धर्मो न हन्तव्यो मा नो धर्मो हतो वधीद् ॥

मनु 8.15

इत्यादि ।

(1) "नन्वर्थस्यापि धर्मकारणतानुभवात् कथं धर्मस्यैव प्राधान्यम्? तदुक्तं भारते—

34. **सर्वथा धर्ममूलोऽर्थो धर्मश्चार्थपरिग्रहः ।**

महाभारत 3.34.29 a-b

तथा—

35. **धर्ममूलं जगद् राजन् नान्यद् धर्माद् विशिष्यते ।**
धर्मश्चार्थेन महता शक्यो राजन् निषेवितुम् ॥

महाभारत 3.34.47

भागवते—

36. **धर्मं च धर्मैकफलम् । इति" ।**

(1) मैवम्, कस्यचिद् यागादिदानादिधर्मस्यार्थसाध्यत्वेऽपि सर्वस्यार्थसाध्यत्वाभावात् । (2) अर्थमन्तरापि जपतीर्थयात्रोपवासादिभ्यो धर्मोदयात्, धर्मं विना चार्थलेशस्याप्यनुदयात् । (3) एवं धर्मस्य प्राधान्ये स एव मुख्यतोऽनुष्ठेयः । तदुक्तमारण्यके—

37. **धर्मं पूर्वं धनं मध्ये जघन्ये काममाचरेत् ।**

महाभारत 3.34.39 a-b

(1) तत्रापि यागदानादिरूपस्य धर्मस्य बहुद्रव्यसाध्यत्वात्, बह्वङ्गकलापवत्त्वाच्चेदानीन्तनैः साङ्गस्य सम्पादयितुमशक्तेः, सपत्नीकसाध्यत्वाद् ऋत्विगादिसहायसम्पाद्यत्वात् सकलवर्णवर्णसंकरजाश्रमानधिकारित्वाच्च तदपेक्षया तीर्थयात्राधर्मोऽतिसुगमः, पूर्वहेतुवैलक्षण्यात् । तदुक्तं भारतमात्स्ययोः—

---

33. रक्षितः P3 रक्षतः । 35. चार्थेन P3 K स्वार्थेन । 37. कामम् P1 P3 C2 L1 L2 धर्मम् । 37.1. –वर्णवर्ण– P1 C1 –वर्ण– ।

38. **ऋषिभिः क्रतवः प्रोक्ता वेदेष्वपि यथाक्रमम् ।**
फलञ्चैव यथातत्त्वं प्रेत्य चेह च सर्वशः ॥
न ते शक्या दरिद्रेण यज्ञाः प्राप्तुं महीपते ।
बहूपकरणा यज्ञा नानासम्भारविस्तराः ॥
प्राप्यते पार्थिवैरेते समृद्धैर्वा नरैः क्वचित् ।
नार्थन्यूनैरवगणैरेकात्मभिरसंहतैः ॥
यो दरिद्रैरपि विधिः शक्यः प्राप्तुं जनेश्वर ।
तुल्यो यज्ञफलैः पुण्यैस्तन्निबोध महीपते ॥
ऋषीणां परमं गुह्यमिदं भरतसत्तम ।
तीर्थाभिगमनं पुण्यं यज्ञैरपि विशिष्यत ॥ इति ।

महाभारत 3.80.34-38
मत्स्यपुराण 112.12-15

(1) 'अवगणैः' सहायरहितैः । (2) 'एकात्मभिर्' अपत्नीकैः । (3) 'असंहतैः' ऋत्विगादिसंघातशून्यैः ।

(4) शूद्रसंकीर्णप्रव्रजितादीनामप्यत्राधिकारोऽस्तीति अधिकारिनिरूपणे निरूपयिष्यते ।

(5) "ननु जपोपवासादिधर्मोऽर्थनिरपेक्षो विद्यत एवेति कथं तीर्थयात्रायामेवातिशयः ?" (6) सत्यम् तथापि तस्य भूयसा शरीरायासेन साध्यत्वाद् विष्टम्बपित्तरोगादियुक्तैश्चानुष्ठातुमशक्तेः सकलानधिकारिकत्वाच्च तद्विलक्षणत्वात् तीर्थयात्रैव श्रेयसी ।

39. **चरन् वै मधु विन्दती— ।**

ऐतरेय ब्राह्मण 33.3.5

(1) त्यादिलिङ्गाच्चायमर्थोऽध्यवसेयः ।

इति श्रीमद्भट्टरामेश्वरसूरिसूनुनारायणभट्टविरचिते त्रिस्थलीसेतौ तीर्थयात्राकर्तव्यतानिरूपणम् ।

38.3. –संघात– P2 –साधन– । 38.5. कथम् LI किम् । 39. –कर्तव्यता– P1 omitted.

अथ सामान्यतस्तीर्थप्रशंसा

शंखः —

40. सर्वतीर्थानि पुण्यानि पापघ्नानि सदा नृणाम् ।
परस्परानपेक्षाणि कथितानि मनीषिभिः ॥

शंख 8.13

(1) परस्परेति प्रत्येकमेव पापघ्नानीत्यर्थः ।

तथा—

41. सर्वे प्रस्रवणाः पुण्याः सर्वे पुण्याः शिलोच्चयाः ।
नद्यः पुण्याः सदा सर्वा जाह्नवी तु विशेषतः ॥

शंख 8.14

गारुडे—

42. पुत्रद्रव्यादि संत्यज्य तीर्थं व्रजति यो नरः ।
ब्रह्माद्या देवतास्तस्य तुष्टिं पुष्टिं ददन्ति हि ॥

गरुडपुराण 2.26.13

भारते—

43. तथा पुण्यानि तीर्थानि पुण्यान्यायतनानि च ।
उपास्य पुण्यं लब्ध्वा च भवत्यमरलोकभाक् ॥

तथा—

44. कीर्तनाच्चैव तीर्थस्य स्नानाच्च पितृतर्पणात् ।
धुनन्ति पापं तीर्थे ये ते प्रयान्ति सुखं परम् ॥

कौर्मे तीर्थानि प्रकृत्य—

45. यत्र स्नानं जपो होमः श्राद्धदानादिकं कृतम् ।
एकैकशो मुनिश्रेष्ठाः पुनात्यासप्तमं कुलम् ॥

कूर्मपुराण 2.34.3 (=304)

---

41. सर्वे प्रस्रवणाः P3 K सर्वप्रस्रवणाः । 41. पुण्याः सदा सर्वा. P1 सर्वास्सदा पुण्या । 42. ददन्ति हि P1 ददन्त्यहो । 43. तथा P2 यथा । 44. सुखं परम् P1 परं सुखम् । 45. यत्र P1 तत्र ।

भारतमात्स्ययोः 'ऋषिभिः क्रतवः प्रोक्ता' इत्यादि 'यज्ञैरपि विशिष्यत' इत्यन्तमुक्त्वोक्तम् —

46. **अनुपोष्य त्रिरात्राणि तीर्थान्यनभिगम्य च ।**
अदत्त्वा काञ्चनं गाश्च दरिद्रो नाम जायते ॥
अग्निष्टोमादिभिर्यज्ञैरिष्ट्वा विपुलदक्षिणैः ।
न तत्फलमवाप्नोति तीर्थाभिगमनेन यत् ॥
महाभारत 3.80.39-40

(1) 'अनुपोष्ये'ति तेन त्रिरात्रोपवासादीनां चतुर्णां प्रत्येकं दारिद्र्याभावः फलमित्यर्थः

तथा—

47. **यान्यगम्यानि तीर्थानि दुर्गानि विषमाणि च ।**
मनसा तानि गच्छेत सर्वतीर्थसमीक्षया ॥
एतानि वसुभिः साध्यैरादित्यैर्मरुदश्विभिः ।
ऋषिभिर्देवकल्पैश्च श्रितानि सुकृतैषिभिः ॥
महाभारत 3.83.88-89

तथा—

48. **इयं राजर्षिभिर्याता पुण्यकृद्भिर्युधिष्ठिर ।**
मन्वादिभिर्महाराज तीर्थयात्रा महाफला ॥
महाभारत 3.90.10

तथा—

49. **अज्ञानेनापि यस्येह तीर्थयात्रादिकं भवेत् ।**
सर्वकामसमृद्धः स स्वर्गलोके महीयते ॥
स्थानं च लभेत नित्यं धनधान्यसमाकुलम् ।
ऐश्वर्यज्ञानसम्पन्नः सदा भवति धर्मवान् ॥
तारिताः पितरस्तेन नरकात् प्रपितामहा । इति ।

(1) 'अज्ञानेने'ति अत्रेदमनुष्ठेयम्, अनेनेदं फलमाप्यत इत्येवंज्ञानाभावेऽपि । बालादेरित्यर्थः ।

46.1. फलम् P3 K omitted. 47. यान्य P1 या न ।

वायुपुराणे—

50. तीर्थान्यनुसरन् वीरः श्रद्दधानः समाहितः ।
कृतपापो विशुध्येत किं पुनः शुद्धकर्मकृत् ॥
तिर्यग्योनिं न गच्छेच्च कुदेशे नैव जायते ।
स्वर्गे वसति वै विप्रो मोक्षमार्गंश्च विन्दति ॥

वायुपुराण 77.125,127

(1) इत्यलं सकलपुराणप्रसिद्धमहिमत्वात् तीर्थानाम् ।

---

50. विशुध्येत P2 विमुच्येत । 50. गच्छेच्च CI गच्छेत ।

अथ तीर्थस्वरूपम्

गारुडे—

51. **रजस्तमोविरहितैस्तपसा धूतकल्मषैः ।**
यदध्यासितमर्हद्भिस्तद्धि तीर्थं प्रचक्षते ॥

भारते—

52. **परिग्रहाच्च साधूनां पृथिव्याश्चैव तेजसा ।**
अतीव पुण्यभागास्ते सलिलस्य च तेजसा ॥

महाभारत 13.111.18

(1) 'तेजसा' प्रभावेण ।

तत् द्विविधम् । तदुक्तं भारते—

53. **लोकेऽस्मिन् द्विविधं तीर्थं स्वच्छन्दं देवनिर्मितम् ।**
स्वयंभूतं प्रभासाद्यं निर्मितं देवनिर्मितम् ॥

(प्र०ख० 1.28.27)

(1) पुनश्च चतुर्विधम् । तदुक्तं ब्रह्मपुराणे —

54. **नारद उवाच—**

कियन्ति तानि तीर्थानि किंफलानि सुरेश्वर ।
सर्वेषामेव तीर्थानां सर्वदा किं विशिष्यते ॥

ब्रह्मोवाच—

चतुर्विधानि तीर्थानि स्वर्गे मर्त्ये रसातले ।
दैवानि मुनिशार्दूल आसुराण्यार्षकाणि च ॥
मानुषाणि च लोकेषु विख्यातानि सुरादिभिः ।
ब्रह्मविष्णुशिवैर्देवैर्निर्मितं दैवमुच्यते ॥
त्रिभ्यो यदेकं जायेत तस्मान्नातः परं विदुः ॥

ब्रह्मपु० 70.15-17, 19

(1) यथा प्रभासपुष्करादीनि त्रिभ्यो जातत्वादतिश्रेष्ठानि ।

---

51. –कल्मषैः P1 किल्बिषैः । 53. स्वयंभूतम् P3 K स्वयंभूत– । 53.1 ब्रह्मपुराणे P3 K ब्रह्माण्डपुराणे ।

55. **गोदावरी भीमरथी तुङ्गभद्रा च वेणिका ।**
तापी पयोष्णी विन्ध्यस्य दक्षिणे तु प्रकीर्तिताः ॥
भागीरथी नर्मदा च यमुना च सरस्वती ।
विशोका च वितस्ता च हिमवत्पर्वताश्रिताः ॥
एता नद्यः पुण्यतमा देवतीर्थान्युदाहृताः ।

ब्रह्मपु० 70.33-35b

तथा—

56. **केनापि न कृतं यद् तद् देवखातमिति स्मृतम् । इति ।**

(1) गयकोलासुराद्यसुरप्रतिष्ठितान्यासुराणि । (2) वसिष्ठादिऋषि-प्रतिष्ठितान्यार्षाणि । (3) मान्धात्रम्बरीषहरिश्चन्द्रादिप्रतिष्ठितानि मानुषाणि । (4) भागीरथ्यादीनां तु सत्यपि दैवत्वे विष्ण्वादिदेवमूर्तित्वादतिवैशिष्ट्यम् । तदुक्तं स्कान्दे रेवाखण्डे—

57. **ब्राह्मी सरस्वती मूर्तिर्गङ्गा मूर्तिस्तु वैष्णवी ।**
नर्मदा शाङ्करी मूर्तिस्तिस्रो नद्यस्त्रिदेवताः ॥

तत्रापि गङ्गा—

58. **गङ्गेयं सरितां श्रेष्ठा सर्वकामप्रदायिनी ।**
त्रिदेवत्या मुनिश्रेष्ठ तदुत्पत्तिमतः शृणु ॥

(1) इत्यादिवचननिचयप्रतिपादितत्रिदेवत्यत्वादिगुणगणवत्त्वाद् अति-श्रेष्ठेति गङ्गामहिमप्रकरणे स्पष्टीभविष्यति ।

(2) पुनर्भौमान्तरिक्षत्रिलोकस्थभेदात् त्रिविधम् । (3) तत्र नैमिषं भौमं, पुष्करं त्वन्तरिक्षस्थं, कुरुक्षेत्रं त्रिलोकस्थम् । तदुक्तं भारते—

59. **पृथिव्यां नैमिषं पुण्यमन्तरिक्षे च पुष्करम् ।**
त्रयाणामपि लोकानां कुरुक्षेत्रं विशांपते ॥

महाभारत 3.81.173

ब्राह्मे—

60. **भौमानां मानसं तीर्थं मया वः परिकीर्तितम् ।**
पुष्करं चान्तरिक्षस्थं मम लोकस्य दुर्लभम् ॥ इति ।

---

55. एता P3 K पूता । 56.1 प्रतिष्ठितान्यासुराणि P3 प्रतिष्ठित्यासुराणि । 56.4–देव– P1 –देवता–। 57. मूर्तिस्तु, C1 मूर्तिश्च । 60. मया वः. P3 K मयाऽत्तः ।

प्रभासखण्डे महादेवः—

61. शृणु देवि प्रवक्ष्यामि तीर्थमाहात्म्यमुत्तमम् ।
पृथिव्यां नैमिषं तीर्थमन्तरिक्षे च पुष्करम् ॥
केदारञ्च प्रयागञ्च —। त्यादि ।

ब्रह्मपुराणे—

62. प्रयागञ्च कुरुक्षेत्रं नैमिषं पुष्करं तथा ।
गङ्गाद्वारञ्च कुब्जाम्रं बदरीसिन्धुसागरम् ॥

इत्यादितीर्थोद्देशः कृतः ।
काशीखण्डे—

63. प्रथमं तीर्थराजं तु प्रयागाख्यं सुविस्तरम् ।
काशीखण्ड 6.21 a-b

इत्यादिना षष्ठाध्याये तीर्थान्युक्तानि ।

64. वाराणस्यां महादेवं प्रयागे तु महेश्वरम् ।

इत्यादिना शिवपुराणे ऽष्टषष्टितीर्थान्युद्दिष्टानि ।

(1) तथा कौर्मे द्वादशेऽध्याये तीर्थोद्देशः कृतः ।

तथा काशीखण्डे—

65. शृणु देवि विशालाक्षि तीर्थं लिङ्गमुदाहृतम् ।
जलाशयेऽपि तीर्थाख्या जाता मूर्तिपरिग्रहात् ॥
मूर्तयो ब्रह्मविष्ण्वर्कशिवविघ्नेश्वरादिकाः ।
लिङ्गं शैवमिति ख्यातं यत्रैतत्तीर्थमेव तत् ॥
वाराणस्यां महादेवः प्रथमं तीर्थमुच्यते । इत्यादि ।
काशीखण्ड 97.5-7b

अन्यत्रापि—

66. शोणः सिन्धुर्हिरण्याक्षः पोष्यलोहितघर्घराः ।
शतद्रुश्च नदाः सप्त पावना ब्रह्मणः सुताः ॥

इत्यादि ।

---

64. द्वादशेऽध्याये P1 द्वादशाध्याये । 65. तीर्थं लिङ्गम् P3 K तीर्थलिङ्गम् ।
66. पोष्य- P2 K कोक- C1 C2 षोष्य- L1 पौष्य- L2 शोण- ।
66. घर्घराः P3 L1 षर्घराः C1 L2 बर्बराः ।

अथ गौणतीर्थानि

67. क्षेत्राग्न्यापः सुरा विप्रा गौर्गुरुस्तीर्थमुच्यते ।
निवासहोमस्नानार्चापोषतोषैः पुनाति तत् ॥

काशीखण्डे—

68. मानसान्यपि तीर्थानि सत्यादीनि च वै विप्रे ।
एतानि मुक्तिदान्येव नात्र कार्या विचारणा ॥
काशीखण्ड 6.26

तथा—

69. **सधर्मिण्युवाच—**

मानसान्यपि तीर्थानि यान्युक्तानि महामते ।
कानि कानि च तानीह ह्येतदाख्यातुमर्हसि ॥

ऋषिरुवाच—

शृणु तीर्थानि गदतो मानसानि ममानघे ।
येषु सम्यङ् नरः स्नात्वा प्रयाति परमां गतिम् ।
सत्यं तीर्थं क्षमा तीर्थं तीर्थमिन्द्रियनिग्रहः ।
सर्वभूतदया तीर्थं तीर्थमार्जवमेव च ॥
दानं तीर्थं दमस्तीर्थं सन्तोषस्तीर्थमुच्यते ।
ब्रह्मचर्यं परं तीर्थं तीर्थञ्च प्रियवादिता ॥
ज्ञानं तीर्थं धृतिस्तीर्थं तपस्तीर्थमुदाहृतम् ।
तीर्थानामपि तत्तीर्थं विशुद्धिर्मनसः परा ॥
न जलप्लुतदेहस्य स्नानमित्यभिधीयते ।
स स्नातो यो दमस्नातः श्रद्धाशुद्धमनोमलः ॥
योऽशुद्धः पिशुनः क्रूरो दाम्भिको विषयात्मकः ।
सर्वतीर्थेष्वपि स्नातः पापो मलिन एव सः ॥

---

67. पोषतोषैः P1 पोषैस्तोषैः P3 तोषशोषैः KL1 तोषपोषैः L2 पोषैः तोषैः ।

69. सधर्मिण्य P1 सहधर्मिण्य ।

न शरीरमलत्यागान्नरो भवति निर्मलः ।
मानसे तु मले त्यक्ते भवत्यन्तः सुनिर्मलः ॥
जायन्ते च म्रियन्ते च जलेष्वेव जलौकसः ।
न च गच्छन्ति ते स्वर्गमविशुद्धमनोमलाः ॥
विषयेष्वतिसंरागो मानसो मल उच्यते ।
तेष्वेव हि विरागोऽस्य नैर्मल्यं समुदाहृतम् ।
चित्तमन्तर्गतं दुष्टं तीर्थस्नानान्न शुध्यति ।
शतशोऽपि जलैर्धौतं सुराभाण्डमिवाशुचि ।
दानमिज्या तपः शौचं तीर्थसेवा श्रुतं तथा ।
सर्वाण्येतान्यतीर्थानि यदि भावो न निर्मलः ॥
निगृहीतेन्द्रियग्रामो यत्रैव वसते नरः ।
तस्य तत्र कुरुक्षेत्रं नैमिषं पुष्कराणि च ॥
ध्यानपूते ज्ञानजले रागदोषमलापहे ।
यः स्नाति मानसे तीर्थे स याति परमां गतिम् ॥
एतत्ते कथितं देवि मानसं तीर्थलक्षणम् ॥

काशीखण्ड 6.28-42b

मात्स्ये—

70. सत्यं तीर्थं दया तीर्थं तीर्थमिन्द्रियनिग्रहः ।
वर्णाश्रमाणां गेहेऽपि तीर्थं शम उदाहृतः ॥

मत्स्यपुराण 22.80

व्यासः—

71 आत्मा नदी संयमतोयपूर्णा सत्यह्रदा शान्ततरा दयोर्मिः ।
तत्राभिषेकं कुरु पाण्डुपुत्र न वारिणा शुध्यति चान्तरात्मा ॥

भारते दानधर्मेषु—

72. अगाधे विमले शुद्धे सत्यतोये धृतिह्रदे ।
स्नातव्यं मानसे तीर्थे सत्त्वमालम्ब्य शाश्वतम् ॥

महाभारत 13.111.3

तथा—

73. तत्त्ववित्त्वनहंबुद्धिस्तीर्थं प्रवरमुच्यते ॥

महाभारत 13.111.6 a–b

---

69. अतिसंरागो C1 अपि संरागो । 69. तीर्थसेवा P1 C2 तीर्थं सेवा । 69. यत्रैव P1 यत्र वै ।69. ध्यानपूते C1 C2 ज्ञानपूते । 69 यः P2 च । 69 एतत्ते C1 एवं ते ।

तथा

74. **स्नाति यो मानसे तीर्थे तत्स्नानं तत्त्वदर्शिनाम् ।**
समारोपितशौचस्तु नित्यं भावसमाहितः ॥
केवलं गुणसम्पन्नः शुचिरेव नरः सदा ।

महाभारत 13.111.13 c-14

(1) सत्यादिषु सत्स्वेव तीर्थफलाधिगमात् सत्त्वशोधकत्वाच्च सत्यादीनां गौणं तीर्थत्वमित्यत्र तात्पर्यम् ।

एवं तीर्थान्युक्त्वोक्तं काशीखण्डे—

75. **एतत्ते कथितं देवि मानसं तीर्थलक्षणम् ।**
भौमानामपि तीर्थानां पुण्यत्वे कारणं शृणु ॥
यथा शरीरस्योद्देशाः केचित् पुण्यतमाः स्मृताः ।
तथा पृथिव्यामुद्देशाः केचित् पुण्यतमाः स्मृताः ॥

(1) 'पुण्यानि सलिलानि चे'ति भारते पाठः

प्रभावादद्भुताद् भूमेः सलिलस्य च तेजसा ।
परिग्रहान्मुनीनाञ्च तीर्थानां पुण्यता स्मृता ॥ (=263)

(2) सलिलस्य तेजसा प्रभावेण सामर्थ्यादित्यर्थः

तस्माद् भौमेषु तीर्थेषु मानसेषु च नित्यशः ।
उभयेषु च यः स्नाति स याति परमां गतिम् ॥ इति ।

काशीखण्ड 6.42-45

(3) भारतेऽपि भीष्मेण 'एतत्ते कथितं राजन्नि'ति सम्बोधनभेदेनेदमेव सर्वमुक्तम् ।

दानधर्मेष्वपि—

76. **मनसश्च पृथिव्याश्च पुण्यास्तीर्थास्तथापरे ।**
उभयोरेव यः स्नायात् स सिद्धिं शीघ्रमाप्नुयात् ॥
यथा बलं क्रियाहीनं क्रिया वा बलवर्जिता ।
नेह साधयते कार्यं समायुक्ता तु सिध्यति ॥
एवं शरीरशौचेन तीर्थशौचेन चान्वितः ।
शुचिः सिद्धिमवाप्नोति द्विविधं शौचमुत्तमम् ॥ इति ।

महाभारत 13.111.19-21

74.1. गौणम् P3 K गौण–। 75. पृथिव्याम् P1 पृथिव्या। 75. मुनीनाञ्च P3 K मुनीनां तु। 75.3 एव सर्वम्। L1 एवम्। 76. पुण्यास्तीर्थास् C1 पुण्यतीर्थास्। 76. अवाप्नोति P2 एवाप्नोति।

अथ तीर्थयात्राधिकारिणः

तत्र—

77. या याः काश्चित् तीर्थयात्रा मुनीन्द्रैः
कृताः प्रयुक्ता ह्यनुमोदिताश्च ।
तां ब्रह्मचारी विधिवत् करोति
सुसंयतो गुरुणा संनियुक्त ॥

(1) इति ब्रह्मपुराणवचनाद् गुरुनियुक्तस्यैव ब्रह्मचारिणोऽधिकारः । (2) इयं चोपकुर्वाणकस्य वेदाध्ययनाविरोधेनैव गुरुनियोगाद् भवति । याज्ञवल्क्येन ब्रह्मचारिणमुपक्रम्य,

78. गुरुञ्चैवाप्युपासीत स्वाध्यायार्थं समाहितः
याज्ञ० 1.26 c-d

(1) इति स्वाध्यायार्थं गुरुमेवोपासीतेति नियमनात्।

(2) नैष्ठिकस्यापि गुर्वनुज्ञातस्यास्त्येवाधिकारः 'ब्रह्मचारी गुरुणा संनियुक्त' इत्यविशेषश्रवणात्।

गृहस्थस्यापि—

79. देहं सुपुष्टं विजरं तु यौवनं
लब्ध्वा न गङ्गानदिषु यान्ति ये नराः ।
स्नात्वा न पश्यन्ति हरिं महेश्वरं
दैवेन ते वै मुषिता नराधमा ॥

इति स्मरणात् ।

(1) "ननु नैतेन वचसा गृहस्थस्य तीर्थयात्रा विधातुं शक्या, तत्पदाश्रवणात्। (2) न च 'यौवनं लब्ध्वे' त्यादिलिङ्गात् तत्परत्वम् । (3) वचनान्तरविरोधेन ब्रह्मचर्यादिविषयत्वेनापि तदुपपत्तेः । तथाहि ब्रह्मपुराणे

80. यस्येष्टिधर्मेष्वधिकारितास्ति
वरं गृहं गृहधर्माश्च सर्वे ।
एवं गृहस्थाश्रमसंस्थितस्य
तीर्थे गतिः पूर्वतरैर्निषिद्धा ॥

78.1. नियमनात् P2 नियमात् । 78.2. अनुज्ञातस्यास्त्ये C1 अनुज्ञयास्त्ये ।

सर्वाणि तीर्थान्यपि चाग्निहोत्र-
तुल्यानि नैवेति वयं वदाम । इति । (=242)

तथा तत्रैव—

81. **यज्ञाधिकारेऽप्यथवा निवृत्ते विप्रस्तु तीर्थानि परिभ्रमेत्तु ।**
तीर्थेष्वलं यज्ञफलं हि यस्मात् प्रोक्तं मुनीन्द्रैरमलस्वभावैः ॥

कौर्मे—

82. **यः स्वधर्मान्परित्यज्य तीर्थसेवां करोति हि ।**
न तस्य तीर्थं फलति इह लोके परत्र चे- । ति" ।

कूर्मपुराण 2.42.20

(1) उच्यते; 'यस्येष्टिधर्मेष्वधिकारितास्ति गृहधर्मश्च सर्वं' इति विशेषोपादानाद्, 'यः स्वधर्मान्परित्यज्ये'ति चोक्तेर्यागाद्यनुष्ठानाशक्तस्य दरिद्रस्य निरधिकारस्य च गृहस्थस्यापि तीर्थयात्राया अविरुद्धत्वात् । (2) अत एव भारते 'ऋषिभिः क्रतवः प्रोक्ता' इत्युपक्रम्य 'न ते शक्या दरिद्रेणे'त्यादीनि पूर्वोदाहृतानि वाक्यान्युक्तानि ।

(3) यद्वा साग्निकस्य सपत्नीकस्यैव गृहस्थस्याधिकारः,

83. **सहाग्निर्वा सपत्नीको गच्छेत्तीर्थानि संयतः ।**
सर्वपापविनिर्मुक्तो यथोक्तां गतिमाप्नुयात् ॥

कूर्मपुराण 2.42.22

इति कूर्मपुराणोक्तेः,

84. **प्रायश्चित्ती व्रजेत्तीर्थं पत्नीविरहितोऽपि वा ।**
यज्ञेष्वनधिकारी वा यश्च वा मन्त्रसाधकः ॥
सहाग्निर्वा सपत्नीको गच्छेत्तीर्थानि संयत ।

इति स्मरणाच्च । अत एव ब्रह्मपुराणे कृकलवैश्योपाख्यानम्—

85. **कश्चित्कृकलो नाम वैश्यः कृततीर्थयात्रो**
'मया पितरस्तारिता' इति कृतार्थमात्मानं
मन्वानः स्वगृहं प्रस्थितो मार्गे सधर्मान्

---

81. परिभ्रमेत् P2 परिश्रमेत् । 82.2. न ते P1 ते न । 85. मन्वानः P1 मन्यमानः ।

पितॄनपश्यत् । 'न ते किञ्चित् तीर्थफलमस्ती'ति
तैरुक्तः 'कुतस्तीर्थफलं मे न जातं कथं न पितरस्तीर्णा'
इति चिन्तामीयिवान् । तमाह धर्मः—
पूतां पुण्यतमां भार्यां यो वा त्यक्त्वा प्रयाति हि ।
तस्य पुण्यफलं सर्वं वृथा भवति नान्यथे– ॥
त्यादि बहूक्त्वा
तया विना यतस्तीर्थे स्नानं दानं कृतं त्विह ।
तेन दोषेण वै बद्धास्तव पूर्वपितामहाः ॥
त्वया सा वञ्चिता मूढ चौरकर्म कृतं त्वया ।
अमी पितामहाश्चौरा यैर्भुक्तं तु तया विना ॥
भार्या पचति चैवान्नं स्वहस्तेनामृतोपमम् ।
तच्चान्नमेव भुञ्जन्ति पितरो हृष्टमानसाः ॥
तस्माद् भार्यां विना सिद्धिः पुरुषस्य न विद्यत ।
इति धर्मेणोक्ते 'कथं मे पितृमोचनं भवेद्' इति कृकलेन पृष्टे धर्म आह—
गच्छ गेहं महाभाग त्वां विना दुःखभागिनीं ।
सम्बोधय सुपुण्यां तां सुफलां धर्मचारिणीम् ॥
श्राद्धदानं गृहे गत्वा तस्या हस्तेन वै कुरु ।
स्मृत्वा पुण्यानि तीर्थानि पूजयस्व सुरोत्तमान् ॥
तीर्थयात्राकृता सिद्धिस्तव चैवं भविष्यति ।
(पद्मपुराण भ०ख० 59.8, 26, 30 b-c, 31-32, 60. 2-3)

(1) इत्येवमाद्युक्तम् । तेन सपत्नीकस्यैव गृहिणोऽधिकारः । (2) एतेन "निरग्निगृहिण एवाधिकारो न तु साग्नेर्" इति निरस्तम् ।

(3) विधुरस्यापि 'यज्ञाधिकारोऽप्यथवा निवृत्त' [81] इति ब्रह्मपुराणवचनादस्त्यधिकारः ।

(4) वानप्रस्थस्यापि

86. ऋणानि त्रीण्यपाकृत्य कुर्यात् तीर्थस्य सेवनम् ।
विधाय वृत्तिं भार्यायाः पुत्रेषु विनिधाय चे– ॥
कू०पु० 2.42.23

---

85. कुतस्तीर्थफलम्, कुतस्तीर्थे फलम् । 85. चौरा P3 चोरा । 85. गत्वा P3 K L2 कृत्वा । 85.1. इत्येवमाद्युक्तम् P3 K omitted. 85.2. निरग्निगृहिण P1 निरग्निकगृहिण । 85.4 वानप्रस्थस्यापि P3 वानप्रस्थोऽपि K वानप्रस्थेऽपि । 86. चेति P3 K वेति ।

ति कौर्मोक्तेः । (1) 'पुत्रेषु विनिधाये'त्यसपत्नीकस्य वानप्रस्थतापक्षे

87. **पुत्रेषु दारान् निक्षिप्य तया वानुगतो वन ।**

मनु 6.3c-d

इति मनुस्मरणात् । (1) 'तया वानुगत' इति पक्षे तु सभार्यस्यैव ।

(2) यतेरप्यस्त्यधिकारः,

88. **मुमुक्षुभिस्तीर्थगतं द्विजेन्द्रैः कार्यं तथा तत्फलकांक्षिभिश्च ।**
मातुः पितुः क्षेप्तुमनास्तथास्थि सुतस्तु कुर्यात् खलु तीर्थयात्राम् ॥

इति काशीखण्डात्, संन्यासमुपक्रम्य,

89. **ग्रामैकरात्रवासिनो नगरे तीर्थे च पञ्चरात्रं वसन्त**

इति कात्यायनेनानुज्ञानाच्च ।

(1) क्षत्रियस्याप्यधिकारः,

90. **सर्वस्वनाशेऽप्यथवा नृपस्तु स ब्राह्मणानग्रत एव कृत्वे– ।**

(1) ति ब्रह्मपुराणे ब्राह्मणपुरःसरस्य नृपस्यापि तच्छ्रवणात्, (2) भारते भीष्मबलभद्रपाण्डवादीनां तीर्थयात्राप्रतिपादनाच्च ।

(3) तथा वैश्यस्यापि ब्रह्मपुराणीयकृकलवैश्योपाख्यानात् । वक्ष्यमानवचनाच्च

(4) शूद्राणामपि भारते पुष्करं प्रकृत्य—

91. **ब्राह्मणः क्षत्रियो वैश्यः शूद्रो वा राजसत्तम ।**
न वियोनिं व्रजन्त्येते स्नातास्तीर्थे महात्मन ॥

महाभारत 3.80.51

इति लिङ्गात्; (1) पूर्वोदाहृतवचसां साधारण्याच्च ।

यत्तु मनुः—

92. **जपस्तपस्तीर्थयात्रा प्रव्रज्या मन्त्रसाधनम् ।**
देवताराधनञ्चेति स्त्रीशूद्रपतनानि षड् । इति

(अत्रि 136c-137b)

तथा —

93. **विप्रसेवैव शूद्रस्य विशिष्टं धर्मलक्षणम् ।**
यदतोऽन्यद्धि कुरुते तद् भवत्यस्य निःफलम् ॥

मनु 10.123

---

87. वन P2 L1 वनम् । 90. पाण्डवादीनाम् P1 पाण्डवानाम् । 90.4. शूद्राणाम् अपि L1 शूद्रस्यापि । 91. स्नाता C1 स्नात्वा । 93. निःफलम् P2 C2 K निष्फलम् ।

(1) इति तद् विप्रसेवाविरोधेन निरन्तरञ्च तीर्थयात्रादि न कार्यमित्येवं परम् । अत एवोक्तं भारते—

94. **शूद्रस्तु द्विजशुश्रूषाविरुद्धं धर्ममाचरन् ।**
नरके पच्यते तद्वद्वेदश्रवणकीर्तनाद् ॥ इति ।

शातातपोऽपि—

95. **निरन्तरं तीर्थसेवा संन्यासो मन्त्रसाधनम् ।**
देवताराधनं ध्यानं तेषां पापावहं परम् ॥

(1) इति शूद्रान् प्रतिलोमजांश्च 'तेषां'शब्देन परामृश्य निरन्तरं तीर्थसेवादि निषेधति । 'यदतोऽन्यद्धी'त्येतद्व्याख्याने

96. **इतरप्रतिषेधो ब्राह्मणसेवास्तुत्यर्थ**

मेधातिथि 10.123

इत्यप्युक्तं मेधातिथिना । (1) तस्माच्छूद्रस्याप्यस्ति द्विजशुश्रूषाऽविरोधेन तीर्थयात्राधिकारः ।

(2) सङ्करजेष्वपि मूर्धावसिक्तादीनामनुलोमजानामस्त्यधिकारः, तेषां द्विजातिजत्वेन द्विजधर्माधिकारात् । (3) प्रतिलोमजानामपि चास्ति,

97. **शूद्राणां तु सधर्माणः सर्वेऽपध्वंसजाः स्मृता ।**

मनु 10.41 c-d

इति स्मरणात् । (1) 'अपध्वंसजा' व्यभिचारजाः ।

(2) स्त्रिया अप्यधिकारः भारते पुष्करं प्रकृत्य—

98. **जन्मप्रभृति यत्पापं स्त्रिया वा पुरुषस्य वा ।**
पुष्करे गतमात्रस्य सर्वमेव प्रणश्यती– ॥

महाभारत 3.80.54

95.1. प्रतिलोमजांश्च P1 प्रति(लोम)ज्(आ)नुलोमजाश्च । 96.2 द्विजातिजत्वेन C1 L2 द्विजातित्वेन । 98. स्त्रिया C1 स्त्रियो ।

ति लिङ्गात् । (1) तत्र विधवाया विशेषतः—

99. **स्नानं दानं तीर्थयात्रां विष्णोर्नामग्रहं मुहुर् ।**

स्क०पुरा०ब्रह्मखण्ड 2.7.72c-d

इति स्कान्दे विधवाधर्मान् प्रकृत्योक्तेः । (1) तत्रापि न स्वातन्त्र्येण किन्तु पुत्रज्ञात्याद्यनुमतेनैव,

100. **बाल्यया यौवनवत्या वा वृद्धया वापि योषिता ।**
न स्वातन्त्र्येण कर्तव्यं किञ्चित् कार्यं गृहेष्वपी –॥

मनु 5.147

ति मनूक्तेः,

101. **रक्षेत् कन्यां पिता विन्नां पतिः पुत्रास्तु वार्धके ।**
अभावे ज्ञातयस्तेषां स्वातन्त्र्यं न क्वचित् स्त्रिया ॥

याज्ञ० 1.85

इति याज्ञवल्क्योक्तेश्च ।

सधवायास्तु भर्त्रा सहैव न पृथक्,

102. **नास्ति स्त्रीणां पृथग् यज्ञो न व्रतं नाप्युपोषणम् ।**
पतिं संसेवते या तु तेन स्वर्गे महीयत ॥

मनु 5.155

(1) इति मनूक्तौ यज्ञादीनामुपलक्षणत्वात्, (2) 'स्त्रीशूद्रपतनानि षड्' इति पूर्वोक्तमनुवचनस्य शूद्रन्यायेन भर्तृशुश्रूषात्यागविषयत्वाच्च ।

(3) तीर्थे मात्राद्यस्थिक्षेप्तुकामस्य सर्वस्यापि, 'मातुः पितुः क्षेप्तुमनास्तथास्थी'ति [88] पूर्वोक्तवाक्यात् ।

(4) कृतपापस्य तु तदपनोदनार्थं सर्वस्याप्यधिकारः,

103. **नृणां पापकृतां तीर्थं पापप्रशमनं भवेत् ।**
यथोक्तं फलदं तीर्थं भवेच्छुद्धात्मनां नृणाम् ॥

का०ख० 6.62 (=127, 178)

---

99. तीर्थयात्राम् K L2 तीर्थयात्रा । 99.1. अनुमतेनैव C1 अनुमत्यैव । 102.3. तथास्थी'ति P1 L1 तथास्थे'ति । 102.4. तदपनोदनार्थम् C2 तदपनोदार्थम् । 103. यथोक्तम् P3 K L1 यथोक्त– ।

इत्युक्तेः,

104. **प्रायश्चित्ती च विबुधस्तथा यायावरो गृही ।**
प्रकुर्यात् तीर्थसंसेवां ये चान्ये तादृशा जना ॥

कू०पु० 2.42.21

इति कौर्मोक्तेश्च । (1) प्रायश्चित्तार्थतीर्थयात्रायां तु गृहस्थस्यापि पत्नी-रहितस्याधिकारः,

105. **प्रायश्चित्ती व्रजेत् तीर्थं पत्नीविरहितोऽपि चे- ।** (=84)

ति वचनात्, (1) अकृतप्रायश्चित्तस्यान्येन सह संसर्गनिषेधाच्च ।

अथ तीर्थफलतारतम्यकारणानि

शङ्खः

106. **तीर्थं प्राप्य प्रसङ्गेन स्नानं तीर्थे समाचरेत् ।**
स्नानजं फलमाप्नोति तीर्थयात्राकृतं न तु ॥

शङ्ख 8.12 (=321)

(1) 'प्रसङ्गेने'ति वाणिज्यराजसेवादिप्रसङ्गेनेत्यर्थः । यत्तु पैठीनसिः—

107. **अर्धं तीर्थफलं तस्य यः प्रसङ्गेन गच्छति ।**
षोडशांशं स लभते यः परार्थेन गच्छती- ॥ (=605)

ति, (1) तत्र 'प्रसङ्गेन' उद्देश्यतीर्थान्तरप्रसङ्गेनेत्यर्थः । (2) 'परार्थेन' वेतनं गृहीत्वेत्यर्थः । (3) प्रभासखण्डे तु 'परान्नेन गच्छती'ति पाठः [प्रभा० खण्ड 1.28.35d] । तत्र परान्नं भुञ्जान इत्यर्थः ।

प्रभासखण्डे—

108. **यश्चान्यं कारयेच्छक्त्या तीर्थयात्रां तथेश्वरः ।**
स्वकीयद्रव्ययानाभ्यां तस्य पुण्यं चतुर्गुणम् ॥

(प्रभा०खण्ड 1.28.23)

(1) विशिष्टनयने त्वष्टगुणम् । तदुक्तं भारते युधिष्ठिरं प्रति—

109. **नेता च त्वमृषीन् यस्मात्तेन तेऽष्टगुणं फलम् । इति ।**

महाभारत 3.83.99c-d

अथ यानविशेषकृतं फलतारतम्यम्

मात्स्यकौर्मयोर्मार्कण्डेयः—

110. कथयिष्यामि ते वत्स तीर्थयात्राविधिं क्रमात् ।
आर्षेणैव विधानेन यथादृष्टं यथाश्रुतम् ॥
प्रयागतीर्थयात्रार्थी यः प्रयाति नरः क्वचित् ।
बलीवर्दसमारूढः शृणु तस्यापि यत्फलम् ।
नरके वसते घोरे गवां क्रोधो हि दारुणः ॥
सलिलञ्च न गृह्णन्ति पितरस्तस्य देहिनः ।

मत्स्यपु० 106.3-5
कूर्मपु० 1.35.1-3

तथा तत्रैव—

111. ऐश्वर्यलोभान्मोहाद् वा गच्छेद् यानेन यो नरः ।
विफलं तस्य तत्तीर्थं तस्माद् यानं परित्यजेत् ॥

मत्स्यपु० 106.7.
कूर्मपु० 1.35.5

तथा—

112. गोयाने गोवधः प्रोक्तो हययाने तु निःफलम् ।
नरयाने तदर्धं स्यात् पद्भ्यां तच्च चतुर्गुणम् ॥

(1) 'पदभ्याम्' इति केवलाभ्यामित्यर्थः ।

(2) "एतेनोपानत्त्यागे फलमधिकम्, तत्परिधानं तु न दोषाय, किन्त्वावश्यकमेव,

113. वर्षातपे सदा छत्री दण्डी रात्र्याटवीषु च ।
शरीरत्राणकामो वै सोपानत्कः सदा व्रजेद् ॥

वि०पु० 3.12.38

(1) इति विष्णुपुराणे 'सदा' शब्दबलात् तीर्थयात्रायामपि शरीररक्षाया आवश्यकत्वात्, निषेधाभावाच्चेति सूचयति,

---

अध्यायशीर्षक, यानविशेषकृतम् P3 K यानविशेषकृत– । 112. निःफलम्; K निष्फलम् । 113. च C2 वा ।

114. **तीर्थानुगमनं पद्भ्यां तपः परमिहोच्यते ।**
तदेव कृत्वा यानेन स्नानमात्रफलं लभेद् ॥

प्रभा०खण्ड 1.28.72

(1) इति प्रभासखण्डे पदगमनमात्रस्योक्तत्वाद् यानस्य च निन्दितत्वात्, (2) सोपानत्कत्वेऽपि पदगमनाक्षतेरुपानहोऽपि यानत्वाभावाच्चे"ति कश्चित् । तन्न,

115. **द्विर्भोजनं तृतीयांशं हरेत्तीर्थफलस्य च ।**
यानमर्धं चतुर्थांशं छत्रोपानहमेव च ॥
तस्मादेतैर्विहीनस्तु सर्वं तीर्थफलं लभेद् ।

इति जाबालिवचनविरोधात्,

116. **यानमर्धफलं हन्ति तदर्धं छत्रपादुके ।**
वाणिज्यं त्रींस्तथा भागान् सर्वं हन्ति प्रतिग्रह ॥

इति वचनविरोधाच्च । (1) यानप्रयुक्तस्तु दोषोऽत्र मा भूत्, विशेषोक्तस्तु छत्रवद् भविष्यति । (2) किञ्च—यद्युपानत्परिधानमावश्यकं तर्हि तत्त्यागे कथं फलाधिक्यम् । (3) प्रत्युत प्रत्यवाय एव भवेत् ।

(4) न च "एतेन 'राजपुपुरोहितौ सायुज्यकामौ यजेयाताम्' इतिवद् द्वन्द्वलभ्यसाहित्यविवक्षया केवलोपानत्परिधाने न चतुर्थांशन्यूनते"ति वाच्यम्, वैषम्यात् । (5) तत्र ह्युपादेयकर्तृगतत्वात् विवक्षा ।(6) इह तूद्देश्यगतत्वाद् 'यस्य पुरोडाशौ क्षायत' इतिवत् साहित्याविवक्षेति । (7)तस्मादुपानत्परिधानं दुष्टमेव ।

(8) "ननु तथापि विरोधः । पद्भ्यां गच्छतश्चतुर्गुणं सोपानत्कस्य चतुर्थांशन्यूनम् । यानान्तरवतस्तु ततोऽपि न्यूनम् (9) तथा च पूर्णफलं कस्य भवतीति ?" (10) उच्यते; 'चतुर्गुण'मित्यत्र गुणशब्दः 'कृते चतुर्गुणो धर्म' इतिवत् पादापरपर्यायचतुर्थांशपरः । (11) तथा च 'पद्भ्यां गच्छतस्तत्फलं चतुर्गुणं चतुश्चरणं पूर्णमि'त्यर्थः ।

(12) अन्ये तु "पादगमनं प्रशंसितुं चतुर्गुणोक्तिर्न तु फलार्थमि"त्याहुः । गोभिलः—

117. **गोभिर्युक्तेन यानेन तीर्थयात्रां करोति यः ।**
स याति नरकं घोरं यावद्गोरोमसंख्यया ॥

114.1 निन्दितत्वात् P1 निराकृतत्वात् । 116.1. प्रयुक्तस्तु दोषो C2 प्रयुक्तदोषो । 116.9. पूर्ण- C2 पूर्णम् ।

(1) तत्सर्वं यानेन सकलमार्गातिवाहने ज्ञेयम् । (2) किञ्चिद्दूरं यान गमने तु क्रोशयोजनादिगणनया फलतारतम्यमूह्यम् ।

अत्र "मात्स्ये—

118. **भगवन्केन विधिना गन्तव्यं धर्मनिश्चयैः ।**
प्रयागे यो विधिः प्रोक्तस्तन्मे ब्रूहि महामते ॥
म०पु० 106.2

(1) इति युधिष्ठिरेण पृष्टे 'कथयिष्यामी'त्युपक्रम्य 'प्रयागतीर्थयात्रार्थी' [110] त्यादिमार्कण्डेयेनाभिधानात् प्रयागप्रकरणत्वावगमाद् याननिषेधो याने विफलत्वाभिधानञ्च प्रयागमात्रविषयमेव । (2) तीर्थान्तरे तु किञ्चित् फलस्य न्यूनतेति" कल्पतरौ ।

(3) तदिदं चिन्त्यम्, गोभिलजाबाल्यादिवाक्यानां सामान्यतीर्थपरत्वात् तदनुसारेण मात्स्यवाक्यानामपि प्रकरणं भित्त्वा प्रकृताप्रकृततीर्थपरत्वस्यौचित्यात्; (4) अवयुत्यानुवादतया प्रकरण एव वा निवेशात् । (5) कश्चित्तु 'विफलं तस्य तत्तीर्थम्' [111] इतिसामान्येनोक्तेः श्रुत्या प्रकरणं बाधित्वा 'प्रयागतीर्थयात्रार्थी'त्यस्यापि [110] तीर्थमात्रोपलक्षणार्थम् अवयुत्यानुवादतेत्यभ्युपगम्य सकलतीर्थपरतां मात्स्यस्याह ।

(6) तन्न, व्रीह्याग्नेय्यादिश्रुतिवत् तीर्थशब्दरूपायाः श्रुतेः प्रकरणानुगुणत्वसम्भवे एकविंशत्याद्यनुवचन इव दर्शपूर्णमासाङ्गत्वप्रापकप्रकरणबाधेन श्रौतप्रतिष्ठादिफलार्थत्वावधारणमूलभूतश्रुतिलिङ्गादिसूत्रस्थसमवायशब्दोक्तविरोधाभावात् । (7) अन्यथा व्रीह्याग्नेयीशब्दादेरपि प्रकरणबाधेन सकलव्रीह्याग्नेयीपरत्वसम्भवाद् भोजनार्थव्रीहीनाम् प्रोक्षणादि अप्रकृततया चाग्नेय्याग्नीध्रोपस्थानं प्रसजत् केन मीमांसकेन वारणीयम् ।(8)इत्यलं भूयसा—प्रकृतमनुसरामः ।

यत् प्रभासखण्डे—

119. **कुरुक्षेत्रादितीर्थानि रथगम्यानि यानि तु ।**
तान्येव ब्राह्मणो यायाद् याने दोषो न तेषु वै ॥ इति,
प्रभा०ख० 1.28.17

तद् अशक्तविषयम्,

117.1 तत् P1 P2 एतत् । 118.5. सामान्येनोक्तेः P1 (+correction of P2) सामान्योक्तेः । 118.5. अनुवादतेत्य P3 K अनुवादेनेत्य । 118.5. –परताम् P1 C1 परता ।

120. **असमर्थस्तु यानेन तीर्थयात्रां समाचरन् ।**
तदुक्तं फलमाप्नोति स्वशक्त्या धर्ममाचरन्नि– ॥

(1) ति गोभिलेन तरय यानाभ्यनुज्ञानात् ।

तथा कूर्मपुराणे—

121. **नरयानं चाश्वतरीहयादिसहितो रथः ।**
तीर्थयात्रास्वशक्तानां यानं दोषकरं नहि ॥

अत्र

122. "**नौकायानमयानं स्याद् ।**

(1) इति वचनान्नौकायाने न दोष" इति कश्चित् । तन्न, साक्षात् स्वशरीरव्यापारासाध्यबुद्धिपूर्वकदेशान्तरप्राप्तिसाधनतया नौकाया अपि यानत्वान्निषेधविषयत्वेन सर्वत्र वर्जनीयत्वे प्रसक्ते यत्र नावा विना गमनमेव न सम्भवति शङ्खोद्धारगङ्गासागरादौ यावति च मार्गप्रदेशे नद्याद्याक्रान्ते तद्व्यतिरेकेण गमनासम्भवस्तत्र दोषाभावप्रतिपादकत्वेन विषयलाभे चरणगम्यतीर्थविषयेऽपि नावायाने दोषाभावे प्रमाणाभावात्, (2) विपर्यये यानत्वेन प्रमाणसत्त्वाच्च ।

(3) कश्चित्तु "पशुरूपाणामपि गवाश्वव्यतिरिक्तानामजादीनां गवाश्वप्रशंसार्थम् 'अपशवो वा अन्ये गोअश्वेभ्यः पशवो गोअश्वा' इति वचनेनापशुत्वकथनवद् अत्रापि यानरूपाया अपि नावोऽश्वादियानप्रशंसार्थमयानत्वकीर्तनमि"त्याह । (4) तन्न, पूर्वोक्तविषयलाभे सम्भवति अर्थवादताकल्पनस्यान्याय्यत्वात् । (5) किञ्च; अश्वादियानप्रशंसायां तेन यातव्यमित्येवापद्येत । (6) अथाश्वादेः प्रशस्तयानत्वात् तत्रैव यानकृतो दोषो नावि तु न कश्चिदल्पो वेत्यभिप्रायः । (7) तदा गतमर्थवादतोपपादनप्रयासेन, यानान्तरतः प्रयासाधिक्याभावेन नाविकस्पर्शादिदोषेण च दोषाधिक्यस्यैवोचितत्वाच्च । (8) न चास्ति यानान्तरनिषेधेनैकवाक्यता येनार्थवादता भवेत् ।

(9) "अथाशक्तविषयमिदं कुतो न भवति ?" (10) न भवति पूर्वोक्तवचनैस्तं प्रति यानान्तराणामप्यनिषेधाद् विशेषेणैतस्यावक्तव्यत्वात्, (11) अवयुत्यानुवादताप्रसङ्गाच्च । (12) तस्मादस्मदुक्त एवास्य विषय, इत्यलं भूयसा ।

---

120. समाचारन् P2 समाचरेत् । 120. तदुक्तम् C1 तदुक्त– । 120.1, तथा C1 अथ । 122.2 यानत्वेन P3 K यानत्वे । 122.3. अयानत्वकीर्तनम् C2 अयानत्वोत्कीर्तनम् । 122.10. न भवति C1 K omitted.

एतेन

123. **आधारतां गतं यत् स्वगत्या देशान्तरं प्रापयति तद्यानम् ।**
रथनौकादि तु न तथेति न तद् यानमतो न तेन गमने दोष

(1) इति महार्णवप्रकाशकारोक्तिः पराकृता, रथनौकयोरपि लक्षण-सत्त्वात् । (2) जलप्रवाहादावतिव्याप्तेश्चेति दिक् । (3) तस्मान्नौकायाने दोष एव ।

(4) तत्रापि अनेकदिनकनौकायानमात्रसाध्यानि यानि तीर्थानि समुद्रद्वीपनिष्ठानि तत्र द्विजैर्न गन्तव्यम्,

124. **द्विजस्याब्धौ तु नौयातुः शोधितस्यापि संग्रह ।**

इति कलिनिषिद्धेषु परिगणनात् । (1) अस्य किञ्चिद् गमनमात्रे पातकाप्रसक्तेः प्रायश्चित्ताख्यशोधनायोगात् तत्प्रसक्तिमदनेकदिनगमनविषयत्वात् ।

(2) येषामपि अङ्गवङ्गादिदेशानां गमनं निषिद्धं तत्रापि तीर्थयात्रो-द्देशेन गमने न निषेधः ।

125. **अङ्गवङ्गकलिङ्गेषु सौराष्ट्रमगधेषु च ।**
तीर्थयात्रां विना यातः पुनः संस्कारमर्हती – ॥

ति स्मृतेः । (1) एवं प्रान्त्यदेशेष्वपि द्रष्टव्यम् ।

इति श्रीमद्भट्टरामेश्वरसूरिसूनुनारायणभट्टविरचिते त्रिस्थलीसेतौ यानविचारः

125.1. प्रान्त्य—, K (+Correction in C2) प्रत्यन्त– । 125.1. मद्भट्ट-रामेश्वरसूरिसूनु– C1 Omitted.

अथ फलतारतम्यप्रसङ्गात् प्रायश्चित्तार्थयात्रायां योजनतारतम्यात् फलतारतम्यं वक्तुं तीर्थप्रत्याम्नाया उच्यन्ते

(125.2) तत्र तावत् तीर्थयात्रायाः पापक्षयार्थत्वे मूलभूतानि वचनानि । (3) तत्र 'तीर्थान्यनुसरन्नि'त्यादीनि [50] तीर्थप्रशंसायामुक्तानि ।

126. **पाण्डवै राज्यलाभाय दुरितोपशमाय च ।**
श्रीकृष्णनारदव्यासश्रीकण्ठेन्द्राजरोमशैः ॥
मार्कण्डेयपौलस्त्याजसप्तर्षिप्रमुखैस्तथा ।
द्वादशद्वादशाब्दानि कृच्छ्राण्यादाय भक्तितः ॥
तीर्थैरकुर्वन्नित्यादिपुराणे श्रूयते कथे—।

(1) त्यादिपुराणोक्तेस्तीर्थयात्रायाः प्राजापत्यकृच्छ्रादिप्रायश्चित्तप्रत्याम्नायतावगम्यते ।

काशीखण्डे च—

127. **नृणां पापकृतां तीर्थं पापप्रशमनं भवेद् । इति ।**
काशीखण्ड 6.62 a-b (=103, 178)

तथा

128. **प्रायश्चित्ती व्रजेत्तीर्थं पत्नीविरहितोऽपि वे–। ति**
(=84, 105)

देवलः—

129. **अभिसंगम्य तीर्थानि पुण्यान्यायतनानि च ।**
प्रमुच्यन्ते नराः पापाद् ब्राह्मणा ये तपस्विनः ॥
सर्वाः समुद्रगाः पुण्याः सर्वे पुण्या नगोत्तमाः ।
सर्वमायतनं पुण्यं सर्वे पुण्या वनाश्रया ॥ इति ।

(1) एवं तीर्थयात्रायाः प्रायश्चित्तार्थतयाचरणे स्मृत्यर्थसाराद्युक्तः प्रकारो लिख्यते । (2) तत्र प्रायश्चित्तविधिना सङ्कल्पपूर्वकं पद्भ्यां षष्टियोजनागतस्य भागीरथ्यां स्नानं षडब्दकृच्छ्रसमम् । (3) अत्रैकैकस्य यात्रयोजनस्य वृद्धा-

---

128. वेति P3 K चेति । 129. ब्राह्मणा ये L1 ब्राह्मणाश्च ।

वर्धकृच्छ्रवृद्धिः परिकल्पनीया । (4) षष्टियोजनागतस्य षडब्दत्वाद् दशयोजनागतस्याब्दप्रायश्चित्तं भवति । (5) एवञ्च तृतीयांशाधिकक्रोशादागतस्य भागीरथ्यां विध्युक्तस्नानेनैकः कृच्छ्रः सिध्यति मध्ये चेत् पर्वतादिव्यवधानम् । (6) तदभावे मार्गस्यादुर्गमत्वे च योजनागतस्य शक्तस्य गङ्गास्नानेनैकः कृच्छ्रः । (7) अशक्तस्य त्वर्धयोजनादागतस्य शक्तस्यापि मार्गस्य दुर्गमत्वेऽर्धयोजनादागतस्येत्येवंकल्पम् ।

(8) पूर्वं सप्तमातृका रक्षोभयान्नद्यो जाताः । भये गते पुनर्देवता अभवन् । ततो नद्यः शुष्काः । तेषु स्थलेषु भागीरथी समभूत् । (9) तासु विष्णुगङ्गादिसप्तमातृकानामासु गङ्गासु स्नानं षष्टियोजनागतस्य षडब्दकृच्छ्रसमम् । (10) प्रयागे वाराणस्यां गङ्गाद्वारे गङ्गासागरसङ्गमे च द्विगुणम् । (11) यमुनायां विंशतियोजनागतस्य स्नानं द्व्यब्दसमम् । (12) मथुरायां द्विगुणम् । (13) सरस्वत्यां चत्वारिंशद्योजनागतस्य चतुरब्दसमम् । (14) प्रभासे द्वारवत्याञ्च द्विगुणम् । (15) यमुनासरस्वत्योर्यात्रायोजनवृद्धौ पादकृच्छ्रवृद्धिः परिकल्प्या । (16) ह्रासस्तु पर्वताद्यभावमार्गसुगमदुर्गमतादौ पूर्वोक्तरीत्यैव कल्प्यः ।

(17) अत्रापि स्नानदिनसंख्या कल्प्या

130. **त्रिभिः सारस्वत्यं तोयं सप्ताहेन तु यामुनम् ।**
सद्यः पुनाति गाङ्गेयं दर्शनादेव नार्मदम् ॥
(पद्मपु० आदिखण्ड 13·7)

इति स्कन्दपुराणवचनात् ।

(1) दृशद्वतीशुतुद्रीविपाशावितस्ताशरावतीमरुद्वृद्धामधुमतीपयस्विनीघृतवतीत्यादिदेवनदीषु स्नानं पञ्चदशयोजनागतस्य त्रिंशत्कृच्छ्रसमम् । (2) चन्द्रभागावेत्रवतीशरयुगोमतीदेविकाकौशिकीमन्दाकिनीनित्यजलासहस्रवक्त्रापौनःपुन्यापूर्णपुन्याबाहुदावारुणीगण्डक्यादिदेवनदीषु स्नानं पञ्चदशयोजनागतस्य पञ्चदशकृच्छ्रसमम् । (3) एतासु महानदीषु परस्परसङ्गमे योजनागतस्य कृच्छ्रत्रयम् । (4) समुद्रगामहानदीभिः पूर्वोक्तदेवनदीनां सङ्गमे योजनागतस्य षट्कृच्छ्रफलम् ।

(5) अनुक्तस्थले यात्रायोजनसंख्यया कृच्छ्रसंख्या विज्ञेया । (6) महानदेषु महानद्यर्धफलम् । (7) शोणमहानदे तु

129.7. कल्पम् L2 वक्तव्यम् । 129.9. –नामासु K –नाम् अप्सु । 129.11 यमुनायाम् P1 यमुनायाञ्च । 129.12 मथुरायाम् P1 मथुरायाञ्च । 129.15 –वृद्धौ; K वृद्ध्यै ।

गङ्गार्धफलम् । (130.8) नदेषु नद्यर्धफलम् ।

(9) माहिष्मत्यादौ नित्यप्रत्यक्षाग्नौ होमे प्राकृताद् दशगुणम् । (10) ज्वालामुख्यामप्येवम् । (11) गणमहानदीसेतुरामेश्वरपद्मनाभश्रीरङ्ग-पुरुषोत्तमकुरुक्षेत्रनैमिषबदर्याश्रमपुण्यारण्यकेदार श्रीशैलमहालयरुद्रकोटिपुष्कर-नर्मदाम्रातकेश्वरकुब्जाम्रप्रभासकोकामुखविजयेशपुरी न्द्रपञ्चनदगोकर्णमथुरायोध्या-द्वारवतीगयाकाञ्चीशालग्रामशम्भलग्रामसंनिहत्यादि मुक्तिक्षेत्राणि संसेव्य गङ्गासमं फलं लभते ।

(12) चतुर्विंशतियोजनागतस्य नर्मदायां स्नानं चतुर्विंशतिकृच्छ्रफलम् । (13) कुब्जिकासंगमे द्विगुणम् । (14) शुक्लतीर्थे चतुर्गुणम् । (15) अष्ट-योजनागतस्य ताप्यामष्टकृच्छ्रसमम् । (16) पयोष्ण्यामप्येवम् । (17) अत्र संगमे द्विगुणम् ।

(18) षष्टियोजनागतस्य गोदावर्यां त्र्यब्दकृच्छ्रसमम् । (19) त्रिशद्योजनागतस्यैकादशतीर्थेषु प्रतिलोमानुलोमस्नानं षष्टिकृच्छ्रसमम् । (20) वञ्जरासङ्गमे द्विगुणम् । (21) सप्तगोदावरे भीमेश्वरे त्रिगुणम् । (22) कुशतर्पणे वञ्जरायां द्वादशयोजनागतस्य द्वादशकृच्छ्रसमम् । (23) प्रणीतायामष्टयोजनागतस्याष्टकृच्छ्रफलम् । (24) पूर्णायां तदर्धम् । (25) कृष्णवेणायां योजनसंख्यया कृच्छ्रसंख्या । (26) तथा तुङ्गभद्रायामपि । (27) पम्पासङ्गमे द्विगुणम् । (28) हरिहरे त्रिगुणम् । (29) भीमरथ्यां योजनसंख्यया कृच्छ्रसंख्या । (30) ककुद्मिनीसङ्गमे दशयोजनागतस्य पञ्चदशकृच्छ्राः । (31) मलापहारिण्यां योजनसंख्यया कृच्छ्रसंख्या । (32) तथा निवृत्यामपि ।

(33) गोदावर्यां यात्रायोजनवृद्धौ पादकृच्छ्रवृद्धिः । (34) सिंहे गुरौ सर्वत्र जाह्नवीसमा । (35) कन्यास्थे गुरौ कृष्णवेणायां सर्वत्र जाह्नव्यर्धम् । (36) तुङ्गभद्रायां तुलास्थे रवौ कर्कस्थे च गङ्गार्धम् । (37) कृष्णवेणायां मलापहारिणीसङ्गमे त्रिशद्योजनागतस्य त्रिश-त्कृच्छ्रसमम् । (38) भीमरथीसङ्गमे द्विगुणम् । (39) तुङ्गभद्रासङ्गमे त्रिगुणम् । (40) निवृत्तिसङ्गमे चतुर्गुणम् । (41) ब्रह्मेश्वर पञ्चगुणम् ।

(42) मल्लिकार्जुनसमीपे पातालगङ्गायां त्रिशद्योजनागतस्य षडब्दसमम् । (43) ततः पूर्वे षष्टिकृच्छ्रसमम् । (44) लिङ्गालये द्विगुणम् । (45) समुद्र-सङ्गमे चैवम् ।

130.8. नदेषु; C1 नदे तु । 130.11. गण–; P3 K गङ्गा–, C1 omitted. 130.11. मथुरा; C1 मधुरा । 130.18. त्र्यब्द–; P2 P3 C2 K L1 अब्द–। 130.28. हरिहरे; L2 हरिद्वारे । 130.33. पाद–; P1 (+correction in P2) सपाद–.

(46) कावेर्यां महानद्यां दशयोजनागतस्य पञ्चदशकृच्छ्राः। (47) ताम्रपर्णीकीर्तिमालापयस्विनीषु द्वादशयोजने द्वादशकृच्छ्राः।

(130.48) सह्याद्रिपादोद्भूता नद्यो योजनमविच्छिन्नप्रवाहरूपाश्च दैर्घ्यानुसारेणयोजनागतस्यैकद्वित्रिकृच्छ्रफलदाः। (49) विन्ध्यश्रीशैलोद्भवा द्विगुणाः। (50) हिमाचलोद्भूतास्त्रिगुणाः। (51) स्मृतिपुराणादिषु यथाकथञ्चिद् अनुक्तकुल्या योजनागतस्य त्रिरात्रफलदाः। (52) अल्पनद्यः कृच्छ्रफलदाः। (53) नद्यो द्विकृच्छ्रफलदाः। (54) महानद्यः कृच्छ्रत्रयफलदाः। (55) एकयोजनगादिषड्योजनगान्ताः स्रवन्त्यः कुल्याः। (56) ततो द्वादशयोजनगान्ता अल्पनद्यः। (57) ततश्चतुर्विंशतियोजनगान्ता नद्यः। (58) तदधिकयोजनगा महानद्यः। (59) समुद्रगाश्च। (60) यत्र च महानदीव्यपदेशः पुराणादिषु ता अपि महानद्यः। (61) उपवासयुक्तं महानदीस्नानं योजनादर्वागपि कृच्छ्रसमम्। (62) शुन्यादिकुत्सितनाम्न्यः पापनद्यश्च कर्मनाशाद्या वर्ज्याः।

(63) समुद्रस्नानं सर्वत्र दर्शे कार्यम्। (64) देवतासमीपे सरोनदीसङ्गमेषु च सर्वदा। (65) समुद्रस्नानं पञ्चदशयोजनागतस्य तावत्कृच्छ्रसमम्। (66) प्रसिद्धदेवतासमीपे द्विगुणम्। (67) तत्र स्नात्वा तद्देवतादर्शने त्रिगुणम।

(68) त्रिंशद्योजनागतस्य सेतुदर्शनं त्रिंशत्कृच्छ्रसमम्। (69) तत्र स्नात्वा रामेश्वरदर्शने द्विगुणम्।

(70) विन्ध्यदेशीयानां सेतुरामेश्वरे जाह्नव्यास्त्रिगुणम्। (71) तद्देशीयानामेव जाह्नवीकेदारयोस्तद्वदेव। (72) दक्षिणदेशीयानां जाह्नव्यां षड्गुणम्। (73) गङ्गादेशीयानां सेतुरामेश्वरे षड्गुणम्। (74) स्कन्ददर्शने विंशतिकृच्छ्रसमं त्रिंशद्योजनागतस्य। (75) यत्र गङ्गा संज्ञास्ति तत्राप्येवम्।

(76) सर्वत्र भाषाभेदपर्वतादिभिर्व्यवधाने मार्गस्य दुर्गमत्वे चोक्तयोजनसंख्यातो योजनसंख्याह्रासेन कृच्छ्रादिफलानि कल्प्यानि, प्रयासाधिक्यात्।

(77) श्रीरङ्गपद्मनाभपुरुषोत्तमचक्रकोटमहालक्ष्मीदर्शनस्थाने लोणारे च त्रिंशद्योजनागतस्य त्रिंशत्कृच्छ्रसमम्। (78) सर्ववैष्णवमाहेश्वरसौरशाक्तेयपीठेषु दर्शनेन योजनसंख्यया कृच्छ्रसंख्या। (79) प्रख्यातेषु द्विगुणम्।

(80) अनुक्तेषु योजनसंख्यया कृच्छ्रसंख्या ज्ञेया। (81) तत्रापि देवदर्शनदेशकालवयःशक्तिनियमविशेषेण विशेषो, न्यूनतया न्यूनता वा ज्ञेया।

130.50. हिमाचलोद्भूतास्; C2 हिमाचलोद्भवास्। 130.53. द्विकृच्छ्र–; L1 द्विगुणकृच्छ्र-। 130.62. शुन्यादि–; P3 C2 Kश्रुत्यादि–। 130.76. चोक्त–; P2 वोक्त—। 130.77. -चक्रकोट–; C1 L1 -चक्रकोटर– ;

(82) यत्र च पुराणादौ यच्च यावच्च विशेषत उक्तं तत् तथैव ग्राह्यम्।

(83) तीर्थतीरस्थितस्यापि योजनपरिमितात् प्रदेशाद् आगमनमन्तरेणापि विधिवत् स्नात्वा धौतं वासः परिधाय केशेषु शुष्केषु पुनः स्नातव्यम्। (84) एवं द्वादशभिः स्नानैरेकः कृच्छ्रो भवति।

(85) यात्रायाम् एकभक्ताधःशयनानृतुब्रह्मचर्याद्या नियमाः पूर्वोक्ता ग्राह्याः। (86) तीर्थे स्नानतर्पणादि। (87) तत्तद्देवतायाश्च पूजनमित्येतदन्ता तीर्थयात्रा सर्वत्र ज्ञेया।

(88) अत्र कृच्छ्रः प्राजापत्यसंज्ञो याज्ञवल्क्योक्तो ग्राह्यः। यथा—

131. **एकभक्तेन नक्तेन तथैवायाचितेन च।**
उपवासेन चैवायं पादकृच्छ्रः प्रकीर्तितः॥
यथाकथञ्चित् त्रिगुणः प्राजापत्योऽयमुच्यते। इति।

याज्ञ० 3.318–319b

(1) एवं चतुरहःसाध्यपादकृच्छ्रस्य त्रिवारावृत्तौ द्वादशाहोरात्रसाध्यतास्य भवति।

योजनपरिमाणञ्च—

132. **तिर्यग्यवोदराण्यष्टावूर्ध्वा वा व्रीहयस्त्रयः।**
प्रमाणमङ्गुलस्योक्तं वितस्तिर्द्वादशाङ्गुलः॥
हस्तो वितस्तिद्वितयं दण्डो हस्तचतुष्टयम्।
तत्सहस्रद्वयं क्रोशो योजनं तच्चतुष्टयम्॥ इति।

इति तीर्थप्रत्याम्नायाः

130.81. वा; P2 च। 130.88. याज्ञवल्क्योक्तो; C2 याज्ञवल्क्योक्तौ। 130.88. यथा; P3 K L2 तथा। 131. चैवायं; LI चैकेन। 131.1. त्रिवारावृत्तौ; P1 C2 त्रिरावृत्तौ।

अथ यात्रायां कालशुद्धिः

133. षष्ठ्यष्टमीद्वादशीषु न गच्छेत् त्रिदिनस्पृशि ।
पूर्णिमाप्रतिपद्दर्शरिक्तावमदिनेषु च ॥

रत्नमालायाम्—

134. हस्तेन्दुमैत्रश्रवणाश्विपुष्य पौष्णश्रविष्ठाश्च पुनर्वसुश्च ।
श्रेष्ठानि धिष्ण्यानि नवप्रयाणे त्यक्त्वा त्रिपञ्चादिमसप्ततारा: ॥
चित्राविशाखानलसार्पयाम्य— वायव्यपित्र्येश्वरदैवतानि ।
यात्रास्वनिष्टान्यपराणि भानि स्मृतानि नेष्टानि न निन्दितानि ॥

रत्नमाला 15.8,13

तथा—

135. वारस्तुषारकरसूर्यसुतावनीजतीक्ष्णत्विषाम् अशुभदः कथितः प्रयाणे

तथा—

136. सोमसौम्यगुरुशुक्रवासराः सर्वकर्मसु भवन्ति सिद्धिदाः ।

तथा—

137. व्यतीपातः परिघार्धं वैधृतियोगश्च विष्टिकरणञ्च
क्रान्तिसमत्वं कुलिका अवमगण्डान्तानि न शुभानि ।

लल्लः —

138. नीचस्थे वक्रसंस्थेऽप्यतिचरणगते बालवृद्धास्तगे वा
संन्यासो देवयात्रा व्रतनियमविधिः कर्णवेधस्तु दीक्षा ।
मौञ्जीबन्धोऽथ चूडापरिणयनविधिर्वास्तुदेवप्रतिष्ठा
वर्ज्या सद्भिः प्रयत्नात् त्रिदशपतिगुरौ सिंहराशिस्थिते च ॥

तथा—

139. रविक्षेत्रं गते जीवे जीवक्षेत्रं गते रवौ ।
वर्जयेत् सर्वकर्माणि व्रतस्वस्त्ययनानि च ॥

---

139. रविक्षेत्रं; P3 K रविक्षेत्र-...... ।

तथा—

140. गुर्वादित्ये गुरौ सिंहे शुक्रे चास्तमुपागते ।
त्यजेद् यानं महादानं व्रतं देवविलोकनम् ॥

तथा—

141. गुर्वादित्ये गुरौ सिंहे नष्टे शुक्रे मलिम्लुचे ।
याम्यायने हरौ सुप्ते सर्वकर्माणि वर्जयेत् ॥

तथा—

142. वापीकूपतडागयागगमनक्षौरप्रतिष्ठाव्रतं
विद्यामन्दिरकर्णवेधनमहादानं वनं सेवनम् ।
तीर्थस्नानविवाहदेवभवनं मन्त्रादि देवेक्षणम्
दूरेणैव जिजीविषुः परिहरेद् अस्तंगते भार्गवे ॥
सिंहस्थितं मघासंस्थं गुरुं यत्नेन वर्जयेत् ।
अन्यत्र सिंहभागेषु विवाहादि विधीयते ॥

तथा—

143. बाले वा यदि वा वृद्धे शुक्रे वास्तगते गुरौ ।
मलमास इवैतानि वर्जयेत् देवदर्शनम् ॥

(1) अत्र प्रकरणे देवदर्शनम् अपूर्वं निषिध्यते ।

अतएव गार्ग्यः

144. अपूर्वदेवतां दृष्ट्वा शुचः स्युर्नष्टभार्गवे ।
मलमासेऽप्यनावृत्ततीर्थयात्रां परित्यजेद् ॥ इति ।

(1) 'अनावृत्ततीर्थयात्राम्' अपूर्वतीर्थयात्राम् ।

तथा—

145. अतिचारगतो जीवस्तं राशिं नैति चेत्पुनः ।
लुप्तः संवत्सरो ज्ञेयः सर्वकर्मसु गर्हितः ॥

---

142. तडाग–; P1 तटाग–। 143. वास्तगते; C2 वास्तंगते, L2 चास्तंगते ।
145. लुप्तः; P1 लुप्त– ।

अस्यापवादः —

146. वृषे मेषे झषे कुम्भे यद्यतीचारगो गुरुः ।
न तत्र काललोपः स्यादित्याह गालवो मुनिर् ॥ इति ।

रत्नमालायाम्—

147. उदयति दिशि यस्यां याति यत्र भ्रमाद् वा
विचरति वा भचक्रे येषु दिग्द्वारभेषु ।
त्रिविधमिह सितस्य प्रोच्यते सम्मुखत्वम्
मुनिभिरुदित एव त्यज्यते च प्रयत्नात् ॥
स्वल्पोऽपि नार्थः प्रतिशुक्रयाने
यियसतां सिद्धिमुपैति नूनम् ।
रत्नमाला 15.17–18b

अस्यापवादो वृत्तशते —

148. नो तेषां प्रतिशुक्रयानमशुभं ये वत्सभृग्वङ्गिरो-
भारद्वाजवसिष्ठकाश्यपकुलोत्पन्नास्तथात्रेः कुले ।
दुर्भिक्षे विषयप्लवे प्रतिसितं न स्याद् विवाहे तथा
तीर्थानां गमने तथैकनगरे ग्रामे च सौम्यं तथे-॥ ति ।

(1) क्वचित्तु गुरुमौढ्यादिदोषाभाव उक्तः —

149. गोदावर्यां गयायाञ्च श्रीशैले ग्रहणद्वये ।
सुरासुरगुरूणाञ्च मौढ्यदोषो न विद्यते ॥

वायुपुराणे —

150. गयायां सर्वकालेषु पिण्डं दद्याद् विधानतः ।
अधिमासे जन्मदिने अस्ते च गुरुशुक्रयोः ॥
न त्यक्तव्यं गयाश्राद्धं सिंहस्थे च बृहस्पतौ ।

(1) अत्र श्राद्धस्य यात्रापूर्वकत्वाद् यात्रापि न निषिद्धेति केचित् ।

---

146. वृषे मेषे; C1 मेषे वृषे । 146. काललोपः; P3 K काले लोपः । 147. भचक्रे; P1 C2 L2 भवचक्रे । 148. –वसिष्ठ–; P1 -वशिष्ठ– । 148. सौम्यं; P3 K सौम्ये ।

तथा—

151. **अधिमासे च जन्मर्क्षे अस्ते च गुरुशुक्रयोः ।**
तीर्थयात्रा न कर्तव्या गयां गोदावरीं विना ॥

(1) अन्येऽपि लग्नलग्नांशशुद्ध्यादयो यात्रोपयोगिनो ज्योतिर्ग्रन्थतद्विद्भ्यो ज्ञेयाः, विस्तरभयात्तु नोच्यन्ते ।

इति त्रिस्थलीसेतौ तीर्थयात्रायां कालशुद्धिः ।

151.1. –ग्रन्थतद्विद्भ्यो; K– ग्रन्थात् तद्विद्भ्यो, LI ग्रन्थत्तदेभियुक्तेभ्यो (sic) ।
151.1. त्रिस्थलीसेतौ; P3 K omitted, Cl तीर्थसेतौ ।

अथ तीर्थगमनविधिः

स्कान्दे —

152. तीर्थयात्रां चिकीर्षुः प्राग् विधायोपोषणं गृहे ।
गणेशञ्च पितॄन् विप्रान् साधून् शक्त्या प्रपूज्य च ॥
कृतपारणको हृष्टो गच्छेन्नियमधृक् पुनः ।
आगत्याभ्यर्च्य च पितॄन् यथोक्तफलभाग् भवेत् ॥

काशीखण्ड 6.56–7

(1) 'आगत्ये'ति तीर्थयात्रां कृत्वा गृहागतेन पुनः श्राद्धं कार्यमित्यर्थः ।

तथा ब्रह्मपुराणे —

153. यो यः कश्चित्तीर्थयात्रां तु गच्छेत् सुसंयतः स च पूर्वं गृहे स्वे ।
कृतोपवासः शुचिरप्रमत्तः संपूजयेद् भक्तिनम्रो गणेशम् ॥
देवान् पितॄन् ब्राह्मणांश्चैव साधून् धीमान् विप्रो वित्तशक्त्या प्रयत्नात् ।
प्रत्यागतश्चापि पुनस्तथैव देवान् पितॄन् ब्राह्मणान् पूजयेच्च ॥
एवं कुर्वंस्तस्य तीर्थाद् यदुक्तं फलं तत्स्यान्नात्र संदिग्धमस्ति ।

(1) श्राद्धञ्चोपवासोत्तरदिने,

154. शुभे तिथौ शुभे वारे शुभे लग्नबले द्विजः ।
उपोष्य रजनीमेकां प्रातः श्राद्धं विधाय च ॥
गणेशं ब्राह्मणान् नत्वा भुक्त्वा प्रस्थितवान् सुधीर् ।

काशीखण्ड 7.39c-40

इति स्कान्दे शिवशर्मोपाख्यानान्यार्थदर्शनात् । (1) अत्र 'शुभतिथ्यादौ प्रस्थितवानि'त्यन्वयः । (2) 'गणेशं ब्राह्मणान् नत्वे'त्यत्र क्रमो न विवक्षितः, उपाख्यायिकारूपतया पाठक्रमस्याविधेयत्वात् । (3) यद्वा श्राद्धपूर्वभाविगणेशपूजातिरिक्तमेव श्राद्धानन्तरं गणेशादिनतिमात्रमत्रोक्तम् ।

(4) श्राद्धानन्तरं कार्पटिकवेशोऽपि कार्यः,

155. **उद्यतस्तु गयां गन्तुं श्राद्धं कृत्वा विधानतः ।**
विधाय कार्पटीवेषं कृत्वा ग्रामं प्रदक्षिणम् ॥
ततो ग्रामान्तरं गत्वा श्राद्धशेषस्य भोजनम् ।
ततः प्रतिदिनं गच्छेत् प्रतिग्रहविवर्जित ॥
(ग०पु० 1.84.1–2)

इति वायुपुराणोक्तेः । (1) केचित्तु "गयायात्रायामेवैष विधिः कार्यः गयामुपक्रम्यैव विधानात्, न तु तीर्थान्तरयात्रायामि"त्याहुः ।

(2) केचिद् "उपवासदिने श्राद्धात् पूर्वं मुण्डनमप्या"हुः,

156. **प्रयागे तीर्थयात्रायां पितृमातृवियोगतः ।**
कचानां वपनं कुर्याद् वृथा न विकचो भवेद् ॥

इति विष्णुवचनात् । (1) "इदञ्च प्रायश्चित्तार्थयात्रायामेव तत्र तस्य विहितत्वादि"त्येके । (2) "कार्पटिकवेषेण तीर्थगमने तदि"त्यन्ये ।

(3) श्राद्धञ्च तीर्थश्राद्धवदेव षड्दैवतं नवदैवतं द्वादशदैवतं वा मतभेदेन पार्वणं कार्यम् ।

(4) "इदञ्च घृतमात्रद्रव्यकं,

157. **गच्छेद् देशान्तरं यस्तु श्राद्धं कुर्यात् स सर्पिषा ।**
यात्रार्थमिति तत्प्रोक्तं प्रवेशे च न संशय ॥

इति विष्णुपुराणोक्तेः । (1) द्रव्यान्तरसाहित्ये 'व्रीहिभिर्यजेते'तिवन्निरपेक्ष-साधनताबोधक'सर्पिषे'तितृतीयाबाधापत्तेरि"ति कश्चित् (2) तन्न, घृतमात्रस्य स्वतन्त्रभक्ष्यत्वाभावेन श्राद्धद्रव्यत्वासम्भवाद् आनर्थक्यप्रतीघातेन श्रुतिसङ्कोचात् । (3) तस्माद् "घृतप्रचुरमि" त्यन्ये । (4) तदपि न, प्राचुर्ये तृतीयाया अविधानात्, लक्षणापत्तेश्च । (5) तस्मात् प्रतिस्पर्धिप्रधानभूतद्रव्यान्तरनिरपेक्षत्वस्यैव तृतीयया बोधनाद् 'घृतेन मुख्यद्रव्येणे'त्यर्थः,

---

155.1 विधिः; LI वेषः । 156. पितृमातृ–; Cl मातृपितृ– । 157. च न; C2 L2 न च । 157.1. –तृतीया–; P3 –तृतीयाया । 157.1. कश्चित्; Cl केचित् । 157.2 -प्रतीघातेन; ClL2 -प्रतिघातेन।

158. **तिलैर्व्रीहियवैर्माषैरद्भिर्मूलफलेन वा ।**
दत्तेन मासं प्रीयन्ते विधिवत् पितरो नृणाम् ॥
द्वौ मासौ मत्स्यमांसेन त्रीन्मासान् हारिणेन त्वि- ।

मनु 3.267–268b

(1) त्यादिमन्वादिवचनस्थ'तिलैरि'त्यादिवत् । (2) सत्यपि हिरण्यशकलोपस्तरणाभिधारणापेक्षत्वे

159. **वपया प्रातःसवने प्रचरन्ति पुरोडाशेन**
माध्यंदिने सवने अङ्गैस्तृतीयसवने ।

इतिवच्च । (1) अतएव स्मृतिरत्नावलीमदनपारिजातकारादिभिरेवमेव व्याख्यातमिति । (2) अत एव ग्रामान्तरे श्राद्धशेषेण घृतनैव पारणं कार्यं तस्यैव मुख्यद्रव्यत्वात् ।

(3) "इदञ्च श्राद्धम् आभ्युदयिकमेवे"ति कश्चित् । (4) तन्न, प्रकृतत्वेनोपस्थितेर्लाघवात् । (5) प्राप्ते पार्वणे विशेषानभिधानाच्च ।

(6) "ब्राह्मणानाञ्च त्रयाणामेव पूजनं कार्यं कपिञ्जलन्यायादि"ति केचिद् । (7) "उद्देश्यगतत्वेन तन्न्यायवैषम्याद् 'विप्रान् शक्त्या प्रपूज्य चे'त्यत्र पूजन इव संख्यायामपि शक्तेरन्वयाच्चानियम"इत्यन्ये ।

(8) तदयमत्रानुष्ठानक्रमः । (9) यात्रामुहूर्तदिनात् प्रपूर्वदिन एकभक्तहविष्यभोजनब्रह्मचर्यादयो नियमाः कार्याः, पूर्वं 'सुसंयत' इति वचनात् । (10) तदुत्तरदिने उपवासः । (11) पक्षे मुण्डनञ्च । (12) तदुत्तरदिने स्नानादि शुचितासम्पादकं नैत्यकं विधाय भक्त्या यथाशक्ति गणेशेष्टदेवते पूजयित्वा घृतमुख्यद्रव्यकं पार्वणश्राद्धं विधाय यथाशक्ति वस्त्रालङ्कारगोभू हिरण्यादिभिर्ब्राह्मणान् सम्पूज्य यात्रासङ्कल्पं विधाय काषाय परिधानादिरूपं कार्पटिकवेषं धृत्वा मुहूर्तवेलायां ग्रामान्निर्गत्य निवासग्रामं प्रदक्षिणीकृत्य क्रोशाभ्यन्तरस्थग्रामान्तरं गत्वा श्राद्धशेषघृतेन पारणं कुर्यात्,

160. **अध्वनि च क्रोशपूरण**

(1) इत्यादिना श्राद्धोत्तरं क्रोशगमननिषेधात् । ततो दिनान्तरे स्नानादि विधाय नियमवान् गच्छेद्

---

159. तृतीय–; P3 K तृतीये । 159.9. –मुहूर्तदिनात्; P1 –मुहूर्तात् । 159.9. –दिन; P1 C1 K –दिने । 159.9. –ब्रह्मचर्यादयो; P1 –ब्रह्मचर्यादि – । 159.12. क्रोशाभ्यन्तरस्थ–; P2 क्रोशाभ्यन्तरस्थं ।

161. **तमपि ग्रामं प्रदक्षिणीकृत्य गच्छेदि—**

(1) ति स्मृतिरत्नावल्याम् ।

(2) "अयञ्च क्रमो यद्युपवासोत्तरदिने पूर्वाह्णे मुहूर्तः स्यात्तदा । (3) यदा त्वपररात्रे स स्याद् तदाऽसमर्थस्तद्दिन एवोपवासश्राद्धादि विधाय मुहूर्तसमये यात्रां विधाय स्थलान्तरे गत्वा प्रातः पार्वणं कुर्यात् प्रधानाविरोधेनैवोपवासस्येष्टत्वादि"ति कश्चित् । (4) तच्चिन्त्यं, पूर्वरात्रेऽपररात्रे वा मुहूर्ते सति तद्दिने उपवासं कृत्वा मुहूर्तसमये ज्योतिःशास्त्रोक्तरीत्या फलवस्त्रादिप्रस्थानं क्वचित् स्थापयित्वा प्रातः श्राद्धादि विधाय गृहान्निर्गत्य तत् प्रस्थानं गृहीत्वा ग्रामं प्रदक्षिणीकृत्य ग्रामान्तरे पारणोपपत्तौ श्राद्धे उपवासोत्तरदिनरूपकालबाधस्यानौचित्यात् । (5) प्रमाणं विना श्राद्धं कृत्वोपवासायोगाच्च । (6) एतादृशविषयार्थमेव हि ज्योतिःशास्त्रे प्रस्थानप्रकार उक्तः ।

(7) अत्र य आतुरादिरुपवासासमर्थ स उपवासप्रतिनिधिं यं कञ्चिच्छक्त्या कुर्यात् । प्रतिनिधयश्च—

162. **नक्तं हविष्यान्नमनोदनं वा फलं तिलाः क्षीरमथाम्बु चाज्यम् ।**
यत् पञ्चगव्यं यदि वापि वायुः प्रशस्तमत्रोत्तरमुत्तरञ्चे- ॥ ति ।

(1) कार्पटिकवेषधारणञ्च यात्राङ्गत्वाद् गमनकाल एव न त्वाह्निकभोजनादिकालेऽपि, 'कर्मकाले नग्नः काषायवाससे'ति काषायवाससो निषेधात् । (2) तद्बाधकमानाभावात् । (3) वेषविधायकवचसो गमनमात्रे वेषविधानेनोपपत्तेः; एवं तीर्थेऽपि तत्तत्क्षेत्राद्यनुसरणे कार्पटिकवेशः । (4) "न तु स्नानश्राद्धादिकालेऽपि, मानाभावादि"ति केचित् । (5) अन्ये तु "उपक्रमादाराभ्य यात्रावसानं यावत् प्रतिग्रहादिनिवृत्तिवद् वेषस्यांङ्गताविधानात् सदा वेषधारणम् । (6) अन्यथा नियमान्तरे का वार्त्ते"त्याहुः ।

(7) तीर्थात् प्रत्यावृत्तोऽपि स्वग्रामसमीपे ग्रामान्तरे कृतोपवासस्तदुत्तरदिने ग्रहान् इष्टदेवताञ्च सम्पूज्य घृतेन पार्वणं विधाय ब्राह्मणान् संपूज्य स्वग्रामं प्राप्य पूर्ववत् प्रदक्षिणीकृत्यवेषस्थाने वेषं त्यक्त्वा स्वगृहं प्रविश्य श्राद्धशेषघृतेन पारणं कुर्यात्, 'प्रत्यागतश्चापि पुनस्तथैव देवान् पितॄन् ब्राह्मणानर्चयेच्चे'तिवचनस्थ'तथा' शब्देन

161.3. अपररात्रे; P2 अपराह्णे । 162.3 गमनमात्रे वेषविधानेनोपपत्तेः ; L1 गमनविधाने विषयमात्रेणोपपत्तेः । 162.7. ब्राह्मणानर्चयेच्चे'ति; P1 ब्राह्मणाश्चे'ति ।

सकलप्रस्थानधर्मातिदेशादि''ति कश्चित् । (8) तन्न, देवादिपूजनधर्मातिदेशेनैव तथाशब्दोपपत्तेः । (9) अत एव स्कान्दे 'आगत्याभ्यर्च्य च पितॄनि'त्येवोक्तम् । (10) शिष्टाचारोऽप्येवमेव ।

(11) अत्र कश्चित् ''यात्रासङ्कल्पे फलोल्लेखः न कार्यः, 'उद्यतश्चेद् गयां गन्तु'' 'फलं स्याद् गच्छतो गयाम्' इत्युपक्रमोपसंहाराभ्यां तादर्थ्यावगमात्, 'उद्देशेन हि तादर्थ्यं विविच्यत' इति न्यायात्,

163. **एवं गच्छन् तस्य तीर्थाद् यदुक्तम्**
फलं तत्स्यान्नात्र सन्दिग्धमस्ती- । (=153)

(1) त्यादिवचनाच्च । अन्यथा प्रतिपदमश्वमेधादिफलाप्तौ तीर्थे वैय्यर्थ्यप्रसङ्गः । (2) यदपि तत्र तत्र यात्रायां स्वर्गराजसूयादिफलाप्तिश्रवणं, तदपि प्रधानफलस्यैवाङ्गे श्रवणन्यायेनार्थवादः ।

''ननु

164. **स्नानजं फलमाप्नोति तीर्थयात्राफलं न त्वि-** (=106)

(1) त्यादिवचनाद् यात्राफलमपि पृथगस्ती''ति चेत् । (2) न, 'तीर्थयात्रया यत्पूर्णं तीर्थफलं तन्नाप्नोति किन्तु स्नानमात्रजमि'त्यर्थकरणात् । (3) 'अर्धं तीर्थफलं तस्य यः प्रसङ्गेन गच्छती'त्यादेरपि [107] इतीर्थस्यैव फलवत्ता । (4) 'तदेव कृत्वा यानेन स्नानमात्रफलं लभेद्' [114] इत्यादिना यानवतस्तीर्थस्यैव वैफल्यं न्यूनफलता वा । (5) यात्राधर्माद्यनुष्ठानादपि तीर्थस्यैव सफलता, न यात्रायाः । (6) 'सम्पूर्णतीर्थफलप्राप्तिकाम' इत्यपि न सङ्कल्पः, यात्रायास्तीर्थफलसाधनत्वाविधानात् । (7) तस्मात्तत्र फलश्रवणं भातृव्याभिभूतिवदर्थवादः ।

(8) प्रायश्चित्तरूपयात्रायां तु पारार्थ्याभावादङ्गत्वानवगतेः स्वतन्त्रं फलम् । (9) तेन तत्रोपक्रमे संकल्प्य पुनस्तीर्थप्राप्तौ न संकल्पस्तीर्थस्नानादेर्यात्रानिर्वर्तकत्वेन तत्रैवान्तर्भावादि''ति ।

(10) एतच्चिन्त्यं, 'गन्तुं' 'गच्छत' इति श्रवणाद् उपक्रमोपसंहारयोर्विरुद्धत्वात् तादर्थ्यानवगतेः (11) गमनस्यैव फलवत्त्वप्रतीतेः ।

163.1. वचनाच्च; P3 K वचनात् । 164.4 लभेद्; P1 भवेद् । 164. तीर्थस्यैव; K तथैव । । 164.4. न्यूनफलता; K फलन्यूनता । 164.6 –विधानात्; L2 –योगात् ।

(12) तीर्थस्य क्रियानाविष्टस्य फलसाधनत्वासम्भवात् क्रियापेक्षायाम् 'एवं गच्छन्नि'ति समानवाक्योपात्तगमनपरित्यागेन स्नानादिधात्वर्थावेशकल्पनायोगाद् गमनस्यैवावच्छेदकत्वप्रतीतेस् 'तीर्थात् तीर्थगमनाद् यदुक्तं फलमि'त्यर्थप्रतीतेर्द्वितीयहेतोरपि विरुद्धत्वात् । (13) एवञ्च तादर्थ्यानवगतौ तत्र तत्र श्रूयमाणस्य स्वर्गादिफलस्याङ्गफलश्रवणन्यायविषयतोच्यत इति महत्साहसम् । (14) किञ्च; 'तीर्थाभिगमनं पुण्यं' [38] 'या याः काश्चित् तीर्थयात्रा मुनीन्द्रैर्' [77] इत्यादिपूर्वोदाहृताधिकारवाक्यपर्यालोचनया यात्राया एव प्राधान्यमवगम्यते । (15) नह्यङ्गे स्वतन्त्राधिकारप्रदर्शनं भवति । (16) एवञ्च 'तीर्थयात्राफलं न त्वि'त्यादेः क्लिष्टकल्पनाव्याख्यानमप्रामाणिकमेव । (17) 'अर्धं तीर्थफलं तस्ये'त्यादावपि [107] अवच्छेदकधात्वर्थापेक्षायां 'गच्छती'तिसमानवाक्योपात्तगमनस्यैवावच्छेदकता । (18) किञ्च; प्रायश्चित्तार्थयात्रायां प्रधानता नान्यत्रेत्यत्र किं नियामकमन्यत्र कोशपानात् ?

(19) तस्मात् सर्वत्र यात्रा फलवती । (20) न च तीर्थवैयर्थ्यप्रसङ्गः ।

165. **कर्मणामल्पमहतां फलानाञ्च स्वगोचरे ।**
विभागः स्थानसामान्यादविभागेऽपि चोदित ॥

त.वा· 1·2·1·7·, p. 130

(1) इति न्यायेनावान्तरवैजात्यकल्पनात् । (2) तादृशस्थलेऽर्थवादत्वाद् वा । (3) तस्मादप्रायश्चित्तार्थापि यात्रा फलवती । (4) स्नानश्राद्धादि च । (5) एतावांस्तु विशेष; स्नानश्राद्धादेरग्निहोत्रवद् ।

166. **एकस्य तूभयत्वे संयोगपृथक्त्वम् ।**

मी.सू. 4.3.3.5

(1) इति न्यायेन काम्यनैमित्तिकतयोभयरूपता, उभयथा वचनसत्त्वात् । (2) ततश्च तीर्थप्राप्तिरूपनिमित्तवान् यदि तन्न करोति तदा यात्राफललाभेऽपि प्रत्यवैति विगीयते च शिष्टैः । (3) अतएव प्रायश्चित्तार्थयात्रायामप्येकं सन्धित्सतो ऽपरप्रच्यवन्यायो मा भूदिति तीर्थकृत्यान्तता। । (4) एवञ्च

164.12. एवं; P3 Cl K एव।164.12. तीर्थात् तीर्थगमनाद्; Cl तीर्थगमनाद् । 164.19. After सर्वत्र; P2 पापवतोऽपापस्य वा । 165. अविभागे; Cl अविभागो । 166.3. ऽपरप्रच्यव–; K ऽपरप्रच्यवन– ।

प्राप्ततीर्थोऽकृतस्नानादिरेव यदि दैवान् म्रियते बलान् म्लेच्छादिनान्यत्र नीयते वा तदा पुरुषापराधाभावान्न प्रत्यवायो नापि यात्रा निःफलेति । (5) तदलं तीर्थयात्रानिःफलेतिजगत्विरुद्धमभिदधानैर्विवादेन ।

(6) अन्ये त्वाहुः; "अस्तु यात्रायाः फलवत्त्वम् । तथापि—

167. **पदे पदेऽश्वमेधस्य फलं स्याद् गच्छतो गयाम् ।**

(1) इति गयायात्रायां श्रुतमपीदमेव फलं सर्वतीर्थयात्रास्वन्वेति,

168. **एकत्र निर्णीतः शास्त्रार्थोऽपरत्रापी—।**

ति न्यायात् । (1) फलाकांक्षायाश्च गमनफलत्वेन श्रुतस्यास्यैवान्तरङ्गतया फलौचित्यात्, विश्वजिन्न्यायात् स्वर्गकल्पने बहिरङ्गत्वेनोपस्थितिगौरवाद्" इति ।

(2) तदप्यतिमन्दं, तत्र तत्र सामान्यतो विशेषतश्च तीर्थयात्रायां फलान्तरश्रवणात् । सामान्यतस्तावत्—

भारते दानधर्मेषु गोलोकं प्रकृत्य;

169. **मनस्विनस्तीर्थयात्रापरायणास्**
ते तत्र मोदन्ति गवां निवासे ।

म. भा. 13.105.44c-d

इति । तथा प्रभासादीन्यनुक्रम्य—

170. **सरस्वतीदृषद्वत्यौ यमुनां येऽनुयान्ति च ।**
तत्र ते दिव्यसंस्थाना दिव्यमाल्यधराः शिवाः ॥
प्रयान्ति पुण्यगन्धाढ्या

म. भा. 13.105.47c–48c

इति (1) वायवीयेऽपि 'तीर्थान्यनुसरन् वीर' [50] इत्यादि ।

विशेषतोऽपि,

कौर्मे —

171. **पुण्डरीकं महातीर्थं ब्राह्मणैरुपशोभितम् ।**
तत्राभिगम्य युक्तात्मा पुण्डरीकफलं लभेद् ॥

कू. पु. 2.36.25

167.1. –यात्रास्वन्वेति; C1 –यात्रास्विति, L1 –यात्रास्वस्ति । 170. पुण्य–; P2 पुण्यं । 171. पुण्डरीकफलं; P2 पुण्डरीकं फल । 171. लभेद्; P1 भवेद् ।

इति । (171·1) एवं सर्वपुराणभारतादिषु तत्तत्तीर्थमुपक्रम्य फलप्रतिपादनं द्रष्टव्यम् । (2) विस्तरभयात्तु न लिख्यते । (3) एवञ्च वाक्यात् प्रकरणाद् वा यथायोगं फले लब्धे तेनैव निराकांक्षत्वात् क्वाकांक्षा क्वतरामन्तरङ्गन्यायः क्वतमामेकत्रेति न्यायः । (4) विपरीतोऽपि चान्तरङ्गभावः विशेषश्रुतस्यै-वान्तरङ्गत्वात् । (5) स्वर्गकल्पनाभावाच्च नोपस्थितिगौरवमपीत्यलं पुराणा-नतिदर्शिभिर्विवादेन ।

इति श्रीमद्भट्टरामेश्वरसूरिसूनुनारायणभट्टविरचिते
त्रिस्थलीसेतौ सामान्यप्रघट्टके तीर्थगमनविधिः ।

171.5. -मद्भट्टरामेश्वरसूरिसूनु-; C1 omitted, L2 –मद्– omitted.

अथ तीर्थयात्रायां नियमाः

भारते—

172. कामं क्रोधञ्च लोभञ्च यो जित्वा तीर्थमाविशेत् ।
न तेन किञ्चिदप्राप्यं तीर्थाभिगमनाद् भवेत् ॥
म.भा. 13.26.60 (=655)

तीर्थानि च यथोक्तेन विधिना सञ्चरन्ति ये ।
सर्वद्वन्द्वसहा धीरास्ते नराः स्वर्गगामिनः ॥
(का० ख० 6.55)

(1) द्वन्द्वानि शीतातपादीनि तत्सहिष्णवः ।

शङ्खपुलस्त्यौ—

173. यस्य हस्तौ च पादौ च मनश्चैव सुसंयतम् ।
विद्या तपश्च कीर्तिश्च स तीर्थफलमश्नुते ॥
शंख 8.15

प्रतिग्रहादुपावृत्तः सन्तुष्टो येन केन चित् ।
अहङ्कारविमुक्तश्च स तीर्थफलमश्नुते ॥
अकल्कको निरारम्भो लघ्वाहारो जितेन्द्रियः ।
विमुक्तः सर्वसङ्गैर्यः स तीर्थफलमश्नुते ॥
अक्रोधनश्च राजेन्द्र सत्यशीलो दृढव्रतः ।
आत्मोपमश्च भूतेषु स तीर्थफलमश्नुते ॥
(प० पु०, सृ० खण्ड 19.8-10)

(1) हस्तसंयमः परताडनपरस्वग्रहणनिवृत्त्या । (2) पादसंयमः पादताडनागम्यदेशगमननिवृत्त्या । (3) मनःसंयमः

174. परद्रव्येष्वभिध्यानं मनसानिष्टचिन्तनम् ।
वितथाभिनिवेशश्च मानसं त्रिविधं स्मृतम् ॥

---

172. च लोभञ्च; LI तथा लोभं ।

इति त्रिविधपापनिवृत्तिः । (1) 'विद्या' तीर्थमहिमज्ञानम् । यत्तु —

175. **विद्या सच्छास्त्रज्ञानम्**

(1) इति स्मृतिदर्पणे, तन्न, प्रकृत्यानुपयोगात् । (2) 'तपः' उपवासैकभक्तादि । (3) 'कीर्तिः' सच्चरिततया प्रसिद्धिस्तेनाभिशस्तता पराक्रियते । (4) प्रतिग्रहव्यावृत्तिर्यात्रोपक्रमानन्तरम् । (5) यत्तु वचनं—

176. **तावदस्य वृथा तीर्थं यावत् तद्धनमश्नुत ।**

इति, (1) "तद् यस्मिस्तीर्थयात्राप्रयोगे प्रतिग्रहः कृतः तत्प्रयोगस्य विफलता, (2) प्रतिग्रहनिवृत्तिरूपाङ्गाभावान्न प्रयोगान्तरस्येत्येतत्परमि"ति कश्चित् । (3) "यात्रारम्भात् प्रागपि दुःप्रतिग्रहार्जितधनविषयमि"ति तु युक्तम् । (4) इयञ्च प्रतिग्रहनिवृत्तिः प्रतिग्रहमन्तरा निर्वहच्छरीरधारणकर्तृ विषया । (5) यतिब्रह्मचार्यादीनां तु भिक्षावस्त्रादिप्रतिग्रहमन्तरा शरीरधारणासम्भवान्न तद्विषया । (6) तेषां संग्रहस्य निषेधात् तत्प्रतिग्रहं विना यात्राया अनिर्वाहाद् आवश्यकत्वात्तस्य । (7) 'येन केनचित् सन्तुष्टः' मिष्टभक्ष्यादावलोलुपः । (8) 'अकल्ककः' निर्दम्भः । (9) 'विराम्भः' क्रय-विक्रयार्थार्जनादिव्यापारशून्यः । (10) 'लघ्वाहारो'ऽबहुभुक् । (11) 'जितेन्द्रियः' एकादशेन्द्रियाणां स्वविषयासक्तिशून्यः । (12) अविहितासक्तिः सङ्गस्तच्छून्यः । (13) 'दृढव्रतः' अङ्गीकृतोपवासादिव्रतक्षतिरहितः । (14) निर्वाह्यमेव तीर्थयात्रायां व्रतं ग्राह्यमिति भावः । (15) सर्वभूतहिते रतः 'आत्मोपमो भूतेषु' ।

तथा—

177. **अश्रद्दधानः पापात्मा नास्तिकोऽच्छिन्नसंशयः ।**
हेतुनिष्ठश्च पञ्चैते न तीर्थफलभागिनः ॥

का० ख० 6.54

(1) 'पापात्मा' बहुपापवान् । (2) तस्य हि पापक्षय एव यात्रया, न तु तीर्थफलं स्वर्गादि,

178. **नृणां पापकृतां तीर्थं पापप्रशमनं भवेत् ।**
यथोक्तफलदं तीर्थं भवेच्छुद्धात्मनां नृणाम् ॥

(=103, 127)

174.1 –महिम–; K L1 L2–महिमा– । 176.6. यात्राया; P1 यात्रायाम् ।

इति काशीखण्डोक्तेः ।

179. "यस्य धर्मध्वजो नित्यं सुराध्वजो इवोच्छ्रितः ।
प्रच्छन्नानि च पापानि बैडालं नाम तद्व्रतम् ॥
मनु 4.195

(1) इति मनूक्तो बैडालव्रतिकः पापात्मे"ति कश्चित् । (2) 'नास्तिकः' पाखण्डः । (3) 'अछिन्नसंशयः' सर्वत्र निश्चयरहितः । (4) फलोपायेतिकर्तव्यार्थ-निश्चयशून्य इत्यन्ये,

180. नायं लोकोऽस्ति न परो न सुखं संशयात्मन ।
म० भा० 6.27.40c-d

इति गीतोक्तेः (1) 'हेतुनिष्ठो' हैतुकः, कुहेतुभिर्धर्मशास्त्रार्थोपप्लावकः । प्रभासखण्डे —

181. येनैकादशसंख्यानि नियतानीन्द्रियाणि वै ।
स तीर्थफलमाप्नोति नरोऽन्यः पापभाग्भवेत् ॥
प्र०ख० 1.28.72.

(1) अत्र ब्रह्मचर्यरूप इन्द्रियनियमः ऋतुकालं विना,

182. तीर्थानि गच्छता नित्यमनृतौ ब्रह्मचारिणे ।

ति स्मृतेः ।

तथा—

183. चित्तमन्तर्गतं दुष्टं तीर्थस्नानैर्न शुध्यति ।
शतशो जलधौतं तु सुराभाण्डमिवाशुचि ॥
व०प्र० (V) 23.4 (=69)

ब्रह्मपुराणे—

184. सर्वेण गाङ्गेन जलेन संयङ
नित्याप्लुतो योऽप्यथ भावदुष्टः ।
आजन्मनः स्नानपरोऽपि नित्यं
न शुध्यतीत्येव वयं वदामः ॥

---

179. प्रच्छन्नानि; Cl प्रपन्नानि । 179.4. –एतिकर्तव्यार्थ–; LI -एतिकर्तव्यतार्थं ।
181. –नियमः; Cl -निग्रहः । 182. स्मृतेः; LI स्मृतौ ।
184. योऽप्य; P3 K वाप्य ।

गङ्गादितीर्थेषु वसन्ति मत्स्या
देवालये पक्षिसंघाश्च राजन् ।
भावोज्झितास्ते न फलं लभन्ते
तीर्थाच्च देवायतनाच्च तस्मात् ॥
भावं ततो हृत्कमले निधाय
तीर्थानि सेवेत समाहितात्मा ।

अन्यत्रापि —

185. **मन्त्रे तीर्थे द्विजे देवे दैवज्ञे भेषजे गुरौ ।**
यादृशी भावना यस्य सिद्धिर्भवति तादृशी ॥

स्क०पु०, रेवाख० 227.20

(1) "तेन भक्तिभावौ मनसि निधाय तीर्थं कुर्याद्" इति भावः ।
(2) एते च हस्तसंयमादयो नियमास्तीर्थयात्रातीर्थस्नानादिसकलकर्माङ्गभूताः 'स तीर्थफलमश्नुत' इति सामान्योक्तेः ।

कूर्मपुराण —

186. **तीर्थयात्रां प्रकुर्वन्ति दम्भेन कपटेन च ।**
तीर्थे मृता न सिध्यन्ति ते नरा वरवर्णिनि ॥

भारते —

187. **भावितैः करणैः पूर्वमास्तिक्याच्छ्रुतिदर्शनात् ।**
प्राप्यन्ते तानि तीर्थानि सद्भिः शिष्टार्थदर्शिभिः ॥

म० भा० 3.83.91

तथा —

188. **संप्रस्थितस्तीर्थयात्रां ब्राह्मणानवमन्यते ।**
नासौ प्रतिनिवर्तेत तदन्तं तस्य जीवितम् ॥

तथा —

189. **तीर्थे गच्छन् चरेत् सन्ध्यास्तिस्र एकत्र मानवः ।**
नास्नातो नाशुचिर्गच्छेन्न भुक्त्वा न च सूतकी ॥

(1) 'तिस्रः सन्ध्या एकत्र चरेद्' इत्यनेन रात्रौ कृतमाध्याह्निकेन प्रात-

---

186. च; L2 वा ।

श्चाकृतनित्यक्रियेण न चलितव्यमित्युक्तं भवति । (2) 'नास्नात' इति शक्तः सन् स्नात्वैव गच्छेदित्यर्थः । (3) 'अशुचिर्' मूत्रं पुरीषं वा कृत्वाऽकृतशौचः । (4) चण्डालोदक्यादिस्पर्शे स्नानाचमनादिनिमित्ते सत्यकृतस्नानाचमनादिश्च । यत्तु षट्त्रिंशन्मते —

190. **देवयात्राविवाहेषु यज्ञेषु प्रकृतेषु च ।**
उत्सवेषु च सर्वेषु स्पृष्टास्पृष्टिर्न दुष्यती– ॥

ति, बृहस्पतिश्च —

191. **तीर्थे विवाहे यात्रायां सङ्ग्रामे देशविप्लवे ।**
नगरग्रामदाहे च स्पृष्टास्पृष्टिर्न दुष्यती– ॥ ति,

बृ० (सं) 27

192. **एतद् यत्राहमनेन स्पृष्ट इति प्रत्यक्षज्ञानं नास्ति तद्विषयं, तन्मात्रापवादे वचनचारितार्थ्याद्**

म० पा०, p. 261

इति मदनपारिजातकारः । (1) अन्ये तु "अनिवार्यस्पर्शे देवपूजायात्रादिमात्रकार्यविषये दोषाभावः, भोजनादौ तु स्नानव्यतिरेकेण नैव शुद्धते"त्याहु : । (2) 'न च सूतकी'ति नाशौचवानित्यर्थः । यत्तु —

193. **प्रारब्धे सूतकं नास्ती–**

ति, (1) तत्परिगणितव्रतादिमात्रविषयं,

194. **व्रतयज्ञविवाहेषु श्राद्धे होमेऽर्चने जपे ।**
प्रारब्धे सूतकं न स्यादनारब्धे तु सूतकम् ॥

इति विष्णुस्मरणात् । (1) अन्यथा पूर्वार्धवैय्यर्थ्यापत्तेः । अत एव

195. **प्रारम्भो वरणं यज्ञे सङ्कल्पो व्रतसत्त्रयोः ।**
नान्दीमुखं विवाहादौ श्राद्धे पाकपरिक्रिये– ॥

लघ्वाश्वलायनस्मृति 15.74

(1) ति तावन्मात्रविषय एवारम्भो विष्णुनोक्तोऽग्रिमवाक्ये । (2) अन्ये तु "यत्र नैरन्तर्येणानुष्ठानं बोधितं मासोपवासादौ तद्विषयमिदं भवतु । (3) न च

---

190. दुष्यतीति; L2 विद्यते । 192. -पारिजातकारः; C1 -पारिजातादयः, P1 —पारिजातः । 192.1.—यात्रादिमात्रकार्यं—; P2 -यात्रादिमात्रकार्यंमात्र—। 192.1. शुद्धते"त्याहुः; L1 शुध्यते"त्याहुः । 195.1.विष्णुनोक्तो; P2 विष्णुनोक्ते ।

तीर्थयात्रायां नैरन्तर्येणानुष्ठानं बोध्यते । (4) तस्मात् प्रारब्धे सूतकाभावो नैतद्विषयः । (5) अत एव सहस्रभोजनादौ सूतकं भवत्येवे"त्याहुः । (6) उभयथापि यात्रामध्ये सूतके सति आशौचकालं तत्रैव परिकलय्य शुद्धौ सत्यां गच्छेदिति सिद्धम् । यत्तु —

196. **विवाहदुर्गयज्ञेषु यात्रायां तीर्थकर्मणि ।**
न तत्र सूतकं तद्वत् कर्मयज्ञादि कारयेद् ॥
(= 315, 385)

(1) इति पैठीनसिवचनं तन्मार्गवैषम्यादिना गत्यन्तराभावे सति तीर्थयात्रायामाशौचं नास्तीत्येवंपरम् ।

(2) अनयैव दिशा रजस्वला स्त्री तत्रैव चत्वारि दिनान्यतिवाह्य पञ्चमेऽहनि व्रजेत्,

197. **दैवकर्मणि पित्र्ये च पञ्चमेऽहनि शुध्यती– ।**

ति वचनात् । (1) यात्रायाश्च दैवकर्मत्वात् ।

(2) एवं नियमेन गच्छतो यद्यन्तरा तीर्थान्तरमापतति तदा तत्र स्नानश्राद्धाद्यवश्यं कार्यं 'अर्धं तीर्थफलं तस्य यः प्रसङ्गेन गच्छती'ति [107] पूर्वमेवोक्तत्वात् । (3) तीर्थप्राप्तिरूपनिमित्ते सति नैमित्तिकस्नानाद्यकरणे प्रत्यवायप्रसङ्गाच्च । (4) "उपवासक्षौरे तूद्देश्यतीर्थ एवे"ति केचित् । (5) एवं तीर्थयात्रायै चलितो यदि दैवात् परावर्तते तदा विशेषो गरुडपुराणे—

198. **तीर्थं चलित्वा यः कोऽपि पुनरायाति वै गृहे ।**
अनुज्ञातः शुभैर्विप्रैः प्रायश्चित्तं समाचरेत् ॥
ग० पु० 2.26.22

(1) सङ्कल्पबाधनिमित्तं प्रायश्चित्तं ब्राह्मणानुज्ञया ग्राह्यमित्यर्थः ।

(2) यदा तु तीर्थं प्रति चलितस्तीर्थमप्राप्यैव मृतस्तत्र विशेषो गरुडपुराणे—

199. **यस्तीर्थसम्मुखो भूत्वा व्रजन्ननशने कृते ।**
चेन्म्रियेदन्तराले तु ऋषीणां मण्डलं व्रजेत् ॥
ग० पु० 2.26.14.

(1) 'अनशने' मासोपवासादिरूपोपवासव्रते च कृत इति चकारोऽध्याहार्यः ।

195.6. परिकलय्य; P3 Cl L1 L2 परिकल्प्य । 196. –दुर्गयज्ञेषु; Cl –यज्ञदुर्गेषु । 197.3. –निमित्ते सति; Cl omitted. 198.1. –निमित्तं; K –निमित्त– ।

(2) विधस्याप्यन्तराले मृतस्य ऋषिलोकप्राप्तिर्भवतीत्यर्थः ।

(3) यदा तु पाश्चात्यानां गयायात्रायां पौरस्त्यानाञ्च काश्यादियात्रायां मार्गे कर्मनाशानाम नदी पतति तदा तज्जलस्पर्शो यथा न भवति तथा केनचिदुपायेन संतरणं कार्यं,

200. **कर्मनाशाजलस्पर्शात् करतोयाविलङ्घनात् ।**
गण्डकीबाहुतरणात् पुनः संस्कारमर्हती– ॥

ति वचनात्। (1) प्राच्यास्तु "'करतोयाजलस्पर्शात् कर्मनाशाविलङ्घनादि'-ति पाठं पठित्वा गङ्गासङ्गममार्गेण नौकया तदुत्तरमार्गेण वा गन्तव्यम्" इत्याहुः । (2) तन्न, कर्मनाशाजलस्पर्शस्यापि तैरनिष्टत्वाङ्गीकारात् तज्जलस्पर्शनिषेधकस्याश्रुतस्यापि वचनान्तरस्य कल्पनापातात्

201. **करतोयां कुरङ्गञ्च त्रिरात्रोपोषितो नरः ।**
अश्वमेधमवाप्नोति विगाह्य प्रयतः शुचिर्– ॥

म० भा० 13.26.11

इति भारते दानधर्मेषु,

202. **करतोयां समासाद्य त्रिरात्रोपोषितो नरः ।**
अश्वमेधमवाप्नोति स्वर्गलोकञ्च गच्छती– ॥

म० भा० 3.83.3

–ति आरण्यकपर्वणि च करतोयास्नानश्रवणविरोधाच्च,

203. **करतोये सदानीरे सरिच्छ्रेष्ठेऽतिविश्रुते ।**
आप्लावयसि पापानां पापं हरकरोद्भवे ॥

(1) इति स्मृतिदर्पणोदाहृतकरतोयास्नानमन्त्रविरोधाच्च । (2) तस्मादस्मयुक्त एव पाठः ।

(3) एवमन्येऽपि शिष्टाचारप्राप्ता यात्राधर्मा ज्ञेयाः ।

इति यात्रानियमाः ।

199.3. तज्जलस्पर्शो; C1 तज्जलस्य स्पर्शो । 200.1. पाठं; P1 omitted. 201. भारते; P1 omitted. 203.3. इति यात्रानियमाः ; P2 इति श्रीमद्भट्टरामेश्वरसूनुनारायणभट्टविरचिते त्रिस्थलीसेतौ तीर्थयात्रानियमाः ।

अथ तीर्थप्राप्तिर्दिनकृत्यम्

(4) तत्र यदि यानारूढः सोपानत्को वा गच्छेत्तदा तीर्थप्राप्तिदिने यावान्मार्गः पादचारेण गन्तुं शक्यस्तावति मार्गे यानोपानहादि परित्यज्य पादचारेण गत्वा तीर्थे दृष्टिपथावतीर्णे साष्टाङ्गं प्रणम्य शिरोवगुण्ठनशस्त्रमाल्यकञ्चुकादि परित्यज्य तीर्थं गच्छेत् । तदुक्तं —

204. **यानानि तु परित्यज्य भाव्यं पादचरैर्नरैः ।**
लुठित्वा लोठनीं तत्र कृत्वा कार्पटिकाकृतिम् ॥

प्र०ख० 1.28.57c-58b

(1) 'लोठनीं लुठित्वे'ति साष्टाङ्गं प्रणम्य । (2) अष्टाङ्गप्रणामस्तु—

205. **पद्भ्यां कराभ्यां जानुभ्यां शिरसा चोरसा तथा ।**
मनसा वचसा दृष्ट्या प्रणामोऽष्टाङ्ग उच्यते ॥

(1) 'कृत्वा कार्पटिकाकृतिमि'ति गन्धमाल्यशस्त्रकञ्चुकादिपरिहार उक्तः । (2) यद्वा यदि यात्राप्रक्रमे कार्पटिकाकृतिर्न कृता तदा प्रवेशदिने कार्येत्यर्थः ।

(3) ततस्तीर्थे प्राप्ते पुष्पाक्षतफलाद्युक्तमञ्जलिम् "अमुकतीर्थाय नमः" इति दद्यात् । (4) यथाशक्ति फलवस्त्रहिरण्यादि चोपढौकनिकं स्थापयेदित्यपि शिष्टाचारः ।

तदनन्तरं—

206. **प्रथमं चालभेत्तीर्थं प्रणवेन जलं शुचि ।**
अवगाह्य ततः स्नायाद् यथावन्मन्त्रयोगतः ॥

प्र०ख० 1.28.123

(1) प्रणवेन तीर्थं स्पृष्ट्वा ततः शुचि जलमवगाहेत् सचैलं स्नायादित्यर्थः, काशीखण्डे शिवशर्मोपाख्याने—

203.4. तीर्थं; LI तीर्थे । 205. जानुभ्यां; LI दृष्टिभ्यां । 205. दृष्ट्या; C1 चैव । 205.4. चोपढौकनिकं; C1 चौपढोकनिकं; P2 चौपठाकसमीपे (sic) । 206. चालभेत्; P3 C1 C2 K चालयेत् ।

207. आगत्य दृष्ट्वा मणिकर्णिकायां
उद्‍गवहां स्वर्गतरङ्गिणीं सः ।
सचैलमाप्लुत्य जलेऽमल

का०ख० 7.72ab, 73a

(1) इति लिङ्गात् । (2) ततो 'मन्त्रयोगतो' मन्त्रमुच्चार्य 'यथावद्' विध्युक्तमार्गेण स्नायात् । मन्त्रश्च प्रभासखण्डे—

208. ओम् नमो देवदेवाय शितिकण्ठाय दण्डिने ।
रुद्राय चापहस्ताय चक्रिणे वेधसे नमः ॥
सरस्वती च सावित्री वेदमाता गरीयसी ।
संनिधात्री भवत्वत्र तीर्थपापप्रणाशिनी ॥
सर्वेषामेव तीर्थानां मन्त्र एष उदाहृतः ।
इत्युच्चार्य नमस्कृत्वा स्नानं कुर्याद् यथाविधि ॥

प्र०ख० 1.28.124–126b

(1) अत्र 'इत्युच्चार्य नमस्कृत्वे'त्युक्तेरयं मन्त्रो न स्नाने करणं किन्तु प्रार्थनमात्रे। (2) स्नानकरणत्वे च मन्त्रलिङ्गबाधोऽपि स्यात्। यद्वायं मन्त्रः —

209. सागरस्वननिर्घोष दण्डहस्तासुरान्तक ।
जगत्स्रष्टर् जगन्मर्दिन् नमामि त्वां सुरेश्वर ॥
तीक्ष्णदंष्ट्र महाकाय कल्पान्तदहनोपम ।
भैरवाय नमस्तुभ्यमनुज्ञां दातुमर्हसि ॥
इमं मन्त्रं समुच्चार्य तीर्थे स्नानं समाचरेत् ।
अन्यथा तत्फलस्यार्धं तीर्थेशो हरति ध्रुवम् ॥

(1) अनयोश्च मन्त्रयोः प्रार्थनाख्यकार्यैकत्वाद् विकल्पः ।

(2) इदञ्च यथाविधि स्नानं वपनानन्तरं कार्यं,

---

207. मणिकर्णिकायां उदग्वहां; L2 मणिकर्णिकायां मुदावहां । 208. संनिधात्री; All but P1 have सन्निधानी (See Critical Apparatus III.B.1.d and III. D.3). 208. भवत्वत्र; C1 L2 भवन्त्वत्र, L1 भवन्त्यत्र । 208. तीर्थ–; P2 तीर्थे; K तीव्र–। 208.1. स्नाने; K स्नान–। 208.2. –बाधोऽपि स्यात्; K बाधोऽपि न स्यात् । 209. त्वां; P3 C2 त्वा। 209. तीर्थे; P3 C2 K तीर्थ–।

210. **पूर्वमावाहनं तीर्थे मुण्डनं तदनन्तरम् ।**
ततः स्नानादिकं कुर्यात् पश्चाच्छ्राद्धं समाचरेद् ॥

इति वचनात् ।

यत्तु–

211. **गत्वा स्नानं प्रकुर्वीत वपनं तदनन्तरम् ।**
(= 282)

(1) इति वचनं, तत्सचैलस्नानविषयम् ।

211.1. After –विषयं; P2 इति तीर्थस्नानं ।

अथ तीर्थोपवासः

(2) तत्र 'स्नानं कुर्याद् यथाविधीत्य् [208] एतदनन्तरं वचः

212. उपवासं ततः कुर्यात् तस्मिन्नहनि सुव्रतः ।
तीर्थोपवासाद् देवेशि अधिकं नास्ति किञ्चन ॥
पापानां पापशमनः सतामीप्सितकारकः ।
उपवासो विनिर्दिष्टो विशेषाद् देवताश्रये ॥
तीर्थोपवासं कुर्वीत तस्मात्तत्र वरानने ।
व्रती च तीर्थयायी च विधवा च विशेषतः ॥
परान्नभोजने देवि यस्यान्नं तस्य तत्फलम् ।

प्र०ख० 1.28.126c-d, 64-65b, 78c-79

काशीखण्डे—

213. तीर्थोपवासः कर्तव्यः शिरसो मुण्डनं तथा ।

का० ख० 6.65a-b (=229, 249)

नारदीये—

214. तीर्थमासाद्य कुर्वीत नरः शुचिरुपोषणम् ।
उपवासविशुद्धात्मा कर्तव्यं कर्तुमर्हसि ॥

अत्र काशीखण्डे—

215. यदह्नि तीर्थप्राप्तिः स्यात् तदह्नः पूर्ववासरे ।
उपवासः प्रकर्तव्यः प्राप्तेऽह्नि श्राद्धदो भवेद् ॥

का० ख० 6.66

(1) इति तीर्थप्राप्तेः पूर्वदिने उपवासो विहितः । (2) ततश्च 'उपवासं ततः कुर्यात् तस्मिन्नहनि सुव्रत इति [212] तीर्थप्राप्तिदिनेन सहास्य विकल्पः । (3) न च काशीखण्डस्य काशीमात्रविषयता, सकलतीर्थसाधारणविधिमुपक्रम्योक्तेः ।

---

213. तथा; LI विना ।

(215.4) अत्र कश्चित्; "पञ्चदशरात्रे तन्त्रेण प्रयोज्यायां सुब्रह्मण्यायां तद्गताग्निष्टुत्संज्ञकप्रथमाहे एकाहाग्निष्टुतो नामातिदेशेनोपसत्कालीन-सुब्रह्मण्याह्वानार्थमाग्नेयी प्राप्ता, द्वितीयादिचतुर्दशस्वहःसु स्वप्रकृत्यनुसारेण प्राप्तयैन्द्रचा बहूनामह्नामनुग्रहाय बाध्यते यथा, तथा प्रस्तुतेऽपि प्राप्तिदिनोप-वासविधायकबहुवाक्यानुरोधात् पूर्वदिनोपवासविधायकैककाशीखण्डवाक्यबाधात् तुल्यबलत्वाभावात् पूर्वदिनोपवासः पापक्षयद्वाराशरीरशुद्ध्यर्थो ग्रहणाद्युपवासवत् । (5) शुद्धान्तःकरणस्यैव यथोक्ततीर्थफलसम्भवात् । (6) न तु तीर्थप्राप्ति-निमित्त" इत्याह ।

(7) तन्न । यदि पूर्वदिनोपवास आवश्यकमङ्गं तदा तीर्थप्राप्तिदिनो-पवासस्यापि नैमित्तिकत्वेनावश्यकत्वाद् उपवासद्वयप्रसक्तौ सकल-शिष्टाचारविरोधः । (8) अथानावश्यकस्तदा नित्यवच्छ्रवणविरोधः । (9) किञ्च, काम्यत्वे एतस्य फलान्तरादृष्टान्तरकल्पनाप्रसङ्गः । (10) किञ्च; प्राप्तिपूर्वदिनरूपकालविशिष्टोपवासान्तरविधौ गौरवम् । (11) अस्मत्पक्षे तु प्राप्त एवोपवासे वैकल्पिकपूर्वदिनरूपकालमात्रविधानाल्लाघवम्, अदृष्टा-न्तरकल्पना च नास्ति ।

(12) न चात्रास्ति प्राप्तिदिनविशिष्टस्यैवोपवासस्य प्राप्तिर्येनोत्पत्ति-शिष्टगुणावरुद्धे उत्पन्नशिष्टो गुणो वाजिनवन्न निविशेत् । (13) 'मुण्डनं चोपवासञ्चे'त्येवमादिवचनैः [231] स्वरूपमात्रविधौ तद्दिनपूर्वदिनरूपकालद्वयस्य वाक्यान्तरैरुत्पन्नशिष्टत्वेन तुल्यबलत्वाद् अग्निहोत्रे पयोदध्यादिवद् विकल्पोपपत्तेः ।

(14) न च "प्राप्तिदिनकर्तव्यमुण्डनानन्तरोक्त्या उपवासस्य तद्दिन-कर्तव्यम् एवोत्पत्तिवाक्येऽवगम्यत" इति वाच्यम्, । (15) पाठ-मात्रकल्पत्वात् । (16) काशीखण्डवाक्यस्थपूर्वदिनशब्दरूपश्रुतिविरोधे च तृतीयस्थानपठितेऽप्याश्विने 'आश्विनो दशमो गृह्यत' इति दशमश्रुतिविरोध इव पाञ्चमिकन्यायेन पाठस्य क्रमाकल्पकत्वात् । (17) एवञ्च पूर्वदिनोपवास-वाक्यस्योक्तयुक्तिभिरानर्थक्यप्रसङ्गाच्च 'आनर्थक्यप्रतिहतानां विपरीतं बलाबलमि'-ति न्यायेन बहुभिरपि तद्दिनोपवासवाक्यैर्बाधानापत्तिः (18) पञ्चदशरात्रे हि बह्वनुरोधादाग्नेयी चोदकेन यद्यपि न प्राप्यते, तथापि तदतिरिक्ताङ्गप्रापणेन चरितार्थ्यं चोदकस्य । (19) इह तु नित्यवच्छ्रुतवाक्यानर्थक्यप्रसङ्ग एव स्यादिति वैषम्यम् ।

215.4. –कालीन–; P3 K –काल– । 215.12. वाजिनवन् न; L1 जनिवन् न (sic) P2 P3 C1 C2 K वाजपेयवन् न (see Critical Apparatus III.B.2b). 215.15. पाठमात्रकल्पत्वात्; C1 C2 L2 पाठमात्रकल्प्यत्वात् । 215.16. पाञ्चमिक–; P3 K वाचनिक– । 215.18. हि; K ऽह्नि ।

(20) किञ्च; काशीखण्डे 'तीर्थोपवासः कर्तव्यः शिरसो मुण्डनं तथे'ति [213] पूर्वमुपवासमभिधायानन्तरवाक्ये 'यदह्नी'ति [215] अस्मिन् पूर्वदिनरूपकालविधानाद् उपक्रमानुरोधेनापि पूर्वदिनोपवासपक्ष एवाभिप्रेतः प्रतीयते। (21) एतेन "तीर्थोपवासपदाश्रवणान्न पूर्वदिनवाक्यं तीर्थोपवासपरं, किन्तु शरीरशुद्ध्यर्थोपवासविधायकम्" इति अपाकृतं भवति, (22) उपक्रम-वाक्ये तीर्थोपवासपदश्रवणाद् एतस्यापि तत्परत्वावगतेः।

(23) यदि तु मीमांसकम्मन्यः कश्चिदेवं वदेत्; "मुण्डनोत्तरोप-दिष्टोपवासस्य प्राग्दिनापकर्षे मुण्डनस्याप्यपकर्षः स्यात्, 'तिष्ठन्तं पशुं प्रयजन्ती'-तिश्रुतप्रयाजापकर्षे प्रयाजप्राचीनाङ्गापकर्षवद्" इति, (24) तदपि न। तत्र हि प्रकृतौ निर्ज्ञातक्रमाणामङ्गानां चोदकेन पशौ प्राप्तानां पश्चात्तन-प्रयाजापकर्षे निर्ज्ञातक्रमानुरोधात् पूर्वेषामप्यपकर्षः! (25) इह तूत्पत्तिवाक्ये स्वरूपमात्रज्ञाने सति क्रमापेक्षायां प्राग्दिनप्राप्तिदिनबोधकवाक्यानां युगपदेव प्रवृत्तेर्निज्ञातक्रमत्वाभावस्योक्तत्वात् दर्शे 'पूर्वेद्युरमावास्यायां वेदिं करोती'ति पूर्वदिनविहितवेदेः पुरोडाशाभिवासनान्तपदार्थानपकर्षकत्ववद् उपवासस्यापि न मुण्डनापकर्षकता स्यात्। (26) एतेन "उपवासस्य पूर्वदिनकर्तव्यत्वे मुण्डनस्यापि तद्दिनकर्तव्यत्वापत्तिरि'त्यपास्तम्। एचञ्च —

216. **आदौ कृत्वा तु वपनं सोमेश्वरसमीपत।**

प्र० ख० 1.29.4 a-b (=250)

इति प्रभासखण्डवचः,

217. **उपवासं ततः कुर्यात्तस्मिन्नहनी—।**

प्र०ख० 1.28.126 c-d (=212)

(1) त्यादीनि च प्राप्तिदिनोपवासवचांसि पाक्षिकत्वेन सर्वाण्युपपन्नानीति न काचिदनुपपत्तिः।

(2) यच्च काशीखण्डे शिवशर्मोपाख्याने 'ततो मायापुरीं प्राप्त' इत्युपक्रम्य—

218. **तीर्थोपवासं कृत्वा स निशि जागरणं तथा।**
प्रातः स्नात्वा च गङ्गायां तर्प्यान् संतर्प्य यत्नतः॥

216. –समीपत; P2 L1–समीप। 217.2. प्राप्त; P1 प्राप्य। 218. तर्प्यान्; K तथा, L2 तीर्थान्।

यावत् स पारणं कर्तुमियेष द्विजसत्तमः ।
तावच्छीतज्वराक्रान्तश्चकम्पेऽत्यर्थमातुरः ॥

का० ख० 7.117–118

(1) इति प्राप्तिदिनोपवास वचनं; तथा तत्रैव कलावत्युपाख्याने माल्यवतो राज्ञः प्राप्तिदिने जागराद्युक्त्वा 'अथ प्रातः समुत्थाये'त्यभिधाय

219. **पारणं कृतवांस्तत** का० ख० 34.113b

इति वचनं ; (1) ब्रह्मवैवर्ते च कामकलोपाख्याने

220. **आगत्य मणिकर्ण्यां तु स्नात्वा दत्त्वा धनं बहु ।**
वपनं कारयित्वा तु स्थिता शुद्धा पयोव्रते– । (=251)

ति वचनम्, (1) तत्सर्वं उपाख्यानरूपत्वात् पक्षे उपपन्नत्वाच्च न पूर्वदिनोपवासविधिं बाधते ।

(2) यत्तु "श्राद्धवद् उपवासस्यापि तीर्थप्राप्तिनिमित्तकस्य तद्दिन एव कर्तव्यतोचिता न तु पूर्वेऽह्नि निमित्तस्याजातत्वात् । (3) अन्यथा 'सति निमित्ते नैमित्तिकम्' इति न्यायविरोधादि"ति, (4) तत्तु मीमांसानतिदर्शन निबन्धनम् । (5) लोके भविष्यन्त्या अपि वृष्टेर्गृहकरणे, वेदे च भविष्यतोऽपि रथन्तरसामत्वादेरैन्द्रवायव्याग्रतादौ निमित्तत्वदर्शनात् । अतएवोक्तं भाष्यकृता—

221. **अथ यदुक्तं 'पूर्वेण निमित्तेन भवितव्यमुत्तरेण नैमित्तिकेने' ति नैतन्नियोगतः । भवति हि भवष्यिदपि निमित्तं यथा 'वर्षिष्यती'ति कृषिगृहकर्मानुष्ठानम् ।** शब० 2.3.1.2, p. 577

इति । भट्टपादा अप्याहुः —

222. **भूतभविष्यवर्तमानां चानियमेन लोके वेदे च निमित्तत्वं दृष्टिमिति रथन्तरभविष्यत्वमचोद्यम्**

त० वा० 2.3.1.2, p. 577

इति । एतद्वार्तिकन्यायसुधाप्यत्रार्थेऽनुसन्धेया;

223. **यदि तु भूतेनैव निमित्तेन भवितव्यमित्याग्रहस्तथापि 'भविष्यती'त्यवधारितत्वेन भूतत्वान्निमित्तता सम्भवत्येव ।**

न्या० सु० 2.3.1.2, p. 896

219.1. ब्रह्मवैवर्ते; L2 ब्रह्मकैवर्ते । 220:5. गृहकरणे, वेदे च; K गृहकरणवद् एव । 220.5. –वायवाग्रतादौ; P2 –वायवग्रहादौ । 221. कृषिगृहकर्मानुष्ठानम्; C1 कृषिकर्मगृहकर्मानुष्ठानम् । 222. चानियमेन; K च नियमेन ।

तदप्याहुर्भट्टपादाः —

224. **यदेकान्तेनावधारितं तन्निष्पन्नमेवे- ।**

त० वा० 2.3.1.2, p. 577

(1) ति तस्मात्पूर्वदिनोपवासो न केवलपापक्षयार्थः किन्तु तीर्थप्राप्तिनिमित्तक एव (2) तेन तीर्थोपवासे प्राप्तिदिनं तत्पूर्वदिनं वेति कालविकल्पः सिद्धः । (3) तत्राद्ये पक्षे तीर्थश्राद्धशेषस्याघ्राणं कृत्वोपवासः, एकादश्यादिवत् ।

(4) "अयञ्च तीर्थोपवासः फलविशेषार्थ एव नत्वावश्यकः,

225. **तीर्थमधिगम्य व्रतोपवासनियमयुक्तस्त्र्यहमवगाहमानस्त्रिरात्र-मुषित्वा सर्वपापेभ्यो मुच्यते स्वस्तिमांश्च भवती–**

(=668)

(1) ति देवलवचने त्रिरात्रोपवासत्र्यहावगाहनयोः सर्वपापविमोकस्वस्ति-मत्त्वफलकत्वाभिधानाद्" इति कल्पतरौ । (2) तन्न, पूर्वोदाहृतनारदाद्यादि-वचनैरावश्यकतया विधानात् । (3) देवलवचनं तु तीर्थोपवासपरमपि त्वति-रिक्तकाम्यत्र्यहोपवासपरम् । (4) तीर्थोपवासविधायकवाक्येषु एकवचना-न्तत्वेन श्रवणात् तस्यैकरात्रोपवासत्वात् । (5) काशीखण्डे शिवशर्मोपाख्याने कलावत्युपाख्याने च तीर्थोपवासे प्रातरेव पारणश्रवणाद् एकाहसाध्यत्वात् । (6) तस्मादावश्यक उपवासः ।

224.2. वेति; L1 चेति । 225. अधिगम्य; C1 अभिगम्य । 225.6. After उपवासः; P2 इति उपवासविचारः ।

अथ तीर्थे मुण्डनम्

देवलः

226. **मुण्डनं चोपवासश्च सर्वतीर्थेष्वयं विधिः ।**
वर्जयित्वा कुरुक्षेत्रं विशालं विरजं गयाम् ॥
(ग०पु० 1.84.4) (=250)

(1) 'विरजम्' उत्कलदेशे, यत्र धर्मराजेन गयासुरनाभौ विरजाद्रिः स्थापितः । तदुक्तं वायवीये—

227. **आक्रान्तं दैत्यजठरं धर्मेण विरजाद्रिणा ।**
नाभिकूपसमीपे तु देवी तु विरजा स्थिते– ॥ ति ।

(1) दक्षिणदेशस्थलोणारक्षेत्रमपि विरजम्, आदित्यपुराणे तस्य विरजत्वोक्तेः —

228. **एवं कृते विधानेऽस्मिन् विरजे विरजो भवेद् ।**

इत्यादि ।

(1) क्वचित्तु 'नैमिषं पुष्करं गयाम्' इति पाठः,
(2) 'विशालं पुष्करं गयाम्' इति वा ।
(3) अन्ये तु 'वर्जयित्वा गयां गङ्गाम्' इति पठन्ति । (4) तत्त्वयुक्तं, बहुनिबन्धेष्वदर्शनात् गङ्गाक्षौरविधायकवक्ष्यमाणबहुवाक्यविरोधाच्च ।

काशीखण्डे—

229. **तीर्थोपवासः कर्तव्यः शिरसो मुण्डनं तथा ।**
शिरोगतानि पापानि यान्ति मुण्डनतो यतः ॥
का० ख० 6.65(=213, 249)

तथा—

230. **उदकं शोणितं दद्यात् पिण्डं दद्यादमेध्यवत् ।**
नोपतिष्ठति तत्सर्वं यो विना मुण्डितं शिरः ॥ (=253)

227.1. -देशस्थ-; CI C2 -देशस्थं ।

स्कान्दे—

231. **मुण्डनं चोपवासञ्चे—**

प्र० ख० 1.29.10

ति देवलवदेव ।

(1) अत्र प्राच्याः " 'सर्वाणि तीर्थानि सन्त्यस्मिन्' इति बहुव्रीहिणा सर्वतीर्थशब्दस्य प्रयागमात्रपरत्वात् तत्रैवोपवासवपने" इत्याहुः । (2) तदसत्, एकवचनेन विग्रहे अन्यपदार्थस्य प्रयागस्य प्रकृत्यर्थस्यैकत्वात् प्रातिपदिकार्थ-बहुत्वाभावात् बहुवचनानुत्पत्तिप्रसङ्गे 'सर्वतीर्थेषु' इति पदस्यासाधुताप्रसङ्गात् । (3) एवञ्च सति यदुच्यते "ग्रहैकत्ववद् अविवक्षितं बहुत्वमि"ति तद् गर्भस्रावेणैव गलितं, बहुवचनस्यैवानुत्पत्तौ विवक्षितत्वाविवक्षितत्वचिन्ता-या निरवकाशत्वात् । (4) 'ग्रहं संमार्ष्टी'त्यत्र हि प्रत्येकं ग्रहेष्वेकत्वस्य वर्तमानत्वाद् एकवचनान्तस्य साधुतायां सर्वग्रहग्रहणार्थमेकत्वाविवक्षोच्यते । (5) नैवं प्रकृतेऽस्ति ।

(6) अथैतद्दोषपरिहाराय 'सर्वाणि तीर्थानि सन्ति येष्वि' ति बहुवचनान्तेन विग्रहः क्रियते। (7) तथापि प्रयागलक्षणानां सर्वतीर्थशब्दप्रतिपाद्यानामनेकेषाम् अभावाद् बहुवचनानुत्पत्तावसाधुता तदवस्था ।

(8) अथ "देवप्रयागादीनि बहूनि प्रयागानि सन्ती"त्युच्येत । (9) तथापि तेषु सर्वतीर्थसत्तारूपावयवार्थाभावाद् बहुव्रीह्यर्थबहुत्वा-भावाद् बहुवचनानुत्पत्तिः सैव भवेत् ।

यदि तु

232. **सर्वतीर्थानि देवाश्च वसन्त्यत्राविमुक्तके ।** (= 237)

233. **सर्वतीर्थमयी गङ्गे—** (= 244)

(1) त्यादिवचनालोचनेन सर्वतीर्थानामनेकेषां सत्त्वात् बहुवचनोत्पत्तिम् उपपाद्य ग्रहैकत्ववद् बहुत्वाविवक्षयाभिप्रेतसिद्धिः क्रियेत, (2) तर्हि सर्वतीर्थ-शब्दार्थानां बहूनां सत्त्वात् क्वैकत्र सर्वतीर्थे वपनादीति सन्देह एव स्यात् । (3) न तु सितासितसम्भेदाख्यप्रयागपरत्वनिर्णयः प्रकरणादेर्निर्णायकस्यात्रा-भावादिति वक्ष्यमाणत्वात् ।

231.3. —चिन्ताया; P2 K—चिन्तायां । 231.4. सर्वग्रहग्रहणार्थम्; P3 C2 K सर्वग्रहणार्थम् । 231.8. उच्येत; L2 उच्यते । 231.9. बहुचनानुत्पत्तिः; P1 बहुवचनानुपपत्तिः । 232. सर्व—; K सर्वे । 233.1. क्रियेत; L2 क्रियते ।

अथ

234. **प्रयागे वपनं कुर्याद् वाराणस्यां तनुं त्यजेद् ।**

(1) इत्यादिनिर्णायकवचनान्तरैः सर्वतीर्थशब्दस्य प्रयागमात्रपरता ।

(2) तन्न, देवप्रयागादीनां बहूनां प्रयागाणां सत्त्वाद् विवक्षितविशेष-निर्णयात् ।

(3) "निरुपपदः प्रयागशब्दस्तेषु नास्तीति एतेन निर्णय" इति चेत्, (4) न । तदा हि 'सर्वतीर्थेष्वि'ति विधेश्चतुर्धाकरणवद् अयमुपसंहारः स्यात्, न च तत् सम्भवति । (5) तत्र हि 'पुरोडाशं चतुर्धा करोतो'ति-सामान्यविधेः पुरोडाशमात्रविषयत्वेनास्पष्टत्वाद् 'आग्नेयं चतुर्धा करोती'ति-विशेषविषयतयोपसंहारो युक्तः । (6) इह तु 'सर्वतीर्थेष्वयं विधिरि'ति-सामान्यविधेः सर्वशब्दबहुवचनबलाद् अशेषतीर्थविषयतया स्पष्टत्वाद् उपसंहारा-सम्भवात् । तदुक्तं—

235. **सामान्यविधिरस्पष्टः संह्रियेत विशेषण ।**

त० वा० 3.4.14.41, p. 977

इति (1) सत्यपि चोपसंहारत्वे वक्ष्यमाणवाक्यैस्तीर्थान्तरेऽपि उपसंहार-सम्भवाच्च ।

(2) नापि पदवाक्यवत् प्रयागवाक्यस्य सर्वतीर्थवाक्यबाधकता । (3) तत्र हि आहवनीयवाक्यस्य पदवाक्येन विषयविशेषे बाधेऽपि होमान्तररूपविषयसद्भावाद् अत्यन्तबाधाभावे वैय्यर्थ्यप्रसङ्गस्याभावाद् बाध्यत्वं युक्तम् । (4) इह तु प्रयागवाक्येन सर्वतीर्थवाक्यस्य बाधे विषयान्तराभावाद् व्यर्थतैवापद्येत ।

(5) किञ्च; सामान्यस्य विशेषणबाधो भवति, न च सर्वतीर्थवाक्यस्य सामान्यता, प्रयागविषयत्वस्य त्वयाङ्गीकारेण विशेषविषयत्वात् ।

(6) किञ्च; उपसंहारे बाधे वोच्यमाने सर्वतीर्थवाक्यस्य सामान्यरूपता-प्रसङ्गात् । (7) प्रयागमात्रपरत्वं सर्वतीर्थशब्दस्योच्यमानं कथं न विरुध्यते ?

(8) यत्तु; " 'प्रयागे वपनं कुर्यादि'त्ययं [234] नापूर्वविधिः, प्रभासखण्डे 'आदौ

234.2. प्रयागाणां; K प्रयागादीनां । 234.3. तेषु नास्तीति; P1 तेषु हि नास्तीति । 234.4. अयं; P2 L2 omitted. 234.4. तत्; P3 स । 234.6. सर्वशब्द—; P2 सर्वशब्दवत् । 235. विशेषण; C1 विशेषत । 235.1. चो—; P2 P3 C1 C2 वो— । 235.5. सामान्यस्य; LI सामान्यार्थस्य ।

कृत्वा तु वपनं सोमेश्वरसमीपत' [216] इति प्रभासे वपनं विधाय 'मुण्डनं चोपवासं चे'ति [226] वाक्यस्य तीर्थान्तरेषु मुण्डनविधायकस्य सत्त्वात् । (9) देवलस्मृतौ चानारम्भ्यविधानात् । (10) नापि नियमविधिः, सर्वतीर्थवाक्येनैव प्राप्तौ अप्राप्तांशाभावेन तत्पूरणाभावात् । (11) नापि परिसंख्या; तदा हि 'प्रयागे वपनमेव नान्यद्' इति वा वचनव्यक्तिः, 'प्रयाग एव वपनम्' इति वा। (12) नाद्यः स्नानादिनिवृत्तिप्रसङ्गात् (13) न द्वितीयः प्राप्तबाधादिदोषत्रयापत्तेर्; । (14) अतोऽवयुत्यानुवादो ऽयं न विधिरि"ति कैश्चिद् दूषितम्; (15) तत्तु विकल्पविभीषिकामात्रम्, अपूर्वविधिता-सम्भवात् । (16) न च देवलादिवचनेनैव प्राप्तेरपूर्वत्वाभावः । (17) ग्रन्थभेदे वक्तृभेदे च समानार्थानामपि विधित्वाक्षतेः । (18) अन्यथाऽनेकशाखास्थानामग्निहोत्रादिविधीनामनेकस्मृतिस्थानाञ्च सन्ध्यावन्दनादि-विधीनामनुवादकताप्रसङ्गात्। (19) प्रयागवाक्यप्राप्तत्वात् तस्य वानुवादकता तद्वाक्यप्राप्तत्वादस्य वेति विनिगमनाविरहश्च । (20) किञ्चैव-मस्यानुवादत्वे वक्ष्यमाणानि तीर्थान्तरमुण्डनवाक्यान्यपि अनुवादकानि समान-न्यायतया भवेयुः (21) न च बहूनामनुवादकता न्याय्या । (22) अनर्थकश्चानुवादः । (23) प्रत्युत प्रतितीर्थं प्रातिस्विकमुण्डनोपवासविधायक-वाक्यप्राप्तार्थस्य समुदायानुवादकता सर्वतीर्थवाक्यस्यैवापद्येतेत्यलं स्वयूथ्य-विवादेन, प्रकृतमनुसरामः ।

(24) अस्य वचनस्याग्निपुराणवायुपुराणयोर्गयाप्रकरणपाठात् स्कन्द-पुराणे च प्रभासप्रकरणपाठात् कैव शङ्का प्रयागपरतायाः ? (25) किञ्च, 'सर्वाणि तीर्थानि सन्त्यत्रे'ति बहुव्रीहौ

236. **दशकोटिसहस्राणि तीर्थानां वै महीपते ।**
सांनिध्यं पुष्करे तेषां त्रिसन्ध्यं कुरुनन्दने- ॥
म० भा० 3.80.42

त्यारण्यकपर्ववाक्यात् पुष्करस्य,

237. **सर्वतीर्थानि देवाश्च वसन्त्यत्राविमुक्तक** ॥ (= 232)

235.15. — विभीषिका —; P2 — विभाषिका— । 235.19. वानुवादकता; P3 C2 K L1 L2 वानुवादता । 235.21. अनुवादकता; P3 C2 K L2 अनुवादता । 235.22. अनर्थकश्; P2 अनर्थश् । 236. महीपते; P1 महामते ।

(1) इति ब्रह्मवैवर्तवचनाच्च काश्या अपि सर्वतीर्थत्वात् तत्रापि प्रसङ्गः। (2) एवं तत्तत्तीर्थेषु प्रशंसार्थानि सर्वतीर्थसद्भावप्रतिपादकानि वाक्यानि सन्ति । (3) तानि तु विस्तरभयान्नोच्यन्ते । तथा—

238. **प्रयागश्चापि तीर्थेन्द्रः सर्वतीर्थार्पितं मलम् ।**
महाधिनां महाघञ्च हरेत् पाञ्चनदाद् बलात् ॥
का० ख० 2.59.16c–17b

(1) इत्यादीनि च पञ्चनदप्रकरणादिषु वाक्यानि विरुध्येरन् सर्वतीर्थानां तत्र सत्त्वे ।

(2) अथ "योगमनपेक्ष्य प्रयागे रूढः सर्वतीर्थशब्द" उच्यते । (3) तन्न, तत्र प्रमाणाभावात् ।

239. **"एवं कुरुष्व कौन्तेय सर्वतीर्थाभिषेचनम् ।**
यावज्जीवकृतं पापं तत्क्षणादेव नश्यती– ॥
म० पु० 108.33

(1) ति मत्स्यपुराणे प्रयागप्रकरणपठितं वचनं तत्र प्रमाणम्" इति चेत्, (2) तन्न । मत्स्यपुराणे हि 'अग्नितीर्थमिति ख्यातम्' [म०पु० 108.27a] इत्युपक्रम्य बहूनि तीर्थान्युक्त्वा

240. **अन्ये च बहवस्तीर्थाः सर्वपापहराः शुभाः ।**
तेषु स्नात्वा दिवं यान्ति ये मृतास्तेऽपुनर्भवाः ॥
एवं कुरुष्व कौन्तेय सर्वतीर्थाभिषेचनम् ।
यावज्जीवकृतं पापं तत्क्षणादेव नश्यती – ॥
म० पु० 108.31,33

(1) त्यन्तेनाभिधानात् प्रकृतसकलतीर्थपरः सर्वशब्दो गम्यते । (2) तत्कथमेतद्बलात् सर्वतीर्थशब्दः प्रयागपरः ?

किञ्च—

241. **सर्वाणि तीर्थानि वसन्ति तत्र**
यत्राच्युतोदारकथाप्रसङ्गः । इति ।

238.1. तत्र; P1 (+correction in P2) तत्रैव । 239. नश्यतीति; C2 नंक्ष्यतीति । 239.1.—पठितं; P3 K —पठित— । 240. नश्यतीत्य्; L2 नंक्ष्यतीत्य्, L1 नक्ष्यतीत्य् । 240.1. अन्तेनाभिधानात्; P3 C1 C2 L2 अन्तेऽभिधानात् ।

242. **सर्वाणि तीर्थान्यपि चाग्निहोत्र-**
तुल्यानि नैवेति वयं वदाम । इति (=80)

243. **सर्वतीर्थेषु यत्पुण्यं सर्वतीर्थेषु यत्फलम् ।** इति

244. **सर्वतीर्थमयी गङ्गे—** (=233)

(1) त्यादौ सर्वतीर्थशब्दोऽनेकतीर्थपरो दृश्यते, न तु प्रयागपरः ।

245. **प्रयागं सर्वतीर्थेभ्यो प्रवदन्त्यधिकं विभो ।**
म० भा० 3.83.74c-d

(1) इति भारवाक्यञ्च विरुध्येत प्रयागस्य सर्वतीर्थतायाम् । (2) अपि च अग्निपुराणे

246. **माहात्म्यं सर्वतीर्थानां वक्ष्ये यद् भुक्तिमुक्तिदम् ।**
अग्नि पु० 109.1a-b

(1) इत्युपक्रम्य गङ्गाकाशीप्रयागादिबहुतीर्थानि बहुभिरध्यायैरभिधायान्ते 'मुण्डनञ्चोपवासश्च सर्वतीर्थेष्वयं विधिर्' [अ० पु० 115.7c-d] [=226] इत्युक्तम् । (2) तेन नानातीर्थविषयता न तु प्रयागमात्रपरतेति ।

(3) किञ्च; यत्रैकतीर्थपरः सर्वतीर्थशब्दः पुराणेषु दृष्टस्तत्रैकवचनान्त एव प्रयुज्यते, यथा सह्याद्रिखण्डे मातृतीर्थप्रकरणे

247. **सह्याद्रेः परमं तीर्थं मातृतीर्थमिति स्मृतम् ।**
मातृतीर्थं परं ज्ञेयं सर्वतीर्थं मुनीश्वराः ॥
तत्र सर्वाणि तीर्थानि यत्र रामोऽथ रेणुके- । ति

248. **सर्वतीर्थस्य च स्नानात् सर्वतीर्थे नृणां स्नानम् ।**
सर्वतीर्थात् परं तीर्थं न भूतं न भविष्यती- ॥

इत्यादौ । (1) न चात्रैकवचनान्तः प्रयुज्यते ।

(2) अपि च; तेषु तेषु तीर्थेषु मुण्डनविधायकवचांसि पुराणेषूपलभ्यन्त एव । (3) तत्र काशीखण्डे 'प्रथमं तीर्थराजं त्वि'त्यादिना [63] ग्रन्थेन बहूनि तीर्थान्युक्त्वा मध्ये च तीर्थयात्राप्रकारमभिधाय

246.1 अभिधायान्ते; K अभिधायान्ते च । 248.2. तेषु तेषु; LI तेषु । 248.3. तीर्थराजं; Pl तीर्थराजस् ।

249. **तीर्थोपवासः कर्तव्यः शिरसो मुण्डनं तथा ।**
शिरोगतानि पापानि यान्ति मुण्डनतो यत ॥ (=213, 229)

(1) इति सामान्येनैव सकलतीर्थविषये मुण्डनमुक्तम् ।

प्रभासखण्डे—

250. **तत्र स्नानं प्रकुर्वीत विगाह्य निधिमम्भसाम् ।**
आदौ कृत्वा तु वपनं सोमेश्वरसमीपतः ॥ (=216)
शङ्करं मनसा ध्यायन् केशांस्तत्र परित्यजेत् ।
तत्र त्यक्त्वाखिलान् केशान् भूयः स्नानं समाचरेत् ॥
यत्किञ्चित् कुरुते पापं पुरुषो वृत्तिकर्षितः ।
तत्ततः पर्वतसुते सर्वं केशेषु तिष्ठति ॥
तस्मात्सर्वप्रयत्नेन केशांस्तत्र परित्यजेत् ।
अश्वमेधसहस्राणां सहस्रं यः समाचरेत् ॥
नासौ तत्फलमाप्नोति वपनाद् यच्च लभ्यते ।
क्षुरकर्म न शस्तं स्याद् योषितां तु वरानने ॥
सभर्तृकाणां तत्रैव विधिं तासां शृणुष्व मे ।
सर्वान् केशान् समुद्धृत्य छेदयेदङ्गुलद्वयम् ॥
प्र०ख० 1.29.3c-6b, 12, 8-9b

(1) इत्येतावता प्रभासीयं मुण्डनं विधायान्ते प्रसङ्गात् सर्वतीर्थेषु मुण्डनोपवासौ विहितौ

250. **मुण्डनञ्चोपवासञ्च सर्वतीर्थेष्वयं विधिर् ।** इति ।
प्र० ख० 1.29.10 (=226)

(2) ब्रह्मवैवर्तेऽपि कामकलोपाख्याने काश्यां मुण्डनोपवासान्यार्थ-दर्शनम् ;

251. **आगत्य मणिकर्ण्यां तु स्नात्वा दत्त्वा धनं बहु ।**
वपनं कारयित्वा तु स्थिता शुद्धा पयोव्रते —॥ ति ।
(=220)

(1) 'पयोव्रता' जलमात्राहारेत्यर्थः ।

249.1. प्रभासखण्डे; Pl Cl omitted. 249.1. प्रभासीयं; C2 K प्रभासीय— ।

अन्यत्रापि—

252. स्नानादिकं विधायादौ तीर्थे मुण्डनमाचरेत् ।
तीर्थोपवासनियमं कृत्वा श्राद्धं समाचरेत् ॥

तथा—

253. उदकं शोणितं दद्यात् पिण्डं दद्यादमेध्यवत् ।
नोपतिष्ठति तत्सर्वं यो विना मुण्डितं शिरः ॥

(=230)

तथा—

254. मुण्डनञ्चोपवासश्च गोभत्यां सिंहगे गुरौ ।
कन्यागते तु कृष्णायां न तु तत्तीरवासिनाम् ॥

तथा गङ्गाविषयेऽपि—

255. यावन्ति नखलोमानि वायुना प्रेरितानि वै ।
पतन्ति जाह्नवीतोये नराणां पापकारिणाम् ॥
तावद्वर्षसहस्राणि स्वर्गलोके महीयते ।

तथा—

256. गङ्गां प्राप्य सरिच्छ्रेष्ठां वपनं यो न कारयेत् ।
स कोटिकुलसंयुक्त आकल्पं रौरवं व्रजेत् ॥

(1) 'गङ्गायां भास्करक्षेत्रे' इति वा पाठः ।

तथा—

257. गङ्गायां भास्करक्षेत्रे मातापित्रोर्गुरोर्मृते ।
आधाने सोमपाने च वपनं सप्तसु स्मृतम् ॥ इति ।

प्र०ख० 1.29.11

तथा—

258. यावन्ति नखलोमानि गङ्गातोये पतन्ति हि ।
तावद्वर्षसहस्राणि स्वर्गलोके महीयते ॥

---

254. गोमत्यां P3 C2 K गौतम्यां, L2 गोतम्यां । 255. स्वर्गलोके; P1 (+correction in P2) ब्रह्मलोके

तथा—

259. **गङ्गां प्राप्य सरिच्छ्रेष्ठां कम्पन्ते पापसञ्चयाः ।**
केशानाश्रित्य तिष्ठन्तस्तस्मात्तान् परिवापयेत् ॥
गङ्गां सम्प्राप्य यो धीमान् मुण्डनं नैव कारयेत् ।
क्रियास्तस्याक्रियाः सर्वास्तीर्थद्रोही भवेन्नरः ॥

(1) एवं तत्तत्तीर्थेषु मुण्डनविधौ श्रूयमाणेऽपि प्रयागादन्यत्र मुण्डनाश्रवणं वदतां महत्साहसम् ।

(2) यदपि गङ्गामुण्डनविधायकवाक्यानां कल्पतरुकारालेखनेन निर्मूलत्वमुक्तं, (3) तदयुक्तम्, अस्थिक्षेपादिविधिवाक्यानां निर्मूलताप्रसङ्गात् ।(4)"कल्पतरुकारादर्शनं निर्मूलतायां मानं न तु तदलेखनम्" इति चेत्, (5) तददर्शने वा किं प्रमाणम् ? (6) न तावत् तदलेखनमेव, पूर्वदोषापत्तेः, (7) इतरेतराश्रयप्रसङ्गाच्च । (8) न चान्यदनिर्वचनात् । (9) सत्यपि वा तददर्शने कथं निर्मूलता ? (10) न हि कल्पतरुकारः सर्वज्ञोऽपर ईश्वर, इत्यलम् ।

(11) यदप्युच्यते, " 'गङ्गायां भास्करक्षेत्रे' [256.1, 257] इति वचो, 'वर्जयित्वा गयां गङ्गां विशालम्' [228.3] इति निषेधान् न सामान्यतो गङ्गापरं किन्तु प्रयागावच्छिन्नगङ्गापरम् । (12) निषेधवचनं तु तदनवच्छिन्नगङ्गापरम्" इति, (13) तदपि निषेधवाक्ये तादृशपाठस्य पूर्वमेवायुक्ततयोक्त्या निरस्तम् । (14) किञ्च "अनेकेषां वचनानां सामान्यरूपाणां विशेषपरता ऽविगीतशिष्टाचारानुरोधाद्" इति त्वयोच्यते । (15) स च वैदिकशिष्टानां मध्यदेशीयानां बहूनामभियुक्तानामाचारेण बाध्यते, (16) अवैदिकानभियुक्ताल्पाचारत्वात् । तदुक्तं भट्टचरणैः—

260. **अतः शास्त्राभियुक्तानामार्यावर्तनिवासिनाम् ।**
या मतिः सैव कर्माङ्गशब्दार्थत्वप्रमा मते— ॥ ति ।

त० वा० 1.3.4.9, p. 220

(1) किञ्च; सर्वतीर्थशब्दस्य प्रयागमात्रपरतायां बहुवचनानुपपत्तिः । (2) न च बहुव्रीहिणा प्रयागमात्रपरतायां 'ग्रहं सम्मार्ष्टी'तिवद् अविवक्षा ।

---

259. तिष्ठन्तस्; Cl तिष्ठन्ति । 259. नैव; Pl यो न ।

(3) बहुव्रीहावसाधुताप्रसङ्गेन विवक्षाऽविवक्षाचिन्ताया निरवकाशत्वस्य पूर्वमेवोदितत्वात् ।

(4) किञ्च; बहुवचनाविवक्षा नास्मत्पक्षविरोधिनी किन्त्वनुकूला । (5) तवैव तु प्रतिकूला । (6) तथा हि 'यस्य पुरोडाशौ क्षायतः,' 'यस्य सर्वाणि हवींपि नश्येयुर्वा दुष्येयुर्वा,' 'प्रयाजशेपेण हवींप्यभिधारयती'त्यादिवद् उद्देश्यगतसंख्याऽविवक्षायामेव प्रतितीर्थं मुण्डनं सिध्यति । (7) विवक्षायां तु समुदाय एव स्यान्नतु प्रत्येकम् ।

(8) कश्चित्तु "संस्कार्यरूपोद्देश्यविशेपणत्वाभावान्न ग्रहैकत्ववद् अविवक्षा । (9) निमित्तरूपोद्देश्यविशेपणत्वाभावाच्च न हविरुभयत्ववद्" इति दूषणमाह । (10) तन्न, नहि तत्र संस्कार्यत्वनिमित्तत्वे न्यायशरीरान्तर्गते, (11) उद्देश्यविशेषणत्वेनैवोभयत्वाविवक्षासिद्धेः ।

(12) उभयात्यधिकरणस्य पौनरुक्त्यं तु "निमित्तस्वरूपान्तर्गतमेवोभयत्वं न तु निमित्तविशेषणम्" इत्यधिकाशङ्काया निराक्रियमाणत्वात् परिहर्तव्यं, (13) न तु संस्कार्यनिमित्तरूपविपयभेदेन । (14) अन्यथा 'यस्य पुरोडाशौ क्षायतः', 'यस्य सर्वाणि हवींपि नश्येयुरि'तिनिमित्तोदाहरणं, 'प्रयाजशेपेण हवींप्यभिधारयती'ति च संस्कार्यहविर्बहुवचनोदाहरणं वार्तिककारीयमसङ्गतं स्यात् । अत एवाहुरुभयात्यधिकरणे पार्थसारथिमिश्राः—

261. **ग्रहाधिकरणन्यायेन 'उद्देश्यविशेषणमविवक्षितमि'ति स्थितमेव न तु निमित्तस्वरूपमविवक्षितम् । इह तु 'यथा नातिमात्रं वा हविर्मात्रं वा निमत्तं, मिलितं तु निमित्तम्, एवमुभयशब्दाम्नानात् त्रयमपि मिलितं निमित्तमस्त्वि'ति ।**

तन्त्ररत्न p. 554

भट्टसोमेश्वरा अपि

262. **उद्देश्यविशेषणविवक्षायां वाक्यभेदापत्तिलक्षणस्य न्यायस्याविवक्षासाधकस्य तुल्यत्वेऽपि, यथोभयपदानर्थक्यपरिहारायोभयत्वस्योद्देश्यान्तर्गतत्वेन विवक्षाशङ्काधिक्यान्नेहोदाहरणत्वम् ।**

इत्याद्याहुः ।

260.3 —चिन्ताया; K —चिन्तायां । 260.4. —पक्ष—; P2—पक्षे । 260.6. क्षायतः; P2 क्षीयतः । 260.6. प्रतितीर्थं; P2 P3 प्रतितीर्थे— । 260.14. क्षायतः; P2 क्षीयतः । 260.14. इति च; P2 इति, C1 L1 इति वा । 262. —लक्षणस्य; C1 —लक्षण— । 262. इत्याद्याहुः; C1 L2 इत्याहुः ।

(262.1) अपि च; असत्यपि निमित्तत्वे संस्कार्यत्वे वा उद्देश्यत्वाद् एव 'प्रयाजशेषं हविःषु क्षारयेद्' इतिवदविवक्षा कथं न भवेत् ? (2) वस्तुतस्तु 'सर्वतीर्थेष्वि'तिनिमित्तरूपतीर्थविशेपणत्वादेव बहुत्वस्योभयत्ववद् एवाविवक्षा संभवत्येव। (3) किञ्च; बहुवचनाविवक्षा कर्मधारयाश्रयणेन प्रतितीर्थमुण्डनपक्षेऽपि न विरुद्धा किन्त्वनुकूलैव। (4) अन्यथा सर्वतीर्थसमुदाय एव मुण्डनं स्यान्न प्रतितीर्थमित्युक्तम्। (5) अतो 'यस्य पुरोडाशौ', 'यस्य सर्वाणि हवींषि,' 'प्रयाजशेषण हवींषी'त्यादिवद् उद्देश्यविशेषणत्वेन बहुत्वाविवक्षाया आवश्यकत्वात् तुल्ययोगक्षेमत्वाच्च प्रयागमात्रमुण्डनवादिनं प्रति अविवक्षान्याया-प्रवृत्तिकथनं विवक्षापादकतया स्वपक्षक्षतिकरत्वेनात्यन्तायुक्तम्।

(6) तस्माद् अस्मदुक्तप्रकारेण निरवकाशतानुकूलताभ्यामेव ग्रहैकत्वाधि-करणन्यायोपन्यासो दूषणीय; (7) इत्यलं स्वपक्षविवादेन।

(8) किञ्च; बहुव्रीहौ पदद्वयार्थस्याप्राधान्यप्रसङ्गाद् अन्यपदार्थलक्षणा-प्रसङ्गाच्च निषादस्थपतिशब्द इव षष्ठीसमासापेक्षया बहुव्रीहितः कर्मधारय एव ज्यायान्, (9) पदार्थद्वयप्राधान्याल्लक्षणाभावाच्च। (10) एतेन 'राजपुरोहितौ सायुज्यकामौ यजेयातामि'त्यत्र तु क्षत्रियस्य पौरोहित्यनिषेधाद् अवेष्ट्यधिकरणसिद्धक्षत्रियवाचिराजशब्दवाच्ययोः पुरोहितत्वासम्भवाद् कर्म-धारयबाधेन द्वन्द्वोऽङ्गीकृतः। (11)इह तु कर्मधारये न किञ्चिद् बाधकमस्ति।

(12) अथ "कर्मधारयमेवाश्रित्यानेकतीर्थरूपत्वात् प्रयाग एव सर्वतीर्थ-शब्दार्थ" इत्यच्युते। (13) तदपि न, तदा हि बहुत्वं विवक्षितमविवक्षितं वा। (14) नाद्यः, उद्देश्यविशेषणत्वेन विवक्षाया असम्भवात्। (15) नान्यः, विवक्षा-व्यतिरेकेणानेकतीर्थसमूहरूपप्रयागालाभात्, प्रतितीर्थं मुण्डनप्रसङ्गाच्च। (16) तस्मान्न बहुव्रीहिः कर्मधारयो वा युज्यते।

(17) अथ "बहुव्रीहेरेकप्रयागार्थत्वेऽपि 'अदितिः पाशान् प्रमुमोक्त्वेतान्' इतिवद् अवयवतीर्थबहुत्वाभिप्रायेण छान्दसं, पूज्यतार्थं वा 'आचार्यास्त्वि'-त्यादिवत् बहुवचनम्" उच्यते। (18) तदप्ययुक्तम्; आञ्जस्येन गतौ सम्भव-त्याम्, अनन्यगतिकछान्दसत्वादिगतेरयुक्तत्वात्। (19) अपि च; तत्राग्निषोमीय-प्रकरणपठितस्य बहुवचनयुक्तस्य मन्त्रस्य प्रकरण एव छान्दसत्वेन बहुवचनं 'वायवः स्थे'तिवद् एकविषयमेवाङ्गीकृत्य, निवेश उत बहुपाशकेषु पशुगणेषूत्कर्ष

262.3. प्रतितीर्थ—; P1 प्रतितीर्थं। 262.10. तु; C1 K omitted. 262.15. नान्यः; P3 C1 K L1 नान्त्यः। 262.15. प्रतितीर्थं; P3 K प्रतितीर्थ—, C2 प्रतितीर्थे।

इति संदिह्य, प्रकरणगतैकपाशे बहुवचनस्यासामर्थ्याद् उत्कर्षं पूर्वपक्षयित्वा, (20) प्रकृत्यर्थस्य पाशस्य विभक्त्यर्थस्य कर्मकारकस्य च प्रकृतौ सत्त्वाद् अप्रधानभूतबहुवचनमात्रानुरोधात् प्रधानभूतस्य प्रातिपदिकस्य कारकवाचि-द्वितीयायाः मन्त्रस्य चोत्कर्षासम्भवान् निर्देशमात्रार्थं बहुवचनं, (21) द्विपत्नीकप्रयोग इव 'पत्नीं संनह्ये'त्येकवचनमवयवाभिप्रायं वेति (22) युक्तं नाव-मिकन्यायेन वक्तुम् । (23) अत्र तूक्तबहुबाधकवशात् प्रयागपरत्वासम्भवात् किमनुरोधेन छान्दसत्वमवयवाभिप्रायता वेति ?

(24) अपि च; सर्वतीर्थवाक्यस्य प्रयागमात्रपरता न तावत् परिसंख्या-व्यतिरेकेण लभ्यते। (25) तत्र च कीदृशी परिसंख्या ? (26) किं 'प्रयाग एव मुण्डनम्' इति वा 'प्रयागे मुण्डनमेवे'ति वा ? (27) न तावदन्त्यः, स्नानादिनि-वृत्तिप्रसङ्गात् । (28) न प्रथमः, पित्रादिमृतौ मुण्डनाभावप्रसङ्गात् ।

(29) अथ "तीर्थाधिकरणकं मुण्डनं प्रयाग एव नान्यत्रे"ति चेत् । (30) काश्यादितीर्थाधिकरणकपित्रादिमृतौ तदभावप्रसङ्गात् ।

(31) अथ "तीर्थनिमित्तकं मुण्डनं प्रयाग एवे"ति चेत् । (32) तथा सति तन्निमित्तकमुण्डनस्य रागतः प्राप्त्यभावाच्छास्त्रतः प्राप्तिः सामान्यतस्-तीर्थमात्रेऽङ्गीकृता स्यात्; (33) इति "तीर्थान्तरे मुण्डनविधानमेव नास्ती"ति वदतो भवतः कथं न स्वोक्तिविरोधः ?

(34) विकल्पद्वयेऽपि प्राप्तबाधादिदोषत्रयापत्तिश्च ।

(35) किञ्च; मुण्डनविधेरस्य प्रयागमात्रविषयत्वे अग्निवायुपुराणयो-र्गयाप्रकरणे पाठो नोपपद्येत ।

(36) किञ्च ; मुण्डनविधौ सर्वपदस्वरसादपि सर्वेषु तीर्थेषु मुण्डनम् । (37) न च "सर्वपदस्यासङ्कोचेऽतिप्रसङ्गः,

263. **प्रभावाददद्भुताद् भूमेः सलिलस्य च तेजसा ।**
परिग्रहान्मुनीनाञ्च तीर्थानां पुण्यता स्मृते- ॥ (=75)

(1) तिभारतस्थभीष्मवाक्येन सातिशयफलस्य स्थलस्य जलस्य च तीर्थत्वाभिधानाद् यत्रक्वचित् स्वदेशान्तर्गतप्रस्रवणादावपि मुण्डनोपवास-

---

262.20. अप्रधानभूत—; P3 L2 अप्रधानकृत— । 262.20. चोत्कर्षा—; C1 C2 L1 वोरकर्षा- । 262.21. वेति; P2 C1 चेति । 262.26. मुण्डनमेवेति वा; P1 P2 मुण्डनमेवेति । 262.29. तीर्थधिकरणकं; P2 तीर्थाधिकरण—। 263.1. भारतस्थ—; C1 L2 भारतस्य । 263.1, स्वदेशान्तर्गत—; K प्रदेशान्तर्गत—।

प्रसङ्गाद्" इति वाच्यम् । (2) पुराणेषु तीर्थोद्देशपरिगणितप्रसिद्धमहातीर्थपरत्वात् सर्वतीर्थशब्दस्य । (3) येष्वेव तीर्थेषु मुण्डनं विशेषवाक्यैर्विहितं तत्परत्वाच्च,

264. **सर्वत्वमाधिकारिकम्**

मी० सू० 1.2.1.16

इति न्यायात् ।

(1) न च "प्रयागातिरिक्ते मुण्डनविध्यभाव एवे"ति वाच्यम् । (2) प्रभासकाश्यादौ तद्विधायकवाक्यानां पूर्वमेवोक्तत्वात् ।

(3) यदपि 'गङ्गायां भास्करक्षेत्र' इति वाक्ये [256.1, 257] भास्करक्षेत्रं प्रयागमभ्युपेत्य सामानाधिकरण्याङ्गीकारेण 'प्रयागावच्छिन्नायां गङ्गायामि'ति कस्यचित् व्याख्यानं, (4) तदप्ययुक्तं, प्रयागस्य प्रजापतिक्षेत्रत्वस्य वक्ष्यमाणत्वाद् भास्करक्षेत्राभावात् ।

265. **तत्र यः सवितुः क्षेत्रे प्राणांस्त्यजति मानवः ।**
स सूर्यलोकमास्थाय देववन्मोदते दिवि ॥

ब्र० पु० 28.62c-63b

(1) इति कोणादित्यादिमाहात्म्यात् तदादेरेव भास्करक्षेत्रतावगमात् ।

(2) किञ्च; विशेषणविशेष्यभावेन व्याख्याने षट्त्वापत्तेः 'सप्तस्वि'तिसंख्यानुपपत्तिश्च । (3) 'गङ्गायामि'त्यस्य व्यर्थताप्रसङ्गश्च ।

(4) किञ्च; वपनविधेः प्रयागमात्रपरत्वे तीर्थान्तरे प्राप्तेरेवाभावाद् 'वर्जयित्वे'तिविशेषनिषेधोऽनुपपन्नः स्यात् ।

(5) यत्तूच्यते; "यथा 'मौद्गश्चरुर्भवती'ति विशेषविधिनैव माषादिनिवृत्तौ सिद्धायां, पुनर् 'अयज्ञिया वै माषा' इति वाक्यं 'प्रतिनिधित्वेनापि माषा न ग्राह्या अत्यन्तायज्ञियत्वाद्' इत्येवंपरम्; (6) तथा गयादिवपननिषेधोऽपि अत्यन्ताप्राशस्त्यपर" इति । (7) तत्र कश्चिदाह "मुद्गविधिशेषत्वात् तत्प्रशंसार्थस्य 'अयज्ञिया' इत्यस्य 'प्रतिनिधित्वेनापि माषा नोपादेया' इत्येवमर्थता न सम्भवति, (8) निन्दाया विधेयस्तुतावेव तात्पर्यात् । (9) तेन 'अनाहुतिर्वै जर्तिलाश्च गवीधुकाश्चे'त्यादिवन् 'नहि निन्दा निन्द्यं निन्दितुं प्रवर्तते, अपि तु

265.1. भास्करक्षेत्रतावगमात्; Cl Ll भास्करक्षेत्रभावगमात् । 265.2 षट्त्वा—; ClLl षट्का-; K षड्धा— । 265.3. —प्रसङ्गश्च; Cl Ll—प्रसङ्गाच्च ।

विधेयं स्तोतुमि'ति न्यायेन मुद्गस्तुतावेव तात्पर्यं, (10) न तु माषाणामत्यन्तायज्ञियत्वे ।

(11) किञ्च; 'अपशवो वा अन्ये,' 'अयज्ञो वा एषः', 'अयज्ञिया वै माषा' इत्यत्र नञा पश्वादिशब्दलक्षितं प्राशस्त्यं निषिध्यत इति अप्राशस्त्यपरता भवति । तदुक्तं—

266. **गवाश्वादिगतं पूर्वमुपादाय प्रशस्तताम् ।**
तदभावोऽन्यपश्वादौ नञ्समासेन कथ्यत ॥ इति ।

त० वा० 1.4.12.23, p. 362.

(1) 'वर्जयित्वेत्य'त्र तु नञो ऽभावान्नाप्राशस्त्यपरत्वं,

267. **श्राद्धं तत्र तु कर्तव्यमर्घ्यावाहनवर्जितम् ।**

इतिवत्,

268. **तीर्थश्राद्धेषु वर्जयेद्**

इतिवच्च ।

(1) किञ्च; वैदिके प्रतिनिध्युपादानस्य वचनं विनाऽभावान् माषाणां प्रतिनिधित्वेनानुपादानं वचनाभावादेव भविष्यति; (2) किम् 'अयज्ञिया माषा' इति प्रतिषेधेन ?

(3) तथा; प्रतिषिद्धस्य प्रतिषेधान्तरमत्यन्तदोष ज्ञापनार्थं भवति । तदुक्तं—

269. **षष्ठ्यादावपि वर्जिते पलमुखे 'मांसाशने पञ्चदश्यभ्यङ्गे च चतुर्दशी'ति कथितं दोषाधिकत्वाय तद् । इति**

(1) प्रस्तुते च निषेधान्तरस्याभावाद् गयादिवपननिषेधस्य नात्यन्ताप्राशस्त्यपरते''ति ।

(2) तदतिबहिर्मुद्रं; षाष्ठतृतीयपादषष्ठाधिकरणे

265.11. अयज्ञो; P2 अयज्ञियो । 268.2. प्रतिषेधेन; P2 निषेधेन ।
269.2. अतिबहिर्मुद्रं; Cl अपि बहिर्मुद्रं ।

270. **प्रतिषिद्धं चाविशेषेण हि तच्छ्रुतिर्--**

मी० सू० 6.3.6.20

(1) इतिसूत्रे, 'अयज्ञिया वै माषा' इत्यस्य प्रतिषेधपरतामङ्गीकृत्य

271. **प्रतिषिद्धश्च न प्रतिनिधातव्यम्**

शब० 7.3.6.20, p. 1420

(1) इति वदता सूत्रकृता भाष्यकृता च प्रतिनिधिप्रतिषेधपरताङ्गीकारात्,

272. **प्रतिषिद्धं प्रत्यवायाद्**

का० श्रौ० सू० 1.129

(1) इत्यत्र सूत्रे कर्काचार्यैरपि निषेधपरताङ्गीकारात् । (2) तथा च कुतो मुद्गविधिशेषता, कुतस्तराम् 'अनाहुतिर्वै जर्तिला 'इतिवत् स्तुतौ तात्पर्यं, कुतस्तराम् 'अपशव' इत्यादिसादृश्यप्रसक्तौ नञ्भावात् तद्वैपम्यप्रतिपादनम् ?

(3) यदपि "वैदिके प्रतिनिध्युपादानं वचनं विना नास्ती"ति तदप्यमीमांसकान् प्रति शोभते । (4) तत्रैव चतुर्थाधिकरणे प्रतिनिधेर्न्यायसिद्धताया उक्तत्वात् कुत्रापि वाचनिकत्वाभावात्,

273. **यदि सोमं न विन्देत पूतीकानभिषुणुयाद् ।**

इत्यादेरपि

274. **नियमार्थः क्वचिद् विधिर् ।**

मी० सू० 6.3.4.16

(1) इति तत्रत्यसूत्र एव नियममात्रार्थत्वस्वीकारात् ।

(2) यदपि "प्रतिषिद्धस्य प्रतिषेधोऽत्यन्तदोषज्ञापनार्थ" इति, (3) तदपि "सर्वतीर्थविधेः परिसंख्यार्थतयाऽन्यत्र वपननिषेधात् पुनर्गयादौ निषेधोऽत्यन्तदोषार्थ" इत्येवाप्राशस्त्यवादिनेष्टापत्त्या सुपरिहरमेव ।

(4) तस्माद् 'अयज्ञिया' इत्येतत् तुल्यत्वं 'वर्जयित्वा गयामि'त्येतस्यैव दूषणीयम् । (5) तत्र हि मुद्गादिमये चरौ विहिते 'मुख्यद्रव्यालाभे तत्सदृशं प्रतिनिधेयमि'ति न्यायान् मुद्गसादृश्येन माषाणां मुद्गाभावे प्रतिनिधिताप्राप्तौ

274.5. वहिते; P3 C2 K विहित— ।

तन्निषेधार्थमयज्ञियताकथनं युज्यते । (6) इह तु गयादौ मुण्डनप्राप्ते-रेवाङ्गीकारान् निषेधायोगात् किमर्थमत्यन्ताप्राशस्त्यकीर्तनम् ?

(7) किञ्च; अप्राशस्त्यकथनं किम् 'अनाहुतिर्वै जर्तिला' इतिविधेयपयः-स्तुत्यर्थमिव विधेयप्रयागवपनस्तुत्यर्थं; (8) किं वा 'अयज्ञिया वै माषा' इतिवद् गयादिवपननिषेधार्थम् ? (9) नान्त्यः, भवतो गयादौ वपनप्रापकाभावान् निषेधायोगात् अस्मन्मतापत्तेश्च । (10) नाद्यः, 'अनाहुतिरि'तिवद् अत्र नञभावाद् अप्राशस्त्यद्वारास्तुत्यप्रतीतेः,

275. **वाक्पाणिपादचापल्यं वर्जयेच्चातिभोजनम्**

इतिवद्, (1) 'अर्घ्यावाहनवर्जितम्' [267] इतिवच्च वर्जयतिना निषेधस्यैव प्रतीतेः, (2) अप्राशस्त्यपरत्वे लक्षणाप्रसङ्गाच्च ।

(3) अथ "प्रयाग एव वपनविधिनाऽन्यत्र तन्निवृत्तावपि दोषाधिक्य-ज्ञापनार्थो गयादिनिषेधः स्यात् । अथवा

276. **सायं प्रातर्द्विजातीनामशनं श्रुतिचोदितम्**

(1) इत्यत्र परिसंख्यावादिनां परिसंख्याविवरणार्थमिव

277. **नान्तरा भोजनं कुर्याद् अग्निहोत्रसमो विधिर्**

—स्मृतिचन्द्रिकायां द्वितीयेऽध्याये p. 609

मनुवचनम्

(1) इत्यस्य गयादिनिषेधस्यापि तद्विवरणार्थता स्यात्" । (2) मैवम्, उभयथापि परिसंख्यात्वापत्तेस्तस्याश्च पूर्वमेव दूषणात् । (3) परिसंख्याविवरणपरतायां गयादिपरिगणनानर्थक्यात् । (4) 'नान्यतीर्थे' इत्येतावन्मात्रस्य वक्तव्यत्वात् ।

(5) " 'नान्तरिक्षे न दिवि चाग्निस्श्चेतव्य' इतिवन्नित्यानुवादः किं न स्यादि"ति चेत्, (6) न, वैषम्यात्; तत्र हि अन्तरिक्षादौ चयनस्यासम्भवादेव नित्यानुवादः । (7) इह तु प्रयागादन्यत्र वपनस्य सम्भवान्न नित्यानुवादता । (8) नामान्तरेणानर्थक्यापातश्च ।

---

276. श्रुतिचोदितम्; C1 श्रु तिनोदितम् । 277.1. गयादि—; C2 गयादौ ।

(9) इत्यलं बहुना कण्ठशोषेण; (10) यद्यपि वाक्यस्वरसादेव 'गयादिव्यतिरिक्तेषु सर्वेषु तीर्थेषु मुण्डनोपवासौ' इत्ययमर्थो ज्ञायत एव, तथापि कुमत्युक्तयुक्तिभिरल्पबुद्धीनां भ्रमो मा भूदिति भूयानयं दूषणप्रयासः कृतः। (11) तत्सिद्धं, कुरुक्षेत्रादिव्यतिरिक्तेषु सर्वेषु प्रसिद्धमहातीर्थेषु मुण्डनोपवासाविति।

(12) इदञ्च मुण्डनं दशमासानन्तरं पुनस्तीर्थप्राप्तौ कर्तव्यं,

278. **संवत्सरे द्विमासोने पुनस्तीर्थं व्रजेद्यदि।**
मुण्डनञ्चोपवासञ्च ततो यत्नेन कारयेद्॥ (=551)

इति स्मरणात्। (1) दशमासोत्तरप्राप्तावेवावश्यं कार्यम्। (2) अन्तरा तु फलेच्छया भवति, न तु नियम इति 'यत्नेने'त्यस्यार्थः। (3) प्रयागे तु विशेषं वक्ष्यामः।

(4) अत्रेदं चिन्त्यं मुण्डने; (5) किं 'वपनं करिष्य' इति सङ्कल्पः, 'कारयिष्य' इति वा ? (6) तत्र केचिदाहुः—"प्रयागे वपनं कुर्याद्' [234] इत्यादिविधिभिस्तीर्थप्राप्तिनिमित्तकवपनस्य विहितत्वप्रतीतेर्, (7) वपनस्य च निमित्तरहितेनैव नापितेन वृत्त्यर्थं क्रियमाणत्वान्नैमित्तिकविध्ययोगात्, (8) 'गङ्गां प्राप्य सरिच्छ्रेष्ठां वपनं यो न कारयेद्' [256] इत्यादिवाक्यस्वरसाच्च, (9) 'कारयेद्' इत्यर्थे 'कुर्याद्' इति णिचो लोपेन निर्देशाद् वापनस्यैव विधानाद्, (10) विहितस्य च फलान्वयात् फलवत एव च कर्तव्यत्वाद् (11) 'यथोक्तफलकामो वपनं कारयिष्य' इति सङ्कल्पः (12) न च "'वपनं कुर्याद्' इति विधानाद् 'विधिशब्द एव च प्रयोज्य' इति न्यायात् 'करिष्य' इति सङ्कल्प" इति वाच्यम्। (13) तस्य न्यायस्य अदृष्टार्थशब्दस्वरूपतात्पर्यकमन्त्रदेवतादिरूपशब्दविषयत्वात्। (14) इह त्वर्थमात्रे तात्पर्यं प्रयाजादिविधिवत्। अत एव

279. **विधिशब्दस्य मन्त्रत्वे भावः स्यात्तेन चोदने—**

मी० सू० 10.4.12.23

(1) ति सूत्रे जैमिनिना 'मन्त्रत्व' इत्युक्तम्। (2) एवञ्च वापनतात्पर्यके विधौ सति 'अरगदामत्ते हि शब्दप्रयोगे'। किमित्यवाचकं प्रयोक्षामहे॥

277.10. ज्ञायत; C2 ज्ञात। 278.4. Before अत्रेदं; K मुण्डने सङ्कल्पः। 278.4. मुण्डने; P3 K वपने। 279.2. तात्पर्यके; K —तात्पर्यक—।

इति न्यायेन 'वपनं कारयिष्य' इति वा सङ्कल्पो 'वापनं करिष्य' इति वा, न तु 'वपनं करिष्य' इतीति "।

(3) एतन्न युक्तं; 'वपनं यो न कारयेत्' [256], 'तस्मात्तान् परिवापयेत्' [259], 'प्रयागे वपनं कुर्याद्' [234] इत्यादिरूपेण विधीनाम् उभयरूपत्वेऽपि

280. **यानि कानि च पापानि ब्रह्महत्यासमानि च ।**
केशानाश्रित्य तिष्ठन्ति तस्मात्केशान् वपाम्यहम् ॥

(1) इति मन्त्रलिङ्गाद् 'वपनं करिष्य' इत्येव सङ्कल्पस्योचितत्वात् । (2) न च बाधाद् अन्वयाप्रतीतेः, केशवियोगसंविधान एव वपनशब्द-प्रयोगाद् बाधाभावात्,

281. **केशश्मश्रुवपने नखानि निकृन्तती—**

त्यादिवत् । (1) ततश्च यथा 'यद् आहवनीये जुहोती'ति वचनाद् आहवनीयाधिकरणकद्रव्यप्रक्षेपस्य होमत्वात् तस्य चाध्वर्युकर्तृकत्वाद् यजमानकर्तृकत्वाभावेऽपि काम्यहोमेषु अध्वर्युकर्तृकत्वपक्षेऽग्निहोत्रहोमे च 'अमुकहोमं करिष्य' इत्येवं सङ्कल्पः; (2) यथा वा समाख्यया चयनस्याध्वर्युकर्तृकत्वेऽपि 'प्रजाकामो नाभिदघ्नं चिन्वीते'त्यादिवचनाद् 'अमुककामश्च चयनं करिष्य' इति सङ्कल्पस्, (3) तथात्रापि । (4) एवञ्च 'अग्निं चितवान्' इत्यग्निचित्पदे विग्रहकथनं वृद्धानां युज्यते ।

(5) एवञ्च तीर्थप्राप्तिरूपनिमित्तवत्यपि संविधानरूपो वपनशब्दार्थो वर्तत एव । (6) यानि तु 'वपनं यो न कारयेद्' [256] इत्यादीनि णिज्गर्भाणि वचनानि, तानि पर्यवसितार्थमादायापि युज्यन्ते ।

(7) यत्तु "अर्थमात्रतात्पर्यकत्वाद् विधिशब्दे तात्पर्याभाव" इति; (8) भवत्ववेम् । तथापि विधिप्रतिसंधानपूर्वकानुष्ठाने बुद्धिस्थत्वाल्लाघवाच्च सङ्कल्पे विधिशब्द एव न्याय्यः । (9) अतएव गुणफलोपबन्धवत् सङ्कल्पादि-व्यवहारोऽपि नामधेयप्रयोजनमवादि मीमांसमांसलैः ।

(10) योऽपि 'अस्मदायत्त' इत्यादिर्न्यायस्तस्याप्ययमविषय; (11) उक्तयुक्त्या प्रत्यायकत्वोपपत्तेरवाचकत्वाभावात्, 'वपाम्यहम्' इतिमंत्रलिङ्गस्यैव नियामकत्वेनास्मदायत्तत्वाभावाच्च ।

280.2. अन्वयाप्रतीते; P2 अन्यथाप्रतीतिः । 281.1. ततश्च; P1 अतश्च । 281.6. णिज्गर्भाणि; K णिजाभाणि (corrected in 'शुद्धिपत्रम्' to णिज्गर्भाणि)। 281.10 इत्यादिर्न्यायस्; P2 C1 इत्यादिन्यायस ।

(12) यद्वा; वपनशब्दो नानार्थः; तत्र कदाचित् केशवियोगसंविधानात्मकं प्रयोजकव्यापारमाह; (13) कदाचिच्च प्रयोज्यव्यापारं, (14) 'मया वपनं कृतं,' 'वपनं कारितम्' इत्युभयथापि प्रयोगात्। (15) तत्र प्रकरणादिवच्छब्दान्तरसमभिव्याहारस्तात्पर्यग्राहकः। (16) यदा कुर्याच्छब्दसमभिव्याहारस्तदा प्रयोजकव्यापारपरता। (17) यदा तु कारयेच्छब्दसमभिव्याहारस्तदा प्रयोज्यव्यापारपरतेति। (18) एवञ्च सति मन्त्रलिङ्गबलात् प्रयोजकव्यापारस्यैव प्रकाश्यत्वाद् 'वपनं करिष्य' इत्येवं सङ्कल्प; (19) इत्यलं बहुना।

(20) "इदञ्च वपनं केशश्मश्रुक्रमेण कार्यं,

282. **गत्वा स्नानं प्रकुर्वीत वपनं तदनन्तरम्।** (=211)
वपेत् केशांश्च श्मश्रूणि नखानि च निकृन्तयेत्॥

इति ब्रह्मपुराणवचनात्,

283. **केशश्मश्रुलोमनखान्युदक्संस्थानि वापयेद्।**

(1) इति अपरार्कलिखितवचने प्रतीतपाठक्रमानुसाराच्च,

284. **स केशश्मश्रु वापयती—**

त्यादिश्रुतौ दर्शनाच्चे" ति केचित्। (1) अन्ये तु "एतानि वचांसि केशादिवपनमात्रविधायकानि न तु तत्क्रमस्यापि गौरवाद् वाक्यभेदप्रसङ्गाच्च। (2) तस्मात् श्मश्रुपूर्वकमेव वपनम्। (3) तथा चापस्तम्बानां केशप्रथमवपननिन्दापूर्वकं श्मश्र्वादिवपनप्रशंसा श्रूयते:

285. **देवा वै यद् यज्ञेऽकुर्वत तदसुरा अकुर्वत। तेऽसुरा ऊर्ध्वं पृष्ठेभ्यो नापश्यन्। ते केशानग्रे ऽवपन्त। अथ श्मश्रूणि। अथोपपक्षौ। ततस्तेऽवाञ्च आयन्। पराभवन्। यस्यैवं वपन्ति अवाङ एति। अथो परैव भवति। अथ देवा ऊर्ध्वं पृष्ठेभ्योऽपश्यन्। त उपपक्षावग्रेऽवपन्त। अथ श्मश्रूणि। अथ केशान्। ततस्तेऽभवन्। सुवर्गं लोकमायन्। यस्यैवं वपन्ति भवत्यात्मना। अथो सुवर्गं लोकमेति। अथैतन्**

281.15. छन्दान्तरसमभिव्याहारस्; P3 छन्दान्तरे समभिव्याहारस्।

मनुर्वप्त्रे मिथुनमपश्यत् । स श्मश्रूण्यग्रेऽवपत । अथोपपक्षौ । अथ केशान् । ततो वै स प्रजायत प्रजया पशुभिः । यस्यैवं वपन्ति प्र प्रजया पशुभिर्मिथुनैर्जायत । इति ।

तै० ब्रा० 1.5.6.1-3

(1) एवञ्च श्मश्रुकूर्चयोरादौ वपने क्षणं म्लेच्छवेशकृता लोकविद्विष्टतापि न भवतीत्ययं बहुसम्मतः पक्षः ।

(2) तत्राप्युदक्संस्थतायै दक्षिणश्मश्रुवपनमादौ । (3) पित्रादिमृतौ तु दक्षिणसंस्थत्वाय वामश्मश्रुवपनं आदावि"ति ।

वपने प्रकारश्चापरार्के—

286. **उदङमुखः प्राङमुखो वा वपनं कारयेत् सुधीः ।**
केशश्मश्रुलोमनखान्युदक्संस्थानि वापयेत् ॥
दक्षिणं कर्णमारभ्य धर्मार्थं पापसञ्चये ।
शिखाद्यं नवसंस्कारे शिखाद्यन्तं शिरो वपेत् ॥

(1) धर्मार्थे तीर्थादिवपने दक्षिणकर्णाद्युदक्संस्थं वपेत् । (2) पापसञ्चयनिमित्तके शिखमादीकृत्याधस्तात् सर्वतो वपेन्नोदक्संस्थम् । (3) 'नवसंस्कारे' चूडाकरणे दक्षिणकर्णाच्छिखान्तं शिखमारभ्य वामकर्णान्तञ्च वपेदित्युत्तरपद्यार्थः ।

(4) इदं वपनं यत्यादिभिः शिखमरक्षित्वैव कार्यं,

287. **यतिः शूद्रश्च विधवा सशिखं वपनञ्चरेद् ।**

इति वचनात् । तत्र यतिभिः

288. **कक्षोपस्थशिखावर्जमृतुसन्धिषु वापयेद् ।**

(1) इति ऋतुसन्धिष्वेवेतिपरिसंख्यानातृतुसन्धिव्यतिरिक्तकाले तीर्थप्राप्तावपि न कार्यम् । (2) यतिशिष्टानामाचारोऽप्येवमेव ।

(3) आहिताग्निभिस्तु पर्वव्यतिरिक्तकालेऽपि तीर्थनिमित्तकं मुण्डनं

285.3. वपने प्रकारश्; P3 C1 C2 K L1 वपनप्रकारश् । 286. धर्मार्थं; K धर्मार्थे । 286.2. आदीकृत्या—; P2 आदिं कृत्वा— । 287. सशिखं; P3 K विशिखं ।

कार्यम् । (4) एतस्य नैमित्तिकतया पित्रादिमरणनिमित्तकमुण्डनवत् पर्व-नियमाभावात्, (5) आचाराच्च ।

(6) जीवत्पितृकेणापि तीर्थे मुण्डनं कार्यं,

289. **विना तीर्थं विना यज्ञं मातापित्रोर्मृतिं विना ।**
यो वापयति लोमानि स पुत्रः पितृघातक ॥

इति वचनात् । (1) अत्र पुत्रपदग्रहणाज्जीवत्पितृकविषयता । (2) अन्यथा 'स पितृघातक' इत्येवावक्ष्यत् । (3)मुण्डनवचनानाञ्च जीवत्पितृकसाधारण्यात् ।

(4) तत्रापि "तीर्थान्तरे आद्ययात्रायामेव । (5) प्रयागे तु प्रतियात्रमि"-त्याहुः ।

(6) तीर्थे च मुण्डनं निषिद्धकालेऽपि कार्यम् । निषेधश्च वृद्धगार्ग्यः——

290. **रव्यारसौरवारेषु रात्रौ पाते व्रताहनि ।**
श्राद्धाहप्रतिपद्रिक्ता भद्राः क्षौरेषु वर्जयेत् ॥

(1) आरो भौमः । (2) सौरः शनिः । (3) पातो व्यतीपातः । (4) रिक्ताश्चतुर्थीनवमीचतुर्दश्यः । (5) भद्रा द्वितीयासप्तमीद्वादश्यः ।

गार्ग्यः—

291. **षष्ठ्यमापूर्णिमापातचतुर्दश्यष्टमी तथा ।**
आसु संनिहितं पापं त्रिषु तैले भगे क्षुरे ॥

व्यासः ——

292. **नक्षत्रे तु न कुर्वीत यस्मिन् जातो भवेन्नरः ।**
न प्रोष्ठपदयोः कार्यं नैवाग्नेये तु भारत ॥
दारुणेषु तु सर्वेषु दुष्टतारान् तु वर्जयेत् ।
म० भा० 13.107.119c-120b (=393)

---

289. इति वचनात्; L2 इति स्मरणात् । 289.6. निषेधश्; L2 निषिद्धश् ।
290. —सौर— ; P1 P2 C2 —सौरि— । 290.2 सौरः; P1 P2 सौरिः ।

तथा—

293. कुम्भे कर्कटके चैव कन्यायां कार्मुके रवौ ।
रोमखण्डं गृहस्थस्य पितॄन् प्राशयते यमः ॥

तथा—

294. विवाहमौञ्जीचूडासु वर्षमर्धं तदर्धकम् ।
अन्तर्वत्न्याञ्च जायायां नेष्यते केशवापनम् ॥

(1) इत्यादि । अस्य सर्वस्यापवादस्तीर्थप्राप्तौ—

295. क्षौरं नैमित्तिकं कार्यं निषेधे सत्यपि ध्रुवम् ।
पित्रादिमृतिदीक्षासु प्रायश्चित्ते च तीर्थके ॥

इति स्मृतेः,

296. नृपविप्राज्ञया यज्ञे मरणे बन्धमोक्षणे ।
उद्वाहेऽखिलवारर्क्षतिथिषु क्षौरमिष्टदम् ॥

(1) इति नारदवचने निमित्तपरिगणनस्योपलक्षणत्वाच्च ।

अत्र

297. "केशानां यावती संख्या छिन्नानां जाह्नवीजले ।
तावद्वर्षसहस्राणि स्वर्गलोके महीयत ॥

(1) इति वचनात् स्थलोपविष्टस्तथा वापयेद् यथा स्वयमेव केशा गङ्गादिषु पतन्ती"ति कश्चित् । अन्ये तु

298. "तुषकेशपुरीषभस्मास्थिश्लेष्मनखलोमान्यप्सु न क्षिपेद्
शंख (K) 87

(1) इति गद्यशंखवचनान् न जले क्षेपः किन्तु तीरे गर्तं कृत्वा केशनखादीनि क्षिपेदि"त्याहुः । (2) अपरे तु—

---

296. —वारर्क्ष—; P3 C2 —वार्क्षे ।

299. "**यावन्ति नखलोमानि वायुना प्रेरितानि वै ।**
पतन्ति जाह्नवीतोये नराणां पुण्यकर्मणाम् ।।

(1) इति वचनात्तादृशे तीरप्रदेशे वपेद् यतो वायुनुन्नाः केशादयस्तीर्थे पतन्ति न तु स्वयं काचित् प्रतिपत्तिः कार्ये"त्याहुः । (2) अत्र यथादेशाचारं व्यवस्था ।

(3) स्त्रीणां सधवानां बालानाञ्च मुण्डने विशेषविचारः प्रयागप्रकरणे करिष्यते ।

इति त्रिस्थलीसेतौ मुण्डनविचारः ।

299.3. After त्रिस्थलीसेतौ; P2 सामान्यप्रघट्टके ।

अथातस्तीर्थस्नानम्

महाभारते—

300. नाव्रतो नाकृतात्मा च नाशुचिर्न च तस्करः ।
स्नाति तीर्थेषु कौरव्य न च वक्रमतिर्नरः ॥

म० भा० 3.83.92

तथा—

301. नानृजुर्नाकृतात्मा च नाविद्यो न च पापकृत् ।
स्नाति तीर्थेषु कौरव्य न च वक्रमतिर्नरः ॥

म० भा० 3.90.11

तथान्यत्राप्युक्तं—

302. नदीसरिद्देवखातगर्तप्रस्रवणेषु च ।
सरःसु चाकृत्रिमेषु शस्तं तीर्थे विशेषतः ॥

(1) स्नानमिति शेषः ।

कौर्मे—

303. पृथिव्यां सर्वतीर्थेषु स्नात्वा पुण्येषु च द्विजः ।
मुच्यते पातकैः सर्वैः समस्तैरपि पूरुषः ॥

कू० पु० 2.33.144

तथा तीर्थानि प्रकृत्य—

304. यत्र स्नानं जपो होमः श्राद्धदानादिकं कृतम् ।
एकैकशो मुनिश्रेष्ठाः पुनात्या सप्तमं कुलम् ॥ (=45)

(1) इदञ्च यत्र स्थलविशेषे विपरीतप्रवाहादि तत्र न कार्यम् ।

---

301. स्नाति तीर्थेषु... नरः; Cl L1 उत्तरार्धं तु समानं । 302. चाकृत्रिमेषु; P2 P3 C1 C2 वाकृत्रिमेषु । 302. तीर्थे; C1 C2 तीर्थं, P2 P3 C2 K L1 तीर्थ— । 304. यत्र; P1 P2 तत्र ।

तदुक्तं—

305. प्रत्यावृत्तोदके स्नानं वर्ज्यं नद्यां द्विजातिभिः ।
तस्यां रजकतीर्थे तु दशहस्तेन वर्जयेत् ॥

तथा—

306. अग्राह्यास्त्वागता ह्यापो नद्याः प्रथमवेगजाः ।
प्रक्षोभिताश्च केनापि तथा तीर्थाद् विनिर्गताः ॥

(1) एतस्य गङ्गायामपवादः —

307. प्रतिस्रोतो रजोयोगो रथ्याजलनिवेशनम् ।
गङ्गायां न प्रदुष्यन्ति सा हि धर्मद्रवः स्वयम् ॥

निषेधान्तरमपि—

308. शाल्मलीतिन्तिणीनिम्बकरञ्जाश्च हरीतकी ।
कोविदारकपित्थार्कबदर्येरण्डशिग्रवः ॥
शेलुश्च खदिरश्चैषां स्नानं छायासु वर्जयेद् ।

(1) इत्यादि । 'बदरी च विभीतिकी'ति वा पाठः ।

(2) यश्च रात्रिसन्ध्यादिषु स्नाननिषेधः सोऽप्याकस्मिकतीर्थप्राप्तौ न प्रवर्तते नैमित्तिकत्वात् । अतएव शातातपः ——

309. रात्रौ स्नानं न कुर्वीत होमं दानञ्च रात्रिषु ।
नैमित्तिकञ्च कुर्वीत स्नानं दानञ्च रात्रिषु ॥

वृद्धयाज्ञवल्क्योऽपि—

310. ग्रहणोद्वाहसङ्क्रांतियात्रार्तिप्रसवेषु च ।
स्नानं नैमित्तिकं ज्ञेयं रात्रावपि तदिष्यते ॥

(1) "एतच्च रात्रौ तीर्थे स्नानमाद्यान्त्यप्रहरद्वयविषयं,

---

305. रजकतीर्थे तु; C1 रजकतीर्थेषु । 306.1. अपवादः; C1 अपवादमाह ।
308.—निम्ब—; P2—लिम्ब— । 308.2. —सन्ध्यादिषु; C1 —सन्ध्यासु ।
310.1 तीर्थे; P2 तीर्थ— ।

311. **महानिशा तु विज्ञेया मध्यस्थं प्रहरद्वयम् ।**
प्रदोषपश्चिमौ यामौ दिनवत् स्नानमाचरेद् ॥

इति पराशरोक्तेरि"ति केचित् ।

(1) अयश्च निषेधाभाव आकस्मिकतीर्थप्राप्तिविषयः । (2)बुद्धिपूर्वकं तु तीर्थप्राप्ती रात्र्यादौ न कार्यैव ।

(3) तथा प्रासङ्गिकप्राप्तौ मलमासेऽपि कार्यं,

312. **तीर्थस्नानं जपो होमो यवव्रीहितिलादिभिर् ।**

इत्युपक्रम्य

कार्याणि मलमासेऽपी-

ति यमेनाभिधानात् । अत्र

313. **तीर्थस्नानं पूर्वोपक्रान्तम्**

म० पा० p. 547

इति मदनपारिजाते,

314. **द्वितीयादी—**

(1) त्यन्यत्र, अपूर्वस्य निषेधात् । (2) "आकस्मिकतीर्थप्राप्तिनिमित्तकम्" इति तु वृद्धाः ।

(3) आशौचेऽप्याकस्मिकतीर्थस्नानं कार्यम् । तदुक्तं पैठीनसिना—

315. **विवाहदुर्गयज्ञेषु यात्रायां तीर्थकर्मणि ।**
न तत्र सूतकं तद्वत् कर्मयज्ञादि कारयेत् ॥

(= 196, 385)

(1) 'सूतकं' मृतकस्याप्युपलक्षणम् । (2) 'तीर्थकर्म' स्नानतर्पणश्राद्धादि ।

(3) परार्थस्नाने विशेषः मार्कण्डेयपुराणे—

316. **मातरं पितरं जायां भ्रातरं सुहृदं गुरुम् ।**
यमुद्दिश्य निमज्जेत अष्टमांशं लभेत सः ॥

(ग० पु० 1.105.121)

311.2. बुद्धिपूर्वकं; P2 बुद्धिपूर्वं । 315.3. परार्थस्नाने; C2 परार्थे स्नाने । 315.3. विशेषः; P2 C1 विशेषो ।

स्मृतिदर्पणे तु—

317. **दशमांशं लभेत सः**

(प्र० ख० 1.28.41)

इति पाठः । स्मृत्यर्थसारे तु

318. **पितामहभ्रातृमातामहमातुलश्वशुरार्थदपोषकाचार्यगुरूपाध्यायार्थं तेषां पत्न्यर्थं मातृष्वसृपितृष्वस्रर्थञ्च स्नात्वाष्टमांशं लभते । मातापित्रर्थं कुर्वंश्चतुर्थांशम् ।**

स्मृत्यर्थसार, p. 154

(1) परस्परार्थं दम्पती अर्धं लभेते ।

(2) विशेषान्तरमाह पैठीनसिः —

319. **प्रतिकृतिं कुशमयीं तीर्थवारिणि मज्जयेत् ।**
मज्जयेच्च यमुद्दिश्य सोऽष्टभागं फलं लभेत् ॥

(अत्रि 50)

तत्र मन्त्रः —

320. **कुशोऽसि कुशपुत्रोऽसि ब्रह्मणा निर्मितः स्वयम् ।**
त्वयि स्नाते स च स्नातो यस्येदं ग्रन्थिबन्धनम् ॥

(1) इति । " 'कुशप्रतिकृतिः' कुशप्रतिमैव कार्या" इति केचित् । (2) अन्ये तु " 'ग्रन्थिवन्धनम्' इति मन्त्रलिङ्गात् तत्तन्नाम्ना ग्रन्थिबन्धनमात्रं प्रतिकृतिरि"त्याहुः ।

(3) "इदं परार्थस्नानं प्रतिकृतिस्थापनञ्च जीवतामजीवतां वोद्देशेन कार्यं सामान्येन विधानाद्" इति कश्चित् । (4) तन्न, मृतानां तर्पणश्राद्धादि-फलभावत्वाज्जीवतामेव फलोद्देशौचित्यात् ।

(5) तथान्योऽपि विशेषः शंखेनोक्तः—

321. **तीर्थं प्राप्यानुषङ्गेण स्नानं तीर्थे समाचरेत् ।**
स्नानजं फलमाप्नोति तीर्थयात्राकृतं न तु ॥

शंख 8.12(= 106)

(1) 'अनुषङ्गेण' वाणिज्यराजसेवादिप्रसङ्गेन ।

(2) विशेषान्तरमाह जाबालिः —

322. **प्रवाहाभिमुखो मज्जेद् यत्रापः प्रवहन्ति वै ।**
स्थावरेषु च सर्वेषु आदित्याभिमुखस्तथा ॥

(1) अन्यन्मृत्तिकास्नानादि ग्रन्थान्तरतो ज्ञेयम् ।

इति तीर्थसेतौ सामान्यप्रघट्टके तीर्थस्नानविधिः

---

322. —आभिमुखस्तथा; P3— आभिमुखस्थितः । 322. मज्जेद्; P1 भूयाद ।
322.1. तीर्थसेतौ; P2 त्रिस्थलीसेतौ ।

अथ तर्पणम्

(2) तच्चादौ स्वशाखानुसारेण स्नानाङ्गं कृत्वा पश्चात्तथैव देवर्षि-तर्पणं कृत्वा पितृणामपि कार्यम्। तदुक्तं स्कान्दे—

323. **अकालेऽप्यथ वा काले तीर्थे श्राद्धं च तर्पणम्।**
अविलम्बेन कर्तव्यं नैव विघ्नं समाचरेद्॥ इति।

का० ख० 6.60. (=386)

(1) पितृतर्पणं तु देवीपुराणेऽप्युक्तं, 'तीर्थे' इति प्रक्रम्य—

324. **प्राप्तैरेव च कर्तव्यं पितृणां चैव तर्पणम्। इति।** (=381)

तथान्यत्र—

325. **यस्तु तीर्थे नरः स्नात्वा न कुर्यात् पितृतर्पणम्।**
पिबन्ति देहनिःस्रावं पितरस्तु जलार्थिनः॥

तथा—

326. **गिरिषु ख्याततीर्थेषु नदीषु च विशेषतः।**
साकांक्षाः पितरो नित्यं तिष्ठन्ति सलिलार्थिनः॥

(1) अत्र च वक्ष्यमाणान् सर्वान् पितॄन् संतर्प्य एक तिलाञ्जलिं सर्वेभ्यो दद्यात्। तत्र विष्णुपुराणे मन्त्राः—

327. **देवासुरास्तथा नागा यक्षा गन्धर्वराक्षसाः।**
पिशाचा गुह्यकाः सिद्धाः कूष्माण्डास्तरवः खगाः॥
जलेचरा भूमिलया वाय्वाधाराश्च जन्तवः।
तृप्तिमेतेन यान्त्वाशु मद्दत्तेनाम्बुनाखिलाः॥

322.1. (Chapter heading) अथ तर्पणम्; P2 अथ तीर्थे तर्पणम् L2 अथ तर्पणविधिः। 324. तथान्यत्र; P3 तथान्यत्। 325. देहनिःस्रावं; P2 P3 L1 देहनिस्रावं। 327. कूष्माण्डास्; P2 कुष्माण्डास्।

नरकेषु समस्तेषु यातनासु च ये स्थिताः ।
तेषामाप्यायनायैतद् दीयते सलिलं मया ॥
येऽबान्धवा बान्धवा वा येऽन्यजन्मनि बान्धवाः ।
ते तृप्तिमखिलां यान्तु ये चास्मत्तोऽभिकांक्षिणः ॥
यत्रक्वचनसंस्थानां क्षुत्तृष्णोपहतात्मनाम् ।
इदमक्षय्यमेवास्तु मया दत्तं तिलोदकम् ॥

वि०पु० 3.11.32-36

वायवीयेऽपि—

328. आब्रह्मस्तबपर्यन्तं देवर्षिपितृमानवाः ।
तृप्यन्तु पितरः सर्वे मातृमातामहादयः ॥
अतीतकुलकोटीनां सप्तद्वीपनिवासिनाम् ।
आब्रह्मभुवनाल्लोकादिदमस्तु तिलोदकम ॥

वा० पु० 110.21-22 (= 337)

एतत्फलञ्च वैष्णवे—

329. कामोदकप्रदानं ते मयैतत् कथितं नृप ।
यद्दत्त्वा प्रीणयत्येतन् मनुष्यः सकलं जगत् ॥
जगदाप्यायनोद्भूतं पुण्यमाप्नोति चानघ ।
दत्त्वा कामोदकं सम्यग् एतेभ्यः श्रद्धयान्वित ॥ इति ।

वि० पु० 3.11.37-38

अत्र

330. पक्षश्राद्धे हिरण्ये चाप्यनुव्रज्य तिलोदकम् ।

(1) इति सौमन्तवाद् वचनात् तीर्थे हेमश्राद्धपक्षे श्राद्धीयब्राह्मणविसर्जनानन्तरं तीर्थनिमित्तं तर्पणमाचरन्ति केचित्, न तु पूर्वम् । (2) तदयुक्तम्, बहुभिर्वाक्यैस्तीर्थस्नानानन्तरमेव तद्विधानात् । (3) सुमन्तुवचनं तु येषां शाखिनां श्राद्धाङ्गभूतं तर्पणमस्ति तेषां हिरण्यश्राद्धे तत्पश्चात् विधत्ते । (4) अत एव प्रयोगपारिजाते श्राद्धांगतर्पणमेव प्रकृत्येदमभिहितम्—

328. —स्तम्बपर्यन्तं; P2 L2 – स्तम्भपर्यन्तं । 330. चाप्यनु— । P2 च अनु— । 330.1 सौमन्तवाद् वचनात्; P2 Cl K सौमन्तवचनात् ।

331. **तस्मात्तीर्थतर्पणं स्नानान्त एव कार्यमिति सिद्धम् ।**

(1) तर्पणेऽन्योऽपि विशेषोऽन्यत्रोक्तः—

332. **पितॄनतर्पयित्वा तु नदीस्तरति यो नरः ।**
तस्यासृक्पानकामास्ते भवन्ति भृशदुःखिता ।। इति ।
(= 670)

(1) अत्र तर्पणे तर्प्यक्रमः—

333. **आदौ पिता ततो माता सापत्नजननी तथा ।**
मातामहाः सपत्नीका आत्मपत्न्यस्ततः परम् ।।
सुतभ्रातृपितृव्याश्च मातुलाश्च सपत्निकाः ।
दुहिता च स्वसा प्रोक्ता दौहित्रो भागिनेयकः ।।
पितृष्वसा मातृष्वसा श्वशुरो गुरुरिक्थदौ ।

(1) 'रिक्थं' धनम् ।

एते स्युः पितरस्तीर्थे तर्पणे च महालये ।।

(2) 'पिते'ति पित्रादित्रयमित्यर्थः । (3) एवं 'माते'त्यत्रापि ।

अन्यत्रापि—

334. **ताताम्बत्रितयं सपत्नजननी मातामहादित्रयम्**
सस्त्रि स्त्रीतनयादि तातजननीस्वभ्रातरस्तत्स्त्रियः ।
ताताम्बात्मभगिन्यपत्यधवयुक् जायापिता सद्गुरुः
शिष्याप्ताः पितरो महालयविधौ तीर्थे तथा तर्पण ।।

(1) इति । 'त्रितय'शब्दस्य ताताम्वाभ्यां प्रत्येकं सम्बन्धः । (2) 'सस्त्री'ति मातामहादित्रयस्य विशेषणम् । (3) अन्ये तु मातामह्यादीनां पृथक्तर्पणमिच्छन्ति श्राद्धवत् । (4) 'स्त्रीतनयादी'ति तर्पयित्रपेक्षया । (5) 'तातजननीस्वभ्रातर' इति तातभ्रातरः पितृव्याः मातृभ्रातरो मातुलाः स्वभ्रातरस्तर्पणकर्तृभ्रातरः । (6) 'तत्स्त्रियः' पितृव्यमातुलस्वभातृस्त्रियः । (7) 'सस्त्रिय' इति वा पाठः । (8) तदा 'तातभ्रात्रादयः

---

331. स्नानान्त; L2 स्नानानन्तर । 332.1 तर्प्यक्रमः; K तर्पणक्रमः । 334.4 तर्पयित्र-पेक्षया; C1 तर्पयितुरपेक्षया ।

सपत्नीका' इत्यर्थः । (9) 'ताते'ति पितृष्वसृमातृष्वसृस्वस्वसारोऽपत्यभर्तृयुक्ताः । (10) ततश्च पितृष्वस्रे यथायोग्यं सभर्तृकायै सापत्यायै इत्येवंप्रकारकं प्रयोगवाक्यमनुसन्धेयम् । (11) 'जायापिता' श्वशुरः । (12) अन्यत्स्पष्टम् । (13) अत्र भ्रातृपितृव्यादीनां पूर्वोक्तक्रमेण सह विकल्पः ।

(14) एवं पूर्वोक्तसकलतर्पणाशक्तौ संक्षेपतर्पणं कार्यं,

335. आब्रह्मस्तम्बपर्यन्तं जगत् तृप्यत्विति ब्रुवन् ।
जलाञ्जलित्रयं दद्यात् कुर्वन् संक्षेपतर्पणम् ॥

इति वचनात् । (1) तच्चेत्थम्—

336. आब्रह्मस्तम्बपर्यन्तं जगत् स्थावरजङ्गमम् ।
मया दत्तेन तोयेन तृप्तं यातु परां गतिम् ॥

इति मन्त्रेण, यद्वा

337. आब्रह्मस्तम्बपर्यन्तं देवर्षिपितृमानवाः ।
तृप्यन्तु पितरः सर्वे मातृमातामहादयः ॥
अतीतकुलकोटीनां सप्तद्वीपनिवासिनाम् ।
आब्रह्मभुवनाल्लोकादिदमस्तु तिलोदकम् ॥ (=328)

(1) इति मन्त्रेण सतिलकुशान् त्रीन् जलाञ्जलीन् दद्याद् इति । (2) अत्र प्रत्यञ्जलि मन्त्रावृत्तिः । (3) "ननु मन्त्रस्य तर्पणकर्मकरणत्वात् संख्याञ्जलिदानस्य चैककर्मत्वान्

338. मन्त्रान्तेन कर्मादिसंनिपातः स्याद्

शब० 11.4.19.53

(1) इति न्यायेन 'अव रक्षो दिवः सपत्नं वध्यासमित्यवहन्ती'तिवद्, 'वेदिरसि बर्हिषे त्वेति त्रिर्वेदिं प्रोक्षती'तिवच्च सकृदेव मन्त्रपाठः स्यात्" । (2) मैवं, प्रत्यञ्जलि ह्यन्यद् अन्यज्जलं दीयते । (3) ततश्च यत्र मन्त्रः प्रयुक्तस्तदर्थ एव स स्यान्न सर्वार्थ इति विशेषग्रहणात् सर्वसंस्कारासिद्धेस्तत्सिद्धये

---

335. -स्तम्बपर्यन्तं; P2 L2 —स्तम्भपर्यन्तं । 336. स्तम्बपर्यन्तं; P2 L2 स्तम्भपर्यन्तं 336. तृप्तं; P1 P2 K L1 तृप्ति । 337.3. संख्याञ्जलि—; Cl K L2 ससंख्याञ्जलि— । 338.3. यत्र; P1 (+correction in P2) यत्र यो ।

निर्वपणलवनादिवत् द्रव्यान्तरत्वेन प्रत्यञ्जल्येव मन्त्रप्राप्तिः । (4) अवघात-प्रोक्षणयोस्तु त एव व्रीहयः पुनरव हन्यन्ते, सैव च वेदिः पुनः प्रोक्ष्यत इति द्रव्यैकत्वात् संस्कारलाभान्न मन्त्रावृत्तिः । (5) तस्मात् सन्ध्यार्घ्यदानवत् प्रत्यञ्जलि मन्त्रावृत्तिः ।

(6) केचित्तु "'इति ब्रुवन्' [335] इति शतृप्रत्ययेन समानकालत्वाव-गमाद् 'युवा सुवासा' इतिवत् क्रियमाणानुवादितया करणत्वाभावात् सकृदेव मन्त्रं पठन्नञ्जलित्रयं दद्याद्" इत्याहुः ।

(7) यश्च तर्पणे तिलनिषेधः—

गार्ग्यः—

339. **भानौ भौमे त्रयोदश्यां नन्दाभृगुमघासु च ।**
पिण्डदानं मृदास्नानं न कुर्यात् तिलतर्पणम् ॥ इति । (=394)

मारीचिः—

340. **सप्तम्यां रविवारे च गृहे जन्मदिने तथा ।**
भृत्यपुत्रकलत्रार्थी न कुर्यात्तिलतर्पणम् ॥
पक्षयोरुभयो राजन् सप्तम्यां निशि सन्ध्ययोः ।
विद्यापुत्रकलत्रार्थी तिलान् सप्तसु वर्जयेत् ॥

स्मृत्यर्थसारे—

341. **विवाहे चोपनयने चौले सति यथाक्रमम् ।**
वर्षमर्धं तदर्धञ्च नेत्येके तिलतर्पणम् ॥
वृद्धौ सत्याञ्च तन्मासि नेत्याहुस्तिलतर्पणम् ।

स्मृत्यर्थसार, p. 30

(1) इति, अयं तीर्थतर्पणे न प्रवर्तते,

342. **तीर्थे तिथिविशेषे च गयायां प्रेतपक्षके ।**
निषिद्धेऽपि दिने कुर्यात्तर्पणं तिलमिश्रितम् ॥

इति वचनात्,

343. **तिथितीर्थविशेषेषु कार्यं प्रेते च सर्वदे—**

स्मृत्यर्थसार p. 30

ति स्मृत्यर्थसारोदाहृतवचनाच्च ।

(1) तर्पणेऽन्यत् सर्वं सामान्यविधानं ग्रन्थान्तरतोऽवसेयम् ।

(2) विधवयापि तीर्थे तर्पणं कार्यं,

344. तर्पणं प्रत्यहं कार्यं भर्तुः कुशतिलोदकैः ।
तत्पितुस्तत्पितुश्चापि नामगोत्रादिपूर्वकम् ॥

स्क० पु०, ब्रह्मखण्ड 2.7.69

(1) इति स्कान्दे विधवाधर्मेषु प्रत्यहमप्यभिधानात् । (2) तीर्थे निमित्तिकतया सुतरां तदधिकारात् । (3) इदञ्च पुत्रपौत्राभावविषयम् । (4) मदनपारिजातेऽप्येवमेव ।

(5) संन्यासिना तु तर्पणं न कार्यं,

345. न कुर्यात् सूतकं भिक्षुः श्राद्धपिण्डोदकक्रियाम् । (= 571)

(1) इति स्मृतेः ।

इति श्रीभट्टरामेश्वरसूरिसूनुनारायणभट्टविरचिते त्रिस्थलीसेतौ सामान्यप्रघट्टके तीर्थतर्पणम्

343.1. ग्रन्थान्तरतोऽत्रसेयम्; P1 ग्रन्थान्तरतो ज्ञे (?) यम्. Cl ग्रन्थान्तरेऽवसेयम्, P2 ग्रन्थान्तरतो विधेयम् । 344. तर्पणं प्रत्यहं; Cl प्रत्यहं तर्पणं । 344.3. -विषयम्; P3 K -विषये । 345 श्राद्ध—; P1 श्राद्धं., L2 श्राद्धे । 345.1. श्रीभट्टरामेश्वर..... विरचिते; Cl omitted.

अथ तीर्थस्नानतर्पणप्रसङ्गान्नदीनां रजोदोषः

देवल:

346. नभोनभस्ययोर्मध्ये सर्वा नद्यो रजस्वलाः ।
तासु स्नानं न कुर्वीत देवर्षिपितृतर्पणम् ॥

अत्रि:

347. सिंहकर्कटयोर्मध्ये सर्वा नद्यो रजस्वलाः ।
न स्नानादीनि कर्माणि तासु कुर्वीत मानवः ॥

(1) इदञ्च महानदीव्यतिरिक्तविषयं,

348. सिंहकर्कटयोर्मध्ये सर्वा नद्यो रजस्वलाः ।
तासु स्नानं न कुर्वीत वर्जयित्वा समुद्रगा ॥

इति व्याघ्रपा क्तेः । (1) महानदीषु विशेषान्तरं भविष्योत्तरे––

349. आदौ तु कर्कटे देवि महानद्यो रजस्वलाः ।
त्रिदिनं तु चतुर्थेऽह्नि शुद्धाः स्युर्जाह्नवी यथे- ॥

ति । (1) महानद्यश्च ब्रह्मपुराणे––

350. गोदावरी भीमरथी तुङ्गभद्रा च वेणिका ।
तापी पयोष्णी विन्ध्यस्य दक्षिणे तु प्रकीर्तिता ॥ इति ।

(–55)

351. भागीरथी नर्मदा च यमुना च सरस्वती ।
विशोका च विहस्ता च विन्ध्यस्योत्तरतः स्थिताः ॥
द्वादशैता महानद्यो देवर्षिक्षेत्रसम्भवा । इति ।

(1) अल्पनदीषु तु अगस्त्योदयावधि रजस्वलात्वमुक्तं मात्स्ये––

352. यावन्नोदेति भगवान् दक्षिणाशाविभूषणम् ।
तावद् रजोवहा नद्यः करतोयाः प्रकीर्तिता ॥ इति ।

(1) 'करतोयाः' स्वल्पतोयाः ।

(2) अन्योऽपि विशेषः कात्यायनेनोक्तः––

353. **याः शोषमुपगच्छन्ति ग्रीष्मे कुसरितो भुवि ।**
तासु प्रावृषि न स्नायादपूर्णे दशवासरे ॥

(1) गङ्गादिविषये तु देवलः —

354. **गङ्गा च यमुना चैव प्लक्षजाता सरस्वती ।**
(1) (कुरुक्षेत्रे या सरस्वती सा प्लक्षजाता ।)
रजसा नाभिभूयन्ते ये चान्ये नदसंज्ञिताः ॥
शोणसिन्धुहिरण्याख्या कोकलोहितघर्घराः ।
शतद्रुश्च नदाः सप्त पावनाः परिकीर्तिताः ॥

स्मृतिसंग्रहे —

355. **तपनस्य सुता गङ्गा गौतमी च सरस्वती ।**
रजसा नाभिभूयन्ते वेणा च नदसंज्ञिताः ॥

(1) 'तपनस्य सुता' यमुना ।

निगमः—

356. **गङ्गा धर्मद्रवः पुण्या यमुना च सरस्वती ।**
अन्तर्गतरजोदोषाः सर्वावस्थासु चामलाः ॥

एवञ्च

357. **प्रथमं कर्कटे देवि त्र्यहं गङ्गा रजस्वले—।**

(1) त्यादि गङ्गादीनां रजोदोषवचांसि अन्तर्गतरजोविषयाणि ।

तथा—

358. **कर्कटादौ रजोदुष्टा गोमती वासरत्रयम् ।**
चन्द्रभागा सती सिन्धुः शरयूर्नर्मदा तथा ॥

(1) अयञ्च नदीनां रजोदोषो न तत्तीरवासिनाम् । अतएव निगमे—

---

354. —संज्ञिताः; Cl —संज्ञकाः । 354. —हिरण्याख्याः; Cl —हिरण्याक्ष—। 357.1. अन्तर्गतरजोविषयाणि; Pl (+correction in P2) अन्तर्गतरजोदोषविषयाणि । 358. शरयूर्; Pl K सरयूर्, Ll शरयुर् ।

359. **न तु तत्तीरवासिनाम्** । (=254)
इत्युक्तम् ।

(1) रजोदुष्टमपि जलं गङ्गादिजलसंयुतं स्वयमदुष्टं भवति, न च गङ्गादि-जलं दूषयति । तदुक्तं मत्स्यपुराणे—

360. **पुण्याम्भसा समायोगाद् दुष्टमप्यम्बु पावनम्** । इति ।

भारते च—

361. **अपवित्रमपि प्राप्य गङ्गां याति पवित्रताम्** । इति ।

अन्योऽपि विशेषः स्मृतिसङ्ग्रहे—

362. **धनुःसहस्राण्यष्टौ तु गतिर्यासां न विद्यते ।**
न ता नदीशब्दवहा गर्तास्ताः परिकीर्तिताः ॥
काले नभस्यशुद्धं स्यात् त्रिरात्रं तु नवोदकम् ।
अकाले तु दशाहं स्यात् पीत्वा नाद्यादहर्निशम् ॥ इति ।

(1) अन्योऽपि विशेषो भविष्ये—

363. **महदम्बु समं वापि यदि तिष्ठेत् पुरातनम् ।**
नवाम्बु मिश्रितं तेन न दुष्टमिति सूरयः ॥

योगयाज्ञवल्क्यः—

364. **रजोदुष्टेऽम्भसि स्नानं वर्ज्यं नद्यादिषु द्विजैः ।**
कदर्थितं रजस्तेषां सन्ध्योपास्तिश्च तर्पणम् ॥

(1) 'कदर्थितं' कुत्सितम् ।

तथा—

365. **अजा गौर्महिषी चैव ब्राह्मणी च प्रसूतिका ।**
भूमेर्नवोदकञ्चैव दशरात्रेण शुध्यति ॥

(1) नूतनखानितकूप्याद्युदकं 'नवोदकम्' ।
(2) केषुचित्तु कर्मसु रजोदोषाभावः । तदाह व्याघ्रपादः—

366. अभावे कूपवापीनामनपायिपयोभृताम् ।
रजोदुष्टेऽपि पयसि ग्रामभोगो न दुष्यती- ॥ ति ।

वसिष्ठः—

367. उपाकर्मणि चोत्सर्गे प्रेतस्नाने तथैव च ।
चन्द्रसूर्यग्रहे चैव रजोदोषो न विद्यते ॥

(गोमिल 1.143)

इत्यादि ।

इति त्रिस्थलीसेतौ नदीरजोदोषः

367. इत्यादि; P2 L2 इति । 367. इति त्रिस्थलीसेतौ नदीरजोदोषः; P2 इति श्रीत्रिस्थलीसेतौ सामान्यप्रघट्टके नदीरजोदोषः ।

अथ तीर्थश्राद्धम्

पाद्मे सृष्टिखण्डे—

368. तीर्थायतनगोष्ठेषु द्वीपोद्यानगृहेषु च ।
विविक्तेषूपलिप्तेषु श्राद्धं देयं विजानता ॥
प० पु०, सृ० खण्ड 9.138c-139b

पाद्ममात्स्ययोः 'तीर्थं पुष्करकं नामे'त्यादिना [म० पु० 22.65a] तीर्थान्यनुक्रम्योक्तम्—

369. एषु तीर्थेषु यच्छ्राद्धं तत्कोटिगुणमिष्यते ।
यस्मात्तस्मात् प्रयत्नेन तीर्थे श्राद्धं समाचरेत् ॥
म० पु० 22.81a; प० पु०, सृ० खण्ड 11.84 a-b, 85a-b

कौर्मे—

370. देशानां तु विशेषेण भवेत्पुण्यमनन्तकम् ।
गयायामक्षयं श्राद्धं प्रयागेऽमरकण्टके ॥
वराहपर्वते चैव गङ्गायाञ्च विशेषतः ।
वाराणस्यां विशेषेण यत्र देवः स्वयं हरः ॥
गङ्गाद्वारे प्रभासे च बिल्वके नीलपर्वते ।
कुरुक्षेत्रे च कुब्जाम्रे भृगुतुङ्गे हिमाचले ॥
केदारे फल्गुतीर्थे च नैमिषारण्य एव च ।
सरस्वत्यां विशेषेण पुष्करेषु विशेषतः ॥
नर्मदायां कुशावर्ते श्रीशैले भद्रकर्णके ।
वेत्रवत्यां विशेषेण गोदावर्यां विशेषतः ॥
एवमादिषु चान्येषु तीर्थेषु पुलिनेषु च ।
नदीनाञ्चैव तीरेषु तुष्यन्ति पितरः सदा ॥
कू० पु० 2.20.28c–29b, 32-36

368. देयं; P2 कार्यं । 369 एषु; P2 येषु । 369. तीर्थे श्राद्धं; P1 P2 तीर्थश्राद्धं । 369. कौर्मे; P2 कौर्म्ये । 370. हिमाचले; P2 L2 हिमालये । 370. तुष्यन्ति; L2 तृप्यन्ति ।

विष्णुः—

371. पुष्करेष्वक्षयं श्राद्धं जपहोमतपांसि च ।
पुष्करे स्नातमात्रस्तु सर्वपापात् प्रमुच्यते ॥

वि० स्मृ० 85.1-3

इत्यभिधाय,

एवमन्येषु तीर्थेषु सरिद्वरासु सङ्गमेषु प्रभवेषु
पुलिनेषु निकुञ्जेषु प्रस्रवणेषु वनेषूपवनेषु चे- ॥ त्यादि ।

वि० स्मृ० 85.57–65

(1) 'प्रभवा' नद्युत्पत्तिदेशाः, 'सरिद्वरासु सङ्गमेष्वि'ति प्रकृत्याभिधानात् ।

देवलः —

372. श्राद्धस्य पूजितो देशो गया गङ्गा सरस्वती ।
कुरुक्षेत्रं प्रयागञ्च नैमिषं पुष्कराणि च ॥
नदीतटेषु तीर्थेषु शैलेषु पुलिनेषु च ।
विविक्तेषु च तुष्यन्ति दत्तेनेह पितामहाः ॥

शंखः—

373. वाराणस्यां कुरुक्षेत्रे भृगुतुङ्गे हिमालये ।
नर्मदाबाहुदातीरे सर्वमानन्त्यमश्नुते ॥
गङ्गाद्वारे प्रयागे च नैमिषे पुष्करे तथा ।
संनिहित्यां गयायाञ्च सर्वमक्षयतां व्रजेत् ॥

शंख (K) 194

(1) अत्र सामान्यतस्तीर्थश्राद्धविधायकवचनबलादेव सर्वत्र श्राद्धप्राप्तौ सत्यामपि विशेषकीर्तनं गुणफलसम्बन्धविधानार्थं, 'दध्नेन्द्रियकामस्ये'त्यादिवत् । (2) न तु विशिष्टश्राद्धान्तरविधिगौरवापत्तेः, 'सोमेन यजेते'त्यादिवद् अगतिकत्वाभावात् ।

तीर्थान्यनुक्रम्य वायुपुराणे—

374. एवमादिषु तीर्थेषु श्राद्धं ये निर्वपन्ति हि ।
पूता भवन्ति ते स्नात्वा दत्त्वा पश्चाद् यथाविधि ॥

---

371. प्रभवेषु; P1 omitted. 371. निकुञ्जेषु; P2 कुञ्जेषु । 372. तीर्थेषु शैलेषु P2 शैलेषु गर्तेषु । 373. हिमालये; C1 हिमाचले । 374. एवमादिषु; P2 एवमन्येषु ।

375. **'दत्त्वे'ति तर्पणविध्युक्तमार्गेण तिलोदकं दत्त्वे—**

ति स्मृतिरत्नावल्याम् ।

विष्णुधर्मोत्तरे—

376. **दक्षिणाप्रवणे देशे तीर्थादौ वा गृहेऽपि वा ।**
भूसंस्कारादिसंयुक्ते श्राद्धं कुर्यात् प्रयत्नतः ॥

यत्तु यमः—

377. **परकीयप्रदेशेषु पितॄणां निर्वपेत्तु यः ।**
तद्भूमिस्वामिपितृभिः श्राद्धकर्म विहन्यते ॥

तथा ब्रह्मपुराणे—

378. **परकीयगृहे यस्तु स्वान् पितॄंस्तर्पयेद् जडः ।**
तद्भूमिस्वामिनस्तस्य हरन्ति पितरो बलात् ॥
अग्रभागं ततस्तेभ्यो दद्यान्मूल्यञ्च जीवताम् ।

(1) स्वीयद्रव्यस्य 'तेभ्यस्' तद्भूमिस्वामिपितृभ्य उत्सृष्टं देयम् । (2) 'जीवतां' स्वामिनां मूल्यं देयमिति । (3) तत्र परकीयप्रदेशाः परगृहादयो निषिद्धाः, न तु तीर्थादयस्तेषामस्वामिकत्वात् । तदुक्तं कौर्मे—

379. **अटव्यः सर्वतः पुण्या नदीतीराणि यानि च ।**
सर्वाण्यस्वामिकान्याहुर्नहि तेषु परिग्रहः ॥

तथा—

380. **वनानि गिरयो नद्यस्तीर्थान्यायतनानि च ।**
देवखाताश्च गर्ताश्च न स्वामी तेषु विद्यते ॥

(1) 'गर्ता' अकृत्रिमाः क्षेत्रविशेषा ब्रह्मयोन्यादयः ।
(2) इदञ्च श्राद्धं स्नानतर्पणाद्यनन्तरमविलम्बेनैव कार्यम् । तदुक्तं देवीपुराणे—

381. **श्राद्धञ्च तत्र कर्तव्यमर्घ्यावाहनवर्जितम् ।** (= 406)
श्वध्वांक्षगृध्रकाकानां नैव दृष्टिहतञ्च यत् ॥

378.1. -द्रव्यस्य; Cl -द्रव्यस् । 378.3. कौर्मे; P2 कौर्म्ये । 381. च यत्; K L1 च तत्, P3 तु तत् ।

श्राद्धं तत् तैर्थिकं प्रोक्तं पितॄणां तृप्तिकारकम् ।
काले वाप्यथवाऽकाले तीर्थे श्राद्धं तथा नरैः ॥
प्राप्तैरेव च कर्तव्यं पितॄणां चैव तर्पणम् । (=324)
पिण्डदानञ्च तच्छस्तं पितॄणाञ्चातिवल्लभम् ॥
विलम्बो न च कर्तव्यो न च विघ्नं समाचरेद् । इति ।

(1) 'प्राप्तैरेवे'ति आवश्यकस्नानतर्पणाद्यनन्तरं, तावतो विलम्बस्य स्नानतर्पणादिविध्यभ्यनुज्ञातत्वात् ।

(2) तीर्थश्राद्धे निषिद्धकालवर्जनमपि नास्तीत्याह शंखः—

382. **तीर्थे द्रव्योपपत्तौ च न कालमवधारयेत् ।**
पात्रञ्च ब्राह्मणं प्राप्य सद्यः श्राद्धं समाचरेत् ॥

तथा भारते आदिपर्वण्यङ्गारपर्णं प्रत्यर्जुनः—

383. **भुक्तो वाप्यथवाभुक्तो रात्रावहनि खेचर ।**
न कालनियमो ह्यस्ति गङ्गां प्राप्य सरिद्वराम् ॥ इति ।
म० भा० 1.1713*.1pr

चित्रपथामाहात्म्ये—

384. **भुक्तो वाप्यथ वाभुक्तो रात्रौ वा यदि वा दिवा ।**
पर्वकालेऽथ वाकाले शुचिर्वाप्यथ वाशुचिः ॥
यदैव दृश्यते तत्र नदी चित्रपथा प्रिये ।
प्रमाणं दर्शनं तस्या न कालस्तत्र कारणम् ॥

(1) 'अशुचिर्' आशौचेनापि ।

अत एव पैठीनसिः—

385. **विवाहदुर्गयज्ञेषु यात्रायां तीर्थकर्मणि ।**
न तत्र सूतकं तद्वत् कर्मयज्ञादि कारयेत् ॥
(=196, 315)

---

384. वा यदि वा; L1 वाप्यथ वा ।

काशीखण्डे—

386. **अकालेऽप्यथवाकाले तीर्थे श्राद्धञ्च तर्पणम् ।**
अविलम्बेन कर्तव्यं नैव विघ्नं समाचरेत् ॥ (= 323)

(1) 'काले' ऽपराह्णादौ भोजनादिराहित्ये च । (2) 'अकाले' रात्र्यादौ कृतभोजनादिनापि । (3) प्राप्ततीर्थस्यैवाधिकारिविशेषणत्वाद् ग्रहणादिवत् सर्वास्ववस्थासु श्राद्धं कार्यमित्याशयः । (4) 'काल' इति तु दृष्टान्ततयोक्तम् । (5) तत्र च 'समुद्रो वा महासत्त्व' इतिवद् वाशब्दो नेयः ।

(6) कश्चित्तु "'अकाले' अमावास्यादिश्राद्धकालव्यतिरिक्तेऽपि न तु रात्र्यादौ निषेधविरोधात् । (7) अत एव 'तीर्थद्रव्योपपत्तौ च न कालमवधारयेद्' [= 382] इति देवलवचने

387. **'न कालमवधारयेद्' अमावास्यामपराह्णं वा न**
प्रतीक्षेत । निषिद्धं तु रात्र्यादि वर्जयेदेवे—

श्रा० वि० p. 66

त्युक्तं शूलपाणिने"त्याह । (1) तन्न, सर्ववारतिथीनां श्राद्धे निषेधाभावेन नैमित्तिकेऽस्मिन् श्राद्धे निमित्तानन्तरभाविनि प्राप्तत्वादेव विधानवैयर्थ्यात् ।

(2) अथोच्येत "सर्ववारतिथिषु श्राद्धस्यानावश्यकत्वाद् यस्मिन् काले प्रतिपदादौ श्राद्धमनावश्यकं तदापि तीर्थप्राप्तौ सत्यां श्राद्धमवश्यं कार्यम्; (3) इत्यावश्यकत्वार्थम् 'अकाल' इत्युक्तम्" इति । (4) तदपि न, नैमित्तिकविधित एव निमित्ते सत्यवश्यकर्तव्यत्वसिद्धेर्गृहदाहेष्टयादिवत् । (5) ततश्च 'अकाल' इत्यस्य सार्थक्याय निषिद्धरात्र्यादिप्रतिप्रसवार्थत्वमेव युक्तम् । (6) अत एव शंखेन 'न कालमवधारयेदि'ति सामान्यत एवोक्तम् । (7) चित्रपथामाहात्म्ये च 'रात्रौ वा यदि वा दिवे'ति [384] स्फुटमेवाह । विष्णुरपि—

388. **ततः सायाह्नदत्तं हि राक्षसैर्विप्रलुप्यते ।**
ग्रहोपरागसंक्रान्तितीर्थश्राद्धादिकं विने- ॥ ति ।

(1) तस्माद् आकस्मिकतीर्थप्राप्तौ सत्यां भुक्तवता रात्र्यादौ वा श्राद्धादि कार्यमिति सिद्धम् ।

(2) यदा तु प्राप्तिदिने दैवो मानुषो वा विघ्नः स्यात्, तदा दिनान्तरे श्राद्धं

386.3. सर्वास्ववस्थासु; P1 सर्वावस्थासु । 386.7. तीर्थ—; C1 C2 तीर्थे ।
387.2. अथोच्येत; P2 अथोच्यते । 388.1. सिद्धम्; C1 स्थितम् ।

कार्यम्। (3) "ननु 'प्राप्तैरेव कार्यमि'ति प्राप्त्यनन्तरकाले कर्तव्यतोक्तेः दिनान्तरे च तदभावात्, अमावास्यायां सूतकादिविघ्ने सति श्राद्धलोपवदत्रापि लोप एव स्यात् । (4) क्षयाहादेस्तु सूतकाद्यनन्तरमप्यनुष्ठानं युक्तं,

389. **तदहश्चेत् प्रदुष्येत केनचित् सूतकादिना ।**
सूतकानन्तरं कुर्यात् पुनस्तदहरेव वे- ।।

त्यादिवचनात् । (1) इह तु वचनाभावाल्लोप एव युक्तः । (2) एवं रात्रौ सन्ध्यायां वा तीर्थप्राप्तौ लोपोऽस्तु रात्रिसन्ध्ययोः श्राद्धनिषेधादुत्तरदिने च प्राप्त्यनन्तरकालाभावात्" ।

(3) सत्यमेवं भवेत्, यद्यमावास्यादिवत् कालविधानं स्यात् । (4) इह तु तीर्थप्राप्तेर्निमित्ततामात्रमुच्यते । (5) तथा च 'निमित्ते सति नैमित्तिकानुष्ठानम् अनन्तरकाल एवासति प्रतिबन्धे कार्यम्' इति न्यायलभ्यः कालः । (6) तेन सति प्रतिबन्धे जातेष्टिवत् कालान्तरेऽप्यनुष्ठानमविरुद्धम् । (7) यथा हि 'वैश्वानरं द्वादशकपालं निर्वपेत् पुत्रे जात' इति विहिता जातेष्टिर्जातकर्मणः पूर्वं क्रियमाणा जातकर्मणः प्राक् स्तनपाननिषेधाद् इष्टिजातकर्मादिव्यवधाने पुत्रविपत्त्यापत्तेरुपजीव्यविरोधापत्तेरनन्तरकाल एव न कार्या, किन्तु जातकर्मण ऊर्ध्वमिति चतुर्थे सिद्धान्तिते, जातकर्मानन्तरं सूतकेनाशुचित्वान्निमित्ताव्यवहितानन्तर्यस्य च बाधित्वान्निमित्तस्य च जातत्वाद् अत्यन्तलोपायोगाच्छुद्धचनुरोधेन सूतकानन्तरे पर्वण्यनुष्ठेयेति तदुत्तराधिकरणे साधितम् । (8) तद्वदत्रापि कालान्तरानुष्ठानमविरुद्धम् ।

(9) इयांस्तु विशेषः; (10) तत्रावश्यको मध्ये प्रतिबन्धः, इह तु कादाचित्क इति ।

(11) यदा तु प्रतिबन्धाद् अकृतश्राद्ध एव वहिर्याति तथा तीर्थरूपदेशाभावात् तन्निमित्तकश्राद्धं लुप्यत एव, मृत इव पुत्रे पूतत्वादिफलाधिकरणाभावाज्जातेष्टिः । (12) यदि स्वबुद्ध्याऽकृतश्राद्ध एव गच्छेत् तदा प्रत्यवेयात् पुरुषापराधात् । (13) अबुद्धिपूर्वे तु प्रतिबन्धे न प्रत्यवैतीत्येतावान् विशेषः ।

(14) रात्रिसन्ध्ययोरपि तीर्थप्राप्तौ पूर्वोक्तवाक्यवशान्निषेधं बाधित्वा

388.3. -काले कर्तव्यतो—; P3 C2 K L1 —कालकर्तव्यतो —। 389. तदहश्चेत् प्रदुष्येत; C1 ततश्चेद् विप्रदुष्येत । 389. एव वेत्यादि—; C1 एव त्वित्यादि- । 389.2. लोपोऽस्तु; P2 C1 लोपोऽस्ति । 389.6. प्रतिबन्धे; C1 प्रतिबन्धके । 389.7. यथा P1; (+correction in P2) तथा । 389.11. जातेष्टिः; C1 जातेष्ट्यादिः ।

तदैव श्राद्धमित्युक्तमेव । (15) स्नानमुण्डनोपवासादावप्ययमेव सर्वो निर्णयः, नैमित्तिकत्वेन साम्यात् । तथा प्रभासखण्डे—

390. **न वारं न च नक्षत्रं न कालस्तत्र कारणम् ।**
यदैव दृश्यते तीर्थं तदा पर्वसहस्रकम् ॥

(1) अतश्च तीर्थश्राद्धे तिथिवासरनक्षत्रादि प्रत्युक्तो निषेधो न प्रवर्तत इत्यभिप्रायः । (2) तन्निषेधश्च गार्ग्यः—

391. **नन्दायां भार्गवदिने त्रयोदश्यां त्रिजन्मनि ।**
एषु श्राद्धं न कुर्वीत गृही पुत्रधनक्षयात् ॥

(1) 'त्रिजन्मनि' जन्मदिननक्षत्रतारासु ।
वृद्धगार्ग्यः—

392. **प्राजापत्ये च पौष्णे च पित्र्यर्क्षे भार्गवे तथा ।**
यस्तु श्राद्धं प्रकुर्वीत तस्य पुत्रो विनश्यति ॥

(1) प्राजापत्यं रोहिणी । (2) पौष्णं रेवती । (3) पित्र्यर्क्षं मघा ।
भारते—

393. **नक्षत्रे च न कुर्वीत यस्मिन् जातो भवेन्नरः ।**
न प्रोष्ठपदयोः कार्यं न चाग्नेये च भारत ॥
दारुणेषु च सर्वेषु प्रत्यरे च विवर्जयेत् ॥ (=292)

म० भा० 13.107.119c–120b

(1) आग्नेयं कृत्तिका । (2) दारुणान्यार्द्राश्लेषाज्येष्ठामूलानि । (3) जन्मर्क्षात् पञ्चमं चतुर्दशं त्रयोविंशश्च प्रत्यरम् ।

(4) एतानि वचनानि यद्यपि प्रेतश्राद्धनिषेधपरतया हेमाद्रिप्रभृतिभिरङ्गीकृतानि; तथापि कैश्चिच्छ्राद्धमात्रनिषेधपरताङ्गीकारादत्रोदाहृतानि ।

(5) तथा पिण्डदानेऽपि निषेधः—

394. **भानौ भौमे त्रयोदश्यां नन्दाभृगुमघासु च ।**
पिण्डदानं मृदास्नानं न कुर्यात् तिलतर्पणम् ॥ (=339)

390.1.—वासर—; P1 P2 —वार— । 392. विनश्यति; P2 भविष्यति ।

रामकौतुके—

395. **नन्दाश्वकामरव्यारभृग्वग्निपितृकालभे ।**
गञ्जे वैधृतिपाते च पिण्डास्त्याज्याः सुतेप्सुभिः ॥

(1) नन्दाः प्रतिपत्षष्ठ्येकादश्यः । (2) अश्वः सप्तमी । (3) कामस्त्रयोदशी । (4) रव्यारौ रविभौमवारौ । (5) भृगुः शुक्रवारः। (6) अग्निपितृकालभानि कृत्तिकामघाभरण्यः । (7) गञ्जो वैधृतिश्च योगौ (8)पातो व्यतीपातः ।

कार्ष्णाजिनिः—

396. **विवाहव्रतचूडासु वर्षमर्धं तदर्धकम् ।**
पिण्डदानं मृदास्नानं न कुर्यात्तिलतर्पणम् ॥
वृद्धिमात्रे तथान्यत्र पिण्डदाननिराक्रिया ।
कृता गर्गादिभिर्मुख्यैर्मासमेकं तु कर्मिणाम् ॥

मनुः—

397. **रात्रौ श्राद्धं न कुर्वीत राक्षसी कीर्तिता हि सा ।**
सन्ध्ययोरुभयोश्चैव सूर्ये चैवाचिरोदिते ॥

मनु० 3.280

वायुपुराणे—

398. **त्रिमुहूर्तं तु सायाह्नस्तत्र श्राद्धं विवर्जयेत् ।**
उपसन्ध्यं न कुर्वीत पितृपूजां कथञ्चन ॥
स काल आसुरः प्रोक्तस्तत्र श्राद्धं विवर्जयेद् ।

इत्यादि । (1) मलमासेऽपि तीर्थश्राद्धं कार्यं,

399. **नित्यं नैमित्तिकञ्चैव श्राद्धं कुर्यान्मलिम्लुच ।**

इति जाबालिवचनात्,

400. **नित्यनैमित्तिके कुर्यात् प्रयतः सन् मलिम्लुचे ।**
तीर्थश्राद्धं गजछायाप्रेतश्राद्धं तथैव चे— ॥

बृ० (श्रा०) 149

ति बृहस्पतिवचनाच्च ।

(1) इदञ्च कृतभोजनादेः सन्ध्यायां रात्रौ मलमासे आशौचेनाशुचेश्च स्नानश्राद्धादिविधानमाकस्मिकतीर्थप्राप्तिविषयं, न तु बुद्धिपूर्वविषयम् । (2) तीर्थप्राप्तिरूपनिमित्तस्य पुरुषप्रयत्नसाध्यतया ग्रहणादिवैलक्षण्यात् ।

(3) ततश्चानिषिद्धकाल एव बुद्धितस्तीर्थप्राप्ति कुर्यात् । (4) आकस्मिक-प्राप्तौ तु निषिद्धकालेऽपि ग्रहणपुत्रजन्मादाविव स्नानश्राद्धादि कुर्यादिति तात्पर्यम् ।

(5) इदञ्चामहेमश्राद्धविषयम् । (6) तावतैव पूर्वोक्तवचनचारितार्थ्यात् । (7) अन्नश्राद्धं तु रात्रिसंध्ययोर्भुक्तवतश्च तीर्थप्राप्तौ द्वितीयदिने । (8) आशौचे तु तीर्थप्राप्तौ आशौचापगमे । (9) तीर्थसम्बन्धस्य तदानीमपि सत्त्वेन ग्रहणादिवैलक्षण्यात् ।

(10) मलमासे तु तीर्थप्राप्तौ विलम्बनिषेधात् तदा श्राद्धं कृत्वा शुद्धमासेऽपि कार्यं, (11) तीर्थप्राप्तेस्तदापि सत्त्वात् कालशुद्धचा फलाधिक्यात्,

401. **यौगादिकं मासिकञ्च श्राद्धं चापरपक्षिकम् ।**
मन्वादिकं तैर्थिकञ्च कुर्यान्मासद्वयेऽपि चे-।।

ति स्मृतिचन्द्रिकालिखितवचनाच्च । (1) अत्र 'अपरपक्षिकं' प्रतिमासं कृष्णपक्षश्राद्धं, न तु महालयश्राद्धं, तस्य तत्र निषेधात् । (2) न चेदं वच उभयत्र तीर्थप्राप्तिविषयम्, एतद्व्यतिरेकेणैव तदा श्राद्धसिद्धेस्तैर्थिकग्रहणानर्थक्यप्रसङ्गा-दिति दिक् ।

(3) श्राद्धीयब्राह्मणे विशेषो देवीपुराणे—

402. **तीर्थेषु ब्राह्मणं नैव परीक्षेत कदाचन ।**
अन्नार्थिनमनुप्राप्तं भोज्यं तं मनुरब्रवीत् ।।

पाद्मे—

403. **ब्राह्मणं न परीक्षेत तीर्थे कालं न चिन्तयेत् ।**
प्राप्ततीर्थो यदा विद्वांस्तदैव श्राद्धमाचरेत् ।।

स्कान्दे—

404. **न परीक्ष्यो द्विजस्तीर्थे ह्यन्नार्थी भोज्य एव तु ।**

का० ख० 6.58a-b

405. **एतच्च श्राद्धार्हब्राह्मणाभावेऽभ्यनुज्ञार्थम् ।**
तत्रापि गुणैरेव न परीक्षेत । पातित्याद्यत्यन्त-
दोषयुक्तस्तु परिहर्तव्य एवे—

ति स्मृतिरत्नावलीकृता व्याख्यातम्

400.3. चानिषिद्ध—; L2 चानिरुद्ध— । 401.2. वच; P3 K वचनं ।

अथ तीर्थश्राद्धे निषिद्धानि

देवीपुराणे—

406. श्राद्धञ्च तत्र कर्तव्यमर्घ्यावाहनवर्जितम् । इति । (= 381)

तथा—

407. अर्घ्यमावाहनञ्चैव द्विजाङ्गुष्ठनिवेशनम् ।
तृप्तिप्रश्नञ्च विकिरं तीर्थश्राद्धे विवर्जयेत् ॥

क्वचित्तु—

408. नावाहनं न दिग्बन्धो न दोषो दृष्टिसम्भवः ।
सकारुण्यञ्च कर्तव्यं तीर्थे श्राद्धं विचक्षणैः ॥

भविष्ये—

409. देवाश्च पितरो यस्माद् गङ्गायां तु सदा स्थिताः ।
आवाहनं विसृष्टिश्च तत्र तेषां न विद्यते ॥

तथा—

410. आवाहनं न तीर्थे स्यान्नार्घ्यदानं तथा भवेत् ।
आहूताः पितरस्तीर्थे कृतार्घाः सन्ति वै यतः ॥

411. अग्नौकरणमपि तीर्थश्राद्धे ने-

ति स्मृतिरत्नावल्याम् ।

देवलः

412. न चात्र श्येनगृध्रादीन् पक्षिणः प्रतिषेधयेत् ।
तद्रूपाः पितरस्तत्र समायान्तीति वैदिकम् ॥

---

407. क्वचित्; Cl कश्चित् । 408. विचक्षणैः; P2 विचक्षणैरिति, Cl विजानता ।
410. कृतार्घाः; P3 Cl K (corrected to कृताघ्र्याः) L1 L2 कृतार्थाः ।
411. देवलः; P2 वसिष्ठः । कृतार्थाः

(412·1) अयञ्चावाहननिषेधस्तीर्थप्राप्तिनिमित्तक एव श्राद्धे न तु तीर्थाधिकरणकश्राद्धमात्रे, (2) 'तत्रे'ति [406] निमित्तसप्तम्या तन्निमित्तकश्राद्धे एव तन्निषेधात्, (3) 'प्राप्तैरेवे'त्युपसंहारे [381] प्राप्तेर्निमित्तत्वकीर्तनाच्च ।

(4) "ननु निमित्तसप्तम्याः पदान्तरसमभिव्याहाराधीनत्वाद् वाक्यगम्यत्वाच्च निमित्तत्वस्याधिकरणसप्तम्येवेयमस्तु; (5) कारकविभक्तित्वेन श्रुतित्वेन च बलवत्त्वात्" ।

(6) न, कारकविभक्तित्वासम्भवेन वाक्यस्यैव निर्णायकत्वसम्भवात् । (7) तथा हि; न तावद् "इयमधिकरणसप्तमी 'अगारे गावो वास्यन्तम्' इतिवत्, 'तप्ते पयसि दध्यानयती'तिवद् वा शेषितया तीर्थस्याधिकरणतां बोधयती"ति युक्तं, (8) श्राद्धेन तीर्थस्य संस्काराद्यतिशयाजनतात् । (9) नापि 'तत्र जयान् जुहुयाद्' इतिवद् अङ्गितया तीर्थस्याविधेयत्वेनेतिकर्तव्यतानाकांक्षत्वात्, (10) फलकरणत्वाभावाच्च । (11) नापि शेषतया 'अग्न्यभावे तु विप्रस्य पाणावेवोपपादयेत्,' 'यद् आहवनीये जुहोती'तिवत् तीर्थस्याधिकरणता, (12) श्राद्धमात्रं प्रति तीर्थस्याङ्गत्वे गृहे क्रियमाणस्य दर्शश्राद्धादेर्वैगुण्यप्रसङ्गात् ।

(13) "तीर्थश्राद्धं प्रति तीर्थमधिकरणतयाङ्गमि"ति चेत्, (14) न, तीर्थश्राद्धयोः सम्बन्धस्याद्याप्यनिर्णयात्, (15) तीर्थश्राद्धशब्दार्थस्यैव निर्णीयमाणत्वात्, (16) तीर्थपदावृत्तिप्रसङ्गाच्च ।

(17) अतो 'भिन्ने जुहोती'तिवत् कारकविभक्तित्वासम्भवान् निमित्तसप्तम्येवेयं 'तत्रे'ति । (18) तत्र तीर्थस्य सदातनत्वेन कादाचित्कत्वाभावान्निमित्तत्वायोगात् प्राप्तत्वेन तस्य निमित्तता, तत्प्राप्तेर्वा निमित्तता 'प्राप्तैरेव तु कर्तव्यम्' [381] इत्यादिवचनालोचनया लभ्यते ।

(19) "ननु तथापि 'तीर्थनिमित्तकं यच्छ्राद्धं तत्रार्घ्यादि वर्जयेदि'त्युद्देश्यश्राद्धविशेषणभूततीर्थाख्यनिमित्तविवक्षायामुभयार्त्यधिकरणोक्तरीत्यावाक्यभेदः । (20) ततश्च श्राद्धमात्रे आवाहनादिनिषेधः स्यादि" ति चेन्, (21) मैवं, उद्देश्यविशेषणविवक्षायां हि वाक्यभेदो, न विशिष्टोद्देश्यतायां, (22) 'मैत्रावरुणः प्रेष्यति चानु चाहे'त्यत्रेव चोक्तसाहित्यविशिष्टप्रैषानुवचनोद्देश्यतायाम् ।

412.8. श्राद्धेन; P1 P2 श्राद्धे च, C2 L1 श्राद्धे तु । 412.11. शेषतया; P2 विशेषतया । 412.19.—विशषणभूत—; C1—विशेषणीभूत— । 412.20.'ततश्च; P2 तच्च । 412.22. Before मैत्रावरुणः; P1 तत्र ।

(23) तत्र च विशिष्टरूपेण प्राकरणिकप्रत्यासन्नप्रमाणोपस्थापिततया बुद्धिविपरिवृत्तिरेव विनिगमहेतुः, (24) प्रैषानुवचनोभयात्मकमन्त्रस्येव पाठेन। (25) ततो न वाक्यभेदः। (26) प्रपञ्चितमेतद् भवदेवेनेति नेहातिप्रपञ्च्यते।

(27) तस्मात् तीर्थप्राप्तिनिमित्तकश्राद्ध एवार्घ्यादिनिषेधो, न तु तदधिकरणश्राद्धमात्रे क्षयाहादावपि; यथा—

413. **अयनद्वितये श्राद्धं विषुवद्वितये तथा।**
सङ्क्रान्तिषु च कर्तव्यं पिण्डनिर्वपनाद् ऋत॥

(1) इति सङ्क्रान्त्यादिनिमित्तक एव पिण्डनिषेधो न तु वार्षिकादौ तद्वत्। तदुक्तं—

414. **न त्वत्रान्यनिमित्तके पितृयज्ञौ पिण्डप्रहाणं भवेद्।** इति

(1) "एवमप्यावाहनस्य संनिधिफलकत्वात् तीर्थे च पितृणां सदासन्निधानात् स्वयंकृतेध्मवेद्योश्छेदनोद्धननादिवत् द्वाराबाधात् तीर्थाधिकरणकश्राद्धमात्र एव वैयर्थ्याद् आवाहनबाधः स्यादि"ति चेत्, (2) मैवं, 'तेन ह्यन्नं क्रियत' इतिवत् संनिधिप्रतिपादनस्य हेत्वर्थवादत्वात्। (3) संनिधानेऽपि चोपचारत्वेनावाहनसंभवाद् बुद्धबोधनवत्। (4) तीर्थनिमित्तके तु निषेधाद् बाधः।

(5) तथा—"न देवतायाः शारीरः संनिधिर्, देवताधिकरणे शरीरनिराकरणात्। (6) नापि बौद्धः, शब्दमात्रस्य देवतात्वाङ्गीकाराद् अचेतनत्वेन तदसम्भवात्। (7) किमर्थं तर्हि अन्यत्राप्यावाहनम्? (8) अदृष्टार्थमित्यवेहि। (9) अत एव नावाहनमन्त्रोहोऽपी"त्यप्याहुः।

(10) अत्र कश्चित्; "न देवताधिकरणे संनिधानं निरस्तं, किन्तु प्राधान्यम्। संनिधानं तु

415. **कर्मारम्भे मन्त्राणां देवता वेदितव्याः**

416. **संन्यस्य मनसि देवतां हविर्हूयत**

(1) इत्यादिभिरुद्देश्यतया कर्तृबुद्धिसंनिध्यवगमान्निषेद्धुमशक्यमेव। (2) किञ्च; अशब्दपूर्वत्वात् तत्र प्राधान्यनिरासः।

412.23. तत्र च; P2 ततश्च। 412.23. विनिगमहेतुः; C1 विनिगमनहेतुः। 412.27—निषेधो; C2 —बाधो। 414. पितृयज्ञौ; C1 K पतृयज्ञे। 414—प्रहाणं; P2 — प्रहरणं, C1 —ग्रहणं, K L2 प्रवाहणं। 414.3. चोपचार—; P2 C2 वोपचार—।

417. **इह चाहं संनिहितस्तत्र पाषाणप्रतिमादिषु**

रामोत्तरतापिनीयोपनिषद्, p. 166 (चतुर्थी खण्डिका)

इति श्रीरामोक्तेः,

418. **शालग्रामशिलायां तु नित्यं संनिहितो हरिर् ।**

(1) इत्याद्युक्तेश्च संनिधानं सर्वसम्मतम् । (2) पितृणामप्य्–।

419. **आच्या जानु दक्षिणतः** (=428)

ऋ० वे० 10.15.6

420. **आसीनासो अरुणीनामुपस्थे**

ऋ० वे० 10.15.7

421. **असावेतत् ते** (=431)

गोभि० गृ० सू० 4.2.35

इत्यादिभिः संनिध्यवगतिः । तथा––

422. **नोद्धरेत् प्रथमं पात्रं पितृणां यद्धि पातितम् ।**
आवृतास्तत्र तिष्ठन्ति पितरः शौनकोऽब्रवीत् ॥

आश्व० गृ० सू० 4.7.14

423. **पूर्वे द्युर्मन्त्रितान् विप्रान् पितरः संविशन्ति वै ।**
यजमानश्च तां रात्रिं वसेयुर्नियतास्तत ॥

(1) इत्यादिभिश्च तदवगतिः ।

(2) किञ्च; नवमे देवताया विग्रहादिपञ्चकनिराकृतिर्न व्यसनितया कृता, किन्तूहसिद्धये गुणत्वाय । (3) तथा हि; प्राधान्ये देवताया निर्वापादिमन्त्राणामग्न्यादिस्वरूपप्रयुक्तौ सत्यां सौर्येऽग्न्यादिदेवताभावान् मन्त्राप्राप्तावूहाभावः प्रसज्येत । (4) तथा न 'न माता वर्धते न पिते'त्याद्यूहदर्शनानुपपत्तिः ।

(5) अपूर्वप्राधान्ये तु, मन्त्राणां तत्प्रयुक्तत्वान् मन्त्रप्रकाशितदेवतः क्रतुरपूर्वं साधयतीति देवतान्तरवत्यां विकृतावूहः सिध्यति । (6) तेन यथा प्रकृतौ देवता प्रकाशिता, एवं विकृतावपीति प्रकृतिवद् भावसिद्धिः ।

(7) तथा––तिरश्चां मण्डूकादीनां पत्रमूलादीनामोषधिवनस्पतीनां हिङ्का-

423.6. देवता; P2 देवताः ।

रादीनां चाश्वचरितानामचेतनानां फलदातृत्वासम्भवाद् अपूर्वमेव प्रधानं, देवता तु गुणभूता ।

(8) "ननु

424. **श्राद्धकृत् सत्यवादी च गृहस्थोऽपि विमुच्यते ।**

425. **स्त्रियः प्रतिपादी—**

पारस्कर गृ० सू०, श्राद्धसूत्र 9

(1) त्यादिवचनैः श्राद्धकर्मण एव फलार्थत्वे शब्दपूर्वत्वात्, पितॄणामपि

426. **अपि वा शब्दपूर्वत्वाद्**

मी० सू० 9.1.4.9

इतिन्यायविषयतैव । (1) न च "मृतपितृकस्यैव श्राद्धाकरणे दोषश्रुतेः श्राद्धं पित्रर्थम्" इति वाच्यम्, (2) तादर्थ्यबोधकविभक्त्यभावेन श्राद्धावश्यकत्वे तात्पर्यात् । (3) तादृशस्यापि च संयोगपृथक्त्वेन फलसाधनत्वोपपत्ते"रिति चेत्, (4) मैवं, यागस्य देवतार्थत्वे प्रमाणाभावात् । (5) श्राद्धस्य तु तदर्थत्वे बहुप्रमाणसत्त्वात् । तथा हि—

427. **अथैनं प्राचीनवीतिनः पितरः सव्यं जान्वाच्योपासीदंस्तानब्रवीन् मासि मासि वोऽशनम्**

श० ब्रा० 2.4.2.2

इति श्रुतिः,

428. **आच्या जानु दक्षिणतः** (=419)

429. **पितॄन् हविषे अत्तव** (=464, 478)

ऋ० वे० 10.16.12d

430. **अत्र पितरो मादयध्वं** (=482)

वा० सं० 2.31a

431. **असावेतत् त** (=421)

---

427. इति श्रुतिः; P2 इति श्रुतेः ।

इत्यादिमन्त्रलिङ्गञ्च,

432. **अग्नौ हुतेन देवस्थाः पितृस्था द्विजतर्पणैः ।**
नरकस्थाश्च तृप्यन्ति पिण्डैर्दत्तैस्त्रिभिर्भुवी- ॥

बृह (श्रा) 110

ति बृहस्पतिः ।

विष्णुपुराणे—

433. **श्राद्धैस्तु पितरस्तृप्तिं प्राप्नुवंस्तत्र वार्षिकीम् ।**

वि० पु० 3.14.7c-d

ब्राह्मे—

434. **पितृभ्यश्च तदा श्राद्धं दत्तमक्षय्यमुच्यते ।**

याज्ञवल्क्यः

435. **ते तृप्तास्तर्पयन्त्येनम् ।**

याज्ञ० 1.47a

(1) एवं तत्र तत्र कात्यायनमन्वादिवचनैः गयादिप्रकरणस्थैश्च वाय्वग्नि-पुराणादिवचनैः पितृतृप्तिरेव श्राद्धाद् गम्यते ।

436. **आयुः प्रजां धनं विद्यां ।**

याज्ञ० 1.269a

437. **ते तृप्तास्तर्पयन्त्येनम् ।** (=435)

(1) इत्यादौ फलदातृतापि तेषां गम्यते ।

438. **यदापिपेषे—।**

श० ब्रा० 12.7.3.21

(1) त्यादि मन्त्रवर्णात् सौत्रामण्या अपि पित्रर्थता ।

439. **शिरस्त्वाद्येन पिण्डेने—।**

438.1. मन्त्रवर्णात्; P1 (+correction in P2) मन्त्रलिङ्गात् ।

(1) त्यादिना प्रेतश्राद्धानामपि पित्रर्थता शरीरसिद्धिद्वारा। (2) अत एव विग्रहस्यापि सिद्धिः।

440. **उद्धरेत् सप्तगोत्राणि**

441. **नरकस्था दिवं यान्ति**

ग० पु० 1.84.30a

442. **मया गयां समासाद्य पितॄणां निष्कृतिः कृता।**

वा० पु० 110.59e-f

(1) इत्यादिवचनैः श्राद्धफलमपि तद्गतम्। (2) अतः श्रुत्यादिवशात् श्राद्धस्य पित्रर्थत्वावगतेर्नात्राशब्दपूर्वत्वम्। (3) न चैते अर्थवादाः, (4) पारार्थ्यशास्त्रदृष्टविरोधाद्यभावात्।

(5) अतः श्राद्धे देवता प्रधानभूता, कर्म तु गुणभूतम्। (6) यागादौ तु विपरीतम्" इति।

(7) तदिदं मीमांसानतिशीलनमूलकम्। (8) तथा हि; यत् तावत् "कर्तृबुद्धिसंनिहितत्वाद् देवतायाः संनिधाननिषेधासम्भव" इति, (9) तन्न, केन वा कर्तृबुद्धिसन्निधिर्विषयताख्यो निषिध्यते ? (10) आवाहनप्रयुक्तो हि संनिधिर्निषिध्यते न चासावाहनप्रयुक्तः। (11) बुद्धिस्थीकृतस्यैवावाहनाद् बुद्धिसंनिधेरावाहनोत्तरभावाभावात्। (12) आवाहनप्रयुक्ते च बुद्धिसंनिधावावाहनबाधवत्युरुक्रमविष्णुयागे तन्निषेधवति च तीर्थश्राद्धादौ बुद्धिसंनिध्यभावप्रसङ्गः। (13) यस्तु आवाहनप्रयुक्तः संनिधिः, स विग्रहादिनिरासान् निरस्त एव गमनागमनादिवत्।

(14) अपिच; "कर्तृबुद्धिसंनिधिर्न निषेद्धुं शक्य इत्युक्त्वा 'अहं संनिहितस्तत्र' 'शालग्रामशिलायां तु नित्यं संनिहितो हरिरि'ति संनिधानप्रमाणोद्भावनं विरुद्धम्। (15) न ह्यनेन कर्तृबुद्धिसंनिधिरुच्यते। (16) यश्च पितृसंनिधानप्रतिपादकोपन्यासः 'आच्या जान्वि'त्यादिः, स तुल्य एव,

443. **आ याहीन्द्र पथिभिरीळितेभिः**

ऋ० वे० खि० 7.55.89

444. **अग्न आ याहि वीतये**

ऋ० वे० 6.16.10

445. **वायवा याहि दर्शत**

ऋ० वे० 1.2.1

446. **ऐभिरग्ने सरथं याहि**

ऋ० वे० 3.6.9

442.2. श्रुत्यादिवशात्; P1 श्रुत्यादेशात्।

447. **इहैवैधि माप च्योष्ठाः**

ऋ० वे० 10.173.2

448. **इन्द्र आगच्छ हरिव आगच्छ**

श० ब्रा० 3.3.4.18

449. **श्वःसुत्यां आगच्छ मघवन्न**

(1) इत्यादिश्रुतिभिर्यागदेवताया अपि संनिध्यवगमात् । (2) तुला-पुरुषादिषु च 'एह्येही'त्यादिबहुतरं देवतासंनिधिप्रतिपादनं, भारतादौ च संवर्तादियज्ञेषु देवतासंनिधिः प्रतिपादिता एव ।

(3) यदपि "नवमे विग्रहादिनिराकरणं देवताया ऊहसिद्धये गुण-त्वार्थम्" इत्यादि, तदपि पितृषु सर्वं तुल्यं, (4) श्राद्धे देवताप्राधान्ये 'यन्मे माता प्रलुलोभे'त्याद्येकवचनान्तपितृपदवतस्तैत्तिरीयशाखास्थमन्त्रस्य, 'शुन्धन्तां पितर' इत्यादेश्च पित्रादिस्वरूपप्रयुक्तौ सत्यां मातामहादिश्राद्धे तदभावान् मन्त्राप्राप्ता-वूहाभावप्रसङ्गात् । (5) तथा च 'मन्त्रोहेन यथान्यायम्' [487] इत्यूहदर्शना-नुपपत्तिः ।

(6) न च "अयं एवोहविधिर्न तु दर्शनम्" इति वाच्यं, (7) मातामह-श्राद्धविधावूहविधौ च वाक्यभेदप्रसङ्गात् । (8) इदञ्च सर्वमनुपदमेव स्पष्ट-यिष्यामः ।

(9) यापि "तिरश्चाम्" इत्यादियुक्तिः, सापि समैव, (10) प्रातिस्विक-स्वकर्मणा नरकस्थानां तिर्यग्योनिगतानां कृमिकीटादिरूपाणां तरुगुल्मादिरूपाणां मुक्तानां वा पित्रादीनां केनापि सचेतनेन प्राधान्यफलदातृतयोरङ्गीकर्तुमशक्य-त्वात् ।

(11) योऽपि "यागस्य देवतार्थत्वे प्रमाणाभावम्" इत्युक्त्वा श्राद्धस्य पित्रर्थत्वे प्रमाणोपन्यासः, सोऽपि तुल्यः ।

(12) तत्र या तावद् 'अथैनं पितर' [427] इति श्रुतिरुपन्यस्ता, तस्याः पूर्वभागोऽयं;

450. **प्रजापतिं वै भूतान्युपासीदन् । प्रजा वै भूतानि । 'व्यु नो धेहि यथा जीवामे'ति । ततो देवा यज्ञोपवीतिनो भूत्वा दक्षिणं जान्वाच्यो-पासीदंस् । तानब्रवीद् 'यज्ञो वोऽन्नममृतं व ऊर्क् सूर्यो वो ज्योतिर्**

श० ब्रा० 2.4.2.1

449.4 श्राद्धे; K श्राद्ध— । 449.10—कर्मणा; P3 C2 K —कर्मणां ।

इति। (1) तदनन्तरम् 'अथैनं पितर' इत्यादि। (2) तत्रैतस्याः श्रुतेः पूर्व-भागात् कथं न यागस्य देवतार्थता ? (3) कथञ्चोत्तरभागाच्छ्राद्धस्य देवतार्थ-त्वमिति कोशपानं विनावैदिकप्रतारणमेवैतत् ।

तथा—

451. **अद्धीदिन्द्र प्रस्थितेमा हवींषी-** । ति
ऋ० वे० 10.116.8

452. **एकया प्रतिधापिबद्**
ऋ० वे० 8.77.4

(1) इति भोक्तृता,

453. **इन्द्रो दिव इन्द्र ईशे पृथिव्याः**
ऋ० वे० 10.89.10

454. **ईशानमस्य जगतः स्वर्दृशम्**
ऋ० वे० 7.32.22c

455. **अहं भुवं वसुनः पूर्व्यस्पतिर्**
ऋ० वे० 10.48.1

(1) इतीशित्वम्,

456. **तृप्त एवैनमिन्द्रः प्रजया पशुभिस्तर्पयति**
तै० सं० 2.5.4.3

457. **स एवैनं भूतिं गमयति**
तै० सं० 2.1.1.1

458. **अहं दाशुषे वि भजामि भोजनम्**
ऋ० वे० 10.48.1d

459. **पुत्रं ददाति दाशुषे**
ऋ० वे० 5.25.5d.

(1) इत्यादि फलदातृता, 'तृप्त एवैनमिन्द्र' [456] इत्यादि तृप्तिः प्रतीयते। (2) पुराणेतिहासेपु तु ईदृशवचसां गणनैव नास्ति। (3) एवं सति यद्येतेषां स्तुत्यादिरूपतया गतिस्तर्हि पितृप्रीत्यादिप्रतिपादकेष्वपि पक्षपातं परिहाय दीयतां दृष्टिः। (4) ततश्च

460. **अपि वा शब्दपूर्वत्वाद् यज्ञकर्म प्रधानं स्याद् गुणत्वे देवतास्तुतिर्**
मी० सू० 11.1.4.9

450.3. चोत्तर—; P1 P2 C1 वोत्तर— ।

(1) इति न्यायविषयतायां न कश्चिद् विशेषो दिव्यदृष्ट्या विनोपपादयितुं शक्यः ।

(2) यदपि 'उद्धरेत् सप्तगोत्राणीत्या- [440]दिपित्रादिगतफलप्रतिपादकोदाहरणं, तत्रापि श्राद्धस्य देवतार्थत्वाभावे न किञ्चिद् विरुध्यते । (3) न हि यज्ञदत्तजनकादय एव श्राद्धदेवताः, किन्तु वस्वाद्याः (4) पित्रादिशब्दस्तु केवलं तेषु तेषु च समानः । (5) न च तावतैक्यं भवति । (6) एवञ्च श्राद्धं न वस्वाद्यर्थम् । (7) त एव तु श्राद्धे गुणभूताः । (8) तद्गुणकञ्च श्राद्धकर्म जनकादितृप्तिं नरकोद्धारं वा करोतीति किमनुपपन्नम् ? तदुक्तं याज्ञवल्क्येन—

461. **वसुरुद्रादितिसुताः पितरः श्राद्धदेवताः ।**
प्रीणयन्ति मनुष्याणां पितॄन् श्राद्धेन तर्पिता ॥ इति ।

याज्ञ० 1.268

(1) अत्र च श्राद्धकर्मगतं प्रीणकत्वं तत्साधनभूतेषु वस्वादिषूपचर्यते, 'तप्त एवैनमिन्द्रः प्रजया पशुभिस्तर्पयन्ती'तिवत् [456] । (2) 'ते तृप्तास्तर्पयन्त्येनम्' इत्यादाव् [435]अप्येवमेवोपचारः ।

(3) न च "श्राद्धेन तृप्तिप्रभृतिफलं जनकादिगतं कथं जायते कर्तृसमवायित्वात् फलस्ये?"ति वाच्यं, (4) जातेष्ट्या पुत्रगतपूतत्वादिवत् प्रमाणेनाकर्तर्येव फलबोधनात् । (5) एतच्च गयाप्रकरणे निपुणमभिधास्यत इति नेह प्रपञ्च्यते ।

(6) किञ्च; पितॄणां संनिध्यङ्गीकृतौ दृष्टे संभवत्यदृष्टाकल्पनाद् आवाहनस्य संनिधिरेव फलमभ्युपेयम् । (7) तथा च तीर्थाधिकरणकश्राद्धमात्रे आवाहनबाधः स्यात्, (8) नित्यसंनिहितत्वेन फलस्यान्यत एव लाभात्,

462. **उदकं तण्डुलास्तत् संसृष्टं प्राजापत्यम्**

(1) इत्यत्र तण्डेलेषु वितुषीभावस्यान्यतः सिद्ध्यावघातबाधवत् ।

(2) न च "नियमादृष्टार्थमावाहनं तत्र भविष्यती"ति वाच्यं, (3) दृष्टार्थानां दृष्टद्वारैवादृष्टजनकत्वात्, कृष्णल इव दृष्टलोपे तस्यापि लोपात्, (4) नियमादृष्टस्यानुनिष्पादिततया वाजिनवद् अप्रयोजकत्वाच्च । (5) तस्मान्न पितॄणां संनिधिसंभवः ।

460.4. तेषु तेषु; P2 P3 C1 तेषु । 461.6. संनिधिरेव फलम्; L2 संनिधिफलम् ।

(6) यदि च पितृष्वङ्गीक्रियते विग्रहादिपञ्चकमभ्युपेत्य तदा––

463. **विरोधः कर्मणीति चेन्न, अनेकप्रतिपत्तेर्दर्शनाद्**

वेदान्तसूत्र 1.3.27

(1) इति व्यासोक्तचतुर्लक्षणीप्राथमिकन्यायेनाङ्गीक्रियतां देवतास्वपि, नाङ्गीक्रियतां वा जैमिनिमुनिमतेन पितृष्वपि, न त्वर्धजरतीयमुचितम् ।

(2) तत्सिद्धमेतत् तीर्थनिमित्तक एव श्राद्धे वचनाद् आवाहनबाधो, न तु तीर्थाधिकरणकश्राद्धमात्र इति ।

(3) यत्तु "किमर्थं तर्हि अन्यत्राप्यावाहनम् ? अदृष्टार्थमित्यवेही" त्युक्त्वा "अत एव नावाहनमन्त्रोहोऽपी"त्युक्तं, (4) तत्तु चिन्त्यम् । आवाहनस्यादृष्टार्थत्वेऽपि मन्त्रस्यानुष्ठेयार्थस्मारणेन दृष्टार्थत्वात् तावतैव चोपपत्तेः । (5) न हि क्रियाया अदृष्टार्थत्वात् तत्साधने मन्त्रे ऊहाभावः । (6) पञ्चमप्रयाजसाधनीभूते स्वाहानिगदे ऊहाभावप्रसङ्गात् ।

अपिच––

464. **पितॄन् हविषे अत्तवे** (=429, 478)

465. **आयन्तु नः पितरः सोम्यास**

वा० सं० 19.58a

(1) इत्यावाहनमन्त्रस्थपितृशब्दस्य प्रकृतिवन् मातामहादिश्राद्धेऽपि समवेतार्थत्वाद् अर्थान्तराभावादेव नोहः प्राप्नोति । (2) तथा हि; द्वेधा ह्ययं पितृशब्दः प्रयुज्यते । (3) क्वचिज्जनकत्वाद्युपाधिना

466. **पिता यस्य तु वृत्तः स्याज्जीवेच्चापि पितामह ।**

मनु 3.221a-b

इत्यादौ । (1) क्वचिच्च सपिण्डीकरणान्तश्राद्धजनितपितृभावोपाधिना स्त्रीपुंससाधारणो गणदेवतावाची, मरुदादिशब्दवद्, अग्निष्वात्तादिशब्दवच्च,

467. **प्रेते पितृत्वमापन्ने सपिण्डीकरणादनु––**

(वि० पु० 3.13.36a-b)

463.6—भूते; P3 C2 K —भूत— । 465.1.—आवाहनमन्त्रस्थ—; P1 P3 K —आवाहनमन्त्रस्य । 466.1. क्वचिच्च; P3 क्वचित् क्वचिच्च । 467. आपन्ने; L1 L2 L3 C2 L1 आपत्ते ।

इति विष्णुस्मृतेः,

468. **ततः प्रभृति वै प्रेतः पितृसामान्यमाप्नुयाद्**

इति हारीतोक्तेश्च । (1) एवञ्चैकोद्दिष्टे आश्वलायनगृह्यपरिशिष्टोदितः पितृशब्दप्रतिषेधोऽप्युपपन्नः ।

(2) अत एव मातामहपितामहादिष्वपि पितृशब्दः साधारणो दृश्यते,

469. **षड्भ्यः पितृभ्यस्तदनु भक्त्या श्राद्धमुपक्रमेद् ॥** इति ।

470. **पितृपात्रेषु प्रेतपात्रं प्रसेचयेद् ।**

याज्ञ० 1.252c-d

इति च । (1) मात्रादिसाधारणोऽपि,

471. **तृप्यन्तु पितरः सर्वे मातृमातामहादय ।** इति ।

(1) यत्तु "पितृपदस्य साधारणवाचकत्वाभावे

472. **द्वौ दैवे प्राक् त्रयः पित्र्ये ।**

याज्ञ० 1.228a

473. **पित्र्ये कर्मणि विद्वद्भिर्ग्राह्या कुतपकालिकी ।**

474. **पितृभ्यो रजतं देयम्**

475. **पितृपात्रं तदुत्तानम्**

याज्ञ० 1.247c

(1) इत्यादिपितृशब्दमादाय विहितं मातामहादिश्राद्धे न प्रवर्तेते"ति दूषणं, (2) तन्न, उपदेशतो ऽप्राप्तावप्यतिदेशतो प्राप्तिसम्भवात् । (3) तस्माद् अस्मदुक्तमार्गेणैव साधारणः पितृशब्दः ।

(4) तथा च पितृभावोपाधिना मातृमातामहादावप्यविकृतस्यैव पितृपदस्य समवेतार्थत्वात् प्रयोगोपपत्तावूहप्रसक्तिरेव नास्तीत्यावाहनादृष्टार्थतया किं निवारणीयम् ?

468.1. -प्रतिषेधोऽप्युपपन्नः; C1 प्रतिषेधो ह्युपपन्नः । 471.1. पितृपदस्य; L2 पितृशब्दस्य । 472. दैवे; P1 P2 C1 L2 देवे । 475.1. प्रवर्तेतेति; P1 P3 C2 K प्रवर्त्ततेति । 475.4. पितृपदस्य; C1 पितृशब्दस्य ।

किञ्च;

476. **पूयति वा एतदृचोऽक्षरं यदेनदूहति तस्मादृचं नोहेद्**

आ० श्रौ० सू० 5.4.8

(1) इति ऋच्यूहनिषेधादपि नात्रोहप्रसक्तिः ।

(2) एतेनेदं निरस्तं, यत् कश्चिदाह,

477. **"यथार्थमूहश्चोदिते; न प्रकृतावपूर्वत्वाद्; विकृतौ वचनाद्**

का० श्रौ० सू० 4.98-100

(1) इति कातीयवचनाद् विकृतिभूतमातामहादिश्राद्धे

478. **पितॄन् हविषे अत्तवे** (=429, 464)

479. **आयन्तु नः पितरः** (=465)

'तिलोऽसी'ति मन्त्रे

480. **स्वधया पितॄन्**

आ० गृ० सू० 4.7.8

'ऊर्जं वहन्तीरि'ति मन्त्रे

481. **तर्पयत पितॄन्** वा० सं० 2.34

482. **अत्र पितरो मादयध्वं** (=430)

483. **नमो वः पितरो रसाय** वा० सं० 2.32a

484. **अमीमदन्त पितरः** वा० सं० 2.31b

485. **एतद् वः पितरो वास** वा० सं० 2.32h

(1) इत्यादिमन्त्रेषु पितृशब्दस्थाने मातामहादिशब्दोहः कार्यः समवेतार्थत्वाये"ति, (2) पितृभावापत्त्युपाधिना प्रवृत्तस्य पितृशब्दस्य मातामहादावप्यविकृतप्रयोगोपपत्तेः, (3) ऋग्रूपेषु निषेधाच्च । (4) कातीयवचस्तु न श्राद्ध-

---

476. एनद्; P3 C2 एतद् । 485.2. Before पितृभावापत्त्....; C1 तन्न ।

प्रकरणपठितं कित्वनारभ्याधीतम् । (5) तन्निर्वापादिप्रकाशकयजुर्मन्त्रविषयत्वेनाप्युपपद्यते ।

(6) न च "एवं 'तिलोऽसी'त्यादिमन्त्रस्थपितृप्रातिपदिकस्य साधारणत्वाद् ऊहाभावेऽपि बहुवचनस्यैकस्मिन् मातामहादावसमवेतार्थत्वाद् एकवद् ऊहः स्यादि"ति वाच्यं, (7) प्रकृतौ बहुवचनस्यासमवेतार्थत्वे विकृतावप्यविकृतस्यैव प्रयोगोपपत्तेः; 'अदितिः पाशान्' इतिवत्, एकस्मिन्नपि चोपरवमन्त्रवद्, 'वायवः स्थे'तिवच्च यथाकथञ्चिद् बहुवचनोपपत्तिः ।

(8) एतेन "बहुवचनान्तपितृशब्दस्य तत्तद्देवताप्रकाशकत्वेन प्रकृतौ समवेतार्थत्वेऽपि प्रतिपुरुषं बहुवचनम्,

486. **'एतद् वः पितरो वास' इति जल्पन् पृथक् पृथग् ।**

इति वचनबलादेव । (1) विकृतौ तु 'यावद् वचनं वाचनिकम्' इतिन्यायाद् वचनाभावाद् एकवचनान्ततयोह" इति निरस्तं, (2) वचनस्य बहुवचनविधौ तात्पर्यकल्पने पितृशब्दप्रयोगविधानेऽप्यविशेषात् तात्पर्यप्रसङ्गे ऊहाभावापत्तौ पितृशब्दोहोक्तिविरोधात् ।

(3) किञ्च; एवं सति वचनादेव बहुवचनस्य प्रकृतावसमवेतार्थत्वाद् विकृतावपि वचनाभावेऽप्यतिदेशात् पाशन्यायेनाविकृतप्रयोग एव भवेदिति नोहः स्यात् ।

(4) किञ्च; 'एतद्व' इत्येतन्मन्त्रमात्रविषयत्वाद् वचनस्य मन्त्रान्तरे का गतिः ? (5) तस्मात् पाठप्राप्तबहुवचनकं मन्त्रमनूद्य वचनं पृथक्शब्दार्थभूतामावृत्तिं विधत्ते । (6) यद्वा सर्वमनूद्य वासोदानमेव विधत्त, इति न वाचनिकं बहुवचनम् ।

(7) "नन्वेमपि पार्वणे जनकपात्रतिलावापादिकार्यमेव प्रकृतिरस्तु । (8) पितामहप्रपितामहसम्बन्धिकार्ये तु विकृती भविष्यतः । (9) जनके च पितृशब्दः समर्थः, वचनमात्रं त्वसमर्थम् । (10) अत उत्तरयोः कार्ययोः पितृशब्दस्थाने पितामहप्रपितामहशब्दावूहितव्यौ, बहुवचनं तु यथास्थितमेव । (11) तथा च मात्रादौ सुतरामूहो भविष्यति । (12) एकश्च पितृशब्दोऽनेकार्थोऽपि न कल्पनीयो भविष्यती"ति चेत्, (13) न, समानप्रकरणे ऐन्द्रानैन्द्रप्रदानन्यायेन प्रकृतिविकृतिभावाभावात् । (14) तथा च त्रिपु समवेतार्थत्वाय पूर्वोक्तयुक्तिभिरनेकार्थताप्यनन्यगतिकतयाङ्गीक्रियत इति ।

485.7. चोपरव—; P2 P3 C2 K वोपरव—। 485.8. प्रतिपुरुषं; P2 प्रतिपूरुषं ।
486.11. भविष्यति; C1 भवति ।

(15) यदि च तत्रोत्तरयोरूहोऽभ्युपगम्येत तर्हि 'शुन्धन्तां पितर' इत्यादित्रयाणां वचनमपार्थकं स्यात् ।

(16) तत्सिद्धमेतत्, पितृशब्दः प्रकृताविव विकृतावपि समवेतार्थत्वान्नोहं याति । (17) बहुवचनञ्च प्रकृतावसमवेतार्थत्वादिति ।

(18) यत्तु विष्णुवचनं—

487. **मातामहानामप्येवं श्राद्धं कुर्याद् विचक्षणः ।**
मन्त्रोहेन यथान्यायं शेषाणां मन्त्रवर्जितम् ॥

त्रि॰ स्मृ॰ 75.7(=614)

इति, (1) तदपि न पूर्वोक्तमन्त्राणामूहार्थं 'यथान्यायम्' इत्युक्तेः । (2) अयं चोहे न्यायः; (3) मुख्यार्थत्वादिविशेषणैः प्रकृतौ प्रयुक्तो मन्त्रो विकृतौ कार्यद्वारातिदिष्टोऽर्थान्तरेऽसमवेतार्थपदवत्तया प्रयुज्यमानः प्रकृतिवत् दृष्टार्थो न स्याद्, अतः समवेतार्थपदवत्तया प्रयोज्य इति । तदाहुर्भट्टपादाः—

488. **मुख्यदृष्टार्थतास्वार्थसमवेतार्थतादिभिः ।**
प्रयुक्ताः प्रकृतौ मन्त्रा गताः कार्यातिदेशतः ॥
विकारेष्वनिषिद्धोहाः कार्यापन्नेषु पञ्चधा।
अर्थान्तरेष्वपूर्वार्थद्वारेणोहं व्रजन्ति न ॥ इति ।

त॰ वा॰ 1.3.8.24, p.263

(1) पञ्चधाकार्यापत्तिश्चोक्ता भट्टसोमेश्वरैः—

489. **प्रत्यक्षविधिनाभावे विधानेन विकारतः ।**
स्वशब्दाच्च निषेधानुवादात् तत्कार्यकारिते- ॥ इति ।

न्या॰ सुधा 1.3.8.24, p.281

(1) पूर्वोक्तमन्त्रेषु च प्रकृतिवद् विकृतावपि पितृशब्दस्य समवेतार्थत्वाद् अर्थान्तरे प्रयोगाभावान्नोहः ।

(2) "कोऽर्थस्तर्हि 'मन्त्रोहेन यथान्यायम्' इत्यस्य ?" उच्यते;

---

488. न; P3 C2 K त । 488.1—कार्यापत्तिश; P2 L1 L2 कार्यापङ्क्तिश् ।
489. स्वशब्दाच्च; P1 स्वशब्दार्थ— ।

490. **शुन्धन्तां पितर**

आ० श्रौ० सू० 2.6.14

(1) इत्यत्र न्यायादूहः । (2) अत्र हि पूर्वोक्तोपाधिना पितृपदप्रवृत्तौ 'शुन्धन्तां पितामहाः' 'शुन्धन्तां प्रपितामहा' इति मन्त्रद्वयपाठोऽनर्थकः स्यात् । (3) अतो जनकत्वाद्युपाधिनैव प्रवृत्तिः । (4) तेन विकृतौ मातृमातामहादिश्राद्धेऽर्थान्तरत्वादूहः ।

(5) सोऽपि प्रातिपदिकमात्रस्यैव । (6) बहुवचनं तु प्रकृतावप्येकस्मिन् पितर्यसमवेतार्थमिति नोह्यम् । (7) ततश्च 'शुन्धन्तां मातरः' 'शुन्धन्तां मातामहा' इत्याद्यूहः । (8) एवं पितामहादावपि ।

(9) 'पितृभ्यः स्वधोच्यताम्' इत्यादि येषां शाखिनां शुन्धनमन्त्रवदेव पाठस्तेषां तत्रापि तद्वदेवोहः । (10) तत्रापि कात्यायनगोभिलाभ्यां 'मातामहेभ्यः स्वधोच्यताम्' इति विशेषतः पठितो मन्त्रोऽतस्तद्विषये नोहः ।

(11) मात्रादौ तु भवति । तथा हि हिरण्यकेशिनां

491. **यन्मे माता प्रलुलोभे--**

हिर० गृ० सू० 2.10.7

(1) त्यादिमन्त्रेषु 'यन्मे मातामही प्रलुलोभ तन्मे रेतो मातामहो वृंक्ताम्' इत्याद्यूहो भवति, (2) पित्रादिशब्दानामेकवचनान्तत्वेन साधारणवाचित्वाभावात् । (3) तथात्वे च 'यन्मे पितामही प्रलुलोभे'त्यादिमन्त्रपाठानर्थक्यप्रसङ्गात् । तदुक्तं भाष्यार्थसंग्रहकृता--

492. **अन्नहोमे तथा स्पर्शे जलपिण्डादिदानके ।**
'यन्मे मातामही'त्यादि तत्रोदाहरणं भवेद् ॥ इति ।

(1) 'उदाहरणम्' ऊहः । (2) 'स्पर्शे'

493. **एष ते तत मधुमान्**

हिर० गृ० सू० 2.13.1

इत्यादिमन्त्रैर्ब्राह्मणभोजनार्थमन्नस्पर्शे । (1) एवमन्यत्रापि यत्र न्याय्य ऊहस्तत्र विचार्य कार्यः ।

490.11. तथा हि; All but P2 have तथा (See Critical Apparatus III. B.1e). 491.3 पितामही; L1 मातामही ।

(2) यत्तु "'मन्त्रोहेन' मन्त्रपाठेन न तु विकाररूपोहेनेत्यर्थ" इति कश्चित्, (3) तन्न, ऊहशब्दस्य पाठेऽप्रसिद्धत्वात्, (4) एवं 'कुर्याद्' इत्यनेनैव धर्मान्तरवन्मन्त्रपाठस्यापि प्राप्तेरेतस्य व्यर्थत्वापातात्, (5) गृहमेधीयाज्यभागन्यायेन वा परिसंख्यापत्तेः, (6) 'यथान्यायमि'त्यस्यानर्थक्यापत्तेश्च। (7) तस्माद् अस्मदुक्त एवास्य विषयः।

(8) 'पितरेतत् तेऽर्घ्यम्' इत्यादिषु तूहानूहविचारो न कार्य एव, (9) एतस्याभिलापमात्रत्वेन मन्त्रत्वाभावात्। (10) तत्त्वे वा 'शेषाणां मन्त्रवर्जितम्' इत्युक्त्याभिलापस्यापि वर्जनप्रसङ्गात्,

494. **अयमेव विधिः प्रोक्तः शूद्राणां मन्त्रवर्जित।**

वराह पु॰ 188.57a-b (=501)

(1) इति वराहपुराणोक्त्या शूद्रस्याप्यभिलापवर्जनोपत्तेः। (2) अतोऽपौरुषेय एव मन्त्रशब्दो मुख्योऽन्यत्र गौणः। (3) अत एवोहप्रवरनाम्नाममन्त्रतेति सिद्धान्त इति।

(4) एष पार्वणे ऊहानूहविवेकः। (5) एकोद्दिष्टे तूच्यते; तत्र पुराणैकोद्दिष्टे पार्वणवदेव, सपिण्डीकरणेन पितृभावापत्तेर्जातत्वात्। प्रेतैकोद्दिष्टे त्व्

495. **एकवन्मन्त्रान् ऊहेतैकोद्दिष्ट**

वि॰ स्मृ॰ 21.2

इति विष्णुवचनादूहः। (1) सपिण्डीकरणाभावेन पितृभावापत्तेरजातत्वात् पितृपदस्थाने प्रेतपदमेकवचनान्तं प्रयोज्यमिति विष्णुवचनार्थः। (2) अत एवाश्वलायनगृह्यपरिशिष्टे पितृपदनिवृत्तिरेकोद्दिष्टे उक्ता। (3) स्मृतिरत्नावलीकारस्तु "बहुवचने एकवचनमात्रमूहितव्यं न तु पितृपदे ऊहः, 'एकवद् ऊहेते'तिवचनात्। (4) इतरथा 'यथार्थमूहेद्' इत्येवावक्ष्यत्। (5) तेन मातृभ्रातृपितृव्यादिश्राद्धे एकवचनमात्रमूह्यं पितृशब्दस्तु यथास्थित एव। (6) तस्य प्रमीतमात्रवचनत्वाद्" इति विष्णुवचनार्थमाह। (7) तन्न, आश्वलायनपरिशिष्टोक्तपितृपदनिवृत्तिविरोधात्, (8) प्रमीतमात्रवाचितत्वे 'शुन्धन्तां पितर' इत्यादौ पूर्वोक्तोहाभावप्रसङ्गात्, (9) अभिलापेऽपि पितृपदस्यैव सर्वत्र प्रसङ्गात्, (10) शिष्टाचारविरोधाच्च। (11) विष्णुना तु 'पितृपदे न्यायादेवोहः प्रप्नोती'-

493.4. एवं; P3 एवञ्च। 495. एकवन्; C1 एकवचनान्। 495.7. आश्वलायनपरिशिष्टोक्त—; P2 L2 आश्वलायनगृह्यपरिशिष्टोक्त—।

ति तमविधाय 'वचनस्य प्रकृतावसमवेतार्थत्वाद् ऊहो न प्राप्नोती' ति तन्मात्रं विहितम् 'एकवन्मन्त्रान् ऊहेते'ति ।

(12) तस्माद् एकवचनान्तः प्रेतशब्द ऊह्यः प्रेतैकोद्दिष्ट इति सिद्धम् ।

(13) 'शेषाणां मन्त्रवर्जितम्' इति विष्णुवचनशेषः । (14) अस्यार्थमाह शूलपाणिः—

496. **पितृव्यमातुलादीनामेकोद्दिष्टे ऊहयोग्यपितृपदवन्मन्त्र एव न प्रयोज्यः, न तूहः कार्यः । न तु पितृपदरहितोऽप्यप्रयोज्योऽप्रकृतत्वाद्**

इति ।

497. **पितृव्यमातुलादीनामावाहनादिमन्त्रवर्जितं कार्यमित्यर्थः**

इति कल्पतरौ (1) युक्तं त्विदम्; अकृतविवाहभोगार्थरक्षितस्त्रीविषयमिदं, पारशवकरणादिशूद्रापुत्रविषयञ्च,

498. **स्त्रीणाममन्त्रकं श्राद्धं तथा शूद्रासुतस्य च ।**
प्राग् द्विजाश्च व्रतादेशात् ते च कुर्युस्तथैव तद् ॥

इति मरीचिस्मरणात् । अत्र

499. **'स्त्रीणा'मित्यकृतविवाहस्त्रीविषयम्**

इति हेमाद्रिः । (1) 'प्राग्' इति अनुपनीता द्विजातयः । (2) ते च स्त्रीपारशवकरणादयोऽसंस्कृतत्वात् संस्कृतानामपि श्राद्धं तथैवामन्त्रकं कुर्युः ।

(3) यद्वा 'शेषाणाम्' इति कर्तरि षष्ठी । (4) ततश्च वर्णशेषाणाम् । (5) शूद्राणां तत्तुल्यानां पारशवकरणानुपनीतस्त्रीणाञ्च कर्त्तव्यं श्राद्धं तैरमन्त्रकं कार्यमित्यर्थः । तदुक्तं श्राद्धं प्रकृत्य पाद्मे सृष्टिखण्डे—

500. **शूद्रोऽप्यमन्त्रकं कुर्यादनेन विधिना नृपे-** । ति ।

प० पु०, सृ० खण्ड 9.193 c-d

(1) मरीचिः—'प्राग् द्विजाश्चे'त्यादि [498] ।

---

4 8. ते च; L2 नैव ।

वराहपुराणे—

501. **अयमेव विधिः प्रोक्तः शूद्राणां मन्त्रवर्जितः ।** (= 494)
अमन्त्रस्य तु शूद्रस्य विप्रो मन्त्रेण गृह्यत ॥ इति ।

वराह पु० 188.57

(1) 'विप्रो मन्त्रेण गृह्यते' सम्बध्यत इत्यर्थः ।

502. **इयञ्च परिभाषा । न च परिभाषा प्रकरणेन नियम्यते । तेनास्य श्राद्धप्रकरण पाठेऽपि शूद्रस्य स्नानदानादावपि विप्रेण मन्त्रः पठनीय**

श्रा० वि०, p. 231

इति शूलपाणिः ।

(1) अत्र 'अमन्त्रकम्' इति वैदिकमन्त्रप्रतिषेधः । (2) तेन पौराणो नामगोत्राद्यभिलापश्च वक्तव्य एव ।

(3) इत्यलं प्रसक्तानुप्रसक्त्या; प्रकृतमनुसरामः ।

(4) तीर्थश्राद्धस्य पार्वणप्रकृतिकतया

503. **पुरूरवार्द्रवौ चैव पार्वणे समुदाहृताव्**

बृह० (श्रा) 93a-b

(1) इति बृहस्पतिवचनात् पुरूरवार्द्रवौ विश्वेदेवत्वेन यद्यपि प्राप्तौ, तथापि तस्य संयोगपृथक्त्वेन काम्यस्यापि सत्त्वाद्, गोदोहनन्यायेन च काम्यस्य नित्य-बाधकत्वान्, नैमित्तिकस्यापि चावश्यकतया नित्यत्वात्,

504. **काम्ये च धुरिलोचनावि—**

बृह० (श्रा) 92d

(1) ति वचनात्तौ बधित्वा धुरिलोचनौ भवतः । (2) न च "तत्र प्रधानभूतेन गोदोहनेन काम्येन नित्याङ्गचमसबाधेऽपीह काम्याङ्गेन कथं नित्याङ्गबाधाऽङ्गत्वसाम्याद्" इति वाच्यं, (3) समानन्यायतया काम्याङ्गस्यापि नित्याङ्गबाधकत्वात्, (4) यज्ञाथर्वणवाक्यविहितकाम्येष्टचङ्गभूतोपांशुत्वस्य जातेष्टौ

505. **मध्यमेन हवींष्या स्विष्टकृत**

आ० श्रौ० सू० 1.5.27

---

501. विप्रो मन्त्रेण; L1 मन्त्रो विप्रेण, L2 विप्रोऽस्य (sic) । 502.1. अमन्त्रकमिति; P3 अमन्त्रस्येति ।

(1) इति वचनविहितचोदकप्राप्तमध्यमस्वरबाधकत्ववत् । (2) अतः काम्यत्वेन तीर्थश्राद्धकरणे धुरिलोचनौ ।

(3) यदा तु कामाभावे केवलनित्यतया करोति तदा पुरूरवार्द्रवौ । यदापि—

506. **हविष्यान्नेन वै मासम्**

याज्ञ० 1.257a

(1) इत्यादिगुणफलाधिकारो गोदोहनवत्, तदापि काम्यश्राद्धाभावेन धुरिलोचनाप्राप्तेर्नित्यकर्माश्रयणेन च गुणफलविधेः कर्मषाड्गुण्याय तावेव ।

(2) न च "अङ्गस्य काम्यगुणस्याष्टमिकन्यायेन पार्वणविकृतौ तीर्थश्राद्धेऽप्रवृत्तिरेवे"ति वाच्यं, (3) प्रकरणमध्यपातिकाम्यगुणविषयत्वात्तस्य ।
(4) हविष्यादयस्तु मन्वादिवचनैः सकलश्राद्धशेषभूता; इत्यलम् ।

इति तीर्थश्राद्धे विहितनिषिद्धानि तत्प्रसङ्गागतश्च ।

505.3. केवल-; Cl K केवलं ।

अथान्नहेमाद्धादिविचारः

गारुडे—

507. तीर्थे गत्वा तु यच्छ्राद्धमामान्नं भोजनं द्विजे ।

गरु० पु० 2.15.36a-b

कात्यायनः—

508. आपद्यनग्नौ तीर्थे च प्रवासे पुत्रजन्मनि ।
आमश्राद्धं प्रकुर्वीत भार्यारजसि संक्रमे ॥

सुमन्तुः

509. पाकाभावेऽधिकारः स्याद् विप्रादीनां नराधिप ।
अपत्नीनां महाबाहो विदेशगमनादिभिः ॥
सदा चैव तु शूद्राणामामश्राद्धं विदुर्बुधाः ।
आत्मनो देशकालाभ्यां विप्लवे समुपागते ॥
आपद्यनग्नौ तीर्थे च प्रवासे पत्न्यसम्भवे ।
चन्द्रसूर्यग्रहे चैव दद्यादामं विशेषतः ॥

तथा—

510. तीर्थे श्राद्धं प्रकुर्वीत पक्वान्नेन विशेषतः ।
आमान्नेन हिरण्येन कन्दमूलफलैरपि ॥
एषामभावे कुर्याच्च श्रद्धयापि जलेन वा ॥

तथा—

511. द्रव्याभावे द्विजाभावे प्रवासे पुत्रजन्मनि ।
हेमश्राद्धं प्रकुर्वीत यस्य भार्या रजस्वला ॥

प्र० ख० 1.206.52

(1) "एवं नानारूपेषु वाक्येषु सत्सु पाकश्राद्धं मुख्यं पाकासम्भवे ब्राह्मणासम्भवे च आमश्राद्धं, तदसम्भवे हेमश्राद्धम्, अपि वा यथाशिष्टाचारं कार्यम्"

---

510. श्रद्धयापि; P1 (+correction in P2) श्राद्धं पिण्डं ।

इति मदनपारिजातदिवोदासाद्याः। (2) प्राच्या अप्येवम्। (3) स्मृतिरत्नावली-कारादयस्तु "ग्रहणे तीर्थादौ चामश्राद्धं हेमश्राद्धं वा मुख्यं पाकश्राद्धं तु न भवत्येवे"त्याहुः। (4) एवं तु युक्तं पश्यामः; तीर्थजलसमीपे आमेन हेम्ना वा

512. **सदैव हि जलान्तेषु आमश्राद्धं प्रशस्यते।**
गृहाद् दशगुणं पुण्यं लभेत् तीर्थे निवापकृत्॥

इति वचनात्। (1) गृहादौ त्वन्नेनैवेति।

(2) दाक्षिणात्यास्तूभयं कुर्वन्ति, पूर्वोक्तात् 'पक्वान्नेन विशेषत' [510] इतिवाक्यात्। (3) अत्र यथादेशाचारं व्यवस्था।

(4) शूद्रेण तु सर्वदामेनैव कार्यं,

513. **सदा चैव तु शूद्राणामामश्राद्धं विदुर्बुधाः।**
न पक्वं भोजयेद् विप्रान् सच्छूद्रोऽपि कदाचन॥
भोजयन् प्रत्यवायी स्यात् न च तस्य फलं लभेत्॥

इति सुमन्तूक्तेः।

(1) आमश्राद्धे च विशेषः—

व्यासः—

514. **आमं ददत् तु कौन्तेय दद्याद् अन्नं चतुर्गुणम्।**

यत्तु—

515. **आमं ददद्धि कौन्तेय आमं तु द्विगुणं भवेत्।**

(1) इति, तच्चतुर्गुणदानाशक्तौ वेदितव्यम्। अत एव स्मर्यते—

516. **आमं ददति चेद् राजन्नामं तद्द्विगुणं भवेत्।**
त्रिगुणं चतुर्गुणं वापि नत्वेकगुणमर्पयेत्॥
ब्राह्मणाय प्रदातव्यं सर्वोपस्कारसंयुतम्। इति।

(1) अत्रोत्तरोत्तरपक्षस्य मुख्यता।

(2) हिरण्यं त्वष्टगुणं चतुर्गुणं द्विगुणं वा दद्यात्। (3) अशक्तौ सममप्यामं हेमं वा दद्यात्। (4) द्वैगुण्यादि च पुरुषाहारापेक्षया।

---

513. लभेत्; L1 भवेत्। 516. ददति; L2 (+correction in K) ददाति।
516. सर्वोपस्कार—; P3 K सर्वोपस्कर—।

उशनाः—

517. आमश्राद्धं यदा कुर्याद् विधिज्ञः श्राद्धदस्तदा ।
हस्तेऽग्नौकरणं कुर्याद् ब्राह्मणस्य विधानतः ॥

तथा—

518. सिद्धान्ने तु विधिर्यः स्याद् आमश्राद्धेऽप्यसौ विधिः ।
(= 525)
आवाहनादि सर्वं स्यात् पिण्डदानञ्च भारत ॥
दद्याद् यच्च द्विजातिभ्यः शृतं वाशृतमेव वा ।
तेनाग्नौकरणं कुर्यात् पिण्डांस्तेनैव निर्वपेत् ॥

तथा—

519. आमश्राद्धं यदा कुर्याद् विधिज्ञः श्रद्धयान्वितः ... ।

(1) उत्तरार्धं पूर्ववत् । (2) आवाहनादिकं ग्रहणादिनिमित्तामश्राद्धे न तु तीर्थश्राद्धे तत्र निषेधस्योक्तत्वात् ।

षट्त्रिंशन्मते—

520. आमश्राद्धं यदा कुर्यात् पिण्डदानं कथं भवेत् ।
गृहपाकात् समुद्धृत्य सक्तुभिः पायसेन वा ॥

(1) पिण्डदानं भवतीति शेषः । (2) आमगृहपाकसक्तुपायसेषु यथालाभं व्यवस्था ।

यत्तु—

521. आमेन पिण्डं दद्याच्चेद् विप्रान् पक्वेन भोजयेत् ।
पक्वेन कुरुते पिण्डमामान्नं यः प्रयच्छति ॥
तावुभौ मनुजप्रोक्तौ नरकार्हौ न संशयः ।

(1) इति, तद् अमावास्यादिपरम् ।

(2) आमश्राद्धे भोजनसम्बद्धा अपोशानादयो लुप्तप्रयोजना निवर्तन्ते, कृष्णलेऽवघातवत् । तदुक्तं —

---

517. विधानतः; L1 विशेषतः । 518. एव वा; P1 P2 L2 एव च । 519.2. षट्त्रिंशन्मते; P2 P3 षड्विंशन्मते । 521. मनुज—; K L2 मनुजौ ।

522. **तृप्तप्रश्नोऽवगाहश्च जुषप्रश्नो यथासुखम् ।**
आमश्राद्धे भवेन्नैतद् अपोशानञ्च पञ्चमम् ॥

(1) 'अवगाहो'ऽङ्गुष्ठनिवेशनम् । (2) ततश्च आमश्राद्धपक्षे एते न भवन्ति । (3) आवाहनादयश्च तीर्थश्राद्धत्वात् । (4) पाकश्राद्धे तु आवाहनादय एव न भवन्तीति विवेकः ।

523. **हेमश्राद्धपक्षे पिण्डनिवृत्तिरपी —।**

ति दिवोदासः । (1) स्मृत्यर्थसारे तु विकल्पः ।

(2) आमश्राद्धे केषाञ्चिन् मन्त्राणामूहोऽपि भवति । अतएव मरीचिः—

524. **आवाहने स्वधाकारे मन्त्रा ऊह्या विसर्जने ।**
अन्यकर्मण्यनूह्याः स्युरामश्राद्धविधिः स्मृतः ॥

(1) आवाहने 'पितॄन् हविषे अत्तव' [429] इति मन्त्रे 'अत्तव' इति-पदस्थाने 'स्वीकर्तवे' इतिपदोहः । (2) स्वधाकारे 'नमो वः पितर इष' इति मन्त्रे 'इष' इतिपदे 'आमाये'त्यूहः । (3) विसर्जने 'वाजे वाज' इति मन्त्रे 'तृप्ता यात पथिभिर्देवयानैरि'त्यत्र 'तृप्ता' इति क्तप्रत्ययस्थाने 'तृप्यते'ति लोट्प्रत्ययोहः कार्यः । (4) यद्यपि 'पूयति वा एतद् ऋचोऽक्षरं यदेनदूहती'ति [476] ऋव्यूहो निषिद्धस्तथापि 'वाजे वाजेऽवते'ति ऋचि वचनाद् ऊहो भवति । (5) एवं 'इदम् अन्नम्' इत्येवमादौ 'इदम् आमम्' इत्याद्यूहो ज्ञेयः । (6) 'अन्यकर्मणि' 'विष्णो हव्यं रक्षस्वे'त्यादौ नोह इति मरीचिवचनार्थः ।

(7) वस्त्रदक्षिणादि यथाशक्ति आमहेमश्राद्धयोरपि देयमेव,

525. **सिद्धान्ने तु विधिर्यः स्याद् आमश्राद्धेऽप्यसौ विधिर्** (=518)

इति सुमन्तुवचनात् ।

(1) यदा तु ब्राह्मणा बहवो न सन्ति तदैकेनापि श्राद्धं कार्यम्,

526. **अन्नाभावे द्विजाभावे तीर्थरूपे महालये ।**
एकस्मिन् दीयते चान्नमर्घ्यान् पिण्डान् पृथक् पृथग् ॥

522. तृप्तप्रश्नो; K तृप्तिप्रश्नो । 524.7. एव; P2 omitted. । 526. अर्घ्यान्; P2 अर्घान्

इति वचनात् ।

(1) यदा तु एकोऽपि न लभ्यते तदा दर्भवटोरुपरि श्राद्धं कार्यम्, अन्नञ्चाग्न्यादौ क्षिपेत्,

527. **पात्राभावेऽखिलं कृत्वा पितृयज्ञविधिं नरः ।
निधाय वा दर्भवटून् आसनेषु समाहितः ॥
प्रैषानुप्रैषसंयुक्तं विधानं प्रतिपादयेत् ।
सर्वाभावे क्षिपेदग्नौ गवे दद्यादथाप्सु वा ॥
नैव प्राप्तस्य लोपोऽस्ति पैतृकस्य विशेषत ।**

इति देवलोक्तेः । (1) 'प्रैषानुप्रैषसंयुक्तम्' इति "श्राद्धं सम्पन्नं ? सुसम्पन्नम्" इत्यादि प्रश्नप्रतिवचने स्वयमेव वदेदित्यर्थः । (2) इदञ्चान्नश्राद्धपक्षे । (3) आमहेमपक्षयोस्तु सर्वं श्राद्धं निर्वर्त्य तद्द्रव्यं कालान्तरे ब्राह्मणाय दद्यात् ।

(4) इदञ्चामश्राद्धं सति सम्भवे पूर्वाह्णे तीर्थप्राप्ति सम्पाद्य तदैव कार्यम्,

528. **आमश्राद्धं तु पूर्वाह्णे एकोद्दिष्टं तु मध्यतः ।
पार्वणं चापराह्णे तु प्रातर्वृद्धिनिमित्तकम् ॥**

इति हारीतोक्तेः । (1) आकस्मिकप्राप्तौ तु प्राप्तिलक्षणनिमित्तानुरोधेन कालान्तरेऽपीत्युक्तं प्राक् ।

(2) यदि तु तीर्थे केनापि प्रकारेण श्राद्धेऽशक्तिस्तदा सक्त्वादिना पिण्डदानमप्यवश्यं कार्यम् । अत एव देवीपुराणे श्राद्धोक्त्यैव पिण्डदानप्राप्तौ

529. **पिण्डदानं तु तच्छस्तं पितृणाञ्चैव वल्लभम् ।** (=381)

(1) इति पुनः पिण्डमात्रं पृथगुक्तम् । (2) अन्यथाङ्गान्तरपरिसंख्यया दोषत्रयं स्यात् ।

देवलः—

530. **पिण्डमात्रं प्रदातव्यमभावे द्रव्यविप्रयोः ।
श्राद्धाहनि तु सम्प्राप्ते भवेन्निरशनोऽपि वे-॥**

526.1. दर्भवटोरुपरि; P1 (+correction in L2) दर्भचटोपरि, C1 दर्भवटूपरि, P2 L1 L2 दर्भवटोपरि । 527. नैव; P3 K न च । 528. हारीतोक्तेः; L2 मरीचिनोक्तेः । 529.1. उक्तम्; P2 उप्तम् । 529.2—परिसंख्यया; P3 —परिसंख्याया ।

ति । विष्णुपुराणेऽपि—

531. **अकुर्वन् वित्तशाठ्यं यः पिण्डान् नो निर्वपिष्यती– ।**

वि० पु० 3.14.22c-d

(1) ति पितृणां वाक्ये पिण्डमात्रमुक्तम् । (2) अत एव ज्ञापकात् तीर्थे पिण्डदानमपि प्रधानमेकोद्दिष्टवत् ।

(3) पिण्डे च द्रव्याणि—

देवीपुराणे—

532. **सक्तुभिः पिण्डदानञ्च संयावैः पायसेन वा ।**
कर्तव्यमृषिभिः प्रोक्तं पिण्याकेनेङ्गुदेन वा ॥

(1) 'गुडेन वे'ति वा पाठः । (2) संयावो गोधूमविकारः । (3) पिण्याकस्तिलकल्कः । (4) इङ्गुदं तापसतरुफलम् । (5) अत्र पूर्वपूर्वासम्भवे उत्तरोत्तरं ज्ञेयम् ।

सत्यव्रतः—

533. **शाकमूलफलान्नैस्तु वासोगोभूमिकाञ्चनैः ।**
अद्भिर्वा विप्रसंवादात् पितृणां प्रीतिमावहेत् ॥

(1) विप्रसंवादः सर्वाभावे विप्रं ब्रूयात् "मयाद्य श्राद्धं कृतमस्तु" "अस्त्व्" इत्येवं विप्रो ब्रूयादित्येवंरूपः ।

(2) पिण्डप्रमाणञ्च अङ्गिराः—

534. **कपित्थबिल्वमात्रान् वा पिण्डान् दद्याद् विधानतः ।**
कुक्कुटाण्डप्रमाणान् वा केषाञ्चामलकैः समान् ॥
बादरेण समान् वापि दद्याच्छ्रद्धासमन्वित । इति ।

(1) अत्राप्यशक्तौ सूक्ष्मप्रमाणा अपि देयाः.

535. **शमीपत्रप्रमाणेन पिण्डं दद्याद् गयाशिर ।**

अग्नि पु० 115.46c-d

533.2. च; C1 चाह ।

इति लिङ्गात् ।

अन्यच्च —

536. **तिलमन्नञ्च पानीयं धूपं दीपं पयस्तथा ।**
मधु सर्पिः खण्डयुक्तं पिण्डमष्टाङ्गमुच्यते ॥

तथा—

537. **अवनेजनं पिण्डदानं पुनः प्रत्यवनेजनम् ।**
दक्षिणा चान्नसंकल्पस्तीर्थश्राद्धेष्वयं क्रम ॥

इति वृद्धश्लोकः ।

(1) तीर्थश्राद्धे पिण्डदानं

538. **पिण्डांस्तु गोजविप्रेभ्यो दद्यादग्नौ जलेऽपि वे- ।**

याज्ञ० 1.256a-b

(1) ति याज्ञवल्क्योक्ता प्रतिपत्तिर्न कार्या किन्तु जल एव क्षेपः ,

539. **तीर्थश्राद्धे सदा पिण्डान् क्षिपेत्तीर्थे समाहितः ।**
दक्षिणाभिमुखो भूत्वा पित्र्या दिक् सा प्रकीर्तिते- ॥

ति वचनात् ।

(1) तीर्थपिण्डदाने नन्दादिप्रयुक्तो निषेधो न प्रवर्तत इति श्राद्धप्रसङ्ग एवाभ्यधायि ।

(2) यदा तु पिण्डदानेऽप्यशक्तिस्तदा तर्पणमप्यवश्यकं कर्त्तव्यं,

540. **तिलैः सप्ताष्टभिर्वापि समवेतं जलाञ्जलिम् ।**
भक्तिनम्रः समुद्दिश्य भुव्यस्माकं प्रदास्यति ॥
यतः कुतश्चित् संप्राप्य गोभ्यो वापि गवाह्निकम् ।

वि० पु० 3.14. 27-28b

इत्यपिशब्दयुक्तपितृवचनात् ।

(1) एवञ्च सत्येप संक्षेपः—(2) शक्तेन तर्पणश्राद्धपिण्डदानानि त्रीण्यपि कार्याणि । (3) अशक्तेन तर्पणपिण्डौ । (4) अशक्ततरेण तर्पणमात्रमपीति ।

---

537. प्रत्यवनेजनम्; P3 प्रत्यवसेचनम् ।

(5) यत्र च काश्यादावेकस्मिन्महातीर्थे अनेकान्यवान्तरतीर्थानि एकदिने गम्यन्ते, तदैकस्मिन्नपि दिने तत्तत्तीर्थप्राप्तिनिमित्तकानि बहूनि श्राद्धानि निमित्तक्रमेण कार्याणि निमित्तभेदात्, दर्शे उपरागश्राद्धवत् । यत्तु प्रचेतसो वचनं—

541. **नैकश्राद्धद्वयं कुर्यात् समानेऽहनि कुत्रचित् ।**
न हन्तेति न होमं च न स्वाध्यायं न तर्पणम् ॥

(1) इति, तत् समाननिमित्तकश्राद्धविषयम् । तदाह जावालिः—

542. **श्राद्धं कृत्वा तु तस्यैव पुनः श्राद्धं न तद्दिने ।**
नैमित्तिकं तु कर्तव्यं निमित्तानुक्रमोदये ॥

कात्यायनोऽपि—

543. **द्वे बहूनि निमित्तानि जायेरन्नेकवासरे ।**
नैमित्तिकानि कार्याणि निमित्तोत्पत्त्यनुक्रमात् ॥

अन्यत्रापि—

544. **एकस्त्वेकनिमित्तमेकदिवसे श्राद्धं न चार्वर्तयेद्** । इति ।

(1) उपवासमुण्डने तु सकृदेव, प्रयागकाश्यादिव्यापकतीर्थोपाध्यवच्छेदेन विधानात् ।

(2) यत्र तु व्याप्यतीर्थावच्छेदेन श्राद्धकरणाद् व्यापकतीर्थश्राद्धमपि सिध्यति, तत्र प्रतिनिमित्तमावत्तिर्न भवति । (3) किन्तु 'इदं कृतं इदं ने'त्यगृह्यमाणविशेषत्वात् तन्त्रेणैव श्राद्धानां सिद्धिर्देशकालकर्त्रैक्यात् द्रव्यदेवतयोरभेदाच्च । (4) यथा गङ्गावेणीप्रयागनिमित्तकानां गङ्गाकाशीमणिकर्णिकानिमित्तकानां चेत्यादि ।

(5) "ननु 'प्राप्तैरेव च कर्तव्यम्' [324] इति वचनात् पञ्चक्रोशाद्यवधि प्राप्तावैव प्रथमं व्यापकतीर्थनिमित्तकं श्राद्धं प्राप्नोति । (6) व्याप्यतीर्थदेशप्राप्तौ तु तन्निमित्तकं पश्चादिति देशकालयोर्भेदात् कथं तन्त्रता ? (7) मैवं, सायंप्रातःपौर्णमास्यमावास्यावावयवशाद् यावज्जीववचनोक्तजीवनाख्यनिमित्तसङ्कोचवन् मणिकर्ण्यादितत्तत्प्रधानतीर्थावच्छेदेन प्राथमिकस्नानश्राद्धादिबोधक-

541. हन्तेति; P1 P2 L1 हन्तंति, P3 K (corrected to हन्तेति) L2 (?) हन्तनि । 544.3. —विशेषत्वात्; L2 — विशेषन्यायात् । 544.5 —निमित्तकं, P1—निमित्तक— ।

वाक्यवशात् 'प्राप्तैरेवे'ति वचनोक्तप्राप्त्याख्यनिमित्तसङ्कोचात् । तथा हि काशीखण्डे व्यासवचः—

545. **निशामय महाप्राज्ञ लोमहर्षण वच्मि ते ।**
यथा प्रथमतो यात्रा कर्तव्या यात्रिकैर्मुदा ॥
सचैलमादौ स्नात्वा तु चक्रपुष्करिणीजले ।
संतर्प्य पितृदेवांश्च ब्राह्मणांश्च यथाविधी- ॥

(1) त्यादि । तथा च मणिकर्ण्याख्यप्रधानतीर्थावच्छिन्नकाशीप्राप्तेर्निमित्तत्वाद् देशकालभेदो नास्तीति युक्ता तन्त्रता । (2) एवं प्रयागादावपि ।

(3) "नन्वेवंविशिष्टस्य निमित्तत्वे निमित्तभेदाभावाद् भिन्नश्राद्धप्रसक्तिरेव नास्तीति केयं तन्त्रता ?" (4) सत्यं, किन्तु मणिकर्ण्यादिश्राद्धेऽपि पृथक्फलप्राशस्त्यबोधकवाक्यैस्तत्प्राप्तेरपि पृथक्श्राद्धनिमित्तत्वम् । (5) तद्यथा पौर्णमास्यमावास्ययोरस्ति च जीवनाख्यनिमित्तावच्छेदकतास्ति च 'य इष्ट्ये'त्यादिवचनात् स्वतन्त्रेष्टिकालता, तद्वदत्रापि द्विविधवचनैर्मणिकर्ण्यादेर्निमित्तावच्छेदकता स्वतन्त्रश्राद्धनिमित्तता च भविष्यति, संयोगपृथक्त्वन्यायात् ।

(6) वस्तुतस्तु निमित्तसङ्कोचे सति प्रतिबन्धकवशान्मणिकर्णिकाद्यप्राप्तौ निमित्तानिष्पत्तेर्नैमित्तिकश्राद्धाननुष्ठानमेव स्यात् । (7) अतः काश्यादिप्राप्तिनिमित्तक एव श्राद्धे मणिकर्णिकादिदेशोऽङ्गत्वेन विधीयते । (8) तथा च निमित्तकतयावश्यकत्वात् तदप्राप्तावपि देशाङ्गविकलमपि श्राद्धं कार्यं निमित्तस्य वृत्तत्वादिति दिक् । (9) तस्मादस्त्यनेकप्राप्तिः ।

(10) "नन्वेकप्रयोगविधिपरिगृहीतेषु प्रयाजाद्यङ्गेष्वेव तन्त्वं दृष्टं, न स्वतन्त्रप्रधानेष्वपी"ति चेत्, (11) अहो यावद्दृष्टग्राही मदः, योऽयं दर्शपूर्णमासराजसूयादौ फलतन्त्रतां, सांनाय्ये च सम्प्रतिपन्नदेवताकत्वेन प्रधानयोरपि देवतोद्देशत्यागात्मयागयोः, यमलपुत्रजन्मनि जातेष्ट्योः, पक्षहोमे अनकहोमानां, युगपदेनकगृहदाहादिनिमित्तेषु क्षामवत्यादीनां, स्मार्ते च संक्रान्त्यमावास्यादिनिमित्तकश्राद्धानाञ्च प्रधानानामपि देशाद्यैक्येनागृह्यमाणविशेषतया सकृदनुष्ठानादेव सर्वापूर्वनिष्पत्तेर्युगपज्जायमानत्वात् तन्त्रभावं नालोचयते, येनेतिकर्तव्यतामात्रविषयतां तन्त्रस्याह ।

(12) तस्मात् 'काशीनिमित्तकं मणिकर्णिकानिमित्तकञ्च श्राद्धं तन्त्रेणाहं करिष्य' इति सङ्कल्प्यैकमेव श्राद्धं कुर्यात् । (13) यदा तु प्रत्यासन्नप्राक्काले गङ्गायामकृतश्राद्धस्तदा 'गङ्गाश्राद्धञ्चे'त्यपि वदेत् । (14) एवं प्रयागगयादावपीति ।

545.11. देवतोद्देश—; C2 देवतोद्देश्य— ।

(15) केचित्तु "काश्यादिव्यापकतीर्थस्यैवोद्देश्यत्वात् तत्प्रकरणे च मणिकर्ण्यादिव्याप्यतीर्थपाठात् तन्मध्यपाताख्यं विशेषग्रहणमस्तीति पश्वर्थानुष्ठितप्रयाजैः पशुपुरोडाशप्रयाजानां काम्याग्निहोत्रेण नित्यस्यापरपक्षिकेण च नित्यश्राद्धस्य प्रसङ्गसिद्धिवद् व्यापककाश्यादिश्राद्धेनैव व्याप्यश्राद्धस्यापि प्रसङ्गत एव सिद्धिमभ्युपेत्य "काशीप्राप्तिनिमित्तकश्राद्धं करिष्य' इत्येव सङ्कल्प" इत्याहुः ।

(16) यत्तु "न तन्त्रं न वा प्रसङ्गः, किन्तु काश्यादिप्राप्तिनिमित्तकमेकमेव श्राद्धं निमित्तसङ्कोचात् । पृथक्फलबोधनं तु पञ्चतीर्थाद्यन्तर्गतमणिकर्ण्यादिश्राद्धविषयं स्वतन्त्रतच्छ्राद्धविषयं वा भविष्यती"ति, (17) तन्न, व्याप्यतीर्थप्राप्तिरूपनिमित्ते सत्यपि तन्निमित्तकश्राद्धबाधे हेत्वभावात् । (18) विपर्यये प्रमाणसत्त्वाच्च । (19) न च पञ्चतीर्थाद्यन्तर्गतमणिकर्ण्यादिश्राद्धविषयं पृथक्फलश्रवणम् । (20) तदन्तर्गतस्नानश्राद्धादेरितरसहितस्यैवसमुदायोपाधिना राजसूयमध्यपतितावेष्ट्यादिवत् समुदायप्रयोगवाक्यगतफलेन निराकांक्षत्वात् पृथक्फलाकांक्षाया अभावात् । (21) नापि स्वतन्त्रश्राद्धविषयं पृथक्फलश्रवणं, फलान्तरार्थं श्राद्धान्तरविधौ गौरवात् । (22) अस्मतपक्षे तु प्राप्त एव प्राप्तिनिमित्तक श्राद्धे ।

546. **संनिधौ त्वविभागात्**

मी० सू० 2.3.13.26

(1) इति न्यायेनावेष्टा'व् 'एतयान्नाद्यकामं याजयेदि'तिवत् फलसम्बन्धमात्रं क्रियत इति लाघवम् ।

(2) तस्मात् मणिकर्ण्यादिश्राद्धमवेष्टिवत् द्विविधम्; (3) इतरैः सह समप्रधानं, स्वतन्त्रञ्चेति । (4) तत्राद्यं पञ्चतीर्थ्याद्यन्तर्गतम् । (5) द्वितीयं तु प्राप्तिनिमित्तकम् । (6) तत्रोत्तरलोपे हेत्वभावाद् उक्तरीत्या तन्त्रेण प्रसङ्गेन वा सिद्धिरित्येव युक्तम् । (7) एकस्यापि चानेकफलसाधनता प्रयोगभेदाद् अवच्छेदकभेदाच्चावेष्टिवदेवोपपादनीया । (8) एवं सर्वत्रेत्यलं बहुना ।

545.15. नित्यस्यापरपक्षिकेण; P2 नित्यापरपक्षिकेण । 545.15. नित्यश्राद्धस्य; C2 नित्यस्य श्राद्धस्य । 545.15. सङ्कल्प; P2 सङ्कल्प्य । 545.17. --प्राप्तिरूपनिमित्ते; P1 P2 --प्राप्तिनिमित्ते । 546.3. चेति; P3 वेति ।

अथ श्राद्धान्तरसमवाये निर्णयः

(9) तत्र यदि तीर्थप्राप्तिदिने वार्षिकं स्यात्तदा पृथगेव कार्यम् । तदुक्तं कालादर्शे—

547. **प्रत्याब्दिकेषु चालभ्ययोगेषु विहितस्य च ।**
सम्पाते देवताभेदाच्छ्राद्धयुग्मं समाचरेद् ॥ इति ।

(1) तत्राप्यादौ तीर्थनिमित्तकं, प्राप्त्यनन्तरमेव कार्यत्वाद् विलम्बायोगात् ।
(2) पश्चाद् वार्षिकम् ।

(3) दार्शिकव्यतीपातयुगादिमन्वादिसंक्रान्त्यादिनिमित्तकानि तु यद्यामेन हेम्ना वा तीर्थश्राद्धं क्रियते तदा पृथगेव कार्याणि, तेषां पक्वसाध्यत्वेन द्रव्यभेदात् प्रसङ्गायोगात् । (4) यदा तु तीर्थश्राद्धं पाकेनैव क्रियते, तदा द्रव्यभेदाभावात् तद्देवतानाञ्च सर्वासां तीर्थश्राद्ध एवेष्टत्वात् प्रसङ्गात् तीर्थश्राद्धेनैव सिद्धिः,

548. **दार्शिकस्य युगादेश्च दार्शिकालभ्ययोगयोः ।**
प्रसङ्गादितरस्यापि सिद्धेरुत्तरमाचरेद् ॥

इति कालादर्शोक्तेः । (1) अत्र दार्शिकशब्दस्तत्समानन्यायानां सर्वेषामुलक्षकः ।

(2) नित्यश्राद्धमपि यद्यामेन हेम्ना वा तैर्थिकं तदा पृथक्, तस्य पक्वद्रव्यत्वात् । यत्तु

549. **नान्दीमुखतीर्थश्राद्धेषु नित्यश्राद्धदेवतानामिष्टत्वात्**
प्रसङ्गसिद्धतया पृथक् नित्यश्राद्धं न कर्तव्यम्

(1) इति हेमाद्रिणोक्तम्, तत् तीर्थश्राद्धस्यान्नेन करणे द्रष्टव्यम् । तदुक्तं नागरखण्डे—

550. **नित्यश्राद्धं न कुर्वीत प्रसङ्गाद्यत्र सिध्यति ।**
श्राद्धान्तरे कृतेऽन्यत्र नित्यत्वात् तन्न हापयेद् ॥

548.2. पक्व—; P3 K पाक— । 549. नित्यश्राद्धं; L2 नित्यपक्वद्रव्यश्राद्धं ।

इति ।

(1) यदा तु केनचिन्निमित्तेनाशक्त्या वा सर्वाणि दार्शिकादीनि आमेन हेम्ना वा चिकीर्षति, तदामिकेन हैमेन वा तीर्थश्राद्धेनैव सिद्धिरित्यादयो निर्णयाः स्वबुद्धया कार्याः ।

(2) इदं तीर्थनिमित्तकश्राद्धं दशमासानन्तरं तीर्थप्राप्तावावश्यकम् । (3) अन्तरा तु फलेच्छया कृताकृतम्,

551. **संवत्सरं द्विमासोनं पुनस्तीर्थं व्रजेद्यदि ।**
मुण्डनञ्चोपवासश्च ततो यत्नेन कारयेद् ॥ (= 278)

(1) इति यत्नपदयुक्तवचनोक्तमुण्डनादिसमानन्यायत्वात्, (2) चकारेणोपसंग्रहाद्वा । (3) स्नानतर्पणादि तु सर्वदा भवतीति वृद्धाः ।

इति श्रीभट्टरामेश्वरसूरिसूनुनारायणभट्टविरचिते
त्रिस्थलीसेतौ सामान्यप्रघट्टके
सपरिकरस्तीर्थश्राद्धविचारः ।

550.2. तीर्थनिमित्तकश्राद्धं; P2 तीर्थनिमित्तकं श्राद्धं ।

अथ श्राद्धाधिकारिणः

तत्र

552. **पितुः पुत्रेण कर्तव्या पिण्डदानोदकक्रिया ।**
पुत्राभावे तु पत्नी स्यात् पत्न्यभावे तु सोदरः ॥
(शंख 188)

इति कात्यायनवचनात्,

553. **पुत्रः पौत्रः प्रपौत्रो वा भ्राता वा भ्रातृसन्ततिः ।**
सपिण्डसन्ततिर्वापि श्राद्धार्हा नृप जायत ॥
वि० पु० 3.13.30c-31b

(1) इति विष्णुपुराणवचनाच्च पुत्रादीनामधिकारः । (2) एवमन्येऽपि सामान्याधिकारिणो ग्रन्थान्तराद् ज्ञेयाः ।

(3) विशेषस्तु; जीवत्पितृकोऽपि तीर्थश्राद्धं कुर्यात् । तदुक्तं मैत्रायणीयपरिशिष्टे—

554. **उद्वाहे पुत्रजनने पित्र्येष्ट्यां सौमिके मखे ।**
तीर्थे ब्राह्मण आयते षडेते जीवतः पितुः ॥
मै० परि०, pp. 236-7

(1) उद्वाहोऽत्र द्वितीयादिः, प्रथमे पितुरेवाधिकारात् । (2) 'पुत्रजनने' जातकर्मणि । (3) इदमपत्यसंस्कारमात्रोपलक्षणम् । (4) 'पित्र्येष्ट्यां' चातुर्मास्यान्तर्गतायाम् । (5) 'सौमिके मखे' तार्तीयसवनिकैः पुरोडाशखण्डैः स्वचमसाधस्तात् पिण्डदाने । (6) 'ब्राह्मण आयते' त्रिमधुस्त्रिसुपर्णक इत्यादिगुणयुतविप्रसम्पदि । (7) 'जीवतः पितुः' पुत्रस्यैते श्राद्धकालाः षडित्यर्थः ।

(8) एवं तीर्थमात्रे श्राद्धे प्रसक्ते गयायामपवादमाह लौगाक्षिः—

555. **दर्शश्राद्धं गयाश्राद्धं श्राद्धञ्चापरपक्षिकम् ।**
न जीवत्पितृकः कुर्यात् तिलैः कृष्णैश्च तर्पणम् ॥

---

554. तीर्थे ब्राह्मण; P2 KL 1 तीर्थब्राह्मण । 554.8. लौगाक्षिः; P2 लौकाक्षि, P3 लोगाक्षिः ।

मैत्रायणीयपरिशिष्टेऽपि—

556. **महानदीषु सर्वासु तीर्थेषु च गयामृते ।**
जीवत्पितापि कुर्वीत श्राद्धं पार्वणधर्मवत् ॥

मै० परि०, p. 237, note 2

(1) मृतमातृकस्य तु प्रासङ्गिकगयाप्राप्तौ मातृश्राद्धे परिशिष्ट एव प्रति-प्रसवः श्रूयते—

557. **आन्वष्टक्यं गयाप्राप्तौ सत्यां यच्च मृतेऽहनि ।**
मातुः श्राद्धं सुतः कुर्यात् पितर्यपि च जीवति ॥

मै० परि० p. 237

(1) अत्रापि 'गयाप्राप्तौ सत्याम्' इत्यनेन प्रासङ्गिकप्राप्तिरुक्ता; (2) तस्यां सत्यां मातृश्राद्धं कार्यं न तूद्दिश्य गत्वा । अत एव स्मृत्यन्तरम्—

558. **गयां प्रसङ्गतो गत्वा मातुः श्राद्धं समाचरेद् ।** इति

(1) ततश्च "गयातिरिक्ततीर्थे जीवत्पितृकेण वक्ष्यमाणोद्देशेन श्राद्धं कार्यम् । (2) गयायां तु यदि प्रसङ्गाद् याति मृतमातृकश्च तदा मातृपार्वणमात्रं कुर्यात् । (3) अमृतमातृकस्तु ने"त्येवं कालादर्शस्मृतिदर्पणकारादयो बहवो मेनिरे । (4) अपरे तु "जीवत्पितृकश्राद्धविधायकवाक्यानां साधारण्याद् गयायामपि जीवत्पितृकेण पितृपित्रादिभ्यो वक्ष्यमाणेभ्यः श्राद्धं कार्यम् । (5) एतस्मिंश्च श्राद्धे मृतमातृकस्य पितृपत्नीत्वेन मातृश्राद्धसिद्धावपि 'आन्वष्टक्यम्' इत्यादि-वचनं मातृत्वादिरूपेण पृथक्पार्वणप्राप्त्यर्थम् । (6) यानि तु गयाश्राद्धनिषेध-वचनानि तानि मृतमातृकेणापि तच्छ्राद्धोद्देशेन गत्वा श्राद्धं न कार्यं, किन्तु प्रासङ्गिकगमन एवेत्येवंपराणीत्ये"वं वचनानां व्यवस्थामाहुः ।

(7) एवमुभयथा वचनव्यवस्थायां सत्यां देशाचाराद् व्यवस्था । (8) उभयथापि तीर्थश्राद्धे जीवत्पितृकस्याधिकारः सिद्धः ।

एवञ्च यत्

559. **सपितुः पितृकृत्येषु अधिकारो न विद्यते ।**
न जीवन्तमतिक्रम्य किञ्चिद् दद्यादिति श्रुतेर् ॥

का० 2.16.12

---

556. सर्वासु; P1 पूर्वासु । 556. पार्वण—; L2 ब्राह्मण— । 557. आन्वष्टक्यं; L2 अन्वष्टक्यं । 558.5. आन्वष्टक्यम् P2 L2 अन्वष्टक्यं ।

इति कात्यायनवचः, यच्च

560 **पित्र्यं जीवत्पितुर्नोक्तम् ।**

(1) इति निगमवचस्तद् विहितकालषट्कातिरिक्तपरं भवति ।

(2) "ननु यदि जीवत्पितृकस्यापि तीर्थश्राद्धेऽधिकारस्तदा पितरि तीर्थवासिनि देशान्तरागतेन पुत्रेण श्राद्धं कर्तव्यं स्यात्, निमित्तस्य वृत्तत्वात् ।" (3) कर्तव्यमेवेति वदामो, बाधकाभावात् । (4) "तर्हि पित्रा सहागतेनापि कुतो न क्रियते ?" (5) उच्यते; वचनात् प्राप्नोत्येव, लोकविद्विष्टत्वात् त्वननुष्ठानम् । तदुक्तम्—

561. **अस्वर्ग्यं लोकविद्विष्टं धर्ममप्यचरेन्न तु ।** इति ।

याज्ञ० 1.156c-d

(1) "पितृकृतेन प्रसङ्गसिद्धेरनुष्ठानं कुतो ने"ति चेत्, (2) न, भिन्नकर्तृके प्रसङ्गाभावात् ।

(3) तत्सिद्धं जीवत्पितृकस्यापि तीर्थश्राद्धेऽधिकारित्वम्

(4) भ्रातरस्तु यदि विभक्ता युगपदयुगपद्वा तीर्थे गतास्तदा प्रत्येकं पृथक् श्राद्धं कुर्युः । (5) अविभक्तेषु तु य एव गतस्तेन कार्यम् । (6) सहगमने तु ग्रहणादिवत् ज्येष्ठेनैव, न तु सर्वैः । तदाह मनुः—

562. **भ्रातॄणामविभक्तानामेको धर्मः प्रवर्तते ।**
विभागे सति धर्मोऽपि भवेत्तेषां पृथक् पृथक् ॥

प्रदीपे—

563. **विभक्तास्तु पृथक् कुर्युः प्रतिसंवत्सरादिकम् ।**
एकेनैवाविभक्तेषु कृते सर्वैस्तु तत्कृतम् ॥

(1) विधवा तु यदि पुत्रवती तीर्थे च गता तदा नैव कुर्यात्,

564. **सपुत्रया न कर्तव्यं भर्तुः श्राद्धं कदाचने- ।**

ति वचनात् । (1) अपुत्रया तु कार्यमेव,

---

559. कात्यायनवचः; L2 कात्यायनवचनं । 560.2.—श्राद्धेऽधिकारस्; P1 —श्राद्धाधिकारस् । 561. धर्मम्; K धर्म्यम् ।

565. **अपुत्रा पुत्रवत्पत्नी--**

ति वचनात् ।

(1) केचित्तु "पुत्रवत्यापि पुत्रासंनिधाने ब्राह्मणादिद्वारा संकल्पश्राद्धं कारणीयम् । (2) साङ्कल्पे च वर्ज्यानि--

वसिष्ठः--

566. **आवाहनं स्वधाशब्दं पिण्डोऽग्नौकरणं तथा ।**
विकिरं पिण्डदानञ्च साङ्कल्पे षट् विवर्जयेत् ॥

(1) " 'पिण्ड' उच्छिष्टपिण्डः" इत्याहुः । (2) तत्र मूलं मृग्यम् ।
(3) अनुपनीतोऽपि तीर्थे श्राद्धं कुर्यात्,

567. **एतच्चानुपनीतोऽपि कुर्यात् सर्वेषु पर्वसु ।**
श्राद्धं साधारणं नाम सर्वकामफलप्रदम् ॥
भार्याविरहितो वापि प्रवासस्थोऽपि भक्तिमान् ।
शूद्रोऽप्यमन्त्रकं कुर्यादनेन विधिना नृपे-॥

--सृ० ख० 9.185-186b

ति पाद्मे सृष्टिखण्डे तीर्थश्राद्वादिकं उपक्रम्योक्तेः । (1) तत्र स्त्रिया अनुपनीतेन च यथादेशाचारं ब्राह्मणद्वारा कारणीयं, स्वयं वामन्त्रकं कार्यम् । तदुक्तं स्मृत्यर्थसारे--

568. **अनुपनीतः स्त्रीशूद्राश्च श्राद्धमृत्विजा कारयेयुः, स्वयं वा अमन्त्रकं नामगोत्राभ्यां कुर्युः, 'देवेभ्यो नमः' 'पितृभ्यः स्वधा नम' इति मन्त्राभ्यां वे-। ति ।**

स्मृत्यर्थसार, p. 56

(1) क्षेत्रजादीनां तु यो विशेषः स नोच्यते,

569. **दत्तौरसेतरेषां तु पुत्रत्वेन परिग्रह ।**

(1) इति पुत्रान्तरनिषेधेन कलावनुपयोगात् ।

---

568. वेति; Cl K L1 L2 चेति ।

तथा—

570. **यो यस्य स्त्रियं धनं वा हरति स तस्य कुर्यात् ।**
स्त्रीहारी धनहारी च कुर्युः पिण्डोदकक्रियाम् ॥

इति कार्ष्णाजिनिवचनात् ।

(1) एवमन्येऽपि ग्रन्थान्तरतोऽधिकारिणो ज्ञेयाः । (2) केचित्तु सम्प्रदाननिर्णयेऽत्रापि स्पष्टीभविष्यन्ति ।

अथाधिकारापवादः

(3) तत्र यतिना न कार्यं,

571. न कुर्यात् सूतकं भिक्षुः श्राद्धं पिण्डोदकक्रियाम् । (=345)
त्यक्तं संन्यासयोगेन गृहधर्मादिकं व्रतम् ॥
गोत्रादिचरणं सर्वं पितृमातृकुलं धनम् ।

इति स्मरणात् ।

(1) पतितोऽपि न कुर्याद्,

572. द्विजातिकर्मभ्यो हानिः पतनम्

इति वचनेन निषेधात् । (1) उपपातक्यादिना तु कार्यमेव, तस्य नित्यनैमित्तिकयोर्निषेधाभावात् ।

इति श्रीभट्टरामेश्वरसूरिसूनुनारायणभट्टविरचिते
त्रिस्थलीसेतौ सामान्यप्रघट्टके
तीर्थश्राद्धाधिकारिणः

---

571. श्राद्धं; C2 श्राद्ध—।

अथ तीर्थश्राद्धे सम्प्रदाननिर्णयः

तत्र —

573. **नदीतीरेषु तीर्थेषु सुभूमौ चैव सानुषु ।**
विविक्तेषु च तुष्यन्ति दत्तेन पितरः सदे- ॥

कू० पु० 2.22.15

ति कूर्मपुराणात्,

574. **सपिण्डीकरणादूर्ध्वं यत्र यत्र प्रदीयते ।**
पार्वणं तत्र कर्तव्यमेकोद्दिष्टं न कर्हिचिद् ॥

(1) इति वचनाच्च पित्रादिपार्वणं तावत्कार्यम् ।
(2) ततो मातामहादिपार्वणमपि

575. **पितरो यत्र पूज्यन्ते तत्र मातामहा अपि ।**
अविशेषेण कर्तव्यं विशेषान्नरकं व्रजेत् ॥

इति गौतमोक्तेः,

576. **कर्षूसमन्वितं मुक्त्वा तथान्यत् श्राद्धषोडशम् ।**
प्रत्याब्दिकञ्च शेषेषु पिण्डाः स्युः षडिति स्थितिर् ॥

कात्या० 3.24.14

इति कात्यायनोक्तेश्च ।

(1) एवं "गयातिरिक्ततीर्थेषु षड्दैवत्यमेवे"ति स्मृतिरत्नावलीकारादयो मेनिरे । (2) अन्ये तु तीर्थादिसामान्यश्राद्धमुपक्रम्य

577. **हविःशेषात् ततो मुष्टिमादायैकैकमादृतः ।**
क्रमशः पितृपत्नीनां पिण्डनिर्वपनं चरेद् ॥

(1) इति देवलवचनान्मातृपार्वणमपीच्छन्ति ।
(2) स्मृत्यर्थसारे तु

578. **तत्र मातृश्राद्धं पृथक् प्रशस्तम्**

स्मृत्यर्थसार, pp. 59-60.

577.2. स्मृत्यर्थसारे; P3 C2 K स्मृत्यर्थसारेण ।

(1) इति वदता कृताकृतत्वमुक्तम् ।

(2) गयायां तु मात्रादिपार्वणमावश्यकमिति तत्रैव वक्ष्यामः ।

579. **एतच्च पित्रादिपिण्डानां पश्चिमभागे देयम्**

इति शांख्यायनः । (1) एवं नवदैवत्यं भवति ।

(2) अन्ये तु "मातामह्यादिपार्वणमपि पृथग्" आहुः,

580. **केचिदिच्छन्ति नारीणां पृथक् श्राद्धं महर्षय ।**

(1) इति चतुर्विंशतिमते नारीणामपि सामान्योक्तेः,

581. **पित्रादिनवदैवत्यं तथा द्वादशदैवतम्**

अग्नि पु० 115.10a-b

इति अग्निपुराणोक्तेश्च । (1) विकल्पार्थस्तथाशब्दः; (2) तथा च द्वादशदैवत्यं भवति । (3) अत्र देशशिष्टसमाचाराद् व्यवस्था ।

(4) तत्र यदा मातृमातामहीपार्वणे पृथङ न स्तस्तदा पित्रादीनां मातामहादीनाञ्च सपत्नीकत्वेन निगमेषु निर्देशः कार्यः,

582. **स्वेन भर्त्रा समं श्राद्धं माता भुंक्ते सुधासमम् ।**
पितामही च स्वेनैव स्वेनैव प्रपितामही-॥

बृह० (श्रा) 75

(1) ति बृहस्पतिना मात्रादीनां पित्रादिसहभावेन देवतात्वोक्तेः,

583. **अन्वष्टका तथा मातृश्राद्धञ्चैव मृतेऽहनि ।**
एकोद्दिष्टं तथा मुक्त्वा स्त्रीषु नान्यत् पृथग् भवेद् ।

शंख (K) 190

(1) इति शंखेन पृथक्श्राद्धं निषेधता अपृथग् भवेदित्यभ्यनुज्ञानाच्च ।

(2) मात्रादीनां पथक्श्राद्धपक्षेऽपि यदि ताः कृतसहगमनास्तदा भार्तारं ताञ्चोद्दिश्य सहैवायुग्मब्राह्मणभोजनम् । (3) पिण्डोऽपि चोभयोद्देशेनैक एव देयः इत्येवं समासेनानुष्ठानं,

---

578.2. मात्रादिपार्वणम्; C2 मातृपार्वणम् । 580.1. अपि; C2 इति । 581. —नवदैवत्यं; P2 P3 C2 L1 नवदेवत्यं । 581. द्वादशदैवतम्; P2 द्वादशदेवतम्। 581.2. द्वादशदैवत्यं; P1 P3 द्वादशदेवत्यं; 582. स्वेनैव; P1 तथैव ।

584. **मृताहनि समासेन पिण्डनिर्वपणं पृथक् ।**
नवश्राद्धं तु दम्पत्योरन्वारोहण एव त्व् ।।

इति लौगाक्षिवचनात् । (1) अयमर्थः; दम्पत्योरन्वारोहणेन निमित्तेन मृततिथ्येकत्वे 'पिण्डनिर्वपणं' पिण्डो निर्वपणं श्राद्धं चोक्तप्रकारेण द्विपितृकश्राद्धवत् समासेन । (2) नवश्राद्धं तु प्राक् सपिण्डीकरणाद् यत् तत् पथक् न तु समासेन । (3) अत्र 'मृताहनी'ति विशेषोपादानान् मृततिथेर्भेदे तु न समासः किन्तु पृथगेव ।

(4) अत्र "नवश्राद्धे एव पृथक्त्वविधानाद् दर्शसांवत्सरिकतीर्थश्राद्धादिषु परिसंख्यया समास एवावगम्यते । (5) एवमनेकासामप्यन्वारोहणे ज्ञेयम् । यच्च स्मृत्यन्तरम्—

585. **एकचित्यां समारूढौ दम्पती निधनं गतौ ।**
पृथक्श्राद्धं तयोः कुर्याद् ओदनञ्च पृथक् पृथग् ।।

(1) इति, तन्नवश्राद्धविषयम्" इत्येवं मदनपारिजातकाराद्याः । (2) हेमाद्रिप्रभृतयस्तु "परिसंख्यापरिहाराय 'मृताहनी'ति यथाश्रुतानुरोधाच्च सांवत्सरिकमात्रविषयमेतत् । (3) तेन तीर्थादौ पृथगेव देयम्" इति ।

(4) तथा सपत्नमातृसपत्नपितामहीसपत्नप्रपितामहीभ्योऽपि तीर्थे दद्यात्,

586. **पितृपत्न्यः सर्वा मातर**

(1) इति सुमन्तुना तास्वपि मातृत्वाद्यतिदेशात् । (2) तत्रापि जनन्यादिस्थानीयब्राह्मणे तत्पिण्डे च तासामप्युद्देशो न तु पृथक्,

587. **अनेका मातरो यस्य तीर्थे चापरपक्षिके ।**
अर्घ्यदानं पृथक् कुर्यात् पिण्डमेकं तु निर्वपेद् ।।

इति गालवोक्तेः । (1) शिष्टास्तु एतस्याशक्तविषयतां मत्वा पृथगेव श्राद्धं पिण्डञ्च कुर्वन्ति । (2) तथा सपत्नमातामहेभ्योऽपि श्राद्धं कार्यं, मातृसपत्नीनां सुमन्तुना मातृत्वेऽतिदिष्टे तत्पितॄणामप्यार्थिकगौणमातामहतासिद्धेः । (3) तदेतत् सर्वमुक्तं श्राद्धकल्पे हेमाद्रिणा ।

---

584. लौगाक्षि—; P2 लौकाक्षि—। 584.1. मृततिथ्येकत्वे; P2 मृततिथ्यैकत्वे ।
587.2. सपत्नमातामहेभ्यो; P2 L2 सपत्नमातामहीभ्यो ।

(4) यदा तु नानापितृतृप्तिकामनया विशिष्टे महालयादिकाले गयादितीर्थविशेषे वा श्राद्धं कुर्यात्, तदा पुत्रवतीनामपुत्राणां वा मातृसपत्नीनामपि श्राद्धं कार्यम् । (5) पुत्रवतीनामपि तासां श्राद्धेषु कृपया स्नेहेन वा सपत्नीपुत्रस्य पाक्षिकाधिकारवत्त्वात् । (6) एतेनैव पितृजननीव्यतिरिक्ताः पितामहपत्न्यः पितामहजननीव्यतिरिक्ताः प्रपितामहपत्न्योऽपि व्याख्याताः । (7) जननीसपत्नीनां गौणमातृत्वनिरूपणेन तज्जनकानामपि गौणमेव मातामहश्राद्धे देवतात्वमित्यपि निरूपितं भवति । (8) यदा तु विशिष्टदेशकालादौ नानापितृतृप्तिकामनया श्राद्धं कर्तुमिच्छेत्, तदा पाक्षिकेणाधिकारेणापि तेषामपि कुर्यादिति स्थितमिति ।

(9) पितृव्यसुतयोरपि कार्यम्; (10) आचार्यादीनाञ्च,

588. **आचार्यगुरुशिष्येभ्यः सखिज्ञातिभ्य एव च ।**
तत्पत्नीभ्यश्च सर्वाभ्यस्तथैव च जलाञ्जलीन् ॥
पिण्डांस्तेभ्यः सदा दद्यात् पृथग् भाद्रपदे नरः ।
तीर्थेषु चैव सर्वेषु माघमासे मघासु चे- ॥

ति चतुर्विंशतिमतात् । (1) ज्ञातयः पितृव्यसुतमातुलाद्याः । (2) भविष्येऽन्योऽपि विशेषः—

589. **दौहित्रपुत्रदाराश्च ये कनिष्ठाः सहोदराः ।**
निःसन्तानमृता ये च तेभ्योऽप्यत्र प्रदीयते ॥

वृद्धशातातपोऽपि—

590. **प्रीत्या श्राद्धं तु कर्तव्यं सर्वेषां वर्णिलिङ्गिनाम् ।**
एवं कुर्वन्नरः सम्यङ्‌ महतीं श्रियमाप्नुयात् ॥

(1) वर्णिलिङ्गिनो ब्रह्मचारियत्यादयः । (2) अत्र सामान्योक्तावपि ज्ञातिभूता एव ते ग्राह्याः ।

(3) 'तत्पत्नीभ्यश्चे'ति चतुर्विंशतिमतवचनादेव पितृव्यादिपत्नीभ्योऽपि पृथग् देयम् ।

(4) एतेषाञ्च सर्वेषामेकोद्दिष्टमेव,

591. **सपिण्डीकरणादूर्ध्वं पित्रोरेव हि पार्वणम् ।**
पितृव्यभ्रातृमातृणामेकोद्दिष्टं सदैव ही- ॥

587.7. मातामहश्राद्धे; P2 मातामहश्राद्ध— । 590. महतीं; L2 कामनां

ति जातुकर्ण्यवचनात्,

592. **सपिण्डीकरणादूर्ध्वं यत्र यत्र प्रदीयते ।**
भ्रात्रे भगिन्यै पुत्राय स्वामिने मातुलाय च ॥
मित्राय गुरवे श्राद्धमेकोद्दिष्टं न पार्वणम् ।

इति सुमन्तूक्तेश्च ।

593. **पूर्ववाक्ये मातृग्रहणं सपत्नमातृविषयं मुख्यमातृपार्वणस्य**
पूर्वमुक्तत्वात्, पितृव्यादिसमभिव्याहाराच्चे-

ति हेमाद्रिः ।

यत्तु वचनं—

594. **पितृव्यभ्रातृमातृणामपुत्राणां तथैव च ।**
मातामहस्यापुत्रस्य श्राद्धादि पितृवद् भवेद् ॥

इति, (1) तदावश्यकतया तुल्यत्वार्थं, न तु पार्वणविधानेन तुल्यत्वार्थम् ।
(2) तथा यस्य यो द्रव्यं हरति तेनापि तस्मै देयमित्यधिकारिपूक्तम् ।
(3) अत्र पार्वणानां निवेशक्रममाह सत्यव्रतः—

595. **पितृणां प्रथमं दानं मातृणां तदनन्तरम् ।**
ततो मातामहानाञ्च पितृव्यस्य सुतस्य च ॥

छागलेयः—

596. **क्षयाहे केवलाः कार्या वृद्धावादौ प्रकीर्तिताः ।**
सर्वत्रैव हि मध्यस्था नान्त्याः कार्यास्तु मातरः ॥

यत्तु वचनं—

597. **पितृमातामहावादौ मातरस्तदनन्तरम् ।**
तर्पणे ऽन्वष्टकाश्राद्धे तीर्थे चायं क्रमः स्मृत ॥

(1) इति स्मृतिरत्नावलीकारोदाहृतं, तत् तेनैव निर्मूलतोक्तेरुपेक्षणीयम् ।

(2) अत एवान्तनिवेशनिषेधमाहोशनाः—

598. **अन्तर्मातामहान् कृत्वा मातॄणां यः प्रयच्छति ।**
स मूढो नरकं याति यावदाभूतसम्प्लवम् ॥

जाबालिः—

599. **अन्ते निवेशयेद् यस्तु मातृः श्राद्धेषु मानवः ।**
स मूढो नरकं याति कालसूत्रमवाक्शिराः ॥

(1) तस्मान्मातृपार्वणं पितृपार्वणानन्तरमेव । (2) अनेनैव न्यायेन मातामह्यादिपार्वणमपि मातामहादिपार्वणानन्तरम् । (3) पत्न्यादीनां तु क्रमस्तर्पणोक्त एव ।

(4) अत्र पितृमातामहपार्वणे नित्ये, तावतैव शास्त्रार्थसम्पत्तेः । (5) अन्यानि तु पार्वणैकोद्दिष्टानि काम्यानीति यावच्छक्ति कार्याणि; न तु सर्वाण्यावश्यकानि । (6) गयायां तु मातृपार्वणमप्यावश्यकमिति तत्रैव वक्ष्यामः ।

(7) एवं पार्वणैकोद्दिष्टानामनेकेषां युगपत्प्राप्तौ तन्त्रेण पाकः कार्यः । तथा चात्रिः—

600. **बहूनामथवा द्वाभ्यां श्राद्धञ्चेत् स्यात् समेऽहनि ।**
तन्त्रेण श्रपणं कृत्वा पृथक् श्राद्धानि कारयेत् ॥

पुलस्त्यः—

601. **महालये गयाश्राद्धे गतासूनां क्षयेऽहनि ।**
तन्त्रेण श्रपणं कृत्वा श्राद्धं कुर्यात् पृथक् पृथक् ॥

(1) तत्रापि पार्वणैकोद्दिष्टयोः क्रममाह मरीचिः—

602. **यद्येकत्र भवेयातामेकोद्दिष्टञ्च पार्वणम् ।**
पार्वणं तत्र निर्वर्त्य एकोद्दिष्टं समापयेत् ॥

(1) एतच्च शक्तौ । (2) अशक्तौ तु पार्वणैकोद्दिष्टानां तन्त्रम् ।

(3) अत्रैकोद्दिष्टेषु शक्तौ प्रत्येकं ब्राह्मणभोजनम् । (4) अशक्तौ त्वेकस्मिन्नपि ब्राह्मणे सर्वाण्येकोद्दिष्टानि । (5) अत एव चतुर्विंशतिमते 'आचार्यगुरुशिष्येभ्यः' [588] इत्याद्युपक्रम्य

597.2. एवान्तनिवेश—; L1 (+correction in P1) एवान्तरनिवेश— ।
602.1. एतच्च; P1 P2 एतत् ।

603. **तीर्थेषु चैव सर्वेषु माघमासे मघासु च ।**
एकस्मिन्ब्राह्मणे सर्वानाचार्यादीन् प्रपूजयेत् ॥

इत्युक्तम् ।

(1) पिण्डदानं तु पृथगेव तीर्थश्राद्धे तस्य प्रधानत्वात् । (2) अत एव ब्राह्मणमात्रैक्यमुक्तं वचने । (3) पित्रादिपार्वणेष्वपि यदि शक्तिस्तदा प्रतिदैवतमेकैकब्राह्मणभोजनम् । (4) दैवं तु सर्वपार्वणानां तन्त्रमेव

604. **कालभेदे न तन्त्रं स्याद् देशभेदे न चैव हि ।**
तस्मात् तन्त्रविधानात्तु यौगपद्यं प्रतीयत ॥

(1) इति संग्रहकारेण देशकालैक्ये दैवतन्त्राभिधानात् । (2) यदा त्वशक्तिस्तदा पित्रादिपार्वणेषु पित्रादित्रयत्रयस्थाने एकैकं भोजयेद् दैवे च तन्त्रेणैकमेवेति निर्णयः ।

(3) यदा त्वन्येन सामदानादिना प्रेरितस्तीर्थं याति, तदा यद्यपि स्वस्य कर्तृत्वं तथाप्यधिकारिणः पूर्णतीर्थयात्राजन्यफलसिद्ध्यर्थं तत्पित्रादीनेवोद्दिश्य प्रथमं श्राद्धं कुर्यात् । (4) तथा च 'यजमानस्य पितृपितामहानाम्' इत्यादिसंकल्पः कार्यः । (5) तदनन्तरं प्रासङ्गिकतीर्थप्राप्तेः स्वपितृश्राद्धनिमित्तभूताया वृत्तत्वात् प्रत्यवायपरिहारार्थं ।

605. **षोडशांशं स लभते यः परार्थेन गच्छती-। (=107)**

(1) ति वचनबोधितपूर्णफललाभार्थञ्च स्वपित्रादिभ्योऽपि श्राद्धं कुर्यात् । (2) यद्यपि स्वाधिकारिकत्वात् स्वपितृश्राद्धमन्तरङ्गतयादौ प्रसज्यते तथापि उद्देश्यत्वाभावाद् यात्रायाः परकीयत्वेन तदनन्तरमुपस्थितत्वभावाच्च स्वपितृश्राद्धं पश्चादेव । (3) उपपादितञ्चैतद्धेमाद्रिणा विस्तरेण श्राद्धकल्प इति नेह प्रपञ्च्यते ।

(4) अतएव वायुपुराणे स्ववचनदानेन प्रेतप्रेरितस्य कस्यचिद् वणिजो गयां गतस्यादौ प्रेतपिण्डदानं तदनन्तरञ्च स्वपितृभ्य इत्युक्तम्—

606. **आदौ गत्वा गयाशीर्षे प्रेतराजस्य पिण्डकम् ।**
स मुदा बन्धुभिः सार्धं स्वपितृभ्यस्ततो ददौ ॥

603.3. प्रतिदैवतम्; P2 L1 L2 प्रतिदेवतम् । 604. -विधानात्तु; P1 (+correction of P2) —प्रधानात्तु । 606. स मुदा; P1 संपाद्य, K (+correction in P3) स तदा ।

वामनपुराणेऽप्येतमेव प्रक्रम्य

607. **पिण्डनिर्वपणं तत्र प्रेतानामनुपूर्वशः ।**
चकार च स्वदायादान् पितॄंश्चक्रे त्वनन्तरम् ॥ इति।

वाम० पु० 57.70

(1) विधवा तु भर्तृपार्वणं स्वपितृपार्वणञ्च कुर्यात्,

608. **स्वभर्तृप्रभृतित्रिभ्यः स्वपितृभ्यस्तथैव च ।**
विधवा कारयेत् श्राद्धं यथाकालमतन्द्रिते- ॥

ति स्मृतिदर्पणलिखितस्मृतेः । (1) 'तथैव' त्रिभ्य एव । (2) 'यथाकालं' यत्र तीर्थमहालयादावनेकदेवत्यं विहितं तत्रेत्यर्थः ।

अत्र

609. **स्वपितुरपुत्रपौत्रत्व एव तत्पार्वणम् ।**

इति दिवोदासीये । (1) तत्र, 'अपुत्रा पुत्रवत्पत्नी'ति [565] वचनस्थवतिना प्रकरणानुरोधाच्छ्राद्धक्रियातुल्यताभिधानात्, पुत्रस्य च स्वपितृमातामहपार्वणयोरधिकाराद्, अपुत्रां प्रति च तत्पित्रादीनां भर्त्रादिरूपत्वात्, तन्मातामहादीनाञ्च पित्रादिरूपत्वात्, पुत्रवतामपुत्राणां वा स्वपित्रादीनां तीर्थश्राद्धादौ पुत्रवदेव विधवाया अप्यधिकारावगमात्; (2) अपुत्राणामेवेति विशेषवचनाभावाच्च ।

(3) "नन्वेनं पुत्रस्य मातामहत्वादिरूपेण तच्छ्राद्धेऽधिकाराद्, एतस्या अपि तत्त्वेनैव स्यान्न तु पितृत्वादिने"ति चेत्, (4) न, एकस्यापि सम्बन्धिभेदेन पत्निधिवत् सम्बन्धितावच्छेदकरूपभेदाद्, यं प्रति येन रूपेण सम्बन्धिता, तं प्रति तेनैवोद्देश्यत्वात् । (5) तावतापि वत्युक्तक्रियातुल्यतानिर्वाहात् । (6) ततश्च यथा पुत्रं प्रति पितृत्वादिनोद्देश्यानामप्येतां प्रति भर्तृत्वादिनोद्देश्यत्वं, तथा मातामहत्वादिनोद्देश्यानामपि पितृत्वादिना भविष्यति । (7) एतद्रूपोद्देश्यतार्थमेव हि 'स्वभर्तृप्रभृती'ति [608] वचः ।

(8) तस्माद् विधवाया भर्तृपार्वणं पितृपार्वणञ्चावश्यकम् । (9) आवश्यकत्वायैव 'अतन्द्रिते'त्याह ।

608.2. अनेकदेवत्यं–; L2 अनेकदैवत्यं । 609.5. तावतापि वत्युक्त—; P1 तावतापितृवत्युक्त—, P2 तावतापि(भ)वन्युक्त—।

यत्तु

610. **भर्तुः श्राद्धं तु या नारी मौढ्यात् पार्वणमाचरेत् ।**
न तेन तृप्यते भर्ता कृत्वा तु नरकं व्रजेद् ॥

(1) इति वचनं, तत्क्षयाहे एकोद्दिष्टपक्षप्रशंसार्थं, न तु सर्वथा पार्वणप्रतिषेधार्थमिति ।

(2) यस्यास्तु श्वशुरो जीवति सा भर्तृतत्पितामहप्रपितामहेभ्यः कुर्यात्; (3) श्वशुरतत्पित्रोर्जीवतोर्भर्तृतत्प्रपितामहवृद्धप्रपितामहेभ्यः ।

(4) "एवं स्वपित्रादिजीवनेऽपी"ति केचित् । (5) प्रामाणिकास्तु "स्वपितरि जीवति द्वारलोपात् तत्पार्वण लोप एवे"त्याहुः ।

(6) मृतश्वश्र्वादेस्तु श्वश्र्वादिपार्वणमपि कृताकृतम् । (7) एवञ्च नवदैवत्यम् । (8) केचिन् "मृतमातृकायाः स्वमात्रादिपार्वणमपीति द्वादशदैवत्यमा"हुः । (9) अपरे "स्वमातामहपार्वणेन पञ्चदशदैवत्यम्" । (10) अन्ये "स्वमातामह्यादिपार्वणेन सहाष्टादशदैवत्यम्" । (11) एतत्त्रयमपुत्रविषयमिति युक्तं भाति । (12) तत्राप्याद्याद्यजीवने द्वारलोपाल्लोप एव ।

(13) भर्तृमातामहादीनां तु श्राद्धप्रसङ्ग एव नास्ति । (14) श्वश्र्वादिमात्रादिपार्वणयोर करणे भर्तृपितृपार्वणयोरेव यथायोग्यं सपत्नीकानामिति वाच्यम् । (15) अन्येषां तु यथासम्भवमेकोद्दिष्टानीति । (16) अत्र तत्तद्देशीयशिष्टाचार एव संदेह सरिदुत्तारणतरिरित्यलम् ।

(17) जीवत्पितृके तु विशेषमाह मनुः—

611. **ध्रियमाणे तु पितरि पूर्वेषामेव निर्वपेद् ।** इति ।

मनु 3.220a-b

स्मृत्यन्तरे—

612. **वृद्धौ तीर्थे च संन्यस्ते ताते च पतिते सति ।**
येभ्य एव पिता दद्यात् तेभ्यो दद्यात् स्वयं सुतः ॥

(1) 'स्वयम्' इति स्वाधिकारिकतोच्यते ।

(2) भविष्यत्पुराणे तु जीवत्पितृकः पितामहप्रपितामहयोरेव दद्यादित्युक्तं–

613. **जीवमाने न देयं स्याद् यस्माद् भारतसत्तम ।**
तस्माज्जीवत्पिता कुर्याद् द्वाभ्यामेव न संशय ॥

610.7. नवदैवत्यम्; P1 P2 नवदेवत्यम् । 610.8. द्वादशदैवत्यम्; C1 द्वादशदेवत्यम्; 610.9. पञ्चदशदैवत्यम्; P3 C2 L1 L2 पञ्चदशदैवत्यताम्, C1 पञ्चदशदेवत्यतम् । 610.10. सहाष्टादशदैवत्यम्; P2 C1 C2 L1 सहाष्टादशदेवत्यम् ।

इति । विष्णुना त्वन्योऽपि विशेष उक्तः—

614. **पितरि जीवति यः श्राद्धं कुर्याद् येषां पिता कुर्यात्तेषां कुर्यात्। पितरि पितामहे च जीवति येषां पितामहः। पितरि पितामहे प्रपितामहे च जीवति नैव कुर्याद्। यस्य पिता प्रेतः स्यात् स पित्रे पिण्डं निधाय पितामहात् पराभ्यां द्वाभ्यां दद्याद् । यस्य पिता पितामहश्च प्रेतौ स्यातां स ताभ्यां पिण्डौ दत्त्वा पितामहपितामहाय दद्याद् । यस्य पितामहः प्रेतः स्यात् स तस्मै पिण्डं निधाय प्रपितामहात् पराभ्यां द्वाभ्यां दद्याद् । यस्य पिता प्रपितामहश्च प्रेतौ स्यातां स पित्रे पिण्डं निधाय प्रपितामहात् परं द्वाभ्यां दद्यात् ।**

मातामहानामप्येवं श्राद्धं कुर्याद् विचक्षणः ।
मन्त्रोहेन यथान्यायं शेषाणां मन्त्रवर्जितम् ॥ इति ।

वि० स्मृ० 75.1–7 (= 487)

(1) 'पितरि जीवती'त्यसाधारणनिर्देशः । (2) पितर्येव जीवतीत्यर्थः । (3) अत एव त्रिषु जीवत्सु 'नैव कुर्याद्' इत्युक्तम् । (4) एवमग्रेऽपि 'मातामहानामप्येवमि'ति । अत्र—

615. **यथा पितरि जीवति येषां पिता कुर्यात्तेषां पुत्रः कुर्यात्, तथा मातामहे जीवति येषां मातामहः । यथा पित्रादिषु त्रिषु जीवत्सु नैव कुर्यात्, तथा मातामहादिषु त्रिषु जीवत्सु नैव कुर्यादित्यादि सर्वमतिदेश्यम् ।**

इति व्याख्यातवान् शूलपाणिः । (1) कालादर्शकारोऽप्येवमाह ।

(2) "मातृजीवनेऽप्येवमेव न्यायसाम्यात् । (3) ततश्च जीवत्पितृकः पितृपित्रादिभ्यस्त्रिभ्यो दत्त्वा, यदि मृतमातृकस्तदा स्वमात्रादिभ्यो; मातृसद्भावे पितामह्यादिभ्यस्तिसृभ्यः, ततः स्वमातामहादिभ्यो; मातामहसद्भावे मातृपितामहादिभ्यस्त्रिभ्यो दद्यादिति फलितम् । (4) न च 'येभ्य एवे'त्यादिवचनविरोधः, (5) मातृमातामहशब्दयोः सम्बंधिशब्दत्वात् पुत्रसम्बद्धानामेव मात्रादीनां मातामहादीनाञ्च मातृमातामहादिशब्दवाच्यत्वेनैक्याद् याः पितुर्देवतास्ता एव पुत्रस्येति व्याख्यानसम्भवात् । (6) ततश्च जीवत्पितृकस्य स्वसम्बन्धिमातृमातामहादीनामेव श्राद्धम्" इति ।

---

614. पितामहात् पराभ्यां; P1 P2 C1 प्रपितामहात् पराभ्यां । 615. पित्रादिषु त्रिषु; P3 C1 K पित्रादिषु ।

(7) इदं त्वयुक्तं, "यच्छब्दवाच्येभ्यस्" "तच्छब्दवाच्येभ्य" इति व्याख्याने यत्तच्छब्दयोर्लक्षणाप्रसङ्गात्; (8) पितृपित्रादिविषये श्रुत्यर्थसम्भवेन युगपद्वृत्तिद्वयप्रसङ्गाच्च। (9) अपिच; अत्र यत्तच्छब्दाभ्यामेव वाक्ये निर्देशः सोऽपि च 'येभ्यः पिते'ति पितृप्रतियोगिकत्वेन, न तु स्वप्रतियोगिकत्वेन। (10) तथा च; क्व सम्बन्धिशब्दबलात् पुत्रसम्बद्धमात्रादिप्राप्तिः ? (11) विष्णुवचने तु 'एवम्' इत्यनेन मातामहश्राद्धे इतिकर्तव्यतामात्रमतिदिश्यत इति।

(12) तस्मात् पितृसम्बद्धा मात्रादयस्तत्सम्बद्धा एव च मातामहादयो जीवत्पितृकस्य तीर्थश्राद्धे देवताः न तु स्वसम्बद्धाः। (13) स्वमातुस्तु पितृपत्नीत्वेनैकोद्दिष्टं, स्वमातामहस्यापि पितृश्वशुरत्वेन। स्वपितुस्तीर्थे तदेकोद्दिष्ट एवाधिकारात् 'येभ्य एव पिता दद्याद्' इत्यस्याविशेषाच्च।

(14) अत्र "जीवत्पितृकोऽपि साग्निरेव तीर्थे श्राद्धं कुर्यान्नानग्निकः,

616. **न जीवत्पितृकः कुर्याच्छ्राद्धमग्निमृते द्विजः।**
येभ्य एव पिता दद्यात् तेभ्यः कुर्वीत साग्निक॥

इति सुमन्तुवचनात्। (1) 'साग्निकः' श्रौतेन स्मार्तेन वाग्निना। (2) तेन साग्नेरेव जीवत्पितृकस्य तीर्थश्राद्धेऽधिकार" इति मदनपारिजातकारादयः। (3) "साग्नीनामपि मैत्रायणीयसूत्रोपजीविनामेव न तु सर्वेषां, 'षडेते जीवतः पितु'रिति [554] पूर्वोक्तवचनस्य तत्परिशिष्ट एव श्रवणादि"ति स्मृतिरत्नावलीकारदिवोदासादयः।

(4) इदं मतद्वयमप्ययुक्तं,

617. **कुर्यादहरहः श्राद्धं प्रमीतपितृको द्विजः।**
साग्निको नाग्निको वापि तीर्थेष्वपि विशेषत॥

इति उशनोवचनविरोधात्। (1) सौमन्तवं तु अग्निरहितः पिण्डपितृयज्ञविधिना श्राद्धं न कुर्यात् साग्निकस्तु तद्विधिना पितृपित्रादिभ्यो दद्यादित्येवंपरम्। (2) 'षड् एत' इति वचनञ्च यद्यपि मैत्रायणीयपरिशिष्ट एव श्रुतं, तथापि उशनोवचनस्य 'वृद्धौ तीर्थे चे'त्यादि [612] प्रागुदाहृतवचसाञ्च साधारण्यात् सर्वशाखिसाधारणतयैव व्याख्येयम्। (3) किञ्च; मैत्रायणीयवाक्यस्य साग्नितच्छाखिमात्रविषयत्वे तद्वाक्योपात्तद्वितीयोद्वाहादौ का वार्त्तेति ?

616.2. After मदनपारिजातकारादयः; P2 कालादर्शेऽपि। 617.2. and 617.3. मैत्रायणीय—; P1 मैत्रावरुणीय—। 617.3. साग्नि—; correction in P1 L2 साग्निक—।

(4) अधिकारविचारोऽप्ययं प्रसङ्गादत्र कृतः। एवं जीवत्पितृकस्याधिकारे सिद्धे स यदि द्रव्यादिदानप्रेरितपुमन्तरवत् पितृनियुक्तस्तत्फलार्थमेव याति, तदा पितुरेवाधिकारित्वाद् 'यजमानस्य पितृपितामहप्रपितामहानामि'त्येवंप्रकारकवाक्यरचनयैकं श्राद्धं कृत्वा, स्वस्यापि श्राद्धहेतुप्रासङ्गिकतीर्थप्राप्तेर्वृत्तत्वात् 'पितुः पितृपितामहप्रपितामहानामि'त्येवंविधवाक्यरचनया श्राद्धानन्तरमपि कार्यम्, (5) देवताभेदात्, 'येभ्यः पिता दद्यात् तेभ्यो दद्याद्' [612] इत्यनेन पितृपितृत्वाद्युपाधिनैव देवतात्वबोधनात्। (6) पूर्वश्राद्धे च पुत्रातिरिक्तसेवकान्तरकर्तृक इव यजमानपितृत्वाद्युपाधिनैव देवतात्वात्। (7) स्वयंशब्देन स्वाधिकारिकतासूचनाद् भिन्नाधिकारिकयोस्तन्त्रेण प्रसङ्गेन वा अनिर्वाहाच्च।

(8) यदा तु पित्रानुज्ञातोऽननुज्ञातो वा स्वफलार्थमेव तीर्थं याति, तदा स्वयंशब्दाक्षिप्तस्वाधिकारिकतानिर्वाहार्थं "मम पितुः पितृपितामहप्रपितामहानामि'त्येवमादिवाक्यरचनया एकमेव श्राद्धं कार्यम्।

(9) अन्योऽपि विशेषः; यदा मृतमातृकः पित्रर्थं गयां याति, तदा प्रथमश्राद्धे यजमानपत्नीत्वेन स्वमात्रे एकोद्दिष्टं कार्यं, स्वपितुस्तस्या एकोद्दिष्ट एवाधिकारात्। (10) द्वितीयश्राद्धे तु पितृपत्नीत्वेनैकोद्दिष्टमेव मातुः कार्यं पूर्वोक्तन्यायादेव। (11) तदनन्तरं गयाप्रसङ्गगमने अधिकारप्रकरणे मातश्राद्धस्यापि कर्तव्यत्वाभिधानान्मात्रादिपार्वणमपि कार्यं,

618. **नान्दीमुखेऽष्टकाश्राद्धे गयायाञ्च मृतेऽहनि।**
पितामह्यादिभिः सार्धं मातुः श्राद्धं समाचरेत्॥

(1) इति शातातपवचनात् स्वस्य तत्पार्वण एव अधिकारात्।

(2) यदा तु प्रसङ्गात् गयां मृतमातृको याति, तदा प्रथमश्राद्धे पितृपत्नीत्वेन स्वमात्रे एकोद्दिष्टं कार्यम्। (3) द्वितीयं तु मात्रादित्वेन पार्वणमेवेति।

(4) कालादर्शादिमते तु गयायां जीवत्पितृकस्य श्राद्धेऽनधिकारात् पित्रर्थं गतस्य द्वितीयं श्राद्धं नास्ति। (5) प्रसङ्गगतस्य त्वाद्यं नास्तीत्येतदधिकार उक्तम्।

(6) गयातिरिक्ततीर्थे तु यथायोगं यजमानपत्नीत्वेन पितृपत्नीत्वेन वा एकोद्दिष्टमेव मातुः कार्यं, न तु पार्वणं, वचनाभावादिति विवेकः। (7) एवं पितृव्यादीनामपि यथायोगं गयायामन्यतीर्थे वा जीवत्पितृकेण यजमानभ्रातृत्वेन पितृभ्रातृत्वेन वा एकोद्दिष्टं कार्यम्। (8) पितृव्यत्वादिरूपेण तु श्राद्धं नास्त्येव, वचनाभावात्। (9) कालादर्शादिमते तु पितृभ्रातृत्वादिनापि नास्ति, जीवत्पितृकस्य गयाश्राद्धे स्वतोऽधिकाराभावात्।

617.4. एवंप्रकारकवाक्य—; P3K एवंप्रकारवाक्य—। 617.4. कार्यम्; P3 K कुर्यात्। 617.8. स्वयं; Cl L2 स्व—। 618.4. पित्रर्थं; P3 Cl K L1 L2 पित्रर्थ—।

(10) "नन्वेवमुपाधिभेदमात्रेण पुनः पुनः श्राद्धकरणे पित्रादेरेवाचार्यत्वादौ सति तदुपाधिनापि पुनः श्राद्धप्रसङ्गः"। (11) उच्यते; 'येभ्य एव पिता दद्याद्' [612] 'गयां प्रसङ्गतो गत्वेत्' [558] एवमादिवचनान्यथानुपपत्त्योपाधिभेदेन पुनः पुनः श्राद्धं न दोषाय। (12) आचार्यादिश्राद्धशास्त्रं तु पित्राद्यतिरिक्ताचार्यादिवन्तमधिकृत्य चरितार्थतया न पुनः श्राद्धं प्रयोजयति।

(13) किञ्च; प्रत्यासन्नासाधारणपितृत्वादिरूपोपाधिप्रयुक्ते प्रथमं श्राद्धे कृते, 'प्रत्यासन्नसाधारणाचार्यत्वादिप्रयुक्तपुनःश्राद्धासम्भवः; (14) निगदे निगदत्वप्रयुक्तोच्चैस्त्वे कृते यजुष्ट्वप्रयुक्तोपांशुत्वासम्भववत्, (15) उपांशुत्ववचनस्येव यजुरन्तरे आचार्यादिश्राद्धवचनस्य केवलाचार्यान्तरे चारितार्थ्याच्चेत्यलं बहुना!

(16) एवं जीवत्पितृकोऽपि पितृदेवताभ्य एव तीर्थे श्राद्धं कुर्यादिति सिद्धम्।

(17) यदा तु मृतपितृकोऽपि जीवन्मातृकस्तदा मातृपार्वणलोप एव। (18) किन्तु यथायोग्यं 'सपत्नीकानामि'ति पित्रादिविशेषणं कार्यम्। (19) एवं मातामहजीवनेऽपि तत्पार्वणलोपः। (20) मातामहीजीवनेऽप्येवमेव। (21) किन्तु पूर्ववद् विशेषणं कार्यम्। तदुक्तं—

619. **पितृवर्गे मातृवर्गे तथा मातामहस्य च।**
जीवेच्चेद् यदि वर्गाद् यस्तद्वर्गं तु परित्यजेत्॥

(1) अत्र 'पितृवर्गे' इत्येतद् अमावास्यादिविषयम्, तीर्थे वचनाज्जीवत्पितृकस्यापि पितृपित्रादिपार्वणस्योक्तत्वात्। (2) एवं 'मातृवर्गे'ऽपि।

(3) एवं यस्य यस्य या या देवता उक्तास्ताभ्यः श्राद्धं पिण्डदानञ्च पृथक् पृथक् कृत्वा सामान्यपिण्डो देयः; यदाह देवलः—

620. **ततः पिण्डमुपादाय संस्कृतासंस्कृतस्य च।**
ज्ञातिवर्गस्य कृत्स्नस्य सामान्यमिति निर्वपेत्॥

(1) 'इती'ति वक्ष्यमाणमन्त्रेण। स च मन्त्रः—

621. **पितृवंशे मृता ये च मातृवंशे च ये मृताः।**
गुरुश्वशुरबन्धूनां ये चान्ये बान्धवा मृताः॥
ये मे कुले लुप्तपिण्डाः पुत्रदारविवर्जिताः।
क्रियालोपगताश्चैव जात्यन्धाः पङ्गवस्तथा॥
विरूपा आमगर्भाश्च ज्ञाताज्ञाताः कुले मम।
तेषां पिण्डो मया दत्तो ह्यक्षय्यमुपतिष्ठताम्॥ ग० पु० 1.85.18-20

618.12—आचार्यादिवन्तम्; P1 (+correction in P2) आचार्यादिवचनम्, P3K आचार्यादिजीवन्तम्। 618.14. उच्चैस्त्वे; P3K उच्चैष्ट्वे। 618.14.-सम्भववत्; P2 -संभवात्। 620. च; P3 C2 K वा। 621. अक्षय्यम्; P3 Cl Cl K Ll अक्षय्य।

(1) इति। अत्र श्लोकत्रयस्यापि एकमन्त्रता, तावतैव वाक्यार्थपरिसमाप्तेः; (2) तथैव च जैमिनिमुनिनैकमन्त्रत्वस्य

622. **अर्थैकत्वादेकं वाक्यं, साकांक्षञ्चेद् विभागे स्याद् ।**

मी० सू० 2.1.14.46

इत्यत्रोक्तत्वात्; (1) 'पिण्डमुपादाये'ति देवलोक्तावेकवचनाच्च ।

तथा—

623. **आ ब्रह्मणो ये पितृवंशजाता**
मातुस्तथा वंशभवा मदीयाः ।
कुलद्वये ये मम दासभूता
भृत्यास्तथैवाश्रितसेवकाश्च ॥
मित्राणि सख्यः पशवश्च वृक्षाः
स्पृष्टाश्च दृष्टाश्च कृतोपकाराः ।
जन्मान्तरे ये मम सङ्गताश्च
तेभ्यः स्वधापिण्डमहं ददामि ॥

(1) इति श्लोकाभ्यां पिण्डान्तरं देयम् । (2) अत्रापि पूर्ववदेकमन्त्रता ।

(3) एवं पिण्डदानं कृत्वा ब्राह्मणानुव्रजनान्तं श्राद्धं स्वस्वसूत्रोक्तविधिना समापयेत् ।

(4) यस्य तु एतावन्तं श्राद्धकलापं प्रत्येकञ्च पिण्डदानं कर्तुमशक्तिः रोगादिना, तावतः कालस्य वाऽभावः स संक्षेपश्राद्धं कुर्यात् । (5) तच्चैवं : 'अशक्त्या संक्षेपश्राद्धमहं करिष्य' इति सङ्कल्प्य

624. **ओं पिता पितामहश्चैव तथैव प्रपितामहः ।**
माता पितामही चैव तथैव प्रपितामही ॥
मातामहस्तत्पिता च प्रमाताभहकादयः ।
तेषां पिण्डो मया दत्तो ह्यक्षय्यमुपतिष्ठताम् ॥

गरु० पु० 1.84.45c–46, 48

(1) इति मन्त्रेणैकं पिण्डं दद्यादिति ।

इति तीर्थश्राद्धे सम्प्रदाननिर्णयः ।

इति श्रीभट्टरामेश्वरसूरिसूनुनारायणभट्टविरचिते
तीर्थसेतौ सामान्यप्रघट्टके तीर्थश्राद्धप्रकरणम् ।

624. अक्षय्यम्; P3 C1 C2 K L1 अक्षय्य । 624.1. तीर्थसेतौ; P1 त्रिस्थलीसेतौ । 624.1. after प्रकरणम्; P2 समाप्तम् ।

अथ तीर्थेऽस्थिप्रक्षेपविधिः

(2) तत्र तीर्थमात्रेऽस्थिक्षेपे विधिपूर्वकं फलमुक्तं ब्रह्माण्डपुराणे—

625. **स्नात्वा ततः पञ्चगवेन सिक्त्वा हिरण्यमध्वाज्यतिलेन योज्य ।**
ततस्तु मृत्पिण्डपुटे निधाय पश्येद् दिशं प्रेतगणोपगूढाम् ॥
'नमोऽस्तु धर्माय' वदन् प्रविश्य तीर्थं 'स मे प्रीत' इति क्षिपेच्च ।
स्नात्वा तथोत्तीर्य दिवाकरञ्च दृष्ट्वा प्रदद्यादथ दक्षिणां तु ॥
एवं कृते प्रेतपुरे स्थितस्य स्वर्गे गतिः स्यात्तु महेन्द्रतुल्या ।

(1) पञ्चगवं पञ्चगव्यम् ।

(2) अत्र यद्यप्यविशेषतः स्वर्गप्राप्तिरुक्ता तथापि तीर्थतारतम्यात् तत्र वैजात्यं ज्ञेयम् । (3) गङ्गायां तु विशेषः; ब्रह्माण्डे—

626. **यस्मिन्काले नृणामस्थि गङ्गायां क्षिप्यते नरैः ।**
तं कालमादितः कृत्वा स्वर्गलोके भवेत् स्थितिः ॥

(1) अत्रोत्तरावधेरनुक्तेः कल्पान्त एवावधिर्योग्यत्वात् । (2) तथा ब्रह्मलोकावाप्तिरपि श्रुता;
यमः—
627. **गङ्गातोयेषु यस्यास्थि क्षिप्यते शुभकर्मणः ।**
न तस्य पुनरावृत्तिर्ब्रह्मलोकात् सनातनात् ॥
यम 90

तथा—
628. **यावदस्थि मनुष्याणां गङ्गातोयेषु तिष्ठति ।**
तावद् वर्षसहस्राणि ब्रह्मलोके महीयते ॥
यम 91

इत्यादि । (1) ब्रह्मलोकाप्तिश्च प्रयागादिक्षेत्रविशेषात् ज्ञेया, सामान्यतः स्वर्गावाप्तेरुक्तत्वात् ।

(2) तत्र कालविशेषः —

624.1. (chapter heading) —प्रक्षेप—; P1—संक्षेप— । 627. क्षिप्यते; C1 C2 प्लवते । 628.2. काल—; P2 L1 L2 काले ।

629. **अस्तंगते गुरौ शुक्रे तथा मासे मलिम्लुचे ।**
गङ्गायामस्थिनिक्षेपं न कुर्यादिति गौतमः ॥

तथा—

630. **अस्थिक्षेपं गयाश्राद्धं श्राद्धञ्चापरपक्षिकम् ।**
प्रथमेऽब्दे न कुर्वीत यदि न स्यात् सपिण्डनम् ॥

(1) 'कृतेऽपि तु सपिण्डन' इति क्वचित्पाठः ।

तथा—

631. **अस्थिक्षेपं गयाश्राद्धं श्राद्धञ्चापरपक्षिकम् ।**
प्रथमेऽब्देऽपि कुर्वीत कृतं यस्योर्ध्वदेहिकम् ।

(1) 'यदि स्याद् भक्तिमान् सुत' इति चतुर्थपादं केचित् पठन्ति ।

(2) दशाहाभ्यन्तरे तु न दोषः,

632. **दशाहाभ्यन्तरे यस्य गङ्गातोयेऽस्थि मज्जति ।**
गङ्गायां मरणं यादृक् तादृक् फलमवाप्नुयाद् ॥

इति वचनात् ।

(1) तथान्योऽपि विशेषः पुराणे—

633. **मातुः कुलं पितृकुलं वर्जयित्वा नराधमः ।**
अस्थीन्यन्यकुलोत्थानि नीत्वा चान्द्रायणञ्चरेत् ॥

(1) इदञ्च द्रव्यादिलोभविषयम् । तथा—

634. **अस्थीनि मातापितृवंशजानि नयन्ति गङ्गामपि ये कदाचित् ।**
सद्बान्धवस्यापि दयाभिभूतास्तेषाञ्च तीर्थानि फलप्रदानि ॥

---

631. यस्योर्ध्वदेहिकम्; C2 यस्यौर्ध्वदेहिकम् ।

अथ प्रकारः

635. शौनकोऽहं प्रवक्ष्यामि अस्थिशुद्धिविधिं क्रमात् ।
ग्रामाद् बहिस्ततो गत्वा स्नानं कुर्यात् सचैलकम् ॥
प्रोक्षयेत् पञ्चगव्येन तत्तन्मन्त्रैर्विचक्षणः ।

(1) यत्रास्थीनि निखातानि सन्ति तां भूमिं प्रोक्षयेददित्यर्थः । (2) 'तत्तन्मन्त्रैः' 'आ प्ययस्वे'त्यादिपयोदध्यादिप्रकाशकैः पञ्चगव्यमन्त्रैः ।

636. उपसर्पादिभिर्मन्त्रैः प्रार्थनं खननं तथा ।
मृत्तिकोद्धरणश्चास्थ्नां ग्रहणञ्च यथाक्रमम् ॥

(1) 'उप सर्पे'ति चतसृणां शंखः पितरस्त्रिष्टुप् । (2) प्रथमाया भूप्रार्थने, द्वितीयायाः खनने, तृतीयाया मृत्तिकोद्धरणे, चतुर्थ्या अस्थिग्रहणे विनियोगः ।
(3) एवमस्थीनि गृहीत्वा

637. ततो जलाशयं गत्वा स्नानं कुर्याद् यथाविधि ।
अस्थिशुद्धि ततः कुर्याद् 'एतो न्विन्द्रे'ति मन्त्रतः ॥
स्पृष्ट्वा स्पृष्ट्वा तथा स्नानं पञ्चगव्येन शुध्यति ।
दशस्नानानि कुर्वीत तत्तन्मन्त्रैर्विचक्षणः ॥
गोमूत्रं गोमयं क्षीरं दधि सर्पिः कुशोदकम् ।
भस्ममृन्मध्वबादीनि मन्त्रस्नानानि वै दश ॥
कुशैः सम्मार्जयेदस्थीन्य् 'अतो देवे'ति मन्त्रतः ।
'एतो न्विन्द्रं' 'शुची वे'ति 'न तमंह' ति त्वथ ॥
पावमानी 'ममाग्ने' च रुद्रसूक्तं यथाक्रमम् ।
एतत् सूक्तं पठेद् विद्वान् शुचिर्भवति नान्यथा ॥
हेमश्राद्धं ततः कुर्यात् पितॄनुद्दिश्य यत्नतः ।
पिण्डदानं प्रकुर्वीत ततश्च तिलतर्पणम् ॥
अजिनं कम्बला दर्भा गोकेशाः शाणमेव च ।
भूर्जपत्रं ताडपत्रं सप्तधा वेष्टनं स्मृतम् ॥

---

637. —मध्वबादीनि; correction in P1 —मधुवारीनि ।

(1) क्वचित्तु 'गोकेशा भूर्जपत्रकम् । ताडपत्रञ्च नेत्रञ्चे-॥ त्यस्थ्नां वेष्टन-सप्तकमि'ति पाठः ।

हेमञ्च मौक्तिकं रूप्यं प्रवालं नीलकं तथा ।
निक्षिपेदस्थिमध्ये तु शुद्धिर्भवति नान्यथा ॥
ततो होमं प्रकुर्वीत तिलाज्येन विचक्षणः ।
'उदीरते'ति सूक्तेन हुनेदष्टोत्तरं शतम् ॥
ततो गत्वा सुतीर्थेषु स्पर्शदोषो न विद्यते ।
मूत्रं पुरीषाचमनं कुर्याद् नास्थीनि धारयन् ॥

काशीखण्डे—

638. **धनञ्जयोऽपि धर्मात्मा मातृभक्तिपरायणः ।**
आदायास्थीन्यथो मातुर्गङ्गामार्गस्थितोऽभवत् ॥
पञ्चगव्येन संस्नाप्य ततः पञ्चामृतेन वै ।
यक्षकर्दमलेपेन लिप्त्वा पुष्पैः प्रपूज्य च ॥
आवेष्टच नेत्रवस्त्रेण ततः पट्टाम्बरेण च ।
ततः सुरसवस्त्रेण ततो माञ्जिष्ठवाससा ॥

(1) सुरसवस्त्रं श्वेतं चीनांशुकम् ।

नेपालकम्बलेनाथ मृदा चाथ विशुद्धया ।
ताम्रसम्पुटके कृत्वा मातुरङ्गान्यहो वणिक् ॥
अस्पृष्टहीनजातिः स शुचिष्मान् स्थण्डिलेशयः ।

का०ख०, 1.30.42-46b.

व्यासः—

639. **पट्टवस्त्रञ्च कौशेयं माञ्जिष्ठं श्वेतवस्त्रकम् ।**
कम्बलं शाणपट्टौ च अजिनञ्च तथोत्तरम् ॥

(1) एतेषाञ्च वेष्टनसाधनानां वेष्टनक्रमाणाञ्च विकल्पः ।

---

637. हेमं; P2 हैमं । 637. शुद्धिर्; P2 C1 शुचिर् । 638. मृदा चाथ; P3 मृदा वाथ

अथास्य प्रयोगपद्धतिः

(639.2) यत्रास्थीनि निखातानि सन्ति तत्र गत्वा सचैलं स्नात्वास्थिनिखननभूमिम् 'आ प्यायस्वे'ति पयसा, 'दधिक्राव्ण' इति दध्ना, गायत्र्या गोमूत्रेण, 'गन्धद्वाराम्' इति गोमयेन, 'घृतं मिमिक्ष' इति घृतेन प्रोक्ष्य तत ('उप सर्पे'ति चतसृणां शंखः पितरस्त्रिष्टुप्, आद्याया भूप्रार्थने, द्वितीयायाः खनने, तृतीयाया मृत्तिकोद्धरणे, चतुर्थ्या अस्थिग्रहणे विनियोगः) इत्युक्त्वा एताभिः क्रमेण एतानि कृत्वा जलाशयेऽस्थिसहितः स्नात्वा पञ्चगव्येनास्थीन्य् 'एतो न्विन्द्रम्' इति सूक्तेन प्रक्षाल्य शुद्धोदकेन स्नापयेत् । (3) ततः सास्थिर्दशस्नानानि कुर्यात्; गायत्र्या गोमूत्रेण, 'गन्धद्वाराम्' इति गोमयेन, 'आ प्यायस्वे' ति पयसा, 'दधिक्राव्ण' इति दध्ना, 'घृतं मिमिक्ष' इति घृतेन, 'आपो हि ष्ठे'ति कुशोदकेन 'मा नस्तोक' इति भस्मना, 'बळित्था पर्वतानाम्' इत्यादिगृह्यपरिशिष्टोक्तमन्त्रैर्, 'अश्वक्रान्ते रथक्रान्त' इत्यादिभिर्वा मृदा, 'मधु वाते' ति मधुना, 'आपो हि ष्ठे'ति शुद्धोदकेन।(4) एवं दशस्नानानि विधाय कुशैरस्थ्नां मार्जनं कुर्यादेभिर्मन्त्रैः —'एतो न्विन्द्रम्' इति सूक्तं, 'शुची वो हव्ये' ति सूक्तं, 'न तमंह' इति सूक्तं, 'इति वा इति मे मन' इति सूक्तं, 'यद् अन्ति यच्च दूरक' इत्याद्याः पावमान्यः, 'ममाग्ने वर्च' इति ऋक्, रुद्रसूक्तञ्च ।

(5) ततो हिरण्यश्राद्धं कृतसपिण्डीकरणस्य त्रिदैवत्यमकृतसपिण्डीकरणस्यैकोद्दिष्टं कुर्यात् । (6) इदञ्च यदीयान्यस्थीनि तद्देवत्यं श्राद्धम् ।

(7) तदनन्तरं तथैव सक्तुपिण्डान् दत्त्वा तथैव तिलतर्पणञ्च कृत्वा यक्षकर्दमादिना लिप्त्वा पुष्पैः प्रपूज्य अजिनादिभिः पूर्वोक्तपक्षचतुष्टयमध्ये केनचित् पक्षेण वेष्टयित्वा सुवर्णमौक्तिकरूप्यप्रवालनीलमणीन् अस्थिषु प्रक्षिपेत् । (8) तत 'उदीरताम्' इति सूक्तेनाष्टोत्तरं शतं तिलाज्यं जुहुयात् । (9) 'उदीरतां' शंखः पितरस्त्रिष्टुप् ।

(10) ततस्ताम्रसम्पुटेऽस्थीनि निधायाकृतचाण्डालपतितादिस्पर्शः शुचिस्तीर्थं गच्छेत् । (11) ततस्तीर्थे सास्थि स्नात्वा पलाशपत्रपुटे स्थापयित्वा

639.2. तत; P3 C2 omitted। 639.2. भूप्रार्थने; L2 भूमिप्रार्थने 639.2. प्रक्षाल्य; P3 L1 L2 प्रक्षाल्य प्रक्षाल्य । 639.4. रुद्रसूक्तञ्च; P1 P2 रुद्रसूक्तम् । 639.6 तद्देवत्यं; L2 तद्दैवत्यं । 639.10. —चाण्डाल—; P3 K —चण्डाल— 1

" अमुकगोत्रस्यामुकशर्मणोऽपुनरावृत्तिकब्रह्मलोकावाप्तयेऽमुकतीर्थेऽस्थिप्रक्षेपमहं करिष्य" इति सङ्कल्प्यास्थीनि पञ्चगव्येन प्रक्षाल्य हिरण्यशकलमधुघृततिल-मिश्रितानि कृत्वा मृत्पिण्डे निधाय दक्षिणतोऽवेक्षमाणो नाभिमात्रे जले स्थित्वा 'नमोऽस्तु धर्मराजाय स मे प्रीतोऽस्त्वि'ति मन्त्रेण तीर्थे प्रक्षिप्य स्नात्वा जलाद् बहिरागत्य सूर्यं दृष्ट्वा नत्वा च हरिं स्मृत्वा "अमुकगोत्रस्यामुकशर्मणो ब्रह्मलोका-वाप्तये कृतस्यास्थिप्रक्षेपस्य साद्गुण्यायेदं रजतं चन्द्रदैवत्यं ब्राह्मणाय सम्प्रददे" इति पितृकृत्यत्वात् रजतं यथाशक्ति दद्यात् । (639.12) इदञ्च सर्वं दक्षिणावर्जम् अपसव्यम् ।

(13) एतच्च तीर्थमात्रे कार्यम् । (14) गङ्गायां विशेषतः पूर्वोदाहृत-वचनेभ्यः । (15) तत्रापि प्रयागे विशेषत इति शिष्टाः । (16) एवं कृते फलं प्रागेवोक्तम् ।

(17) अत्र "एतत् कृत्वा सर्वस्तीर्थविधिः कार्य" इति दिवोदासादयः । (18) अपरे तु "नित्यानित्यसंयोगविरोधात्त्यास्थिक्षेपस्य तीर्थकृत्यान्तःपाता-भावाच्छ्राद्धादौ च विलम्बनिषेधादनावश्यकेनैतेन स्नानादिनेव विलम्बानभ्य-नुज्ञानाद्, अनन्तरमेव कर्तव्यत्वे वचनाभावाद् 'आगन्तूनामन्ते निवेश' इति न्यायाच्च स्नानादितीर्थकृत्यं निर्वर्त्यानन्तरमस्थिप्रक्षेपः कार्य" इति मेनिरे । (19) न्यायविदस्तु "अस्थिप्रक्षेपजन्यफलोद्देशेन तीर्थं गतेनादौ स एव कार्यः, उद्देश्यकृत श्राद्धादिविलम्बस्य तच्छास्त्रेणाभ्यनुज्ञातत्वात्, तीर्थकृत्यस्य नान्तरीय-कत्वेनोद्देश्ये विलम्बकारित्वायोगाच्च । (20) अत एव तीर्थनिमित्तकं सविधिस्नानमपि पश्चादेव । (21) यस्तु तीर्थफलोद्देशेन गच्छन्ननुषङ्गादस्थीनि नयति स सकलतीर्थकृत्यानन्तरं तानि क्षिपेद्" इत्याहुः । (22) एवं सत्यत्र शिष्टा एव प्रमाणम् ।

इति श्रीतीर्थसेतौ सामान्यप्रद्यट्टकेऽस्थिक्षेपणविधिः ।

639.15. विशेषत; P1 P3 C1 C2 K L1 विशेष । 639.18 नित्यानित्यसंयोग—; P2 C1 L2 नित्यसंयोग— । 639.19. तीर्थं गतेनादौ; C2 L1 तीर्थंगतेनादौ ।

अथ प्रकीर्णकास्तीर्थधर्माः

देवलः

640\. तर्पणं पितृदेवानां श्राद्धदानं सदक्षिणम् ।
तीर्थे तीर्थे च गोदानं नियतः प्राकृतो विधिः ॥
विशिष्टख्यातलिङ्गेषु वृषदानं विधीयते ।
स्नानं विलेपनं पूजां देवतानां समाचरेत् ॥
ब्राह्मणानां भूमिदानं देवपूजाकराय वा ।
सर्वत्र देवयात्रायां विधिरेष प्रवर्तते ॥

तथा—

641\. देवानां दर्शनं पुण्यं दर्शनात् स्पर्शनं वरम् ।
स्पर्शनादर्चनं श्रेष्ठं घृतस्नानमतः परम् ॥
अष्टकृत्वो मन्त्रजपैः सुप्रभूतसुगन्धिभिः ।
प्राहुर्गङ्गाजलैः स्नानं घृतस्नानसमं बुधाः ॥

(1) घृतग्रहणं पञ्चामृतोपलक्षणम् । (2) अर्चने च तत्तद्देवेष्वनिषिद्धानि गन्धपुष्पादीनि ग्राह्याणि ।

(3) भानौ तु विशेषः —

642\. अर्घद्रव्यविशेषेण गङ्गातोयेन यः सकृत् ।
मागधप्रस्थमात्रेण ताम्रपात्रस्थितेन च ॥
भानवेऽर्घं प्रदद्यात्तु स्वकीयपितृभिः सह ।
पुत्रपौत्रैश्च संयुक्तः स्वर्गलोके महीयते ॥

का० ख० 27.96-97

(1) अर्घश्चाष्टाङ्गः स्कान्दे—

643\. आपः क्षीरं कुशाग्राणि घृतं मधु गवां दधि ।
रक्तानि करवीराणि रक्तचन्दनमित्यपि ।
अष्टाङ्गोऽर्घोऽयमुद्दिष्टस्त्वतीव रवितोषणः ॥

का० ख० 27.98-99b

642\. अर्घं—; P2 K L1 अर्घ्यं— । 642.1 अर्घश; C2 L2 अर्घ्यंश ।
643\. ऽर्घो; K ऽर्घ्यो ।

(1) प्रदक्षिणायां तु विशेषः—

644. **एकां चण्ड्यां रवेः सप्त तिस्रो दद्याद् विनायके ।**
चतस्रो विष्णवे देयाः शिवस्यार्धप्रदक्षिणम् ॥

तथा—

645. **शिवं प्रदक्षिणं कुर्वन् सोमसूत्रं न लंघयेत् ।**

(1) सोमसूत्रादिपरिमाणं विश्वेश्वरादौ दोषाभावश्च काशीप्रकरणे वक्ष्यामः ।

(2) नमस्कारेऽपि विशेषः—

646. **अग्रे पृष्ठे वामभागे समीपे गर्भमन्दिरे ।**
जपहोमनमस्कारान्न कुर्याद् देवतालये ॥
अग्रे मृत्युमवाप्नोति पृष्ठे त्वपचयः स्मृतः ।
वामभागे भवेन्नाशो दक्षिणे सर्वकामदः ॥

(1) शिवे त्वग्रेऽपि कार्यः—

647. **पशोः पशुपतेरग्रे दण्डवत् पततो भुवि ।**
पतन्ति पातकाः सर्वे नोत्तिष्ठन्ति तदा सहे- ॥ ति ।

अन्यच्च देवीपुराणे—

648. **देवमाल्यापनयनं देवागारसमूहनम् ।**
स्नापनं सर्वदेवानां गोप्रदानफलं स्मृतम् ॥

(1) समूहनं सम्मार्जनादि पतितस्योत्थापनञ्च ।

तथा पाद्मे—

649. **द्रव्यमन्नं फलं तोयं शिवस्वं न स्पृशेत् क्वचित् ।**
लङ्घयेन्नैव निर्माल्यं कूपे सर्वं विनिक्षिपेत् ॥
मक्षिकापादमात्रं यः शिवस्वमुपजीवति ।
लोभान्मोहात् स पच्यते कल्पान्ते नरके नरः ॥

ब्राह्मे तु—

650. ब्रह्माङ्गलग्नं विप्रेभ्यो वैष्णवञ्च प्रदापयेत् ।
रुद्राङ्गलग्नमग्नौ च दहेत् सर्वञ्च तत्क्षणात् ॥
अन्येभ्यस्त्वथ देवेभ्यो यत् तद् दीनेषु निक्षिपेत् ।
विप्रेभ्यस्त्वथ तद्देयं मातृभ्यो यन्निवेदितम् ॥
वाडवेभ्यस्तु तद्देयं गणेशादिनिवेदितम् ।

(1) विश्वेश्वरादौ त्वपवादं वक्ष्यामः ।

(2) तीर्थे प्रतिग्रहादिनिवृत्तिश्च कार्या । पाद्मे —

651. जीवनार्थं हतं तीर्थं जीवनार्थं हतं व्रतम् ।
असत्या च तथा वाणी तथा पैशुन्यवादिनी ॥
न तीर्थे प्रतिगृह्णीयात् प्राणैः कण्ठगतैरपि ।
अपि कामातुरो जन्तुरेकां रक्षति मातरम् ॥
तीर्थे प्रतिग्रहो यस्तु तीर्थविक्रय एव सः ।
विक्रीतायां तु गङ्गायां विक्रीतः स्याज्जनार्दनः ॥
जनार्दने च विक्रीते विक्रीतं भुवनत्रयम् ॥ इति ।

652. यस्तु लौल्याद् द्विजः क्षेत्रे प्रतिग्रहरुचिर्भवेत् ।
नैव तस्य परो लोको नायं लोको दुरात्मनः ॥
महादानानि ये विप्रा गृह्णन्ति ज्ञानदुर्बलाः ।
वृक्षास्ते द्विजरूपेण जायन्ते ब्रह्मराक्षसाः ॥
न वेदबलमाश्रित्य प्रतिग्रहरुचिर्भवेत् ।
अज्ञानाद् वा प्रमादाद्वा दह्यते कर्म नेतरत् ॥
स्थितो वै नृपतेर्द्वारि न कुर्याद् वेदविक्रयम् ।
हत्वा गावं परं मांसं भक्षयीत द्विजाधमः ॥
अथ चेत् प्रतिगृह्णाति ब्राह्मणो वृत्तिकर्षितः ।
दशांशमर्जितं दद्यादेवं तन्न प्रहीयते ॥

प्र० ख० 1.28.30c–31b, 43-44, 47e–48b, 31c-f

---

650. दीनेषु; P1 P3 दानेषु ।

कौर्मे 'प्रतिगृह्णीयाद्' इत्युपक्रम्य

653. **स्वकार्येऽप्यन्यकार्ये वा देवताभ्यर्चनेऽपि वा ।**
निःफलं तस्य तत्तीर्थं यावत्तत्फलमश्नुते ॥
अतस्तीर्थे न गृह्णीयात् पुण्येष्वायतनेषु च ।
निमित्तेषु च सर्वेषु अप्रमत्तो द्विजो भवेत् ॥
कू० पु० 1.34.43-44

(1) मात्स्येऽपीदं वचनद्वयं पठितम् ।

(2) अत्र "यावत् प्रतिगृहीतं धनमुपभुंक्ते तीर्थकृतप्रतिग्रहस्य पुंसो यावत् तीर्थोपार्जितधने स्वत्वानुवृत्तिस्, तावत् तीर्थदानादिषु कोटिगुणत्वादिलक्षणं फलं न जनयति । (3) तद्धनत्यागात्तु स्वं फलं जनयत्येवे"ति कल्पतरौ । (4) "इदमपि प्रभुनिर्बन्धादिनाऽकामकृते; कामकृते तु तीर्थविक्रयान्नैव फलमि"ति कश्चित् ।

पाद्मे सृष्टिखण्डे—

654. **यदन्यत्र कृतं पापं तीर्थे तद्याति लाघवम् ।**
न तीर्थकृतमन्यत्र क्वचित् पापं व्यपोहति ॥
(प्र० ख० 1.28.51)

भारते—

655. **कामं क्रोधं च लोभं च यो जित्वा तीर्थमावसेत् ।**
न तेन किञ्चिन्न प्राप्तं तीर्थाभिगमनाद् भवेत् ॥ (≈172)

पाद्मे उत्तरखण्डे—

656. **न तीर्थे पातकं कुर्यात् त्यजेत्तीर्थोपजीवनम् ।**
तीर्थे प्रतिग्रहस्त्याज्यस्त्याज्यो धर्मस्य विक्रयः ॥
दुर्जरं पातकं तीर्थे दुर्जरश्च प्रतिग्रहः ।
तीर्थे तु दुर्जरं सर्वं नरके याति तद्विधः ॥
(आदि० ख० 31.70-71)

गारुडे—

657. **संन्यासिनं तीर्थगतं रक्षन्ति धनदेवताः ।**
मम दूता विशेषेण न याम्यास्तस्य चान्तिकाः ॥

653. निःफलं; C2 K L1 निष्फलं । 653.3. स्वं; P1 P3 स्व— । 653.4 सृष्टिखण्डे; P2 पातालखण्डे ।

सेवितेऽपि सदा तीर्थे अन्यत्र म्रियते यदि ।
शुभे देशे कुले धीमान् स भवेद् वेदविद् द्विजः ॥
गं० पु० 2.26.17, 19

तथा—

658. गृहे तु यत्कृतं पापं तीर्थस्नानैर्विशुध्यति ।
तत्र दानानि दत्त्वा च अक्षयाणि सदा खग ॥
कुरुते तत्र पापं चेद् वज्रलेपसमं हि तत् ।
क्लिश्येत् स नात्र संदेहो यावच्चन्द्रार्कतारकम् ॥
गं० पु० 2.26.25-26

तथा—

659. न काष्ठे विद्यते देवो न शिलायां कदाचन ।
भावे हि विद्यते देवस्तस्माद् भावं समाश्रयेत् ॥
गं० पु० 2.28.11

नारदीये—

660. पुण्यक्षेत्राभिगमनं पुण्यतीर्थनिषेवणम् ।
यज्ञो वा विविधो ब्रह्मंस्त्यक्ताचारं न रक्षति ॥

देवलः—

661. न नदीषु नदीं ब्रूयात् पर्वतेषु च पर्वतम् ।
नान्यत् प्रशंसेत् तत्रस्थस्तीर्थेष्वायतनेषु च ॥

तथा—

662. यत्र स्थानेषु यत् तीर्थं नदी पुण्यतमा च या ।
तां ध्यायेन्मनसा वापि अन्यत्रेच्छाविचिन्तनम् ।।

(1) इदं स्नानविषयम् । (2) इदं द्वयमपि गङ्गातिरिक्तविषयं; यथोक्तं स्कान्दे—

663. स्नानकालेऽन्यतीर्थेषु जप्यते जाह्नवी जनैः ।
विना विष्णुपदीं क्वान्यत् समर्थमघशोधने ॥

---

657. तथा; P1 P2 omitted. 658. खग; L2 सुखी; 659. समाश्रयेत्; P2 हि कारणम् (corrected to समाश्रयेत्) । 663. अघशोधने; P1 L1 L2 अघशोधनं; P2 अवशोधनं ।

ब्राह्मेऽपि—

664. अन्यतीर्थेषु गङ्गायाः स्मरणं कार्यते नृभिः ।
तस्माद् गङ्गासमं तीर्थं न हि ब्रह्माण्डगोलक ॥ इति ॥

(1) कृतश्च तीर्थयात्रादि विष्णावर्पणीयम् । तदुक्तं ब्राह्मे—

665. यानि यानि च तीर्थानि दानव्रततपांसि च ।
तानि सर्वाणि सिध्यन्ति विष्णोः पादार्पणेन वै ॥
नार्पयन्ति हरौ लोके पुण्यानि विविधानि च ।
विफलानि भवन्तीह श्रम एव फलं भवेत् ॥

देवलः—

666. अरण्यं देवतास्थानं तीर्थान्यायतनानि च ।
तस्मात् तेषु वसन् लोकान् याति नाकं दिवौकसाम् ॥

तथा—

667. श्रौतस्मार्तक्रियाः कर्तुं यो न शक्नोति मानवः ।
तेन तीर्थानि सेव्यानि व्रतानि च तपांसि च ॥

(1) यात्रार्थगतस्य तु साधारण्येन तीर्थे दिनत्रयं वासः,

668. तीर्थमधिगम्य व्रतोपवासनियमयुक्तस्त्र्यहम्
अवगाहमानस्त्रिरात्रमुषित्वा सर्वपापेभ्यो मुच्यत । (≈225)

इति देवलवचनात् । (1) यत्र चाधिकता विशेषत उक्ता सापि ग्राह्या ।

(2) यदा मार्गगामिनोऽन्तरा सरस्वतीव्यतिरिक्ता नदी पतति तदा परपारे स्नानादि कार्यं; सरस्वत्यास्त्वर्वाक्तीरे । तदुक्तं—

669. मार्गेऽन्तरा नदीप्राप्तौ स्नानादि परपारतः ।
अर्वागेव सरस्वत्या एष मार्गगतो विधिः ॥

यत्तु

670. पितॄनतर्पयित्वा तु नदीस्तरति यो नरः ।
तस्यासृक्पानकामास्ते भवन्ति भृशदुःखिता ॥ (—332)

---

665. विफलानि; P2 विकलानि । 665 भवेत्; C1 लभेत् । 666. लोकान्; P3 लोको । 667.1. यात्रार्थगतस्य; P2 यात्रार्थं गतस्य ।

(1) इति वचनं, तत्सरस्वतीविषयम् । (2) तासामपि बहूनां सत्त्वाद् बहुवचनोपपत्तेः । (3) यद्वा तरणमतिलंघ्य गमनं; तेन मार्गपतितायामपि नद्यां स्नानतर्पणाद्यकृत्वा न गच्छेदित्यर्थः । अतएव शंखः—

671. **न स्रवन्तीमतिक्रमेदनवसिच्य-**

(1) त्यतिक्रमनिषेधमाह । (2) 'अनवसिच्य' तर्पणमकृत्वा । (3) अत्र वचनद्वयेऽपि तर्पणं स्नानस्याप्युपलक्षणं, तर्पणस्य तदनन्तरभावित्वात् ।

(4) प्रसिद्धनद्यां मार्गपतितायां श्राद्धमपि कार्यं समानन्यायत्वात् ।

(5) इदञ्च नदीषु परपारे स्नानमर्वाक्तीरे विशिष्टतीर्थाभावे ज्ञेयं; तत्सत्त्वे त्वर्वागेव स्नानादि, तदवगणनायां दोषापत्तेः । (6) सरस्वत्यां तु परपारे तीर्थविशेषसत्त्वेऽर्वाक्तीरे कृत्वा परपारेऽपि कार्यमिति विवेकः ।

(7) अथ प्रतिग्रहादिप्रतिषेधार्थं तीर्थगर्भादि कथ्यते । तत्र ब्रह्मपुराणे—

672. **प्रवाहमवधिं कृत्वा यावद्धस्तचतुष्टयम् ।**
तत्र नारायणः स्वामी नान्यः स्वामी कदाचन ॥
तत्र न प्रतिगृह्णीयात् प्राणैः काण्ठगतैरपि ।

(1) अत्र 'प्रवाहम्' इति जलावध्युपलक्षणम् । (2) तेन पुष्करादौ तडागवाप्यादिरूपेऽपि तीर्थे सर्वत्रैव जलमवधीकृत्य हस्तचतुष्टयाभ्यन्तरेति निषेधः ।

दानधर्मे—

673. **भाद्रशुक्लचतुर्दश्यां यावदाक्रमते जलम् ।**
तावद् गर्भं विजानीयात् तदूर्ध्वं तीरमुच्यते ॥

(1) अत्र भाद्रशुक्लचतुर्दश्यां कदाचिद् वृष्ट्यभावेन जलवृद्ध्यभावेऽपि किञ्चिद्वर्षभाविवृद्धचैव

674. **लक्षणं हि पुरोडाशाव—**

मी० सू० 10.8.18.69

इतिन्यायेन देशविशेष उपलक्ष्यते ।

(1) तीरावधिश्च ब्रह्मपुराणे—

675. **साधं हस्तशतं यावद् गर्भतस्तीरमुच्यते ।**

671.3. तदनन्तरभावित्वात्; P1 P2 तदनन्तरं भावित्वात् । 675. साधं; P2 साधं—।

स्कान्दे—

676. **तीराद् गव्यूतिमात्रं तु परितः क्षेत्रमुच्यते ।**
अत्र दानं जपो होमो गङ्गायां नात्र संशयः ॥

(1) तटद्वये प्रत्येकं क्रोशद्वयाख्यगव्यूतिमात्रं क्षेत्रम् । अतएवोक्तं भविष्ये—

677. **गङ्गासीमान्न लंघन्ति सर्वपापान्यशेषतः ।**
दिशो दश पलायन्ते सिंहं दृष्ट्वा यथा मृगाः ॥
एकयोजनविस्तीर्णा क्षेत्रसीमा तटद्वयम् ॥ इति ।

(1) अत्र गर्भे प्रतिग्रहनिषेधः प्रसिद्धनदीषु । (2) प्रसिद्धतरगण्डक्यादिनदीषु तु उभयतः सार्धहस्तशतमिते तीरेऽपि निषेध इति शिष्टाः । (3) क्षेत्रे तु निषेधो गङ्गाविषयस्तत्रैव क्षेत्रकथनात् ।

यत्तु ब्रह्मपुराणे—

678. **यत्र गङ्गा महाराज शम्भुस्तत्र तपोवनम् ।**
सिद्धिक्षेत्रं च तद् ज्ञेयं समन्तात् तु त्रियोजनम् ॥

(1) एकैकस्मिन् पार्श्वे सार्धयोजनमिति 'समन्तात् त्रियोजनम्' इत्यर्थ इति तन्मरणेऽतिशयार्थं न तु प्रतिग्रहप्रतिषेधार्थम् । (2) यदा तु 'समन्तादर्धयोजनम्' इति पाठः, तदा स्कान्देन तुल्यार्थतैव ।

(3) अथ लिङ्गाद्यर्चने विशेषः । नारदीये—

679. **यः शूद्रेणार्चितं लिङ्गं विष्णुं वा प्रणमेन्नरः ।**
न तस्य निष्कृतिर्ह्यस्ति प्रायश्चित्तायुतैरपि ॥
तथैव शूद्रसंस्पृष्टं लिङ्गं वा हरिमेव वा ।
स सर्वयातनाभोगी यावदा चन्द्रतारकम् ॥
पाखण्डपूजितं लिङ्गं नत्वा पाखण्डतां व्रजेत् ।
आभीरपूजितं लिङ्गं नत्वा नरकमश्नुते ॥
योषिद्भिः पूजितं लिङ्गं विष्णुं वापि नमेत्तु यः ।
स कोटिकुलसंयुक्त आकल्पं रौरवे वसेत् ॥

---

679. शूद्रेणार्चितं; K शूद्रेणार्पितं । 679. पाखण्डतां; Cl पाषण्डतां ।
679. रौरवे; P2 रौरवं ।

(1) एतत्सर्वं इदानीन्तनप्रतिष्ठितलिङ्गादिविषयं, न तु पुराणप्रसिद्ध-महिमविषयं,

680. यदा प्रतिष्ठितं लिङ्गं मन्त्रविद्भिर्यथाविधि ।
तदा प्रभृति शूद्रश्च योषिद् वापि न संस्पृशेत् ॥

इति तत्रैवोक्तत्वात् । अतएव स्कान्दे काशीलिङ्गं प्रकृत्योक्तम्—

681. अदृश्यान्यपि दृश्यानि दुरवस्थान्यपि प्रिये ।
भग्नान्यपि च कालेन तानि पूज्यानि सुन्दरी- ॥

क० ख० 73.24c–25b

(1) ति । 'दुरवस्थानि' अस्पृश्यस्पृष्टानि ।

(2) तथान्योऽपि विशेषस्तत्रैव;

682. स्त्रीणामनुपनीतानां शूद्राणाञ्च नरेश्वर ।
स्थापने नाधिकारोऽस्ति विष्णोर्वा शङ्करस्य वा ॥
यः शूद्रसंस्कृतं लिङ्गं विष्णुं वापि नमेन्नरः ।
इहैवात्यन्तदुःखानि पश्यत्यामुष्मिके किमु ॥
शूद्रो वानुपनीतो वा स्त्रियो वा पतितोऽपि वा ।
केशवं वा शिवं वापि स्पृष्ट्वा नरकमश्नुते ॥

इत्यादि । (1) अन्योऽपि विशेष :—

683. महातीर्थस्य गमनमुपवासव्रतानि च ।
संवत्सरं न कुर्वीत महागुरुनिपातने ॥

तथा—

684. तीर्थस्नानं महादानं परान्नं तिलतर्पणम् ।
अब्दमेकं न कुर्वीत महागुरुनिपातने ॥
वपनं मैथुनं तीर्थं वर्जयेद् गुर्विणीपतिः ।
श्राद्धञ्च सप्तमान् मासादूर्ध्वञ्चान्यत्र वेदवित् ॥

---

681. दुरवस्थान्य्; P2 दुःखस्थान्य्, P3 C1 दुखस्थान्य् । 681.1. दुरवस्थानि; P2 दुःखस्थानि, P2 C1 दुखस्थानि । 683. महातीर्थस्य गमनम्; P1 (+correction in P2) महातीर्थाभिगमनम् ।

(1) 'श्राद्धं' श्राद्धभोजनम् ।

लल्लः—

685. **उपप्लवे शीतलभानुभान्वो-**
रर्धोदये वा कपिलाख्यषष्ठ्याम् ।
सुरासुरेज्यास्तमयेऽपि तीर्थे
यात्राविधिः संक्रमणेऽपि शस्तः ॥

(1) उपप्लवो ग्रहणम् । (2) गुरुशुक्रास्तमय उपलक्षणम् । (3) तेन निषिद्धकालान्तरेऽपि ग्रहणादौ न दोष इत्यर्थः ।

(4) अस्थिप्रक्षेपार्थयात्रायामाद्यवर्षेऽपि न दोष इत्याहुः ।

तथा धर्मविवृत्तौ—

686. **उपवासो व्रतं होमस्तीर्थस्नानजपादिकम् ।**
विप्रैः सम्पादितं यस्य सम्पन्नं तस्य तत्फलम् ॥

तथा—

687. **नार्वाक् संवत्सरात् प्रोक्तं क्षौरं तीर्थनिवासिनाम् ।**
देशान्तरगतानाञ्च क्षौरं नैमित्तिकं विना ॥

तथा—

688. **अम्बुमध्ये गवां गोष्ठे तीर्थेष्वपि च पर्वसु ।**
राहोर्दर्शनकाले च सूतकं नैव विद्यते ॥

(1) इदं शीघ्रमन्यत्रगमनसम्भावनायां दानादिविषये द्रष्टव्यम् ।

तथा—

689. **गृहे दशगुणं दानं गोष्ठे शतगुणं भवेत् ।**
पुण्यतीर्थेषु साहस्रमनन्तं शिवसन्निधौ ॥

अन्यच्च—

690. **येषु तीर्थेषु ये देवा येषु तीर्थेषु ये द्विजाः ।**
येषु तीर्थेषु यत्तोयं विचार्याक्तसेन्न तत्र तु ॥

---

685. P1 तीर्थ—, P3 तीर्थं । 686. सम्पन्नं; P2 सम्पूर्णं । 688. पर्वसु; P1 (+ correction in P2) कर्मसु ।

(1) एतेषूपहतेष्वपि न दोष इत्याशयः ।

तथा—

691. न देवः पर्वताग्रेषु न देवो विष्णुसद्मनि ।
देवश्चिदानन्दमयो दिवि भावेन दृश्यते ॥
यत्र यत्र दृढा भक्तिर्यदा यस्य महात्मनः ।
तत्र तस्य महादेवः प्रसादमुपगच्छति ॥

(1) इत्यादि । बहुनालम्!

इति श्रीमद्विद्वन्मुकुटमाणिक्यश्रीमद्भट्टरामेश्वरसूरिसूनुनारायणविरचिते त्रिस्थलीसेतौ सामान्यप्रघट्टके प्रकीर्णकतीर्थधर्मप्रकरणं समाप्तम् ।

समाप्तश्च प्रघट्टकः ।

इतः परं प्रयागप्रकरणं भविष्यति ।

691.1.—प्रकीर्णक—; P2—प्रकीर्ण—। 691.1 समाप्तश्च...भविष्यति; P2 P3 Cl K omitted.

APPENDICES TO THE TEXT

I. Interpolated Passages

K: After 144.1, this text is added in the 'शुद्धिपत्रम्' of K :

सौदामनी वर्षणगर्जितेषु
नाकालजेषु प्रवसेन्नरेन्द्रः ।
आ सप्तरात्राद् ध्रुवमद्भुतेषु
दिव्यान्तरिक्षक्षितिजेषु चैव

P2 : after 148 :

उपप्लवे शीतलभानुभान्वोर्.....इत्यादि (as in text, 685).

K: After 141.1 :

सदा कृतयुगश्चात्र महापर्वसमोऽत्र वै ।
न च ग्रस्तोदयकृतो दोषो विश्वेश्वरालये ॥
अस्तादावपि काशीयात्रा न निषिध्यते । तथा.....

P1 and K: In 156.3 after 'तीर्थश्राद्धवद् एव' :

तीर्थे महालये चैव गयायां प्रेतपक्षके ।
(K पितृपक्षके)
ज्ञेयं द्वादशदैवत्यं शेषं षट्पौरुषं विदुः ॥
इति स्मृतिरत्नावल्याम् ।

L2 : After 285 (इति) :

अत्र श्मश्रुशब्दः कूर्चस्याप्युपलक्षकः ।

P2 : In 639.2, after 'इत्युक्त्वा', the full text of the four मन्त्र-s is written out.

P2: 639.7, after 'वेष्टयित्वा' :

अजिनं 'अग्ने विश्वेभिर्' इति कम्बलं 'देवस्य त्वे'ति कुशान् 'केश्याग्निम्'
इति, गोवालान् 'शन्नो इन्द्राग्नी'ति शाणसूत्रं भूर्जपत्रं ताडपत्रञ्च 7.
ततो होमं प्रकुर्वीत तिलाज्येन विचक्षणः
उदीरतेति मन्त्रेण हुनेदष्टोत्तरं शतम्
अत्र दशदानवैतरणी ऋणमोक्षपापधेनुदानमुक्तं दिवोदासीये ।

APPENDICES TO THE TEXT

II. अनुक्रमणिका-ऽ

A. अनुक्रमणिका included at end of MS. P2.
(Figures represent folios of P2.)

श्रीगणेशाय नमः । त्रिस्थलीसेतुरनुक्रमणिका ।

अथ मङ्गलाचरणं
धर्ममाहात्म्यं
अर्थप्रशंसा
कामप्रशंसा
मोक्षप्रशंसा
धर्मानुष्ठानमुख्यत्वं
धर्ममध्ये यात्राप्राधान्यं
तीर्थयात्रा कर्त्तव्यतानि०

6. सामान्यतीर्थप्रशंसा
पुत्रादित्यागेन तीर्थगम०
गमनाभावे मनसा गम०
अज्ञानपूर्वकं तीर्थगमने तत्फलप्राप्तिः

7. तीर्थस्वरूपनिरूपणं
तीर्थद्वैविध्यं
तीर्थानां चतुर्विधत्वं

9. अथ गौणतीर्थानि
मानसानि तीर्थानि
मानसतीर्थफलं
भौमतीर्थमाहात्म्यं
तीर्थयात्राधिकारिणः
ब्रह्मचारिणोधिकारः
गृहस्थस्याधिकारः
कृकलोपाख्यानं
सपत्नीकस्यैवाधिकारः
साग्निकस्याप्यधिकारः

संन्यासिनोधिकारः
क्षत्रियस्याधिकारः
वैश्याधिकारः
शूद्रस्य द्विजशुश्रूषाविरोधेन यात्राधिका०
सङ्करजेष्वनुलोमजानाधिकारः (sic)
प्रतिलोमजानामपि
स्त्रीणां अधिकारः
विधवानां विशेषेण
सधवानां भर्त्रा सहैव
पित्राद्यस्थिक्षेपार्थं सर्वेषामधिकारविषयः
प्रायश्चित्तार्थंसर्वेषां
तीर्थफलतारतम्यकार०
यानविशेषकृतं फलता०
असमर्थस्तु यानेन तीर्थयात्रां समा०
तीर्थप्रत्याम्नाया उच्यन्ते

24. यात्रायां कालशुद्धिः

26. तीर्थगमनविधिः
तदयमनुष्ठानक्रमः
कार्पटिकवेशधारणञ्च यात्राङ्गत्वाद् गमनकाल एव न त्वन्यदापि

33. तीर्थयात्रायां नियमाः

38. तीर्थप्राप्तिदिनकृत्यं

39. तीर्थोपवासः
अयञ्चोपवासः फलविशेषार्थ एव, न त्वावश्यकः

44. तीर्थमुण्डनं
तत्सिद्धं कुरुक्षेत्रादिव्यतिरिक्तेषु प्रसिद्धतीर्थेषु मुण्डनोपवासाविति। इदञ्च मुण्डनं दशमासानन्तरं पुनस्तीर्थप्राप्तौ कर्त्तव्यं। अत्रेदं चिन्त्यं मुण्डने किं वपनं करिष्ये इति संकल्पः कारिष्ये (sic) इति वा विचारः।
वपनं करिष्ये इत्येव सं०
तस्माश्छश्रुपूर्वकमेव वपनं
इदञ्च वपनं यत्यादिभिः शिखामरक्षित्वैव कार्यं
आहिताग्निभिस्तु पर्वव्यतिरिक्तकालेपि तीर्थप्राप्तौ मुण्डनं कार्यं
जीवत्पितृकेणापि तीर्थप्राप्तौ मुण्डनं कार्यं

तीर्थे च मुण्डनं निषिद्धकालेपि कार्यं
निषेधश्च
तीरे एव वपनं कार्यं

63. अथ तीर्थस्नानं
प्रत्यावृत्तोदके स्नाननिषेधः
रजकतीर्थे स्नाननिषेधः
एतस्य गङ्गायामपवादः
तीर्थाद् बहिर्गतोदके स्नाननिषे०
वृक्षछायायां स्नाननिषेधः
रात्रिसन्ध्यादिषु स्नाननिषेधः आकस्मिकतीर्थप्राप्तौ न प्रासङ्गिक-तीर्थप्राप्तौ
मलमासेपि कार्यं
आशौचेपि कार्यं
परार्थस्नाने विशेषः
अनुषङ्गिकतीर्थगमने स्नानफलप्राप्तिः
नद्यादौ प्रवाहाभिमुखः स्नायात्
तर्पणं
तर्पणे देवताक्रमः
अशक्तस्य संक्षेपतर्पणं तद्विधिश्च
तर्पणे तिलनिषिद्धोभा०
विधवयापि तीर्थतर्पणं कार्यं पुत्रपौत्रवत्यानिषे०
नदीनां रजोदोषविचारः
अथं तीर्थश्राद्धं
श्राद्धे तीर्थविशेषः
परगृहादौ श्राद्धनिषेधः
तीर्थश्राद्धाङ्गतर्पणं
श्राद्धात् पूर्वं स्नानतर्पणानन्तरमविलम्बेन कार्यं
तीर्थश्राद्धे निषिद्धकालवर्जं
तीर्थप्राप्तौ अशौचादिनिषेधः
रात्रौ सन्ध्यायाञ्च तीर्थप्राप्तौ तदेव मुण्डनादि काय
तीर्थश्राद्धे निषिद्धकालेपि पिण्डदानविचारः
तीर्थे ब्राह्मपरीक्षाविचाराभावः

तीर्थश्राद्धे निषिद्धा०
देवतायाः स्वरूपवि०
आवाहनविचारः
पार्वणे ऊहविचारः
एकोद्दिष्टे ऊहविचारः
स्त्रीशूद्रानुपनीतादिभिः आमन्त्रकं श्राद्धं का०
तीर्थश्राद्धे धुरिलोचनौ विश्वेदेवौ
अन्नाभावे हेमश्राद्धविचारः
शूद्रस्य आमश्राद्धमेव
आमश्राद्धे विशेषः
आमश्राद्धादौ ऊहविचारः
आमश्राद्धकालः
तीर्थश्राद्धे पिण्डानां तीर्थ एव प्रक्षेपः
तीर्थे पिण्डदाने नन्दादिनिषेधाभावः
तीर्थे शक्तेन तर्पणश्राद्धपिण्डदानानि त्रीण्यपि कार्याणि
अशक्तेन तर्पणपिण्डौ अशक्ततरेण तर्पणमात्र कार्यं
यत्र काश्यादौ एकस्मिन् महातीर्थे अनेकान्यवान्तरतीर्थानि गम्यन्ते
तदा एकस्मिन्नपि दिनेऽनेकश्राद्धानि कर्त्तव्यानि
अनेकतीर्थप्राप्तौ तन्त्रप्रसङ्गविचारः
अथ श्राद्धान्तरसमवाये निर्णयः
तीर्थप्राप्तिदिने वार्णिकं (sic) स्यात्तदा पृथगेव कार्यं
तीर्थवार्षिकादिश्राद्धसम्पाते तीर्थश्राद्धं प्रथमं कार्यं
इदं तीर्थश्राद्धं दशमासानन्तरं तीर्थप्राप्तौ आवश्यकं अतरा
(sic) तु फलेच्छया कर्त्तव्यं
तीर्थश्राद्धाधिकारवि०
जीवत्पितृकस्यापि श्राद्धाधिकारः
विभक्तभ्रातृणां युगपत्तीर्थप्राप्तौ तीर्थश्राद्धं पृथक् कर्त्तव्यं
अविभक्तभ्रातृणां युगपत्तीर्थप्राप्तौ ज्येष्ठेनैव कर्त्तव्यं
विधवायाः
पुत्रवत्यास्तीर्थप्राप्तौ श्राद्धविचारः
साङ्कल्पश्राद्धे वर्ज्यानि

अनुपनीतस्य श्राद्धाधिकारविचारः
स्त्रिया अनुपनीतेन च ब्राह्मणेन च कारणीयं स्वयं वा अमन्त्रकं कुर्यात्
अथाधिकारापवादः
तीर्थश्राद्धे सम्प्रदाननिर्णयः
पार्वणानां निवेशक्रमः
यदा अन्येन प्रेरितःस्तीर्थं गछति तदा यजमानस्य पित्रादीन् उद्दिश्य श्राद्धं कुर्यात् ।
जीवत्पितृके विशेषः
अशक्तस्य संक्षेपश्रा०
अथ तीर्थेस्थिप्रक्षेपविधिः
गङ्गायां विशेषः । अस्तादौ निषेधः । प्रथमाद्बे अस्थिप्रक्षेपविचारः
दशाहाभ्यन्तरे विशेषः
अस्थिशुद्धिविधिः प्रयोगश्च
प्रयागेस्थिप्रक्षेपे विशेषः तीर्थे अस्थिप्रक्षेपश्राद्धयोः पूर्वापरीभावविचारः
अथ प्रकीर्णकास्तीर्थधर्माः
शिवादिप्रदक्षिणाविचारः
शिवादिनिर्माल्यप्रतिपत्ति । तीर्थे प्रतिग्रहनिषेधः
मार्गेन्तरा तीर्थप्राप्तौ परतीरे एव स्नादि०
सरस्वत्यास्तु पूर्वतीरे
तीरनिर्णयः
अथ लिङ्गाद्यर्चने विशेषः
इति त्रिस्थळी अनुक्रमणिका समाप्तः । (sic) श्रीकृष्णार्पणमस्तु ।
एवं ग्रन्थसंख्या 52 ।
इति त्रिःस्थळी अवर्तणिका समाप्तः । (sic)

B. अनुक्रमणी at end of P3. (Figures represent folios of P3.)

प्रघट्टकस्यानुक्रमणिका

1. प्रथमं यात्राकर्त्तव्यता
4. तीर्थस्वरूपं तीर्थप्रशंसा
5. अथ गौणतीर्थानि

6. अथ तीर्थयात्राधिकारः
7. अथ तीर्थफलतारतम्यं
7. अथ यानविशेषकृतफलतारतम्यं
11. अथ तीर्थप्रत्याम्नायाः
14. अथ यात्रायां कालशुद्धिः
17. अथ तीर्थगमनविधिः
18. अथ तीर्थयात्रायां नियमाः
21. अथ तीर्थप्राप्तिदिनकृत्यं
23. अथ तीर्थोपवासः
25. अथ तीर्थे मुण्डनं
37. अथ तीर्थस्नानं
48. अथ तीर्थश्राद्धनिषिद्धानि
57. अथामहेमश्राद्धादिविचारः
60. अथ श्राद्धान्तरसमवायनिर्णयः
61. अथ श्राद्धाधिकारिणः
63. अथ तीर्थश्राद्धे सम्प्रदाननिर्णयः
70. अथ तीर्थे अस्थिप्रक्षेपविधिः
72. अथास्य प्रयोगः
72. अथ प्रकीर्णकास्तीर्थधर्माः
75. अथ तीर्थे प्रतिग्रहविचारः
76. अथ तीर्थमर्यादाप्रासङ्गिकं
77. इति तीर्थप्रघट्टानुक्रमणी छ छ छ छ
ग्रन्थसंख्या 2300 छ इति त्रिस्थलीसेतौ
तीर्थप्रघट्टकप्रकरणमिदं प्रथमम् छ ।

TRANSLATION :

THE GENERAL SECTION

OF THE

BRIDGE TO THE THREE HOLY CITIES

BY NĀRĀYAṆA BHAṬṬA

INTODUCTORY VERSES

Here begins the First Section, called 'The Section on Pilgrimage,' of the Bridge to the Three Holy Places. Homage to Lord Gaṇeśa. Homage to the feet of the Noble Bhaṭṭarāmeśvara.

1. We bow to Sarasvatī, so that she may remove every difficulty. The highest understanding comes to those who set their minds on her alone.
2. Homage to you, Lord of Obstacles; destroy all obstacles. Grant us your generous bounty and bestow on us purity of mind.
3. I worship Rāma, whose eyes are like lotuses with a hundred opened petals. Friend of Sugrīva, famed for his marvelous deeds, his body is the color of a deep blue sapphire; he is Lord of his line, and husband of Kamalā.
4. Son of the Noble Bhaṭṭagovinda, the Noble Bhaṭṭarāmeśvara triumphs first in the rolls of the wise, the one sun to make bloom the lotus of knowledge. He is like a full moon over the ocean of the Viśvāmitra clan, a treasure of arts [or 'digits' (of the moon)], whose nectar has been stored up by his students and their students in all their literary compositions.
5. There is no city more revered than Vārāṇasī, and when he settled there, it became like another Mountain of Gold (Mount Meru).
6. His son Nārāyaṇa, well-read in the sacred texts, who learned śruti, smṛti and the ways of the land from his own father, now composes his 'Bridge to the Three Holy Places' at Avimukta (Vārāṇasī).
7. If I were to say that there are many good things in this book—who would not say that of his own book? Therefore, good people, I beg of you with hands joined in reverence at my head : please correct whatever I say here, be it good or bad.

8. Of cynics, I ask only this : please cease to be cynics (to me). Turn your minds to improving this work, and not to disparaging it.
9. First, the general rules for tīrthas will be properly described, and after that, the rules for the three tīrthas, beginning with Prayāga : this is the scheme of this book.

PRAISE OF THE PURPOSES OF MEN

(1) For men revolving in this wheel of saṃsāra, four purposes in life, known as Dharma, Artha, Kāma, and Mokṣa, are declared in all the smṛtis, itihāsas, and purāṇas to be worthy of pursuit. Thus in the MAHĀBHĀRATA, Bhīmasena says to Yudhiṣṭhira :

10. O best of orators : The wise man who knows the proper times should properly pursue all of these—Dharma, Artha, and Kāma, dividing them according to their appropriate times. Or else, O king, he may pursue Mokṣa, which is the ultimate good for men who seek happiness.

(1) Here it is really happiness and the absence of suffering which are primarily the purposes of men; for they are sought by men as the object of their essential desires. Only in a secondary sense are the *means* of achieving happiness and the absence of suffering considered the purposes of men. (2) This being so, Dharma and Artha are conventionally regarded as purposes of men in a figurative sense only; for they are (merely) the means for achieving happiness and the absence of suffering respectively. (3) Therefore also Dharma, which is of two kinds, consisting of spiritual progress and cessation, was declared by those of old to be a means for achieving the purposes of men :

11. In the Dharma known as 'progress' the benefit is considered to be elevation; in that called 'cessation,' the ultimate good (i.e. mokṣa).

In the SKANDAPURĀṆA also :

12. From Dharma come both happiness and knowledge. So that he may attain both of these, the wise man should abandon everything and practice Dharma. Whatever happiness there may be in both the worlds is attained by Dharma. Therefore one should practice Dharma alone, to achieve all his desires and goals.

And in the MAHĀBHĀRATA :

13. Religion alone is the raft; there is no other. (By it), Draupadī, we may go to heaven.

The śruti text

14. By means of Dharma one drives away sin,

(1) shows that Dharma is also a means to the absence of suffering, by driving off the sin which is the cause of suffering.

And in the SKANDAPURĀṆA :

15. O great ascetic : by austerity long-practiced, the desires of those whose sins are wiped out by Dharma are fulfilled.

MANU says :

16. With Dharma as his helper, one crosses the uncrossable darkness. It leads the religious man whose sins have been destroyed by asceticism, who is luminous and embodied, swiftly to the higher ethereal worlds.

(1) (Thus) it is well-known from all śruti, smṛti, and purāṇas that that Dharma which consists of penances and the like is also a means for eliminating suffering by means of wiping out evil. (2) Artha, also, is a means for achieving happiness and the absence of suffering, as is proven by experience, and by sacred texts, from the words of the mantra :

17. The givers of sacrificial fees dwell on high in heaven. Those who give horses dwell with the sun. Those who give gold enjoy immortality. Those who give clothing, O Soma, increase their lives;

and from the smṛti,

18. A giver of gold instantly becomes pure.

(1) The texts which prescribe the tulā-puruṣa and other religious gifts also constitute a proof of this. (2) Thus it is established that Dharma and Artha are purposes of men in a figurative sense. (3) Kāma, however, is a primary purpose of

men, because it consists of happiness. That it consists of happiness is declared in the ĀRAṆYAKA PARVAN of the MAHĀBHĀRATA:

19. The delight which arises in material things, wealth, sensation, and sexual contact, is Kāma, a conception of the mind; it has no body.

Also :

20. One seeking Artha, O king, desires great Dharma; and he desires Artha. One who desires Kāma does not desire anything other than Kāma. For no other desire is obtained by Kāma; it is its own result.

And also :

21. The delight which arises in the five senses, the mind and the heart, when they are applied to their respective objects—that is Kāma, so I think, the ultimate result of actions.

(22.1) In these passages, (it is seen that) Kāma consists of happiness, because this word 'delight' (prīti) is included among the synonyms of 'happiness' (sukha) enumerated in the lexicon :

22. 'Joy' (mud), 'delight' (prīti), 'rejoicing' (pramada), 'pleasure' (harṣa)...;

and because Kāma is said to have no other result than itself; and because it is described as its own result. Thus in the comment on the Section (of the MĪMĀṂSĀ SŪTRAS) on the Smṛti:

23. Anything connected with Dharma and Mokṣa is derived from the Veda; but whatever relates to Artha or happiness (sukha) is based on temporal custom,

(1) Kāma is denoted by the word 'happiness.'

Also in (the comment on) the Section on Explanatory Passages :

24. The result [of the words of the MAHĀBHĀRATA, etc.] is to establish a means for (understanding) the goal, namely Dharma, Artha, Kāma, and Mokṣa, and (their opposites,

namely) non-Dharma, non-Artha, suffering (duḥkha) and saṃsāra; establishing the means to the first four as a contributing factor to adopting them, and the latter four to renouncing them,

(1) the author of the comment, in speaking of suffering (duḥkha) as its opposite, considers Kāma, as a purpose of men, to be simply 'happiness' (sukha).

(25.1) As for the repudiation of Kāma, taken as a means for obtaining the happiness called 'delight of the senses,' in the BHĀGAVATAPURĀṆA passage

25. As long as a man lives, he will not obtain delight of the senses, the result of Kāma;

and the description of Kāma elsewhere as a means of achieving delight;

26. From Dharma comes Artha; from Artha, Kāma; from Kāma, the ultimate delight;

(1) these are to be explained as taking the word 'pleasure' (Kāma) in a secondary sense, insofar as it is the *means* of achieving that happiness which is known as 'Kāma' in reference to the enjoyment of its objects.[1] (2) Or else, (it may be explained thus:) in this passage also the word 'Kāma' does indeed mean 'happiness'; (3) but that word 'delight of the senses' (indriyaprīti) refers to satisfaction of the (desires of) the senses;[2] for 'delight', taken as another synonym of 'happiness', is not a phenomenon applicable to the senses.

(4) Therefore it is established that Kāma is a primary purpose of man, because it consists of happiness.

(5) Mokṣa too is a primary purpose of man, because it consists, according to different opinions, of either happiness or of the absence of suffering.

1. That is, in these two verses (25 and 26) the word kāma is used with a secondary meaning, in the context of the sense-organs, so that it denotes a *means to* happiness; while the primary meaning of kāma applies to the objects of the senses, so that it denotes happiness itself.

2. I.e., 'delight' is *not* meant as a synonym of 'happiness.'

(6) The application of the term 'purposes of men' in common to (all) four is figurative, like the use of the word 'umbrella-bearer' (='king') in reference to a group of people including the umbrella-bearer and others who are not umbrella-bearers;[1] and like the use of the words 'sṛṣṭi' and 'prāṇabhṛt' in reference to groups (of bricks) which include both sṛṣṭi (-bricks) and non-sṛṣṭi (-bricks), and prāṇabhṛt (-bricks) and non-prāṇabhṛt (-bricks).[2]

(7) Then among these four purposes of men, Dharma is the chief purpose, because it promotes the other purposes, and also promotes such qualities as wisdom. Thus it is said in the KŪRMAPURĀṆA:

27. Artha arises from Dharma, Kāma arises from Dharma, and the Supreme Brahman comes from Dharma alone. Therefore one should practice Dharma.

(1) 'Supreme Brahman' means liberation.

Also:

28. I shout with arms raised high, and no one listens to me. From Dharma come Artha and Kāma; why is it not practiced?

Also:

29. The ultimate good [liberation] is considered to be the result of that Dharma of cessation.

In the MAHĀBHĀRATA:

30. Wisdom and wealth, beauty and strength, high birth, good health, and the cause of cessation of saṃsāra; these are said to arise from Dharma alone.

In the SKANDAPURĀṆA:

31. From Dharma come sovereignty, wealth, and happiness; from non-Dharma arises sorrow. Thus for the sake of happiness one should practice Dharma and shun evil.

1. This usage is known as the 'Chatri-nyāya' (see MK p. 1725b).
2. This figurative usage is explained in Śab.I.4.12.23.

YĀJÑAVALKYA:

32. With act, mind, and speech one should practice Dharma zealously.

MANU:

33. Dharma, when harmed, harms; when protected, it protects. Thus Dharma is not to be harmed, lest it, when harmed, destroy us;

and so on.

(1) "But", it is objected, "it is known from experience that Artha also is a cause of Dharma; so how can Dharma alone be supreme? Thus, it is said in the MAHĀBHĀRATA:

34. Artha is always rooted in Dharma, and Dharma depends on Artha.

Also:

35. Thus the whole world is rooted in Dharma, O king. Nothing is better than Dharma; and Dharma may be cultivated by means of great wealth (Artha), O king.

In the BHĀGAVATAPURĀṆA:

36. Dharma is the sole benefit of wealth."

(1) Not so; because, although certain forms of Dharma, such as sacrifices and donations, can be carried out by means of Artha, Dharma in its entirety cannot be carried out by means of Artha. (2) For Dharma can be increased without wealth, by means of prayer, pilgrimage, fasting, etc.; but without Dharma Artha cannot be increased in the slightest. (3) Thus since Dharma is supreme, it alone is to be practiced above all. Thus it is said in the ĀRAṆYAKA PARVAN (of the MAHĀBHĀRATA):

37. One should practice Dharma first, then Artha, and lastly Kāma.

(1) Within Dharma, the kind of Dharma which consists of sacrifices, donations, etc., cannot be practiced in full detail.

nowadays, because it requires much material expense, and because it consists of many and various parts; and not all the varṇas, mixed varṇas, and life-stages are authorized to practice it, because it can be carried out only by a married man, and completed with the aid of a ṛtvij and other priests. Thus, as compared to those kinds of Dharma, the Dharma of pilgrimage to tīrthas is much easier to perform, for it is quite different in respect to the reasons just mentioned. Thus it is said in the MAHĀBHĀRATA and the MATSYAPURĀṆA:

38. The sacrifices were proclaimed by the sages in the Vedas, in proper order; and they also truly proclaimed their results always, both here and in the afterlife. But these sacrifices cannot be achieved by a poor man, O Lord of the Earth; sacrifices require many instrumen s and vast provisions of various sorts. They are achieved by kings or sometimes by wealthy men; but not by poor men, lone men, single men, nor unaccompanied men. But hear, O Lord of the Earth, that way which can be performed even by poor men, and which, O Lord of the Earth, is equal to the meritorious benefits of sacrifices. This is the supreme secret of the sages, O Mightiest of the Bharatas: Travelling to tīrthas is meritorious, better even than sacrifices.

(1) 'Lone men' means men without assistants. (2) 'Single men' means unmarried men. (3) 'Unaccompanied men' means men without the company of ṛtvij's and other priests.

(4) It will be explained in the discussion of who is authorized[1] that even śūdras, mixed castes, and mendicants are authorized (to conduct pilgrimages).

(5) "But," it is objected, "the sort of Dharma which consists of prayer, fasting, etc., is also known to be independent of Artha; so why does this special excellence apply to pilgrimage only?"

(6) This is true; but because (that form of Dharma) must be carried out with greater bodily exertion, and thus cannot be performed by those afflicted with paralysis, bilious disease, and

1. See 90.4ff.

other maladies, and because all people are not authorized for it, pilgrimage, being dissimilar in these respects, is better. And this fact can be ascertained from the indication of the words:

39. Travelling about, he finds honey...[1]

THUS ENDS THE DISCUSSION OF THE ADVISIBILITY OF PILGRIMAGE IN THE BRIDGE TO THE THREE HOLY PLACES BY NĀRĀYAṆA BHAṬṬA, SON OF THE NOBLE BHAṬṬARĀMEŚVARA SŪRI.

1. This verse, 'Travelling about he finds honey, travelling about, the sweet udumbara. Behold the greatness of the sun, who tires not in travelling' —is often taken as a praise of pilgrimage. Cf. Sāyaṇa's comment on AitBr 33.3.2.

PRAISE OF TĪRTHAS IN GENERAL

ŚAṄKHA says :

40. All tīrthas are said by the wise to be auspicious; they destroy men's sins always, and do not depend on one another.

(1) By 'one another' it is meant that each one by itself destroys sin.

Also :

41. All springs are auspicious ; all mountains are auspicious ; all rivers are always auspicious, but especially the Jāhnavī.

In the GARUḌAPURĀṆA :

42. Brahmā and the other gods bestow satisfaction and prosperity on him who leaves his sons, wealth, etc., and goes to a tīrtha.

In the MAHĀBHĀRATA :

43. Thus worshipping auspicious tīrthas and shrines, one gains merit and comes to enjoy the heavenly world.

Also:

44. They reach the supreme happiness who erase their sins at a tīrtha by singing the praises of that tīrtha, by bathing, and by satiating their ancestors.

In the KŪRMAPURĀṆA, referring to tīrthas :

45. When performed there, O Best of Sages, bathing, prayer, oblations, śrāddha, donations, etc., each purify unto the seventh generation.

In the MAHĀBHĀRATA and the MATSYAPURĀṆA, after the statement [38] beginning, "The sacrifices were proclaimed by the sages..." and ending..."better even than sacrifices," it is said :

46. If one neither fasts for three nights, nor goes to tīrthas, nor gives gold and cows, he is reborn as a pauper. By performing the agniṣṭoma and other sacrifices with huge fees one does not get the benefit that he gets by going to tīrthas.

(1) By 'If one neither fasts...' it is meant that any one of these four activities, three-nights' fasting, etc., has as its result freedom from poverty.

Also :

47. One should go in his mind to those tīrthas which cannot be reached or which are inaccessible and dangerous, with the desire to see all tīrthas. These tīrthas are frequented by the Vasus, Sādhyas, Ādityas, Maruts, Aśvins, and the god-like sages desirous of merit.

Also :

48. This pilgrimage of great benefit, O Yudhiṣṭhira, has been made by Manu and the other sage-kings of meritorious deeds, Great king.

Also :

49. Whoever makes a pilgrimage here, even without knowing it, becomes fulfilled in all desires and rejoices in heaven; and he reaches that place eternally full of wealth and food. He is always endowed with mastery and knowledge and possessed of Dharma. He saves his parents and his ancestors from hell.

(1) 'Without knowing it' means even without knowing "such and such will be done here, whereby such and such a benefit is obtained." This refers to children and the like.

In the VĀYUPURĀṆA :

50. Going to tīrthas, faithful and devout, a man is purified even if he be a sinner; how much more a man of pure

actions! He will not be born as an animal, nor in an evil land; he dwells in heaven as a brāhmaṇa and finds the path of liberation.

(1) Enough said!—for the greatness of tīrthas is well-known in all the purāṇas.

THE NATURE OF TĪRTHAS

In the GARUḌAPURĀṆA :

51. That place they call a tīrtha, which was frequented by those worthy ones, free of passion and ignorance, whose sins were wiped out by austerities.

In the MAHĀBHĀRATA :

52. Because they were frequented by holy men, and because of the efficacy of their land and water, these (places) are exceedingly auspicious.

(1) 'Efficacy' means power.

(Tīrthas) are of two kinds. Thus it is said in the MAHĀBHĀRATA :

53. In this world there are two kinds of tīrthas : natural, and created by the gods. Prabhāsa and others came into being by themselves. Those which were made by the gods are created.

(1) Then again, tīrthas are of four kinds. Thus it is said in the BRAHMAPURĀṆA :

54. Nārada spoke :

'How many are these tīrthas, and what are the benefits to be gained from them, O Lord of the Gods ? Of all these tīrthas, which is always the best ?

Brahman spoke :

Four kinds of tīrthas have been proclaimed by the gods and others : those of the gods, O Lion of Sages; those of the asuras, and those of the seers, in heaven, hell, and the mortal world ; and the human tīrthas among men. Those are called godly, which were made by Brahman, Viṣṇu, and Śiva; nothing better is known than one born of these three.

(1) For example, Prabhāsa, Puṣkara, etc., are the most excellent, because they were born of those three.

Also :

55. The Godāvarī, Bhīmarathī, Tuṅgabhadrā, Veṇikā, Tāpī, and Payoṣṇī are the renowned rivers to the south of the Vindhya mountains. The Bhāgīrathī, Narmadā, Yamunā, Sarasvatī, Viśokā, and Vitastā rise from the Himavat mountains. These most auspicious rivers are cited as tīrthas of the gods.

Also :

56. That (tīrtha) which was not made by anyone is said to be 'constructed by the gods.'

(1) Those tīrthas established by asuras such as Gaya and Kola, etc., are called 'asuric'. (2) Those established by seers like Vasiṣṭha, etc., are 'of the seers' (ārṣa). (3) Those established by Māndhātṛ, Ambarīṣa, Hariścandra and others are human.

(4) The Bhāgīrathī and certain others, though divine, are even more outstanding because they embody gods such as Viṣṇu, etc. This is expressed in the REVĀKHAṆḌA of the SKANDAPURĀṆA :

57. The Sarasvatī is an embodiment of Brahman; the Gaṅgā, of Viṣṇu; the Narmadā, of Śaṅkara (Śiva). The three rivers are the three gods.

(58.1) And among these, the Gaṅgā is the most excellent, due to its many special qualities, such as having been created by the three gods; this is established by many sayings such as :

58. This Gaṅgā is the best of rivers, which fulfills every desire; so hear now how it was created by the three gods, O Best of Sages.

This will be clarified in the chapter on 'The Greatness of the Gaṅgā.'[1]

1. Prayāga Pra. pp. 61ff. Note especially 'Brahmaviṣṇuśivadevarūpiṇī Gaṅgā,' p.64.

(2) Then again, tīrthas are threefold, divided into 'earthly', 'atmospheric, 'and 'located in the three worlds.' (3) In this classification, Naimiṣa is earthly, Puṣkara is in the atmosphere, and Kurukṣetra is in all three worlds. Thus it is said in the MAHĀBHĀRATA :

59. On earth, Naimiṣa is auspicious, and in the atmosphere, Puṣkara. In all the three worlds, Kurukṣetra (is auspicious), O Lord of Peoples.

In the BRAHMAPURĀṆA :

60. Of earthly tīrthas, Mānasa-tīrtha I have proclaimed to you. Puṣkara is located in the atmosphere, and difficult for my people to reach.

In the PRABHĀSAKHAṆḌA, Mahādeva says :

61. Listen, goddess, I will proclaim the supreme greatness of tīrthas. Naimiṣa is a tīrtha on earth, and in the atmosphere are Puṣkara, Kedāra, and Prayāga.

In the BRAHMAPURĀṆA the tīrthas are enumerated thus :

62. Prayāga and Kurukṣetra, Naimiṣa and Puṣkara, Gaṅgādvāra and Kubjāmra, Badarī, Sindhusāgara,

etc.

In the sixth chapter of the KĀŚĪKHAṆḌA, the tīrthas are listed, beginning with :

63. First is the king of tīrthas, called Prayāga, very wide...

In the ŚIVAPURĀṆA, sixty-eight tīrthas are mentioned, beginning with :

64. At Vārāṇasī (they know me as) Mahādeva; at Prayāga, Maheśvara...

(1) The tīrthas are also enumerated in the twelfth chapter of the KŪRMAPURĀṆA. Also in the KĀŚĪKHAṆḌA :

65. Listen, O Long-eyed Goddess; a liṅga is said to be a tīrtha. The title 'tīrtha' may apply also to bodies of water,

> by their taking the embodiment (of a god). Such embodiments are of Brahman, Viṣṇu, Arka (the Sun), Śiva, Vighneśvara (Gaṇeśa), and others. The liṅga is said to be Śiva's (embodiment); wherever it is, that is a tīrtha. At Vārāṇasī, Mahādeva is said to be first tīrtha,

and so on. Elsewhere also :

> 66. The Śoṇa, Sindhu, Hiraṇyākṣa, Koka, Lohita, Gharghara, and Śatadru; these are the seven purifying male rivers, the sons of Brahman;

and so on.

SECONDARY TĪRTHAS[1]

67. Fields, fire, and water, gods and brāhmaṇas, cows and gurus are said to be tīrthas. A tīrtha purifies one who lives there, performs oblations, bathes, worships, feeds and satiates others.

In the KĀŚĪKHAṆḌA :

68. There are tīrthas of the mind as well; truthfulness, and so on, O wise one. These surely provide liberation, there is no doubt of this.

Also :

69. His good wife spoke :

These tīrthas of the mind which you have spoken of, O Great-minded One—which are they here? Please tell me this.

The sage spoke :

Hear the tīrthas of the mind as I tell them, O Faultless One; properly bathing in them, a man goes to the supreme way. Truthfulness is a tīrtha. Patience is a tīrtha. Restraint of the senses is a tīrtha. Compassion for all creatures is a tīrtha. Honesty, too, is a tīrtha. Charity is a tīrtha. Self-control is a tīrtha. Contentment is said to be a tīrtha. Chastity is the supreme tīrtha, and gentle speech is a tīrtha. Knowledge is a tīrtha. Firmness is a tīrtha. Austerity is declared to be a tīrtha. Complete purity of mind—that is the tīrtha of tīrthas. 'Bathing' does not refer to a body immersed in water; he is bathed, who bathes in self-control and has purified with faith the impurities of his mind. A

1. Gauṇatīrtha could also be interpreted as 'tīrtha of good qualities (guṇa)'. However, I have accepted the interpretation of commentators such as Mitramiśra; see TīPra p. 11.

man who is impure, slanderous, cruel, hypocritical, and attached to sense-objects, though bathed in all the tīrthas remains sinful and impure. A man does not become pure by getting rid of bodily impurities; but when mental impurities are abandoned, then he becomes immaculate within. Fish are born and die in the waters (of tīrthas); but they do not go to heaven, for the impurities of their minds are not removed. Excessive attachment to the objects of sense is known as impurity of mind; detachment from them is called purity of mind. Evil in the mind is not purified by bathing at tīrthas; though washed with water a hundred times it remains, like a wine-jug, impure. Charity, sacrificing, austerity, purity, frequenting tīrthas, and knowledge—these are no tīrthas if the mind is not pure. Wherever a man lives, that place is Kurukṣetra, Naimiṣa, and the Puṣkaras for him, if all his senses are restrained. He goes to the supreme way who bathes in that tīrtha of the mind, which is purified by meditation, whose water is knowledge, and which wipes away passion, sins, and impurities. So have I told you the nature of the tīrthas of the mind, O Goddess.

In the MATSYAPURĀṆA :

70. Truthfulness is a tīrtha. Compassion is a tīrtha. Control of the senses is a tīrtha. Even in the place of the castes and life-stages,[1] tranquillity is said to be a tīrtha.

VYĀSA :

71. The soul is a river, full of the water of restraint; most tranquil, with pools of truth and waves of compassion. Bathe therein, O Son of Pāṇḍu; not by (ordinary) water is the inner self purified.

In the DĀNADHARMA section of the MAHĀBHĀRATA :

72. Always maintaining self-control, one should bathe in the tīrtha of the mind, deep, clear, and pure, with waters of truth and pools of self-control.

1. I.e., in the lay world.

Also :

73. The knower of truth who is free of egoism is said to be the finest tīrtha.

Also :

74. Whoever bathes in the tīrtha of the mind, his is the bathing of the seers of truth. And he who has made himself pure, constantly concentrated in mind, and endowed only with good qualities, this man is forever pure.

(1) The point here is that truthfulness, etc., are tīrthas in a secondary sense, because the benefit of (earthly) tīrthas is realized, and those tīrthas purify one's essence, *only* when one has these qualities of truthfulness, etc.

Thus after listing the tīrthas [69], it is said in the KĀŚĪKHAṆḌA :

75. So have I told you the nature of the tīrthas of the mind, O Goddess. Now listen to the cause of the auspiciousness of earthly tīrthas also. As certain parts of the body are considered most auspicious, so too are certain parts of the earth considered most auspicious.

(1) In the MAHĀBHĀRATA, the reading (of the last phrase) is "and waters are auspicious."[1]

> Tīrthas are said to be auspicious because of the extraordinary power of their earth, and the efficacy of their water, and because they were frequented by the sages.

(2) In 'by the efficacy of their waters,' 'efficacy' means power; i.e., because of its special capability.

> Therefore he goes to the supreme way, who bathes always in both the earthly tīrthas and those of the mind.

(3) This whole passage also appears in the the MAHĀBHĀRATA spoken by Bhīṣma with a different address : "So have I told you O King..."[2]

1. MBh, 13.111.18.
2. Cf. MBh 13.111.16-19; but this phrase does not appear in the extant text of the MBh.

Also in the DĀNADHARMA section of the MAHĀBHĀRATA :

76. Auspicious are the tīrthas of the mind and of the earth, and others as well. Whoever bathes in both of them quickly attains success. When strength is sufficient but action is not taken, or when action lacks strength, then one does not achieve his purpose; but when action is joined with strength one succeeds. In the same way, when endowed with both bodily purity and the purity of tīrthas, one is pure and attains success; for two-fold purity is the best.

THOSE WHO ARE AUTHORIZED TO MAKE PILGRIMAGES

According to the words of the BRAHMAPURĀṆA :

77. Whatever pilgrimages were made, commanded, and assented to by the great sages, those a well-controlled celibate student makes according to rule, when commanded by his guru,

(1) a celibate student is authorized to make a pilgrimage only when commanded by his guru. (2) This pilgrimage is permitted for a temporary celibate student [upakurvāṇa] at the command of his guru only if it does not interfere with his study of the Veda, according to the restriction given by YĀJÑAVALKYA in reference to the celibate student, (78.1) that he should approach his guru alone for instruction in the Veda :

78. And he should attentively approach his guru alone for instruction in the Veda.

(2) The permanent celibate student [naiṣṭhika] is also authorized [by 77] when permitted by his guru; for it says "A celibate student...commanded by his guru," without differentiation (as to different types of celibate student).

(3) A householder is also authorized, according to the smṛti passage.

79. Those who, having attained young-manhood, their bodies well-nourished and youthful, do not go to Gaṅgā, etc., nor bathe there and see Hari and Maheśvara—those most unfortunate men are cheated by fate.

(1) "But," it is objected, "this text [79] cannot prescribe pilgrimage for the householder, because it does not contain that word ('householder'). (2) Nor does it necessarily refer to them because of the words 'having attained young-manhood'. (3) For authorization of the householder would be in conflict with other

statements; so that statement must have been made with reference to celibate students and the like. Thus, for example, in the BRAHMAPURĀṆA :

80. For one who is authorized for the duties of sacrifice, the home and all the duties of the home are preferable. Thus for one who is in this life stage of a householder, travelling to tīrthas has been forbidden by the elders. And this we say : 'All the tīrthas together are not equal to an agnihotra sacrifice.'

Also, in the same text :

81. Or else, when his authority to sacrifice has ceased, a brahman may wander about to tīrthas. For tīrthas have been said by the great sages of immaculate nature to be equal to the benefits of sacrifice.

And in the KŪRMAPURĀṆA :

82. If someone abandons his own duties and frequents tīrthas, the tīrtha does not benefit him, neither here nor in the next world."

(1) To this it is replied : The authorization of a householder does not conflict with these statements, because, according to the specific statement 'For one who is authorized for the duties of sacrifice...and all the duties of the home'; and also according to the saying 'If someone abandons his own duties...', a householder who is poor and unable to perform sacrifices, etc., or is not authorized to perform them, is *not* prohibited from practicing pilgrimage. (2) Wherefore were spoken the previously cited words of the MAHĀBHĀRATA [38], beginning 'The sacrifices were proclaimed by the sages,' which say 'These (sacrifices) cannot be achieved by a poor man,' etc.

(3) Or else, it may be held that a householder who keeps the sacred fire *is* authorized to make a pilgrimage, but only together with his wife, according to the KŪRMAPURĀṆA :

83. Or else, a self-controlled keeper of the sacred fire *may* go to tīrthas together with his wife. Freed from all sins, he would (then) achieve that way described before;

and according to the smṛti passage :

84. Or else a penitent may go to a tīrtha, even without his wife, or one who is not authorized to make sacrifices, or one who is a practitioner of mantras. A self-controlled keeper of the sacred fire may also go to tīrthas together with his wife. (=105, 128)

Wherefore is told in the BRAHMAPURĀṆA the tale of Kṛkala the Vaiśya, as follows :

85. There was a certain Vaiśya named Kṛkala, who had made a pilgrimage. He considered himself to have fulfilled his life's purpose : 'I have delivered my ancestors.' Setting off on the road to his home, he saw his ancestors with the god Dharma. They said to him, 'You have received no benefit from the tīrtha.' He began to wonder, 'Why have I not gotten the benefit of the tīrtha? Why have my ancestors not been delivered ?' Then Dharma spoke to him, saying, 'All one's meritorious benefits are in vain, if one goes forth leaving behind a pure and most meritorious wife; it is not otherwise than this'; and much more. 'Since you have made gifts and bathed at this tīrtha without her, by this very fault your ancestors are held back. You have cheated her; you fool, you have done the work of a thief. These ancestors of yours have become thieves also, who have eaten without her. A wife cooks with her own hand food which is like divine nectar; and the ancestors eat only that food, with delighted hearts. Therefore without his wife a man can have no success.' When Dharma has thus spoken to him, Kṛkala asked, 'How may my fathers be freed ?' Dharma said, 'Go home, O Lucky One, and awaken her who is miserable without you, who is so meritorious and fruitful, a keeper of the Dharma. Go home, and make a śrāddha offering by her own hand. Recalling the auspicious tīrthas, worship the greatest gods. Thus the benefit created by pilgrimage will be yours.'

(1) By this story a householder is authorized for pilgrimage only together with his wife. (2) Thus the idea that "Only a householder without a sacred fire is authorized, but not one

with a sacred fire" is refuted.

(3) A widower is also authorized, according to the words of the BRAHMAPURĀṆA, "Or else, when his authority to sacrifice has ceased."[1] [81]

(4) A forest-dweller is also authorized, according to the saying of the KŪRMAPURĀṆA :

86. Having removed the three debts[2], one should frequent tīrthas after arranging maintenance for his wife and leaving her with his sons.

(1) 'Leaving her with his sons' applies to the alternative of becoming a forest-dweller without one's wife, according to the saying of MANU :

87. Entrusting his wife to his sons, or accompanied by her, one may go to the forest.

(1) But in the alternative of being 'accompanied by her,' he is authorized for pilgrimage only together with his wife.

(2) An ascetic is also authorized for pilgrimage, according to the KĀŚĪKHAṆḌA :

88. Travel to tīrthas should be done by the twice-born, by those who desire liberation,[3] and by those who desire the benefits of that (pilgrimage). A son who wants to throw the bones of his mother or father (into a tīrtha) may also make a pilgrimage;

and also by the permission of KĀTYĀYANA, speaking of mendicancy :

89. Those (ascetics) who stay one night in a village stay five nights in a city or at a tīrtha.

(1) A kṣatriya is also authorized for pilgrimage :

90. Or else a king, if all his worldly property is lost, (may make a pilgrimage), letting brāhmaṇas lead the way.

(1) Thus this authority is given in the BRAHMAPURĀṆA even for a king, preceded by his brāhmaṇas; (2) and also in the

1. By the death of his wife.
2. The debts that every man has to the gods, sages, and ancestors.
3. I.e., ascetics.

MAHĀBHĀRATA, wherein a pilgrimage is made by Bhīṣma, Balabhadra, the Pāṇḍavas, and other (kṣatriyas).[1]

(3) A Vaiśya is also authorized for pilgrimage, according to the Kṛkala story in the BRAHMAPURĀṆA [85], and a text to be quoted below [91].

(4) Śūdras are also authorized for pilgrimage, as is indicated in the MAHĀBHĀRATA, in connection with Puṣkara :

91. Whether a brāhmaṇa, kṣatriya, vaiśya, or śūdra, O Most Powerful of Kings—these great souls will never have a low birth if they have bathed in the tīrtha.

(1) Śūdras are also authorized because the previously quoted words are of general application.[2]

MANU, however, says :

92. Prayer, austerity, pilgrimage, renunciation, practice of mantras, and adoration of deities : these six practices are sins for women and śūdras.

Also :

93. Service to brāhmaṇas alone is the best form of Dharma for a śūdra; for whatever he does other than that yields him no benefit.

(1) These statements mean that pilgrimage is not to be made by a śūdra if it interferes with his service to brāhmaṇas, or is done constantly. Thus it is said in the MAHĀBHĀRATA :

94. A śūdra who practices a Dharma which conflicts with obedience to brāhmaṇas burns in hell; and also if he listens to or recites the Veda.

ŚĀTĀTAPA too prohibits constant pilgrimage, etc. ;

95. Constant pilgrimage, renunciation, practice of mantras,

---

1. In the Tīrthayātrā Parvan of the Vana Parvan.
2. This refers to words such as those of Śaṅkha (40), "All tīrthas are ...auspicious; they destroy men's sins always..."

propitation of deities, meditation—these practices bring great sin on them.

(1) By the word 'them' he refers to śūdras and pratilomajas. In commenting on MANU's words, "For whatever he does other than that," [93] MEDHĀTITHI says :

96. The prohibition of other practices is meant (only) to eulogize service to brāhmaṇas.[1]

(1) Therefore a śūdra is also authorized for pilgrimage if it does not interfere with his service to the twice-born.

(2) Among mixed castes too, the anulomajas, such as mūrdhāvasiktas, are authorized. For being of twice-born caste, they are authorized to practice the Dharma of the twice-born. (3) Pratilomajas also are authorized, according to the smṛti:

97. All born in violation of the law[2] are said to have the same Dharma as śūdras.

(1) 'Born in violation of the law' means born as a result of misconduct.

(2) Women too are authorized, as is indicated in the MAHĀBHĀRATA, in connection with Puṣkara:

98. Whatever sins have been committed from birth by a man or woman, all of them vanish just by going to Puṣkara.

(1) Among women, widows especially are authorized, as is said in the SKANDAPURĀṆA in giving the religious duties of a widow :

99. Bathing, donation, pilgrimage, repeating the name of Viṣṇu...

(1) Even in the case of a widow pilgrimage is not to be made of her own accord, but rather only with the consent of her sons, relatives, etc., according to the saying of MANU:

---

1. It is not to be taken literally.
2. I.e., pratilomajas.

100. Nothing, even in the home, is to be done by a woman of her own accord, be she a girl, young woman, or old;

and according to the statement of YĀJÑAVALKYA :

101. The father should protect a young daughter; the husband a married woman; in her old age, her sons should protect her. If she has no sons, their relatives protect her. Women are never independent.

(1) Married women are authorized to make pilgrimage only with their husbands, not alone; for in the words of MANU:

102. Women may not sacrifice alone, nor practice vows, nor fast. But a woman who serves her husband rejoices with him in heaven,

(1) sacrifice etc. also implicitly includes pilgrimage. (2) The previously quoted words of MANU, 'These six practices are sins for women and śūdras' [92] refer, as in the case of the śūdras, only to cases in which she abandons her duty to her husband.

(3) Anyone who desires to throw the bones of his mother etc. into a tīrtha is authorized to make a pilgrimage according to the previously quoted words, 'Who wants to throw the bones of his mother or father...' [88].

(4) Anyone who has committed a sin is also authorized to make a pilgrimage in order to remove that sin, according to the saying:

103. For men who have committed sins, a tīrtha is the atonement for their sins. For men of pure souls, a tīrtha gives the benefit ascribed to it; (=127, 178)

and according to the saying of the KŪRMAPURĀṆA,

104. A penitent, a wise man, a mendicant, a householder, and other such people should frequent tīrthas.

(1) If the pilgrimage is made as a penance, even a householder is authorized to go without his wife, according to the saying:

105. Or a penitent may go to a tīrtha, even without his wife, (= 84, 128)

(1) and because one who has not done his penance is forbidden to have contact with any other person.

THE CAUSES OF VARYING DEGREES OF BENEFIT FROM TĪRTHAS

ŚAṄKHA :

106. One who arrives at a tīrtha incidentally should bathe in the tīrtha; he gets the benefit of bathing, but not that of a pilgrimage.

(1) 'Incidentally' here means incidentally to merchantry, royal service, or other travel. But in the statement of PAIṬHĪNASI :

107. He gets half its benefit, who goes to a tīrtha incidentally. He gets a sixteenth part of the benefit, who goes on behalf of someone else, (= 605)

(1) 'incidentally' means incidentally to another tīrtha which was the intended goal of his journey. (2) 'On behalf of someone else' means receiving pay. (3) In the PRABHĀSAKHAṆḌA, however, the reading is 'who goes with someone else's food': this means eating someone else's food.

In the PRABHĀSAKHAṆḌA :

108. And if a powerful man by his influence causes another to make a pilgrimage with his own supplies and vehicle, his merit is four-fold.

(1) And if one leads distinguished men on a pilgrimage, his merit is eight-fold. This is said to Yudhiṣṭhira in the MAHĀBHĀRATA :

109. Because you lead the sages, your benefit is eightfold.

VARYING DEGREES OF BENEFIT CAUSED BY PARTICULAR VEHICLES

In the MATSYA and KŪRMAPURĀṆAS, MĀRKAṆḌEYA says :

110. I will tell you, my dear, the rule of pilgrimage in proper order, in the manner of the sages themselves, as it was seen and heard. When a man sets out for a pilgrimage to Prayāga mounted on a bull--hear what befalls him ! He dwells in a fearful hell; for fierce is the anger of bulls. And the ancestors of that person get no water.

A'so, in the same places :

111. If a man, whether from vainglory or from ignorance, travels by vehicle, the tīrtha yields him no benefit. Therefore one should avoid vehicles.

Also :

112. If one travels by bullock-cart, that is said to be equal to killing a bull; if in a horse-cart, the pilgrimage has no benefit; if in a man-drawn vehicle, the benefit is halved; but if by foot, it is four-fold.

(1) 'By foot' means with bare feet.

(2) A certain author has said : "Thus (the text 112) indicates that for discarding shoes the merit is increased; but wearing them does not cause a diminution, but rather is a necessity; for by virtue of the word 'always' in the VIṢṆUPURĀṆA text

113. One who desires to protect his body should go with an umbrella in heat and rain always, with a staff at night and in forests, and always with shoes,

(1) protection of the body is necessary even on a pilgrimage; moreover, there is no specific prohibition (of wearing shoes).[1] And also in the PRABHĀSAKHAṆḌA text :

---

1. Cf. TiCi pp. 8-9.

114. Going to tīrthas on foot is said to be the greatest austerity; for going by vehicle one gets only the benefit of bathing there,

(1) merely 'going by foot' as such is mentioned, while vehicles are censured; (2) and going with shoes does not cancel 'going by foot,' nor is a shoe a vehicle."

But this is not so; for it contradicts the words of JĀBĀLI:

115. Eating twice a day takes away a third part of the benefit of a tīrtha; a vehicle, one half; umbrella or footwear, a fourth part. Therefore going without these one may gain the complete benefit of a tīrtha.

It also contradicts these words :

116 A vehicle destroys half the benefit of a tīrtha; an umbrela or footwear, half of that half. Carrying on trade ruins three parts (of four); accepting gifts, all of it.

(1) The fault here (in wearing footwear) should not be taken as that which is caused by a vehicle; rather it will be a specially prescribed fault, like that of using a umbrella. (2) Furthermore: if putting on shoes is a necessity, then how could there be an *increase* of benefit for taking them off? (3) To the contrary, there would be a decrease of merit.[1]

(4) Nor should it be said: "According to this text there is no diminution of benefit by one-fourth if *only* shoes are put on (but not an umbrella), for the intention is to express the combination (of shoes and umbrella) understood in a copulative compound ;[2] as in the sentence 'A king and a chief priest, desiring communion, should sacrifice.' "[3] For this is a different case. (5) For in that case, there is an intention to express combination because (the duality) refers to the grammatical agent, which is to be taken in a combined sense.

1. For not doing what is required.

2. I.e., only if one both wears shoes *and* carries an umbrella does he ose one-fourth of the benefit.

3. This example of 'intention to express combination' is discussed in Śab 6.6.2.12-15.

(6) Here, however, there is no intention to express combination, because (the duality) refers to the intended aim of the sentence; as in the sentence, '(Either of) whose two sacrificial cakes burn.'[1] (7) Therefore, wearing shoes is bad by itself.

(8) "But," it is objected, "there is still a contradiction. One going by foot gets a four-fold benefit; with shoes the normal benefit is less by one fourth. Those going by other vehicles get still less. (9) So who gets the full benefit?"

(10) It is replied: in the phrase 'four-fold' [112], the word '-fold' (guṇa) is used as a synonym of the word 'quarter', meaning 'a fourth part'; as in the saying 'In the kṛta-era, Dharma has four quarters.'[2] (11) Thus the meaning is that for one going by foot, the benefit is 'four-fold,' that is, four-quartered, or 'full.'

(12) Others, however, say " 'Four-fold' is said as a metaphorical praise of going by foot, and not to (literally) specify the benefit."

GOBHILA says :

117. A person who makes a pilgrimage in a wagon yoked with bulls goes to a fearful hell for as many (years) as the bull has hairs.

(1) All such statements as these are to be understood as referring to covering the whole way by wagon. (2) If one goes only a certain distance by wagon, the variation in benefit is to be calculated according to the distance travelled in krośas, yojanas, etc.

In this connection it is said in the KALPATARU : "In the MATSYAPURĀṆA, when asked by Yudhiṣṭhira

118. By what rule should those who are resolute in Dharma go on pilgrimage? Tell me, Great-minded One, the rule which is prescribed for going to Prayāga,

---

1. Śab 3.1.7.13-15 explains that a grammatical number which refers to the intended aim of the sentence (uddeśya) is not intended to be taken literally (the Graha-nyāya).

2. I.e., it is complete.

(118 1) Mārkaṇḍeya says 'I will tell you...When a man sets out for a pilgrimage to Prayāga,' etc. [110]. Thus because these words are found in the context of Prayāga, the prohibition of vehicles and the statement that pilgrimage is without benefit if a vehicle is used apply only to Prayāga. (2) In a pilgrimage to another tīrtha, however, there is only a partial diminution of benefit for using a vehicle."

(3) This view is dubious; since the words of GOBHILA and JĀBĀLI [117,115] and others refer to tīrthas in general, it is reasonable to hold that, like those others, these words of the MATSYAPURĀṆA too, expanding beyond their immediate context, refer to both the tīrtha being discussed and those not being explicitly discussed. (4) Or it may be that these words are placed in the particular context (of Prayāga) by way of being a supplementary passage which singles out a particular instance (avayutyānuvādatā).

(5) In this connection, a certain author has taken the statement 'When a man sets for a pilgrimage to Prayāga' [110] also as a supplementary passage singling out (Prayāga), meant to imply any tīrtha, by cancelling the context (Prayāga) by the direct statement of the general saying 'The tīrtha yields him no benefit' [111]; and thus he has declared that the statement of the MATSYAPURĀṆA [118] refers in this way to all tīrthas.

(6) But this is not so; for as in the cases of the direct statement of rice in an Agni-hymn,[1] the direct statement in the

---

1. 'The direct statement of rice' refers to the injunction in connection with the Darśa-Pūrṇamāsa sacrifice, 'Vrīhīn prokṣati' (He sprinkles the rice). Here the direct statement of just 'rice' as such is not ascribed any quality at all different from the particular rice which is be inferred from the context; that is, the rice which is used as an offering in the Darśa-Pūrṇamāsa. Therefore there is no conflict between literal statement and contextual statement, so the former can not be taken as overruling the latter.

Similarly, 'the direct statement of an Agni-hymn' refers to the injunction in connection with Jyotiṣṭoma sacrifice, "Āgneyyāgnīdhram upatiṣṭhate' (He approaches the fire-place with an Agni-hymn). In MS 3.2.8.21-24, it is determined that in this case only those Agni-hymns which are otherwise mentioned in connection with the Jyotiṣṭoma—i.e. those which are contextually inferrable—are to be used, and not just any Agni-hymns.

form of the word 'tīrtha' (in 'That tīrtha yields h m no benefit') being comparable in all its qualities with the context (Prayāga), there would not be any such conflict as that which is expressed by the words 'in the case of a conjunction' in the sūtra 'Direct statement, indication...'[1]; whereas there is such a coflict in the case of the repetition of the twenty-one (Sāmidhenī verses), etc., in which case that sūtra is the basis for determining that those repetitions are done for the sake of such benefits as the directly stated 'establishment,' by overruling the context which would establish that those repetitions are mere subsidiaries of the Darśa-Pūrṇamāsa sacrifice.[2] (118.7) Otherwise, by overruling the context of such words as 'rice' and 'an Agni-hymn' also, those words could then apply to all rice or all Agni-hyms, and it would follow that rice meant for eating (and not for

---

Again, since the direct statement of just 'an Agni-hymn' does not conflict in any way with the contextual inference of 'an Agni-hymn connected with the Jyotiṣṭoma,' the direct statement does not overrule the context.

1. The reference is to the important MS 3.3.7.14, 'Śruti-liṅga-vākya-prakaraṇa-sthāna-samākhyānāṃ samavāye pāradaurbalyam arthaviprakarṣāt, which prescribes the order of predominance of the six different kinds of interpretation—direct statement, indication, syntax, context, etc.—in case of a 'concurrence' (samavāya), that is, a conflict (virodha), between them. But in the case at hand, of a direct statement of 'a tīrtha' and a context of 'Prayāga,' there is no such conflict, because 'a tīrtha' does not involve any special qualities not attributable to Prayāga; likewise in the other examples, of rice, etc. Thus since there is no conflict there is no scope for the overruling of context by direct statement; and to do so would cause the undesirable results explained in the next sentence of the text.

2. In connection with the Darśa-Pūrṇamāsa sacrifice, it is prescribed 'Ekaviṃśatim anubrūyat pratiṣṭhākāmasya, caturviṃśatim anubrūyāt brahmavarcasakāmasya...' (He should repeat twenty-one (Sāmidhenī verses) for one who desires establishment; he should repeat twenty-four for one who desires the glory of Brahma...'). Here the question is whether these repetitions are merely a subsidiary of the Darśa-Pūrṇamāsa, or whether they are done for their own purpose. According to the context, they are merely a part of the Darśa-Pūrṇamāsa; but according to the ı: statement of their prescription, they are separate acts to be done for their own particular benefits ('establishment' etc.), separate from the benefit of the Darśa-Pūrṇamāsa. Thus in this case there *is* a conflict between context and direct statement, and according to the sūtra cited the direct statement prevails; unlike the cases of 'rice,' 'Agni-hymn,' and 'tīrtha,' where there is no such conflict. See TV 3.3.7.14, p. 835.

ritual use) would be sprinkled, etc., and that the approch to the fireplace would be done with an inappropriate Agni-hymn;[1] how could any Mīmāṃsaka avoid this? (8) Enough of this! We return to the subject at hand.

The statement in the PRABHĀSA KHAṆḌA :

119. A brāhmaṇa may go by vehicle to those tīrthas— Kurukṣetra, etc.—which can be reached by a chariot. In going to them by vehicle there is no fault,

(1) refers to the handicapped; (120.1) for they are permitted by GOBHILA to use vehicles :

120. But a handicapped person may make a pilgrimage by vehicle. Performing the Dharma to the best of his ability, he obtains the specified benefit.

Also in the KŪRMAPURĀṆA :

121. Man-drawn vehicle, or chariot drawn by she-mule, horse, etc.; for the handicapped person on pilgrimage, such a vehicle does not cause any fault.

In connection with this, a certain author has said : "According to the saying

122. A ship is not a vehicle,

there is no fault in going by ship."

(1) This is not so; a ship also is clearly a vehicle, insofar as it is a means whereby one may reach an intended foreign land which cannot by reached by the an exertion of his body alone. Therefore it falls within the range of the prohibition of vehicles,

---

1. If one accepts the mode of interpretation proposed in 118.5, which involves the overruling of context by direct statement even when there is no conflict between the two, it leads to this result of inappropriate ritual actions, since the ritual acts may be applied to objects not appropriate to the context of the particular ritual.

Thus although the conclusion of the proposition in 118.5—that statements such as 118 which concern Prayāga in fact apply to all tīrthas—is the proper one, the mode of argumentation used is logically defective; so only the interpretation of 118.3-4, 'breaking through,' rather than 'cancelling' the context, is acceptable.

and it follows that it is to be avoided in all cases. But that statement [122] establishes that there is no fault in a case where travel is impossible without a ship, such as to Śaṅkhoddhāra, Gaṅgāsāgara, and where, the area of the road being flooded by rivers, etc., it is impossible to go without a ship. Thus the statement in question finds its application in these cases, and so does not constitute evidence that there is no fault in going by ship to tīrthas which can be reached on foot. (122.2) And there is proof to the contrary (that there is a fault in going by ship), inasmuch as it *is* a vehicle.

(3) A certain author, however, has said : "Saying a ship is a non-vehicle, while in fact it does have the form of a vehicle, is like saying that goats and other animals other than cows and horses are 'non-animals', although they *do* have the form of animals, in order to praise cows and horses ; as in the saying 'Animals other than cows and horses are non-animals; cows and horses are animals.' The ship is said to be a non-vehicle, in order to praise other vehicles such as horses, etc." (4) This is not so : Since the statement [122] has already found its application (as a prescription), it is not right to consider it as an explanatory passage.[1] (5) And further, if that statement were a praise of horse chariots, etc., then it would follow that one ought to travel by that (i.e. by ship). (6) Then the idea would be 'Horses, etc., being praised vehicles, the fault caused by a vehicle would apply to them, but no fault, or a lesser fault, would apply to a ship.' (7) Then the attempt to establish this statement as explanatory is ruled out; because as a matter of fact there is a *greater* fault in going by ship, as it involves no greater effort than other vehicles, and an additional fault arises from contact with sailors,[2] etc. (8) Nor is this phrase to be construed along with the prohibition of other vehicles, whereby it would be an explanatory passage.[3]

---

1. See arthavāda in "Glossary of Mīmāṁsā and Other Technical Terms."
2. Who are considered impure.
3. A commendatory statement which constitutes a single sentence together with a prescription is taken as an arthavāda; but such is not the case here.

(9) "Then why does this statement not apply to the handicapped?" (10) It does not, because there is no need to mention a ship specially, as it has already been established by the previously cited sentences [119-121] that other vehicles are not forbidden for the handicapped. (11) Thus this statement would have to be taken as a supplementary passage singling out a particular instance[1]. (12) Therefore it refers to just what we have said it does. Enough of this !

Thus this statement by the author of the MAHĀRṆAVAPRAKĀŚA :

> 123. It is taken as the basis of the discussion that that is a vehicle, which by its own motion brings one to another place.[2] But chariots, ships, etc., are not such, and thus are not vehicles; so there is no fault in going by them,

(1) is disproven; for a chariot and ship do also have the characteristics of a vehicle. (2) Also, his definition of a vehicle would be overextensive, as it would apply to such things as the current of a river. (3) Therefore there is in fact a fault in going by ship.

(4) Also in this connection : Twice-born men should not go to those tīrthas in the ocean or on islands which can be reached only by a ship-journey of many days; for travelling by ship is included in the things which are forbidden in the Kali-era :

> 124. A twice-born man who travels by ship, even if he undergoes purification, is included (in the things forbidden in the Kali-era).

(1) For this saying must refer to a boat-journey of many days, which results in a sin, and not to a short journey, because that does not result in that sin, so that purification—that is, penance—would not apply to it.

(2) Those who are forbidden to go to Aṅga, Vaṅga, and other such lands, are not forbidden to go even there when their intention is to make a pilgrimage, according to the smṛti :

---

1. Rather than as a prescription, which would be preferable.
2. Such as a horse or bullock.

125. One who goes to Aṅga, Vaṅga, Kaliṅga, Saurāṣṭra, or Magadha, unless it be for a pilgrimage, must re-do his consecration ceremonies.

(1) The same consideration applies to the frontier countries.

THUS ENDS THE DISCUSSION OF VEHICLES IN THE BRIDGE TO THE THREE HOLY PLACES BY NĀRĀYAṆA BHAṬṬA, SON OF THE NOBLE BHAṬṬARĀMEŚVARA SŪRI.

TĪRTHAS AS EQUIVALENT SUBSTITUTES

In connection with the Varying Degrees of Benefit, TĪRTHAS AS EQUIVALENT SUBSTITUTES will be described, in order to explain the varying degrees of benefit caused by different numbers of yojanas travelled on a pilgrimage made for the sake of penance.

(2) Now the basic statements on this subject are those concerned with pilgrimage being made in order to wipe out sins. These have been quoted in The Praise of Tīrthas: "Going to tīrthas..." [50], etc.

From the statement of the ĀDITYAPURĀṆA:

126. With the Pāṇḍavas, to gain their kingdom and to end ill fortune, together with Śrīkṛṣṇa, Nārada, Vyāsa, Śrīkaṇṭha, Indra, Aja, and Romaśa, and with Mārkaṇḍeya, Pulastya, and Aja, the foremost of the seven sages, taking on themselves twenty-four years of penances devoutly, they carried them out by means of tīrthas: this story is told in the Ādi Purāṇa,

(1) it is understood that pilgrimage is an equivalent substitute for such penances as the prājāpatya.

Also in the KĀŚĪKHAṆḌA :

127. For men who have committed sins, a tīrtha is the atonement for their sins. (=103, 178)

Also :

128. Or else a penitent may go to a tīrtha, even without his wife. (=84, 105)

DEVALA says :

129. Coming to tīrthas and auspicious shrines, men who are diligent brāhmaṇas are freed from sin. All rivers are

auspicious, all great mountains are auspicious; every shrine is auspicious, all forest dwellings are auspicious.

(129.1) Thus the method of calculation when a pilgrimage is to be made for the sake of penance, described in the SMṚTYARTHASĀRA and other texts,[1] is given here. (2) In this connection, bathing in the Bhāgīrathī after coming sixty yojanas on foot with a declaration of intent made beforehand according to the rule for penances, is equal to six years of kṛcchra penance. (3) For each increase of one yojana, an increase of one-half of a kṛcchra is to be added. (4) Since one who comes sixty yojanas has six years of penance, one who comes ten yojanas will have one year of penance. (5) And thus one who comes one and one-third krośas achieves one kṛcchra[2] by bathing in the Bhāgīrathī according to rule, if there are mountains and other obstacles en route. (6) If there are no such obstacles, and the road is not difficult, then by bathing in the Gaṅgā (= Bhāgīrathī) after coming one yojana a healthy person achieves one kṛcchra instead of three. (7) But for a handicapped person coming one-half of a yojana, and, if the road is difficult, for a healthy person coming one-half of a yojana, the result is the same (one kṛcchra).

(8) Of old, the seven divine mothers, fearing the demons, became rivers. When they were no longer afraid, they became deities again; then the rivers dried up. In their place there came to be the Bhāgīrathī. (9) Bathing in the Gaṅgās which are named for the seven divine mothers, Viṣṇugaṅgā, etc., after coming sixty yojanas, is equal to six years of kṛcchras. (10) At Prayāga, Vārāṇasī, Gaṅgādvāra, and at the confluence of the Gaṅgā with the ocean (Gaṅgāsāgara), it is equal to twice that. (11) Bathing in the Yamunā after coming twenty yojanas is

---

1. SAS pp. 150ff.; MP pp. 755ff.

2. One prājāpatya kṛcchra takes twelve days, so one year of kṛcchras = 30 kṛcchras. Thus

60 yojanas = 6 years of kṛcchras = 180 kṛcchras

10 yojanas = 1 year of kṛcchras = 30 kṛcchras

and 1 yojana = 3 kṛcchras.

Since 1 yojana = 4 krośas,

$1\frac{1}{3}$ krośa = 1 kṛcchra.

equal to two years of kṛcchras; (12) at Mathurā, twice that. (13) Bathing in the Sarasvatī after coming forty yojanas is equal to four years of kṛcchras; (14) at Prabhāsa and Dvāravatī, twice that. (15) On pilgrimages to the Yamunā and Sarasvatī, for an increase of one yojana, an increase of one quarter of a kṛcchra is to be figured. (16) The decrease in benefit in case of the relative ease of the road due to the absence of mountains, etc. is to be figured just as previously described [129.6].

(17) Also in this connection the number of days of bathing is to be taken into account, according to the words of the SKANDAPURĀṆA :

> 130. The water of the Sarasvatī purifies in three days; of the Yamunā, in seven. Gaṅgā water purifies instantly; that of the Narmadā, merely by the sight of it.

(1) Bathing in the Dṛṣadvatī, Śutudrī, Vipāśā, Vitastā, Śarāvatī, Marudvṛdhā, Payasvinī, Ghṛtavatī, and other divine rivers after coming fifteen yojanas is equal to thirty kṛcchras. (2) Bathing in the Candrabhāgā, Vetravatī, Śarayū, Gomatī, Devikā, Kauśikī, Mandākinī, Nityajalā, Sahasravaktrā, Paunaḥpunyā, Pūrṇapuṇyā, Bāhudā, Vāruṇī, Gaṇḍakī, and other divine rivers after coming fifteen yojanas is equal to fifteen kṛcchras. (3) Bathing at the confluence of two of these great rivers is equal to three kṛcchras for one who has come one yojana. (4) Bathing at the confluence of the above-mentioned divine rivers with the great rivers that flow to the ocean has the benefit of six kṛcchras for one who has come one yojana.

(5) At places not mentioned, the number of kṛcchras is equal to the number of yojanas of the journey. (6) For bathing in the great male rivers,[1] the benefit is half that of the great female rivers; (7) but in the great male river Śoṇa, half the benefit of the Gaṅgā. (8) For bathing in the male rivers, one gets half the benefit of the female rivers.

(9) If an oblation is made in a eternally visible fire such as that at Māhiṣmatī,[2] ten times the basic benefit is obtained; (10) and likewise at Jvālāmukhī.

1. These are enumerated in 66.
2. I.e. in a live volcanic opening in the earth.

(130.11) Frequenting such places of liberation as Gaṇa, Mahānadī, Seturāmeśvara, Padmanābha, Śrīraṅga, Puruṣottama, Kurukṣetra, Naimiṣa, Badaryāśrama, Puṇyāraṇya, Kedāra, Śrīśaila, Mahālaya, Rudrakoṭi, Puṣkara, Narmadā, Āmrātakeśvara, Kubjāmra, Prabhāsa, Kokāmukha, Vijayeśa, Purīndra, Pañcanada, Gokarṇa, Mathurā, Ayodhyā, Dvāravatī, Gayā, Kāñcī, Śālagrāma, Śambhalagrāma, and Saṃnihatī, one obtains a benefit equal to that of the Gaṅgā.

(12) For one who has come twenty-four yojanas, bathing in the Narmadā has the benefit of twenty-four kṛcchras; (13) at the confluence with the Kubjikā, twice that; (14) at Śuklatīrtha, four times. (15) For one who has come eight yojanas, bathing in the Tāpī is equal to eight kṛcchras; (16) likewise in the Payoṣṇī; (17) at the confluence of the two, twice that.

(18) For one who has come sixty yojanas, bathing in the Godāvarī is equal to three years' kṛcchras. (19) For one who has come thirty yojanas, bathing both with and against the current at the eleven tīrthas is equal to sixty kṛcchras; (20) at the confluence with the Vañjarā, twice that; (21) at Saptagodāvara and Bhīmeśvara, three times. (22) For one who has come twelve yojanas, bathing at Kuśatarpaṇa and at the Vañjarā is equal to twelve kṛcchras. (23) Bathing in the Praṇītā is equal to eight kṛcchras for one who has come eight yojanas; (24) in the Pūrṇā, half of that. (25) For bathing in the Kṛṣṇaveṇā, the number of kṛcchras is the same as the number of yojanas; (26) likewise in the Tuṅgabhadrā; (27) twice that, at the confluence with the Pampā; (28) three times, at Harihara. (29) For bathing in the Bhīmarathī, the number of kṛcchras is the same as the number of yojanas. (30) To one who has come ten yojanas and bathes at the confluence with the Kakudminī, fifteen kṛcchras accrue., (31) For bathing in the Malāpahāriṇī, the number of kṛcchras is the same as the number of yojanas; (32) likewise in the Nivṛtti.

(33) For bathing in the Godāvarī, there is an increase of one quarter of a kṛcchra for each increase of a yojana in the journey. (34) When Jupiter is in Leo, bathing in the Godāvarī is everywhere equal to bathing in the Jāhnavī (Gaṅgā). (35) When

Jupiter is in Virgo, bathing in the Kṛṣṇaveṇā is everywhere equal to half the benefit of the Jāhnavī. (130.36) Bathing in the Tuṅgabhadrā when the Sun is in Libra or Cancer has half the benefit of the Gaṅgā. (37) For one who has come thirty yojanas, bathing in the Kṛṣṇaveṇā at the confluence with the Malāpahāriṇī is equal to thirty kṛcchras; (38) at the confluence with the Bhīmarathī, twice that; (39) at the confluence with the Tuṅgabhadrā, three times that; (40) at the confluence with the Nivṛtti, four times; (41) at Brahmeśvara, five times.

(42) For one who has come thirty yojanas, bathing in the Pātālagaṅgā near Mallikārjuna is equal to six years of kṛcchras; (43) to the east of that, sixty kṛcchras; (44) at Liṅgālaya, twice that; (45) likewise at the confluence with the ocean.

(46) To one who has come ten yojanas and bathed in the great river Kāverī accrue fifteen kṛcchras; (47) to one who has come twelve yojanas and bathed in the Tāmraparṇī, Kīrtimālā, and Payasvinī, twelve kṛcchras.

(48) The rivers which rise at the foot of the Sahyādrī mountains, and whose flow is continuous for at least a yojana, give the benefit of one, two, or three kṛcchras, according to their length, to one who has come one yojana. (49) The rivers which arise from the Vindhya and Śrīśaila mountains have twice that benefit; (50) those arising from the Himācala, three times that. (51) Small streams which are not mentioned at all in the smṛtis, purāṇas, and other texts give to one who has come one yojana the benefit of three nights (one fourth of a kṛcchra). (52) Such small rivers[1] give the benefit of one kṛcchra; (53) rivers, two kṛcchras; (54) great rivers, three kṛcchras. (55) Those rivers which flow from one yojana up to six yojanas are called 'small streams'; (56) from there up to twelve yojanas, 'small rivers'; (57) from there up to twenty-four yojanas, 'rivers'; (58) those which flow more yojanas than that, 'great rivers'; (59) and also those which flow to the sea. (60) Also, whatever river is mentioned as a 'great river' in the purāṇas, etc., is also a great river. (61) Bathing in a great river, accompanied by fasting, is equal to one kṛcchra, even if the distance travelled is less than a yojana. (62)

1. I.e., those not mentioned in smṛtis, purāṇas, etc.

Rivers such as the Śunī whose names are bad,[1] and evil rivers such as the Karmanāśā are to be avoided.

(130.63) Bathing in the ocean should be done everywhere on a new moon day; (64) and it is always to be done at the confluence of rivers and lakes, or near a deity. (65) For one who has come fifteen yojanas, bathing in the ocean is equal to just that many kṛcchras; (66) twice that, if nearby a famous deity. (67) If one beholds that deity after bathing, he gets three times that benefit. (68) For one who has come thirty yojanas, beholding Setu is equal to thirty kṛcchras. (69) If after bathing, one beholds Rāmeśvara, he gets twice that.

(70) For natives of the Vindhya the benefit of bathing at Seturāmeśvara is triple that of the Jāhnavī. (71) And bathing in the Jāhnavī and at Kedāra is likewise tripled for them. (72) For natives of the south, the benefit of bathing in the Jāhnavī is six-fold. (73) For natives of the Gaṅgā region, the benefit of bathing at Seturāmeśvara is six-fold. (74) Beholding Skanda is equal to twenty kṛcchras for one who has come thirty yojanas. (75) Likewise, wherever (a river) is called 'Gaṅgā.'

(76) In all cases, when there is an obstacle by way of difference of language, mountains, etc., or where the road is difficult, the (same) benefits in kṛcchras etc., are to be figured with a decrease in the number of yojanas to be travelled from the number of yojanas specified, because of the greater effort expended.

(77) At Śrīraṅga, Padmanābha, Puruṣottama, Cakrakoṭa and Mahālakṣmīdarśanasthāna, and at Loṇāra, bathing is equal to thirty kṛcchras for one who has come thirty yojanas. (78) For beholding deities at all Vaiṣṇava. Māheśvara, Saura, and Śākta shrines, the number of kṛcchras is the same as the number of yojanas; (79) at famed shrines, twice that.

(80) At other places not mentioned, the number of kṛcchras is to be understood as equal to the number of yojanas.

---

1. Because the word 'Śunī' means 'bitch'. Other such rivers—Caṇḍālī, Kaṣṭagā, etc.—are given in SAS, p.153.

(81) At those places also, an extra benefit is to be understood because of special factors, such as beholding gods, one's homeland, age, physical strength, and voluntary restrictions; and a lesser (benefit) is to be understood in the absence of such factors. (82) And wherever, whatever, and however much (benefit) is specially mentioned in the Purāṇas, etc., that is to be taken just so.

(83) A person who is on the bank of a tīrtha, though he has not come from a place distant by at least a yojana, should bathe properly and put on clean clothes; when his hair is dry, he should bathe again. (84) By bathing in this way twelve times, he obtains the benefit of one kṛcchra.

(85) The previously mentioned restrictions like eating only once a day, sleeping on the ground, observing chastity outside the normal time, etc., are to be practiced on the journey. (86) At the tīrtha, bathing, tarpaṇa, etc. are to be performed. (87) The pilgrimage should always be considered as ending with the worship of one or another deity.

(88) The kṛcchra referred to here is to be taken as the one called 'Prājāpatya,' described by YĀJÑAVALKYA as follows :

131. Eating once a day, eating by night only, eating unasked-for food only, and fasting; this is said to be a Pāda-kṛcchra. When managed three times, it is called Prājāpatya.

(1) Thus since the Pāda-kṛcchra, which is completed in four days, is repeated three times, the Prājāpatya-kṛcchra is completed in twelve days and nights.

The measure of a yojana is as follows :

132. Eight barley corns, or three grains of rice put lengthwise, are said to be a finger's measure. Twelve finger's measures are a vitasti. A pair of vitastis is a hand's measure. Four hand's measures are a rod (daṇḍa). Two thousand of these are a krośa; and four of these, a yojana.

THUS ENDS 'TĪRTHAS AS EQUIVALENT SUBSTITUTES'

PURITY OF TIMES FOR A PILGRIMAGE

133. On the sixth, eighth, or twelfth days of a fortnight one should not travel, nor on a 'tridinaspṛś'[1] day; nor on a full-moon day, the first day of a fortnight, a new-moon day, a 'riktā' day,[2] or an 'avama' day.

In the RATNAMĀLĀ :

134. Hastā, Indu, Maitra, Śravaṇa, Aśvin, Puṣya, Pauṣṇa, Śraviṣṭha, and Punarvasu are the best asterisms for a new journey; avoiding the third, fifth, first, and seventh stars.[3] Citrā, Viśākhā, Anala, Sārpa, Yāmya, Vāyavya, Pitrya, Īśvara, and Daivata are undesirable for journeys. The other asterisms are said to be neither favourable nor unfavourable.

Also :

135. The days of the moon, Saturn, Mars, and the sun[4] are said to be inauspicious for a journey.

Also :

136. The days of the moon, Mercury, Jupiter, and Venus[5] yield success in all rites.

Also :

137. Vyatīpāta, parighārdha, vaidhṛtiyoga, viṣṭikaraṇa, krāntisamatva, kulikas, avama, and gaṇḍānta are not auspicious.

LALLA :

138. When Jupiter is in Nīca (=Makara, Capricorn), in

---

1. For this and other terms in this chapter, see the "Glossarial Index of Sanskrit Terms in the Translation."
2. See 290.4 below.
3. In relation to one's birth-star.
4. Monday, Saturday, Tuesday, and Sunday.
5. Monday, Wednesday, Thursday, and Friday.

reversed motion, in accelerated motion, or new, old,[1] or set, then renunciation, religious journey, the rites of vows and voluntary restrictions, the ear-piercing ceremony, initiation, the tying of the mauñjī-cord, tonsure, and marriage ceremonies, the dedication of a building or a god-image should be avoided scrupulously by good people; and also when Jupiter is in Leo.

Also :

139. When Jupiter is in the house of the sun, or the sun in the house of Jupiter, one should avoid all religious rites, and vows and benedictions.

Also :

140. When there is a conjunction of Jupiter and the sun, when Jupiter is in Leo, and when Venus is set, one should avoid vehicles, major donations, vows, and beholding gods.

Also :

141. When there is a conjunction of Jupiter and the sun, when Jupiter is in Leo, when Venus is set, in an intercalary month, and when the sun is dormant on its southward course, one should avoid all religious rites.

Also :

142. Ponds, wells, tanks, sacrifice, travelling, shaving, dedications, vows, the house of knowledge, the ear-piercing ceremony, major donations, the forest, service, bathing at tīrthas, marriage, temples, mantras etc., beholding gods—these one should shun afar, if he desires to live, when Venus is set. One should carefully avoid Jupiter when in Leo and in Maghā. (When Jupiter is) in the other sections of Leo, marriage is prescribed.[2]

---

1. For definitions of 'new' and 'old' Venus and Jupiter, see MuCi 5.27-28.

2. See MuCi 1.49

Also :

143. When Venus or Jupiter is new or old or set, one should avoid these for beholding gods, as in an intercalary month.

(1) In this context, it is beholding gods which has not been previously done which is prohibited. Thus GĀRGYA :

144. If, when Venus is invisible, one looks on a god previously unseen, there will be grief for him. In an intercalary month also one should avoid non-repeated pilgrimage.

(1) 'Non-repeated pilgrimage' means pilgrimage not previously made.

Also :

145. If Jupiter in accelerated motion does not re-enter that asterism (which it left prematurely), the year is considered to be dropped, forbidden for all religious rites.

The exception to this :

146. If Jupiter is in accelerated motion into Taurus, Aries, Pisces, or Aquarius, then the time would not be dropped: so says the sage Gālava.

In the RATNAMĀLĀ :

147. In which direction it rises, or where it goes due to the movement (of the globe), or to which of the stars (Kṛttikā, etc.) of the doors to the directions[1] among the circle of stars it goes : Venus is said to be opposing in three ways. Especially (where it is) risen, it is avoided scrupulously by the sages. Not even the slightest purpose of those who wish to travel attains success at this time, in a journey opposed to Venus.

The exception to this is given in the VṚTTAŚATA :

1. See MuCi 5.40, 47.

148. A journey opposed to Venus is not inauspicious for those who are born in the families of Vatsa, Bhṛgu, Aṅgiras, Bharadvāja, Vasiṣṭha, and Kaśyapa; and also in the family of Atri. In case of famine or a flood of the region, there would be no opposition to Venus, nor at a wedding; in going to tīrthas. or (a journey) of one city or village. it is benign.

(1) At certain places faults like misplacement of Jupiter are said not to occur :

149. At the Godāvarī, at Gayā, and Śrīśaila, and at the two eclipses,[1] the fault of misplacement of Jupiter and Venus is not observed.

In the VĀYUPURĀṆA :

150. At Gayā one should offer piṇḍas according to the rule at all times, (even) in an intercalary month, on one's birthday, and when Jupiter and Venus are set. Nor should the śrāddha offering at Gayā be dropped when Jupiter is in Leo.

(1) Regarding this, some say that since śrāddha (at Gayā) presupposes a pilgrimage, pilgrimage also is not prohibited at these times. Thus :

151. In an intercalary month, or one's birth star, and when Jupiter and Venus are set, pilgrimage should not be made, except to Gayā or the Godāvarī.

(1) Also other matters such as the auspiciousness of the zodiacal signs and sections of these signs as they apply to pilgrimage may be learned from those familiar with astrological texts; but they are not mentioned here, as it would take too long.

THUS ENDS 'PURITY OF TIMES FOR A PILGRIMAGE.'

---

1. I.e., of the sun or the moon.

THE WAY OF GOING TO TĪRTHAS

In the SKANDAPURĀṆA :

152. One who intends to go to a tīrtha should first fast in his home and worship Gaṇeśa, his ancestors, brāhmaṇas, and holy men to the best of his ability. Then after breaking his fast he should go joyfully, keeping to the observances. Having arrived and paid homage to his ancestors, he will obtain the specified benefit.

(1) 'Having arrived' etc., means that one who has made a pilgrimage should perform śrāddha again when he returns to his home. Thus in the BRAHMAPURĀṆA :

153. Any wise brāhmaṇa who goes on a pilgrimage should first worship Gaṇeśa in his own home, well-controlled, fasting, pure, vigilant, bowing with devotion; and he should honor the gods, ancestors, brāhmaṇas, and holy men zealously, with as much money as he can. And when he returns home he should once again honor the gods, ancestors, and brāhmaṇas in the same way. Doing so, he obtains the specified benefit from the tīrtha; there is no doubt of this.

(1) The śrāddha is to be done on the day after the fast :

154. On an auspicious month-day, an auspicious weekday and an auspicious moment, after fasting one night and, performing a śrāddha in the morning, bowing to Gaṇeśa and the brāhmaṇas, and eating, the twice-born man set out with resolute mind,

according to this other exposition of this matter in the story of Śivaśarma in the SKANDAPURĀṆA. (1) Here the order is to be construed as 'He set out on an auspicious month-day,' etc. (2) The order of the phrase 'Bowing to Gaṇeśa and the brāhmaṇas' is not intended; since the passage is merely a story, the order of the reading is not meant to be prescriptive. (3) Or else, only that bowing to Gaṇeśa etc. which is done after the śrāddha is referred to here, and not the worship of Gaṇeśa which comes before the śrāddha.[1]

(4) After the śrāddha, one should also put on the pilgrim's dress, according to the statement of the VĀYUPURĀṆA :

155. When setting out to go to Gayā, one should perform a śrāddha according to the rule, put on a pilgrim's dress, and circumambulate his village. Then on reaching another village he should eat the leftovers from the śrāddha. Thereafter he should travel every day without accepting gifts.

(1) Some, however, say that "This rule is to be observed only on a pilgrimage to Gayā, since it is prescribed in connection with Gayā. It is not to be observed on pilgrimages to other tīrthas."

(2) Some say that shaving of the head is also to be performed before the śrāddha on the day of the fast, according to the words of VIṢṆU :

156. On a pilgrimage to Prayāga, or because of separation from one's mother and father,[2] one should shave his hair. One who has shaven would not act in vain.

(1) Some say this applies only to a pilgrimage undertaken for the sake of penance, since shaving is prescribed in connection with that (penance). (2) Others say it applies (only) when one goes to the tīrtha in a pilgrim's dress.

(3) The śrāddha (done before leaving), like the śrāddha at the tīrtha, should be a pārvaṇa-śrāddha, with six, nine, or twelve deities, according to different opinions.

(4) A certain author says : "This śrāddha has ghee alone as its offering-material, according to the words of the VIṢṆUPURĀṆA:

---

1. The phrase quoted comes after 'Performing a śrāddha', whereas normally homage should be made to Gaṇeśa *before* the śrāddha; for Gaṇeśa is the god of auspicious beginnings, and is worshipped at the beginning of any important undertaking.

2. I.e., at their death.

157. Whoever goes to a foreign land should perform a śrāddha with ghee. That is said to be 'for the journey'. And upon re-entering (his home, he should) certainly (perform another śrāddha).[1]

(1) If it were combined with other substances, that would cancel the sense of the instrumental case of 'with ghee,' which denotes an independent means, as in the phrase 'One should sacrifice with grains of rice.'"

(2) This is not so, because the literal statement ('with ghee') must be restricted in order to avoid a meaningless statement; for ghee alone cannot be the (only) material for a śrāddha, because it cannot be eaten by itself.

(3) Thus others say : '(The śrāddha-offering consists) *mainly* of ghee." (4) This also is not so; because the instrumental case is not used to prescribe 'plenitude'; and because this would constitute indirect expression (lakṣaṇā). (5) Therefore the meaning is 'with ghee as the principal material', because the instrumental case indicates that ghee is not dependent on any other equally important main material; just like 'with sesamum seeds,' etc., in the words of MANU and others :

158. With sesamum seeds, with rice and barley, with māṣa-beans, with water, or with roots and fruit, the ancestors of men are satisfied for one month when they are properly given; with the meat of fish, for two months; with that of a deer, for three months,

etc.;[2] and as (the instrumental case is used) in the words

159. In the morning pressing, they perform it with marrow; in the midday pressing, with a sacrificial cake; in the third pressing, with limbs,

even though the pouring of ghee above and below a piece of

1. For the interpretation of this verse see VM, TīPra p. 25, line 8, and Śrāddha Prakāśa p. 332.

2. Each of these materials, sesamum seeds etc., can serve as an independent main material, without any of the others.

gold is required.[1] (159.1) For these reasons this very explanation has been given by the authors of the SMṚTIRATNĀVALĪ, the MADANAPĀRIJĀTA, and others.[2] (2) Therefore when one has gone to another village the fast should be broken with that very ghee which was left from the śrāddha, since that was its principal material.

(3) A certain author has said : "This śrāddha is an ābhyudayika śrāddha." (4) Not so; because (pārvaṇa śrāddha), being the basic (śrāddha), most readily comes to mind; (5) so a pārvaṇa is assumed, and no particular specification to the contrary is made.

(6) Some authors say : "Only three brāhmaṇas should be worshipped, according to the 'Partridge-rule.'"[3] (7) Others say "There is no such restriction; for it is a different case here than in that rule, because here the reference is to the intended aim of the sentence. In the phrase 'worship brāhmaṇas to the best of his ability,' [152] as in respect to the 'worshipping' so also in respect to the number of brāhmaṇas there is no restriction, either from the literal sense or from the construction."[4]

(8) This, then, is the order of performance : (9) Two days before the day of the auspicious moment for the journey, the observances of eating once a day, eating sacrificial food, celibacy, etc., should be followed, according to the previously quoted word 'well-controlled' [153]. (10) On the day after that, a fast

1. See KātŚrSū VI.7.20ff., where the pouring of ghee on a piece of gold in the Nirūḍha-paśu sacrifice is described. The main materials, marrow etc., are prescribed with the instrumental ending which denotes that each of the three main materials are independent of each other, although the subsidiary piece of gold is required with each of them. Likewise, ghee is prescribed for the śrāddha by an instrumental which denotes it as the only *main* material, though other subsidiary materials must still be used.

2. See MP p. 478.

3. According to this rule, given in Śab XI.1.8.43, a plural number indicates three things if there is no indication to the contrary.

4. The 'intended end' (uddeśya) of a sentence must not be restricted or else the undesirable consequence of 'split of the sentence' (vākyabheda) results. See under vākyabheda in 'Glossary of Mīmāṃsā and other Technical Terms.'

is to be observed, (11) and shaving may optionally be performed. (12) On the day after that, after performing the obligatory actions such as bathing, etc. which effect purity, worshipping Gaṇeśa and one's chosen deity with devotion and to the best of his ability, performing a pārvaṇa-śrāddha with ghee as its principal substance, honoring brāhmaṇas to the best of his ability with clothing, ornaments, cattle, land, gold, etc., making a declaration of a journey, and putting on the pilgrim's dress consisting of the red cloak, etc., at the auspicious moment one should go out from his home village and circumambulate it, go to another village within a krośa's distance, and break his fast with the ghee left over from the śrāddha. (160.1) This is in accordance with the prohibition of travelling a krośa after a śrāddha :

160. (And after performing a śrāddha, one should not go) on a road extending for a krośa.[1]

(2) Then on the next day, having performed his bathing, etc., he should go on, keeping to the observances.

161. He should go after having circumambulated that village also;

(1) so it is said in the SMṚTIRATNĀVALĪ.

(2) A certain author has said : "This order is to be followed if the auspicious moment is in the morning of the day after the fast. (3) But if it is in the latter part of the night, then, being unable (to follow this order), after performing the fast, śrāddha, etc. on the day of that night, one should begin the journey at the auspicious time, go to another place, and break his fast in the morning; for a fast is desirable only insofar as it does not interfere with the main activity.[2]" (4) This is doubtful; for when the auspicious moment is in the earlier or later night, it is possible to perform a fast on the

1. The full śloka is quoted in a slightly different form in Nirṇayasindhu p.1774 (commentary) as 'Śrāddhaṃ kṛtvā na gaccheta adhvani krośapūraṇe. NB apparently knew the śloka as '...na gacchetādhvani ca krośapūraṇe.'

2. I.e., the journey.

day of that night, and at the auspicious time, according to the manner described in the astrological science, to leave in a certain place a deposit of fruit and clothing, etc.; and in the morning, having performed the śrāddha, etc., to leave one's house, take the deposit, circumambulate the village, and break one's fast in another village; so, this being possible, it would not be proper to cancel the proper time for the śrāddha, namely the day after the fast. (5) Also, fasting after performing a śrāddha is not proper unless there is an explicit authority for it. (6) It is for just such cases as this that the technique of deposit is proclaimed in the astrological science.[1]

(7) In this connection, someone who is ill or incapable of performing a fast for some other reason should perform some substitute for the fast. The substitutes are :

162. Eating only by night, eating sacrificial food, or food without condiments, fruit, sesamum seeds, milk, water, ghee, the five cow-products, or wind. Among these, each one is more praiseworthy than the preceding.

(1) The wearing of the pilgrim's dress, being a subsidiary of the journey, is to be done only during travel, but not at the time of the daily meal, etc., because of the prohibition of the red cloak, 'At the time of a religious rite, one should be bare of the red cloak'; (2) for there is no authority to overrule this. (3) Because the statement prescribing that clothing prescribes it for any travel whatever, the pilgrim's dress is to be worn at the tīrtha also while going to this and that place within the tīrtha. (4) Some say : "But not at the time of bathing, śrāddha, etc., as there is no authority for that." (5) Others, however, say : "From the beginning until the end of the pilgrimage the pilgrim's clothing is worn all the time, since the clothing is prescribed as a subsidiary of the pilgrimage, just like refraining from accepting gifts, etc. (6) If it were otherwise,

---

1. See MuCi XI.92ff. A 'deposit' (prasthāna) is an offering which constitutes a symbolic departure when for some reason beyond his control a person cannot actually leave at the auspicious time for beginning his journey.

what would serve as prescriptive authority for other observances ?"[1]

(162.7)A certain author has said: "Again when returning from the tīrtha, having fasted at another village near his own village, on the following day, after worshipping the planets and his chosen deity and performing a pārvaṇa śrāddha with ghee and honoring brāhmaṇas, reaching his own village, one should circumambulate it as before, leave his clothing in its place, enter his own house, and break his fast with ghee left from the śrāddha. This is established by the transfer of the entire body of rules for setting out, in accordance with the words 'in the same way' in the statement 'And when he returns home he should once again honor the gods, ancestors, and brāhmaṇas in the same way' [153]".[2] (8) This is wrong; for the words 'in the same way' are given in connection with the transfer only of the ceremonies of honoring the gods, etc. (9) Thus in the SKANDAPURĀṆA it is said 'Having arrived (home) and paid homage to his ancestors ...'[152]. (10) And such, indeed, is the practice of refined people.

(11) In this connection, a certain author has said : "In the declaration of a journey, no mention should be made of a benefit; for it is seen from the introductory and concluding statements 'If one sets out to go to Gayā' and 'One would get that benefit, going to Gayā'[3] that (the journey) is made for the sake of the (tīrtha); this is according to the rule 'Because it is intended for something, (an act) is determined to be for the sake

1. If the prescription of pilgrim's dress is taken to apply only to the actual act of travelling, the same qualification would apply to other rules such as the cessation of accepting gifts, which are prescribed together with the pilgrim's dress (in 155). But these other restrictions are meant to apply to the pilgrimage in its entirety, so the pilgrim's dress must be taken in the same way.

2. Cf. TiCi p. 10.

3. The above statements are from the Vāyu Purāṇa passage quoted above (in slightly different form), 155. The last half-śloka, not quoted there, is 'Pade pade 'śvamedhasya phalaṃ syād gacchato Gayām.' It is quoted below in 167.

of that thing.'[1] This is also seen from the saying

163. Thus going, he obtains the specified benefit from the tīrtha; there is no doubt of this. (≈153)

(1) If it were otherwise than this, then the benefit of an aśvamedha sacrifice being obtained at every step of the journey,[2] the tīrtha itself would be purposeless. (2) Although it is proclaimed in various texts that pilgrimage has such benefits as heaven or the benefit of a rājasūya sacrifice, these are explanatory passages made in accordance with the rule of proclaiming the benefit of the main matter by attributing it to a subsidiary of the main matter.[3]

If it is objected : "But, according to the saying,

164. He gets the benefit of bathing, but not that of a pilgrimage (≃106),

(1) the pilgrimage also has a separate distinct benefit"—(2) not so, because the meaning is to be construed as 'He does not obtain the benefit of the tīrtha which is fulfilled by the pilgrimage, but only that of bathing.' (3) Also according to such statements as 'He gets half its benefit, who goes to a tirtha incidentally,' [107], it is the tīrtha which provides the benefit. (4) According to statements such as 'For going by vehicle one gets only the benefit of bathing' [114], it is the tīrtha which has no benefit, or a reduced benefit, for one who goes by vehicle. (5) As a result of the performance of the duties of the journey etc. also, it is the tīrtha, not the journey, which is beneficial. (6) Nor should there be a declaration such as 'Desiring to obtain the full benefit of the tīrtha I will journey to it,' because pilgrimage is not prescribed as a means to obtain the benefit of a tīrtha. (7) Therefore the proclamation of the

1. Thus the journey is 'intended for' something else—namely the tīrtha, in this case Gayā—so that it does not have a benefit of its own, but is done only for the sake of the tīrtha. Therefore one should not, in declaring his intention to journey to a tīrtha, make mention of a benefit he hopes to derive from the journey.

2. See note on 162.11.

3. The main matter=the tīrtha. The subsidiary=the journey. According to this rule, as given in MS IV.3.1.1, a text which attributes a benefit to a subsidiary is merely an explanatory or commendatory passage, for the benefit actually results from the main matter.

benefit of the journey is an explanatory passage, like that of 'overcoming of rivals.'[1]

(164.8) In a pilgrimage undertaken as a penance, however, the benefit of the journey *is* independent, because, not being for the sake of anything else, the pilgrimage is not a subsidiary. (9) Therefore, having made a declaration at the beginning of the journey, another declaration is not made upon reaching the tīrtha, since the bathing, etc. done at the tīrtha concludes the journey, and thus is included in it."

(10) This [162.11-164.9] is doubtful : because of the use of the words 'to go' and 'going' in the introductory and concluding statements,[2] it cannot be concluded that (the journey) is for the sake of (the tīrtha); (11) for the very act of going is seen to be beneficial. (12) The second reason[3] is also ruled out; for a tīrtha itself without being endowed with any verbal action cannot be a means for achieving any benefit. As regards this necessity for a verbal action, you may not construe it by endowing (the tīrtha) with the meaning of a verb root such as 'to bathe', discarding (the verbal action) 'thus going' which is expressed in that very same sentence [163]. Thus that action 'going' is clearly the delimiting factor (in respect to the verbal action).[4] So it is understood that the sense of [163] is 'The specified benefit from the tīrtha—i.e. from *going* to the tīrtha...' (13) And since it is seen that the journey is *not* for the sake of something else, it is a great distortion to say that its benefit—heaven, etc.—proclaimed in various texts falls within the scope of the rule of proclaiming the benefit of the main matter by attributing it to a subsidiary. (14) Further : by considering the previously quoted sentences which authorize (pilgrimages), 'Travelling to tīrthas is meritorious' [38], 'Whatever pilgrimages (were made)...by the

1. This is one of the examples of benefits attributed by explanatory passages to a subsidiary, cited by Śab. in IV.3.1.1. (Cf. note on 163.2 above.)

2. Above, 162.11.

3. Above, 163-163.1.

4. A tīrtha yields benefit only as a result of some action. Since the sentence in question (163) contains the verb 'go', it is clear that it is this action and not some other which causes the benefit mentioned therein.

great sages...' [77] etc., the journey itself is seen to be the main matter; (15) for authorization is not proclaimed separately for a subsidiary. (16) Thus also, the explanation by a forced construction of the sentence, '...but not the benefit of the pilgrimage,' [164] etc., is not legitimate. (17) And in such sentences as 'He (gets) half of the benefit...,' [107] etc., if we look for the delimiting verbal root-meaning, the delimiter is the verbal act of going, expressed in the very same sentence by the word 'goes'. (18) Further : What decisive authority, other than an arbitrary decision,[1] is there for saying 'Only in a pilgrimage undertaken as a penance is (the journey) the main matter, not elsewhere'? (19) Therefore the journey is beneficial in every case. (20) Nor does it follow then that the tirtha is purposeless; for according to the rule

> 165. Greater and lesser actions and their benefits can be divided in their respective ranges, according to the similarity of their rank, even when no differentiation (of the benefit) is prescribed

(1) a mutual difference in quality may be construed.[2] (2) Or else, in such a case as this [167] (the benefit attributed to the journey) may be a commendatory passage (arthavāda).

(3) Therefore a journey is beneficial even if it is not undertaken as a penance; (4) and so are bathing, śrāddha, etc. (5) But to this extent there is a difference : like the agnihotra sacrifice, bathing and śrāddha, etc. have a dual character, being both optional and occasional, according to the rule,

---

1. 'Kośapāna,' literally 'drinking of sacred water,' is a procedure used as an ordeal to determine criminal guilt, and also as an oath to seal an agreement or alliance. Here it is evidently used idiomatically to express the notion of an arbitrary decision which must be taken on faith, rather than on logical grounds. Cf. 450.3.

2. In this verse Kumārila explains that different ritual actions may have different results corresponding to their importance; and even when different acts are declared to yield the same benefit, the benefit may be considered to vary in amount or quality according to the importance of the act. Thus, although the benefit ('an aśvamedha at every step') is enjoined in reference to the act of going, it may be considered that the tirtha itself further increases the benefit of the journey.

166. If the one (act) is both (mandatory and occasional, the reason is) separateness of connection;[1]

(1) for there are authoritative statements to establish them in both ways. (2) And therefore if one does not do that bathing etc. when he is subject to the occasioning factor in the form of arriving at a tīrtha, then he commits an offense and is reviled by refined people, even though he obtains the benefit of the journey. (3) Therefore a journey undertaken as a penance also is concluded with the performance of the tīrtha-rites, lest the saying 'In trying to join the one the other is lost'[2] take effect.[3]

(4) Thus also if one who has reached the tīrtha but has not yet bathed etc. by chance dies or is taken by force elsewhere by barbarians, etc., then, since there is no human fault, there is no offense nor lack of benefit from the journey. (5) Now, enough of this arguing with those who say 'Pilgrimage has no benefit' —a statement which is denied by the whole world !

(6) Others, however, say : "So be it; the journey is beneficial. But nevertheless, this same benefit which is proclaimed for a journey to Gayā

167. One going to Gayā gets at every step the benefit of an aśvamedha sacrifice,

(1) applies to *all* pilgrimages, according to the rule

168. The meaning of a sacred text determined in one place (applies) elsewhere also.

(1) When the benefit of a pilgrimage is to be specified, it would be appropriate that this same benefit already mentioned be

1. According to this rule the agnihotra sacrifice can be both mandatory (nitya) and occasional (naimittika), because there are separate prescriptions of it in these two forms; and it has a separate connection with each of these prescriptions. See Śab. on IV.3.3.5.

2. For a discussion of this nyāya see Col. Jacob's Laukikanyāyāñjali, Pt. 1 pp. 9 10.

3. Bathing and śraddha are occasional to, and therefore mandatory in, a normal pilgrimage. In a pilgrimage undertaken as a penance, they are optional, but nevertheless they should be done, lest one lose the opportunity to gain merit by doing these rituals while at the tīrtha.

that benefit, as it is closely connected in that it is also a benefit of 'going'. Postulating the benefit to be heaven by invoking the rule of the viśvajit sacrifice would involve an excessive effort in bringing that rule to mind, because it is only remotely connected to this case.[1]"

(2) This too is sheer foolishness; for in various places the benefits of pilgrimages are mentioned, both in general and specifically; in general, as follows :

In the Dānadharma section of the MAHĀBHĀRATA, referring to the cow-heaven :

169. The wise who are diligent in pilgrimage rejoice there in the land of the cows.

And after listing the tīrthas beginning with Prabhāsa, it is said (in the Dānadharma section),

170. Those who go to the Sarasvatī, Dṛṣadvatī, and Yamunā go there (to the cow-heaven), bearing divine forms and wearing divine garlands, fortunate, full of auspicious fragrance.

(1) Also in the VAYŪPURĀṆA: 'Going to tīrthas, a man...' etc. [50]. Also specifically, in the KŪRMAPURĀṆA :

171. One who goes with self-control to the great tīrtha Puṇḍarīka, which is adorned by brāhmaṇas, would obtain the benefit of the Puṇḍarīka sacrifice.[2]

(1) Thus we may refer to the benefits which are established in connection with the various tīrthas in all the purāṇas, the Mahābhārata, etc.; (2) but these are not all copied here, as it

---

1. According to the viśvajin-nyāya(Śab.IV.3.7.15-16), when the benefit of an act is not specified, it should be assumed to be heaven. But, according to this pūrva-pakṣin, this rule applies only remotely to the question at hand, namely pilgrimage; whereas the benefit specified in connection with Gayā applies closely, since it is concerned specifically with the benefits of pilgrimage. Thus it is preferable to generalize the Gayā-rule to pilgrimages to all tīrthas, rather than to apply the viśvajin-nyāya.

2. In commenting on a similar phrase in Gayā Prakaraṇa, p. 378, NB explains 'Puṇḍarīka' as 'yāgaviśeṣaphalam.'

would take too long.(171.3)And thus, the benefit being established appropriately from either syntactic or contextual interpretation, there is therefore no lack (of specified benefit). Then why speak of such lack, and why, moreover, bring in the rule of close connection; and why, above all, apply the rule 'In one place' [168]? (4) Besides, the close connection is quite the opposite (of what was proposed), for a specific statement certainly constitutes close unection.[1] And since there is no postulation of heaven (as the benefit),[2] there is no excessive difficulty in bringing to mind (the benefit). Enough, then, of arguing with those who cannot see deeply into the purāṇas !

THUS ENDS 'THE WAY OF GOING TO TĪRTHAS' IN THE GENERAL SECTION OF THE BRIDGE TO THE THREE HOLY CITIES BY NĀRĀYAṆA BHAṬṬA, SON OF THE NOBLE BHAṬṬARĀMEŚVARA SŪRI.

1. The benefits of pilgrimage to various tīrthas are surely more closely connected with the specific statements of them in the passages quoted above and the many others not quoted, than with the statement of the benefit of pilgrimage to Gayā.

2. As there would be if the viśvajit rule were invoked; see 168.1 and note.

OBSERVANCES ON A PILGRIMAGE

In the MAHĀBHĀRATA :

172. If one enters a tīrtha after overcoming desire, anger, and greed, there is nothing which he could not attain by going to that tīrtha. And those men who go to tīrthas in the prescribed manner can withstand all pairs of opposites; they are resolute, and go to heaven.

(1) They are able to withstand 'pairs of opposites' such as heat and cold.

ŚAṄKHA and PULASTYA :

173. He whose hands and feet and mind are well-controlled, who is endowed with wisdom, austerity, and renown—he attains the benefit of a tīrtha. Refraining from accepting gifts, satisfied with anything at all, free of egoism—he attains the benefit of a tīrtha. Deceitless, not undertaking business, eating lightly, conquering the senses, devoid of all attachments—he attains the benefit of a tīrtha. Free from anger, truthful, firm in his vows, treating all creatures as himself—he, O Lord of Kings, attains the benefit of a tīrtha.[1]

(1) Control of the hands is achieved by refraining from striking others and taking the property of others; (2) control of the feet by refraining from kicking and from going to forbidden places; (3) and control of the mind is refraining from the three-fold sins :

174. Cherishing the property of others, considering in the mind undesirable matters, and wrong application of the mind; mental sins are said to be threefold.

(1) 'Wisdom' is knowledge of the greatness of tīrthas. As for what is said in the SMṚTIDARPAṆA :

1. Commentary on these verses continues through 176.15.

175. Wisdom is the knowledge of the three sacred texts,

(1) that is not so, as it does not apply to the subject at hand. (2) 'Austerity' is fasting, eating once a day, and so on. (3) 'Renown' is the reputation of being of good conduct; this excludes those who have a bad name. (4) Ceasing to accept gifts starts immediately on beginning the journey. (5) Concerning the saying :

> 176. As long as he obtains that money, so long is the tīrtha without benefit for him,

(1) one author has said : "That means that that undertaking of pilgrimage is without benefit, during which gifts are accepted; (2) but not any other undertaking (made before the beginning of the pilgrimage), because that would not entail the feature of ceasing to accept gifts." (3) But the correct interpretation is that this applies to wealth obtained by improper acceptance of gifts even before the beginning of the journey.[1] (4) And this refraining from accepting gifts applies to those who succeed in maintaining their bodies without accepting gifts. (5) It does not apply to ascetics, celibate students, etc., since they cannot maintain their bodies without accepting gifts of alms, clothing, etc. (6) Since accumulation of provisions is forbidden to them, the journey cannot be carried out without accepting gifts; thus acceptance of gifts is necessary. (7) 'Satisfied with anything at all' means not desirous of sweet foods, etc. (8) 'Deceitless' means free of hypocrisy. (9) 'Not undertaking business' means not engaging in such activities as buying, selling, and obtaining property. (10) 'Lightly eating' means not consuming much. (11) 'Conquering the senses' means free of attachment of the eleven sense organs to their respective objects. (12) ('Devoid of all attachments' means) free of attachment; 'attachment' is clinging to improper things. (13) 'Firm in vows' means not breaking the vows of fasting etc. which one has taken on himself; (14) the idea is that only those vows which can actually

---

1. The quotation means that a pilgrimage has no benefit if during it one uses ill-gained money. NB interprets 'that money' as referring to improperly obtained money.

be carried out on a pilgrimage should be taken up. (15) 'Treating all creatures as himself' means delighting in the benefit of all creatures.

Also :

177. The faithless one, the evil-souled, the atheist, the doubter, and the skeptic—these five do not share in the benefit of a tīrtha.[1]

(1) 'Evil-souled' means one who has committed many sins. (2) For him, only the expiation of his sins is achieved by the pilgrimage, but not such benefits of the tīrtha as heaven, etc.; this, according to the words of the KĀŚĪKHAṆḌA :

178. For men who have committed sins, a tīrtha is the atonement for their sins. For men of pure souls, a tīrtha gives the benefit ascribed to it. (= 103, 127).

(179.1) One author has said that 'evil-souled' means the 'cat-like one' described by MANU :

179. He whose flag of Dharma is always raised like a wine shop's flag, and whose sins are hidden; his conduct is called 'cat-like'.

(2) 'Atheist' means a heretic. (3) 'Doubter' means one who is undecided about all matters; (4) others say it means lacking decision as to benefits, means, duties and goals,[2] according to the saying of the GĪTĀ,

180. A doubter has neither this world nor the next, nor any happiness.

(1) 'Skeptic' means a cynic who attacks the meaning of the books of the Dharma with false reasons.

In the PRABHĀSAKHAṆḌA :

181. He who controls his eleven sense organs obtains the benefit of the tīrtha; anyone else would partake of sin.

1. Commentary on this verse continues through 180.1.
2. Cf TiCi p.4.

(1) Here, suppression of the sense-organs in the form of celibacy does not apply at the prescribed time for intercourse (ṛtukāla), according to the smṛti text:

182. Constantly going to tīrthas, practicing celibacy except at the prescribed time...

Also:

183. Evil in the mind is not purified by bathing at tīrthas; though washed with water a hundred times, it remains impure, like a wine-jug. (. 69).

In the BRAHMAPURĀṆA:

184. 'One who is evil in mind, though constantly bathed properly in all the water of the Gaṅgā, though always given to bathing from his birth, is not purified': just so we say. Fish dwell in the tīrthas of the Gaṅgā and other rivers, and flocks of birds in the abode of the gods, O King; lacking love, they obtain no benefit from the tīrtha, nor from that place of the gods. Therefore fixing love in the lotus of the heart, one should frequent tīrthas with steadfast soul.

Elsewhere also:

185. As deep as is one's faith in mantra, tīrtha, brāhmaṇa, god, prophet, doctor, or guru, so great is one's success.

(1) Thus the idea is "One should make a journey to a tīrtha with devotion and love fixed in his heart." (2) And these restraints—control of the hands and feet and so on—are (required) subsidiaries of all the actions of pilgrimage, such as bathing at the tīrtha, etc., by virtue of the general statement 'He attains the benefit of a tīrtha...' [173].

In the KŪRMAPURĀṆA:

186. O Fair-faced One, men who make a pilgrimage with cheating or deceit die at the tīrtha and do not achieve their goal.

In the MAHĀBHĀRATA :

187. These tīrthas are attained by good people who perceive proper purposes, with their senses previously purified by faith and the study of the sacred lore.

Also :

188. He who shows disrespect to brāhmaṇas when setting out on a pilgrimage does not return; his life ends there.

Also :

189. A man going to a tīrtha should perform three sandhyā-rituals in one place. He should not go unbathed, nor after eating, nor when impure because of the birth of a child.[1]

(1) By 'He should perform three sandhyā-rituals in one place,' it is meant that one should not set out in the evening after having performed the mid-day sandhyā, nor in the morning without having performed the obligatory duties.[2] (2) 'Not unbathed' means that he should go only after bathing, if possible. (3) 'Impure' means not having purified himself after passing urine or faeces, (4) and not having bathed and sipped purifying water when there arises an occasion to do so, as when he has been touched by an untouchable, a menstruating woman, etc. As for what is said in the ṢAṬTRIṂŚANMATA :

190. On a divine pilgrimage, at weddings, at sacrifices while in progress, and at all festivals, one who comes in contact with others[3] is not polluted,

and by BṚHASPATI :

191. At a tīrtha, a wedding, a journey, in battle, during a

1. Commentary on this verse continues through 197.1.
2. Including the morning sandhyā.
3. For the formation of the bahuvrīhi compound 'spṛṣṭāspṛṣṭiḥ' see Pāṇini II.2.27, V.4.127, and VI.6.137.

regional disaster, and when a town or village is burning, one who comes in contact with others is not polluted,

192. "This rule applies where there is no clear awareness that 'I have been touched by him'; for the rule retains its significance (even) with that exception";

so says the author of the MADANAPĀRIJĀTA. (1) Others, however, say "There is no fault only in case of unavoidable contact during such activities as worship of gods or a journey; but when it occurs during eating, etc., one cannot become pure without bathing." (2) 'Nor when impure because of the birth of a child,—this means 'Nor one who carries such an impurity.'[1] As for the saying :

193 When (a religious activity) has already begun, there is no birth-impurity,

(1) that applies only to certain vows etc. specifically enumerated according to the VIṢṆUSMṚTI :

194. When a vow, sacrifice, wedding, śrāddha, oblation, worship, or prayer has already begun, there is no birth impurity. But if it has not begun, then there is birth-impurity.

(1) If it were not so, the first half of this sentence[2] would lack any purpose. (195.1) For the same reason, the 'beginning' referred to by VIṢṆU in the preceding sentence [194] refers to just these rituals :

195. 'The beginning' is the choosing of the participants in a sacrifice; the declaration in a vow or sattra; the Nāndīmukha offering at a wedding etc., and the preparation of the food at a śrāddha.

(2) Others, however, say : "This [193] applies where performance is prescribed as uninterrupted, as in the

1. For a ten day period after the birth of a child, both of its parents are considered ritually impure; this impurity is called 'sūtaka.'

2. Which enumerates those activities to which the rule (193) applies.

month's fast, etc.; (3) but uninterrupted performance is not prescribed for a pilgrimage. (4) Therefore, the absence of birth-impurity when the activity has already begun does not apply here (in the case of pilgrimage). (5) For the same reason, there is birth-impurity in such rites as the feeding of a thousand brāhmaṇas."[1]

(6) In either case[2] it is established that when a birth impurity arises during a pilgrimage, it is considered an impure time, and only when purity is re-established should one proceed. As for the words of PAIṬHĪNASI :

196. At weddings, in inaccessible places, and during sacrifices, on a journey and in the tīrtha ritual, there is no such birth-impurity; one should perform the ritual, sacrifice, etc., (=315,385)

(1) that means that there is no impurity on a pilgrimage when there is no alternative (but to proceed onwards), because of such factors as difficulty of the road.[3]

(2) In the same way, a menstruating woman should pass four days just where she is, and proceed on the fifth day, according to the saying

197. During a ritual for the gods or the ancestors, she becomes pure on the fifth day;

(1) for a pilgrimage is a ritual for the gods.

(2) If one going thus with the proper observance comes on another tīrtha (than the intended one) en route, then he must mandatorily perform bathing, śrāddha, etc., there; as has been previously said, 'He gets half of its benefit, who goes to a tīrtha incidentally, [107]; (3) and because, if he does not perform the specially occasioned bathing etc. when the special occasion, namely arrival at a tīrtha, arises, he would incur an offense.

---

1. For a description of this ritual see *Bodhāyana Gṛhya Sūtra* 3.17-18.
2. Whether one accepts the explanation in 193.1ff or that in 195.2ff.
3. Cf. Nāgojī Bhaṭṭa's *Tīrthenduśekhara* p. 5; 'Mārgavaiṣamyādinā sthātum aśaktau tu yātrāyāṃ nāśaucam.'

(4) Some, however, say that fasting and shaving of the head are to be done only at the intended tīrtha.

(5) A special rule is given in the GARUḌAPURĀṆA for a case where someone who has set out for a pilgrimage by some chance returns :[1]

198. Whoever returns to his home after setting out to a tīrtha must perform a penance with the assent of pure brāhmaṇas.

(1) The idea is that a penance for violating a declaration (of pilgrimage) must be undertaken with the permission of brāhmaṇas.

(2) A special rule is given in the GARUḌAPURĀṆA for a case when someone sets out for a tīrtha, but dies before reaching it :

199. If someone were to die in the meantime while going toward a tīrtha, (or) while keeping a fast, he would go to the land of the seers.

(1) With 'while keeping a fast,' the word 'or' (ca) has to be supplied; thus it means 'or having made a vow of a fast such as the month's fast.' (2) The meaning is that in either of these two cases one who dies in the meantime attains the world of the seers.[2]

(3) When westerners on a pilgrimage to Gayā, or easterners on a pilgrimage to Kāśī, etc., come on the way upon the river called Karmanāśā, then they must cross it in some way whereby they do not touch its water, according to the saying :

200. For touching the water of the Karmanāśā, crossing the Karatoyā, or fording the Gaṇḍakībāhu, one must re-do his consecration ceremonies.

(1) But the easterners have the reading 'For touching the water of the Karatoyā, crossing the Karmanāśā...,' and say that

1. Before completing the pilgrimage.
2. That result occurs when one dies in the middle of either a fast or a pilgrimage.

one should go by ship by the route of the confluence of the Gaṅgā (with the Karmanāśā) or by the route to the north of there.[1] (2) But this is not so; for, since they also agree that the touch of the water of the Karmanāśā is undesirable, it becomes necessary to postulate another sentence, which is not actually found, to prohibit touching the waters of the Karmanāśā. (202.1) And also, their reading conflicts with the mention of bathing in the Karatoyā in the Dānadharma section of the MAHĀBHĀRATA :

201. A self-controlled pure man who fasts three nights at the Karatoyā and Kuraṅga and bathes there obtains (the benefit of) an aśvamedha sacrifice,

and in the ĀRAṆYAKAPARVAN,

202. Reaching the Karatoyā and fasting three nights, a man obtains the (benefit of an) aśvamedha sacrifice, and goes to heaven.

(203.1) Their reading also conflicts with the mantra for bathing in the Karatoyā quoted in the SMṚTIDARPAṆA :

203. O Karatoyā, O Sadānīrā, O Best of Rivers, widely famed, Born from the hand of Hara (Śiva), you wash away the sins of sinners.

---

1. The Karmanāśā (modern Karamnas) River flows from south to north through the Bhojpur (formerly Shahabad) District of Bihar and the Mirzapur District of Uttar Pradesh, entering the right bank of the Ganges near Chausa. Thus if an easterner going to Benares or a westerner going to Gayā had to avoid crossing it, he would have to travel by boat on the Ganges past the confluence with the Karmanāśā, or by road to the north of the confluence.

The Bābur-Nāma (translated by Annette Susannah Beveridge, London 1922, vol. II pp. 659-60) confirms that (contrary to NB's views) this was the actual practice: "About the waters of [the Karmanāśā] Hindūs are understood to be extremely scrupulous. They do not cross it, but go past its mouth by boat along the Gang (Ganges)." This account, written in A.D. 1529, is nearly contemporary with the TSS.

(2) Therefore the reading given by us is the only proper one.

(3) Other religious duties of pilgrimage also are to be observed, as they are learned from the practice of refined people.

THUS ENDS OBSERVANCES ON A PILGRIMAGE

DUTIES ON THE DAY OF ARRIVAL AT A TĪRTHA

(4) If one goes by a vehicle or wearing shoes, then on the day on which he will reach the tīrtha he should discard his vehicle, shoes, etc. and go on foot for as much of the way as he is able; and when the tīrtha comes into sight, he should bow with eight limbs, discard his head covering, sword, garland, armor, etc., and go to the tīrtha. Thus it is said :

204. Discarding vehicles, men should go by foot after rolling on the ground there and putting on the garb of a pilgrim.

(1) 'Rolling on the ground' refers to bowing with eight limbs. (2) The eight-limbed bow is :

205. With the feet, hands, knees, head and chest, with mind, speech, and sight, the bow is said to be eightfold.

(1) 'Taking on the pilgrim's garb' prescribes discarding fragrances, garland, sword and armor, etc.; (2) or else it means that if the pilgrim's garb was not put on at the beginning of the journey, then it should be put on on the day of entering the tīrtha.

(3) Then when one reaches the tīrtha, he should give an offering of flowers, unhusked rice, and fruit, saying 'Homage to such-and-such a tīrtha.' (4) And it is also the practice of refined people that one should place an offering of respect (upaḍhaukanika) containing as much fruit, clothing, gold, etc. as possible.

After that :

206. First he should touch the tīrtha with the syllable 'Oṃ' (praṇava); then, entering the pure water, he should bathe properly with a mantra.

(1) This means 'Touching the tīrtha with the syllable 'Oṃ', he should enter the pure water; i.e., he should (first) bathe with

his clothes on.' This is indicated in the story of Śivaśarma in the KĀŚĪKHAṆḌA :

207. Arriving at Maṇikarṇikā and seeing its heavenly waves flowing upwards, entering in the immaculate waters with his clothes on...

(1) Then 'with a mantra'—that is, after pronouncing a mantra —he should bathe 'properly', i.e., in the prescribed manner.[1] And the mantra is given in the PRABHĀSAKHAṆḌA :

208. 'Om ! Homage to the God of Gods, the Dark-Throated One, the Wielder of the Staff, Rudra. Homage to the Bow-handed, Discus-bearing Creator. And may Sarasvatī, daughter of Savitṛ, mother of the Vedas, most revered, destroyer of sins at a tīrtha, be present here.' This is said to be the mantra for all tīrthas. After thus pronouncing it and paying homage one should bathe according to the rule.

(1) Because it says here 'After thus pronouncing it and paying homage,' this mantra does not effect bathing, but is only for the supplication (of the gods); (2) if it did effect bathing, that would contradict the indication of the mantra itself.[2]

Alternatively, this mantra may be used :

209. 'O Ocean-roarer! O Staff-handed Asura-slayer! O Creator of the World, Destroyer of the World! I bow to you, O Lord of Gods. O Sharp-fanged, Great-bodied One, who are like the fire at the end of an eon! Homage to you, O Bhairava! May you please give your consent.' Having recited this mantra, one should bathe in the tīrtha; otherwise, the Lord of Tīrthas will certainly take away half of its benefit.

(1) There is an optional choice between these two mantras, since they serve the same purpose, namely supplication.

---

1. That is, he should bathe again (this time without clothes).
2. Because the mantra itself (i.e. the words up to pāpapraṇāśinī) contains only supplicatory statements, and does not mention bathing.

(2) This bathing according to rule[1] is to be done directly after shaving, according to the saying,

> 210. First to be done at a tīrtha is the invitation of the deities; after that, the tonsure; then one should do bathing, etc.; lastly he should perform śrāddha.

As for the saying

> 211. Having gone there, he should bathe, and after that shave,

(1) that refers to bathing with the clothes on.[2]

1. The second bathing, without clothes.
2. The first bathing, which is done immediately upon arriving at the tīrtha (206.1).

FASTING AT A TĪRTHA

(2) After the words, 'one should bathe according to the rule' [208] it says (in the PRABHĀSAKHAṆḌA) :

212. Then on that day the strict observer should keep a fast. There is nothing greater than fasting at a tīrtha, O Queen of the Gods. Fasting is proclaimed to be atonement for the sins of sinners and the realization of the desires of the good; especially so at an abode of the gods. Therefore, O Fair-faced One, one should keep a fast there at the tīrtha; especially a keeper of vows, a pilgrim, and a widow. If he eats another's food, O Goddess, the benefit of the fast goes to him whose food it is.

In the KĀŚĪKHAṆḌA :

213. Fasting is to be done at the tīrtha, and shaving of the head. (=229, 249)

In the NĀRADĪYAPURĀṆA :

214. Reaching a tīrtha, a pure man should keep a fast. You should do your duties with a soul purified by fasting.

Concerning this, in the KĀŚĪKHAṆḌA :

215. A fast should be kept on the day before one arrives at a tīrtha. On the day of arrival, one should offer śrāddha,

(1) the fasting is prescribed for the day *before* reaching the tīrtha. (2) Therefore there is an optional choice between this day and the day of reaching the tīrtha as prescribed in 'Then on that day (on which he arrives at a tīrtha) the strict observer should keep a fast' [212]. (3) Nor do the words of the KĀŚĪKHAṆḌA refer to Kāśī alone; for the statement is made in the context of the general rules for all tīrthas.

(215.4) In reference to this one author has said: "In the pañcadaśarātra sacrifice, when the Subrahmaṇyā recitation is performed in combination,[1] a mantra to Agni which is used to call up the Subrahmaṇyā recitation at the time of the upasad rite would be used on the first day of that pañcadaśarātra, which is denoted as agniṣṭut by transferral of the name from the one-day agniṣṭut sacrifice. But this Agni-mantra is superseded by an Indra-mantra which is established in accordance with the archetype (the dvādaśāha sacrifice) for the remaining fourteen days, from the second day on, of the pañcadaśarātra. This is done so that the many (i.e. the fourteen) days may be beneficial (rather than the one).[2] Now in just the same way in the present case also, the single sentence of the KĀŚĪKHAṆḌA prescribing the fast on the preceding day is superseded, since its force is not equal, by the accordance of the many sentences which prescribed the fast on the day of arrival. Therefore the fast on the previous day is done in order to purify the body by means of eliminating sins, as are fasts at eclipses, etc. (5) For the benefit of the tīrtha as described comes about only for one whose mind is purified. (6) But that fast on the previous day is not the one occasioned by the arrival at a tīrtha."

(7) This is not so : If the fast on the previous day were a mandatory subsidiary of the pilgrimage, then, since the fast on the day of arrival at the tīrtha also is specially occasioned, and therefore mandatory, there would then result a double fast; and this is in conflict with the practice of all refined people. (8) Now, if it is non-mandatory, that would conflict with its being mentioned as if it were regular (i.e. mandatory) [215]. (9) Moreover :

---

1. I.e., it is done once in combination for all fifteen days.

2. This comparison refers to the discussion of complex sacrifices in MS XII.2.7.22 and commentaries. The pañcadaśarātra ('fifteen nights' sacrifice') has more than one archetype; its first day is equal to an agniṣṭut sacrifice, wherein the Subrahmaṇyā recitation is made with an Agni-mantra. But the main part of the pañcadaśarātra is a modification (vikṛti) of the archetypal (prakṛti) dvādaśāha sacrifice, wherein the Subrahmaṇyā is done with Indra-mantras. In such a case, the Indra-mantras of the dvādaśāha should be used, rather than the Agni-mantra of the agniṣṭut, because a greater number of details will thereby be in accordance with the archetype, and therefore a greater benefit will be realized.

If it were optional, there would result the postulation of another invisible result, namely another benefit.[1] (215.10) Moreover : If that were a prescription of another fast with a modification as to the time, i.e., 'on the day before arrival,' this would be overloading of sense.[2] (11) But in our position, by taking it as a prescription merely of an alternative option as to time, i.e. the previous day, for the already established fast, there is simplicity of interpretation (lāghava) and there is no postulation of another invisible result.

(12) Nor is the fast initially established with the particularity of being done only on the day of arrival, by which particularity a qualification given in respect to the already originated prescription could not enter into an act which is restricted by the qualification given in the originative prescription, as in the case of the whey.[3] (13) Since fasting as such (without any qualification) is prescribed by such sentences as 'Shaving and fasting' [226], both of the times for it—the day of arrival and the day before—are given in respect to a prescription already originated by other sentences. Thus their authority

---

1. An act may have only one 'invisible' or 'transcendental' result. If this previous day's fast were optional, then it would give an invisible result separate from that of the mandatory pilgrimage rites. But it is always desirable to avoid the postulation of an invisible result.

2. Caused by both prescribing and modifying something in the same sentence, which is contrary to the laws of Mīmāṃsā interpretation.

3. A qualification given in the originative prescription (utpattiśiṣṭaguṇa) is weightier than one given separately in connection with a previously originated prescription (utpannaśiṣṭaguṇa). But such is not the case here, as will be explained in the following sentence. The example of whey (vājina) refers to the Guṇādhikaraṇa of the MS (II.2.9.23). In connection with the prescription 'Tapte payasi dadhy ānayati sā vaiśvadevy āmikṣā vājibhyo vājinam' ('He puts the curd in the hot milk; that mixture is āmikṣā for the Viśvedevas. The whey is for the Vājins'), it is determined that the offering of the whey is not a variant of the āmikṣā offering, but rather a separate act. This is taken by later commentators as a typical instance where a qualification of an already originated act cannot outweigh the originative qualification; for example *Parimala* quoted in MK p.1108 col.2 : 'Utpattivākyaśiṣṭāmikṣā'varuddhe yāge vākyāntareṇa vājinaṃ niveśanaṃ na labhate.'

is equal, and an optional alternative becomes possible, like that of milk or curd in the agnihotra sacrifice.[1]

(215.14) Nor can it be said : "Since the fast is mentioned immediately after the shaving, which is to be done on the day of arrival, it is understood from the originative sentence that the fast should be done on that day only"; (15) for that is construed only on the basis of (the order of) reading. (16) And since it contradicts a direct statement, namely the word 'on the day before' in the sentence in the KĀŚĪKHAṆḌA [215], the (order of) reading does not determine the order of performance, according to the rule of the fifth (book of the Mīmāṃsā Sūtras). This is as in the case of the Aśvins', (cup); although in reading it is in the third place, this does not determine the order of performance, because it contradicts the direct statement 'the tenth' in 'The Aśvins' (cup) is taken as the tenth.'[2] (17) And thus, since by the reasons given the sentence concerning the fast on the previous day would be meaningless, it cannot be cancelled by the sentences prescribing the fast on that day of arrival, though they are many; this, according to the rule 'The relative strength and weakness of (different sorts of evidence) are reversed if they are ruled out because they would cause something to be purposeless.'[3] (18) To be sure, in the pañcada-

1. The agnihotra is originally established by the unqualified prescription 'Agnihotraṃ juhoti' ('He offers the agnihotra'). Concerning this, there are two separate prescriptions of accessories (guṇavidhi), 'Dadhnā juhoti' and 'Payasā juhoti' ('He offers with curd' and 'He offers with milk'). Since neither of these are originative prescriptions, they are equal in strength, and there is an optional choice. See MNP, 60-61.

2. The example is given in MS V.4.1.1. In the texts describing the jyotiṣṭoma sacrifice, the cup devoted to the Aśvins is mentioned in the third place. But since there is a sentence which specifically says that it should be taken as the tenth, this, rather than its place in the reading, determines the order of performance. Likewise in the case at hand, a direct statement of order outweighs an inference based on order of mention.

3. Thus normally the greater number of sentences prescribing fasting on the day of arrival would be taken as authoritative; but in this case it would result in making the prescription in the Kāśīkhaṇḍa of fasting on the previous day purposeless. This must be avoided, as no sentence may be considered purposeless; so the normal strength of different sorts of evidence must be reversed, and the single sentence must be considered in this case to be as strong as the many others.

śarātra, although the Agni-mantra is not obtained by the rule of transfer because of the accordance (of the Indra-mantra) with a greater number (of details), the rule of transfer does become purposeful by establishing subsidiaries other than that Agni-mantra. (215.19) But this case is different, for it would actually result in a sentence which is prescribed as mandatory becoming purposeless.

(20) Moreover : the KĀŚĪKHAṆḌA first mentions fasting, saying : 'Fasting is to be done at the tīrtha, and shaving of the head' [213]; then in the next sentence it says 'On the day before one arrives at the tīrtha...'[215]. Since the time, namely the previous day, is prescribed in this latter sentence, it is evident that it is the alternative of a fast on the previous day which is intended; for (a later text) is to be taken in accordance with a preceding statemen . (21) Therefore this statement : "Since in the second sentence, which prescribes the fast on the previous day, the word 'fast of the tīrtha' is not used, this sentence is not concerned with the fast of the tīrtha, but rather prescribes (another) fast for the sake of purifying the body"—is rejected; (22) for, since that word 'fast of the tīrtha' *is* used in the introductory statement, this latter statement also is understood to be concerned with that.

(23) And if someone who fancies himself a Mīmāṃsaka were to say this : "If the fast, which is prescribed as coming *after* the shaving, is drawn back to the preceding day, then the shaving would also be drawn back; just as when the pre-sacrifices are drawn back, as is expressed by the sentence 'They offer pre-sacrifices for the living animal,' then the other subsidiaries which precede the pre-sacrifices are also drawn back"[1];

1. See MS V.1.12.23-24. When the pre-sacrifices (prayāja) are drawn back—i.e., done earlier than their normal sequence in the sacrifice as a whole—then all the subsidiary acts which precede the pre-sacrifices are drawn back with it (the 'Tadantāpakarṣanyāya'). The sentence 'They offer the standing animal. . .' indicates drawing back (apakarṣa) of the pre sacrifices in the agnīṣomiya sacrifice, because normally these are not performed until after the offering material is prepared—i.e. the animal is slaughtered. But here the animal is evidently still alive at the time of the pre-sacrifices.

(24) this too is not so; for in that case the order of the subsidiaries of the ceremony was pre-determined in the archetype and transferred in conjunction with the animal by the rule of transfer. Thus when the pre-sacrifices which come after them are drawn back, then the preceding subsidiaries also are drawn back, in accordance with the pre-determined order. (25) But in this case (of the shaving), only the basic form (shaving) as such is known from the originative sentence, and, as far as the order of performance is concerned, the sentences which prescribe the day before and those which prescribe the day of arrival function simultaneously. Therefore no pre-determined order is mentioned and thus the fast cannot draw back the shaving; just as in the darśa sacrifice the altar, prescribed for the previous day by the sentence 'In the moon-less day sacrifice he makes the altar on the preceding day,' does not draw back the various items performed before the covering of the sacrificial cake with ashes.[1] (26) Therefore the statement that "If the fast is to be done on the previous day, then the shaving would also have to be done on that day" is refuted. And thus the text of the PRABHĀSAKHAṆḌA :

216. Having first shaved nearby Someśvara

and other texts which mention a fast on the day of arrival, such as

217. Then he should observe a fast on that day on which he arrives at the tīrtha—

(1) all these are acceptable as providing an optional choice. There is no incompatibility in fasting on the previous day.

---

1. This rule, given in MS V.1.16.29, is one of the exceptions to the Tadantāpakarṣanyāya (see note on 215.23). The construction of the altar is prescribed for the darśa and pūrṇamāsa sacrifices after the covering with ashes of the offering material (the sacrificial cake, puroḍāśa). However, in relation to the amāvāsyā (=darśa) offering only, the altar is to be made on the preceding day. But in this case the drawing back of the altar does not condition the drawing back also of the covering with ashes and other subsidiaries which precede it, because the darśa offering is not a modification of an archetype, but is rather being described for the first time; so the drawing back of the subsidiaries, which is based on the order of procedure of an archetype, does not apply in this case.

(2) As for the statement in the story of Śivaśarma in the KĀŚĪKHAṆḌA, which describes fasting on the day of arrival :

218. Then after reaching Māyāpurī...keeping a fast at the tīrtha and a vigil through the night, and in the morning bathing in the Gaṅgā, and assiduously satisfying those (ancestors) who need to be satisfied, as long as that best of twice-born men wished to break his fast, so long was he stricken with a fever-chill and shivered, severely afflicted;

(1) and also the statement in the same text, in the story of Kalāvatī, after telling of the vigil etc., of king Mālyavat on the day of his arrival :

219. Then rising in the morning...he broke his fast;

(1) and the statement in the BRAHMAVAIVARTAPURĀṆA, in the story of Kāmakalā :

220. Having reached Maṇikarṇī, bathed, and given away much money, and having had her hair shorn, she stood purified, keeping the water vow;[1] (= 251)

(1) all these texts, being in the form of stories, and being acceptable as providing an option, do not rule out the prescription of fasting on the previous day.

(2) As for the argument : "Since, like the śrāddha, the fast also is occasioned by arrival at a tīrtha, it is proper that it be done on that very day of arrival, and not on the preceding day. For in the latter case the occasioning factor has not yet arisen. (3) If this were not so, it would conflict with the rule 'The occasioned act (is done) when the occasioning factor arises'"; (4) this argument is the work of one lacking deep insight into the Mīmāṃsā. (5) For in worldly matters, one finds occasion for building a house because of rain that is yet to come, and in the Veda one sees occasion for taking (the cups) of Indra

1. See 251.1.

and Vāyu first because there is a Rathantara-sāman which is yet to be recited.[1] Therefore the commentator (ŚABARA) says :

221. As for what was said, that 'The occasioning factor must be first, the occasioned act afterwards'—this is not necessarily so. For there is such a thing as an occasioning factor in the future; as for instance, plowing or building a house because it is going to rain.

BHAṬṬAPĀDA (Kumārila) also says :

222. In both worldly matters and in the Veda, an occasioning factor may be past, present, or future without restriction; thus there can be no objection on the ground that the Rathantara-sāman is in the future.

(1) In this connection the commentary of the NYĀYASUDHĀ on this Vārtika should be noted :

223. Even though one may be inclined to say that 'An act can come about only by a past occasioning factor,' still it is possible that something be considered an occasioning factor because it is 'past' inasmuch as it is ascertained that it will (certainly) come about.

BHAṬṬAPĀDA also says this :

224. That which is definitely ascertained (may be considered) as having actually occurred.

(1) Therefore, the fast on the previous day is not merely done for the sake of destroying sin, but rather is actually

---

1. See MS II.3.1.1-2 In connection with the jyotiṣṭoma sacrifice, it is said that if the soma is to be addressed with the Rathantara-sāman, the cups of Indra and Vāyu should be taken first. But, it is objected, the cups are taken up before the recitation of the sāman; so how can the latter condition the former ? In connection with this it is established that an act can be occasioned by a factor which has not yet come about, but which definitely will come about. This is explained in the four following quotations.

occasioned by the arrival at the tīrtha.[1] (2) Thus it is established that there is an optional choice as to the time for the tīrtha-fast, viz. on the day of arrival or the day before that. (3) In the first alternative, one should fast while smelling the remains of the tīrtha-śrāddha, as in the eleventh-day fast and others.[2]

(4) "This tīrtha-fast is for a special benefit only; it is not mandatory. For in the words of DEVALA :

225. Having arrived at the tīrtha, keeping vows, fasts, and voluntary observations, bathing for three days and staying there (fasting) for three nights, one is freed from all sins and becomes prosperous, (≈668)

(1) it is said that the three nights, fast and the three days, bathing produce the result of liberation and prosperity"—so says the KALPATARU.[3] (2) This is not so : for the fast is prescribed as mandatory by the previously quoted words of the NĀRADĪYAPURĀṆA [214], etc. (3) The words of DEVALA, on the other hand, do not refer to the fast of the tīrtha, but rather to a separate, optional three-day fast. (4) Since in the sentences which prescribe the tīrtha-fast, it is referred to with the singular ending, the tīrtha-fast is a one-night fast. (5) And since in the stories of Śivaśarma and Kalāvatī in the KĀŚĪKHAṆḌA [218,219] the breaking of the fast is said to be on the very morning after the tīrtha-fast, that (tīrtha-fast) is to be completed in one day. (6) Therefore the fast *is* mandatory.[4]

---

1. Since it has been proven that an occasioned act may be performed even before its occasioning factor (arrival at the tīrtha) actually comes about.

2. On such days as the eleventh day of a fortnight (ekādaśī) there is a mandatory fast. When one also performs a śrāddha on such a day, instead of eating the remnants of the offerings as in a normal śrāddha, he should only smell them, thereby symbolically partaking of them without breaking his fast. (See *Śrāddha-mayūkha*, p.100, last line.)

3. TVK p. 11 (not a literal quote).

4. Since it is not the same as the three-days' fast described by Devala, which is not mandatory.

SHAVING AT A TĪRTHA

DEVALA says :

226. Shaving and fasting; this is the rule at all tīrthas, except Kurukṣetra, Viśāla, Viraja, and Gayā.

(1) 'Viraja' is in the Utkala country (Orissa), where Dharmarāja set Mount Viraja on the navel of the demon Gaya. This is described in the VĀYUPURĀṆA :

227. Dharma crushed the demon's stomach with Mount Viraja. The goddess Virajā was placed next to the hollow of his navel.

(1) The land of Loṇāra in the south is also 'Viraja,' as it is so called in the ĀDITYAPURĀṆA :

228. When this rule is thus carried out at Viraja, one would becomes faultless (Viraja).

(1) In some texts, however, the reading [of 226] is '...(except) Naimiṣa, Puṣkara, and Gayā', (2) or else '...(except) Viśāla, Puṣkara, and Gayā.'

(3) Other authors read '...except Gayā and the Gaṅgā.' (4) But this reading is incorrect, since it is not observed in most compendia, and because it conflicts with many sentences which will be quoted below which do prescribe shaving at the Gaṅgā. Thus the text in the KĀŚĪKHAṆḌA :

229. Fasting is to be done at the tīrtha (Kāśī), and shaving of the head; for sins which are in the head disappear with shaving. (=213,249)

Also :

230. He would give water red with blood; he would give a contaminated piṇḍa. He does not get all that (benefit), whose head is not shaven. (=253)

And in the SKANDAPURĀṆA :

231. Shaving and fasting...,

etc., the same as the text of DEVALA[1] [226].

(1) Concerning this quotation of DEVALA, the easterners say : "The word 'All-tīrthas', being analyzed as a bahuvrīhi compound meaning 'all tīrthas are in this one,' refers only to Prayāga; and thus shaving and fasting are to be done there only." (2) This is untrue : if the compound is analyzed as singular ('in this one'), there would be no occasion for a plural in the nominal stem, because the basic meaning of the object referred to by the bahuvrīhi compound, namely Prayāga, is singular; therefore the word 'at all tīrthas' would be grammatically incorrect (if it referred only to Prayāga). (3) And since this is so, the argument that "The plural number here is not actually intended, as in the case of the singularity of the cups"[2] is disproven by its own basic premise:[3] since there is no plurality (of Prāyagas), there can be no occasion for questioning whether or not the plurality is intended. (4) For in the sentence 'He cleanses the cup,' the singular ending is appropriate; thus the singular number is said to be 'not actually intended,' in order to express the taking of all the cups (one at a time). (5) But it is not so in the case at hand.[4]

(6) Then, in order to avoid this fault, the compound is analyzed with a plural ending : 'In which (tīrthas) are all tīrthas.' (7) Then still, since there is no plurality of places

1. Except that here upavāsa is neuter, whereas in Devala it is masculine. Both forms are grammatically acceptable.

2. In MS III.1.7.13-14 it is explained that in the phrase 'He cleanses the cup,' the singular ending of the word 'cup' is 'not really intended'; the phrase applies to each one of the many individual cups, so that ultimately a plurality is really expressed by the singular 'cup' (the Grahaikatvanyāya).

3. Literally, 'is verily aborted'.

4. In the case of the cups, we may say that the singular ending is 'not really intended', because there actually are many cups, although they are considered individually when the singular ending is used. But in the case of Prayāga, there cannot be in any sense a plurality of Prayāgas, so there can be no discussion of whether or not a plurality is 'really intended'. Thus the Grahaikatvanyāya (note 2 above) is irrelevant to this case.

which are characterized as 'Prayāga' and which can be denoted by the word 'all-tīrtha,' there would be no occasion for the plural number; so that that form (with the plural) would be incorrect.

(8) Then it may be said, "There are many Prayāgas, such as Deva-Prayāga, etc."[1] (9) Still then, the meaning of the component parts (of the bahuvrīhi compound), which is 'being all-tīrthas' does not apply to those other Prayāgas, so there is no plurality of the meaning of the bahuvrīhi; and thus there would be no occasion for the plural number.[2]

(233.1) But what if the intended interpretation is made by establishing plurality on the grounds that there *are* many 'all tīrthas,' because of such saying as:

232. All the tīrthas and the gods reside here at Avimuktaka (=237)

233. The Gaṅgā is made of all tīrthas (=244)

and so on, so that there may indeed be a non-intention to express the plural, like the non-intention to express the singularity of the cups?[3] (2) In that case, there being many meanings for the word 'all-tīrtha,' the problem would arise "At wha particular all-tīrtha is shaving etc. to be done?" (3) Nor can it be determined that it refers to that Prayāga which is known as 'The Confluence of the Light and Dark Waters,'[4] because in this case there is no determinant such as context, etc., as will be explained below.[5]

---

1. There are several other tīrthas located at confluences of rivers which are called 'Prayāga,' such as Deva-Prayāga (at the confluence of the Bhāgirathī and the Alakanandā), Rudra-Prayāga, Skanda-Prayāga, etc.

2. It is true that there are many tīrthas called 'Prayāga,' such as Devaprayāga (see note 1 above). But those other Prayāgas are not 'all-tīrthas', so there would still be no occasion for a plural bahuvrīhi.

3. This is intended to avoid the refutation of the invocation of the Grahaikatvanyāya given in 231.3-5.

4. I.e. the main Prayāga, at the confluence of the 'light' Gaṅgā and the 'dark' Yamunā.

5. See 235.25ff.

(234.1) "Then the word 'all-tīrtha' refers to Prayāga because of other determining sentences such as

234. At Prayāga one should shave, at Vārāṇasī one should leave one's body."

(2) This is wrong, because, there being many 'Prayāgas,' such as Deva-Prayāga and others, there is no determination of which particular Prayāga is intended here.

(3) And if it is said : "This is determined on the grounds that there is no 'Prayāga' among those (other Prayāgas) without a modifying word"? (4) No, for then that statement would be a restrictive statement of the general prescription 'at all tīrthas,' as in the case of the dividing in four (of the sacrificial cake);[1] but that cannot be. (5) For in the case of the sacrificial cake, the general prescription 'He divides in four the sacrifical cake' is unclear because it has as its object just 'the sacrificial cake' as such. Thus a restrictive statement is appropriate in that it specifies the object; thus 'He divides in four (the sacrificial cake) *of Agni*.' (6) But in this case, the general prescription 'This is the rule at all tīrthas' is clear, as its object is every tīrtha as is seen from the force of the plural number of the word 'all'; so there would be no occasion for a restrictive statement. Thus it is said :

235. A general prescription which is not clear may be restricted to a particular object.

(1) And even if it were a restrictive statement, there would be other restrictive statements in reference to other tīrthas too, according to the sentences to be quoted below.[2]

(2) Nor would a sentence prescribing Prayāga [234] supersede a sentence prescribing all tīrthas, as in the case of the

1. See MS III.1.15. 26-27 (the 'Upasaṃhāra-nyāya').

2. Even if this qualification ('There is no 'Prayāga' among them....' 234.3) can be taken as a restrictive statement of the rule 'at all tīrthas,' then other sentences, namely those quoted below, 250ff., which prescribe shaving at various tīrthas other than Prayāga, are also restrictive statements of that rule; and thus the interpretation of 'all-tīrthas' as referring to Prayāga only is destroyed.

sentence prescribing the footstep.[1] (235.3) For in that case, although the sentence prescribing (the offering) in the āhavanīya fire is superseded in a particular context by the one prescribing offering in the footstep, this supersession is permissible because (the original prescription 'He offers in the āhavanīya fire') still has an application in another offering, so that it is not *completely* superseded, and thus does not become purposeless. (4) In this case, however, if the sentence prescribing all tīrthas is superseded by the sentence prescribing Prayāga, then it (the all-tīrtha sentence) would become purposeless, because it could have no other object.

(5) Furthermore : The general is superseded by the specific; but the 'all-tīrtha' sentence is not general, but rather—since you have accepted that its object is Prayāga—it has a specific object.

(6) Furthermore : When you speak of either a restrictive statement or a supersession, then the all-tīrtha sentence would have to be of a general form; (7) but how would this not contradict what you are saying, that the word 'all-tīrthas' refers to Prayāga only?

(8) As for the refutation[2] given by some, that : "The sentence 'At Prayāga one should shave' [234] is not an absolute prescription; for in the PRABHĀSAKHAṆḌA, after first prescribing shaving at Prabhāsa—'Having first shaved nearby Someśvara' [216]—the sentence 'Shaving and fasting...' [231] which prescribes shaving at the other tīrthas is then given. (9) And this latter sentence is given in the DEVALA SMṚTI[226] as a generally applicable prescription. (10) Nor is it [234] a delimiting prescription; for the (full prescription) being established by the 'all tīrthas' sentence [226], there is no unestablished part; so it [234] does not complete the 'all-tīrtha' prescription. (11) Nor is it a prescription of exclusion; for then the expanded form of the sentence would be either 'At Prayāga only shaving is done and

1. See Mīmāṃsābālaprakāśa, p. 132, and MK, pp.2432-3. The injunction 'He offers in the āhavanīya fire' is superseded, in a particular context, by the injunction 'He offers in the footstep of the one year old cow.'

2. Of the 'shaving only at Prayāga' doctrine.

nothing else', or 'Only at Prayāga is shaving done.' (235.12) The first alternative is wrong, since it would rule out bathing etc. (13) The second is wrong, because the three faults (of a prescription of exclusion), namely superseding what has already been established etc., would result.[1] (14) Therefore, this [234] is a partial supplementary passage, and not a prescription." (15) This refutation is merely a frightening display of alternatives; (the prescription of shaving at Prayāga [234]) may in fact be an absolute prescription. (16) Just because it is also established by the words of DEVALA and others, does not mean that it cannot be an absolute prescription. (17) For the sentences of different authors and in different books are not prevented from being prescriptions, even though they may have the same meanings. (18) Otherwise, it would result that the different prescriptions of the agnihotra sacrifice etc. in the various schools of the Veda, and the different prescriptions of the sandhyā-worship etc. in the various smṛtis, would be supplementary passages (and not prescriptions). (19) And then there would be no way of deciding whether that sentence [226] is the supplementary passage, the prescription being obtained by the prescription of Prayāga [234], or this sentence [234] is the supplementary passage, the prescription being obtained by that sentence [226]. (20) Furthermore, if in this way this sentence [234] is a supplementary passage, then the other sentences to be quoted [250ff.] which prescribe shaving at other tīrthas also would be supplementary passages, according to the same rule; (21) and it is not proper that these many sentences be supplementary passages.

(22) And also, a supplementary passage has no meaning (of its own). (23) But in the other alternative[2] the sentence prescribing all tīrthas [226] would be a supplementary passage to a group of sentences, and it *would* have a meaning of its

1. A prescription of exclusion (parisaṃkhyā) is said to always involve three faults, namely departure from what is literally stated (śrutahāni), construing what is not literally stated (aśrutakalpanā), and superseding what has been already established (prāptabādha).

2. If the general injunction 226 is taken to be the supplementary passage to the various separate prescriptions of shaving at various tīrthas.

own derived from the sentences prescribing shaving and fasting separately for each tīrtha. Enough, then, of arguing with one who is on our side ![1] We return to the main question.

(24) Since this sentence [226] is found in the Gayā chapters of the AGNI- and VĀYUPURĀṆAS, and in the Prabhāsa chapter of the SKANDAPURĀṆA, how can there be any question of its referring to Prayāga? (25) Moreover: if the compound 'all tīrthas' is interpreted as a bahuvrīhi, i.e., 'All tīrthas are in it,' (237.1) then it follows that Puṣkara and Kāśī are also included in that compound; for they too are 'all-tīrthas' according to the words of the ĀRAṆYAKA PARVAN :

236. There are ten thousand times ten million tīrthas, O Lord of the Earth; they are all present in a triple form at Puṣkara[2] O Kurunandana;

and according to the words of the BRAHMAVAIVARTAPURĀṆA :

237. All the tīrthas and the gods reside here at Avimuktaka. (=232)

(2) And there are other such sentences intended to praise this or that tīrtha, which establish them as 'all-tīrthas'; (3) but they are not quoted here, lest it take too long.

Also, such sentences in the chapter on Pañcanada in the KĀŚĪKHAṆḌA and in other places, as :

238. And Prayāga is the Lord of Tīrthas; by the power of Pañcanada it would remove the impurities deposited at all the tīrthas, and the great sins of great sinners,

(1) would be contradicted, if all tīrthas were there at Prayāga.

(2) Then it is said : "The word 'all-tīrthā' is applied conventionally to Prayāga, regardless of its etymological mean-

---

1. The proposition given in 235.8-14 is meant to achieve our purpose—i.e. to show that the sentence 'He should shave at Prayāga' does not mean that one should shave at Prayāga only. But we disagree with the method used therein to establish the proper conclusion.

2. Puṣkara is said to consist of three lakes (hence it is often referred to in the plural number, as in 370-372 below).

ing." (3) This is not so, because there is no evidence for it. If it is said : "The sentence given in the section on Prayāga in the MATSYAPUPĀṆA :

239. Thus, O Kaunteya, anoint yourself at all-tīrthas; from that very moment, all sins done your life-long will vanish,

(1) is the evidence for it"—(2) this too is not so. For this passage in the MATSYAPURĀṆA is given after listing many tīrthas, beginning with 'Known as Agnitīrtha...' and then ending :

240. There are many other auspicious tīrthas which take away all sins. Those who bathe at them go to heaven when they die, and they do not return. Thus, O Kaunteya, anoint yourself at all tīrthas; from that very moment, all sins done your life-long vanish.

(1) Thus the word 'all' is seen to refer to all the (different) tīrthas which are being discussed in the passage. (2) How then, by the force of this passage, can the word 'all-tīrtha' refer to Prayāga?

Furthermore : In the sentences :

241. All the tīrthas reside at that place which is connected with the story of Acyutodāra

242. And this we say : 'All the tīrthas together are not equal to an agnihotra sacrifice' (=80)

243. The auspiciousness in all tīrthas, the benefit in all tīrthas...

244. The Gaṅgā is made of all tīrthas, (=233)

(1) and in others as well, the word 'all tīrthas' is seen to refer to many tīrthas, not to Prayāga. And the sentence in the MAHĀBHĀRATA :

245. They say, O Mighty one, that Prayāga is greater than all the tīrthas,

(1) would be contradicted, if Prayāga were itself all tīrthas.

(2) Furthermore : In the AGNIPURĀṆA, after beginning

246. I will proclaim the greatness of all tīrthas, which provides happiness and liberation,

(1 and then mentioning many tīrthas such as Gaṅgā, Kāśī, Prayāga, etc., it is finally said 'Shaving and fasting; this is the rule at all tīrthas' [=226]

(2) Therefore the objects of this latter sentence are the various tīrthas, not Prayāga only.

(3) Furthermore : Wherever the word 'all-tīrtha' is observed in the purāṇas in reference to one particular tīrtha, it is used there with a singular ending only; as in the chapter on Mātṛtīrtha in the SAHYĀDRIKHAṆḌA, in such sentences as :

247. The greatest tīrtha of Sahyādri is known as Mātṛtīrtha. Mātṛtīrtha is to be known as the supreme tīrtha, O Lords of the Sages! All tīrthas are there, where are Rāma and Reṇukā,

(and)

248. By bathing in an all-tīrtha, men bathe in every tīrtha. There never was a tīrtha greater than an all-tīrtha, nor will there ever be.

(1) But here [in 226] the singular ending is not used.

(2) Furthermore : Sentences which prescribe shaving at various tīrthas are indeed found in the purāṇas. (3) Thus in the KĀŚĪKHAṆḌA, after listing many tīrthas in sequence, beginning 'First the king of tīrthas...', in the middle of the passage the manner of making a pilgrimage is mentioned :

249. Fasting is to be done at the tīrtha, and shaving of the head; for sins which are in the head disappear with shaving. (=213, 229)

(1) Thus shaving is mentioned in general in connection with all tīrthas.

In the PRABHĀSAKHAṆḌA :

250. There one should bathe, after entering the waters. Having first shaved nearby Someśvara (=216), meditating on Śaṅkara in his heart, he should leave his hair there. After leaving all his hair there he should bathe again. Whatever sin a man does when hard pressed for sustenance, all that then stays in his hair, O Daughter of the Mountain. Therefore with all his effort one should leave his hair there. He who performs a thousand thousands of aśvamedhas does not obtain that benefit which is gained from shaving. But, O Fair-faced One, the act of shaving is not recommended for women. Hear from me the rule for married women there : holding all her hair, she should cut off two-fingers' length.

(1) After shaving at Prabhāsa was prescribed to this extent, at the end of this passage shaving and fasting is prescribed incidentally for all tīrthas :

Shaving and fasting; this is the rule at all tīrthas (=226)

(2) Also in the story of Kāmakalā in the BRAHMAVAIVARTA-PURĀṆA, there is another exposition of shaving and fasting at Kāśī :

251. Having reached Maṇikarṇī, bathed, and given away much money, and having had her hair shorn, she stood, purified, keeping the water vow. (=220)

(1) 'Keeping the water vow' means eating nothing but water. Elsewhere too :

252. Having first carried out bathing, etc., one should perform shaving at the tīrtha. After fulfilling the observances of the tīrtha-fast, he should perform a śrāddha.

Also :

253. He would give water red with blood; he would give a contaminated piṇḍa. He does not get all that (benefit), whose head in not shaven. (=230)

Also :

254. Shaving and fasting (should be done) at the Gomatī when Jupiter is in Leo, and at the Kṛṣṇā, when it is in Virgo; but not by those who dwell on its banks.

And also in connection with the Gaṅgā :

255. As many nails and hairs of men who commit sins, tossed by the wind, fall into the waters of the Jāhnavī, for so many years does one rejoice in the heaven-world.

Also :

256. If one arrives at the Gaṅgā, best of rivers, and does not have himself shaved, he and tens of millions of others go to the Raurava hell until the end of the eon.

(1) Or the reading (of the first quarter) may be: 'At the Gaṅgā, in Bhāskarakṣetra...'

257. At the Gaṅgā, in Bhāskarakṣetra, at the death of mother, father, or guru, at a fire-piling ceremony, and when soma is drunk; at these seven occasions, shaving is recommended.

258. As many of his hairs and nails fall into the water of the Gaṅgā, for so many thousands of years he rejoices in heaven.

Also :

259. When one reaches the Gaṅgā, best of rivers, his accumulated sins tremble, taking refuge in his hair. Therefore he should have them shaved off. If a wise man did not have himself shaved upon reaching the Gaṅgā, all his religious works would be nothing; he would offend the tīrtha.

(1) Thus it is a great distortion on the part of those who say that shaving is not mentioned elsewhere than Prayāga, when in fact the prescription of shaving is given in connection with these various tīrthas.

(2) Concerning the statement that the words prescribing shaving at the Gaṅgā [255ff.] are baseless because they are not recorded by the author of the KALPATARU[1]; (3) that is incorrect. For it would then follow that the sentences prescribing, for instance, the throwing of bones into a tīrtha, which are seen in all the purāṇas and in a great many compendia, but which are not recorded by him, are also baseless. (4) If it then is said : "The fact that the author of the KALPATARU did not *see* them is the proof of their baselessness, rather than that he did not record them" ? (5) What is the proof that he did not see them ? (6) The fact that he did not record them is certainly no proof of this ! For then the previous fault results again,[2] (7) and also because that would be circular reasoning. (8) Nor, is there any other proof, for such proof is nowhere mentioned. (9) And even if they were not seen by him, how does that prove that they are baseless ? (10) For the author of the KALPATARU is not the supreme omniscient Lord ! Enough of this !

(11) Concerning what is said, that "The words 'At the Gaṅgā, in Bhāskarakṣetra... (shaving is recommended),' [256.1, 257] do not refer to the Gaṅgā in general, because of the prohibition 'Except Gayā, Gaṅgā, and Viśāla' [228.3]; rather they refer to the Gaṅgā as delimited by Prayāga (= Bhāskarakṣetra). (12) The prohibition (of the Gaṅgā) refers to the Gaṅgā (in general) without that delimitation" (13)—this is refuted, because it has already been shown [228.4] that such a reading of the prohibitive phrase is wrong. (14) Moreover, you have said yourself, "Many sentences which are general in form may (be taken to) refer to some particular object, in accordance with the unanimous practice of refined people." (15) And that reading (restricting shaving at the Gaṅgā in general) is ruled out by the practice of the many diligent residents of mid-India who are versed in the Veda : (16) it is the practice of non-Vedic, undiligent, low people. Thus it is said by BHAṬṬACARAṆA (Kumārila) :

260. Thus only the view of the residents of the lands of the Aryans who are versed in the scriptures is considered

---

1. TīCi p. 16 : 'Gaṅgāmuṇḍanavidhāyakavākyānām amīṣāṃ Kalpatarukārādibhiḥ sarvair evānibaddhatvena nirmūlataiva.'

2. That then the other rituals not 'seen' by him are also baseless.

authoritative as to the significance of words related to ritual acts and details.

(260.1) Moreover : As has been said previously [231.2-5], if the word 'all-tīrtha' refers to Prayāga only, there is no occasion for a plural number. (2) Nor, if it refers as a bahuvrīhi to Prayāga only can the plural be 'not actually intended,' as in the sentence 'He cleanses the cup.' (3) For if it is taken as a bahuvrīhi, the plural number is inappropriate, and then there is no occasion for questioning whether or not the plurality is 'actually intended.' (4) Moreover : The non-intention to express plurality (even if it were applicable in this case) is not opposed to our view, but rather is favorable to it : (5) instead, it is unfavorable to *yours*. (6) For as in the sentences 'Whose two sacrificial cakes burn up,' 'All of whose offerings are ruined or defiled,' and 'They sprinkle the offerings with the remnant of the pre-sacrifice,' if in fact the grammatical number attached to the intended aim of the sentence is 'not actually intended,' shaving at *each* tīrtha is established. (7) But if the plural were actually intended, shaving would be done at the sum of all tīrthas, not at each one.[1] (8) A certain author has proposed this refutation : "There is here no non-intention to express plurality, as there *is* in the case of the singularity of the cup, because (in the passage in question the number) does not particularize an intended aim which is an object to be consecrated, as in the case of the singularity of the cup. (9) Nor is there a non-intention to express plurality as there is in the case of the duality of the offerings, because (the number of the passage in question) does not particularize an intended aim which is an occasioning factor." (10) This is not so, for (the qualification that the intended aim must be) an object to be consecrated or an occasioning factor are not included in that rule. (11) The non-intention of expressing

1. In MS III.1.7.13-15 it is explained in connection with the examples quoted here than any grammatical number applied to the 'intended aim' (yad uddiśya kriyā vidhīyate) is 'not actually intended.' Thus in this case ('all tīrthas') the plural is 'not actually intended'; if it were, it would mean that one must shave at all the tīrthas together, which is obviously impossible. But as it is, the plural not being really meant, one must shave at any one of the tīrthas.

number is established in both cases simply by the number being a particularizer of an intended aim of whatever sort.[1]

(260.12)(The contention that) the Section of the Ruining of Both Offerings is merely a restatement (of the Section on the Cleansing of the Cups) is to be refuted on the grounds that it removes a further objection (concerning the sentence 'Both of whose offerings are ruined...'), namely that "The duality is actually an essential part of the form of the occasioning factor, and not a modifier of it." (13) (The contention that the Section on the Ruining of Both Offerings is merely a restatement) is *not* to be refuted on the grounds that it differentiates the objects (of the Cup-rule) on the basis of their being 'objects to be consecrated' or 'occasioning factors.'[2] (14) For if it were not so, then the citation by the author of the Vārtika of occasioning factors, in 'Whose two sacrificial cakes burn up...' and 'All of whose offerings are destroyed...,' and his citation in the plural number of the offering, which is an 'object to be consecrated,' in 'He sprinkles the offerings with the remnant of the pre-sacrifice,'

1. The proposal says that the number is not intended only when it modifies an intended aim which is an object to be consecrated, as in the case of the cup, or an occasioning factor, as in the case of the ruining of both offerings (see note 2 below). But it is replied that the rule of non-intention of the number applies to a number which modifies any intended aim without restriction. The fact of being an object to be consecrated or an occasioning factor is irrelevant to this rule.

2. The Section of the Ruining of Both Oflerings (Ubhayārtyadhikaraṇa, also called Ārtyadhikaraṇa, etc., MS VI. 4.6.22-23) discusses the sentence 'Yasyobhayaṃ havir ārtim ṛcchet ...' ('Both of whose offerings are ruined ...'). The question is, does this mean 'If both of his offerings are ruined,' or 'If (either of) his two offerings is ruined'? The siddhānta view is that the latter interpretation is correct, because the duality is a modifier of the intended aim of the sentence, which, according to the Cup-rule, is 'not really meant.'

The problem here is : What is the purpose of the Section on the Ruining of Both Offerings? What does it add to the Section on the Cups (MS III.1.7.13-14) so that it is not a mere repetition of it? The pūrvapakṣin says that it specifies the object of the Cup-rule as 'objects to be consecrated' and 'occasioning factors' (260.8-9). But actually, the purpose of the section is to rule out the incorrect notion that the duality in the sentence 'Both of whose offerings...' is actually an essential part of the occasioning factor, rather than a mere modifier of the intended aim (which modifier is 'not actually intended.').

would be improper.[1] Thus PĀRTHASĀRATHIMIŚRA on the Chapter on the Ruining of Both Offerings says :

261. It is established by the Section on the Cups itself that a modifier (such as a grammatical number) of the intended aim is 'not actually intended.' But is not (established that) the form of the occasioning factor is (also) 'not really intended.'[2] But here it may be (proposed as a preliminary argument) that "Just as neither the ruining itself, nor the offering itself is the occasioning factor, but rather the two combined constitute the occasioning factor, thus also, since the word 'both' is used, all three combined should be the occasioning factor."[3]

BHAṬṬASOMEŚVARA too says :

262. Although the rule (i.e. the Cup-rule) which establishes that a split of the sentence results when there is an intention to express a modifier of the intended aim of a sentence is the same in both cases, in that it proves that there is not such an intention, (nevertheless) this (Section on the Ruining of Both Offerings) is not a mere restatement (of that Cup-rule), because (it refutes) the further objection that "The duality (in the sentence 'Both of whose offerings...') must be an intrinsic part of the intended aim of the sentence, as otherwise the word 'both' would be pointless."

(1) Moreover : Even if (the tīrtha) is neither an 'occasioning

---

1. In this Vārtika on the Section on the Cups (TV III.1.7.13, p. 699) Kumārila cites these passages which contain 'objects to be consecrated' and 'occasioning factors' as their intended aims. If the purpose of the Section on the Ruining of Both Offerings, which comes later, is to differentiate the range of the Cup-rule into these two factors, then Kumārila would not have cited them here in the Cup Section. Therefore this differentiation is not the true function of the Section on the Ruining.

2. I.e. establishing this will be the function of the Section on Ruining of Both Offerings.

3. The point is that the function of the Section on Ruining of Both Offerings is to refute such an interpretation as this. This quotation is excerpted from a longer passage in the *Tantraratna*, p.554.

factor' nor an 'object to be consecrated,' why could there not be non-intention to express (the plurality) on the grounds that it is the intended aim of the sentence, as in 'He should sprinkle the remnant of the pre-sacrifice on the offerings'? (262.2) But as a matter of fact, because 'at all tīrthas' is indeed a modifier of the tīrtha, which is the occasioning factor, there *is* no intention to express the plurality, as in the case of the duality (of the offerings).[1]

(3) Moreover : Taking the compound ('at all tīrthas') as a karmadhāraya (instead of a bahuvrīhi), the non-intention to express the plural number is still not opposed to the position that shaving is to be done at every tīrtha, but rather is favorable to it. (4) Otherwise (if the plural were 'actually intended'), shaving would be done at the sum of all tīrthas only, not at each tīrtha : this has been said previously.[2] (5) Thus it would be completely wrong for the supporter of shaving only at Prayāga to claim that the rule of 'non-intention to express' does *not* apply, since that would destroy his own position, as the plural would then actually be meant ; for the non-intention of expressing plurality is unavoidable, as it (the plural) is a modifier of the intended aim, as in 'Whose two sacrificial cakes', 'All of whose offerings,' and 'With the remnant of the pre-sacrifice (they sprinkle) the offerings'; and it is the same whether he accepts (the non-intention) or adopts (intention).[3] (6) Therefore the use (by the objector) of the Rule of The Singularity of the Cups is to be refuted in the way described by us, i.e. because there is no occasion for it [231.3] and because it actually is favorable to our side. (7) Thus, enough of arguing with our own side.[4]

---

1. But even if 'at all tīrthas' were *not* a modifier of an occasioning factor, its plurality would still not be 'actually intended.'

2. 260.6-7.

3. If the proponent of shaving at Prayāga only accepts (kṣema) that the plural is 'not really meant', then his position is refuted, as 'sarvatīrtheṣu' would mean 'at each and every tīrtha.' If he adopts (yoga) the position that the plural *is* meant, then also his position is destroyed, as an intended plural certainly could not refer to Prayāga only.

4. 'Our own side' is that the Cup-rule, establishing the non-intention to express grammatical number, does not apply (231.3-5). But we have

(262.8) Moreover: A karmadhāraya compound is preferable to a bahuvrīhi, because in it the two objects are themselves principal and thus there is no indirect expression; just as the compound 'Niṣāda-chief' is preferably taken as a karmadhāraya, rather than as a genitive (tatpuruṣa).[1] (9) For in a bahuvrīhi, the two objects mentioned in the compound are not themselves principal, and there is an indirect expression of another object. (10) Then in the case of 'A king and a chief priest, desiring communion, should sacrifice', it is accepted that the compound 'A king and a chief priest' is a dvandva compound, because a karmadhāraya ('The two king-chief priests') is ruled out; for it is not possible that the two persons referred to by the word 'king' can be chief priests, as it is established in the 'Aveṣṭi-section' that the word 'king' denotes a kṣatriya;[2] and a kṣatriya cannot be a head-priest.[3] (11) In the case at hand, however, there is nothing which rules out a karmadhāraya.[4]

(12) Then it is said : "Taking it as a karmadhāraya, the meaning of the word 'all-tīrthas' is Prayāga, because Prayāga consists of many tīrthas." (13) This too is not so; for then the plurality would be either 'actually intended' or 'not actually intended'. (14) It is not the first, because, being a modifier of the intended aim, (the plurality) cannot be 'actually intended.' (15) Nor can it be the other, because unless the (plurality) is 'actually intended' Prayāga cannot be taken as consisting of a group of tīrthas; and also, there would then be shaving at every tīrtha (not just Prayāga). (16) Therefore, neither a bahuvrīhi nor a karmadhāraya is correct (if 'all tīrthas' is taken to mean Prayāga).

(since 260.4) been 'arguing with our own side' in order to show that even if the Cup-rule was applicable, it would still favor our interpretation that shaving should be done at all tīrthas, not at Prayāga only.

1. This is established in MS VI.1.13.51.

2. In Śab. II.3.2.3 it is determined that the word 'rājan' applies only to kṣatriyas, and not to brāhmaṇas who serve as kings.

3. See MS VI.6.2.14.

4. By the 'Niṣādasthapati rule,' it is established that if a compound is ambiguous, it is best to take it as a karmadhāraya, unless, as in the case of 'rājapurohitau,' there is some factor which rules out a karmadhāraya. But in 'sarvatīrtheṣu' there is nothing which rules out a karmadhāraya, and therefore it should be taken as such.

(262.17) Then it is said : "Even if the bahuvrīhi signifies a single Prayāga, the plural number is a Vedic usage, like 'May Aditi release these bonds,'[1] with reference to the plurality of its component tīrthas; or it is a plural denoting venerability, as in 'But the teacher(s) (say)...' ."[2] (18) This too is incorrect; for when there is a way of explaining something directly, it is wrong to resort to explaining it by Vedic usage etc., which is to be used when there is no other way. (19) Furthermore : In that case (of the 'bonds'), it is first accepted that the plural number of that mantra containing the plural, being a Vedic form, applies to a single object, like 'You are the winds,'[3] only in the context in which it is recited, namely in connection with the animal offered to Agni and Soma. It is then considered whether the mantra is to be included (in the sacrifice with just one animal and one bond), or should be excluded (and used only) where there are (in a modified sacrifice) a group of animals with a plurality of bonds. It is first proposed that the mantra be excluded, because the plural number cannot refer to the single bond which is present in this context. (20) (But this is rejected), and the plural is said to be simply for the sake of indication (of the bond), (and thus the mantra is to be used); because the single bond, which is the object expressed by the nominal stem ('bond'), and the syntactic function of direct object, which is what is expressed by the (accusative) inflection, *are* present in the original sacrifice. Thus the nominal stem (of the word 'bond'), which is the principal item, and the accusative inflection which expresses the syntactic function,

1. In MS IX.3.5.15-19, it is discussed whether the mantra 'Aditiḥ pāśān pramumoktv etān' ('May Aditi release these bonds') may be used in an Agnī-ṣoma offering consisting of only one animal and one bond. It is concluded that it may be so used, because the basic meaning of the word 'bond' and the accusative case function will be in accord with the actual procedure, while only the plural number, which is of less importance, is not in accordance. The pūrvapakṣin says that there is a similar case here, and that the plurality of 'sarvatīrtheṣu' may be disregarded.

2. Cf. JNMV XI.4.26, Ekasminn api bahuvacanaṃ pūjārtham ācāryādiṣv iva.'

3. The mantra 'You are the winds' is recited for a single sacrificial animal, despite its plural endings. See Uvaṭa's commentary on VS I.1.1.1 (p.4, col. 2 of the Kāśī Sanskrit Series edition). Also cf. 485.7 and note.

and the mantra (itself) would not be removed simply to accord with the plural number only, which is after all not a principal item. (262.21) Or, as in the case of the phrase 'Dressing up his wife'[1] being used in a procedure where (the sacrificer) has two wives, the singular number is said to be 'denoting each part separately'. (22) In such cases, it is proper to invoke such kinds of singulars and plurals by the rule of the ninth book.[2] (23) But in this case, in accordance with what is (the plural of 'sarvatīrtheṣu') a Vedic usage, or used in reference to its component parts? For by the many reasons already given, the passage does not refer to Prayāga (alone).[3]

(24) Moreover : The sentence about 'all tīrthas' [226] cannot refer to Prayāga alone unless it is a prescription of exclusion. (25) Then what sort of prescription of exclusion would this be ? (26) Would it be "At Prayāga only there is shaving," or "At Prayāga there is only shaving"? (27) Surely not the second, for that would rule out bathing, etc; (28) nor the first, for then one could not shave at the death of his father, etc.[4]

(29) Then it is said : "The shaving which is (specified as being) located at a tīrtha may be done at Prayāga only, not elsewhere;" (30) then it would follow that one could not perform shaving if his father died at Kāśī or any other tīrtha !

(31) Then if it is said: "Shaving *occasioned by* a tīrtha is done at Prayāga only"? (32) If this were so, since this shaving

1. See MS IX.3.7.21.

2. (of the MS)—i.e., the rule given here, that in such cases the grammatical number may be disregarded.

3. In the cases given in the Mīmāṃsā texts, only the grammatical number in a mantra is not in accord with the actual procedure, while all the other main factors such as stem and case are in accordance; so it is reasonable to apply the rule of the ninth book and, in effect, disregard the grammatical number. In the case at hand, however, it is *not only* the plural number of 'sarvatīrtheṣu' which is not in accord with the actual practice, if 'sarvatīrtha' is interpreted as referring to Prayāga alone; there are also many other reasons, which have already been cited, that show that 'sarvatīrtha' does not refer to Prayāga alone. Thus one is not justified to invoke the rule of the ninth chapter which permits the use of a plural mantra in a singular procedure, or vice versa.

4. As is requried by 257.

occasioned by a tīrtha is not established by natural inclination, it must be established by a sacred text ; which establishment would be given generally, in connection with tīrthas as such.[1] (33) Thus how would you not contradict your own words, who say "There is no prescription of shaving at other tīrthas (than Prayāga)"?

(34) In either of the two alternatives (of prescriptions of exclusion) there would result the triple fault of superseding what has been already established, etc.[2]

(35) Furthermore : If this prescription of shaving applied only to Prayāga, it would not be found in the Gayā chapters of the AGNI and VĀYUPURĀṆAS.

(36) Moreover; According to the very sense of the word 'all' in the prescription of shaving [226], shaving is to be done at all tīrthas. (37) Nor should this be said : "If there is no limitation at all on the word 'all', the statement would over-apply. Since the words of Bhīṣma in the MAHĀBHĀRATA :

> 263. Tīrthas are said to be auspicious because of the extraordinary power of their earth, and the efficacy of their water, and because they were frequented by the sages, (=75)

(1) say that (any) land or water with special benefits is a tīrtha, one would then shave and fast in (any) spring, etc., anywhere in one's own country."[3] (2) (This is wrong) because the word 'all tīrthas' refers to the famous and great tīrthas enumerated under the designation 'tīrtha' in the purāṇas; (3) and it also refers only to those tīrthas at which shaving is laid down by specific prescriptions, according to the rule :

---

1. If a specific act is established by men's natural inclinations, it may be prohibited by a special prescription; thus, for example, the prohibition of eating red garlic (kalañja). (See rāgataḥ prāpti in Glossary of Mīmāṁsā and other Technical Terms) But here shaving at a tīrtha is not established by men's natural inclination, so it must first be established by a general rule, before specific instances of it can be prohibited.

2. See note on 235.13.

3. This proposition is nearly a word-for-word quote from TīCi pp.14-15.

264. 'All' depends on authorization.[1]

(1) Nor should it be said, "There are no prescriptions for shaving at places other than Prayāga"; (2) for sentences prescribing shaving at Prabhāsa, Kāśī, and other places have already been cited [250ff.].

(3) As for the explanation by one author, that in the sentence 'At the Gaṅgā, in Bhāskarakṣetra...' [256.1, 257], Bhāskarakṣetra is taken as Prayāga, so that the meaning is 'At the Gaṅgā as delimited by Prayāga,' since they (Gaṅgā and Bhāskarakṣetra) are grammatically coordinated— (4) that also is incorrect, because Prayāga is mentioned (elsewhere) as 'Prajāpatikṣetra,' and thus it is not Bhāskarakṣetra. Thus from the (Chapter on) the Greatness of Koṇāditya in the BRAHMAPURĀṆA :

> 265. A man who leaves his life there at the field of the sun (Savituḥ kṣetra = Bhāskarakṣetra) reaches the sun-world and rejoices like a god,

(1) it is seen that only such places as Koṇāditya are 'Bhāskarakṣetra'.

(2) Moreover : If (the words 'At the Gaṅgā, in Bhāskarakṣetra') [257] are explained as the one modifying the other, then there would be six occasions, and the number 'at these seven' would not be appropriate.[2] (3) And also, the phrase 'at the Gaṅgā' would be purposeless.

(4) Moreover : If the prescription of shaving referred only to Prayāga, then it would not apply at all to other tīrthas, and thus the special prohibition 'except..' would not appear.[3]

(5) As for the proposition : "Although it is established by the specific prescription 'The oblation is of mudga-beans' that māṣa-beans etc. are not used, the further sentence 'Māṣa-beans are unworthy of sacrifice' means that māṣa-beans are not to be

1. The meaning of the sūtra is that 'all' in such sayings as 'Such-and-such a ritual yields all benefits' means 'all to which one is entitled.' Thus in the context of 'sarvatīrtheṣu,' this rule means that 'all' denotes 'all those tīrthas at which shaving, etc., is appropriate' (namely the great tīrthas, and those at which shaving is specifically prescribed).
2. 257, '. . .at these *seven* occasions, shaving is recommended.'
3. In 226 ('except Kurukṣetra. . .').

used even as a substitute (for mudga-beans), because they are completely unworthy of sacrifice.[1] (6) In just the same way, the prohibition of shaving at Gayā etc. refers to the complete unworthiness (of those places for shaving)."[2] (7) In answer to this proposition, one author has said :[3] "The sentence '(Māṣa-beans) are unworthy of sacrifice' is for the purpose of commending the prescription of mudga-beans, since it completes that prescription. It does not mean that 'Māṣa-beans are not to be used, even as a substitute'; (8) for the intention of a depreciatory statement is only to praise the prescribed material. (9) Therefore its aim is only to praise the mudga, according to the rule 'A depreciatory statement does not serve to depreciate the object of depreciation, but rather to praise what is prescribed'; as in such sentences as 'The offering is not wild sesamam, nor gavīdhuka.'[4] (10) Its aim is *not* to declare that māṣa-beans are completely unworthy of sacrifice.

(11) Moreover: In the sentences 'The others are non-animals', 'This is unworthy of sacrifice,' and 'Māṣa-beans are unworthy of sacrifice,'[5] the worthiness characterized by the words 'animal' etc. is prohibited by the privative particle 'non-' or 'un-'[6]; thus these sentences *are* meant to indicate complete unworthiness. Thus it is said :

266. First the worthiness of cows etc. is mentioned. The absence of that in other animals etc. is indicated by the privative compound ('non-animals' etc.).

(1) In this case, however, of 'except...' [226], since there is

1. This refers to the example discussed by Śab. in VI. 3.6.20.

2. It is established by the first part of 226 that shaving is done only at Prayāga; the specific exclusion of Gayā etc. shows that at such places *especially* shaving should not be done. This proposition is virtually a literal quotation from TīCi p.17.

3. In 265.7-269.1, a refutation of the proposition in 265.5-6 is given. Then in 269.2-274.3 this refutation is refuted, and finally in 274.4-275.2 the correct refutation of 265.5-6 is given.

4. These sentences are cited in Śab.X.8.4.7.

5. These sentences are cited in Sab. 1.4.12.22 (p.362).

6. The Sanskrit privative particle nañ (=a- or an-).

no privative particle, the sentence does not indicate unworthiness; just as the sentences :

267. A śrāddha should be performed there, except for (= without) the water offering and invitation,

and

268. One should except that at tīrtha-śrāddhas,

(do not indicate unworthiness of the water-offering etc.).

(1) Moreover : Because there is in Vedic usage no application of a substitute without a sentence (specifically prescribing it), māṣa-beans would not be used as a substitute, for lack of a sentence (prescribing their use). (2) How then would the sentence 'Māṣa-beans are unworthy of sacrifice' prohibit that (which has not been prescribed)?

(3) And also : A further prohibition of something already prohibited is for the purpose of demonstrating an extreme fault. Thus it is said :

269. Although meat etc. have already been prohibited on the sixth and other days of a fortnight,[1] "The fifteenth brings one to ruin if he eats meat on it, and the fourteenth, if he anoints himself with oil on it"[2] is said in order to show an extra fault.

(1) But in the sentence in question the prohibition of shaving at Gayā etc. does not indicate that it is completely unworthy, because it is not prohibited elsewhere."

(2) This is far off the mark. For both the author of the (Mīmāṃsā) sūtras (JAIMINI), in the sūtra in the sixth section of the third chapter of the sixth book :

270. That which was prohibited is also (not to be substituted); for the declaration of that (prohibition) was without qualification,

---

1. As in 291 below, where oil (for anointment) is prohibited on the sixth, fourteenth, and other days. Also cf. *Samaya-mayūkha* p.105, line 3.

2. For this śloka (in a slightly different form) see *Kāla-viveka* p. 333 (where it is attributed to Manu).

(1) and the commentator (ŚABARA), who, accepting that the sentence 'Māṣa-beans are unworthy of sacrifice' is intended as a prohibition, says :

271. That which is prohibited is not to be used as a substitute,

(1) accept that (the sentence 'Māṣa-beans are unworthy...') is meant as a prohibition (of using māṣa-beans) as a substitute. And in the sūtra :

272. A prohibited substance (may not be substituted), because that would cause an offense,

(1) it is accepted by KARKĀCĀRYA also that this indicates a prohibition.[1] (2) And thus, how does that sentence complete the mudga-prescription ?; and how, moreover, is it intended to praise, like the sentence 'Wild sesamum is not the offering'?; and how, above all, when it is so similar to sentences like '(The others are) non-animals,' is it to be differentiated from them (merely) on the grounds of the absence of the privative particle ?

(3) As for the statement [268.1] that "There is no application of a substitute in Vedic usage without a sentence specifically prescribing it"; that also would appeal to non-Mīmāṃsakas. (4) For in that same (book and chapter), in the fourth section, substitution is declared to obtain in accordance with the rule whenever there is no explicit prescription for it. Thus such sentences as

273. If he does not find soma, he may press pūtika-plants (instead),

(274.1) are taken in that sūtra as being meant only to delimit (a prescription) :

274. Sometimes a prescription is made to delimit (another prescription).

1. In his commentary on this sūtra, Karkācārya cites 'Ayajñiyā vai māṣāḥ' as an example of a prohibited substance.

(274.2) As for : "A further prohibition of something already prohibited is for the purpose of demonstrating an extreme fault" [268.3]; (3) this is readily refutable on the grounds that it would establish the result desired by the one who maintains that Gayā etc. are (completely) unworthy (for shaving).[1] (For he would reply:) "Since the rule for all-tīrthas (i.e., Prayāga) is meant as a prescription of exclusion, shaving at other places is already prohibited; and thus a further prohibition in respect to Gayā etc. would be for the sake of showing an extreme fault."

(4) Thus what is to be refuted is the content on that '(Māṣa-beans are) unworthy of sacrifice' is similar to 'except Gayā..'.[2] (5) For in the former, it is proper to hold that the declaration that māṣa-beans are unfit for sacrifice is meant as a prohibition, because they would (otherwise) become a substitute for mudga-beans, due to their similarity to mudgas (an offering having already been prescribed as being made of mudga-beans), according to the rule 'In case of a lack of the preferred material, something similar to it should be substituted.' (6) But in this case, since it is not accepted at all that there is shaving at Gayā etc., thus there will be no reason for the application of a prohibition; then what purpose is there in saying that (Gayā etc.,) are completely unworthy ?

(7) Moreover : (If the purpose of the exception of Gayā is to proclaim that Gayā is unworthy,) is this proclamation made for the sake of praising the shaving at Prayāga which is prescribed, as 'Sesamum is not an offering' is said in order to praise the milk which is prescribed ? (8) Or is it to prohibit shaving at Gayā etc., like 'Māṣa-beans are unworthy of sacrifice' ?(9) It is not the latter, since, for you, there is nothing which establishes that there *is* shaving at Gayā, and thus there is no occasion to prohibit it; and (if you accept the latter alternative)

---

1. The proponent of 268.3 is on the side of the author, and thus is opposed to the proponent of the idea that Gayā is completely unworthy of shaving. Thus he should not make this statement, which would support the contention of their opponent.

2. Here NB returns to the main subject, the refutation of the proposition given in 265.5-6. See note on 265.7.

you would be taking our position.[1] (10) Nor is it the former, for one does not observe here a praise of one thing by means of mentioning something else which is unworthy, as is observed in '...not an oblation.' As in

> 275. One should avoid unsteadiness of speech, hand, and foot and over-eating,

(1) and in 'Avoiding (=without) the water-offering and invitation' [267], prohibition (rather than unworthiness) is indicated by the verb 'avoid'. (2) If the exception of Gayā were meant to indicate unworthiness, then it would have to be by way of indirect expression.[2]

(3) Then it is proposed : "Even though shaving is already eliminated elsewhere by the prescription of shaving at Prayāga only, the prohibition of Gayā etc. may be for the sake of showing a greater fault. (277.1) Or else this prohibition of Gayā may be for the sake of amplifying the prescription of exclusion 'At all tīrthas...'; just as the sentence

> 277. He should not eat in between; this rule is equal to the agnihotra sacrifice,

(276.1) is an amplification of a prescription of exclusion according to those who say that

> 276. Eating is prescribed by the sacred texts for the twice-born in the morning and in the evening

is a prescription of exclusion." (277.2)—Not so! For in either case it follows that the sentence 'At all tīrthas' is a prescription of exclusion, and that has previously been refuted [262.24ff]. (3) And if the prohibition of Gayā etc. were an amplification of a prescription of exclusion, the specific enumeration of Gayā etc. would be purposeless; (4) for in that case it would be necessary only to say 'not at other tīrthas.'

1. If you agree that it is necessary to prohibit Gayā, then you agree with our position, that Gayā is not ruled out by the phrase 'at all tīrthas'.

2. Which is always undesirable.

(5) If it is said: "Why can the prohibition of Gayā not be a supplementary reference to a known fact, like 'The fire should not be built in the atmosphere, nor in heaven'?"[1] (6) It cannot, because that is a different case. In that case, there is a supplementary reference to a known fact, because building a fire in the atmosphere etc. is quite impossible. (7) But in this case, since shaving at places other than Prayāga is possible, there is no supplementary reference to a known fact; (8) and without mentioning names the statement would be purposeless.

(9) Enough of all this throat-drying! (10) Although this fact is known from the very sense of the words themselves, that "There is fasting and shaving at all tīrthas excepting Gayā etc.," nevertheless, lest those of lesser intelligence be confused by the false reasonings uttered by the false-minded, this lengthy effort of refutation has been made. (11) Therefore it is established that there is shaving and fasting at all the great and famous tīrthas excepting Kurukṣetra, etc.

(12) This shaving may be done if one arrives again at the tīrtha within ten months, according to the smṛti :

> 278. If one should go to the tīrtha again with a year less two months, then he should carry out shaving and fasting assiduously. (≈551)

(1) Only when the arrival is after more than ten months is the shaving to be done mandatorily. (2) But within ten months, it is done for the sake of its special benefit; this is not an obligatory rule. This is the sense of 'assiduously.' (3) In connection with Prayāga, we will mention a special rule.[2]

(4) Now in connection with shaving, this is to be considered : (5) Is the declaration 'I will perform shaving,' or 'I will have myself shaved'?[3] Concerning this some say : (11) "The

1. This is discussed in MS I.2.2.18 and commentaries. See *nityānuvāda* in Glossary of Mīmāṃsā and other Technical Terms.

2. See below 289.4-5, and Prayāgaprakaraṇa, pp.19-21.

3. In this section (278.4-281.19) it is discussed whether the declaration of intent to shave is to be made with the simple form of the verb 'to perform, (kṛ) or with the causative form. The pūrvapakṣin (278.4-279.2) maintains the causative form; the siddhānta view is that the simple form is correct.

declaration is 'Desiring the specified benefit, I will have myself shaved,' for the following reasons : (6) Such prescriptions as 'At Prayāga one should shave' [234] are understood as prescribing shaving occasioned by arrival at a tīrtha. (7) And since that shaving is performed by a barber, who is not at all affected by that occasioning factor, simply in order to make his living, therefore the prescription of the specially occasioned act does not apply to him. (8) Because of these reasons, and from the very form of sentences such as 'If one arrives at the Gaṅgā, best of rivers, and does not have himself shaved' [256], (9) it is 'having oneself shaved by another' (vāpanam) which is prescribed by the word 'one should shave', which actually indicates 'one should have oneself shaved,' with a dropping of the causative affix. (10) Also, a prescribed act has as its consequence some benefit, and only that which is beneficial should be performed.[1] (12) Nor should it be said that "The declaration is 'I will perform (shaving)' because of the prescription 'One should shave' [234], on the grounds of the rule 'Only the word of the prescription is to be used.'" (13) For that rule applies only to words expressing an invisible purpose and words such as the (name of) the deity of a mantra which express the form (of the deity). (14) In this case, however, the reference is only to the meaning of the word (not its actual form), as in the prescription of the pre-sacrifices etc. For this reason in the sūtra :

279. In connection with a mantra (the indication of the deity) should be made by the word in the prescription; for by that word prescription (is made),

(1) JAIMINI specifies 'in connection *with a mantra*.'

(2). And thus since the prescription refers to 'having oneself shaven,' by the rule 'When the use of the word is up to us, why should we use a non-appropriate form ?,' the declaration may be 'I will have myself shaved (by someone),' or else 'I will have shaving-done-by-someone'[2]; but not 'I will perform shaving.'"

1. This is the reason for the phrase in the declaration 'Desiring the specified benefit.'

2. That is, the causality may be expressed either in the causative verb form kārayiṣye or else in a noun vāpanam derived from the causative form of the verb 'vap' 'to shave.' The distinction cannot be adequately rendered in English.

(3) This is not correct. For although the prescriptions do have both forms, in such forms as 'If one does not have himself shaved,' [256], 'Therefore he should have them (his hairs) shaved off' [259], and 'At Prayāga one should shave' [234], nevertheless by the indication of the mantra :

280. Whatever sins there are, even if they are equal to the killing of a brāhmaṇa, they take refuge in the hair; therefore I shave that hair,

(1) only the declaration 'I will perform shaving' is proper. (2) Nor should the actual sense not be accepted on the ground that there is something to rule it out; for since the word 'shaving' is used to mean simply 'an arrangement for removing the hair', there is nothing to rule it out; as in such sayings as

281. In shaving the hair and beard, he cuts his nails.[1]

(1) And thus it is just as in this example : Although, according to the sentence 'When (the adhvaryu-priest) offers in the āhavanīya fire,' the throwing of the offering-material in the āhavanīya fire is an oblation, and that oblation is done by the adhvaryu and not by the sacrificer; nevertheless for both optional oblations, and for the agnihotra sacrifice, wherein the actual action is done by the adhvaryu, the declaration is 'I (the sacrificer) will offer such-and-such an oblation'. (2) Or as in this example : Although according to its designation[2] the piling is done by the adhvaryu, still, according to the sentence 'Desirous of offspring, (the sacrificer) should pile it, reaching to his navel' the declaration is 'Desiring such-and-such I (the sacrificer) will perform the piling up.' (3) It is just so in the case at hand. (4) And thus the word 'fire-piler' is properly analyzed by the elders as 'he who has piled the fire.'[3]

---

1. That is, 'cuts' (nikṛntati) is a synonym of 'shaves'. Thus 'shaving' (vapanam) means simply 'cutting off,' without any specification as to agency (see also 281.12ff. below).

2. That is, 'piling' is among those Vedic acts specifically enumerated as 'of the adhvaryu' (ādhvaryava). Cf. Śab. III.3.6.13 and III.7.19.40.

3. I.e., the sacrificer, even though the adhvaryu actually does the physical act of piling up.

(281.5) Thus the meaning of the word 'shaving' as an arrangement (for removing the hair) does indeed apply to shaving which is occasioned by arrival at a tīrtha. (6) As for the sentences like '(If he) does not have himself shaved,' [256] which contain the causative form, they are also appropriate when the word ('shaving') is taken in the sense which we have determined for it.

(7) As for the statement that "Because it is meant to express just the meaning as such, the word of the prescription is not meant to express (a particular verb form)"—(8) so be it. But nevertheless, in a performance which includes the recollection of its prescriptive sentence, the word of the prescription itself is proper, since it is readily in mind and is the simplest way. (9) For this reason, like a connection of an accessory and a benefit, so also the act of declaration has been declared by those strong in Mīmāṃsā to be a function of denomination.[1]

(10) As for the rule, 'When it is up to us...'[279.2]; that too does not apply to this case. (11) For by the previously mentioned reason (the simple form of the verb) is not inappropriate, as it does express the intended idea. And also, it is not a matter of 'up to us,' since the indication of the mantra 'I shave...' is definitive (as to the verb form to be used in the declaration).

(12) Or else it may be explained : The word 'shaving' has various meanings. Among them, sometimes it denotes the action of the one who institutes the action, which consists of an arrangement for removing the hair; (13) and sometimes it

1. See Śab. and Kumārila on MS 1.4.1.2 (p. 326). Śab. explains that one of the functions of 'Nāmadheya' or 'denomination' (i.e. the name of a sacrificial act) is in a prescription of a particular detail or benefit belonging to that act (e.g. 'Svargakāmo darśapūrṇamāsābhyāṃ yajeta'). Kumārila adds that in a declaration like 'I will sacrifice with this (sacrificial act)' ('Anenāhaṃ yakṣye'), the denomination is the only simple (laghu) means of denoting the act.

Thus, as in a declaration one should use the actual name of the act to be done, so also one should use the exact phrasing of the sentence which prescribes the act, as that is the simplest and most efficient means of expression.

denotes the action of the one who is employed to do it. (14) For it is used in both these ways, as in 'Shaving has been done by me' and 'Shaving has been caused to be done (by me).' (15) In such a case, its co-mention with other words—the context, and so on — reveals its sense. (16) When (the word 'shaving') is co-mentioned with the word 'he should perform,' then it refers to the action of the one who institutes it. (17) But when it is co-mentioned with the word 'he should cause to be performed,' then it refers to the action of the one who is employed to do it. (18) And in such a case as this, by force of the indication of the mantra [280], it is the action of the causer that is to be illustrated, and thus the declaration can only be 'I will perform shaving.' (19) Enough of this!

(20) Some say : "This shaving is to be done in the order of hair and then beard, according to the words of the BRAHMAPURĀṆA :

282. Having gone there, he should perform bathing, and after that shaving. He should shave his hair and his beard, and cut off his nails ;

(283.1) and in accordance with the order of reading seen in the words cited by APARĀRKA :

283. He should have his hair, beard, and nails shaven, finishing to the north;

and from the observation in the sacred text :

284. He has his hair and beard shaven."

(1) Others, however, say : "These words prescribe only the shaving of the hair etc. as such, but not also the order of that shaving; because that would be overloading of the meaning, and because there would then be splitting of the sentence.[1] (2) Therefore the shaving should only be done with the beard first.

1. Caused by enjoining something and modifying it in the same sentence, which is forbidden in Mīmāṃsā.

(3) And thus it is recorded that the Āpastambas[1] recommend shaving the beard first, and criticize shaving the hair first :

285. Whatever the gods did in the sacrifice, that the demons did also. Those demons did not see (that shaving should be done) upward from their backs. They shaved their hair first; then their beards; then their armpits. Therefore they went down. They were overcome. He for whom they shave thus, goes down. He is overcome.

The gods saw (that shaving should be done) upward from their backs. They shaved their armpits first; then their beards, then their hair. Then they were (dominant). They went to the heaven-world. He for whom they shave thus he himself is (dominant).

Then Manu saw this pair (of methods) for the shaver. He shaved his beard first; then his armpits; then his hair. Then he multiplied with offspring, with cattle. He for whom they shave thus multiplies with offspring, with cattle, with pairs.

(1) And also, if you shave the mustache and beard first you are not despised by people for wearing a barbarian's dress, even for a moment;[2] this is the view generally agreed to.

(2) There too, the shaving of the right half of the beard is done first, so that it finishes to the north.[3] (?) But in the case of (shaving because of) the death of one's father, etc., shaving of the left half of the beard is done first, so that it finishes on the south "[3]

The manner of shaving is given in APARĀRKA :

286. Facing north or east, a wise man should have himself shaved. He should have his head-hair, beard, body-hair,

1. The Taittirīya Brāhmaṇa, in which this passage appears, belongs to the Āpastamba śākhā.

2. Barbarians are described as wearing a full beard and shaven or half-shaven head (cf. Rājataraṅgiṇī IV.179). Thus if one shaves the head hair first, he wears the barbarians' style for a moment, until he shaves his beard. But if he shaves the beard first, there is no danger of this.

3. Because one stands facing east while shaving.

and nails shaved, finishing to the north; for the sake of Dharma, beginning with the right ear; (in a rite to remove) an accumulation of sins, beginning with the top-knot; in the early consecration ceremony, he should shave his head beginning and ending with the top-knot.

(1) In shaving at a tīrtha etc., (which is an act) 'for the sake of Dharma,' one should shave beginning at the right ear, finishing to the north. (2) In shaving occasioned by an accumulation of sins, one should begin with the top-knot and shave from there down in all directions, not finishing to the north. (3) In a ceremony of early consecration, that is, in the tonsure ceremony, one should shave from the right ear to the top-knot, and from the top-knot to the left ear. This is the meaning of the latter verse.

(4) This shaving is to be done by ascetics etc. without preserving the top-knot, according to the words :

287. An ascetic, śūdra, and widow should perform shaving including the top-knot.

In this connection, in the statement :

288. He should have himself shaved excluding the armpits, crotch, and top-knot at the junctures of the seasons,

(1) according to the exclusive prescription 'at the junctures of the seasons (only),' (this type of shaving) is not to be done by ascetics at times other than the junctures of the seasons, even when he arrives at a tīrtha. (2) And this is in fact the practice of ascetics and refined people.

(3) The shaving occasioned by a tīrtha is to be done by fire-keeping brāhmaṇas even at a time other than a parvan; (4) because, this shaving being specially occasioned, it is not restricted to a parvan, like the shaving occasioned by the death of one's father etc.; (5) and this is the common practice.

(6) Shaving at a tīrtha is also to be done by one whose father is living, according to the words :

289. He who has his body-hair shaved without (an occasion

such as) a tīrtha, a sacrifice, or the death of his mother or father—that son is a murderer of his father!

(1) From the use of the word 'son' (it is seen that) the subject is a son whose father is living; (2) otherwise it would have said only '*He* is a killer of his father.' (3) And (shaving is to be done by one whose father is living) also because the words prescribing shaving apply equally to such a person.

(4) Also in this connection, they say that "Shaving is to be done at other tīrthas on the first pilgrimage only ; (5) but at Prayāga on every pilgrimage."

(6) This shaving at a tīrtha is to be performed even at a prohibited time. The prohibitions are given as follows; VṚDDHAGĀRGYA says :

290. On the days of Ravi (Sunday), Āra (Wednesday), and Sauri (Saturday), at night, at a pāta, and on the day of a vow, (one should avoid shaving); and for shaving one should avoid the day of a śrāddha, the new moon day, rikta-days, and bhadra-days.

(1) 'Āra' is Bhauma (Mars). (2) 'Sauri' is Śani (Saturn). (3) 'Pāta' is a vyatīpāta. (4) 'Rikta-days' are the fourth, ninth, and fourteenth days (of the fortnight). (5) 'Bhadra-days' are the second, seventh, and twelfth days (of a fortnight).

GĀRGYA says :

291. The sixth, moon-less, and full-moon days, a pāta-day, the fourteenth, and the eighth; on these days there is evil in these three things : oil, the vulva, and the razor.

VYĀSA says :

292. A man should not perform (shaving) in that asterism in which he was born. It should not be done in the two Proṣṭhapadas, nor in Āgneya, O Bhārata, nor in all the Dāruṇas. One should avoid unfavorable stars.[1]

1. See 393-393.3 for a more detailed explanation.

Also :

293. When the sun is in Aquarius, Cancer, Virgo, and Sagittarius, Yama feeds to the ancestors the householder's shorn hair.

Also :

294. After a wedding, mauñjī-ceremony, and tonsure, for a year, half-year, and a half of that (half), and while one's wife is pregnant, shaving of hair is not desirable.

(1) The exception to all this is when one arrives at a tīrtha, according to the smṛti :

295. Shaving which is specially occasioned—at an initiation or the death of one's father etc., during a penance, and at a tīrtha—should definitely be done, even if there is a prohibition at that time.

And a tīrtha is excepted also because in the words of NĀRADA :

296. With the consent of a king or brāhmaṇa, on the occasion of a sacrifice, a death, a release from imprisonment, and a wedding, shaving yields one's wish on all weekdays, under all stars, and on all month-days,

(1) the enumeration of occasions includes by implication (a tīrtha also).

In this connection, someone says : "According to the words :

297. Whatever number of shorn hairs (fall) in the waters of the Jāhnavī, for that many thousands of years one rejoices in the heaven-world,

(1) one should have oneself shaved while sitting in such a place that his hairs will of themselves fall into the Gaṅgā etc." Others, however, say : "According to the prose text of ŚAṄKHA :

298. One should not throw into water chaff, hair, excrement, ashes, bones, phlegm, nails, and body hair,

(1) one should not throw his hair, nails, etc., in the water, but rather should dig a hole in the bank and put them there." (2) Yet others say : "According to the words :

299. As many nails and body-hairs of men of auspicious acts, driven by the wind, fall into the water of the Jāhnavī...,

(1) one should shave at such a place on the place on the bank that his hair etc., driven by the wind, fall into the tīrtha; but he should not cause this himself in any way." (2) In respect to this (divergence of opinion) one's decision should be made according to local custom.

(3) A special discussion of the shaving of women, married women, and children will be presented in the section on Prayāga.[1]

THUS ENDS THE CONSIDERATION OF SHAVING IN THE BRIDGE TO THE THREE HOLY CITIES.

1. See Prayāga-prakaraṇa pp. 21-22.

BATHING AT A TĪRTHA

In the MAHĀBHĀRATA :

300. Neither the impious man, nor the man of uncontrolled spirit, nor the impure man, nor the thief bathes in tīrthas, O Kauravya ; and neither does the false-minded man.

Also :

301. Neither the dishonest man, nor the man of uncontrolled spirit, nor the ignorant, nor the evil-doer bathes in tīrthas, O Kauravya; and neither does the false-minded man.

Also elsewhere it is said :

302. In rivers, streams, natural caves, and springs, and in natural ponds, and especially at a tīrtha, it is recommened.

(1) Here 'bathing' is understood.

In the KŪRMAPURĀṆA :

303. And a twice-born man, having bathed in all the auspicious tīrthas, is freed from each and every sin.

And, referring to tīrthas :

304. When performed there, O Best of Sages, śrāddha, gifts, etc. each purify unto the seventh generation.

(1) This bathing is not to be done in any place where there is a reversed current, etc. Thus it is said :

305. The twice-born man should avoid bathing in water with a reversed flow. And in a river he should avoid a washer's ford for a distance of ten hands' measures.

Also :

306. Those waters of a river which come in the first flood,[1] which are stirred up by anything, or which come out from a tīrtha are not to be used (for bathing).

(1) The exception to this is in the Gaṅgā :

307. A reversed current, contact with impurities, and the entry of water from a road do not cause impurity in the Gaṅgā; for that river is the stream of Dharma itself.

(1) There is also another prohibition :

308. The śālmalī, tintiṇī, nimba, and karañja; the harītakī, kovidāra, kapittha, arka, badarī, eraṇḍa, and śigru, the śelu and the khadira : one should avoid bathing in the shade of these trees.

(1) Or else, the reading may be '...the badarī and the vibhītakī...'

(2) And as for the restriction against bathing at night and at the sandhyā times; that also does not apply to an unexpected arrival at a tīrtha, since bathing is then specially occasioned. Thus, ŚĀTĀTAPA says :

309. One should not bathe at night, nor make oblations and gifts at night. But one should perform specially occasioned bathing and gift-giving at night.

And VṚDDHAYĀJÑAVALKYA also :

310. At the time of an eclipse, a wedding, an astronomical passage, a journey, a disease, or a birth, bathing is to be considered as specially occasioned; it is desirable (to perform it) even at night.

(1) Some say that "This night-bathing at a tīrtha applies only to two watches, the first and the last, according to the words of PARĀŚARA :

311. The middle of the night is defined as the two watches in the middle. During the morning and evening twilight watches, one may bathe as during the day."

---

1. This refers to the flow at the beginning of the rainy season, which is considered contaminated.

(1) This cancellation of the prohibition on bathing at night applies only to an unexpected arrival at a tīrtha. (2) But one should never intentionally arrive at a tīrtha at night, etc.

(3) And in the case of an incidental arrival at a tīrtha, bathing is to be done even during an intercalary month, according to the words of YAMA :

312. Bathing at a tīrtha, prayer, oblation with barley, rice, and sesamum...should be done even during an intercalary month.

In commenting on this, it is said in the MADANAPĀRIJĀTA :

313. 'Bathing at the tīrtha' (refers to bathing) which was begun previously.

Elsewhere it is said

314. ('Bathing at the tīrtha') refers to one's second and later tīrtha-bathings,

(1) because bathing which has not been done before is prohibited. (2) But the elders say "It refers to bathing occasioned by an unexpected arrival at a tīrtha."

(3) The bathing at the unexpected tīrtha is to be done even if one carries an impurity. Thus it is said by PAIṬHĪNASI:

315. At weddings, in inaccessible places, and during sacrifices, on a journey and in the tīrtha ritual, there is no such birth-impurity; one may perform the ritual, sacrifice, etc. (= 196, 385)

(1) 'Birth-impurity' implicity suggests death-impurity also. (2) The 'tīrtha ritual' is bathing, tarpaṇa, śrāddha, etc.

(3) There is a special rule concerning bathing for another's sake in the MĀRKAṆḌEYAPURĀṆA :

316. One who bathes for the sake of either mother, father, wife, brother, friend, or guru obtains an eighth part (of the benefit).

But in the SMṚTIDARPAṆA, the reading is

317. ...obtains a tenth part.

But in the SMṚTYARTHASĀRA :

318. One who bathes for the sake of his grandfather, brother, grandmother, maternal uncle, father-in-law, benefactor, keeper, preceptor, guru, or instructor, or for the sake of their wives, or for the sake of his mother's sisters or father's sisters, obtains an eighth part (of the benefit). Bathing for the sake of his mother or father, he obtains a fourth part.

(1) A husband and wife bathing for each other's sake each get half (the benefit).

(2) PAIṬHĪNASI gives another special rule :

319. One should bathe a representation made of kuśa-grass in the water of the tīrtha; and the one for whom one bathes it obtains one eighth of the benefit.

The mantra for this is :

320. 'You are kuśa, you are the son of kuśa, formed by Brahma himself. When you are bathed, he too is bathed, for whom this knot is tied.'

(1) Some say "The words 'a representation made of kuśa-grass' indicate that an actual image in kuśa-grass is to be made." (2) Others, however, say "The representation is simply a knot (in the kuśa-grass) tied with the name of so-and-so, according to the words 'this knot is tied' in the mantra."

(3) One author has said : "This bathing for another's sake and placing of a representation (in the water of the tīrtha) is to be done for the sake of either the living or the dead, since these rites are prescribed generally." (4) This is not so; since the dead enjoy the benefits of such rites as tarpaṇa and śrāddha, it is proper that the benefits of these rites be directed to the living only.

(5) Another special rule is given by ŚAṄKHA :

321. One who arrives at a tīrtha incidentally should bathe

in the tīrtha. He gets the benefit of bathing, but not that of a pilgrimage.

(1) 'Incidentally' means 'in connection with trade, official service, etc.'

(2) JĀBĀLI gives another special rule :

322. Where the water flows one should bathe facing the current. In all still waters, one should bathe facing the sun.

(1) Other matters, such as a bathing with earth etc., may be learned from other books.

THUS ENDS THE WAY OF BATHING AT A TĪRTHA IN THE GENERAL SECTION OF THE BRIDGE TO THE THREE HOLY CITIES.

TARPAṆA

(2) After first performing that tarpaṇa which is a subsidiary of bathing[1] according to the texts of one's own Vedic school, thereafter one should perform tarpaṇa for the gods and seers, and then also for his ancestors. Thus it is said in the SKANDAPURĀṆA :

323. Whether at an appropriate or inappropriate time, śrāddha and tarpaṇa should be done without delay at a tīrtha. One ought not interfere with them. (=386)

(1) The tarpaṇa of the ancestors is also mentioned in the DEVĪPURĀṆA :

324. At a tīrtha...tarpaṇa for the ancestors is also to be done by men as soon as they have arrived there. (≈381)

Elsewhere also :

325. If a man bathes at a tīrtha and does not perform tarpaṇa for his ancestors, thirsting for water, they drink the flow from his body.

Also :

326. On mountains, at renowned tīrthas, and especially in rivers, ancestors always dwell, anxiously thirsting for water.

(1) After giving tarpaṇa to all the ancestors who will be specified below [333], one should give a single handful of sesamum for all of them. The mantras for this are given in the VIṢṆUPURĀṆA :

---

1. Tarpaṇa may be either a subsidiary to the act of bathing, or an independent act (pradhāna) in itself. Thus, after having performed the subsidiary tarpaṇa during bathing, one must then carry out the independent tarpaṇa also.

327. The Gods and Demons, Nāgas, Yakṣas, Gandharvas, Rākṣasas, Piśācas, Guhyakas, Siddhas, Kuṣmāṇḍas, and trees and birds; and the creatures which move in water, dwell on land, and live in the air—may they all quickly find satisfaction with this water that I give. This water is also given by me to nourish those who dwell in all the hells and purgatories. May those who are not my relatives and those who are, and those who were relatives is another birth, find complete satisfaction; and whoever else desires (water) from us. Let this sesamum water given by me go eternally to those who are stricken by hunger and thirst, wherever they may be.

Also in the VĀYUPURĀṆA:

328. From Brahma down to a clump of grass, may the gods, seers, forefathers, and humans, and all my ancestors, mother, mother's father, etc., be satisfied. Let this sesamum-water go to tens of millions of past generations, dwelling on the seven continents, unto that world which is the abode of Brahma. (= 337)

And the benefit of this is told in the VIṢṆUPURĀṆA :

329. I have told you, O King, of giving this water-offering. In giving this, a man pleases the entire world. One obtains, O Sinless One, that benefit caused by nourishing the world, when, endowed with faith, he properly gives the water offering to them.

In this connection, some people, according to the words of SUMANTU :

330. In the śrāddha of the (latter) fortnight and in a gold (-śrāddha), after following (the brāhmaṇas), (one gives) the sesamum-water...

(1) perform the tarpaṇa occasioned by the tīrtha after the discharging of the śrāddha-brāhmaṇas[1] in the case of a gold-śrāddha at a tīrtha, rather than before (the śrāddha).

1. I.e., after completion of the śrāddha.

(2) This is incorrect; for tarpaṇa is prescribed by many texts as coming immediately after the tīrtha-bathing. (3) The words of SUMANTU, however, prescribe tarpaṇa after the gold-śrāddha for those whose Vedic schools have a tarpaṇa as a subsidiary of the śrāddha. (4) Therefore this is said in the PRAYOGA-PĀRIJĀTA, in connection with this tarpaṇa which is a subsidiary of the śrāddha :

331. Therefore it is established that tarpaṇa at a tīrtha should be done right after bathing.

(1) Another special rule in regard to tarpaṇa is mentioned elsewhere :

332. If a man crosses rivers without performing tarpaṇa for his ancestors, they are sorely pained and desire to drink his blood. (=670)

(1) The order of recipients in tarpaṇas is :

333. First the father; then the mother, and the mother of one's half-brothers; the mother's ancestors and their wives, and after them one's own wives; sons, brothers, and paternal uncles; maternal uncles, and their wives; daughter and sister are next prescribed; daughter's son and sister's son; father's sister, mother's sister, father-in-law, guru and any giver of inheritance.

(1) 'Inheritance' means wealth.

These are the ancestors at a tīrtha, in tarpaṇa and in a Mahālaya (-śrāddha).

(2) 'Father' here means the three ancestors beginning with the father.[1] (3) Likewise 'mother' also.[1]

Elsewhere also :

334. The three fathers and mothers,[1] mother of half-brothers, the three maternal ancestors beginning with the grand-

1. That is, father, grandfather and great-grandfather; mother, grandmother, and great-grandmother.

father, with their wives; wives and children, etc.; father's, mother's and one's own sisters with their offspring and husbands; wife's father; honored guru; students and friends. These are the ancestors in the procedure of Mahālaya (-śrāddha), at a tīrtha, and in tarpaṇa.

(1) The word 'three' applies to both 'mother' and 'father' separately. (2) 'With their wives' modifies 'the three maternal ancestors, beginning with the grandfather.' (3) Others, however, say that the maternal grandmother etc. desire tarpaṇa separately, as in case of śrāddha. (4) 'Wives and children, etc.' refers to the wives and children of the performer of the tarpaṇa. (5) In 'father's, mother's and one's own brothers,' the father's brothers are the paternal uncles; the mother's brothers are the maternal uncles, and one's own brothers are the brothers of the performer of the tarpaṇa. (6) 'Their wives' are the wives of the paternal uncles, maternal uncles, and one's own brothers; (7) or else the reading may be '*with* their wives', (8) in which case the meaning is 'the father's brother' etc. together with their wives.'[1] (9) 'Father's (etc., sisters)' means the father's sisters, mother's sisters, and one's own sisters, together with their offspring and husbands. (10) Thus for the father's sisters, a procedural statement of the type 'with her husband and with her children' is to be supplied wherever appropriate. (11) 'Wife's father' means father-in-law. (12) The rest is clear. (13) There is an optional choice between this order [334] and the previously given order [333] with respect to the brothers, paternal uncles, etc.[2]

(14) If one is unable to perform the entire tarpaṇa as previously described, then an abbreviated tarpaṇa may be done, according to the statement :

335. When performing an abbreviated tarpaṇa, one should

---

1. That is, if this alternate reading is accepted, tarpaṇa is performed for the brother's wives together with the tarpaṇa for the brothers, not separately.

2. In 333, tarpaṇa is done first for brothers and then for paternal uncles. In 334 this order is reversed.

give three handfuls of water, saying 'May the world, from Brahma down to a clump of grass, be satisfied.'

(1) And this abbreviated tarpaṇa is as follows : With the mantra :

336. With this water which I give, may the entire world, both moving and unmoving, from Brahma down to a clump of grass, be satisfied and go to the supreme way;

or with this mantra :

337. From Brahma down to a clump of grass, may the gods, seers, forefathers, and humans, and all my ancestors, mother, mother's father, etc., be satisfied. Let this sesamum-water go to tens of millions of past generations, dwelling on the seven continents, unto that world which is the abode of Brahma, (=328)

(1) one should give three handfuls of water with sesamum and kuśa-grass. (2) In this procedure the mantra is repeated with each handful. (3) "But," it may be objected, "since the mantra effects the act of tarpaṇa, and since the act of giving handfuls in a certain number constitutes a single act, (338.1) the mantra would be recited only once, according to the rule :

338. The beginning of the act coincides with the end of the mantra;

as in 'He strikes down, saying 'May I strike down the Rakṣas, rival of heaven',[1] and as in 'He wipes the altar thrice, saying 'You are the altar, you, for the sacrifical grass...'".[2] (2) This is not so; for with each handful, different water is being given. (3) For a distinction (between the acts) is perceived on the grounds that 'Wherever a mantra is used, it is for the sake of

---

Cited in Śab. XI.4.12.42.

2. Cited in Śab. XI.4.15.46-47. In both this and the preceding example, an act is repeated several times but the mantra which incites the act is recited only once.

that item only, not for the sake of all the items,'[1] so that the entire consecration is not accomplished (by a single recitation of the mantra); thus in order to accomplish that consecration the mantra is applied with each handful, as those handfuls are separate substances, as in the case of 'putting in' (handfuls of rice)' and 'cutting (bunches of grass),' etc.[2] (4) But in the case of striking (the rice) and wiping (the altar), the same grains of rice are struck again, and the same altar is wiped again; thus, the substance being the same, there is no repetition of the mantra, as the consecration is completed (by a single recitation of the mantra). (5) Therefore in this case the mantra *is* repeated with each handful, as in the giving of water at the sandhyā-times.

(6) Some, however, say that "Because of the present participial form in 'saying' [335], this recital of the mantra is seen to be simultaneous (with the act); thus being like the mantra 'A young man with beautiful clothing...' a supplementary reference to what is being done,[3] it does not effect the act. Therefore one should give three handfuls reciting the mantra once only."

(7) As for the prohibition of sesamum in tarpaṇa, as given by GĀRGYA :

339. In the sun, Mars, the thirteenth day, in Nandā, Bhṛgu, and Maghā, one should not give piṇḍas, bathe with earth, or perform tarpaṇa with sesamum; (=394)

and MARĪCI :

340. On the seventh day, on a Sunday, in one's house, and on one's birthday, one desirous of servants, sons, or wives would not perform tarpaṇa with sesamum. And on the seventh day of both fortnights of the month,

1. Cf. Śab. XI.4.12.42, 'Yena karmaṇā saṃnipatito mantras tadarthaḥ.'

2. These acts of the darśa-pūrṇamāsa sacrifices are discussed in Śab. XI.4.14.44-45.

3. Śab. XII.3.16.36-7 describes this mantra (RV III.8.4) as 'a supplementary reference to what is being done, (kriyamāṇānuvāditvāt). It merely describes the action being performed, rather than stimulating the performer to action, as do mantras in general.

O King, at night, and at the sandhyā-times; at these seven times one desirous of knowledge, sons, or wives should avoid sesamum;

and in the SMṚTYARTHASĀRA :

341. After a wedding, initiation, or tonsure ceremony respectively, for a year, a half-year, and a half of that (half), some say there should be no tarpaṇa with sesamum. They also say there should be no tarpaṇa with sesamum if there is an auspicious occasion in that month;

(1) this prohibition does not apply to tarpaṇa at a tīrtha, according to the words,

342. At a tīrtha, on a special month-day,[1] at Gayā, and in the half-month of the pretas,[2] one should give tarpaṇa mixed with sesamum even on a prohibited day,

and according to the words quoted in the SMṚTYARTHASĀRA :

343. On special month-days[1] and at tīrthas, (tarpaṇa with sesamum) should always be done for a preta.

(1) All the rest of the general rules for tarpaṇa may be determined from other texts.

(2) Tarpaṇa is to be done at a tīrtha by a widow also, (344.1) as it is mentioned in the 'Widow's Dharma' section of the SKANDAPURĀṆA as worthy of being performed every day :

344. She should do tarpaṇa with kuśa-grass, sesamum, and water every day for her husband, his father, and his father's father, with their personal and gotra names.

(2) Since tarpaṇa is (already) occasioned by a tīrtha, she is all the more entitled to perform it there. (3) But this applies only

---

1. Such as aṣṭakā days (*Śrāddha-mayūkha* p.115).
2. The dark fortnight of Gauṇa Āśvina.

in the case that she has no sons or grandsons. (4) This same thing is said in the MADANAPĀRIJĀTA.

(5) But tarpaṇa is not to be done by an ascetic, according to the smṛti passage :

345. One carrying a birth-impurity and a mendicant should not perform the rites of śrāddha, piṇḍas, and water.[1] (≃571)

THUS ENDS TARPAṆA AT A TĪRTHA IN THE GENERAL SECTION OF THE BRIDGE TO THE THREE HOLY PLACES BY NĀRĀYAṆA BHAṬṬA, SON OF THE NOBLE BHAṬṬARĀMEŚVARA SŪRI.

1. 'Water' here refers to a tarpaṇa offering.

DEFILEMENT OF RIVERS

DEVALA :

346. Between the months Nabhas (Śrāvaṇa, = July-August) and Nabhasya (Bhādra, = August-September) all rivers are defiled;[1] one should not bathe in them nor perform tarpaṇa for gods, seers, and ancestors.

ATRI :

347. Between Leo and Cancer, all rivers are defiled. A man should not bathe or perform other ritual acts in them.

(1) This applies to rivers other than the 'great rivers,' according to the words of VYĀGHRAPĀDA :

348. Between Leo and Cancer, all rivers are defiled, except those which go to the ocean; one should not bathe in them.

(1) Another specification with regard to the great rivers is given in the BHAVIṢYOTTARAPURĀṆA :

349. At the beginning of Cancer, O Goddess, the great rivers are defiled for three days; but on the fourth day they become as pure as the Jāhnavī.

(1) The great rivers are enumerated in the BRAHMAPURĀṆA :

350 The Godāvarī, Bhīmarathī, Tuṅgabhadrā, Veṇikā, Tāpī and Payoṣṇī are the renowned rivers to the south of the Vindhya mountains. (=55)

351. The Bhāgīrathī and Narmadā, Yamunā and Sarasvatī, Viśokā and Vihastā are located north of the Vindhya

1. 'Rajasvalā' means both 'dirty' and, when applied to women, 'menstruating.' The muddy flow of rivers during the rainy season is metaphorically considered as a menstrual flow, and thus is contaminated; but those rivers which are (grammatically) masculine are exempted (see below, 354-355).

mountains. These are the twelve great rivers, which rise in the land of the gods and seers.

(1) But small rivers are said in the MATSYAPURĀṆA to be defiled until the rising of Agastya:[1]

352. Until the Lord Ornament of the Southern Direction rises, shallow (literally, 'hand-water') rivers are said to be defiled.

(1) 'Shallow' rivers are those with very little water.

(2) Another special rule is mentioned by KĀTYĀYANA :

353. In the rainy season one should not bathe in those lesser rivers of the earth which dry up in the hot season until ten days are past.

(1) But in regard to the Gaṅgā etc., DEVALA says :

354. Gaṅgā and Yamunā, and the Sarasvatī born of the fig-tree,

((1) The Sarasvatī in Kurukṣetra is called 'born of the fig-tree')

are not affected by defilement; nor are those others which are known as male rivers (nada). The Śoṇa, Sindhu, and Hiraṇyākhya, and the Koka, Lohita, Gharghara and Śatadrū are famed as the seven purifying male rivers (nada).[2]

In the SMṚTISAMGRAHA :

355. The daughter of the sun, the Gaṅgā, Gautamī, and Sarasvatī are not affected by defilement, nor is the Veṇā, nor those known as male rivers (nada).[2]

(1) 'The daughter of the sun' is the Yamunā.

---

1. The rising of the star Agastya (Canopus) marks the end of the rainy season and the beginning of the cool season. See KKT, Niyatakālakāṇḍa (Gaekwad's Oriental Series no. CXI, 1950), Introduction. pp.50-51.

2. See note on 346.

NIGAMA says :

356. In the Gaṅgā, the stream of the Dharma, in the auspicious Yamunā, and in the Sarasvatī, the defilement disappears, and they are immaculate at all times.

Likewise, such words as :

357. At the beginning of Cancer, O Goddess, the Gaṅgā is defiled for three days,

(1) which mention defilement of the Gaṅgā etc., refer to this defilement which disappears. Likewise:

358. At the beginning of Cancer the Gomatī is defiled for three days; and so are the pure Candrabhāgā, Sindhu, Śarayū, and Narmadā.

(1) This defilement of rivers does not apply to those people who dwell on their banks. Therefore it is said in NIGAMA :

359. ...but not for those who dwell on their banks.

(1) Even water which is defiled, when mixed with water of such rivers as the Gaṅgā itself becomes undefiled; nor does it defile the water of the Gaṅgā etc. This is said in the MATSYA-PURĀṆA :

360. By contact with auspicious water, even defiled water becomes purifying.

And in the MAHĀBHĀRATA :

361. Even impure (water) which contacts the Gaṅgā becomes pure.

(1) Another specification is given in the SMṚTISAṂGRAHA :

362. Those (waters) which do not flow for a distance of eight thousand bows do not carry the name 'river'; they

are called 'streams' (garta). New water at the normal time, in the month of Nabhas (Śrāvaṇa)[1], would be impure for three nights. But at an abnormal time, it would be impure for ten days; after drinking it, one should not eat for a day and a night.

(1) Another specification is given in the BHAVIṢYAPURĀṆA :

363. If a greater or equal amount of water stands stagnant, fresh water mixed with it is not defiled by it; so say the sages.

YOGAYĀJÑAVALKYA says :

364. The twice-born should avoid bathing in the water of rivers etc., which is defiled. The defilement of these (bodies of water) is despised. Sandhyā-worship and tarpaṇa in them are also to be avoided.

(1) 'Despised' means condemned.

Also :

365. A she-goat, cow, buffalo, and a brāhmaṇa woman who have recently given birth, and new water from the earth, become pure in ten nights.

(1) Water from a newly excavated well etc., is 'new water'.

(2) In certain rituals, however, there is no defilment. VYĀGHRAPĀDA says this :

366. In the absence of wells and ponds or of lasting clouds, the use (of the water of a river) in a village is not contaminating, even if the water (of the river) is defiled.

VASIṢṬHA says :

1. I.e., the first rains of the rainy season, which begin on the first day of Śrāvaṇa.

367. In the opening and closing ceremonies of a study-term,[1] and in bathing for the deceased and also at an eclipse of the sun or moon, there is no defilment.

THUS ENDS DEFILEMENT OF RIVERS IN THE GENERAL SECTION OF THE BRIDGE TO THE THREE HOLY CITIES.

1. Which two ceremonies take place in the month of Śrāvaṇa, during which rivers are normally defiled (above, 346).

ŚRĀDDHA AT A TĪRTHA

In the SṚṢṬIKHAṆḌA of the PADMAPURĀṆA :

368. At tīrthas, shrines, cow-pens, on islands, in parks and houses, at pure and anointed places, a wise man should perform śrāddha.

In the PADMA and MATSYAPURĀṆAS, after listing the tīrthas, beginning 'A tīrtha, Puṣkaraka by name...,' it is said :

369. The value of śrāddha performed at the tīrthas is multiplied by ten million; therefore one should zealously perform śrāddha at a tīrtha.

In the KŪRMAPURĀṆA :

370. In connection with certain places, the auspiciousness (of śrāddha) would be infinite. At Gayā, śrāddha is eternal; and at Prayāga, and Amarakaṇṭaka; at Varāha-parvata, and especially at the Gaṅgā; at Vārāṇasī especially, where dwells Lord Hara himself; at Gaṅgā-dvāra, Prabhāsa, Bilvaka, and Nīlaparvata; at Kurukṣetra, Kubjāmra, Bhṛgutuṅga, and Himācala; at Kedāra, Phalgutīrtha, and Naimiṣāraṇya; at the Sarasvatī especially, and so too at the Puṣkaras; at Narmadā, Kuśāvarta, Śrīśaila, and Bhadrakarṇaka; at the Vetravatī especially, and the Godāvarī likewise. At these and other such tīrthas, shores, and riverbanks, the ancestors are always satisfied.

VIṢṆU says :

371. Śrāddha, prayer, oblation, and austerities at the Puṣkaras are eternal. One who merely bathes at Puṣkara is freed from all sin...likewise at other tīrthas, pure rivers, confluences, springs, shores, bowers, streams, forests, and groves...

(1) 'Springs' means the places where rivers arise, as it is mentioned in connection with 'pure rivers, confluences...' DEVALA says :

372. A place sanctified for śrāddha is Gayā, and the Gaṅgā, and the Sarasvatī; and so are Kurukṣetra, Prayāga, Naimiṣa and the Puṣkaras. On the banks of rivers, at tīrthas, on mountains, on shores, and at pure places; the ancestors are satisfied by what is given there.

ŚAṄKHA says :

373. At Vārāṇasī, Kurukṣetra, Bhṛgutuṅga, Himālaya, on the banks of the Narmadā and Bāhudā, everything becomes infinite. At Gaṅgādvāra and Prayāga, at Naimiṣa and Puṣkara, at Saṃnihitī and Gayā, everything becomes eternal.

(1) Although it is established by the force of the words which prescribe śrāddha at tīrthas generally that śrāddha is to be done everywhere, the praise of particular tīrthas in these sentences is for the sake of prescribing the connection of an accessory and a benefit, as in 'For one desirous of power (he should offer) with curd.' (2) It is not a modified prescription of another śrāddha, for that would be over-reading of the sense; for that latter is not the only possible interpretation, as it is in the case of 'One should offer with soma.'[1]

In the VĀYUPURĀṆA, after listing the tīrthas, it is said :

374. Those who offer śrāddha at these and other such tīrthas are purified, after bathing and then offering properly.

375. 'After offering' means after offering sesamum-water in the manner given in the rules for tarpaṇa;

---

1. The sentence 'Somena yajeta' is the standard Mīmāṃsā example of a modified prescription (viśiṣṭavidhi). But a prescription should not be considered as modified unless it can be interpreted in no other way, because a modified prescription always includes an 'implied possessive sense' (matvarthalakṣaṇā), and implied statements of any kind are considered undesirable. 'Dadhnendriyakāmasya...' is a standard example of a prescription of a detail and a benefit. (See MNP § 13 ff.)

so says the SMṚTIRATNĀVALĪ.

In the VIṢṆUDHARMOTTARAPURĀṆA :

376. One should carefully perform śrāddha on land sloping to the south, or at a tīrtha etc., or in the home, prepared with the earth-purifying sacraments.[1]

As for what YAMA says :

377. If one offers śrāddha to his ancestors on another person's lands, his effort is ruined by the ancestors of the owner of that land;

and what is said in the BRAHMAPURĀṆA :

378. If an ignorant person were to satiate his own ancestors in someone else's house, the ancestors of the owner of that land seize his (offering) by force. Therefore he should give the first part to them, and a payment to the living;

(1) a gift of his own property is to be given 'to them'—i.e., to the owners of that land, (2) and 'to the living' owners a fee is to be given. (3) In these sentences, lands belonging to other people, such as another person's house, are prohibited; but not tīrthas etc., for they have no owner. This is said in the KŪRMAPURĀṆA :

379. Forest lands are auspicious everywhere, and the banks of rivers; all these they say to be ownerless, for they cannot be taken.

Also :

380. Forests, mountains, rivers, tīrthas, shrines, and natural caves—these have no owners.

(1) 'Caves' are special natural places such as Brahmayoni.

(2) This śrāddha is to be done immediately after bathing, tarpaṇa, etc., without any delay. This is said in the DEVĪPURĀṆA:

1. Nīlakaṇṭha Bhaṭṭa explains these sacraments as 'sweeping, anointing with cow-dung etc.' ('Mārjanalepanādiḥ'; *Śrāddha-mayūkha* p. 30).

381. Śrāddha should be done there without the water-offering and invitation [=406]. That śrāddha which is not ruined by the sight of dogs, gulls, vultures, or crows[1] is called the tīrtha-śrāddha, which brings satisfaction to the ancestors. Śrāddha is to be done at a tīrtha by men as soon as they have arrived there, whether at an appropriate or inappropriate time; likewise, tarpaṇa for the ancestors (≃324). Giving piṇḍas then is recommended; it is most dear to the ancestors. No delay should be made, nor should one interfere with it.

(1) By 'as soon as they have arrived (at the tīrtha)' is meant that śrāddha is to be done right after the mandatory bathing and tarpaṇa, for this much delay is permitted by the prescriptions of bathing and tarpaṇa, etc.

(2) In tīrtha-śrāddha there is also no exception for prohibited times; so says ŚAṄKHA :

382. At a tīrtha, or when materials becomes available, one should not consider the time. Having found a brāhmaṇa as recipient, one should perform śrāddha immediately.

And, in the ĀDI-PARVAN of the MAHĀBHĀRATA, Arjuna says to Aṅgāraparṇa :

383. Having eaten or not, at night or in day-time—O Flying One, there is no restriction as to time when one has reached the Gaṅgā, best of rivers.

In the CITRAPATHĀMĀHĀTMYA :

384. Having eaten or not, whether at night or by day, at a parvan time or an inappropriate time, whether pure or impure—whenever this river Citrapathā is seen, my dear, the sight of it is sufficient reason (for performing a śrāddha). The time is not the cause of it.

---

1. At a normal śrāddha, such unclean animals must be kept out of view; but this rule does not apply to tīrtha-śrāddha. The reason for this is given in 412.

(1) 'Impure' means even when affected by some impurity. Therefore PAIṬHĪNASI says :

385. At weddings, in inaccessible places, and during sacrifices, on a journey and in the tīrtha ritual, there is no such birth-impurity; one should perform the ritual, sacrifice, etc. (=196,315)

In the KĀŚĪKHAṆḌA :

386. Whether at an appropriate or inappropriate time, śrāddha and tarpaṇa should be done without delay at a tīrtha. One ought not interfere with them. (=323)

(1) 'At an appropriate time' means, for instance, in the afternoon, and without having eaten. (2) 'At an inappropriate time' means, for instance, at night, and after eating. (3) Since 'having reached a tīrtha' is the only necessary qualification for authority to perform a śrāddha, the śrāddha should be done in all situations, as in the case of an eclipse, etc.[1]; this is the purport. (4) 'At an appropriate time' is said by way of example only. (5) The word 'or' there is to be taken as in 'The ocean, or a great being...'

(6) A certain author, however has said: " 'At an inappropriate time' means even at times other than the usual times for śrāddha, such as the moon-less day; but not at night, etc., for that (śrāddha at night) would contradict a specific prohibition. (7) Therefore in commenting on the words of DEVALA, 'At a tīrtha, or when materials become available, one should not consider the time,'[2] ŚŪLAPĀṆI says :

387. 'One should not consider the time' means that one should not wait for the moon-less day or the afternoon; but one must avoid prohibited times such as the night."

---

1. The rituals which are to be done when an eclipse occurs must be done regardless of any other circumstances such as time, date, etc., because the eclipse itself is the only necessary condition, and it overrules all others; likewise in the case of the tīrtha-śrāddha.

2. Cf. 382, where this phrase is quoted as Śaṅkha's.

(1) This is not so; for, since there is no prohibition of śrāddha on all week- and month-days, this specially occasioned (tīrtha-) śrāddha would be done (on any day) as soon as the occasioning factor arises. Thus that prescription would be unnecessary, (its result) having been already brought about (by the absence of a prohibition of śrāddha on any particular day).[1]

(2) Then it may be said : "Since śrāddha is not mandatory on all week- and month-days, then even on those days such as the new-moon day when it is (normally) non-mandatory, it is to be done mandatorily if one arrives at a tīrtha (on that day). (3) Thus 'at an inappropriate time' is said to show that the śrāddha becomes mandatory at such times." (4) This also is not so; for by its very prescription as a specially occasioned act, it is established that an act is to be done mandatorily when the occasioning factor comes about; as in the case of the offering made at the burning of a house.[2] (5) Therefore, for 'at an inappropriate time' to have any meaning, it can properly be taken only as a counter-exception to the otherwise prohibited night-time, etc. (6) Therefore ŚAṄKHA says 'One should not consider the time' without any specifications; (7) and in the CITRAPATHĀMĀHĀTMYA it is said clearly 'whether at night or by day' [384]. VIṢṆU too says :

388. Thus what is given in the evening is stolen by Rākṣasas, except at an eclipse of the sun or moon, an astronomical passage, a tīrtha-śrāddha, etc.

(1) Therefore it is established that when there is an unexpected arrival at a tīrtha, śrāddha etc. is to be performed (even) by one who has eaten and (even) at night, etc.

1. In the interpretation proposed in 386.6-387, the sentence 386 establishes only that tīrtha-śrāddha may be done on any *day*, but not that it may be done at night. But this is wrong, because no particular week- or month-days are prohibited for śrāddha, so that, with the proposed interpretation, 386 would not establish anything otherwise unknown, and would thus be purposeless. But if it is taken as permitting tīrtha-śrāddha even at night (which is otherwise a forbidden time for śrāddha) then it does have a purpose.

2. The Kṣāmavatī offering made when a house burns down is cited by Mādhavācarya (JNMV VI. 3. 2, p. 319) to show that a specially occasioned (naimittika) act is mandatory.

(2) When, however, on the day of arrival there is a divine or human interruption, then the śrāddha should be done on the next day. (3) "But," it is objected, "it has been said that '(śrāddha) is to be done by men as soon as they have arrived there,' [381] so that it must be done in the time immediately after reaching the tīrtha; since the following day is not such a time, in this case (when there is an interruption) the śrāddha should be omitted entirely; just as when there is an interruption such as birth-impurity on the moon-less day, the śrāddha of that day is omitted. (4) The performance of the Death-day and other śrāddhas after the (cessation of) birth-impurity, etc., is proper, because of the words

> 389. If that day is defiled by some (impurity) such as birth-impurity, then one should perform (the śrāddha) after the birth-impurity (ceases); or he may perform it on the same date (of the next month).[1]

(1) But in this case, since there are no such prescriptive sayings it is correct to omit the śrāddha entirely. (2) Therefore if one arrives at a tīrtha at night or at the sandhyā-times, let the śrāddha be omitted, since śrāddha at night or at sandhyā-times is prohibited, and the next day is not 'the time immediately after arrival.' "

(3) This would be true, if this were a prescription of time, like the (prescription of) the moon-less day, etc. (4) But in this case, arrival at a tīrtha is being mentioned simply as an occasioning factor. (5) And thus the proper time can be determined according to the rule, 'When the occasioning factor arises, the performance of the specially occasioned act is to be done in the time immediately afterwards, if there is no obstacle.'
(6) Therefore if there *is* an obstacle, the performance even at another time is not forbidden; as in the case of the birth offering, (7) as follows: It is established in the fourth (book of the *Mīmāṃsā Sūtras*)[2] that the birth-offering, prescribed by the words 'When a son is born, he should give an offering with

1. For the interpretation of this śloka see *Samaya-Prakāśa* (vol. 13 of the *Vīramitrodaya*), p. 195.

2. MS IV. 3. 16. 39 (2nd varṇaka).

twelve sherds to Viśvānara,' should not be done in the time immediately after birth, but rather after the birth-ceremony; for if it were done *before* the birth-ceremony, there would result a danger to the child in the interval taken up by the offering and the birth-ceremony, because he would be cut off from his sustenance; for he is forbidden to drink from the breast before the birth-ceremony. Then in the following section[1] it is proven that the birth-offering should be performed in the parvan immediately following the (end of the father's) birth impurity, in accordance with the requirements of purity. For immediately after the birth-ceremony, the father becomes impure by reason of birth, and the time directly after the arising of the occasioning factor is ruled out; but since the occasioning factor has arisen, it would not be appropriate to omit the occasioned act altogether.[2] (389.8) In the same way, in this case also, the performance of the ceremony at a later time is not forbidden.

(9) There is, however, this much difference : (10) In that case, the obstacle intervening is inevitable: in this case, it is incidental.

(11) But when someone goes out (from the tīrtha) without

1. In Śab. this discussion is part of the same adhikaraṇa (16), but later authors such as Pārthasārathimiśra and Mādhavācārya treat it as a separate adhikaraṇa.

2. The birth-offering is an example where a specially occasioned act is not performed immediately after the occasioning factor (the birth) arises, because of an obstacle to so doing—namely the rule that a baby cannot drink his mother's milk until after the birth-ceremony is completed. (If the birth-offering was done before the birth-ceremony, the child could not drink until after both rites were completed, and he might become ill or die in the meantime.) Likewise in the case at hand, the prescription of śrāddha due to a particular occasioning factor is not primarily meant to enjoin a particular time for the śrāddha, but only the śrāddha itself. In the words of Jaimini MS IV.3.16.39) : 'The connection of the subsidiaries (e.g., the birth-offering) with an event (e.g., the birth of a son) is meant to indicate an occasioning factor (and not the time of the act).' Thus the śrāddha should be done as soon as possible after arriving at the tīrtha, but it does not necessarily have to be done immediately after arrival, if some obstacle arises.

having done the śrāddha because of some obstacle, then, since the place (to which he goes) is not a tīrtha, the śrāddha is omitted entirely; as the birth-offering is dropped when the child dies, because there ceases to be any recipient for its benefits of purity etc.[1] (12) If he goes intentionally without having performed the śrāddha, he would incur a sin, because that would be a human offense. (13) But if there is an unintentional obstacle, he does not commit a sin; such is the difference.

(14) If one arrives at a tīrtha at night or at sandhyā-times, the (usual) prohibition being cancelled by force of the previously quoted words [382ff], the śrāddha is to be done at that very time; this has already been said. (15) This same determination applies also to bathing, shaving, fasting, etc., since these are the same as śrāddha inasmuch as they are specially occasioned. Thus in the PRABHĀSAKHAṆḌA:

390. Neither the week-day, nor the asterism, nor the time is the cause for that (tīrtha-śrāddha). Whenever a tīrtha is seen, then there are a thousand parvans.

(1) And therefore the prohibition with respect to month-day, week-day, asterism, etc., does not apply to tīrtha-śrāddha; this is the sense. (2) And that prohibition is:

GĀRGYA:

391. In Nandā, on Friday, on the thirteenth day, in the three birth-times; at these times a house-holder should not perform śrāddha, lest he destroy his sons and wealth.

(1) 'The three birth-times' are the day, asterism, and star of one's birth.

---

1. This refers to the passage (TS II. 2.5.3-4) immediately following the prescription of the birth-offering quoted above (389.7): 'Yasmin jāta eva etām iṣṭiṃ nirvapati pūta eva sa tejasvy annāda indriyāvī paśumān bhavati.' ('He at whose birth this offering is made becomes pure, glorious, an eater of food, powerful, an owner of cattle.')

VṚDDHAGĀRGYA :

392. If one performs śrāddha in Prājāpatya, Pauṣṇa, Pitrarkṣa, or Venus, his son dies.

(1) Prājāpatya is Rohiṇī. (2) Pauṣṇa is Revatī. (3) Pitrarkṣa is Maghā.

In the MAHĀBHĀRATA :

393. A man should not perform (śrāddha) in the asterism in which he was born. It should not be done in the two Proṣṭhapadas, nor Āgneya, O Bhārata; and in all the Dāruṇas, and in Pratyara one should avoid it.

(1) Āgneya is Kṛttikā. (2) The Dāruṇas are (the asterisms) Ārdrā, Āśleṣā, Jyeṣṭhā and Mūla. (3) Pratyara is the fifth, fourteenth, or twenty-third (asterisms) from the asterism of one's birth.

(4) Although these sentences are taken by HEMĀDRI and others as referring to prohibitions on preta-śrāddha, nevertheless they are quoted here because they have been taken by some as referring to prohibitions on śrāddha in general.

(5) Likewise, the prohibition in respect to the giving of piṇḍas (does not apply at a tīrtha[1]) :

394. In the sun, Mars, the thirteenth day, Nandā, Bhṛgu, and Maghā, one should not give piṇḍas, bathe with earth, or perform tarpaṇa with sesamum. (=339)

In the RĀMAKAUTUKA :

395. In the Nandās, Aśva, Kāma, Ravi, Āra, Bhṛgu, Agni, Pitṛ, and Kālabha, and in gañja, vaidhṛti, and in a pāta, piṇḍas are to be avoided by those who desire sons.

(1) The Nandās are the new-moon, sixth, and eleventh days. (2) Aśva is the seventh day. (3) Kāma is the thirteenth. (4) Ravi and Āra are Sunday and Tuesday. (5) Bhṛgu is Friday. (6) Agni,

1. Cf. *Nirṇaya-sindhu* (commentary), p. 1788, lines 16-18.

Pitṛ, and Kālabha are (the asterisms) Kṛttikā, Maghā, and Bharaṇī. (7) Gañja and vaidhṛti are particular conjunctions. (8) Pāta is a vyatīpāta.

KĀRṢṆĀJINI says :

396. At a wedding, vow, and tonsure, for a year, half-year, and a half (of that half) one should not give piṇḍas, bathe with earth, or offer tarpaṇa with sesamum. After any other auspicious occasion, the giving of piṇḍas was forbidden by the great sages such as Garga for the performers of the rituals for one month.

MANU says :

397. One should not perform śrāddha as night; for night is said to belong to the Rākṣasas. And likewise one should not perform it at the two sandhyā-times, nor when the sun is just risen.

In the VĀYUPURĀṆA :

398. During the three muhūrtas of evening one should avoid śrāddha. One should never worship the ancestors around sandhyā-times. That time is said to belong to the demons; one must avoid śrāddha then.

(1) Tīrtha-śrāddha should be done even in an intercalary month, according to the words of JĀBĀLI :

399. One should perform the regular and specially occasioned śrāddhas during an intercalary month,

and according to the words of BṚHASPATI :

400. A zealous man should perform regular and specially occasioned acts during an intercalary month, and also tīrtha-śrāddha, preta-śrāddha, and śrāddha at a gajachāyā.

(1) This prescription of bathing, śrāddha, etc. by one who has eaten etc., and at sandhyā-times, at night, in an intercalary month, and by one who is affected by some impurity, applies to unexpected arrival at a tīrtha, but not to an intentional arrival;

(2) for the occasioning factor, namely arrival at a tīrtha, being achievable by human effort, is unlike eclipses etc.[1] (3) Therefore one should intentionally arrive at a tīrtha only at a non-prohibited time. (4) But in case of an unexpected arrival at a tīrtha, as in the case of an eclipse, the birth of a son, etc., one should perform bathing, śrāddha, etc., even at a prohibited time; this is the intent of these rules.

(5) And this applies to śrāddha with uncooked food and with gold; (6) for by applying to just them the previously cited sentences fulfill a function. (7) The cooked-food śrāddha, however, is to be done on the next day, if the arrival at the tīrtha is at night or sandhyā-times, or after one has eaten. (8) But if there is some impurity at the time of the arrival at the tīrtha, then it is to be done when that impurity ends; (9) for, unlike the case of an eclipse etc., there is still then a connection with the tīrtha.

(10) But in the case of arrival at a tīrtha during an intercalary month, one should perform the śrāddha then, since it is forbidden to delay it, and should then perform it again during a pure month also. (11) For there is an arrival at the tīrtha even then[2], and because of the purity of the time[3] the benefit is increased; and according to the words written in the SMṚTICANDRIKĀ :

> 401. One should perform the śrāddha of yugādi-days, the monthly śrāddha, that of the latter fortnight of the month, that of manvādi-days, and that of the tīrtha in both months.

(1) Here the '(śrāddha of the) latter fortnight of the month' is the monthly śrāddha of the dark half of the month; but not the Mahālaya-śrāddha, for that is forbidden at that time (an intercalary month). (2) This sentence [401] does not refer to arrival at the tīrtha at both times (i.e. months), for then the word 'that of the tīrtha' would lose its significance, as a śrāddha

1. See note on 386.3.
2. In the intercalary month.
3. In the pure month.

would be established anyway without that (sentence)[1]; this is the sense.

(3) In respect to the śrāddha-brāhmaṇa, a special rule is given in the DEVĪPURĀṆA :

402. One should never examine a brāhmaṇa at tīrthas.[2] Manu said that (a brāhmaṇa) who has been found desiring food is to be fed.[3]

In the PADMAPURĀṆA :

403. One should not examine a brāhmaṇa at a tīrtha, nor consider the time. A wise man should perform a śrāddha whenever he reaches a tīrtha.

In the SKANDAPURĀṆA :

404. A twice-born man is not to be examined at a tīrtha; if he desires food, he should just be fed.

405. This is stated to permit (another brāhmaṇa) in case there is no brāhmaṇa (properly) worth of śrāddha. Even then, it is only about specific qualities that one should not examine the brāhmaṇa. But a brāhmaṇa who has extreme faults such as being outcaste must still be avoided;

(1) so explains the auther of the SMṚTIRATNĀVALĪ.

---

1. If the sentence in question (401) referred to arriving at a tīrthá twice (in an intercalary and in a normal month), there would be no purpose in its specifying śrāddha *of a tīrtha*, as those śrāddhas would be occasioned by the arrivals anyway, without any special mention. Therefore the purpose of the word 'at a tīrtha' is to prescribe two śrāddhas occasioned by a single arrival during an intercalary month.

2. Normally, the brāhmaṇas who are chosen as recipients of the śrāddha feeding are to be carefully examined as to their purity, learning, etc.; but for a tīrtha-śrāddha this procedure is suspended.

3. See Mauu III. 243.

PROHIBITED ELEMENTS IN TIRTHA-ŚRĀDDHA

In the DEVĪPURĀṆA :

406. Śrāddha should be done there without the water-offering and invitation. (=381)

Also :

407. In a tīrtha-śrāddha one should omit the water-offering, the invitation, the placing of the brāhmaṇa's thumb in the food, the question about satisfaction, and the scattering of rice.

In a certain text, however, it is said :

408. There is no invitation, nor closing off the directions, nor fault arising from the sight (of unclean beasts).[1] Śrāddha at a tīrtha should be done by the intelligent with compassion (for their ancestors).

In the BHAVIṢYAPURĀṆA :

409. Since the gods and ancestors are always at the Gaṅgā, there is no invitation or dismissal of them there.

Also :

410. Invitation should not be made at a tīrtha, nor should there be offering of water; for ancestors are (always) invited to a tīrtha, and they have (already) received the water-offering.

In the SMṚTIRATNĀVALĪ :

411. There is also no fire-oblation in a tīrtha-śrāddha.

DEVALA says :

412. Nor in this (tīrtha-śrāddha) should one drive away hawks, vultures, and other such birds; for the ancestors

---

1. See 381 and note, and 412.

come together there in the form of these birds; so says the Vedic scripture.

(412.1) This prohibition of invitation etc. refers to śrāddha which is specially occasioned by arrival at a tīrtha, but not to any śrāddha which is located at a tīrtha; (2) for the prohibition of that invitation etc. applies only to śrāddha specially occasioned by that arrival, according to the causal-locative 'there' [406]; (3) and because the arrival is described as the occasioning factor in the concluding statement 'By them, as soon as they have arrived there...' [381].[1]

(4) "But," it is objected, "a causal locative is dependent on co-mention with another word, and can be undestood (only) from the sentence (as a whole). Therefore this must be a locative of location[2]; (5) for it has force as the inflection for an (independent) case function,[3] and as an independent expression."

(6) This is not so; for the sentence alone can be the determinant, since the word 'there' cannot be the inflection for a case function, (7) as follows : It is not correct to say "This is a locative of location which indicates that the tīrtha is the locus (of the śrāddha) as the recipient of a supplement, as in the sentence 'Let the cattle be lodged in the stable' or 'He puts the curd in the hot water.' " (8) For the śrāddha does not produce any improvement, such as consecration, of the tīrtha.[4] (9) Nor is this a locative as the recipient of a subsidiary, as in 'He should offer with the 'Jaya' mantras'[5]; for the tīrtha,

1. This statement follows the verse in question in the Devī Purāṇa; see 381.

2. This objection and the following discussion is based on Tī Ci pp. 11ff.

3. A causal locative (nimitta-saptamī) is a special type of locative absolute (sat-saptamī), which is not considered to be a case function (kāraka).

4. A supplement (śeṣa) is defined as 'that which assists (the main matter)' (Śab. III. 7.1.2, 'yad yasyopakaroti tat tasya śeṣabhūtam), and is said to apply to such secondary matters as consecrations, etc. (Śab. III. 1.3.3, "Badarir ācāryo dravyaguṇasaṃskāreṣv eva śeṣaśabda iti mene').

5. In reference to the text 'Yena karmaṇertsyet tatra jayān juhuyāt' ('He should offer with the 'jaya' mantras in that act by means of which he

not being a prescribed element, does not require any details of performance; (412.10) and because (the śrāddha) does not bring about any benefit (to the tīrtha).[1] (11) Neither is the tīrtha the locus as a supplement, as in 'In the absence of fire, he should place in the hand of a brahman,' and 'When he offers in the āhavanīya-fire;' (12) for if the tīrtha were a subsidiary to śrāddha in general, then such śrāddhas as the new-moon śrāddha which are done in the home would be devoid of value.[2]

(13) If it is said : "In relation to *tīrtha*-śrāddha, the tīrtha is a subsidiary, namely the locus," (14) this is not so because the relation of tīrtha and śrāddha (performed at a tīrtha) has not yet been determined. (15) For it is the meaning of that very word 'tīrtha-śrāddha' which is now being determined. (16) Also, if that were so, the word 'tīrtha' would have to be repeated.[3]

(17) Thus the word 'there' is in fact a causal locative, like 'When it is broken, he offers,'[4] because it cannot have the inflection of a case function.[5] (18) In this connection, since a tīrtha is permanent, it cannot be occasional, and thus the term 'occasioning factor' does not apply to it; rather it is an occasioning factor only in respect to its 'being arrived at;' or else, the

---

would succeed'), 'jayān' is taken by Śab. as an instance of a 'subsidiary' (aṅga) in his comments on MS VII.2.1.3 (also see MS III.4.9.25). Thus 'jayān' being the aṅga, 'tatra' is the 'aṅgin.' Concerning these 'jaya' mantras, see TS III. 4.4.1 and III. 4.6.1, and Sāyaṇa's comments thereon.

1. A subsidiary (aṅga) is that which makes the main matter fruitful (Śab. XII. 3.5.16, 'Aṅgaṃ nāma tat yat pradhānaṃ phalavat karoti'). That is also considered a subsidiary, which supplies details of procedure (itikartavyatā) to another prescribed element (see Śab. IV. 4.11.34).

2. Because a special rule prevails over a general rule. If 'there (at a tīrtha)' is taken as a special rule, then the tīrtha would be a necessary subsidiary of śrāddha, and śrāddhas other than tīrtha-śrāddhas would be useless (which is obviously untrue).

3. That is, 406 would then read '*Tīrtha*-śrāddha should be done there...'

4. This is commonly cited in the Mīmāṃsā as an instance of causal locative (nimitta-saptamī), e.g. in Ṭupṭīkā IX. 1.1.1 (p. 1639).

5. The gist of the argument (412. 6ff) is this : if 'there' is a local, rather than causal locative, it must be either the locus of a supplement (śeṣin, 412.7), the locus of a subsidiary (aṅgin, 412.9), or a supplement (śeṣa, 412.11); for these are the possible functions of a locative in a prescription. But each of these interpretations is shown to be improper, so that the only remaining alternative is to take 'there' as a causal locative.

arrival at it is the occasioning factor. This can be seen by considering such sentences as '(Śrāddha) is to be done by men as they have arrived there (the tīrtha)' [381].

(412.19) "But still," it is objected, "if in saying 'One should omit the water-offering etc. in that śrāddha which is occasioned by a tīrtha,' one intends to express the occasioning factor, namely the tīrtha, which is a particularizer of the intended aim, (namely) the śrāddha, then there will be a split of the sentence in the manner explained in the 'Section on the Ruining of Both Offerings.'[1] (20) And thus there would be a prohibition of the invitation etc. in any śrāddha at all.[2]" (21) Not so!—for there is a split of the sentence when there is the intention to express a particularization of the intended aim; but not when the intended matter is already particularized, (22) as in the sentence 'The Maitrāvaruṇa priest pronounces the praiṣa and the anuvacana,' wherein the intended aim is the praiṣa and the anuvacana which are particularized by the word 'and'.[3]

(23) And therefore, since the sentence in question is established by the contextually appropriate and suitable evidence as a particularized prescription, the only solution to the problem is (for you) to change your mind; (24) as (in the other case, the sentence in question is established as a particularized pre-

---

1. In the Section on Ruining of Both Offerings (MS VI. 4.6.22-23), it is explained that a modifier of the intended aim (uddeśya) of a sentence cannot be 'actually intended' (vivakṣita), or else 'split of the sentence' (vākyabheda) results. See note on 260.13.

2. A modifier of the intended aim of the sentence cannot be taken as 'intended' (vivakṣita), lest the fault of vākyabheda result. Thus what appears to be such a modifier must be considered 'not actually intended,' and should be overlooked. So in this case the modifier, 'at a tīrtha,' of the intended aim, 'śrāddha,' must be passed over, and the original prescription (406) would prohibit invitation etc. at any śrāddha. But this is obviously wrong, so the interpration of 'tatra' (=tīrtha) as a nimitta must be dropped.

3. So that there would be no split of the sentence. It is discussed in MS III. 7.21.43-45 whether this sentence means that the Maitrāvaruṇa priest recites all the praiṣas and anuvacanas, or only those mantras which serve as both praiṣa and anuvacana (namely the puronuvākyās). It is determined that the latter is correct, because the word 'and' modifies the two so as to indicate 'those which are combined (praiṣa and anuvacanas).'

scription) with the recitation of a mantra which is at once both a praiṣa and an anuvacana (i.e., the puronuvākya). (25) Therefore there is no split of the sentence. (26) This will not be further expounded, as it has been previously expounded by BHAVADEVA.

(27) Therefore the prohibition of the water-offering etc. applies only to śrāddha occasioned by arrival at a tīrtha, not to any śrāddha, such as the death-day śrāddha, which may be located there; just as in :

413. At the two solstices, at the two equinoxes, and during astronomical passages, śrāddha is to be done without the offering of piṇḍas,

(1) the restriction of piṇḍas applies only to the śrāddha specially occasioned by astronomical passages etc., but not to yearly and other śrāddhas (which may happen to be done at that time). Thus it is said (in comment on this verse) :

414. But this omission of piṇḍas would not apply to an offering to the ancestors occasioned by something else.

(1) If it is said : "Even so, since the result of the invitation is the presence (of the ancestors), and since the ancestors are always present at a tīrtha, the reason (dvāra) (for the invitation) would be ruled out, as in the case of the chopping and turning up of the natural firewood and altar.[1] Thus because the invitation serves no purpose at a tīrtha, the cancellation of the invitation would apply to any śrāddha at all located at a tīrtha"; (2) not so!—for, as in 'For food is made by that,' the 'bringing about of presence' is a commendatory statement of cause[2];

1. In the Maitrābārhaspatya oblation of the rājasūya sacrifice, the altar is prescribed as being 'self-made', i.e., a natural, unprepared piece of ground (Svayaṃkṛtā vedir bhavati), whereas in the archetypal rite the earth of the altar is to be turned up (Sphyenottamāṃ tvacam uddhanti). Since the altar of the modified rite is to be unprepared, the reason (dvāra) for turning up the earth is eliminated, so that the act of turning up (uddhanana) is dropped. Similarly, if the firewood is to be unprepared, the act of chopping it is dropped. See Śab. on MS X. I.1.3 (1st varṇaka), JNMV X.1.1, and *Veda-Prakāśa* pp. 21-2.

2. A 'commendatory statement of cause' (hetvarthavāda) is a passage which appears to give the cause for a prescription, but which is actually a

(414.3) and because an invitation may be made as a courtesy, even when the person is already present; just as one may explain a thing to someone who already understands it. (4) But in a śrāddha occasioned by a tīrtha the invitation is cancelled, because it is specifically forbidden (by 381 etc.).

(5) Furthermore, certain authors have said this :[1] "The presence of the deity is not physical, for the existence of bodies of the gods is disproven in the Section on Deities.[2] (6) Nor is it mental; for it is agreed that it is just the word (the name of the deity) which is 'the deity'; and thus the deity is non-sentient, and so cannot be mentally present.[3] (7) What purpose, then, would the invitation have at a place other than a tīrtha? (8) Consider that it has an invisible purpose. (9) For this reason there would also be no modification of the invitation mantra.[4]"

(10) In respect to this, one author says :[5] "In the Section on Deities, what is disproven is not that deities are present, but

---

metaphorical praise of the act or thing prescribed. Thus in the example 'He offers with the winnowing basket, for food is made by that,' (MS I. 2.3.26ff) the latter clause is not actually part of the prescription 'He offers with the winnowing basket,' but rather is a praise of it. Thus NB interprets passages which state that the invitation of the ancestors actually causes their presence as such metaphorical praises of the invitation, rather than as statements of fact.

(This type of arthavāda is also known, more explicitly, as hetuvadarthavāda, 'commendatory statement of what seems like the cause' (e.g. JNMV I. 2.3).)

1. This is virtually a verbatim quote from TīCi, p. 11.

2. MS IX. 1.4.6-10. See note on 423.2 below.

3. This concept of 'deity' presented by Śab. in X. 4.12.23 is characteristic of the extreme formality of Mīmāṃsā, in which gods and deities are important only insofar as they aid the sacrifice, which is the real subject of Mīmāṃsā thought. But even some Mīmāṃsakas found this notion repugnant, and disputed Śabara's view on this point; e.g. Bhaṭṭasomeśvara in NS p. 643. See also MK pp. 2140-41 and Introduction to Vol. 1, pp. 25-26.

4. The subject of Modification (ūha) will be discussed at length in the following passages. (See note on 423.6.) In the quotation from Kumārila (488) below, it is stated that only mantras with a visible purpose (dṛṣṭārtha) can undergo modification.

5. This pūrvapakṣa continues through 442.6.

rather that they are the main matter of the ritual. Their presence, however, cannot be denied; for, from such statements as :

415. At the beginning of the ritual, the deities of the mantras are to be known,

416. Placing the deity in one's mind, the offering is offered,

(1) it is seen that the deity is present in the mind of the performer of the ritual as the object of his acts. (2) Furthermore: It is disproven there (in the Section on Deities) that the deities are the main matter, because there is no verbal evidence for it. But because of the words of Lord Rāma :

417. I am present here, and I am present there in stone-images etc.,

and such words as :

418. Hari is always present in the rock of Śālagrāma,

(1) the presence of deities is agreed to by everyone. (2) And it can be seen that the ancestors too are present, from such words as :

419. With knees bent, to the right ... (=428)

420. Sitting in the lap of the red (flames)...

421. This is yours...[1] (=431)

(423.1) This is also understood from such statements as :

422. One should not raise that first receptacle, which was placed for the ancestors. The ancestors stay there, covered over : so says Śaunaka;

423 The ancestors enter the brāhmaṇas who were consecrated

1. These three mantras are all addressed to the ancestors.

on the previous day, and they would dwell that night fixed in the sacrificer.

(423.2) Furthermore: The refutation in the ninth (book of the Mīmāṃsā Sūtras) of the five items, body etc., of a deity[1] is not made just because of fondness (for argumentation), but rather in order to establish (the deity as) secondary, so that modification may take place. (3) That is to say : If the deity were the main matter, the mantras of oblation etc. would not apply in a (modified) ritual for Sūrya, etc., where the deities such as Agni are not involved; then there could not be (the necessary) modification of the mantra (to a different deity).[2] (4) And also, there would be no occasion for the observation of modification in such texts as 'The mother does not grow, nor the father.'[3]

(5) But if the transcendental result[4] is the main matter, then since the mantras are used for its sake, the sacrifice whose

---

1. In MS IX 1.4.6-10 it is determined that the body, fist, neck, arms, and eyes of Indra mentioned in various mantras do not literally exist.

2. See note on 423.6 below.

3. This Vedic sentence is taken by Mīmāṃsakas as a proof of the existence of ūha. It is prescribed in reference to the text (Tai. Br. III.6.6.1) 'Anv enaṃ mātā manyatām anu pitā...' ('May. the mother consent to that (sacrificial animal), may the father.') Śab. I.2.4.44 explains that the sentence cannot refer to the physical growth of the mother and father, since they obviously do grow physically. Therefore it must refer to 'growth of the word' (śabdasya vṛddhiḥ); that is, it prescribes that in the sentence 'Anv enaṃ...' the words 'mother' and 'father' do not change to dual or plural. This specific prohibition of a modification of the words mātā and pitā implies that, in a modified sacrifice involving two or many sacrificial animals, the pronoun enam *does* change to enau or enān. Thus there is a Vedic text which at least implicitly recognizes ūha, as explained in 423.3. Therefore the implicit Vedic sanction of ūha proves that the deity is not the main element in a sacrifice.

A clear exposition of this argument can be found in Sāyaṇa's introduction to his commentary on RV (vol. 1 p.6).

4. The 'transcendental result' (apūrva) of the properly performed ritual is the central concept of the Mīmāṃsā. It is this invisible potency which brings about the various benefits of sacrifices, such as going to heaven, rather than the deities of the sacrifices, who are merely subordinate parts of the ritual.

deity is illustrated by the mantra brings about the transcendental result; thus modification in a modified ritual is established. (6) Therefore, as the deity was illustrated in the original ritual, so also it is illustrated in the modified ritual; thus their presence there, as in the original, is established.[1]

(7) And also : Animals such as frogs, plants and trees consisting of leaves and roots, and the neighing and other acts done by horses, being non-sentient things, cannot be the givers of benefits[2]: therefore the transcendental result only is the main matter, and the deity is secondary.

(8) "But," it is objected,[3] according to such words as

424. If he performs śrāddha and speaks the truth, even a householder may be liberated,

425. Women (are the desire which is achieved by the performance of śrāddha) on the new-moon day,

(1) there is verbal testimony to the effect that the act of śrāddha itself is done for the sake of its benefit. Therefore the ancestors also (being the deities of śrāddha) do indeed come under the rule :

426. But rather, (the sacrificial act is the main matter), as it is so established by verbal testimony; (the deity is praised as a subsidiary).[4]

---

1. Modification (ūha) of a mantra occurs in certain precisely defined cases when a mantra used in an original or archetypal ritual (prakṛti) is transferred to a modified ritual based on the original (vikṛti). Thus in the example in the text, the original ritual is the Āgneya rite of the darśa-purṇamasa sacrifice, which contains certain mantras addressed to Agni. In the modified form of this sacrifice called sauryayāga, which is dedicated to Sūrya, there mantras undergo modification (ūha) by having 'Agni' changed to 'Sūrya'. (See MS VIII. 1.16.27-28). Such a modification in the name of the deity would be permissible only if the deities were a secondary feature of the sacrifice, which is in fact the case.

2. All these non-sentient items are addressed as 'deities' in various Vedic mantras. Frogs are the devatā of RV VII. 103. Plants and trees and their component parts are addressed in TS VII. 3.19.1 and VII. 3.20.1. The neigh and other acts of the horse are addressed in VS 22.7.

3. This objection (423.8-426.3) is a counter-objection to the pūrvapakṣa 414.10-442.6, and contains within itself a further counter-objection (426.1).

4. Here the sūtra (MS IX.1.4.9) is partially quoted. It is quoted in full in 460, q.v.

(1) Nor should it be said, "Because a fault for non-performance of śrāddha is proclaimed only for one whose father is dead, śrāddha is done for the sake of the father"[1]; (2) for the intention there is (only) to indicate that śrāddha is mandatory; for there is no (dative) inflection which would indicate that it is for the sake of the father. (3) And even if śrāddha were (for the sake of the father), it would still be done for the sake of its benefit, because of the separateness of its connections.[2]"

(4) Not so!—for there is no proof that sacrifice is for the sake of the deity; (5) but there is abundant proof that śrāddha is for the sake of its (deity, namely the ancestors). There is the sacred text :

427. Then the ancestors sat before him, wearing their sacred thread on their right shoulders, with their knees bent to the left. He said to them : "From month to month you will have food";

(1) and the words of such mantras as :

428. With knees bent, to the right...(=419)

429. ...the ancestors, to eat the offering... (=464, 478)

430. O Ancestors, rejoice here (=482)

431. This is yours... (=421)

Also, BṚHASPATI says :

432. Those (ancestors) dwelling among the gods are satisfied by an oblation in fire; those dwelling among the ancestors by tarpaṇa by the twice-born; those in hell, by three piṇḍas given on earth.

---

1. In such ślokas as 'Śrāddhaṃ kuryād avaśyaṃ tu pramītapitṛko dvijaḥ' ('A twice-born man whose father is deceased must mandatorily perform śrāddha'), quoted in *Śrāddha-Mayukha*, p. 6.

2. Śrāddha may be both for the sake of the father and for that of the performer, because it has separate and different connections with each. See also note on 166.

In the VIṢṆUPURĀṆA :

433. The ancestors are satisfied for a year by śrāddhas done at that time.

In the BRAHMAPURĀṆA :

434. The śrāddha given to the ancestors then is said to be eternal.

YĀJÑAVALKYA says :

435. Being satisfied, the (ancestors) satisfy him. (=437)

(1) Likewise from statements in various places in KĀTYĀYANA, MANU, and others, and from the words in the Gayā and other chapters in such texts as the VĀYU and AGNIPURĀṆAS, it is seen that that the ancestors are in fact satisfied by śrāddha. And in such sentences as :

436. (The ancestors, when satisfied, offer) long life, offspring, wealth and wisdom,

437. Being satisfied, the (ancestors) satisfy him, (=435)

(1) it is seen that they are also the givers of benefits.

And according to the wording of such mantras as

438. While I pressed...

(1) the sautrāmaṇī sacrifice is also for the sake of the ancestors.[1] Because of such texts as :

439. With the first piṇḍa, a head...

(1) the preta-śrāddhas also are for the sake of the ancestors,

---

1. This mantra, given in the ŚBr in connection with the sautrāmaṇī sacrifice, reads

Yad āpipeṣa mātaraṃ putraḥ pramudito dhayan /
Etat tad Agne anṛṇo bhavāmy ahatau pitarau mayā //

('While as a child, happily sucking, I pressed my mother, so now, O Agni, I become free of debt; my parents are not hurt by me').

because they give them a body.[1] (2) Therefore they do indeed come to have a body.[2]

According to such words as :

440. He would raise up seven gotras[3]

441. Those in hell go to heaven

442. Reaching the Gaṅgā, I have made atonement for my ancestors,

(1) the benefits of śrāddha also apply to the (ancestors). (2) Therefore, since it is seen from the sacred texts and other sources that śrāddha is for the sake of the ancestors, there is no lack of textual evidence for that. (3) Nor are these statements quoted above explanatory passages, (4) for they are not made for the sake of something else, nor do they contradict anything given in the sacred texts, etc.[4]

(5) Therefore, the deity is the main matter in śrāddha, and the ritual is secondary; (6) but in sacrifices etc., the opposite is true."[5]

---

1. This mantra is recited at śrāddha done for a recently dead person (preta). It reads:

Śiras tv ādyena piṇḍena pretasya kriyate sadā /
Dvitīyena tu karṇākṣināsikās tu samāsataḥ //

and so on. ('With the first piṇḍa, a head is always made for the preta; with the second, the ears, eyes and nose all together.') For the full text, see *Nirṇayasindhu* p. 2012.

2. Unlike the gods; see 414.5 and 423.2.

3. This is another part of the śloka partially quoted in 535. The seven gotras are explained in the *Gayā Prakaraṇa* (p. 327) as those of the father, mother, wife, sister, daughter, and the mother's and father's sisters.

4. Such being the defining characteristics of explanatory passages (arthavāda).

5. Thus ends the pūrvapakṣa which began in 414.10. Its intent is to prove that śrāddha, unlike sacrifice, is done for the sake of its deities (the ancestors), and that therefore their presence at a śrāddha is both real and necessary. The implied connection with the original point of controversy, the function of 'tatra' in 406, is as follows: Since the presence of the ancestors is real and necessary, the invitation has a visible purpose (not an invisible one, as maintained in 414.8), namely to bring about their

(442.7) Now, this argument [414.10—442.6] is based on a superficial acquaintance with the Mīmāṃsā. (8) That is to say : What you have said, that "Presence of the deity cannot be denied, because the deity is present in the mind of the performer" [416.1], (9) is wrong. For who has denied that the deity is present in the mind of the performer, in that the deity is within the range (of the performer's thoughts)? (10) For it is the presence *caused by the invitation* which is denied; this presence (at the tīrtha) is not caused by the invitation. (11) Only a deity who is already in mind can be invited, so the presence in mind cannot be a condition which follows after the invitation.[1] (12) If the presence in mind were caused by the invitation, then there would be no presence of the deity in the mind in the offering to Urukrama-Viṣṇu in which invitation is ruled out,[2] nor in the tīrtha-śrāddha, in which invitation is prohibited. (13) As for the supposed presence caused by the invitation, that is eliminated, as is their going and coming, by the elimination of a body etc. of the deities.[3]

(14) Furthermore : After saying "The presence of the deity in the mind of the performer cannot be denied," [414.10] you then cited as evidence for such presence the words 'I am present there...' [417] and 'Hari is always present in the rock of Śālagrāma' [418]. This is incorrect; (15) for these words do not express presence in the mind of the performer. (16) As for the citation of 'With knees bent...' [428] to establish the presence of the ancestors, that applies just as well (to gods in sacrifices); for from such passages in sacred texts as :

---

presence. But since the ancestors are always present at a tīrtha (414.1), the invitation is unnecessary at *any* śrāddha done at a tīrtha, whether occasioned by the tīrtha or not. Therefore 'tatra' in 406 is a locative of location, not of cause.

1. The invitation of a deity does not *cause* its presence in the mind of the performer, but rather reinforces it.

2. See MS X.1.1.1-3, 3rd varṇaka (pp. 1802-03). In connection with an offering to the Viśvedevas, there is also an optional offering to Viṣṇu-Urukrama ('Viṣṇu the wide-stepping'). It is determined that it is not necessary to summon Viṣṇu there (Viṣṇur urukramo nāvāhayitavya iti).

3. See 414.5 and 423.2. There can be no question of a (physical) presence produced by the invitation, since the deities have no bodies etc. to begin with.

443. Come, O Indra, by the praised paths...

444. Come, O Agni, to eat...

445. Come, O beautiful Vāyu...

446. Come, O Agni, together in your chariot with these...

447. Remain here; do not go away...

448. Come, O Indra, come, O Harivat...

449. Come O Maghavan, to the evening pressing...

(1) it is seen that the deity is also present (at sacrifices). (2) And in such rituals as the tulā-puruṣa gift the presence of the deity is established repeatedly with the words 'Come, Come;'[1] and in the MAHĀBHĀRATA and other texts, the presence of the deity at Saṃvartta's and other sacrifices is definitely established[2].

(3) As for what you said, that "The refutation in the ninth (book of the Mīmāṃsā Sūtras) of the body etc. of a deity is made to establish (the deity) as secondary, so that modification may take place" [423.2]; all that too is the same with respect to the ancestors. (4) For if the deity were the main matter in śrāddha, the mantra of the Taittirīya school 'When my mother lusted..,' which has the word 'father' with the singular ending, and such mantras as 'Let the ancestors be purified,' which are used in their original forms in connection with the father etc., would not apply in a śrāddha to the maternal grandfather and others, as the father is not present in them; and then (the prescribed) modification would not occur.[3] (5) And also,

1. In the prescribed ritual for the tulā-puruṣa, several deities are invoked with different mantras, each beginning with 'Ehy ehi'. These are given in *Aparārka* on Yāj. I. 208 (part I p. 316 ff.).

2. This refers to the sacrifice performed by the sage Saṃvartta on behalf of Marutta, to which Indra and the other gods came, as described in chapter 10 of the Aśvamedha parvan. Note especially verses 18-21, containing such phrases as 'Ayam Indro haribhir āyāti rājan...mantrāhutaḥ' and 'Yajño 'dyāyaṃ saṃnihite tvayīndra śośubhyate.'

3. These mantras are prescribed in the Gṛhya Sūtras as having also modified forms, with the substitution of 'grandfather' etc. for 'father'; see below

there would be no occasion for observation of a modification (in the śrāddha) as prescribed in '...with modification of the mantras according to the rule' [487].

(6) Nor should it be said, "This is a prescription of modification, not an observation of it"; (7) for then there would be a split of the sentence between the prescription of the śrāddha to the maternal grandfather and the prescription of modification.[1] (8) We will clarify this word for word (later on).[2]

(9) As for the reasoning concerning animals etc. [423.7], that also is the same (with respect to the ancestors); (10) for it cannot be accepted by an intelligent person that the ancestors, who may by the fruits of their own actions be situated in hell, or born in the womb of an animal, or as a worm, insect, etc., or as a tree or bush, or who may be liberated, can be the main object or the giver of the benefits of the śrāddha.

(11) As for the statement [426.4-5] that there is no evidence that the sacrifice is for the sake of the deity, but that there is evidence that the śrāddha is for the sake of the ancestors; that too is the same (in respect to the deities of sacrifice).[3]

(12) Then as for the sacred text 'Then the ancestors... '[427] which was given there; this is the first half of that passage :

450. The beings sat before Prajāpati. The beings are his offspring. 'Give to us, that we may live !' Then the gods, wearing the sacred thread, with their knees bent to the right, sat before him. He said to them : 'The sacrifice is your food, ambrosia your drink, the sun your light.'

489.2—490.4 and 491—491.3. The mantra 'When my mother...'(491) appears in the Hiraṇyakeśin Gṛhya Sūtra, which belongs to the Taittirīya śākhā of the black Yajur Veda.

1. The pūrvapakṣin says that the verse 487 (q.v.) simply prescribes modification in general, rather than giving an instance of it. But in such an interpretation, the passage is taken as both prescribing something and modifying it in the same sentence, and this causes the fault of vākyabheda.

2. See 489.2ff.

3. That is, in the same way that it can be maintained that the śrāddha is for the sake of the ancestors, it can also be held that the sacrifice is for the sake of the gods.

(1) After this comes 'Then the ancestors...' (2) Thus how can it be that from the first part of this sacred text the sacrifice is not for the sake of the deity, (3) and from the latter part that the śrāddha *is* for the sake of its deities (the ancestors), unless, it be by an arbitrary decision?;[1] that is a non-Vedic distortion.

Further: The deity is seen to be the enjoyer (of the sacrificial offerings) from the passages

451. O Indra, eat these offerings which are set forth...

452. With one draught (Indra) drank...

He is seen to be the Lord, from the passages

453. Indra rules over heaven, Indra over the earth...

454. Lord of this world, seer of heaven...

455. I am the first Lord of riches...

He is seen to be the giver of benefits, from the passages

456. When he is himself satisfied, Indra satisfies him with offspring and cattle...

457. He alone leads him to prosperity...

458. I bestow food on the worshipful one...

459. He gives a son to the worshipful one...;

(1) and he is seen to be satisfied (by the sacrificial offerings) from 'When he is himself satisfied, Indra...' [=456]. (2) Such sentences in the purāṇas and epics cannot even be counted. (3) This being the case, if these sentences are to be taken as (metaphorical) eulogies etc. (rather than as prescriptive passages), then let us also look at those passages which establish the pleasing etc. of the ancestors (in the same way), without partiality. (4) And thus the (ancestors too) are subject to the rule :

1. Kośapāna; see note on 164.18.

460. But rather, the sacrificial act is the main matter, as it is so established by verbal testimony; the deity is praised as a subsidiary; [cf.426]

(1) so no difference at all (between the function of the gods and of the ancestors) can be established—unless it be by superhuman vision !

(2) As for the citation of examples such as 'He would raise up seven gotras...' [440] which establish the benefit for the father etc.; there too there is no contradiction, even if śrāddha is not for the sake of the deity. (3) For the father etc. of so-and-so are not the only deities of the śrāddha; the Vasus etc. are (also deities of śrāddhas).[1] (4) It is only certain words such as 'ancestor' (pitṛ) which are applied commonly to both of them; (5) but this does not constitute identity. (6) And thus śrāddha is not for the sake of the Vasus etc.; (7) they are merely subordinates in the śrāddha. (8) Thus what is wrong in saying "The act of śrāddha, in which (the Vasus) are subordinates, causes the satisfaction of the father etc., or their uplifting from hell"? This is said by YĀJÑAVALKYA :

461. The (divine) ancestors, who are the Vasus, Rudras, and the sons of Aditi, are the deities of a śrāddha. When they are satisfied by śrāddha, they satisfy the ancestors of mortals.

(1) Here the capability of the śrāddha to please (the ancestors) is figuratively applied to the Vasus etc., who are really only instruments (of that capability); as in "When he is himself satisfied, Indra satisfies him with offspring and cattle" [456]. (2) This same figure of speech is also used in sentences like "Being satisfied, the (ancestors) satisfy him" [435].

(3) Nor should it be said : "How can a benefit such as satisfaction of one's progenitors be produced by the śrāddha? For the benefit (of an act) is inherently connected with the

1. A śrāddha, though directed to one's own ancestors, has also for its deities the gods known as Vasus, Rudras, and Ādityas; (see Kane, *History of Dharmaśāstra*, Vol. IV, p. 335). The word 'ancestor' (pitṛ) applies both to one's actual progenitors (e.g. 'the father of so-and-so'), and to these particular gods or 'divine fathers.'

performer." (4) For the benefit of certain acts is legitimately ascribed to one who was not the performer, as for instance such benefits as the purity which accrues to the son by the performance of the birth offering (by the father) [1] (5) This will be explained at length in the Gayā Section, so it will not be propounded here.[2]

(6) Furthermore: If the presence of the ancestors is accepted, then the result of the invitation must be considered to be that very presence; for when there is a visible (purpose), it is not permissible to construe an invisible one. (7) And in that case invitation would be cancelled in any śrāddha located at a tīrtha[3]; (8) for its result would obtain anyway (without the invitation) in another way, since (the ancestors) are always present (at a tīrtha); just as in :

462. Curd, honey, milk, ghee, barley, water, threshed rice grains—these, mixed together, are the offering for Prajāpati,

(1) the threshing (of the rice) is cancelled because (its result, namely) the rice grains being free of husks is obtained anyway in another way.[4]

(2) Nor should it be said : "The invitation there (at a tīrtha) must have an invisible purpose connected with the restriction upon it."[5] (3) For acts which have visible purposes generate

---

1. See above, 389.11 and note.

2. See Gayā Prakaraṇa pp. 317ff.

3. But this has been disproven above (412.1—414.4). It might be charged here that NB is guilty of faulty argumentation; for he uses his own conclusion to refute the position of an opponent who would not necessarily support that position. However, NB's logic may be defended on the grounds that the subject of the present discussion (beginning from 414.10) is merely the sub-topic of whether or not there is a presence of ancestors caused by the invitation, and not the original question of whether invitation is omitted from all śrāddhas done at a tīrtha, or only at a śrāddha occasioned by a tīrtha.

4. Because they have been threshed already, taṇḍula being by definition threshed rice. Thus when the offering is threshed rice (as here, in the Prajāpati offering of the Citrā sacrifice; see MS I.4.2.3) the usual prescription of threshing the rice ('Vrīhīn avahanti') is cancelled.

5. According to Mīmāṃsā theory, even acts with a visible purpose carry with them an invisible purpose related to the restrictions or specifications (as

an invisible result only through their visible result; for, as in the case of the gold piece,[1] when the visible result is dropped, that (invisible result) is also dropped. (462.4) And also, an invisible purpose connected with a restriction does not cause (an act), because, like the whey,[2] it is (merely) co-produced (along with the visible result). (5) Therefore it is not possible that the ancestors are present (at a tīrtha).[3]

(6) Furthermore, concerning the five elements of body etc.;[4] if they are accepted in connection with the ancestors,

---

to time, place, etc.) placed upon them. Thus TV I.3.8.27 (p. 283) 'Dṛṣṭe saty api sarvatra niyamādṛṣṭam iṣyate' (Even when there is a visible purpose, an invisible purpose of the restriction is always to be sought for), and JNMV VI. 2.10, 'Dṛṣṭārtheṣv api vihiteṣu niyamādṛṣṭaṃ sambhavati' (Even when visible purposes are prescribed, there is an invisible purpose to the restriction).

1. See MS X.1.1.1-3 (varṇaka 2). In the archetypal rite, the offering of corn undergoes threshing (avaghāta), which act obviously has a visible result. In a modified ritual wherein gold pieces are substituted for corn, the act of threshing, which does not apply to gold pieces, is cancelled. Thus along with the visible result of being free of husks, whatever invisible result was caused by the restrictions on the original act is also cancelled.

2. Śab. on MS IV.1.9.22-24 discusses the text 'Tapte payasi dadhy ānayati, sā vaiśvadevy āmikṣā, vājibhyo vājinam' (He puts the curd in the hot milk; that mixture is āmikṣā for the Viśvedevas. The whey (which is also produced) is for the Vājins.) It is determined that the production of āmikṣā is the main purpose of the act of putting the curd in the milk. The āmikṣā is the cause (prayojaka) of the act, while the whey is merely an incidental by-product. Similarly, the invisible result produced by the restriction on an act with a visible purpose is merely a by-product, and cannot be considered the reason for doing the act.

3. It has been shown in the preceding paragraph of the text that the invitation cannot have a visible purpose, namely the presence of the ancestors, because then the invitation would be cancelled at any śrāddha done at a tīrtha; but this has been disproved above (412.1—414.4). The objector, who still wishes to prove that the ancestors are present at a tīrtha-śrāddha, proposes that the invitation has some invisible purpose caused by the restrictions on it, and that this invisible purpose would account for the cancellation of invitation only at a śrāddha occasioned by a tīrtha. But this is rejected, because such an invisible purpose is merely incidental to the visible purpose, and cannot of itself regulate the performance of ritual acts. Thus this proposal cannot account for the special regulation concerning invitation, and it remains that the invitation must have an invisible purpose, rather than the visible purpose of the presence of the ancestors at the tīrtha; and therefore the ancestors are not present at the tīrtha.

4. See above, 423.2.

then according to the rule of the first section of the CATURLAKṢAṆĪ (Vedānta Sūtras) expounded by VYĀSA :

> 463. If it is said that there would be an obstacle to sacrificial acts, that is not so, because (the gods) are observed to assume numerous (bodily forms),[1]

(1) the body etc. must be accepted in connection with the divinities also; or else, according to the opinion of the sage JAIMINI, it must not be accepted in connection with the ancestors either; but you may not have it both ways.[2]

(2) Thus it is established that the restriction on the invitation applies only to śrāddha which is occasioned by a tīrtha, because there is an explicit statement to that effect; but not to any śrāddha which is located at a tīrtha.

(3) As for what was said, "What purpose, then, would the invitation have at a place other than (a tīrtha) ? Consider that it has an invisible purpose. For this reason there would also be no modification of the invitation mantra" [414.7-9]; (4) this is doubtful. For even if the invitation is invisible in purpose, the mantra has a visible purpose in that it calls to mind the ritual to be performed, and therefore it may be modified.(5) For modification in a mantra is not ruled out just because the action to which it is an instrument has an invisible purpose.

---

1. According to the Vedānta view expressed in this sūtra, gods such as Indra do have bodies and minds. An objector protests that if Indra had a body, he could not be present at all the different sacrifices which are being offered to him at the same time. This argument is rejected on the grounds of such Vedic passages as 'Sa ekadhā bhavati tridhā bhavati'(He is single, he is threefold) (Chāndogya Upaniṣad VII.26.2), which prove that the gods can have multiple bodily forms.

2. Ardhajaratīya, 'the law of half of an old woman,' is the practice of maintaining one side of an argument in one connection and the other in another; that is, "trying to have it both ways." The objector above, who maintained one position in respect to gods and another in respect to the ancestors, is guilty of this logical fault. For one may accept either the Vedānta view that both men and gods have bodies, or the Mīmāṃsā (Jaimini's) view that neither the gods nor the ancestors have bodies; but one may not accept half of one and half of the other.

For a discussion of the ardhajaratīya-nyāya and its literal sense, see Colonel Jacob's *Laukika-nyāyāñjali*, part 1, p. 6.

(6) If that were so there would be no modification in the svāhā-formula which is an instrument of the fifth pre-sacrifice.[1]

Moreover : Modification of the word 'ancestor' in the invitation mantras

464. ...the ancestors, to eat the offering...(=429,478)

and

465. May our beloved ancestors come...

(1) does not obtain, because the word 'ancestor' has a suitable meaning in the (modified) śrāddha to the maternal grandfather also, just as it has in the archetypal (śrāddha to the father), and therefore there is no difference of meaning at all. (2) That is to say : this word 'ancestor' (pitṛ) is used in two senses. (3) Sometimes 'ancestor' is used with the particular sense of 'father' etc., as in such sayings as

466. Whose father is alive, and whose grandfather is living...

(1) And sometimes it is used with the particular sense of the state of ancestor-hood brought about by a śrāddha ending with the sapiṇḍīkaraṇa[2] ceremony, in which use the word is common to both males and females, and expresses the gaṇa deities (of the śrāddha), like the words 'Marut' etc., and the words 'Agniṣvātta'[2] etc.; thus, according to the VIṢṆUSMṚTI :

467. When the preta has become an ancestor (pitṛ) after the sapiṇḍīkaraṇa ceremony...

---

1. Thus, the reason for the absence of modification is not the spiritual purpose of the invitation-mantra (as claimed in 414.9), but rather the reasons given in the following passage.

The example refers to the fifth pre-sacrifice of the darśa-pūrṇamāsa, as described in ĀśSrSū. I.5.24 : 'Svāhāmuṃ svāhāmum iti yathāvāhitam anudrutya devatā yathācoditam anāvāhita svaha devā...' The pre-sacrifice has an invisible purpose, but nonetheless its mantra is modified for each deity. (In the performance the name of the particular deity is to be substituted for the pronoun amum, 'so-and-so.')

2. For definitions of these terms see Appendix D, Glossary of Sanskrit Terms.

and according to the words of HĀRĪTA

468. From then (the sapiṇḍīkaraṇa ceremony) onward, the preta becomes the same as an ancestor.

(1) Thus also is occasioned the prohibition mentioned in the ĀŚVALĀYANA-GṚHYA-PARIŚIṢṬA of the word 'pitṛ' in the śrāddha intended for one person.[1]

(2) Therefore the word 'ancestor' (pitṛ) is seen to be common to maternal and paternal grandfathers etc. also; thus

469. After that, one should begin a śrāddha to the six ancestors[2] with devotion

and

470. He should pour out the receptacle of the preta into the receptacle of the ancestors.

(1) It is also common to the mother etc. :

471. May all the ancestors—mother, maternal grandfather, etc.—be satisfied.

(1) As for the refutation "If the word 'ancestor' did not express a common meaning, then whatever is prescribed with the word 'ancestor(s)', such as

472. Two (brāhmaṇas) facing east in a divine ritual, three in an ancestral...

473. (The moonless or new-moon day) at the kutapa-time is to be used by the wise for an ancestral offering[3]

1. In *Āśvalāyana-gṛhya-pariśiṣṭa* 3.10 (p. 170) it is said: 'Athaikoddiṣṭavidhiḥ....na dhūpadīpau na svadhā pitṝn namaḥ śabdenāvāhanam.' (This is the rule of the ekoddiṣṭaśrāddha....no incense and lights, no invitation with the words 'Svadhā, the ancestors, homage.') Also note Kumārila's kārikā on ekoddiṣṭa-śrāddha (p. 221), 'Pitṛśabdo namaḥśabdaḥ sūktādiśravaṇaṃ na ca,' and a quotation attributed to the ĀśGṛ Pariśiṣṭa in Śrāddha-kāṇḍa of the KKT, p. 245: 'Pitṛśabdaṃ na kurvīta....'

2. Maternal and paternal father, grandfather, and great-grandfather.

3. Cf. Śrāddhakāṇḍa of *Smṛticandrikā*, p. 82.

474. Silver should be given to the ancestors

475. Then (turning) that receptacle of the ancestors upward...

(1) would not apply in a srāddha to the maternal grandfather etc."; (2) this is wrong, for even something not established by explicit prescription may be established by extension. (3) Therefore the word 'ancestor' is common in just the way described by us.[1]

(4) Thus the word 'ancestor', with the particular sense of '(having attained) the state of being an ancestor,' (which word is not modified even when used in connection with the mother, paternal grandfather, and others) has an appropriate meaning, so that it does not follow that it is modified at all when it is used (in connection with the mother etc.); how is this to be disproven on the grounds that the invitation has an invisible purpose?[2]

Furthermore: Also because of the prohibition of modification of ṛc's;

476. This syllable of a ṛc is defiled, when one modifies it.
Therefore one should not modify a ṛc,

(1) there is no modification here (in the invitation mantra).[3]

(2) Thus this statement by a certain author is refuted : "According to the words of KĀTYA (KĀTYĀYANA),

477. Modification should be applied appropriately to the prescribed matter; not in the archetype, for that is unprecedented, but in the modified rite, according to an authoritative statement,

1. This argument (471.1-475.1), although it supports our position, is not the correct way of proving that the word 'ancestor' applies commonly to the various ancestors, as the usage described may be explained by the principle of extension by inference (atideśa). Our explanation (465.2-468.1), however, irrefutably proves the commonness of meaning of the word 'ancestor.'

2. Thus we have shown that the absence of modification is due to the variability of the meaning of the word 'ancestor' (pitṛ) and not, as was said in 414.7-9 (representing the view of Vācaspati Miśra), because the invitation mantra has an invisible purpose.

3. Because the invitation mantra 'Pitṝn haviṣe attave' (464) is a ṛc.

(1) in the śrāddha to the maternal grandfather etc., which is a modified rite, in such mantras as :

478. ...the ancestors, to eat the offering... (=429, 464)

479. May our ancestors come (=465);

in the mantra 'You are the sesamum,' in the phrase

480. With nectar, the ancestors...,[1]

and in the mantra 'Bearing strength,' in the phrase

481. Satisfy the ancestors;[2]

and in the mantras

482. O ancestors, rejoice here (=430)

483. Homage to you, O ancestors, for drink...

484. The ancestors rejoiced

and

485. This is your clothing, O ancestors,

(1) the word 'maternal grandfather' etc. should be substituted in the place of the word 'ancestors,' in order to achieve an appropriate meaning." (2) This is refuted because the word 'ancestor', occurring in the particular sense of 'having attained the state of being an ancestor (by sapiṇḍīkaraṇa),' is used in an unmodified form in respect to the maternal grandfather etc. also; (3) and because of the prohibition (of modification) of mantras which have the form of ṛc's. (4) These words of KĀTYA are not found in the context of śrāddha, but appear in a general context. (5) They also appear in connection with the Yajur

---

1. The full text of this mantra is :
Tilo'si somadevatyo gosave devanirmitaḥ /
Pratnavadbhiḥ prattaḥ svadhayā pitṝn imāṃl-
lokān prīṇayāhi naḥ svadhā namaḥ //
2. The full text of this mantra is :
Urjaṃ vahantīr amṛtaṃ ghṛtaṃ payaḥ kīlālaṃ parisrutam /
Svadhā stha tarpayata me pitṝn //

Veda mantras which manifest oblations etc.[1]

(6) Nor should this be said : "Even though there is no modification of the nominal base 'ancestor' in such mantras as 'You are the sesamum' [480] because it is common in meaning, still it would be modified into the singular number, because the plural number (in the original mantra) cannot have an appropriate sense in respect to a single maternal grandfather." (7) For when the plural number is not appropriate in the original, then (the mantra) is used in an unmodified form in the modified ritual also; as in '(May) Aditi (release) the bonds,' and as in the use of the uparava-mantra for a single uparava-pit,[2] and as in 'You are the winds,'[3] the plural number does appear, for various reasons.

(8) Thus this position is rejected : "While the word 'ancestors' with the plural ending does indeed have an appropriate sense in the archetypal rite, as it illustrates each deity (i.e. ancestor) separately, this is a plural denoting the separate persons one at a time. This, according to the text :

486. Muttering separately for each one, 'This, O ancestors, is your clothing.'

(1) But in the modified rite the word 'ancestor' is modified to the singular, because there is no statement (indicating plurality therein), according to the rule 'Only as much as is actually stated is significant."[4]

---

1. Kātyāyana's discussion of transfer from archetype to modified ritual, and of the modification consequent from this (described in 477) is made in a general context, not with specific reference to śrāddha rites. According to Karkācārya's commentary it can also be taken in reference to such Yajur Veda mantras as 'Sauryaṃ caruṃ nirvapet brahmavarcasakāmaḥ' and 'Agnīsomīyam ajam ālabheta,' which manifest the acts of oblation (nirvāpa) and sacrifice (ālambhana) (comm. on sūtra IV.78).

2. See Śab. on IX.3.5.15 and XI.4.17.52-53. In both of these cases, a mantra with a plural number (pāśān, Vaiṣṇavān [uparavān]) is employed in a ritual act with a single object.

3. This mantra is used in connection with a single sacrificial animal, even though it has plural endings. Note Uvaṭa's commentary on VS I.1.1.1 (see above, 262.19, note):'Ekasyāpi vatsasyopasparśane sarveṣāṃ saṃskāro bahuvacanopadeśāt, pūjyārthaṃ vā bahuvacanam.'

4. This rule is used, for example, by Śab. in V.3.4.12: "Yāvad vacanaṃ vācanikaṃ na sadṛśam upasaṃkrāmati' (Only as much...; the statement does

(486.2) This is rejected because if that sentence is taken as intended to prescribe a plural number, it must also be taken as prescribing the use of the word 'ancestor,' as these (the word 'ancestor' and the plural number) are not distinguished (in that sentence); thus there would be no modification. But this conflicts with your statement that there *is* modification of the word 'ancestor'.[1]

(3) Furthermore : It being so, that according to that very text [486] the plural number in the archetype does not have an appropriate sense, so also in the modified rite, even though there is no specific statement, by extension the procedure is unmodified, according to the rule of the bonds.[2] Thus there would be no modification (of the mantra).

(4) Furthermore : Since it applies only to the mantra 'This is your (clothing, O ancestors),' how can that text [486] apply to another mantra ? (5) Therefore, that sentence is meant to prescribe a repetition—this is the sense of the word 'separately'—repeating the mantra with the plural number as found in the original reading. (6) Or else, it may be that it is meant simply to prescribe the giving of the clothing repeating the whole (mantra); thus the plural number is not significant.[3]

(7) If it is said : "Even so, in the pārvaṇa śrāddha, let only such acts as setting the sesamum in the receptacle of the father

---

not extend to a similar case). Thus the appropriateness of the plural number indicated by 486 applies only to the archetypal śrāddha, namely the pārvaṇa śrāddha to the father, grandfather, and great-grandfather, in reference to which that statement 486 was made. But the statement cannot be extended to apply to the modified śrāddha to a single ancestor, and thus the word 'ancestors' must be modified to the singular 'ancestor'.

1. If the sentence 486 is taken as prescribing the plural number of the word 'pitṛ' in the offering to each of the three ancestors in the pārvaṇa śrāddha, then it must also be taken as prescribing the word pitṛ itself for each of these offerings. But this contradicts the opponent's previously stated position (477-485.1) that the word 'pitṛ' is modified in the offerings to the ancestors other than the father.

2. This rule refers to the use of the mantra 'Aditiḥ pāśān...' (cited above, 485.7) in a ritual where only one bond is used. A mantra with a plural number, though not strictly appropriate, may be used in connection with a singular object.

3. The intention of the śloka (486) is only to prescribe the giving of clothes, so other details such as the plural number are not to be taken literally. Details prescribed along with the main matter (uddeśya) of a prescription are not to be taken literally (cf. above 412.19).

be the archetype. (486.8) Then the same activities in connection with the paternal grandfather and great-grandfather will be the modified rite. (9) Now the word 'ancestor' (pitṛ) is capable to denote 'the father'; it is only the (plural) grammatical number which is not capable (to denote him). (10) Thus in the latter two activities, in place of the word 'father' (pitṛ) the words 'grandfather' and 'great-grandfather' are to be substituted by way of modification, but the plural number is to remain just as it appears.[1] (11) Likewise in connection with the mother etc., modification will occur all the more. (12) And thus although the word pitṛ has several meanings, it will not need to be so construed;" (13) this is not so, because an archetypal and a modified rite cannot both be given in the same context, according to the rule of the Indra-offering and the non-Indra-offering.[2] (14) And thus, in order for it to have an appropriate sense for the three ancestors, it is accepted for the reasons given previously that (the word pitṛ) has several meanings; for there is no other way to take it.[3]

---

1. It is only the grammatical number—that is, the plural—which is not appropriate in the archetype, and therefore not subject to modification. The noun stem 'pitṛ' however is appropriate, and thus is modified in the modified rites. Compare the commentary on ĀśGṛSū II.5.8 (p. 72), which contains a similar discussion.

2. See MS. III.2.11.28-29 and III.2.11.44. In connection with the act of feeding the remnants of the Indra-offering (aindrapradāna) and the Mitrāvaruṇa-offering (=anaindrapradāna) in the jyotiṣṭoma sacrifice, a mantra is prescribed which contains a characterization of the offering at 'drunk by Indra (Indrapītasya). The question is whether this mantra can also be used in connection with the 'non-Indra' offering. The pūrvapakṣa view is that it should not be so used (sūtra 28), or that it may be so used, but with modification of the word 'Indrapītasya' to 'Mitrāvaruṇapītasya' (sūtra 29). Thus a distinction of an archetypal and modified rite (prakṛti and vikṛti), and the consequent modification (ūha), is discerned within a single rite. But in the siddhānta sūtra (III.2.11.44) this interpretation is not accepted.

Likewise in the present text, the proponent of 486.7-12 wishes to discern a prakṛti and vikṛti within the single pārvaṇa śrāddha to the three ancestors, and to apply ūha to the vikṛti. But as in the case of the jyotiṣṭoma, it is not proper to divide a single ritual into prakṛti and vikṛti, even though the ritual contains several parts.

3. It would be preferable not to have to resort to interpreting the same word 'pitṛ' in different ways. But the alternative interpretation being ruled out, it must be so taken.

(15) And if it were accepted that there is modification for the latter two ancestors, then the statement prescribing the three mantras 'May the fathers be purified', etc., would have no purpose.[1]

(16) Thus it is established that the word 'ancestor' is not subject to modification, because it has an appropriate sense in both the archetype and in the modified rite as well. (17) And the plural number (remains in the modified rite) because it does not have an appropriate sense (even) in the original.

(18) As for the words of VIṢṆU :

> 487. A wise man should thus perform śrāddha for his maternal grandfathers also, with modification of the mantras according to the rule; and for the rest (of his ancestors) without mantras;[2]

(1) this also is not meant to provide for modification of the previously cited mantras, because of the words 'according to the rule.' (2) For this is the rule for modification (of mantras) : (3) when a mantra which is used in the archetype with such qualities as being for the sake of the main object is extended to the modified rite by the (extension of) the act (in which it is used), and is so employed in connection with a different object (than in the archetype) that it contains a word which is not appropriate, and thus would not realize its meaning as it did in the archetype—then it should be used with a word which does have an appropriate meaning. Thus BHAṬṬAPĀDA (Kumārila) says :

> 488. Those mantras which are not prohibited from undergoing modification,[3] which are used in the archetypal rite with a primary and visible purpose, for their own purpose and with an appropriate sense, and which are

---

1. I.e., the mantras 'May the fathers...' 'May the grandfathers...' and 'May the great-grandfathers....' (see below, 490.2) If modification occurred according to the principles proposed, then such a text which explicitly prescribed it in a certain case would actually serve no purpose. But since every authoritative text must have a purpose, the principles proposed must be wrong.

2. For an alternative interpretation of this last phrase, see below, 499.3ff.

3. I.e., ṛc's; see above, 476.

transferred to modified rites by the transfer of their functions to apply to different objects; for us these mantras undergo modification in functional circumstances of five sorts, by virtue of their being used for the sake of the transcendental result of the rite.[1]

(1) And BHAṬṬASOMEŚVARA gives the five-fold functional circumstances :

489. On the grounds of an evident prescription, or of a prescription of something in the case of the absence (of something else); because of an alteration of procedure; according to the words (of a prescription themselves); and according to a supplementary passage of prohibition, (an item in the modified rites) performs the function of an (item of the archetype).[2]

(1) In the previously cited mantras the word 'ancestor' has an appropriate sense in the modified rite as well as in the archetype and thus is not used in connection with a different object, so there is no modification of the mantra.

(2) "What, then, is the purpose of the statement '...with modification of the mantras according to the rule [487]?" It is replied : In the mantra

490. May the fathers be purified,

(1) there is modification according to the rule. (2) For in this mantra, if the word pitṛ were used in the previously mentioned particular sense (expressing 'ancestor' as well as 'father'), then the reading in the text of the two mantras 'May the grandfathers be purified' and 'May the great-grandfathers be purified' would be purposeless.[3] (3) Thus it must

1. NB uses the reading which is followed in the *Nyāyasudhā* (pp. 279-282), and which is undoubtedly the better one. The Ānandāśrama edition of the TV has instead of 'Vikāresv aniṣiddhohāḥ' 'Vikāre'tha niṣiddhohāḥ', which reading deprives the śloka of its proper sense.

2. For examples and explanations of each of these circumstances, see NS p. 281 or *Mīmāṃsā-Bāla-Prakāśa*, pp. 129-130.

3. The full text of ĀśŚrSū II.6.14 is 'Mekṣaṇam anupahṛtya prācīnāvītī lekhaṃ trir udakenopanayacchundhantāṃ pitaraḥ śundhantāṃ pitāmahāḥ śundhantāṃ prapitāmahā iti.'

be used here with the particular sense of 'father'. (4) Therefore, in the modified rite, namely the śrāddha to the mother, maternal grandfather etc., there is modification of this mantra, because it applies to a different object.

(5) This modification is only of the nominal stem itself; (6) but the plural number does not apply to a single ancestor even in the original, so it is not to be modified (in the modified rite). (7) Therefore the modification is : 'May the mothers be purified,' 'May the maternal grandfathers be purified,' etc. (8) Thus also in connection with the paternal grandfather and the others.

(9) For those in whose Vedic schools the mantra 'Let svadhā be said to the ancestors' is recited in just the same way as the mantra of purification,[1] they should make that same modification in that mantra too. (10) With reference to the same mantra, the mantra 'Let svadhā be said to the maternal grandfathers' is specifically given by KĀTYĀYANA and GOBHILA; therefore in connection with those mantras there is no modification.[2]

(11) But in connection with the mother etc., there is modification. Thus in such mantras of the followers of the HIRAṆYAKEŚIN GṚHYA SŪTRA as

491. When my mother lusted...

(1) the words are modified to 'When my maternal grandmother lusted, may my maternal grandfather accept that sperm as his own'; (2) for the words 'father' etc., having a singular ending (in the original), cannot be expressive of the general (notion of 'ancestors'). (3) If it were so, then the reading of the mantras such as 'When my paternal grandmother lusted'[3] would be purposeless. Thus it is said by the author of the BHAṢYĀRTHASAṂGRAHA :

---

1. I.e. where the mantra is prescribed with different forms mentioning the father, grandfathers, etc. separately.

2. The text 'Pitṛbhyaḥ pitāmahebhyaḥ prapitāmahebhyo mātāmahebhyo pramātāmahebhyo vṛddhapramātāmahebhyaś ca svadhocyatām iti' appears in the *Gobhila* [Gṛhya Sūtra] *Pariśiṣṭa*, Śrāddhakalpa 2.34, and in paragraph 3 (p. 598) of the appendix called *Śrāddha-sūtra* to the *Pāraskara Gṛhya Sūtra*. (The *Pāraskara Sūtras* are attributed to Kātyāyana.)

3. The mantra in question (*Hiraṇyakeśin Gṛhya Sūtra* II.10.7) reads 'Yan me mātā pralulobha caraty ananuvratā/Tan me retaḥ pitā vṛṅktām' etc. (When my mother lusted, wandering against her vows, may my father accept

492. In the food offering and the touching, and in the giving of water, piṇḍas, etc., there should be citation of 'When my grandmother...'

(1) 'Citation' here means modification (ūha). (2) 'In the touching' means in the touching of the food for the feeding of the brāhmaṇas, with mantras like

493. This...for you, O father, honey-like...[1]

(1) And likewise elesewhere, modification of the mantra is to be made wherever proper, after due consideration.

(2) As for what one author has said, that "'With 'ūha' of the mantra' [487] means 'with recital of the mantra,' and not 'with 'ūha' in the sense of modification'";[2] (3) this is not so. For the word 'ūha' is not generally known to mean 'recital.' (4) And also, by the very words 'He should perform (śrāddha)' [487], the recital of the mantra, like the other parts of the rite, is already established, so that (this phrase, taken as 'recital of the mantra') would be purposeless. (5) Or (if this śrāddha is taken as an original act), by the rule of the gṛhamedhīya-ājya-bhāga offerings, this would then be a prescription of exclusion.[3] (6) Also, in this interpretation, the phrase 'according to the rule' would be purposeless. (7) Thus this phrase applies to just what we have said.

(8) In connection with such phrases as 'This, O father, is

---

that sperm as his own). The HirGṛSū prescribes that it should be repeated a second and third time, changing 'mātā' to 'pitāmahī' and 'prapitāmahī,' implying that 'pitā' should be changed to 'pitāmaha' and 'prapitāmaha.' Therefore 'pitā' in this mantra must have the specific sense of 'father' or 'progenitor,' and thus is subject to modification; and thus other modified forms with '*maternal* grandmother' etc. also should be used when appropriate.

Incidentally, the *Śāṅkhāyana Gṛhya Sūtra* (III.13.5) specifies that this mantra is to be used only by an illegitimate son; but the *Hiraṇyakeśin* and other Sūtras do not specify any such restriction, implying that no one can be certain of his own legitimacy! Thus Manu (9.20) cites this mantra as a proof of the undependability of all women.

1. The mantra continues 'Eṣa te tata madhumān ūrmiḥ sarasvān' (This honey-like, juicy wave is for you, O father).

2. I.e. 'ūha' is not to be taken here in the technical Mīmāṃsā sense of 'modification of a mantra.'

3. See MS X.7.9.24-33. In connection with the offering to the Gṛhamedhin Maruts, it is prescribed 'Ājyabhāgau yajati.' It is determined that this

your water-offering,'[1] one should not even consider the question of modification or the absence of it; (9) for this is not a mantra, but simply the declaration of the object of the rite (abhilāpa). (10) For if it were a mantra, then according to '...for the rest without mantras' [487] the declaration of the object of the rite would also have to be excluded;[2] and according to the words of the VARĀHAPURĀṆA :

494. This very way, without mantras, is prescribed for śūdras,

(1) this declaration would be excluded also for śūdras. (2) For the word 'mantra' applies primarily only to words of non-human origin (i.e., Vedic words), and to other words (only) figuratively.[3] (3) Therefore modifications and gotra and personal names are not mantras; this is the established view.[4]

(4) This consideration of modification and the absence of it applies to the pārvaṇa śrāddha. (5) Now that consideration is

---

prescription is intended to prescribe this Gṛhamedhīya offering as an original (apūrva) and not a modified sacrifice (vikṛti). Thus rather than carrying over details from its archetype, the offering in question involves only the details specified, namely the two ājyabhāgas; and this constitutes a prescription of exclusion (parisaṃkhyā). Likewise, if the sentence 487 is taken as prescribing an original śrāddha, then the phrase 'with modification of the mantras' would be an exclusive prescription. But a prescription of exclusion is always to be avoided if possible.

For other examples of this application of the *Gṛhamedhīyā-ājyabhāga-nyāya* see MK pp. 1609b and 1610a.

1. Various phrases of this type are prescribed for different parts of the śrāddha in the different Śrauta- and Gṛhya-sūtras; see for example ĀśŚrSū II 6.15. In the discussion of ūha in the commentary on ĀśGṛSū II.5.8 cited above (note to 486.10), various modifications of such a phrase are given; but NB disagrees, saying that such phrases are not subject to modification at all.

2. In a śrāddha to relatives other than those mentioned in 487.

3. The term 'mantra' is sometimes used loosely to apply to non-Vedic formulae, which are human in origin. But strictly speaking mantras proper are only non-human, Vedic sounds, and the rules of ūha only apply to these. See also 502.1-2.

4. This refers to MS II.1.9.34 'Anāmnāteṣv amantratvam...' (i.e., Words which are not so enumerated by tradition are not mantras), and to Śab's comments thereon:'Ūhapravaranāmadheyeṣu saṃśayaḥ: mantrā uta na?....Na te mantrāḥ' (In connection with modifications and clan and personal names (used in rituals), it is to be considered: are they mantras, or not?... They are not mantras.)

offered in respect to the ekoddiṣṭa śrāddhas. Among them, in the purāṇaikoddiṣṭa, (there is no modification), just as in the pārvaṇa, because in it the state of being an ancestor has already come about by sapiṇḍīkaraṇa. But in a pretaikoddiṣṭa there is modification, according to the words of VIṢṆU :

495. One should modify the mantra to the singular in the ekoddiṣṭa.

(1) Since sapiṇḍīkaraṇa has not yet been performed, the state of being an ancestor has not come about; so in place of the word 'pitṛ' the word 'preta' with a singular ending should be used; this is the meaning of VIṢṆU's words. (2) For this reason it is said in the ĀŚVALĀYANAGṚHYAPARIŚIṢṬA that the word 'pitṛ' is not used in the ekoddiṣṭa.[1] (3) The author of the SMṚTIRATNĀVALĪ, however, says this is the meaning of VIṢṆU's words : "Only the singular number is to be used as a modification, in place of the plural number; there is no modification of the word 'pitṛ'; this according to the words 'one should modify (the mantras) to the singular.'(4) Otherwise (VIṢṆU) would have said simply 'One should modify (the mantras) as is appropriate.' (5) Thus in a śrāddha to the mother, brother, paternal uncle, etc., only the singular number is to be used as a modification, but the word 'pitṛ' is to be left as it stands; (6) for that word merely denotes 'the deceased.' " (7) This is not so, because it contradicts the omission of the word 'pitṛ' mentioned in the ĀŚVALĀYANA (GṚHYA) PARIŚIṢṬA[1], (8) and because if 'pitṛ' denoted merely 'the deceased' then the previously mentioned modification (of the word 'pitṛ') in 'May the fathers be purified,' etc. would not take place; (9) and also because the word 'pitṛ' would then appear in every declaration of the object of a śrāddha; (10) and because this conflicts with the practice of refined people. (11) VIṢṆU does not prescribe the modification with respect to the word 'pitṛ', because it obtains (anyway) according to the rule; he only prescribes that one should modify the mantras to the singular because that modification would not (normally) obtain, since the grammatical

1. See note on 468.1.

(plural) number does not have an appropriate sense in the archetype.[1]

(12) Therefore it is established that the word 'preta' with the singular ending is to be substituted in the pretaikoddiṣṭa.

(13) The rest of VIṢṆU's words [487] was "(A śrāddha) for the rest (is done) without mantras." (14) ŚŪLAPĀṆI says the meaning of that is :

> 496. In an ekoddiṣṭa to the paternal uncle, maternal uncle, etc., it is only a mantra containing the word 'pitṛ' which is susceptible to modification that is not to be used; modification is not to be made. But a mantra without the word 'pitṛ' need not be unused, for that is not under consideration here.

In the KALPATARU it is said :

> 497. The meaning is that śrāddha to the maternal and paternal uncles etc., is to be done without the mantras of invitation etc.

(1) But this the correct interpretation : This applies to women who are unmarried or who are kept for the sake of pleasure, and to the sons of śūdra women, such as pāraśavas and karaṇas, according to the MARĪCISMṚTI :

> 498. Śrāddha is without mantras for women and for the son of a śūdra woman; and the twice-born before their investiture should also perform it in this way.

Concerning this HEMĀDRI says :

> 499. 'For women' refers to unmarried women.

(1) 'Before,' etc., refers to the twice-born who have not yet been initiated. (2) And those women, pāraśavas, karaṇas, etc., because they are not consecrated, should also perform such a

---

1. That is, Viṣṇu intends that there be modification of both the nominal base 'pitṛ' and of its plural number, but he only specifies the latter, because it would not normally follow from the general rules for modification.

mantra-less śrāddha, even if it is for those who are consecrated.

(3) Or else, the phrase in question [in 487] may be taken as a genitive denoting the agent—'(The śrāddha) by the rest'. (4) Then it would mean 'by the rest of the varṇas.' (5) The sense is : a śrāddha to be done by śūdras, or by those equal to śūdras, viz. pāraśavas, karaṇas, the uninitiated, or women, should be done by them without mantras. This is said in the SṚṢṬIKHAṆḌA of the PADMAPURĀṆA, in speaking of śrāddha :

500. A śūdra also should perform (śrāddha) by this rule, without mantras, O king.

(1) MARĪCI says 'The twice-born before their investiture,' and so on [498].

In the VARĀHAPURĀṆA :

501. This very way, without mantras, is proclaimed for śūdras. For the mantra-less śūdras, a brāhmaṇa is taken with the mantra.

(1) 'A brāhmaṇa is taken with the mantra' means 'He is charged with it.'

ŚŪLAPĀṆI says :

502. This is a definitive precept; and a definitive precept cannot be restricted by context. Therefore although the rule is given in the context of śrāddha, also in bathing, gift-giving, etc., by a śudra the mantra is to be recited by a brāhmaṇa.

(1) Here 'without mantras' prohibits Vedic mantras. (2) Thus a purāṇic mantra and the declaration of name, gotra, etc.[1] should indeed be pronounced by a śūdra.

(3) Enough, then, of digressions and sub-digressions;[2] we return to the main subject.

---

1. See above, 494.1-3.

2. This discussion of mantra-less śrāddha is a sub-digression from the discussion of modification of mantras, which was itself a digression which came up in connection with the main subject of the section, namely the restrictions on tīrtha-śrāddha.

(4) Since tīrtha-śrāddha is patterned on the pārvaṇaśrāddha, according to the words of BṚHASPATI :

503. Purūrava and Ārdrava are proclaimed for the pārvaṇa,

(1) Purūrava and Ārdrava are established as the Viśvedevas[1] in a tīrtha-śrāddha. However, tīrtha-śrāddha is also an optional act, by the separateness of its connections;[2] and by the rule of the cow's milk vessel, an optional act supersedes a regular act.[3] Now although tīrtha-śrāddha is an occasional act, it is (also) a regular act, insofar as it is mandatory; (504.1) and therefore Dhuri and Locana become the Viśvedevas of the tīrtha-śrāddha, superseding Purūrava and Ārdrava, according to the statement

504. Dhuri and Locana (are the Viśvedevas) in an optional srāddha.

(2) Nor should it be said : "Although in that case the soma-vessel which is a subsidiary of the regular act is superseded by the optional cow's milk vessel which is a principal element,[4] how in this case can a subsidiary of the regular act be superseded by a subsidiary of the optional act, since they are both equal, in that they are subsidiaries?" (3) For the subsidary of the optional act also can supersede the subsidiary of the regular act, since they come under the same rule; (4) just as the low tone, which is a subsidiary of oblations as prescribed by the sentence concerning the sacrificial Ātharvaṇa,[5] (505.1) supersedes in the birth offering the middle tone established by the transfer rule, having been prescribed with the words

1. Every śrāddha has as its deities, besides the performer's own ancestors, two of the class of gods called Viśvedeva. See Kane, *History of Dharmaśāstra* vol. IV, p. 457. Also cf. Yāj. I.269.

2. By which an act may have a two-fold character. See above, 166 and note.

3. The rule of the cow's milk vessel (godohana) is expounded in MS III. 6.3.10 in reference to the prescription 'Camasenāpaḥ praṇayed godohanena paśukāmasya' (He should bring forth the water with a soma vessel, (but) with a cow's milk vessel for one who desires cattle). It is determined that in this case the optional element (the cow's milk vessel)overrules the regular element (the soma vessel). Therefore an element prescribed as optional overrules that which is prescribed as regular.

4. Because it is directly connected with the benefit (obtaining cattle).

5. This is the prescription, cited in Śab. III.8.19.34, 'Yajñātharvaṇaṃ vai kāmyā iṣṭayaḥ, tā upāṃśu kartavyāḥ.'

505. The oblations until the sviṣṭakṛt offering are made with a middle tone.

(2) Thus Dhuri and Locana are the Viśvedevas in the performance of the tīrtha-śrāddha, because it is an optional act.

(3) When, however, one performs (tīrtha-śrāddha) without any special desire, but simply as a regular act, then Purūrava and Ārdrava are the Viśvedevas. And although there are prescriptions of eligibility for an accessory and a benefit such as

506. With sacrificial food, (the ancestors are satisfied) for a month...,

(1) like that of the cow's milk vessel,[1] still those same ones (Purūrava and Ārdrava) are the Viśvedevas for the act to be successful; for this is not an optional śrāddha, so that Dhuri and Locana are not established, and that prescription of an accessory and a benefit can be taken as applying to the regular act.

(2) Nor should it be said : "The subsidiary which is an optional accessory (of the archetypal act) would not apply at all in the tīrtha-śrāddha, which is a variant of the pārvaṇa śrāddha according to the rule given in the eighth (book of the Mīmāṃsā Sūtras)."[2] (3) For that (rule) applies to an optional accessory which occurs within the context (of the description of the archetypal act). (4) But such elements as sacrificial food are, according to the words of MANU etc.,[3] supplements to every śrāddha. Enough of this!

THUS ENDS PRESCRIBED AND PROHIBITED ELEMENTS IN TĪRTHA-ŚRĀDDHA AND THE DETAILS CONNECTED WITH THEM.

---

1. (A prescription of) entitlement to an accessory and a benefit (guṇaphalādhikāra (vidhi)) prescribes an optional accessory to an act and the benefit resulting from it. Thus for instance the prescription 'Godohanena paśukāmasya praṇayet' prescribes an accessory, the cow's milk vessel, and its benefit, cattle.

2. In MS VIII.1.14.23-24, it is established that an optional detail, such as the cow's milk vessel, of an archetypal act is not transferred to the modified rite.

3. See Manu III.267 (quoted above, 158). Also note *Mitākṣarā* on Yāj. I. 257.

DISCUSSION OF ŚRĀDDHAS WITH COOKED FOOD, RAW FOOD, AND GOLD, AND OTHER MATTERS

In the GARUḌAPURĀṆA :

507. The śrāddha which (one gives) when he comes to a tīrtha, feeding raw food to a brāhmaṇa...

KĀTYĀYANA :

508. In an emergency, if there is no fire,[1] at a tīrtha, on a journey abroad, at the birth of a son, during the wife's menses, and during an astronomical passage, one may perform śrāddha with raw food.

SUMANTU says :

509. When there is no cooked food, then brāhmaṇas and others would be allowed (to give śrāddha with raw food) O Lord of Men; as would those who are without their wives, O Great-armed One, because they are travelling abroad, etc. And the wise know that the raw-food śrāddha is for śūdras at all times. One may especially give raw food when a disaster has struck one's country and time, in an emergency, if there is no fire, at a tīrtha, on a journey abroad, if one has no wife, and at an eclipse of the sun or moon.

Also:

510. At a tīrtha especially one should perform śrāddha with cooked food, and with raw food, gold, or bulbs, roots, and fruits. Or if these are not available, one may even perform śrāddha devotedly with water.

---

1. Nīlakaṇṭha (*Śrāddhamayūkha* p. 120) explains that this refers to the case in which the performer of śrāddha is not a keeper of a sacred fire, and not to the case of an absence of a fire with which to cook the food ('śrautasmārtāgnyabhāve iti yāvat, na tv iha pākādyartham laukikāgniparam...' etc.)

Also

511. In the absence of (other) substances or of a brāhmaṇa, on a journey abroad, or at the birth of a son, one should perform śrāddha with gold, as should one whose wife is menstruating.

(1) "Since there are various sentences to this effect, the cooked-food śrāddha is the principal; in the absence of cooked food or of a brāhmaṇa, the raw-food śrāddha is to be done, and in the absence of that, the gold śrāddha; or else one may act in accordance with the practice of refined people." So say the MADANAPĀRIJĀTA, DIVODĀSA, and others;[1] (2) likewise, the easterners. (3) The author of the SMṚTIRATNĀVĀLĪ and others, however, say : "At an eclipse and at a tīrtha and so on, raw food śrāddha or gold śrāddha is the principal; there is no cooked food śrāddha at all." (4) But we consider it proper that (śrāddha be done) near the water of a tīrtha with raw food or with gold, according to the words

512. Raw food śrāddha is always recommended nearby water. He who offers it at a tīrtha gets ten times the merit he would get at home.

(1) But at home etc., śrāddha should be done only with cooked food.

(2) The southerners, however, do both,[2] according to the previously cited 'Especially with cooked food' [510]. (3) In respect to this, one's decision should be made according to tocal practice.

(4) A śūdra, however, must always perform (śrāddha) with raw food only, according to the words of SUMANTU :

513. The wise know that the raw-food śrāddha is for śūdras at all times. Even a good śūdra may never feed cooked food to brāhmaṇas. If he so fed them, he would incur a sin, and would not obtain the benefit of that (śrāddha).

1. See MP p. 481.

2. That is, they perform śrāddha at a tīrtha with both cooked and raw food.

(1) There is this special rule in connectton with the raw-food śrāddha: VYĀSA says

514. But when giving raw food, O Kaunteya, one should give four times as much food.

As for what is said,

515. When giving raw food, O Kaunteya, the raw food should be doubled,

(1) that is to be understood as applying when it is not possible to give fourfold. Therefore it is said in the Smṛti:

516. If one gives raw food, O King, the raw food should be doubled, or threefold, or fourfold; but one should not offer a single portion. It should be given to brāhmaṇas with all the condiments.

(1) Here, each alternative in succession is preferable.

(2) But one should give gold eightfold, fourfold, or twofold. (3) Or, if this is impossible, one may give an equal amount of raw food or gold. (4) This doubling etc., is in comparison to a single meal.

UŚĀNAS says :

517. When the giver of śrāddha who knows the rule would perform the raw food śrāddha, he should make the fire-oblation properly in the hand of a brāhmaṇa.[1]

Also :

518. The rule which applies to cooked food is also the rule for raw food (=525). All the invitation and so on are to be done, and the giving of piṇḍas, O Bhārata. Whatever food one gives to the twice-born, whether cooked or uncooked, with that one should perform the fire-oblation, and with just that he should offer piṇḍas.

---

1. I.e., the oblation which is poured into the fire in a cooked food śrāddha is poured into a brāhmaṇa's hand in the raw-food śrāddha.

Also :

519. When he would perform the raw food śrāddha, knowing the rule, endowed with faith...

(1) The latter half of this verse is the same as the preceding verse. (2) The invitation etc. applies to raw food śrāddha occasioned by eclipses and so on, but not to tīrtha-śrāddha, for it has already been explained that invitation etc. is forbidden in them [406ff].

In the ṢAṬTRIṂŚANMATA :

520. When one does the raw food śrāddha, how are the piṇḍas given ? With grits, or with rice pudding, taken from home-cooked food...,

(1) Supply here '...thus the piṇḍas are given'. (2) The decision between raw food and home-cooked food such as grits and rice pudding is to be made according to their availability.

As for the text :

521. If one gives a piṇḍa of raw food and feeds the brāhmaṇas with cooked food, or if one gives a piṇḍa with cooked food and offers raw food (to the brāhmaṇas), both of these are said by men to merit hell, without a doubt,

(1) this refers to the moon-less day and other (śrāddhas, but not to tīrtha-śrāddha). (2) In the raw food śrāddha, the apośāna ceremony[1] and other acts connected with the feeding are omitted, since their function is dropped; like the threshing of a gold-piece.[2] Thus it is said :

---

1. This term also appears in the forms āpośana, apośana, and āpośāna, and is variously interpreted. The best known occurrences of this word are in Yāj. I.31 and I. 106. The *Mitākṣarā* takes it as the act of spreading a seat (upastaraṇa) for the food . Aparārka, however, explains it as a formula of invitation ('Apo 'sānety upanetā māṇavakaṃ preṣyati'. The *Bālakrīḍā* (I.105) refers to apośāna as 'ācamana,' sipping of water. In any case, it would seem that Aparārka's etymology of apośāna is correct; i.e. that it is a noun formed from the phrase 'Apo'śāna'(Drink water!). (Compare the formation of such nouns as itihāsa from 'iti ha āsa.') Thus apośāna is the correct spelling of the word.

2. See 462.3.

522. The questioning of the satisfied,[1] the plunging, the request to enjoy, (the words) 'to your contentment,'[2] and the apośāna as fifth; these are not done in the raw food śrāddha.

(1) 'The plunging' is the placing of the thumb (in the food). (2) Thus these are not done in the case of the raw food śrāddha; (3) nor is the invitation etc., since this is a tīrtha-śrāddha. (4) But in the cooked food śrāddha, it is only the invitation etc. which are not done; this is the proper analysis.

523. In the case of the gold-śrāddha, the piṇḍas are also left out;

so says DIVODĀSA. (1) In the SMṚTYARTHASĀRA, however, there is an optional choice.[3]

(2) Also, in the raw food śrāddha some mantras are modified. Thus, MARĪCI :

524. In the invitation, the saying of 'svadhā,' and the discharging, the mantras are to be modified. In other actions they are not to be modified. This is the rule proclaimed for raw food śrāddha.

(1) 'In the invitation'; in the mantra '...the ancestors, to eat the offering,' [429] in place of the word 'to eat' the word 'to receive' is substituted. (2) 'In the saying of 'svadhā'; in the mantra 'Homage to you, O Ancestors, for drink...' (Maitrāyaṇī Saṃhitā I. 10. 3 etc.), in place of the word 'for drink' the word 'for raw food' is substituted. (3) 'In the discharging'; in the phrase 'Go, satisfied, by the paths which are the ways of the gods' in the mantra 'In every battle' (RV VII. 38.8),[4] in place of the past participial suffix in 'satisfied', the imperative ending is to be substituted; 'Be satisfied!'. (4) Although

1. Wherein the sacrificer asks the brāhmaṇas 'Tṛptāḥ stha ?' and the brāhmaṇas reply 'Tṛptāḥ smaḥ' ('Are you satisfied'? 'Yes, we are.')

2. In a cooked food śrāddha, the sacrificer says to the brāhmaṇas 'Yathāsukhaṃ juṣadhvam' (Enjoy to your contentment).

3. See SAS p. 60.

4. The full text of this ṛc is: Vāje vāje'vata vājino no dhaneṣu viprā amṛtā ṛtajñāḥ/Asya madhvaḥ pibata mādayadhvam tṛptā yāta pathibhir devayānaiḥ//

according to the text 'This syllable of a ṛc is defiled, when one modifies it' [476] modification of a ṛc is (in general) forbidden, nevertheless there is modification of this ṛc 'Protect us in every battle' because of an express statement(prescribing it). (5)Also, in place of 'This is food' and so on, modification to 'This is raw food' etc. is to be understood. (6) 'In other actions' means that there is no modification in such mantras as 'O Viṣṇu, guard the oblation'(TS I.1. 3.1, etc.).[1] This is the meaning of MARĪCI's words.

(7) In the śrāddhas with raw food or gold also,[2] clothing, sacrificial fees, and so on are to be given to the best of one's ability, according to the words of SUMANTU :

> 525. The rule which applies to cooked food is also the rule for raw food. (=518)

(1) When there are not many brāhmaṇas, then śrāddha may be performed with just one brāhmaṇa, according to the saying :

> 526. In the absence of food, or of brāhmaṇas, in a tīrtha- or a mahālaya-(śrāddha), food is given to one(brāhmaṇa). (One should give) the water-offering and piṇḍas (to him) one by one.

(1) If even one brāhmaṇa is not found, śrāddha should be done over a model of a brāhmaṇa made of a clump of grass, and one should throw the food in the fire etc., according to the words of DEVALA :

> 527. If there is no recipient (brāhmaṇa), one may perform the whole ceremony of worship of the ancestors (without them) ; or, placing model brāhmaṇas made of clumps of grass in the seats, one may carry out the ceremony with the call and response. If everything is lacking, one should throw (the food) in the fire, or give it to a cow, or put it in the water. What has been established, especially a ritual to the ancestors, is never dropped.

---

1. 523.2-524.3 and 524.6 are taken virtually verbatim from MP p. 483.
2. As in the cooked-food śrāddha.

(1) 'With the call and response' means that one should himself speak the question and answer 'Is the śrāddha done?', and 'Yes, well done.' (2) This (disposition of the food) refers to cooked food śrāddha. (3) In the case of raw food and gold śrāddhas however, after finishing the entire śrāddha one should give materials from it to a brāhmaṇa at some other time.

(4) This raw food śrāddha should be done, if possible, in the forenoon after arriving at the tīrtha, according to the words of HĀRĪTA:

528. The raw food śrāddha should be performed in the forenoon, the ekoddiṣṭa at midday, the pārvaṇa in the afternoon, and the śrāddha occasioned by an auspicious occasion (vṛddhiśrāddha) in the early morning.

(1) But in the case of an unexpected arrival at a tīrtha, it may be done even at another time, in accordance with the occasion, namely the arrival. This has been said previously.[1] (2) If for some reason one is unable to perform śrāddha at the tīrtha, then he still must make a gift of piṇḍas with grits etc. Thus in the DEVĪPURĀṆA:

529. Giving piṇḍas then is recommended, and it is dear to the ancestors, (=381)

(1) piṇḍas alone are mentioned separately, even though the giving of piṇḍas has been previously established by the mention of śrāddha itself. (2) Otherwise, this would be an exclusive prescription of a separate subsidiary, and thus the three faults would result.[2]

DEVALA says:

530. In the absence of brāhmaṇas or materials, a piṇḍa alone may be given. Or when the day of the śrāddha is reached, one may go without food at all.

Also in the VIṢṆUPURĀṆA:

531. Who will offer piṇḍas to us without being stingy with money...

1. See 388.1.
2. See note on 235.13.

(1) In this sentence spoken by the ancestors, piṇḍas alone are mentioned. (2) Therefore according to this implicatory rule,[1] the offering of piṇḍas also is a principal act at a tīrtha, as in the ekoddiṣṭa śrāddha.

(3) The materials for a piṇḍa are :[2]

In the DEVĪPŪRĀṆA :

532. The offering of piṇḍas is proclaimed by the seers to be done with grits, wheat-cake, rice pudding, oil-cake, or iṅguda-fruit.

(1) Or else the reading may be '...or with raw sugar.' (2) 'Wheat-cake' is a preparation of wheat. (3) 'Oil-cake' is sesamum paste. (4) 'Iṅguda' is the fruit of the tāpasa tree. (5) Here each succeeding substance is to be used when the preceding one is unavailable.

SATYAVRATA says :

533. One should bring pleasure to the ancestors with edible leaves, roots, and fruits, with clothes, cows, land, and gold; or, with the permission of brāhmaṇas, with water.

(1) 'The permission of brāhmaṇas' is as follows : If all these substances are lacking, one should say to a brāhmaṇa, 'Let me perform a śrāddha today (without the usual substances).' The brāhmaṇa should say, 'So be it'.

(2) AṄGIRAS prescribes the size of the piṇḍa :

534. Endowed with faith, one should give according to rule piṇḍas the size of kapittha fruit or bilva fruit, or the size of hen's eggs, or, according to some, equal to āmalaka fruits; or one may give them the size of badara fruit.

---

1. A 'jñāpaka' is a precept which contains an added implication besides what is explicitly given. Thus this statement, which explicitly only mentions the offering of piṇḍas, implicitly establishes this offering as a principal and therefore independent rite.

2. This section is referred to in the Gayā Prakaraṇa, p. 346.

(1) In this case too, if one is unable to do this, piṇḍas of even smaller size may be given, as is indicated in :

535. He may give a piṇḍa the size of a śamī leaf at Gayāśira.[1]

Another rule :

536. Sesamum, cooked food, water, incense, lamp oil, milk, honey and ghee with treacle; the piṇḍa is said to have eight parts.

Also, VṚDDHAŚLOKA says :

537. Ablution, giving of piṇḍas, then ablution again, the sacrificial fee, the declaration of the food;[2] this is the order for tīrtha-śrāddhas.

(1) In a tīrtha-śrāddha, the piṇḍas should not be disposed of according to the saying of YĀJÑAVALKYA,

538. He should give the piṇḍas to cows and brāhmaṇas, or (throw them) in the fire or water,

(1) but rather they should *only* be thrown in the water, according to the saying :

539. In a tīrtha-śrāddha, one should always carefully throw the piṇḍas in the water, while facing the south; for that is said to be the direction of the ancestors.

(1) The prohibition caused by the stars Nandā etc. does not apply to giving piṇḍas at a tīrtha; this has been said already in connection with the śrāddha.[3]

(2) But if one is not able to perform the giving of piṇḍas at all, then tarpaṇa at least must be done, according to the sentence spoken by the ancestors, with the word 'even' :

1. Pāda c of this same verse (as given in the Agni Purāṇa) is quoted in 440.

2. Wherein the sacrificer asks 'Annaśeṣaḥ kiṃ kriyatām?' (What should be done with the rest of the food?), and the brāhmaṇas reply 'Iṣṭaiḥ saha bhujyatām' (Eat it with whom you wish).

3. See 390ff.

540. Bowing with devotion on the earth, he may *even* give a handful of water with seven or eight sesamum seeds, declaring it for us; or he may even give a cow's daily food, obtained from anywhere at all, to cows (on our behalf).

(1) Here is the summary for all this : (2) If one is able, he should do all three, tarpaṇa, śrāddha, and the giving of piṇḍas. (3) If he is unable to do that he should give tarpaṇa and piṇḍas. (4) And if he is unable to do even that, he should still give just tarpaṇa.

(5) When, as for instance at Kāśī, one goes in one day to several secondary tīrthas within a single great tīrtha, then he should perform the many śrāddhas occasioned by the arrival at the various tīrthas in that one day, in the order of the occasions. For the occasions are separate, like the (additional) śrāddha occasioned by an eclipse on a new moon day. As for the words of PRACETAS :

541. One should nowhere perform a pair of śrāddhas on the same day, nor (twice) say 'hanta' (as a reception to a guest), nor (twice) perform oblations, nor study, nor tarpaṇa,

(1) that refers to śrāddhas having the same occasion. Thus JĀBĀLI says :

542. One who has done a śrāddha should not do it again on the same day; but specially occasioned śrāddhas should be done in the order that the occasions arise.

KĀTYĀYANA too says :

543. Two or many occasions may arise in one day. The occasioned acts should be done in the order that the occasions arise.

Elsewhere too :

544. One person should not repeat a śrāddha which has one occasion on one day.[1]

1. The implication being that if there is more than one occasion, one should repeat the śrāddha.

(544.1) Fasting and shaving, however, are to be done only once, as they are prescribed with the particular condition that the tīrtha have the title 'comprehensive tīrtha,' such as Prayāga, Kāśī, etc.

(2) In such places, however, where the śrāddha of the comprehensive tīrtha is also completed by the performance of the śrāddha characterized as that of the comprehended tīrtha, there the śrāddha is not repeated for each occasion. (3) Rather the śrāddhas are accomplished in combination, because no differentiation like 'This one has been done, and this one not' is perceived; for the place, time, and agent are the same, and the materials and deities are not different. (4) Thus, for example, those śrāddhas occasioned (simultaneously) by Gaṅgā, Veṇī,[1] and Prayāga, or by Gaṅgā, Kāśī, and Maṇikarṇikā, (are completed in combination).[2]

(5) "But," it is objected, "according to the words '(śrāddha) is to be done by men as soon as they have arrived (at a tīrtha)' [381], the first śrāddha occasioned by the comprehensive tīrtha results as soon as one arrives within the limit of, for example, five krośas.[3] (6) But the śrāddha occasioned by the comprehended tīrtha comes afterwards, when he arrives within the area of the comprehended tīrtha. Thus how can there be combined performance, as the time and place are different?" (7) Not so ! For the occasion, namely the arrival, given in the words 'by men as soon as they have arrived' is delimited by the force of the words (quoted below) which prescribe the first bathing, śrāddha, etc. with the qualification of one or another *main* (sub-) tīrtha such as Maṇikarṇī; just as that occasion of 'living' given in the words 'As long as one lives (he should perform...)' is delimited by the force of the sentences (which prescribe the times) of morning and evening, and the full-moon day and the

1. The confluence of the Gaṅgā and Yamunā at Prayāga.

2. Thus if one goes to Maṇikarṇikā, he need perform only one śrāddha, which suffices as a śrāddha for Gaṅgā and Kāśī as well. But if he goes on the same day to another sub-tīrtha at Kāśī, he would then have to perform another śrāddha, according to what was said in 543.

3. The example refers to the tīrtha of Gayā, which is said to extend for a distance of five krośas.

new-moon day.[1] Thus the words of Vyāsa in the KĀŚĪKHAṆḌA :

> 545. Listen, O Great Wise Lomaharṣaṇa, I will tell you from the beginning how pilgrimage is to be done joyfully by pilgrims. First he bathes with his clothes on in the water of Lake Cakra[2]; then he satisfies the gods, ancestors, and brāhmaṇas according to rule...

(1) Thus since the occasion, which is the arrival at Kāśī, is particularized by the main (sub-) tīrtha, namely Maṇikarṇī, there is no difference in time or place; and thus combined performance is appropriate. (2) Thus also at Prayāga etc.

(3) "But," it is objected, "if the occasion is (a tīrtha) thus qualified, there are no separate occasions, and thus there will be no separate śrāddhas at all. So of what acts would there be combined performance?" (4) True; but because of the sentences which state that śrāddha is recommended at Maṇikarṇī etc. because it produces an extra benefit, arrival there also is an occasion for a separate śrāddha. (5) Just as the full moon day and new moon day are both restrictions on the occasion of 'being alive,' and also are of themselves separate times for offering, according to the words 'Who with an oblation...,'[3] just so here also, according to two different sorts of sentences Maṇikarnī etc. will be both restrictions on (other) occasions, and of themselves occasions for śrāddha, according to the rule of separateness of connections.[4]

---

1. See MS VI.2.7.23-26. The agnihotra and darśa-pūrṇamāsa offerings are prescribed in the sentences 'Yāvajjīvam agnihotraṃ juhoti' (As long as he lives he offers the agnihotra) and 'Yāvajjīvaṃ darśapūrṇamāsābhyāṃ yajeta (As long as he lives he should offer the darśa-pūrṇamāsa). But these offerings are elsewhere prescribed as to be offered in the morning and evening and on the new and full moon days respectively. Thus it is determined in sūtra 25 that one is to perform these offering at those specified times, and not constantly throughout one's life.

2. The Cakra lake at Maṇikarṇī is the main (sub-) tīrtha of the comprehensive tīrtha Kāśī, and it is at one's arrival there that one first bathes, not at arrival at the larger, comprehensive tīrtha Kāśī, which includes it.

3. This refers to the prescription, cited in Śab. XII.2.9.25, 'Ya iṣṭyā paśunā somena vā yajeta so 'māvasyāyāṃ pūrṇamāsyāṃ vā yajeta' (He who would offer with an oblation, an animal, or soma should offer them on the full moon day and new moon day).

4. Cf. above, 166 and 503.1 and notes.

(545.6) But as a matter of fact, there being such a restriction on the occasion, if because of some obstacle one does not reach Maṇikarṇikā etc. then the occasioned śrāddha would not be performed at all, because its occasion does not arise. (7) For this reason, places such as Maṇikarṇikā are prescribed as subsidiaries in the śrāddha actually occasioned by the arrival at Kāśī etc. (8) And thus because, being occasional, it is mandatory, śrāddha should be done even if one does not reach there (Maṇikarṇikā), even though it is lacking the subsidiary feature of (the prescribed) place; for the (main) occasion has come about; this is the idea. (9) Thus there is a multiplicity of arrivals (at the various tīrthas).

(10) "But," it is objected, "combined performance is only observed in connection with subsidiary acts such as pre-sacrifices, which are included within a single procedural prescription; but not also in connection with several independent main acts." (11) O you fool, who understand only as far as you see!—who do not perceive that there is a combination of benefit in such sacrifices as the darśa-pūrṇamāsa and rājasūya;[1] and that there is a combined performance in the sāṃnāyya offering of the two sacrifices consisting of giving up something on behalf of a deity, even though they are both principal acts, because they have the same deity (Prajāpati);[2] and in the birth-offering for the birth of twin sons; and of the several oblations in the fortnight's oblation; and of Kṣāmavatī offerings when there are several simultaneous occasions such as the burning of a house; and, in the smārta (non-Vedic) ritual, of the (several) śrāddhas occasioned by (several occasions, such as) an astronomical passage and a new moon day; which, though they are all main acts, are performed only once, because no difference of place etc. is perceived, so that the entire transcendental result is produced simultaneously; wherefore (because you do not see this) you say that combined performance applies only to details of performance, (and not to main acts).

---

1. In MS XI.1.1.1 (the 'Tantra-nyāya') it is explained that the benefits of the component parts of sacrifices such as the darśa-pūrṇamāsa are attained 'combinedly' (tantram).

2. Cf. *Bhāṭṭadīpikā* V.1.4. and *Śrāddha-mayūkha* p. 131.

(545.12) Therefore first declaring 'I will do this śrāddha occasioned by Maṇikarṇikā, and this one occasioned by Kāśī, with a combined performance,' one should perform just one śrāddha. (13) But when one has not done a śrāddha at the Gaṅgā in the recent past, one should also say '...and the śrāddha of the Gaṅgā.' (14) Likewise also at Prayāga etc.

(15) Some, however, say "The declaration is only 'I will perform the śrāddha occasioned by arrival at Kāśī'; because the śrāddha of the comprehended tīrtha (Maṇikarṇikā) is also achieved incidentally (prasaṅgataḥ) by the śrāddha of the comprehensive tīrtha, such as Kāśī. For Kāśī etc., being the comprehensive tīrtha, alone is intended, and Maṇikarṇī etc. is referred to as the 'comprehended' tīrtha in connection with Kāśī. Thus a difference is perceived, namely that the one falls within the other; just as the pre-sacrifices of the animal's cake are achieved incidentally by the pre-sacrifice performed for the animal,[1] and the regular agnihotra is achieved incidentally by the optional one, and the regular śrāddha is achieved incidentally by the śrāddha of the latter fortnight of the month.

(16) As for the statement : "There is neither combined performance, nor incidental performance; but rather there is just a single śrāddha occasioned by Kāśī etc., because the occasion is restricted to (Kāśī etc. alone). The mention of the separate benefits must refer to śrāddha at Maṇikarṇikā (as) included among the Five Tīrthas[2] etc., or to śrāddha performed there independently"; (17) this is not so; because, even when the occasion is the arrival at a comprehended tīrtha, there is no cause to cancel the śrāddha occasioned by it. (18) Rather,

1. This instance of 'prasaṅga' is discussed in MS XII.1.1.1-6. In the agniṣomīya offering, a sacrificial cake for the animal is to be given. The subject of discussion is whether the normal subsidiary acts such as pre-sacrifices of such an offering must be performed separately, or whether those subsidiaries can be considered to have been already achieved incidentally (i.e. by prasaṅga) by the similar acts performed for the animal itself. The siddhānta view is that the subsidiaries *are* achieved by prasaṅga; thus sūtra 3: 'Tantramadhye vidhānād vā mukhyatantreṇa siddhiḥ syāt. . . .' (Rather, it would be accomplished as it is prescribed within the (main) procedure...). This feature of one act *coming within* another is characteristic of prasaṅga, as opposed to tantra.

2. 'The Five Tīrthas' are Asisambheda, Daśāśvamedha, Pādodaka, Pañcanada, and Maṇikarṇī; see Kāśī Prakaraṇa, p. 261.

there is evidence to the contrary. (19) Nor does the proclamation of separate benefits refer to Maṇikarṇikā etc. as included in the Five Tīrthas; (20) for bathing, śrāddha, etc. within (the Five Tīrthas) do not require any separate benefit to be prescribed, since their benefits are fully established in the sentence (describing) the combined procedure, as they are qualified as combined with one another; like, for example, the aveṣṭi offering within the rājasūya sacrifice.[1] (21) Nor does the proclamation of the separate benefit refer to (another) independent śrāddha; for the prescription of a separate śrāddha for a separate benefit would be unnecessary verbiage. (22) But according to our position, the śrāddha occasioned by the arrival having been established already, it is merely connected with its benefit, according to the rule

> 546. But in (such) proximity, (the repetition of the prescription is made in order to express the benefit); for there can be no differentiation (of acts);[2]

(1) as in connection with the aveṣṭi offering it is said, 'One should have the one desirous of food sacrifice with this' :[3] thus the minimum of verbiage is achieved.

(2) Therefore śrāddha at Maṇikarṇikā etc. is, like the aveṣṭi offering, of two kinds: (3) Equally important to the others, and independent. (4) The first of these is the (śrāddha) within the Five

---

1. The aveṣṭi offering is of two types. One is included in the rājasūya sacrifice, the other is an independent offering. In the first, a specification of a benefit is not necessary, as its benefit is included in that of the rājasūya. Similarly, śrāddha at Maṇikarṇikā as part of the Five Tīrthas does not require the specification of a benefit, as its benefit is included in that of śrāddha at the Five Tīrthas as a whole. The independent aveṣṭi, however, does have a separate benefit, as specified in the sentence '...one desirous of food...' Likewise, śrāddha at Maṇikarṇikā as a separate act has a separate benefit. For the aveṣṭi offering, see MS II.3.2.3.

2. This sūtra means that a benefit which is mentioned immediately after (in proximity to) the prescription of an act does *not* indicate another, separate act; like the sentence 'Etayānnādyakāmaṃ yājayet' which comes immediately after 'Āgneyo' ṣṭakapālaḥ puroḍāśo bhavati' etc. (the prescription of the aveṣṭi offering).

3. See note 1 above.

Tīrthas etc.; (546.5) the second is the one occasioned by arrival (at the tīrtha). (6) Since there is no reason for omitting the latter, it is achieved by combined performance or incidentally, in the manner explained; this is the only correct interpretation. (7) Even one (act) can become a means for several benefits, on the grounds of a difference in procedure or in qualification; just like the aveṣṭi offering. (8) This is so in every case; enough of this!

DETERMINATION IN THE CASE OF THE COINCIDENCE (OF THE TĪRTHA-ŚRĀDDHA) WITH OTHER ŚRĀDDHAS

(9) In this connection, if on the day of arrival at the tīrtha there is a yearly śrāddha, then it should be done separately. Thus it is said in the KĀLĀDARŚA :

547. In case of the concurrence of the prescribed (śrāddha) with a yearly (śrāddha) or a śrāddha occasioned by a rare (alabhya) conjunction,[1] one should perform a pair of śrāddhas, because of the difference in their deities.

(1) Of these, the śrāddha occasioned by the tīrtha should be performed first, because it must be done immediately after the arrival, delay being improper. (2) The yearly śrāddha is to be done afterwards.

(3) If the tīrtha-śrāddha is done with raw food or gold, the śrāddhas occasioned by the new moon day, a vyatīpāta, yugādi days, manvādi days, astronomical passages, and so on are to be done separately, because they should be done with cooked food, and thus there is a different material, wherefore incidental performance is not possible. (4) But when the tīrtha-śrāddha is done with cooked food, then they can be performed incidentally with the tīrtha-śrāddha itself, because there is no difference in materials, and because all the deities of these śrāddha are invoked in the tīrtha-śrāddha itself; this, according to the saying in the KĀLĀDARŚA :

548. Of the new moon day and yugādi (śrāddhas), or of the new moon day śrāddha and the śrāddha occasioned by a rare conjunction,[1] one should perform the latter, as the other is also achieved incidentally.

1. Such as vyatīpāta or kapilaṣaṣṭhī (see below, 685, and *Samaya-Prakāśa*, p. 145).

(1) Here the word 'new moon day (śrāddha)' implies all the others which come under the same rule.

(2) The regular śrāddha also is to be performed separately if the tīrtha-śrāddha is done with raw food or gold, because it should be done with cooked good. As for what HEMĀDRI said,

549. The regular śrāddha is not be done separately, as it can be achieved incidentally, since the deities of the regular śrāddha are invoked in the Nāndīmukha and tīrtha-śrāddhas,

(1) that is to be observed when the tīrtha-śrāddha is done with cooked food. Thus it is said in the NĀGARA KHAṆḌA (of the SKANDAPURĀṆA) :

550. One should not perform the regular śrāddha when it is achieved incidentally. (But) when another śrāddha (of the same kind) is not done, one must not omit it, because it is regular.

(1) But when, because of some special reason or because one is unable to do otherwise, one intends to do all the new moon day and other śrāddhas with raw food or gold, then they are achieved by that same tīrtha-śrāddha with raw food or gold; this and other such determinations one may make for one's self.

(2) This śrāddha occasioned by the tīrtha must be done mandatorily if one arrives (again) at the tīrtha after ten months. (3) Within that period, it may be done or not, according to one's desire for its benefits :

551. If one should go to the tīrtha again within a year less two months, then he should carry out shaving and fasting assiduously. ($\simeq$278)

(1) For śrāddha is governed by the same rules as shaving etc., which are mentioned in this sentence with the word 'assiduously';[1] (2) or because the word 'and' (in 'shaving and...') is all-

1. Cf. 278.2 above.

inclusive.[1] (3) Bathing and tarpaṇa, however, are always done (even within ten months); so say the ancients.

THUS ENDS THE CONSIDERATION OF TĪRTHA-ŚRĀDDHA AND ITS DETAILS IN THE GENERAL SECTION OF THE BRIDGE TO THE THREE HOLY CITIES BY NĀRĀYAṆA BHAṬṬA, SON OF THE NOBLE BHAṬṬA RĀMEŚVARA SŪRI.

1. I.e., it suggests the entire tīrtha ritual.

THOSE WHO ARE AUTHORIZED TO PERFORM TĪRTHA-ŚRĀDDHA

(553.1) Sons and others are authorized (for tīrtha-śrāddha) according to the words of KĀTYĀYANA :

552. A son should perform the offering of piṇḍas and the water ceremony for his father. If there is no son, the wife should do them; if there is no wife, his co-uterine brother,

and of the VIṢṆUPURĀṆA :

553. The son, grandson, or great-grandson, brother or brother's children, or (other) descendants who offer the same piṇḍas are worthy (to perform) śrāddha, O King.

(2) Thus also the others who are generally authorized can be learned in any other text.

(3) There is, however, a special rule. Even (a son) whose father is alive may perform tīrtha-śrāddha. Thus it is said in the MAITRĀYAṆĪYA-PARIŚIṢṬA :

554. At a wedding, the birth of a son, an ancestral offering, a soma sacrifice, a tīrtha, or when a brāhmaṇa is present; these are the six (times for śrāddha) when one's father is alive.

(1) Here 'wedding' refers to the second and subsequent weddings; for at the first only the father is authorized (for śrāddha). (2) 'At the birth of a son' means during the birth ceremony; (3) this implicitly includes any consecration ceremony for the son. (4) 'At an ancestral offering' refers to the one included in the cāturmāsya offering.[1] (5) 'At a soma sacrifice' refers to the giving of piṇḍas consisting of pieces of the sacrificial cake

1. The cāturmāsya offering includes an offering to the ancestors called Mahāpitṛyajña. See ĀśŚrSū I.19.1ff. Also see Kane, *History of Dharmaśāstra* vol. II part 2 pp. 1101-03.

of the third soma pressing (by the various priests) from below (i.e. to the south of) their own soma vessels.[1] (6) 'When a brāhmaṇa is present' means when one is fortunate enough to have a brāhmaṇa who possesses such qualities as knowing the three madhus[2] and the three suparṇakas.[3] (7) 'When one's father is alive' means that these are the six times for śrāddha by the son.

(8) Śrāddha at tīrthas in general having been established, LAUGĀKṢI mentions an exception for Gayā :

555. One whose father is living should not perform the new moon day śrāddha, śrāddha at Gayā, the śrāddha of the latter fortnight of the month, nor tarpaṇa with sesamum or kṛṣṇa-berries.

Also in the MAITRĀYAṆĪYA-PARIŚIṢṬA :

556. Even one whose father is living may perform śrāddha by the rules of the pārvaṇa śrāddha at all great rivers and at tīrthas except Gayā.

(1) But in the case that one whose mother is dead arrives unexpectedly at Gayā, a suspension of the general rule is mentioned in that same PARIŚIṢṬA :

557. Even if his father is living, a son may perform an ānvaṣṭakya śrāddha, or, when he arrives at Gayā or when it is her death day, a (pārvaṇa) śrāddha for his mother.[4]

(1) Here too, 'when he arrives at Gayā' refers to an unexpected arrival. (2) When this is the case, śrāddha should be done for the mother; but not if one has gone intentionally. Therefore it is said in another smṛti:

---

1. This procedure in the agniṣṭoma sacrifice is described in ĀśŚrSū V. 17.5, and in Kane, op. cit., p. 1193.
2. The three mantras beginning with 'madhu,' RV I.90.6-8.
3. The three mantras RV X.114.3-5. With this comment (554.6) compare Yāj. I. 217, 219, and 221 and *Mitākṣarā* thereon; 'Brāhmaṇāḥ....śrāddhasampadaḥ śrāddheṣv akṣayyaphalasampattihetavaḥ (*Mitākṣarā* I.221).
4. Cf. Gayā Prakaraṇa, p. 345.

558. Coming to Gayā unexpectedly, one should perform śrāddha for his mother.

(1) Thus the authors of the KĀLĀDARŚA, SMṚTIDARPAṆA, and many others are of the opinion that "At a tīrtha other than Gayā, one whose father is alive should perform śrāddha with the intended recipients who will be specified below.[1] (2) But at Gayā, if he comes unexpectedly, and if his mother is dead, then he should perform only the pārvaṇa śrāddha for his mother; (3) but not if his mother is alive." (4) Others, however, explain these sentences in this way: "Since the sentences which prescribe śrāddha by one whose father is alive apply generally, even one whose father is alive should perform śrāddha at Gayā for his father's father and other relatives who will be specified below.[1] (5) Sentences like '...an ānvaṣṭakya śrāddha...' [557] are meant to establish a separate pārvaṇa śrāddha for the mother as such, even though a śrāddha for the mother of one whose mother is dead is already established in that śrāddha (to the father's father etc.) inasmuch as she is the father's wife. (6) As for the sentences prohibiting śrāddha at Gayā, they are meant to express that śrāddha is not to be done even by one whose mother is dead if he has come with the intention of performing śrāddha, but only if he has come unexpectedly."

(7) Thus since these sentences are interpreted in both ways, the decision should be made according to local custom. (8) But either way it is established that one whose father is alive is authorized to perform tīrtha-śrāddha.

Thus what is said by KĀTYĀYANA:

559. He who has a father is not authorized to perform ancestral rites; he may not give anything, passing over his living (father); so say the sacred texts,

and what is said by NIGAMA,

560. Ancestral rites are not prescribed for one whose father is alive,

1. See the following section on The Determination of the Beneficiaries in the Tīrtha-Śrāddha (573ff.)

(1) these refer to times other than the six prescribed [in 554]. (2) "But," it is objected, "if even one whose father is living is entitled to perform tīrtha-śrāddha, then if his father lived at a tīrtha, the son would have to perform a śrāddha when he arrived there from another place, because the occasion (for śrāddha) would then have occurred." (3) Let it be done, we say; for there is nothing to rule it out. (4) "Then would not the son have to perform śrāddha even if he was accompanied by his father?" (5) We answer; (strictly) according to the word, it would indeed so occur. But it would not (actually) be performed, as it is universally condemned. As it is said:

561. But if it is not conducive to heaven and is universally condemned, one should not even follow the law.

(1) If it is said: "Could it (the son's śrāddha) not be performed by being achieved incidentally with the śrāddha done by the father?" (2) No, because there can be no incidental performance when the performer is different.

(3) Therefore it is established that even one whose father is alive is authorized to perform tīrtha-śrāddha.

(4) Concerning brothers : if they have divided the patrimony, they should each perform a separate śrāddha when they go to a tīrtha, whether together or separately. (5) But if they have not yet divided, then whoever of them goes should perform it (for all of them). (6) If they go together, then it is to be done by the eldest only, not by all, as in the case of an eclipse etc. Thus MANU said:

562. For brothers who are undivided a single law prevails. When division has been made, the law is for each of them separately.

In the PRADĪPA:

563. When (brothers) are divided, they should each perform the yearly and other (śrāddhas). But when they are undivided, it is done by only one of them; when done by him, it is done by all.

(1) If a widow has a son, and she goes to a tīrtha, she should not perform (śrāddha) at all, according to the words:

564. Śrāddha for the husband should never be performed by a woman who has a son.

(1) But if she has no son, then she should indeed do it, according to the words:

565. A wife without sons (should perform the son's duties) like a son.[1]

(1) Some, however, say: "Even (a widow) with a son may have an 'intended śrāddha' (saṃkalpa-śrāddha) performed by a brāhmaṇa etc., if her son is not near."

(2) The elements to be omitted from an intended śrāddha are: VASIṢṬHA:

566. In an intended (śrāddha) one should leave out these six: The invitation, the saying of 'svadhā,' the piṇḍa, the fire-oblation, the scattering of rice, and the giving of the piṇḍas.

(1) (Some) say that "'The piṇḍa' means 'a remnant piṇḍa'." (2) No authority for this is to be found.

(3) One who has not been initiated may also perform śrāddha at a tīrtha, according to the statement in the SṚṢṬI-KHAṆḌA of the PADMAPURĀṆA concerning tīrtha-śrāddha etc.:

567. The uninitiated also may perform this (śrāddha) at all parvans. Śrāddha is truly common to all; it gives as its benefit all desires. A man without a wife, or a devoted man on a journey may also perform it. Even a śūdra may perform it by this rule without mantras, O King.

(1) Thus a woman or uninitiated man may have a śrāddha performed with the aid of a brāhmaṇa, or perform it himself without mantras, according to local custom. Thus it is said in the SMṚTYARTHASĀRA:

568. The uninitiated, women, and śūdras should have śrāddha performed by a ṛtvij priest, or perform it them-

1. The full saying reads 'Aputrā putravat patnī putrakarma samācaret.'

selves without mantras, with the personal and gotra-names, or with the mantras 'Homage to the gods' and 'Homage to the ancestors, svadhā !'

(1) The special rule concerning kṣetrajas etc. is not mentioned, (569.1) because it does not apply in this Kali-era, as children other than sons are prohibited here:

569. Accepting as sons (children) other than those adopted or born of one's self (is prohibited in the Kali-era).

Also; according to the words of KĀRṢṆĀJINI:

570. Whoever inherits someone's woman or wealth should do śrāddha for him; and that inheritor of women and wealth should do the rites of piṇḍa and water.

(1) Other such persons authorized to perform śrāddha may be known from other books. (2) Some of them, however, will be clarified here too in the (section on) 'The Determination of the Beneficiaries.'[1]

1. See 611ff.

EXCEPTION TO THOSE WHO ARE AUTHORIZED TO PERFORM TĪRTHA-ŚRĀDDHA

(570.3) Śrāddha is not to be done by an ascetic, according to the smṛti:

571. One carrying a birth-impurity and a mendicant should not perform śrāddha or the rites of piṇḍa and water (≈345). For by taking on renunciation, one abandons the vows of the domestic law etc., all of one's gotra, caraṇa, etc., and the mother's and father's families, and wealth.

(1) Nor may an outcaste perform śrāddha, according to the prohibition by the words

572. Outcasting is separation from the religious rites of the twice-born.

(1) Śrāddha may, however, be performed by one who has committed a minor sin etc., for he is not forbidden to perform regular and occasional rites.

THUS ENDS 'THOSE WHO ARE AUTHORIZED TO PERFORM TĪRTHA-ŚRĀDDHA' IN THE GENERAL SECTION OF THE BRIDGE TO THE THREE HOLY CITIES BY NĀRĀYAṆA BHAṬṬA, SON OF THE NOBLE BHAṬṬA RĀMEŚVARA SŪRI.

DETERMINATION OF THE BENEFICIARIES IN THE TĪRTHA-ŚRĀDDHA

According to the KŪRMAPURĀṆA:

573. The ancestors are always pleased by what is given at river-banks, tīrthas, and good land, and on mountain tops and pure places,

and according to the words:

574. Whenever (an offering) is given after sapiṇḍīkaraṇa, it should be made as a pārvaṇa śrāddha, never an ekoddiṣṭa,

(1) a pārvaṇa śrāddha should be done for the father etc. then (after sapiṇḍīkaraṇa).

(2) A pārvaṇa for the maternal grandfather etc., also should be done, according to the saying of GAUTAMA:

575. When the father etc. are worshipped, then the maternal grandfather etc. also should be worshipped. (Śrāddha) must be done without distinction; for making a distinction, one goes to hell,

and according to the saying of KĀTYĀYANA:

576. Except for that (śrāddha) which includes trenches,[1] the other sixteen śraddhas,[2] and the annual śrāddha, in the rest the piṇḍas are six;[3] this is the law.

(1) Thus the author of the SMṚTIRATNĀVALĪ and others hold that śrāddha has six deities at tīrthas other than Gayā. (2)

---

1. According to the *Caturviṃśatimatasaṃgraha*, p. 163, and others, this refers to the sapiṇḍīkaraṇa śrāddha. But according to Mitramiśra, it refers to the anvaṣṭakā śrāddha, because Gobhila prescribes that 'one should dig trenches' in preparation for that śrāddha. See Mitramiśra's discussion of this point in *Śrāddha-prakāśa*, p. 13. Since NB's own sūtra (ĀśGṛSū II.5.6) also mentions 'karṣū' in connection with the anvaṣṭakya, this is probably the interpretation he would have favoured.

2. For an enumeration of the 'sixteen śrāddhas,' see SAS p. 95, lines 11ff.

3. For the father, paternal grandfather and great-grandfather, and the maternal grandfather, great- and great-great-grandfather.

Others, however, (577.1) call for a (separate) pārvaṇa for the mother also, according to the words of DEVALA, speaking of tīrtha- and other śrāddhas in general:

577. Then respectfully taking a handful from the remains of the offering, he should offer piṇḍas in order, one by one, to the wives of his ancestors.

(2) But in the SMṚTYARTHASĀRA that (mother's pārvaṇa) is described as to be done or not (optionally), with the words

578. Śrāddha for the mother there is praised separately.

(1) But at Gayā, pārvaṇa for the mother etc. is required: we will explain this there (in the Gayā section).[1]

ŚĀṄKHĀYANA says:

579. And this (śrāddha to the mother etc.) is to be given behind the piṇḍas for the father etc.

(1) Thus this śrāddha has nine deities.[2]

(2) Others, however, say that the pārvaṇa for the maternal grandmother etc. is separate, (580.1) according to the genera statement on women in the CATURVIṂŚATIMATA:

580. Some, O Great Seers, call for separate śrāddha for women,

and according to the statement of the AGNIPURĀṆA:

581. (This śrāddha) has nine deities, the fathers etc., and it has twelve deities.[3]

(1) Here the word 'and' indicates an optional choice: (2) 'and also it may have twelve deities.' (3) In this question, the decision is made according to the local practice of refined people.

---

1. Gayā Prakaraṇa, p. 349.
2. The six mentioned previously, plus the mother and paternal grandmother and great-grandmother.
3. The nine mentioned previously, plus the maternal grandmother, great- and great-great-grandmother.

(4) In the case where the pārvaṇa for the mother and maternal grandmother are not done separately, then they are to be mentioned when the names of the deities are spoken as the wives of the fathers and of the maternal grandfather etc. (582.1) This is according to the statement of BṚHASPATI which describes the mother etc. as deities by way of their concomitance with the father etc.:

582. The mother enjoys the śrāddha, which is like nectar, together with her own husband; and so does the paternal grandmother with hers, and the paternal great-grandmother with hers;

(583.1) and according to ŚAṄKHA, who, while prohibiting separate śrāddha (for women), agrees that it may be combined:

583. (In a śrāddha done on) an anvaṣṭakā day, the śrāddha to the mother, and (śrāddha done on) the day of death (śrāddha is done separately for women). There is no other separate śrāddha for women, except for the ekoddiṣṭa.

(2) In the case of separate śrāddha for the mother etc.; if they have gone with their husbands,[1] then the feeding of an uneven number of brāhmaṇas is done together, intended for both her husband and her. (3) And also a single piṇḍa is to be given, intended for both of them. Thus the performance is combined, according to the words of LAUGĀKṢI :

584. Because the husband and wife ascended (the funeral pyre) together, the offering of piṇḍas on the date of their death is done in combination; but the new śrāddha is done separately.

(1) Here is the meaning of this : If the day of their death is the same by reason of the wife and husband ascending the funeral pyre together, the 'offering of piṇḍas'—that is, the piṇḍa, the offering, and the śrāddha—are done in combination, as described, like a (single) śrāddha to two ancestors. (2) But the new

---

1. I.e., performed satī.

śrāddha, which is done before the sapiṇḍīkaraṇa, is done separately, not in combination. (3) Because of the special mention in this sentence of 'on the day of their death', the performance can only be separate and not combined if the day of their death is different.

(4) Commenting on this verse, the author of the MADANA-PĀRIJĀTA and others say : "Since only the new śrāddha is prescribed here as separate, combined performance only is seen to apply in new moon, yearly, tīrtha, and other śrāddhas, because of the exclusive prescription.[1] (5) The same interpretation is to be understood when several wives ascend the funeral pyre together with the husband. As for the other passage from the law-books :

> 585. If the husband and wife mounted on the same pyre and died there, one should perform separate śrāddha and give cooked rice to them separately,

(1) that applies to the new śrāddha." (2) But HEMĀDRI and others say that, "In order to avoid an exclusive prescription and in accordance with the text 'on the date of their death' as it is given, this statement [584] must refer to the yearly śrāddha only.[2] (3) Therefore at tīrthas etc., śrāddha is to be given separately."

(4) Furthermore : One should also give śrāddha to the co-wives of one's father, paternal grandfather, and paternal great-grandfather at a tīrtha, (586.1) because 'motherhood' etc. applies by extension to them also, according to SUMANTU :

> 586. All of one's father's wives are one's mothers.

(2) And in this case, these co-wives, etc. are represented in the brāhmaṇa who represents the mother etc., and in his piṇḍa; they are not represented separately, according to the saying of GĀLAVA :

---

1. That is, the mention of the new śrāddha is to be taken as an exclusive prescription: 'In the new śrāddha, and in the new śrāddha only....'

2. In this interpretation, the mention of the new śrāddha in 584 is not an exclusive prescription, so that separate performance also applies at tīrtha- and other śrāddhas.

587. At a tīrtha or in the śrāddha of the latter fortnight of the month, one who has several mothers should give the water offering separately, but should offer a single piṇḍa (for them).

(1) However, refined people, considering this to apply only to those who are unable to do otherwise, do give the śrāddha and piṇḍa separately. (2) Similarly, śrāddha should also be done for one's maternal grandfathers through his father's co-wives; for, since the co-wives to the mothers are included by SUMANTU [586] by extension as mothers, so too their fathers are established as maternal grandfathers in an implied secondary sense. (3) All this is explained by HEMĀDRI in the ŚRĀDDHAKALPA.

(4) When one performs śrāddha with the desire to satisfy his various ancestors at a special time such as the mahālaya, or at a special tīrtha such as Gayā, then he should perform śrāddha for his mother's co-wives also, whether or not they have sons. (5) For even if they have sons of their own, the son of their co-wife is optionally entitled to perform śrāddha for them out of sympathy or affection for them. (6) In the same way the wives of the paternal grandfather other than the mother of the father, and the wives of the paternal great-grandfather other than the mother of the grandfather are also accounted for. (7) Since the co-wives of one's mother have been determined to be mothers in a secondary sense, so their fathers also are deities in a secondary sense in the śrāddha for the maternal grandfather; this has already been determined [in 587.2]. (8) But when one may wish to perform a śrāddha at a special place or time etc., with the desire of satisfying various ancestors, then he may perform it (separately) for them also by his optional authority; thus it is established.

(9) Śrāddha should also be done for the paternal uncle and his son, (10) and for one's teacher etc., according to the CATURVIṂŚATIMATA :

588. In Bhādrapada a man should always give handfuls of water and piṇḍas separately to his teacher, guru, and students, friends and relatives, and also to all their

wives; likewise at all tīrthas, in the month of Māgha and in maghā.

(1) 'Relatives' are paternal and maternal uncles, sons and so on.

(2) Another special rule is given in the BHAVIṢYAPURĀṆA :

589. Śrāddha is also given here to sons, daughter's sons, and wives, and to one's younger co-uterine brothers, and to those (relatives) who died without sons.

VṚDDHAŚĀTĀTAPA also says :

590. Śrāddha should be done with affection for all those who bear the marks of celibacy. For thus acting properly one achieves much good fortune.

(1) 'Those who bear the marks of celibacy' are religious students, ascetics, etc. (2) Although they are mentioned here in general, this is to be understood to refer only to those who are one's relations.

(3) According to the words 'and to their wives' in the CATURVIṂŚATIMATA [588], śrāddha is also to be given separately to the wives of the paternal uncle etc.

(4) For all of these relatives, only ekoddiṣṭa śrāddha is to be done, according to the words of JĀTUKARṆYA :

591. After sapiṇḍīkaraṇa, pārvaṇa śrāddha is done for the parents only. For the paternal uncles, brothers, and mothers, ekoddiṣṭa is always done,

and according to the statement of SUMANTU :

592. After sapiṇḍīkaraṇa, whenever śrāddha is given to a brother, sister, son, husband, maternal uncle, friend, or guru, it is an ekoddiṣṭa, not a pārvaṇa.

593. In the first sentence [591], the word 'mother' refers to one's co-mothers,[1] because pārvaṇa for one's actual mother has already been prescribed, and because the

1. I.e., one's mother's co-wives.

word 'mother' is mentioned in connection with the paternal uncle etc.;

so says HEMĀDRI.

As for the words :

594. For paternal uncles, brothers, and mother, and also those (relatives) who have no sons, and for a maternal grandfather who has no sons, the śrāddha and other rites are done as for the father,

(1) that is to say that they are the same insofar as they are mandatory, not they are the same by way of being pārvaṇa śrāddhas.

(2) Also, it has already been mentioned in the section on 'Those who are Authorized to Perform Śrāddha' that whoever inherits wealth from someone should give śrāddha to him also.[1]

(3) SATYAVRATA gives this order of placement (of the recipients) of the pārvaṇas :

595. First the offering to the fathers; after that, to the mothers; then the maternal grandfathers etc., the paternal uncle, and son.

CHĀGALEYA says :

596. In the death-day śrāddha, the mothers alone are made (the objects); in the śrāddha on an auspicious occasion they are offered to first. They are always (in other śrāddhas) in the middle; they should not be put at the end.

As for the sentence :

597. First, the paternal and maternal grandfather, after them the mothers; this is the order proclaimed for tarpaṇa, anvaṣṭakā-śrāddha, and at a tīrtha,

---

1. See 570.

(1) which is quoted by the author of the SMṚTIRATNĀVALĪ, that he himself rejects as being baseless. (2) Therefore UŚANAS prohibits placing the mother at the end :

598. The fool who puts the maternal grandfathers in the middle and offers (last) to the mothers goes to hell until the destruction of creation.

JĀBĀLI says :

599. The foolish man who places mothers at the end of the śrāddhas goes to the Kālasūtra hell hanging head down.

(1) Therefore the pārvaṇa śrāddha for the mother is right after the pārvaṇa to the father. (2) By this same rule, the pārvaṇa for the maternal grandmother etc. also is done just after the pārvaṇa for the maternal grandfather etc. (3) But the order for the wife etc. is the same as was given in the order for tarpaṇa [333ff].

(4) Here the pārvaṇas for the father and maternal grandfather are regular, for by them alone the purpose of the text [575] is fulfilled. (5) The other pārvaṇa and ekoddiṣṭa śrāddhas are optional, and thus are to be done to the best of one's ability; but they are not all mandatory. (6) At Gayā, however, the pārvaṇa for the mother is also mandatory; we will explain this there (in the Gayā Section).[1]

(7) Further : When several pārvaṇa and/or ekoddiṣṭa śrāddhas are to be done at the same time, the cooking of the offerings may be done in combination. Thus ATRI says :

600. If there be śrāddha for two or many relatives on the same day, one should boil the offerings in combination and perform the śrāddhas separately.

PULASTYA says :

601. In a mahālaya śrāddha, a śrāddha at Gayā, or on the death day of those who have passed away, one should

1. See Gayā Prakaraṇa, p. 349.

boil the offerings in combination and perform the śrāddhas separately.

(1) Also in this connection, MARĪCI gives the order of pārvaṇa and ekoddiṣṭa :

602. If there be an ekoddiṣṭa and a pārvaṇa at the same time, then one should complete the ekoddiṣṭa after finishing the pārvaṇa.

(1) This applies if one is able to do so. (2) If not, the pārvaṇa and ekoddiṣṭa are combined.

(3) If one is able to, he should feed one brāhmaṇa in each of the ekoddiṣṭas. (4) But if not, he may perform all the ekoddiṣṭas with just one brāhmaṇa. Thus it is said in the CATURVIṂŚATIMATA, after 'to his teacher, guru, and students...' [588],

603. Likewise at all tīrthas, in the month of Māgha and in maghā, one should honor all his teachers etc. through one brāhmaṇa.

(1) The giving of piṇḍas, however, is separate (for each ancestor), because that is the main part of the tīrtha-śrāddha. (2) Therefore in that sentence singularity is specified in connection with the brāhmaṇa only. (3) Also in the pārvaṇas to the father etc., if one is able he should feed a different brāhmaṇa for each deity. (4) But the offering to the divinities[1] is done in combination in all the pārvaṇas; (604.1) for the author of the SAṂGRAHA mentions the combination of the divinity offering if the time and place are the same :

604. If the time is different, there is no combination; nor if the place is different. Thus simultaneity (of the divinity-offerings) is understood according to the rule of combination.

(2) When, however, one is unable (to carry out the full procedure), then he may feed one brāhmaṇa in place of each

1. That is, the offerings to the Viśvedevas, such as Dhuri and Locana. See above, 502.4ff.

three ancestors, and feed just one brāhmaṇa in the divinity-offering, as a combined performance; so it is decided.

(3) But when someone goes to a tīrtha induced by someone else by means of persuasion, gifts, etc., then, even though he himself performs the rite, he should perform the first śrāddha for the sake of the ancestors of the other person, in order to produce the full benefit to be realized from the pilgrimage for that one who authorized him. (4) And thus the declaration is to be made as 'For the father, grandfather, and great-grandfather of the sacrificer'.[1] (5) After that (first śrāddha), he should perform a śrāddha to his own ancestors also, in order to avoid an offense (by not performing it), since an incidental arrival at a tīrtha, which is an occasion for śrāddha to one's own ancestors, has occurred; (605.1) and in order to obtain the full benefit described in the words

605. He gets a sixteenth part (of the benefit), who goes on behalf of someone else. (=107)

(2) Although, since he himself is entitled to perform śrāddha, a śrāddha for his own fathers would normally be done first as that act is more closely connected to him, nevertheless the śrāddha for his own ancestors is only done afterward, because that was not the intended purpose of the journey; and because, the journey being for another's sake, one's own śrāddha need not follow immediately after (arrival). (3) This was proven at length by HEMĀDRI in the ŚRĀDDHAKALPA, and therefore will not be expounded here.

(4) Thus in the VĀYUPURĀṆA, a certain merchant, who had gone to Gayā induced by a preta with a gift of his own money, first performed the offering of piṇḍas to the preta, and after that to his own ancestors. Thus it is said :

606. Having come to Gayāśirṣa, and having first offered piṇḍas happily to the King of the Pretas together with his kinsmen, he then offered to his own ancestors.

In the VĀMANAPURĀṆA too, speaking of the same man :

607. There he made an offering of piṇḍas to the pretas one

1. The one who induces the other to go on his behalf.

after another, and thereafter made an offering with his own ancestors as recipients.

(1) A widow should perform a pārvaṇa for her husband and for her own ancestors, according to the law-book quoted in the SMṚTIDARPAṆA :

608. A widow should untiringly have śrāddha done for the three ancestors beginning with her own husband and also to her own ancestors at the appropriate time.

(1) 'And also (to her own ancestors)' means to just three (of her own ancestors, as to her husband's). (2) 'At the proper time' means when an offering to several deities is prescribed, as at a tirtha, on the mahālaya day, etc.

Commenting on this, it is said in the DĪVODĀSĪYA that

609. She does a pārvaṇa for her own father only if he has no sons or grandsons.

(1) This is not so; because in the saying 'A wife without sons (should perform the son's duties) like a son' [565], the word 'like' (vati = vat) indicates, according to the context, equality (of the sonless widow to a son) in respect to the act of śrāddha; and a son is entitled to perform pārvaṇa śrāddha for his own father and maternal grandmother. Now for a sonless widow, the father etc. of the son (whose place she takes) is her husband etc.; and his maternal grandfather etc. is her own father etc.; so that a widow also is seen to be authorized to perform tīrtha-śrāddha etc. for her own fathers, whether or not she has sons.[1] (2) That statement [609] is also incorrect because there is no specification 'Only for those (widows) without sons.'

(3) If it is said : "But since the son is authorized to perform

1. Thus Divodāsa is wrong in saying that a widow does śrāddha to her father etc. only if he has no sons, because a widow who herself has no sons performs the rites that her son, if she had one, would have performed. Therefore she does śrāddha for her own father (as he is her hypothetical son's maternal grandfather), whether or not he has sons.

śrāddha for them as his maternal grandfather etc., then she too (the widow) would be authorized (to do śrāddha for them) as just that (the grandfather etc.), and not as her father etc."; (4) this is not so, for the same one thing can be different in respect to the determining characteristic of its relationship when there is a difference in that to which it is related, as in the case of the wooden stick;[1] so a person is to be denoted in relation to another in just that way in which he is related to him. (5) The equality in respect to action expressed by the word 'like' [in 565] is realized in just this way. (6) And thus, just as those who are denoted in respect to the son as father etc. are denoted in respect to her as husband etc., so also those who are denoted as grandfather etc. will be denoted as father etc. (7) The words 'beginning with her own husband' [608] are meant to indicate just this sort of denotation.

(8) Therefore the pārvaṇa for her husband and her father are mandatory for a widow. (9) The word 'untiringly' [in 608] is meant to indicate that these are mandatory.

As for the statement :

> 610. A woman who foolishly performs a pārvaṇa śrāddha for her husband goes to hell, and her husband is not satisfied by that śrāddha,

(1) that is intended to praise the alternative of performing an ekoddiṣṭa on his death day, and not to entirely rule out the pārvaṇa.

---

1. The reference is to the example of MS XII.2.10.26. In the cāturmāsya sacrifice, a paridhi (wooden stick normally used to enclose the sacrificial fire) is substituted for the archetypal yūpa (sacrificial post) to which the sacrificial animal is tied. It is declared in the sūtra ('Paridhir dvyarthatvād ubhayadharmā syāt') that both the ritual details applicable to the archetypal yūpa, and those applicable to the paridhi in its normal function, are to be applied to this substitutive paridhi. The reason is that this paridhi serves a dual function; it functions as a yūpa in relation to the sacrificial animal, and as a paridhi in relation to the sacrificial fire. Thus the same thing can become different in respect to its relations with different objects. Just as the paridhi is related to the animal as a yūpa and thus is treated as such in respect to the animal, so the sonless woman is related to her father as a daughter and thus functions as such in relation to him.

(2) A widow whose father-in-law is living should perform śrāddha to her husband and his paternal grandfather and great-grandfather. (3) When the father-in-law and *his* father are living, she should perform śrāddha for the husband and his paternal great-grandfather and great-great-grandfather.

(4) Some say it is the same when her own father etc. are living. (5) But the reliable authorities say that when her own father is living, the pārvaṅa for him is simply dropped, since the reason (dvāra) for going it is dropped.[1]

(6) For (a widow) whose mother-in-law etc. are dead, the pārvaṇa for the mother-in-law etc. also may or may not be done. (7) Thus, her śrāddha has nine deities. (8) Some say that if (a widow's) mother is dead, then pārvaṇa is to be done for her own mother etc. also; and thus the śrāddha has twelve deities. (9) Others say that with the pārvaṇa for her own maternal grandfather, it has fifteen deities. (10) Others say that, with the pārvaṇa for her own maternal grandmother etc. it has eighteen deities. (11) It would seem that these three statements apply if those relatives are sonless. (12) In each of these, if the first member is living, his śrāddha is dropped, since the reason for doing it is dropped.[1]

(13) There is no incidental achievement of śrāddha for the husband, maternal grandfather, etc. (14) If the pārvaṇas for the mother-in-law, mother, etc. are not done, one should say '(for these,) together with their wives,' in the pārvaṇa for the husband and father, whenever appropriate. (15) For the others, ekoddiṣṭas should be done as far as possible. (16) In these matters, let the practice of the refined people of the various lands be the boat for crossing the river of uncertainty. Enough of this !

(17) MANU mentions a special rule for one whose father is alive :

611. But while his father is living, he should offer only to those before him.

---

1. If the father is alive, there is no reason to perform śrāddha for him, nor for his ancestors, since he will perform it for them.

In another law-book :

612. At a tīrtha, and when his father is old, has renounced the world, or is outcaste, then the son should himself give (śrāddha) to the same ancestors to whom the father would give.

(1) 'Himself' indicates that the son is authorized on his own.

(2) But in the BHAVIṢYAPURĀṆA it says that the son whose father is living should offer only to his paternal grandfather and great-grandfather :

613. Since, O Best of the Bharatas, śrāddha is not to be given for one who is alive, a son whose father is alive should offer only to two ancestors; there is no doubt of this.

Another special rule is mentioned by VIṢṆU :

614. If someone performs śrāddha while his father is living, he should do it for those for whom his father would do it; when his father and paternal grandfather are living, for those for whom his grandfather would do it. When his father, paternal grandfather, and paternal greatgrandfather are living, he should not perform it at all. One whose father is a preta should offer a piṇḍa to his father, and give (śrāddha) to the two beyond his grandfather. One whose father and grandfather are pretas should give piṇḍas to them and give (śrāddha) to his grandfather's grandfather. One whose grandfather is a preta should offer a piṇḍa to him and give (śrāddha) to the two ancestors beyond his great-grandfather. One whose father and great-grandfather are pretas should offer a piṇḍa to his father and give (śrāddha) to the two beyond his great-grandfather.

A wise man should thus perform śrāddha for his maternal grandfathers also, with modifications of the mantra according to the rule, and for the rest (of his ancestors) without mantras.

(1) 'While his father is living' is a restrictive rule; (2) it means 'while *only* the father is living.' (3) Therefore it is said that while the three (father, grandfather. and great-grandfather) are living, 'he should not perform it at all.' (4) After that, 'Thus...to his maternal grandfathers also' is also (a restrictive rule). Commenting on this, ŚŪLAPĀṆI explained:

615. As a son, when his father is alive, should perform śrāddha for those for whom his father performs it, so when his maternal grandfather is alive, he should perform it for those for whom his grandfather performs it. As when the three, his father etc., are living, he should not perform it at all, so also when the three, maternal grandfather etc. are living, he should not perform it at all; all this and the rest is to be understood by extension.

(1) The author of the KĀLĀDARŚA also says the same thing.

(2) "The case is the same when the mother is alive, as the same rule applies. (3) Thus it follows that one whose father is alive should give to three, his father's father etc., and, if his mother is dead, to his own mother etc.; if his mother is alive, to the three beginning with the paternal grandmother, and then to his own maternal grandfather etc.; if his maternal grandfather is alive, to the three beginning with his mother's paternal grandfather. (4) Nor does this contradict the words 'to the same ancestors (to whom the father would give)' [612]. (5) For it may be explained that those same ones who are the deities of the father (in the śrāddha) are those of the sons (also); for 'mother' and 'maternal grandfather' being words of relationship, those who are mothers etc. and maternal grandfathers etc. in relation to the son are the same (as those of the father) in that they are denoted by the words 'mother' and 'maternal grandfather.' (6) And thus the son whose father is alive performs śrāddha for his own mother, maternal grandfather, etc."

(7) This [615.2-6] is wrong; for in explaining the relative and co-relative pronouns (in 612) as 'those who are denoted by the

same terms of relationship',[1] there would be indirect expression by the relative and co-relative pronouns. (8) It is also wrong because (these words) would then function in two different ways simultaneously, since the literal meaning must apply to the father's father etc.[2] (9) Moreover: (these ancestors) are denoted in the sentence only by the relative and co-relative pronouns; and the denotation is 'to whom the father...' as relative to the father, not relative to one's self (i. e., the son). (10) Also: how does it come about that the mother etc. is referred to in relation to the son simply by virtue of a word denoting relationship? (11) Rather, by the word 'thus' in the words of VIṢṆU [614] 'A wise man should thus perform...', it is only meant that the details of the performance (and not the specification of the beneficiaries) are to be applied by extension to the śrāddha to the maternal grandfather.

(12) Thus only the mother etc. of the *father*, and *his* maternal grandfather etc. are the deities in a tīrtha-śrāddha by one whose father is alive; not his own mother etc. (13) He may do an ekoddiṣṭa śrāddha for his own mother as the wife of his father, and also for his own maternal grandfather as the father-in-law of his father. For his father is authorized to do an ekoddiṣṭa for them at a tīrtha; and this does not diverge from the words '(He should give śrāddha) to the same ancestors to whom the father would give' [612].

(14) Concerning this, the author of the MADANAPĀRIJĀTA and others say "One whose father is living may offer śrāddha at a tīrtha only if he keeps a fire, and not if he has no fire; according to the words of SUMANTU :

616. A brāhmaṇa whose father is alive should not offer śrāddha

1. In the proposed interpretation, the relative and co-relative pronouns are taken to signify not their literal sense, which is 'to whom' meaning 'to the grandfather' etc., but rather to signify 'to him who may be denoted by the words 'grandfather' etc.' This sort of explanation involves an indirect use of the words (lakṣaṇā), and it is always preferable to avoid such an interpretation.

2. The literal interpretation of 'to whom' etc. applies to the father's ancestors. But according to the proposed interpretation, those words also apply to the mother's ancestors; but the same words cannot have two different functions at the same time.

without a fire. One who has a fire should offer only to those to whom his father would offer.

(1) 'One who has a fire' means one with a sacred fire of the Vedic or non-Vedic (smārta) rituals. (2) Thus one whose father is alive is authorized to perform tīrtha-śrāddha only if he keeps a fire."[1] (3) The author of the SMṚTIRATNĀVALĪ, DIVODĀSA, and others say : "Even of those who keep a fire, only those who follow the Maitrāyaṇīya sūtra are authorized, not all fire-keepers; for the previously quoted text 'These are the six (times for śrāddha) when one's father is alive' [554] appears only in the appendix to that Maitrāyaṇīya sūtra." (4) But both of these opinions are wrong, for they contradict the words of UŚANAS :

617. A brāhmaṇa whose father has passed away should perform śrāddha daily, especially at tīrthas, whether he keeps a fire or not.

(1) SUMANTU's words [616] mean only that one without a fire may not perform śrāddha according to the procedure of the piṇḍapitṛyajña, while one with a fire may offer to his father's father etc. by that rule. (2) And although the words 'These are the six' [554] appear only in the appendix to the Maitrāyaṇīya sūtra, nevertheless this should be explained as being common to all schools, because the words of UŚANAS, and previously quoted words such as 'At a tīrtha, and when (his father) is old...' [612] apply generally. (3) Moreover, if that sentence of the Maitrāyaṇīyas applied only to followers of that school who keep the fire, what would provide the information about the second wedding etc. which is mentioned in that sentence ?[2]

(4) Although this discussion concerns authorization, it has been given here as incidental (to the subject at hand)[3]. Thus

---

1. See MP p. 544.

2. See 554.1. It is clear from 612 that others than Maitrāyaṇīya fire-keepers may perform śrāddha while their fathers are alive. But the sentence in the Maitrāyaṇīya Pariśiṣṭa (554) must still be taken as applying to people of other śākhās, because only that sentence explains the specific instances in which such śrāddha is permitted.

3. Rather than in its proper place in the chapter on "Those Who are Authorized to Perform Tīrtha-Śrāddha."

it is established that one whose father is alive is authorized. If he goes (to a tīrtha) commissioned by his father for the sake of his (the father's) benefit only, like any other man who is induced by money or other gifts, he should (first) perform one śrāddha construing the sentence (of the declaration) as 'For the father, grandfather, and great-grandfather of the sacrificer;'[1] for his father is the authority in that śrāddha. Then he should perform another śrāddha construing the sentence (of the declaration) as 'For the father, grandfather, and great-grandfather of my father'; for an occasion for him to perform śrāddha himself, namely an incidental arrival at a tīrtha, has also arisen. (617.5) (These śrāddhas are done separately) because their deities are different; for, according to 'He should himself give to the same ancestors to whom the father would give,' [612] (those ancestors) are described as the deities only in the sense that they are the father's father etc.; (6) while in the first śrāddha, they are the deities only in the sense that they are the father etc., of the sacrificer, just as if the actual performer were some servant (of the sacrificer) rather than his son. (7) Also, (two actions) which have different authorities cannot be performed in combination or incidentally; and the word 'himself' [612] indicates that (the son) himself is the authority (in the second śrāddha).

(8) But when (a son) goes to a tīrtha for the sake of his own benefit, with or without his father's assent, then he should perform a single śrāddha only, construing the sentence (of the declaration) as 'For my father's father, grandfather, and great-grandfather,' in order to carry out his own authority invested by the word 'himself' [in 612].

(9) Another special rule : If (a son) whose mother is dead goes to Gayā for the sake of his father, then in the first śrāddha he should perform an ekoddiṣṭa to his own mother as the wife of the sacrificer (the father); for his father is authorized only to perform an ekoddiṣṭa for her. (10) Then in the second śrāddha, he should perform (another) ekoddiṣṭa to his mother as the wife of his father, according to the rule previously mentioned. (11) After that, he should also perform a pārvaṇa for the mother etc.,

1. Cf. 604.4.

as it is said in the section on 'Who is Authorized' that in the case of an incidental arrival at Gayā a śrāddha to the mother is also to be done.[1] For according to the words of ŚĀTĀTAPA,

618. In a Nāndīmukha śrāddha, an aṣṭakā śrāddha, at Gayā, and on the death day, one should perform śrāddha for his mother together with his paternal grandmother etc.,

(1) the son is himself authorized for that pārvaṇa for her.

(2) But when one whose mother is dead goes to Gayā incidentally, then for the first śrāddha he should do an ekoddiṣṭa for his mother as his father's wife. (3) For the second śrāddha, he should do a pārvaṇa for her as his mother.

(4) But in the opinion of the KĀLĀDARŚA, if he goes for the sake of his father he should not perform a second śrāddha at Gayā. (5) But if he goes there incidentally, he should not perform the first; this was explained in connection with the authority (for śrāddha).[2]

(6) But at tīrthas other than Gayā, only an ekoddiṣṭa is to be made for the mother, as the wife of the sacrificer, or as the wife of the father, as is appropriate; but not a pārvaṇa, as there is no statement prescribing that. This is the correct interpretation. (7) Similarly, at Gayā or another tīrtha, one whose father is alive should perform an ekoddiṣṭa for his paternal uncles etc. also, as brothers of the sacrificer or as brothers of the father, as is appropriate. (8) But there is no śrāddha for them just as paternal uncles etc. as such, because there is no text prescribing that. (9) But in the opinion of the KĀLĀDARŚA and others, there is no śrāddha for them even as the father's brothers, since one whose father is alive has no authority of his own for śrāddha at Gayā.

(10) "But," it is objected, "if the śrāddha (for the same person) is repeated over and over in this way, just because there is a difference in his specific qualification, then if, for instance, one's own father is also one's teacher, then by that special qualification also there would be another śrāddha for him." (11) It is replied : The repetition of śrāddha because of a difference in the particular qualification does not cause any

1. See 558ff.
2. See 555-557.2.

fault, if it does not produce any contradiction of such sentences as 'to the same ancestors to whom the father would offer' [612], and 'Coming to Gayā unexpectedly (one should perform śrāddha for his mother)' [558]. (12) But the text prescribing śrāddha to one's teacher etc. does not cause another śrāddha (in this case), since it fulfills its purpose by reference to a person who has as a teacher someone other than his father etc.

(13) Moreover : When the first śrāddha, which is caused by the proximate and specific qualification, namely of being the father, has been done, then there is no repetition of the śrāddha caused by the more remote and general qualification of being the teacher. (14) For in the case of a nigada prayer, when it is established that it is spoken loudly because it is a nigada, it is not pronounced softly because it is a yajus. (15) Just as the sentence prescribing soft pronunciation achieves its purpose in connection with a different yajus,[1] so the sentence prescribing śrāddha for the teacher etc. achieves its purpose in connection with another person who is only one's teacher. Enough of this !

(16) Thus it is established that even one whose father is living may perform śrāddha at a tīrtha for the deities of his father only.

(17) But when one's mother is alive, even through his father is dead, the pārvaṇa for the mother is omitted. (18) Instead, the father etc. are to be qualified as 'Together with their wives,' whenever appropriate. (19) Likewise when the maternal grandfather is alive, the pārvaṇa for him is omitted, (20) and the same when the maternal grandmother is alive; (21) but as before, a qualification (of the grandfather etc.) is to be made. Thus it is said :

619. If someone in the line of the father, or of the mother, or of the maternal grandfather, is alive, one should omit that line (from the śrāddha).

(1) Here 'in the line of the father' applies to such śrāddhas as that of the moonless day. For it has already been said that

1. See MS II.1.13.38-43. Especially note the last sentence of Śabara's commentary on sūtra 42.

according to a specific prescription, one whose father is alive does a pārvaṇa for the father's father etc. at a tīrtha. (2) Likewise in respect to the mother's family.

(3) Then, after performing śrāddha and giving piṇḍas separately to each of those who are prescribed as the deities for him, one should give a common piṇḍa, as DEVALA says :

> 620. Then taking a piṇḍa he should offer it in this way, common to his entire group of relatives, both those who have been consecrated and those who have not.

(1) 'In this way' means 'with the following mantra'; and that mantra is:

> 621. Those in my father's family who have died, and those in my mother's family who have died, and those other relatives of my guru, father-in-law and friends who are dead; and those in my family who get no piṇḍas, having no sons or wives; and those who are excluded from sacred rites, who are blind from birth, or lame, deformed, miscarried, both known and unknown, in my family—to them I give this piṇḍa. May it serve them forever !

(1) Although this is three verses, it constitutes one mantra, because by those three verses one entire sentence-meaning is fulfilled; (2) for the sage JAIMINI has defined the unity of a mantra as:

> 622. Unity of meaning establishes one sentence. If the sentence is lacking something (then that) is (placed) before the division (of the sentence);

(1) and also because of the singular number in the words of DEVALA 'Taking a piṇḍa...' [620].

(623.1) Then another piṇḍa is to be given with these two verses:

> 623. Those who were born in my father's family, up to Brahma, and those who were born in my mother's family; and those who have been slaves in both of my families, and servants, subjects, and attendants; friends, companions, animals, trees; those whom we touched, or

saw, or who have aided us; and those whom I have met in another life; to them I give this piṇḍa of ancestral food!

(2) Here too, as in the preceding, this is only one mantra (although it has two verses).

(3) After giving the piṇḍas in this way, one should conclude the śrāddha according to the rule given in the sūtras of his own school, ending by following the brāhmaṇas as they depart.

(4) But if one is not able to perform such a multitude of śrāddhas, nor to give each piṇḍa, because he is ill or does not have enough time, he may perform an abbreviated śrāddha. (5) That is as follows: after declaring, "Because of my inability (to carry out the complete rites) I will perform an abbreviated śrāddha," (624.1) he should give a single piṇḍa with the mantra:

624. Om! My father and grandfather and great-grandfather; my mother and paternal grandmother and great-grandmother; my maternal grandfather, and his father, and my maternal great-grandfather, and so on—to them I give this piṇḍa. May it serve them forever!

THUS ENDS THE DETERMINATION OF THE BENEFICIARIES IN THE TĪRTHA ŚRĀDDHA.

THUS ENDS THE SECTION ON TĪRTHA-ŚRĀDDHA IN THE GENERAL SECTION OF THE BRIDGE TO THE THREE HOLY CITIES BY NĀRĀYAṆA BHAṬṬA, SON OF THE NOBLE BHAṬṬARĀMEŚVARA SŪRI.

THE RULE OF THROWING BONES IN A TĪRTHA

(624.2) The benefit for throwing bones in any tīrtha according to rule is given in the BRAHMĀṆḌAPURĀṆA:

625. Having bathed and anointed (the bones) with the five cow-products, and mixed with them gold, honey, ghee and sesamum, then placing them in the hollow of a ball of clay, he should look in the direction embraced by the pretas.[1] Saying 'Homage to you, O Dharma', he should enter the tīrtha, and saying '(May he be) pleased with me,' should throw in the bones. Then bathing and coming out, looking at the sun, he should give the priest's fee. So doing, (even) one who is in the city of the pretas would find a place in heaven like Mahendra.

(1) 'The five cow-products' (pañcagava) is the same as the five cow-products called 'pañcagavya.'

(2) Although the attainment of heaven is mentioned here without any specification, nevertheless it is to be understood that there are different degrees of it, caused by the differences between various tīrthas. (3) There is a special rule for the Gaṅgā; in the BRAHMĀṆḌAPURĀṆA:

626. When men throw the bones of others into the Gaṅgā, from that time onward they would dwell in heaven.

(1) Since the future limit is not mentioned here, the limit must be the end of the eon, as that would be appropriate. (2) The attainment of the Brahma-world also is mentioned (as a benefit); YAMA says:

627. If the bones of a man who did auspicious deeds are thrown into the waters of the Gaṅgā, he does not return again from the eternal Brahma-world.

1. The south.

Also:

628. As long as a man's bones remain in the waters of the Gaṅgā, for so many thousands of years he rejoices in the Brahma-world.

(1) The attainment of the Brahma-world is to be considered as applying to a special place such as Prayāga, since the attainment of heaven is ascribed generally (to other tīrthas).

(2) A special rule concerning the time for that (throwing of bones):

629. One should not perform the throwing of bones into the Gaṅgā when Jupiter or Saturn are set, or in an intercalary month; so says Gautama.

Also:

630. One should not perform the throwing of bones, nor śrāddha at Gayā, nor śrāddha in the first year (after death), if sapiṇḍana has not been done.

(1) In some texts, the reading is '...even if sapiṇḍana has been done.'

Also:

631. One may perform the throwing of bones, śrāddha at Gayā, and the śrāddha of the latter fortnight even in the first year (after death) for one whose funeral ceremonies have been done.

(1) Some read the fourth quarter of the verse as '...if his son is devoted.'[1]

(2) But (if the throwing of the bones is done) within ten days (after death), then there is no fault (even though sapiṇḍīkaraṇa has not been done), according to the words:

632. If a person's bones sink in the water of the Gaṅgā within ten days (after his death), then he will obtain a benefit equal to that of dying at the Gaṅgā.

---

1. For an explanation of this reading, see Gayā Prakaraṇa, p. 347.

(1) Also, another special rule is given in a PURĀṆA:

633. That lowest of men who neglects his mother's and father's family and takes the bones of another's family must perform the cāndrāyaṇa penance.

(1) This refers to (one who does so) out of greed for money etc.

Also:

634. The tīrtha yields its benefits to those who, overwhelmed by sympathy, at any time take the bones of their mother's and father's families to the Gaṅgā, and also those of their good friends.

THE MANNER (OF THROWING BONES IN A TIRTHA)

635. I, Śaunaka, will tell the way to purify bones, step by step. After going out of his village, one should bathe with his clothes on. Then the wise man should sprinkle (the bones) with the five cow-products, with various mantras.

(1) This means that he should sprinkle the ground wherein the bones had been buried. (2) 'With the various mantras': with the mantras of the five cow products, 'Increase...' (RV I.91.16) etc.,[1] which manifest the milk, curds, etc.

636. Then come the digging and petitioning, with the mantras 'Approach...' etc. (RV X. 18. 10-13), and the removing of the earth and the taking of the bones in proper order.

(1) Śaṅkha is the seer, the ancestors are the deities, and triṣṭubh is the meter of the four mantras beginning with 'Approach...' (2) The first is used in petitioning the earth, the second in digging it, the third in removing the earth, and the fourth in taking the bones.

(3) Then, having taken the bones in this manner,

637. Going to a body of water, he should bathe properly, and then purify the bones with the mantra 'Come now, (let us praise) Indra...' (RV VIII. 95. 7), touching each of them. Then he bathes; and he is purified by the five cow products. The wise man should perform ten baths with the various mantras. Cow's urine, cow's faeces, milk, curds, ghee, water with kuśa grass, ashes, earth, honey, and water—ten are the mantra-baths. He should brush the bones with kuśa grass, with the mantra 'From this, the gods...' (RV I. 22. 16), and then with 'Come now, (let us praise) Indra,' 'May your oblations be pure,' (RV VII. 56. 12), 'Let evil not (reach) this man' (RV

1. See below, 639.2.

X. 126.1), the Pāvamānī hymn,[1] 'Mine, o Agni...' (RV X. 128.1), and the Rudra hymn (RV I. 43), in order. A wise man should recite this hymn; he thus becomes pure, nor can it be otherwise. Then he should assiduously perform a gold śrāddha for the ancestors and then give an offering of piṇḍas, and tarpaṇa with sesamum. Antelope skin, blankets, clumps of (kuśa) grass, cow's hair, hemp-cloth, birch leaf, and palm leaf; the wrapping (of the bones) is declared to be seven-fold.

(1) In some texts, however, the reading is '...cow's hairs and birch leaf, palm leaf, and netra cloth; thus, the seven items for wrapping the bones.'

He should deposit among the bones gold, pearl, silver, coral, and sapphire; thus they become pure, nor can it be otherwise. Then the wise man should give an oblation with sesamum-butter. With the hymn 'May they rise...' (RV X. 15.1) he should make the offering, (repeating the hymn) one hundred and eight times. Then, going to excellent tīrthas, there is no impurity from his touch. He should not perform excretions or washing while holding the bones.

In the KĀŚĪKHAṆḌA:

638. Dhanaṃjaya too, a religious soul, intently devoted to his mother, took her bones and set off on the road to the Gaṅgā. He bathed them with the five cow products and the five immortal foods, anointed them with perfumed ointment[2] and worshipped them with flowers, and covered them with netra cloth and then with silk cloth, then with sweet-smelling cloth and red-dyed cloth,

((1) 'Sweet-smelling cloth' is white China-silk.)

and with a Nepal blanket, and with purified clay. Then that merchant, who slept on bare earth, who had not

---

1. The hymn IX.67.21; see below, 639.4.
2. For a full description of 'yakṣakardama', see Kāśī Prakaraṇa p. 226, lines 25-27.

touched a low-born man, and was pure, putting the limbs of his mother in a bronze casket...

VYĀSA says:

639. Silk cloth, kauśeya-silk, red-dyed cloth, white cloth, a blanket, silk and hemp cloth, and antelope skin after that...

(1) There is an optional choice as to these wrapping materials and the order of wrapping (the bones with them).

THE GUIDE FOR THIS PROCEDURE

(639.2) One should go to wheie the bones were buried, bathe with his clothes on and sprinkle the earth where the bones were buried with milk with the mantra 'Increase...' (RV I. 91.16), with curds with the mantra 'Of Dadhikrāvan' (RV IV. 39. 6), with cow's urine with the Gāyatrī mantra (RV III. 62. 10), with cow's dung with the mantra 'By the smell...' (RV Kh V. 87. 9), and with ghee with the mantra 'I pour the ghee' (RV II. 3. 11). Then reciting the four mantras beginning with 'Approach..' (RV X.18.10-13) (of which mantras (the seer) is Śaṅkha, (the deities) are the ancestors, (and the meter) is triṣṭubh, the use of the first is in petitioning the earth, of the second in digging it, of the third in removing the dirt, and of the fourth in taking the bones) and doing these actions with these mantras in order, he should bathe in the body of water holding the bones, and wash them with the five cow-products with the hymn 'Come now, (let us praise) Indra' (RV VII. 95.7), and bathe them with pure water. (3) Then he should perform the ten baths with the bones; with cow's urine with the Gāyatrī; with cow's dung with 'By the smell...'; with milk with 'Increase...'; with curds with 'of Dadhidrāvan...'; with ghee with 'I pour the ghee'; with water with kuśa grass with 'For you, O waters, are...' (RV X. 9. 1); with ashes with 'Not on our young ones...' (RV I. 114.8); with clay with the mantras mentioned in the Gṛhyapariśiṣṭa such as 'Truly, thus, of the mountains...' (RV V. 84.1), or with the mantras 'Travelled by horses, travelled by chariots...' (TA X. 1. 8) etc.; with honey with 'The winds (rain) sweet...' (RV I. 90. 6); and with pure water with 'For you, O waters, are...' (4) After thus doing the ten baths, he should wipe the bones with kuśa grass with these mantras: the hymn 'Come now, (let us praise) Indra'; the hymn 'May your oblations be pure' (RV VII. 56. 12); the hymn 'Let evil not (reach) this man;' the hymn 'Thus indeed my mind...' (RV X. 119. 1); 'Which is near and which is far...' (RV IX. 67. 21) and other Pāvamānī hymns; the ṛc 'Mine, O Agni, be your glory'; and the Rudra hymn (RV I. 43).

(639.5) Then he should do a gold śrāddha, with three deities for an ancestor who has had the sapiṇḍīkaraṇa done for him, or as an ekoddiṣṭa for an ancestor who has not. (6) This deity of this śrāddha is the one whose bones (are being used).

(7) After this he should give piṇḍas of grits in the same way, also perform tarpaṇa with oil in the same way, and anoint (the bones) with fragrant paste etc., worship them with flowers, wrap them with the antelope skin etc. in one of the four ways previously mentioned,[1] and place on the bones gold, pearls, silver, coral and sapphires. (8) Then he should make a sesamum-butter offering (repeating) the hymn 'May they rise...' (RV X. 15. 1) one hundred and eight times. (9) Of the hymn 'May they rise,' (the seer is) Śaṅkha, (the deities are) the ancestors, (and the meter is) triṣṭubh.

(10) Then, putting the bones in a bronze casket, he should go to the tīrtha pure, without touching an untouchable, an out-caste, or the like. (11) Then after bathing in the tīrtha with the bones and placing them in a folded palāśa-leaf, he should declare "I am throwing the bones of so-and-so Śarma,[2] of such-and-such a gotra, into such-and-such a tīrtha, that he may reach the Brahma-world and never return." Then he should wash the bones with the five cow-products, mix them with a piece of gold, honey, ghee, and sesamum, put them in a ball of clay, and, looking to the south, standing in water to his navel, throw them into the tīrtha with the mantra 'Homage to King Dharma ! May he be pleased with me !' Then he should bathe, come out of the water, look at the sun, bow, and thinking of Hari say "I give this silver, sacred to the moon, to a brāhmaṇa, for the success of this throwing of bones, done so that so-and-so Śarma of such-and-such a gotra might reach the Brahma-world." He should give as much silver as he can, since this is an ancestral rite.[3] (12) All this is to be without facing the south, and with the sacred thread on the right shoulder (apasavyam).

(13) This is to be done at any tīrtha, (14) but especially at

1. In 637, 637.1, 638, and 639.

2. Śarma is used in rituals as the last name of any brāhmaṇa. For 'so-and-so' (amuka) the personal name of the deceased is to be substituted.

3. Silver is the appropriate material for offerings in ancestral rites, as opposed to gold in divine rites. Cf. 474 above.

the Gaṅgā, according to the previously quoted words [626ff.]. (639.15) Refined people say that this is also to be done especially at Prayāga. (16) The benefit arising from such an action has been previously stated [625ff].

(17) Concerning this, DIVODĀSA and others say: "After doing this, the whole (rest of) the procedure of a tīrtha is to be done." (18) Others, however, think that "The throwing of the bones cannot fall within the ritual of the tīrtha, since that would cause a contradiction in the form of a combination of regular and non-regular acts; and since it is prohibited to delay the śrāddha etc., it is not permissible to delay that (śrāddha) by this action which is non-mandatory, as (it is possible to delay it) by bathing etc.[1] And there is no statement prescribing that it must be done immediately after (arrival at the tīrtha). Therefore by the rule 'Incidentals are placed at the end,' the throwing of the bones is to be done immediately *after* finishing the tīrtha rites of bathing and so on." (19) Those who know the rules, however, say "If one goes to the tīrtha with the benefit caused by throwing the bones as his intended purpose, then it is to be done first: for that text (which prescribes śrāddha) permits a delay in the śrāddha etc. if it is caused by the intended purpose (of the pilgrimage); nor can the intended purpose be said to cause a delay in the tīrtha ritual, as that (intended purpose) is included within the tīrtha ritual itself. (20) Therefore, the bathing according to the rule which is occasioned by the tīrtha[2] is also to be done only *after* (the throwing of the bones). (21) But if someone goes with the benefit of the tīrtha as his intended purpose, and takes the bones along in addition, he should throw them in after performing the whole tīrtha ritual." (22) Such being the case, the refined people are the authority in this matter.

THUS ENDS THE RULE OF THROWING BONES IN THE GENERAL SECTION OF THE BRIDGE TO THE HOLY CITIES.

---

1. See above, 381.1.
2. See above, 207.1 and 209.2 (note).

MISCELLANEOUS LAWS OF TĪRTHAS

DEVALA says:

640. Tarpaṇa of the gods and ancestors, giving of śrāddha with fees, and giving cows; this is the basic fixed rule for every tīrtha. At especially famous liṅgas, giving of bulls is prescribed, and one should perform there bathing, anointment, and worship of the deities, and should give land to brāhmaṇas or the one who performs worship. This rule applies in every divine pilgrimage.

Also:

641. Beholding the gods is auspicious; touching them is better than beholding them. Worshipping them is greater than touching them; bathing them with ghee is greater yet. The wise say that bathing with Gaṅgā water is the same as bathing (the gods) with ghee, with mantras muttered eight times and with great amounts of incense.

(1) The word 'ghee' implies the five immortal foods. (2) In 'worshipping' such substances as scents, flowers, etc. which are not prohibited for the various gods are to be used.
(3) For the sun there is a special rule:

642. Whoever gives the water offering once to the sun with Gaṅgā water, the best substance for the water offering, measuring a Magadhan prastha,[1] and placed in a bronze cup—he rejoices in heaven with his own ancestors and his sons and grandsons.

(1) The water offering has eight ingredients; in the SKANDAPURĀṆA:

643. Water, milk, tips of kuśa grass, ghee, honey, cow-curds, red oleander, and red sandal; this water offering with eight parts is said to be extremely pleasing to the Sun.

1. According to the commentary on this śloka in the Skandapurāṇa, a Magadhan prastha is equal to 12 1/2 palas.

(1) There is a special rule for circumambulation:

644. One should make one (circumambulation) for Caṇḍī, seven for the Sun and three for Vināyaka (Gaṇeśa). Four are to be made for Viṣṇu, and for Śiva half of a circumambulation.

Also:

645. When making a circumambulation for Śiva, one must not cross the soma-sūtra.

(1) We shall give in the Kāśī section the measurement of the soma-sūtra, and explain that there is no fault (for crossing the soma-sūtra if the circumambulation is) for Viśveśvara etc.[1]

(2) There is also a special rule for paying homage:

646. One should not perform prayer, oblation, or homage in a temple in front, behind, on the left side, nearby, or in the inner chamber. (If one does these) in front, he dies; in back, he suffers a loss, it is said; on the left, he is destroyed. But on the right, (homage) yields all desires.

(1) For Śiva, however, it may be done in front also:

647. Falling on the ground like a rod in front of Paśupati, Lord of Beasts, all the sins of a creature fall away, and do not rise up with him.

Another rule is given in the DEVĪPURĀṆA:

648. Removing the wreaths from the gods, cleaning up the god's chamber, and bathing all the gods is said to have the benefit of giving a cow.

(1) 'Cleaning up' means sweeping etc., and also restoring any thing that has fallen down.

Also in the PADMAPURĀṆA :

---

1. See Kāśī Prakaraṇa pp. 210-212.

649. One must never touch the money, food, fruit, or water belonging to Śiva, nor may one violate the remains of his offerings. One must throw them all in a well. A man who, out of greed or foolishness, lives off what belongs to Śiva, even as much as a fly's foot, burns in hell till the end of the eon.

But in the BRAHMAPURĀṆA :

650. What is placed on the body of Brahma and on that of Viṣṇu, one should give to brāhmaṇas; but one should immediately burn in the fire all of what is placed on the body of Rudra (Śiva). Whatever was (offered) to other gods one should give to the destitute. What was dedicated to the Mothers should be given to brāhmaṇas; and what was dedicated to Gaṇeśa and others should also be given to brāhmaṇas (vāḍava).

(1) We will mention (later) an exception in the case of Viśveśvara.[1]

(2) At a tīrtha one must refrain from accepting gifts etc. In the PADMAPURĀṆA :

651. A tīrtha can be ruined for the sake of survival ; a vow can be ruined for the sake of survival. False and slanderous speech are also ruinous. One must not accept gifts at a tīrtha, even with his dying breaths. Even a creature mad with desire protects at least his mother; but acceptance of gifts at a tīrtha is the same as selling the tīrtha. When the Gaṅgā is sold, then Janārdana (Viṣṇu) is sold; when Janārdana is sold, the three worlds are sold.

652. If a brāhmaṇa out of greed wishes to accept gifts in a sacred place, there is no world beyond for that evil one, nor even this world. Brāhmaṇas weak in wisdom who accept great gifts (there)—those Brahma-demons are born as trees with a brāhmaṇa's form. One must not desire to accept gifts, relying on the strength of the

1. See Kāśī Prakaraṇa p. 213, lines 16ff.

Veda. Whether because of ignorance or foolishness, his ritual acts are burnt up; this cannot be avoided. Standing at the king's door, one would not sell the Veda; the lowest of twice-born men should rather kill a cow and eat its flesh. And if a brāhmaṇa accepts a gift when he is hard pressed for sustenance, he should give away a tenth part of what he has received; then it is not lost.

In the KŪRMAPURĀṆA :

653. Should he accept a gift..., whatever benefit he would gain from it in his own rites, or in those of another, or in the worshipping of a god, that tīrtha bears no benefit for him. Therefore one must not accept gifts at a tīrtha or at auspicious shrines, or on all special occasions;[1] a brāhmaṇa must be vigilant.

(1) These two verses also appear in the MATSYAPURĀṆA.

(2) Concerning this, it is said in the KALPATARU: "As long as a man enjoys the wealth accepted as a gift (at a tīrtha), as long as a man who has accepted gifts at the tīrtha continues to keep possession of that wealth obtained there, for so long he cannot generate the benefit of donations etc. at a tīrtha, which benefit is characterized by such qualities as being multiplied by ten million. (3) But by discarding that wealth he does generate that proper benefit for himself." (4) Someone else says that "This also applies only when it is not done willfullye when, for example, some powerful person insists (that one accept a gift); but if it is done willfully, there can be no benefit at all, because he has sold the tīrtha."

In the SṚṢṬIKHAṆḌA of the PADMAPURĀṆA :

654. A sin committed elsewhere becomes insignificant at a tīrtha; but nothing elsewhere removes a sin committed at a tīrtha.

In the MAHĀBHĀRATA :

---

1. The TiCi (p. 45) explains 'special occasions' as 'astronomical passages etc.'

655. If one dwells at a tīrtha after overcoming desire, anger, and greed, there is nothing which he could not attain by going to that tīrtha. ($\approx$172)

In the UTTARAKHAṆḌA of the PADMAPURĀṆA :

656. One should not commit a sin at a tīrtha; one should avoid living off the tīrtha. Accepting gifts at a tīrtha is to be avoided, as is selling of the Dharma. A sin committed at a tīrtha is hard to atone for, and so is acceptance of gifts (there). Everything done at a tīrtha is hard to atone for; one who does such things goes to hell.

In the GARUḌAPURĀṆA :

657. The forest deities protect a mendicant who goes to a tīrtha. My emissaries especially are near to him, not those of Yama. If, though he always stayed at a tīrtha, he dies somewhere else, he is born in an auspicious land as a wise, Veda-knowing brāhmaṇa.

Also :

658. A sin committed in the home is cleansed by bathing in a tīrtha. But if, after always giving everlasting gifts there, one commits a sin there, that, O Bird, (sticks to him) like cement. Surely, he will suffer (for that) as long as the sun, moon, and stars remain.

Also :

659. A god is never found in wood or rock; for god is found in love. Therefore one should rely on love.

In the NĀRADĪYA PURĀṆA :

660. Going to auspicious places, frequenting auspicious tīrthas, and sacrifices of all kinds do not, O Brahma, protect a man who has abandoned proper conduct.

DEVALA says :

661. At rivers, one should not speak of (another) river; on

mountains, one should not speak of (another) mountain. When present at tīrthas and holy places, one should not praise another place.

Also :

662. That tirtha among (all) places, and that most auspicious river; one should meditate on these in his mind, without conceiving a desire for another place.

(1) This applies during bathing. (2) These two sayings refer to places other than the Gaṅgā, as is said in the SKANDAPURĀṆA :

663. When bathing at other tīrthas, people pray to the Jāhnavī (=Gaṅgā). Except for the Viṣṇupadī (Gaṅgā), what other place can cleanse sins ?

Also in the BRAHMAPURĀṆA :

664. At other tīrthas, men call to mind the Gaṅgā. Therefore there is no tīrtha like the Gaṅgā in the whole universe.

(1) After the pilgrimage etc. is done, it should be dedicated to Viṣṇu. Thus it is said in the BRAHMAPURĀṆA :

665. Whatever tīrthas (one has visited), and whatever gifts, vows, and austerities (one has made), they all become successful by being dedicated to the feet of Viṣṇu. People in this world do not dedicate their various auspicious acts to Hari. Those acts are fruitless here; their only result is exhaustion.

DEVALA says :

666. A forest is the place of the deities, as are tīrthas and shrines. Therefore a person who lives in them goes to the heaven world of the gods.

Also :

667. A man who is unable to perform the rites of sacred texts and law-books should frequent tīrthas and practice vows and austerities.

(1) One who goes for the sake of the journey generally stays at the tīrtha for three days, according to the words of DEVALA :

668. Having arrived at the tīrtha, keeping vows, fasts, and voluntary observations, bathing for three days and staying there (fasting) for three nights, one is freed from all sins. (≈ 225)

(1) But where a longer (stay) is specifically mentioned, that too is to be done.

(2) If one comes en route upon a river other than the Sarasvatī, then he should bathe etc. on the farther side; but on the nearer side of the Sarasvatī. Thus it is said :

669. If one comes en route upon a river, he should bathe etc. on the farther side; but on the nearer side of the Sarasvatī; this is the rule concerning the route.

As for the sentence :

670. If a man crosses rivers without performing tarpaṇa for his ancestors, they are sorely pained and desire to drink his blood, (≈332)

(1) that refers to the Sarasvatī. (2) The plural number ('rivers') is used because there are many of them (rivers named 'Sarasvatī'). (3) Or else, 'crossing' here means 'going in violation'; then the meaning is 'One should not proceed without having performed bathing, tarpaṇa etc., even at a river which he has come upon (unintentionally) en route. (671.1) Thus ŚAṄKHA prohibited passing over (a river) :

671. One should not pass beyond a stream without having sprinkled water.

(2) 'Without having sprinkled water' means without having performed tarpaṇa. (3) In both of these sentences, 'tarpaṇa' implies bathing also, since tarpaṇa comes immediately after it.

(4) When one comes en route upon a famous river, he should also perform śrāddha, as the same rule applies (to śrāddha).

(5) This bathing on the farther bank of rivers applies when there is no special tīrtha on the nearer side. When there is, one should bathe etc. on the nearer side; for if he were to ignore that (tīrtha), he would incur a fault. (6) But if there is a special tīrtha on the farther side of the Sarasvatī, he should perform bathing etc. on the farther bank also after (first) performing it on the nearer side; this is the correct interpretation.

(7) Now, for the sake of the (correct application of) the prohibition of accepting gifts etc., the interior and other sections of a tīrtha are defined. Thus in the BRAHMAPURĀṆA :

672. Taking the current as the limit, for a distance of four hands Nārāyaṇa is the owner; there is never any other owner. And there one may not accept gifts, even with his dying breaths.

(1) Here 'current' implies the limit of (still) water.[1] (2) Therefore this prohibition applies within four hands from the limit of the water of every tīrtha, including those such as Puṣkara which have the form of a tank, pool, etc.

In the Dānadharma (section of the MAHĀBHĀRATA) :

673. As far as the water advances on the fourteenth day of the bright half of the month of Bhādra, that is to be known as the interior (of the tīrtha); beyond that it is called the bank.

(1) Even though sometimes because of a lack of rain there is no increase in the amount of water on the fourteenth day of the bright half of the month of Bhādra, still this particular area (the interior) is implicitly indicated by that increase which will occur in some future year, according to the rule

674. The two sacrificial cakes are (merely) an indication.[2]

---

1. That is to say, this rule implicitly applies to standing as well as to flowing water.

2. The upāṃśuyāja of the darśa-pūrṇamāsa sacrifice is prescribed as being done between the offerings of the two sacrificial cakes. In MS X.8.18.62-70, it is determined that these two cakes are merely an indication of the time

(1) The limit of the bank is given in the BRAHMAPURĀṆA :

675. (The area) for one hundred and fifty hands, up to the interior, is called the bank.

In the SKANDAPURĀṆA :

676. (The area) measured by a gavyūti from the bank in all directions is the field. At the Gaṅgā donation, prayer, and oblations are surely to be done there.

(1) The field measures for a gavyūti, which is two krośas, on each of the two banks. Therefore it is said in the BHAVIṢYA-PURĀṆA :

677. All sins without exception cannot cross the limit of the Gaṅgā; they flee (from it) in ten directions, like deer who have seen a lion. The field on both banks extends for one yojana.[1]

(1) The prohibition of accepting gifts applies in the interior at renowned rivers. (2) But at especially renowned rivers such as the Gaṇḍakī the prohibition applies also on the bank which measures one hundred and fifty hands on both sides; so say the refined people. (3) But the prohibition in the field applies only to the Gaṅgā, since the field is discussed only in connection with the Gaṅgā [676-677].

As for what is said in the BRAHMAPURĀṆA:

678. Wherever is the Gaṅgā, there is Śambhu (Śiva), (and) a forest for practice of austerities: the area for three yojanas around is considered a field of success,

---

for the upāṃśuyāja, rather than the defining characteristic of that time; so that even when only one cake is used the upāṃśuyāja is not dropped. Likewise, the water on the fourteenth bright day of Bhādra is merely an indication of the 'interior' of a tīrtha. Thus even in a year in which the normal increase of water at this time fails to occur, the 'interior' is still the same as it is in a normal year.

1. 1 yojana= 4 krośas= 2 gavyūtis. Thus 1 gavyūti on each bank gives a total of yojana.

(1) by 'for three yojanas around' is meant for one and one half yojanas on each side. This is meant to express the special virtue of dying there (in the field of success), not to (indicate the application of) the prohibition of accepting gifts there. (2) But when the reading is '..for half a yojana around,' then the sense is the same as that of the SKANDAPURĀṆA passage [676].[1]

(3) Now, the special rule for worshipping liṅgas etc.; in the NĀRADĪYAPURĀṆA:

679. If a man bows to a liṅga or a Viṣṇu-image which has been worshipped by a śūdra, he cannot make atonement, even with tens of thousands of penances. Likewise if he bows to a liṅga or an image of Hari which has been touched by a śūdra, he experiences all the torments for as long as the moon and stars remain. Bowing to a liṅga worshipped by heretics, he becomes a heretic; bowing to a liṅga worshipped by Ābhīras, he goes to hell. But he who bows to a liṅga or a Viṣṇu-image worshipped by women lives in the Raurava hell till the end of the eon, together with tens of millions of others.

(1) All this refers to liṅgas etc. erected in modern times, not to those ancient ones of great fame; for it is said in the same text:

680. When a liṅga is erected correctly by those who know the mantras, from then on a śūdra or a woman cannot touch it.

Thus it is said in the SKANDAPURĀṆA, concerning the liṅga of Kāśī:

681. Those which are attractive and those which are not, O Dear One, and those which are in bad condition, and which are broken by time; (all) these are to be worshipped, O Beautiful One !

(1) Here 'in bad condition' means touched by untouchables.

---

1. That is to say that the distance specified applies on *each* bank, so that the total measurement is double the figure given, as in th Skandapurāṇa passage quoted above.

(2) There is also another special rule given in the same text:

682. Women, the uninitiated, and śūdras do not, O Lord of men, have the authority to erect figures of Viṣṇu or Śaṅkara (Śiva). A man who would bow to a liṅga or Viṣṇu image consecrated by a śūdra sees extreme sorrow even in this world—and how much more in the next ! A śūdra or a non-initiate, a woman or an outcaste who touches Keśava (Viṣṇu) or Śiva goes to hell.

(1) Another special rule:

683. For a year after the death of his father,[1] one should not make a trip to a great tīrtha, nor perform fasts and vows.

Also:

684. For one year after the death of his father one should not bathe at a tīrtha, give great gifts, eat another's food, or perform tarpaṇa with sesamum. A Veda-knowing husband of a pregnant woman would avoid shaving the head, sexual intercourse, tīrthas, and śrāddha anywhere after the seventh month.

(1) 'Śrāddha' refers to eating of śrāddha offerings.

LALLA says:

685. When there is an eclipse of the sun or moon, a half-rising,[2] or the sixth day known as 'kapilā'[3] the rule of pilgrimage to a tīrtha is recommended, even if Jupiter or Venus is set, or if there is an astronomical passage.

(1) 'Upaplava' is the same as 'grahaṇa', 'eclipse.' (2) The setting of Jupiter and Venus is an implicative state-

1. 'Mahāguru' is to be taken here as 'father'; cf. *Nirṇayasindhu* p. 2104

2. A 'half-rising' day is a moon-less day (amā) in the months of Pauṣa or Māgha which falls on a Sunday, whose nakṣatra is Śravaṇa, and on which there is a vyatīpāta. See *Samaya-mayūkha*, p. 67.

3. A 'Kapilā-sixth' is a sixth day of the dark half of the month Bhādra which falls on a Tuesday, whose nakṣatra is Rohiṇī, and on which there is a vyatīpāta. See *Samaya-mayūkha*, p. 24.

ment; (3) thus it means that when there is an eclipse etc., there is no fault (in doing pilgrimage) at other forbidden times as well.[1]

(4) They say there is no fault in a pilgrimage whose purpose is throwing bones even if it is done during the first rain.[2]

Also, in the DHARMAVIVṚTTI:

686. He gets the complete benefit, whose fasting, vow, oblation, tīrtha-bathing, prayer etc. is effected for him by brāhmaṇas.

Also:

687. Shaving is not prescribed for those who live at a tīrtha within a year (since their last shaving); nor for those who come (to the tīrtha) from another place, unless it is specially occasioned.

Also:

688. In the midst of water, in a cowpen, at tīrthas, and during parvans, and also at the time of seeing Rāhu (i.e. at an eclipse), there is no birth-impurity at all.

(1) This is considered to apply to donations etc. when one intends to go to another place immediately.[3]

Also:

689. A gift is tenfold in the home; in a cowpen, one hundredfold; at auspicious tīrthas, one thousandfold; in the presence of Śiva, it is infinite.

Further:

690. One should not worry there about which gods are at which tīrtha, or which brāhmaṇas are at which tīrtha, or what water is at what tīrtha.

---

1. For the prohibition of pilgrimage when Venus or Jupiter are set and at other times, see above, 138ff.
2. Otherwise a prohibited time; see above, 346ff.
3. I.e., in such a case one should do the donation etc. even while sūtaka still applies; but otherwise he should wait to perform it until the impurity has ceased.

(1) The sense is that there is no fault even if they (the gods etc.) are overlooked.

Also:

691. God is not on the peaks of mountains; God is not in the abode of Viṣṇu. God who consists of consciousness and bliss is seen in heaven through love. Wherever and whenever the devotion of a great-souled man is strong, there the Great God is pleased with him;

and so on.

(1) Enough of this:—

THUS ENDS THE CHAPTER ON THE MISCELLANEOUS LAWS OF THE TĪRTHA
IN THE GENERAL SECTION OF THE BRIDGE TO THE THREE HOLY CITIES
BY NĀRĀYAṆA BHAṬṬA, SON OF THE REVERED
BHAṬṬA RĀMEŚVARA SŪRI, THE REVERED CROWN-JEWEL IN
THE CROWN OF THE WISE;
AND THE GENERAL SECTION IS FINISHED.
AFTER THIS WILL COME THE SECTION ON PRAYĀGA.

BIBLIOGRAPHY

A. *Sanskrit Texts and Translations*

AGNI PURĀṆA. Ed. by the paṇḍits of the Ānandāśrama. Ānandāśrama Sanskrit Series 41. Puṇyākhyapattana (Poona): Ānandāśramamudraṇālaya, 1900.

AṄGIRAḤ SMṚTI. In SMṚTĪNĀṂ SAMUCCAYAḤ, pp.1-8.

ATRI SMṚTI. In SMṚTĪNĀṂ SAMUCCAYAḤ, pp. 9-27.

APARĀRKA. See YĀJÑAVALKYA.

AMARAKOŚA. See NĀMALIṄGĀNUŚĀSANA.

ĀŚVALĀYANA GṚHYA SŪTRA. Ed. Puruṣottama Śāstrī Rānaḍe, with the commentary of Nārāyaṇa, the Gṛhya-pariśiṣṭa, and the kārikās of Bhaṭṭa Kumārila. Ānandāśrama Sanskrit Series 105. Puṇyākhyapattana (Poona): Ānandāśramamudraṇālaya, 1936.

ĀŚVALĀYANA ŚRAUTA SŪTRA. Ed. Rāmanārāyaṇa Vidyāratna, with the commentary of Gārgya Nārāyaṇa. Bibliotheca Indica work 49. Calcutta: Asiatic Society, 1874.

UŚANAS (AUŚANASA SMṚTI). In SMṚTĪNĀṂ SAMUCCAYAḤ, pp. 46-48.

ṚG VEDA SAṂHITĀ. The Sacred Hymns of the Brāhmans, together with the commentary of Sāyaṇāchārya. Ed. F. Max Müller. Varanasi: The Chowkhamba Sanskrit Series Office, 1966. (1st Indian edition.)

AITAREYA BRĀHMAṆA with the commentary of Sāyāṇācārya. Ed. Kāśīnātha Śāstrī Āgāśe. Ānandāśrama Sanskrit Series 32. Puṇyākhyapattana (Poona): Ānandāśramamudraṇālaya, 1896. 2 vols.

KĀTYĀYANA ŚRAUTA SŪTRA, with the commentary of KARKĀCĀRYA. Ed. Vidyāratna Śarmā. Chowkhamba Sanskrit Series 19. Benares: Chowkhamba Sanskrit Series Office, 1933-34.

KĀTYĀYANA SMṚTI, In DHARMAŚĀSTRASAṄGRAHA, vol. 1, pp. 603-644.

KĀLAVIVEKA, (A Part of DHARMARATNA), A Treatise on Hindu Law and Rituals by Jīmūtavāhana. Ed. Pan. Pramathanātha Tarkabhūṣaṇa, Bibliotheca Indica work 136. Calcutta: Asiatic Society of Bengal, 1905.

THE KŪRMA PURĀṆA. Critically edited by Anand Swarup Gupta. Varanasi: All-India Kashiraj Trust, 1971.

KṚTYAKALPATARU of Bhaṭṭa Lakṣmīdhara. Ed. K. V. Ramaswami Aiyyangar. Gaekwad's Oriental Series 92, 98, 100, 101, 102, 106, 110-112, 119, 123. Baroda: Oriental Institute, 1941-53. 11 vols.

GARUḌA PURĀṆA. Ed. Jīvānanda Vidyāsāgara. Calcutta: Sarasvatī Press, 1890.

GOBHILA GṚHYA SŪTRA with a commentary by the Editor. Ed. Chandrakānta Tarkālaṃkāra. Bibliotheca Indica work 73. 2nd ed., Calcutta: Asiatic Society of Bengal, 1880. 2 vols.

GOBHILA [GṚHYA SŪTRA] PARIŚIṢṬA. Ed. Chandrakānta Tarkālaṃkāra. Bibliotheca Indica work 183. 2nd ed., Calcutta: Asiatic Society of Bengal, 1909.

GOBHILA SMṚTI. In SMṚTĪNĀṂ SAMUCCAYAḤ, pp. 49-71.

CATURVARGACINTĀMAṆI of Hemādri. Ed. Paṇḍita Bharatachandra Śiromaṇi et al. Bibliotheca Indica work 72. Calcutta: Asiatic Society of Bengal, 1873-1911. 4 vols.

CATURVIṂŚATIMATASAṂGRAHA by Bhaṭṭoji Dīkṣita. Ed. Paṇḍit Devidatta Parājuli. Benares Sanskrit Series 33. Benares: Messrs. Braj B. Das & Co., 1907.

CHĀNDOGYOPANIṢAD, with the commentary of Rangarāmānuja. Ed. Gaṇeśa Śāstrī Gokhale. Ānandāśrama Sanskrit Series 63. Puṇyākhyapattana (Poona): Ānandāśramamudraṇālaya, 1910.

JAIMINĪYA NYĀYAMĀLĀ, with the author's own commentary VISTARA, by Mādhavācārya. Ed. Śivadatta Śarmā. Ānandāśrama Sanskrit Series 24. Puṇyākhyapattana (Poona) : Ānandāśramamudraṇālaya, 1892.

The TANTRARATNAM of Pārthasārathimiśra. Ed. Ganganatha Jha et. al. Princess of Wales Saraswati Bhavana Texts 31. Benares: Government Sanskrit Library, 1930-63. 3 vols.

TANTRAVĀRTIKA of Kumārila Bhaṭṭa. In MĪMĀṂSĀDARŚANA, q. v.

TANTRAVĀRTIKA of Kumārila Bhaṭṭa, translated into English by Gaṅgānātha Jhā. Bibliotheca Indica work 161. Calcutta: Asiatic Society of Bengal, 1924. 2 vols.

TĪRTHAKAMALĀKARA: See LAGHU-TRISTHALĪSETUḤ.

TĪRTHACINTĀMAṆI of Vācaspati Miśra. Ed. Kamalakrishna

Smrititirtha. Bibliotheca Indica work 195. Calcutta: Asiatic Society of Bengal, 1912.

TĪRTHATATTVAM (or TĪRTHAYĀTRĀTATTVAM) of Raghunandana Bhaṭṭācārya. Ed. Bama Charan Kavyatirtha Bhattacharya. Sanskrit Sahitya Parishad Series 12. Calcutta: Sanskrit Sahitya Parishad, [1925?]. (Bengali characters.)

TĪRTHAPRAKĀŚA of Mitramiśra. Vol. 10 of VĪRAMITRODAYA, q. v.

TĪRTHAVĪVECANAKĀṆḌA. Vol. 8 of KṚTYAKALPATARU, q. v.

TĪRTHENDUŚEKHARA by Nāgeśabhaṭṭa. Ed. Surya Narayana Sukla. Princess of Wales Saraswati Bhavana Texts 66. Benares: Government Sanskrit Library, 1936.

TAITTIRĪYA BRĀHMAṆA with the commentary of Sāyaṇācārya. Ed. Nārāyaṇa Śastrī Goḍabole. Ānandāśrama Sanskrit Series 37. Puṇyākhyapattana (Poona): Ānandāśramamudraṇālaya, 1898. 3 vols.

TAITTIRĪYA SAṂHITĀ with the commentary of Sāyaṇācarya. Ed. Kāśīnātha Śāstrī Āgāśe. Ānandāśrama Sanskrit Series 42. Puṇyākhyapattana (Poona): Ānandāśramamudraṇālaya, 1900. 8 vols.

TAITTIRĪYĀRAṆYAKA, with the commentary of Sāyaṇācārya and the Pariśiṣṭa. Ed. Bābāśāstrī Phaḍke. Ānandāśrama Sanskrit Series 36. Puṇyākhyapattana (Poona): Ānandāśramamudraṇālaya, 1898. 2 vols.

The TAUTĀTITAMATATILAKA of Śrī Bhavadeva. Ed. Pt. A. Chinnaswamy Sastri. Princess of Wales Saraswati Bhavana Texts 79. Benares: Government Sanskrit Library, 1942-44. 3 vols.

TRISTHALĪSETU of Nārāyaṇa Bhaṭṭa. Ed. Gaṇeśa Śāstrī Gokhale. Ānandāśrama Sanskrit Series 78. Puṇyākhyapattana (Poona): Ānandāśramamudraṇālaya, 1915.

TRISTHALĪSETUPRAGHAṬṬAKE SARVATĪRTHAVIDHIPRAGHAṬṬĀKHYAḤ PRATHAMO BHĀGAḤ [i.e. the Sāmānya-praghaṭṭaka of the Tristhalīsetu] by Nārāyaṇa Bhaṭṭa. Ed. Śrī Vāpu Ācārya and Bhāvu Ācārya. Kāśī [Benares]: Published by the editors at the Candraprabhā Press, 1908.

TRISTHALĪSETUSĀRASAṂGRAHA by Bhaṭṭoji Dīkṣita. Ed. Surya Narayana Sukla. Princess of Wales Saraswati Bhavana Texts 65. Benares: Government Sanskrit Library, 1936.

DEVALA SMṚTI. In SMṚTĪNĀṂ SAMUCCAYAḤ, pp. 85-89.

DEVĪ PURĀṆA. Ed. with Bengali translation by Pañcānana Tarkaratna. Calcutta: Vangavāsī Press, 1896. (Bengali characters.)

DHARMAŚĀSTRASAṂGRAHA. Ed. Jīvānanda Vidyāsāgara Bhaṭṭācārya. Kalikātā (Calcutta): Sarasvatīyantrālaya, 1876. 2 vols.

The NĀMALIṄGĀNUŚĀSANA (AMARAKOŚA) of Amarasiṃha with the commentary of Bhānuji Dīkṣita. Ed. Pandit Śivadatta of Jaypur. 6th ed., revised by Nārāyaṇ Rām Ācharya "Kāvyatīrtha". Bombay: Published by Satyabhāmābāi Pāṇḍuraṅg for the Nirṇaya Sāgara Press, 1944.

NIRṆAYASINDHU of Kamalākara Bhaṭṭa, with a commentary by Kṛṣṇaṃ Bhaṭṭa. Ed. Pandit Gopāl Śāstrī Nene. Chowkhamba Sanskrit Series 52. Benares: Chowkhamba Sanskrit Series Office, 1930.

NYĀYAKOŚA, or Dictionary of Technical Terms of Indian Philosophy, by Bhīmācārya Jhaḷakīkara, revised and re-edited by Vāsudeva Shāstri Abhyankar. Bombay Sanskrit and Prakrit Series 49. Poona: Bhandarkar Oriental Research Institute, 1928.

NYĀYARATNAMĀLĀ of Pārthasārathimiśra. Ed. Śrī Gaṅgādhara Śāstrī Mānavalli. Chowkhamba Sanskrit Series 7. Kāśī (Benares): Tārāyantrālaya, 1900.

NYĀYASUDHĀ, a commentary of *Tantravārtika*, by Paṇḍit Someśvara Bhaṭṭa. Ed. Paṇḍit Mukunda Śāstrī. Chowkhamba Sanskrit Series 14. Benares: Chowkhamba Sanskrit Book-Depôt. 1909.

PADMA PURĀṆA. Ed. Viśvanātha Nārāyaṇa Rāvasāheba Maṇḍalīka. Puṇyākhyapattana (Poona): Ānandāśramamudraṇālaya, 1893. 4 vols.

PADMA PURĀṆA. Bombay: Veṅkaṭeśvara Press, 1927.

PĀṆINI'S GRAMMATIK [AṢṬĀDHYĀYĪ], herausgegeben, übersetzt, erläutert...von Otto Böhtlingk. Leipzig: H. Haessel, 1887.

PĀRASKARAGṚHYASŪTRAM, PARIŚIṢṬAKAṆḌIKĀ CA. Ed. and published by Paṇ. Devanāthaśarmā Cāturmāsyayājī and Paṅ. Bālamukunda Śarmā Bhaṭṭa Adhvaryu, with Paṇ. Hanumaddatta Śarmā. Kāśī (Benares): Saṃvat 1952 [=A. D. 1896].

PRAYOGARATNA (NĀRĀYAṆABHAṬṬĪ) and ANTYEṢṬIPADDHATI

(UTTARANĀRĀYAṆĪ) of Nārāyaṇa Bhaṭṭa. Ed. Vāsudeva Śarmā Paṇaśīkara. Bombay: Nirṇaya Sāgara Press, 1937.

The Yājñavalkyasmṛti with the Commentary BĀLAKRĪḌĀ of Viśvarūpācārya. Ed. T. Gaṇapati Sāstrī. Trivandrum Sanskrit Series 74. Trivandrum: Government Press, 1922.

BṚHASPATI SMṚTI (Reconstructed) by Rangaswamy Aiyangar. Gaekwad's Oriental Series 85. Baroda: Oriental Institute, 1941.

BODHĀYANA GṚHYA SŪTRA. Ed. R. Shama Sastri. Mysore Sanskrit Series 32 and 55. Mysore: University of Mysore, 1920.

BRAHMA PURĀṆA. Ed. by the paṇḍits of the Ānandāśrama. Ānandāśrama Sanskrit Series 28. Puṇyākhyapattana (Poona): Ānandāśramamudraṇālaya, 1895.

BRAHMA PURĀṆA. Bombay: Veṅkaṭeśvara Press, 1906.

BRAHMAVAIVARTA MAHĀPURĀṆA. Bombay: Veṅkaṭeśvara Press, 1889.

BRAHMĀṆḌA PURĀṆA. Ed. Ācārya Jagadīśa Śāstrī. Delhi: Motilal Banarsidass, 1973.

BHAGAVAD GĪTĀ. In MAHĀBHĀRATA, q. v., VI. 23ff.

BHAVIṢYA MAHĀPURĀṆA. [Ed. Govinda Paraśurāma Bhaṭṭa]. Bombay: Śrīveṅkaṭeśvara Press, 1197.

BHĀṬṬADĪPIKĀ of Khaṇḍadeva. Ed. Chandrakānta Tarkālaṃkāra and Pramathanātha Tarkabhūṣaṇa. Bibliotheca Indica work 143. Calcutta: Asiatic Society of Bengal, 1912. 2 vols.

MATSYA PURĀṆA. Ed. by the paṇḍits of the Ānandāśrama. Ānandāśrama Sanskrit Series 54. Puṇyākhyapattana (Poona): Ānandāśramamudraṇālaya, 1907.

The MADANAPĀRIJĀTA, A System of Hindu Law, by Madanapāla. Ed. Paṇḍit Madhusūdana Smṛtiratna. Bibliotheca Indica work 114. Calcutta: Asiatic Society of Bengal, 1893.

The MAHĀBHĀRATA. Ed. by Vishnu S. Sukthankar et al. Poona: Bhandarkar Oriental Research Institute, 1933-1972. 19+6 vols.

MĀNAVA DHARMAŚĀSTRA: The Code of Manu. Original Sanskrit Text Critically Edited...by J. Jolly. London: Trübner and Co., 1887.

MĀRKAṆḌEYA PURĀṆA. Ed. K. M. Banerjea. Bibliotheca Indica work 29. Calcutta: Asiatic Society of Bengal, 1862.

The Yājñavalkyasmriti or the Institutes of Yājñavalkya with the commentary MITĀKṢARĀ of Vijñāneshvara. Ed. Bapu Shastri Moghe. 3rd ed., Bombay: Janārdan Mahādev Gurjar, 1882.

MĪMĀṂSĀKOṢAḤ. Ed. Kevalānanda Sarasvatī. Wai [Maharashtra], Prājña Pāṭhaśālā Maṇḍala, 1952-66. 7 vols.

MĪMĀṂSĀDARŚANAM of Jaimini [comprising the MĪMĀṂSĀ SŪTRAS of Jaimini, the BHĀṢYA of Śabara, and the ŚLOKAVĀRTIKA, TANTRAVĀRTIKA, and ṬUPṬĪKĀ of Kumārila Bhaṭṭa]. Ed. Subbaśāstrī Tīrthahaḷḷī. Ānandāśrama Sanskrit Series 97. Puṇyākhyapattana (Poona): Ānandāśramamudraṇālaya, 1929-34. 6 vols.

The MĪMĀṂSĀ-NYĀYA-PRAKĀŚA or ĀPADEVĪ: A Treatise on the Mīmāṃsā System by Āpadeva. Ed. and trans. Franklin Edgerton. New Haven: Yale University, 1929.

MĪMĀṂSĀBĀLAPRAKĀŚA of Śrī Śaṅkara Bhaṭṭa. Ed. Paṇḍit Mukunda Shāstri. Chowkhamba Sanskrit Series 16. Benares: Chowkhamba Sanskrit Book-Depot, 1902.

MĪMĀṂSĀ SŪTRAS. See MĪMĀṂSĀDARŚANAM.

MĪMĀṂSĀ-SŪTRAS: The Aphorisms of the Mīmāṃsā. Ed. Paṇḍita Maheśachandra Nyāyaratna. Bibliotheca Indica work 45. Calcutta: Asiatic Society of Bengal, 1873-1889. 2 ʌols.

The MUHŪRTACINTĀMAṆI of Śrī Rāmadaivajña. Ed. with 'Maṇiprabhā' Hindi commentary by Pt. Kapileśvara Śāstrī. Haridas Sanskrit Series 185. 2nd ed., Varanasi (Benares): Chowkhamba Sanskrit Series Office, 1969.

MEDHĀTITHI: In MĀNAVA-DHARMA-ŚĀSTRA with the commentaries of Medhātithi, Sarvajñanārāyaṇa, Kullūka, Rāghavānanda, Nandana, and Rāmachandra. Ed. Vishvanath Nārāyan Mandlik. Bombay: Ātmārām Kanoba, 1886. 2 vols.

MAITRĀYAṆĪYA PARIŚIṢṬA: In Caland, *Altindische Ahnencult*, pp. 228-39, as MĀNAVAŚRĀDDHAKALPA+PARIŚIṢṬA.

MAITRĀYAṆĪ SAṂHITĀ. Ed. Leopold von Schroeder. Leipzig: Deutsche Morgenländische Gesellschaft, 1881-86. 4 parts.

YAMA SMṚTI. In SMṚTĪNĀṂ SAMUCCAYAḤ, pp. 112-16.

YĀJÑAVALKYA SMṚTI with the commentary of APARĀRKA. Ed. by the paṇḍits of the Ānandāśrama. Ānandāśrama Sanskrit Series 46. Puṇyākhyapattana (Poona), Ānandāśramamudraṇālaya, 1903. 2 vols.

RATNAMĀLĀ. Ed. Rasikamohana Caṭṭopādhyāya. Calcutta: Jyotiṣa Prakāśa, 1321 [Bengali Saṁvat=1915 A. D.].

RĀJATARAṄGIṆĪ of Kalhaṇa. Ed. Vishva Bandhu. Hoshiarpur: Vishveshvaranand Vedic Research Institute, 1963-65. 2 vols.

RĀMATĀPANĪYOPANIṢAD with Commentaries by Ānandavana. Ed. Gopi Nātha Kavirāja. Princess of Wales Saraswati Bhavana Texts 24. Benares: Government Sanskrit Library, 1927.

LAGHU-TRISTHALĪSETUḤ by Kamalākara Bhaṭṭa. Benares: Rājarājeśvarī Press, 1952 [Saṃvat = 1895 A. D.].

LAGHVĀŚVALĀYANA SMṚTI. In SMṚTĪNĀṂ SAMUCCAYAḤ, pp. 142-181.

VARĀHA PURĀNA. Bombay: Veṅkaṭeśvara Press, Śaka 1845 [= A. D. 1923].

VASIṢṬHA SMṚTI. In SMṚTĪNĀṂ SAMUCCAYAḤ, pp. 187-231.

VĀCASPATYAM (Bṛhatsaṃskṛtābhidhānam) by Śrī Tārānātha Tarkavācaspati Bhaṭṭācārya. Chowkhamba Sanskrit Series 94. Vārāṇasī (Benares): Chowkhamba Sanskrit Series Office, 1962. 6 vols.

VĀJASANEYĪ SAṂHITĀ in Mādhyandina and Kāṇva-śākhā, with the Commentary of Mahīdhara. Chowkhamba Sanskrit Series 103. 2nd ed., Varanasi: Chowkhamba Sanskrit Series Office, 1972.

VĀJASANEYĪ SAṂHITĀ of the White Yajur-Veda with the commentaries of Uvvaṭa and Mahīdhara. Ed. Pandit Ram Sakala Misra. Kāśī Sanskrit Series 34. Benares: Chowkhamba Sanskrit Book Depot, 1912-15. 4 pts.

VĀMANA PURĀṆA. Bombay: Veṅkaṭeśvara Press, 1903.

VĀYU PURĀṆA. Ed. by the paṇḍits of the Ānandāśrama. Ānandāśrama Sanskrit Series 49. Puṇyākhyapattana (Poona): Ānandāśramamudraṇālaya, 1905.

ŚRĪ VIṢṆU PURĀṆA (with Hindi translation by Śrī Muni Lāl Gupta). Gorakhpur: Gītā Press, [1967].

VIṢṆU SMṚTI with the Commentary Keśavavaijayantī of Nandapaṇḍita. Ed. Pandit V. Krishnamacharya. Adyar Library Series 93. Madras: Adyar Library, 1964. 2 vols.

VĪRAMITRODAYA of Mitra Miśra. Ed. Parvatīya Nityānanda Śarmā et al. Chowkhambā Sanskrit Series 30. Benares: Chowkhambā Sanskrit Book-Depôt, 1913-36. 21 vols.

VEDAPRAKĀŚA of Śrī Satyajñānānandatīrtha. Ed. Paṇ. Paṭṭābhirāma Śāstrī. Chowkhamba Sanskrit Series 77. Benares: Chowkhambā Sanskrit Series Office, 1939.

VEDĀNTADARŚANAM [VEDĀNTA SŪTRAS], with a Commentary called

Brahmāmṛtavarṣiṇī by Śrī Rāmānanda Sarasvatī Swāmī. Ed. Prajñānānanda Sarasvatī Swāmī. Chowkhambā Sanskrit Series 36. Benares: Chowkhambā Sanskrit Book Depôt, 1911.

VYAVAHĀRAMAYŪKHA of Bhaṭṭa Nīlakaṇṭha, with an Introduction, Notes and Appendices. Ed. P. V. Kane. Bombay Sanskrit and Prakrit Series 80. Bombay: Bhandarkar Oriental Research Institute (Poona), 1926.

The VYAVAHĀRA MAYŪKHA in Original, with an English Translation...Ed. Vishvanāth Nārāyan Mandlik. Bombay: Education Society's Press, 1880.

ŚAṄKHA SMṚTI. In SMṚTĪNĀṂ SĀMUCCAYAḤ, pp. 374-395.

Dharma-sūtra of ŚAṄKHA-LIKHITA. Ed. P. V. Kane in *Annals of the Bhandarkar Institute* VII (1926) pp. 101-128 and VIII (1926) pp. 93-132.

ŚATAPATHA BRĀHMAṆA in the Mādhyandina-Śākhā with extracts from the Commentaries of Sāyaṇa, Harisvāmin, and Dvivedagaṅga. Ed. Albrecht Weber. Chowkhamba Sanskrit Series 96. 2nd ed., Varanasi (Benares): Chowkhamba Sanskrit Series Office, 1964.

ŚABARA BHĀṢYA: See MĪMĀṂSĀDARŚANAM.

SHABARA-BHĀṢYA, translated into English by Ganganatha Jha. Gaekwad's Oriental Series 66, 70, 73. Baroda: Oriental Institute, 1933-36. 3 vols.

ŚABDAKALPADRUMA by Rādhākānta Bāhādur. Chowkhambā Sanskrit Series 93. Vārāṇasī: Chowkhamba Sanskrit Series Office, 1961. 5 vols.

ŚĀNKHĀYANA GṚHYA SŪTRA. Ed. Hermann Oldenberg in *Indische Studien* XV, pp. 1-166. Leipzig : F. A. Brockhaus, 1878.

ŚĀTĀTAPA SMṚTI. In SMṚTĪNĀṂ SAMUCCAYAḤ, pp. 396-410.

ŚRĀDDHAKĀṆḌA: Vol. 4 of KṚTYAKALPATARU, q. v.

ŚRĀDDHAPRAKĀŚA: Vol. 9 of VĪRAMITRODAYA, q. v.

ŚRĀDDHAMAYŪKHA of Nīlakaṇṭha Bhaṭṭa. Ed. M. G. Bakre and V. R. Lele. Bombay: Gujarātī Press, 1920.

ŚRĀDDHAVIVEKASAṀGRAHA of Śūlapāṇi. Ed. Mathurānātha Tarkaratna. Calcutta: Prākṛtayantra, 1886. (Bengali characters.)

SAMAYAPRAKĀŚA: Vol. 13 of VĪRAMITRODAYA, q. v.

SAMAYAMAYŪKHA of Nīlakaṇṭha Bhaṭṭa. Ed. Mahadeva Gangadhar Bakre and Vyankatesha Ramachandra Lele. Bombay: Gujarati Press, 1918.

SKANDA PURĀṆA. Bombay: Veṅkaṭeśvara Press, Śaka 1830 [= A. D. 1908]. 6 vols.

SMṚTICANDRIKĀ of Devanabhaṭṭa; Śrāddhakāṇḍa. Ed. L. Srinivasacharya. Oriental Research Institute Sanskrit Series 52. Mysore: Oriental Research Institute, 1918.

Aṅgiraḥprabhṛtibaudhāyanāntānāṃ saptaviṃśatisaṃkhyāmitānāṃ SMṚTĪNĀṂ SAMUCCAYAḤ. Ed. by the paṇḍits of the Ānandāśrama. Ānandāśrama Sanskrit Series 48. Puṇyākhyapattana (Poona): Ānandāśramamudraṇālaya, 1905.

SMṚTYARTHASĀRA OF Śrīdhara. Ed. Ranganātha Śāstrī Vaidya. Ānandāśrama Sanskrit Series 70. Puṇyākhyapattana (Poona): Ānandāśramamudraṇālaya, 1912.

HIRAṆYAKEŚI-GṚHYA-SŪTRA, with Extracts from the Commentary of Matṛdatta. Ed. J. Kirste. Vienna: Alfred Holder, 1889.

B. *Works in Western Languages*

Apte, V. S.: *The Practical Sanskrit-English Dictionary*. Poona: Prasad Prakashan, 1957. 3 vols.

Aufrecht, Theodor: *Catalogus Catalogorum: An Alphabetical Register of Sanskrit Works and Authors*. Wiesbaden: Franz Steiner Verlag, 1962. 2 vols.

Banerji, Sures Chandra: *A Glossary of Smṛti Literature*. Calcutta: Punthi Pustak, 1963.

Bloomfield, Maurice: *Vedic Concordance*. Harvard Oriental Series 10. Cambridge : Harvard University, 1906.

Böhtlingk, Otto, and Roth, Rudolph: *Sanskrit-Wörterbuch*. St. Petersburg: Kaiserliche Akademie der Wissenschaften, 1855-75. 7 vols.

Caland, W.: *Altidische Ahnencult: Das çrāddha nach den verschiedenen Schulen mit Benützung handschiftlicher Quellen dargestellt*. Leiden: E. J. Brill, 1893.

Eggeling, Julius: *Catalogue of the Sanskrit Manuscripts in the Library of the India Office*, vol. I part 1. London: India Office Library, 1887.

Garge, Vishnu Damodar: *Citations in Śabara-bhāṣya (A Study)*. Deccan College Dissertation Series 8. Poona: Deccan College, 1952.

Hazra, R. C.: *Studies in the Purāṇic Records on Hindu Rites and Customs*. Dacca: University of Dacca, 1940.

Jacob, Colonel G. A.: *Laukikanyāyāñjaliḥ: A Handful of Popular Maxims Current in Sanskrit Literature*. Bombay: Tukārām Jāvajī (Nirṇaya Sāgara Press), 1900-04. 3 vols.

Jha, Ganganatha: *Pūrva-Mīmāṁsā in its Sources*. Library of Indian Philosophy and Religion, Vol. 1. Benares: Benares Hindu University, 1942.

Kane, Pandurang Vaman: *History of Dharmaśāstra (Ancient and Medieval Religious and Civil Law)*. Poona: Bhandarkar Oriental Research Institute, 1930-62. 5 vols.

Katre, S. M.: *Indian Textual Criticism* (with Appendix II by P.K. Gode). Poona: Deccan College, 1954.

Mitra, Rajendralal: *Notices of Sanskrit Manuscripts*. Calcutta: Government of Bengal, 1871-1900. 12 vols.

Monier-Williams, Sir Monier: *A Sanskrit-English Dictionary*. New Edition. Oxford: Clarendon Press, 1899 (reprint 1960).

Poleman, H.I.: *A Census of Indic Manuscripts in the United States and Canada*. American Oriental Series 12. New Haven: American Oriental Society, 1938.

Renou, Louis: *Vocabulaire du rituel védique*. Paris: Librairie C. Klincksieck, 1954.

Salomon, Richard : "The Three Cursed Rivers of the East, and their Significance for the Historical Geography of Ancient India", *Adyar Library Bulletin* XLII (1978), pp. 32-60.

Salomon, Richard : "*Tīrtha-pratyāmnāyāḥ* : Ranking of Hindu Pilgrimage Sites in Classical Sanskrit Texts", *Zeitschrift der Deutschen Morgenländischen Gesellschaft* CXXIX, 1979, pp. 102-28.

Shastri, Haraprasad: "Dakshini Pandits at Benares," *Indian Antiquary* XLI (1912), pp. 7-13.

Shastri, Haraprasad: *A Descriptive Catalogue of Sanskrit Manuscripts in the Government Collection under the Care of the Asiatic Society of Bengal;* Vol. III: *Smṛti Manuscripts*. Calcutta: Asiatic Society of Bengal, 1925.

APPENDIX A

INDEX OF TĪRTHAS AND OTHER GEOGRAPHICAL NAMES

(The main sources for the geographical identification of tīrthas, cited below, are Nundo Lal Dey's *Geographical Dictionary of Ancient and Medieval India* (London 1927), and the "List of Tīrthas" in P. V. Kane's *History of Dharmaśāstra*, vol. IV, pp. 723-825).

AGNITĪRTHA: A tīrtha on the south bank of the Yamunā (Kane p. 731). 239.2.

AMARAKAṆṬAKA: A mountain in eastern Madhya Pradesh, source of the rivers Narmadā and Son. 370.

AYODHYĀ: Modern Ayodhya on the Gharghara, near Faizabad, Uttar Pradesh. One of the seven holy cities of India. 130.11.

AVIMUKTA(KA): = Vārāṇasī. 6, 232, 237.

ĀMRĀTAKEŚVARA: Probably a sub-tīrtha of Vārāṇasī. 130.11.

KAKUDMINĪ: Probably the modern Kumadvati River, a tributary of the Tuṅgabhadrā near Harihara, Karnataka. 130.30.

KARATOYĀ (= SADĀNĪRĀ): A river in north Bengal (now Bangla Desh). 200, 200.1, 202, 203, 203.1.

KARMANĀŚĀ (not a tīrtha !): The modern Karamnas, flowing between Bhojpur District of Bihar and Mirzapur District of Uttar Pradesh. See text and translation, 199.3 ff. 130.62, 199.3, 200, 200.1, 200.2.

KĀÑCĪ: Modern Kanchipuram in Tamil Nadu. One of the seven holy cities. 130.11.

KĀVERĪ: The modern Cauvery River in Karnataka and Tamil Nadu. 130.46.

KĀŚĪ (= Vārāṇasī): 237.1, 246.1, 250.2, 262.30, 264.2, 540.6, 544.1, 544.4, 545.1, 545.7, 545.12, 545.15 (2X), 545.16, 680.

KĪRTIMĀLĀ: The modern Vaigai River in Tamil Nadu, on which is situated the city of Madurai. 130.47.

KUBJĀMRA: A Himalayan tīrtha, = Māyā (Haridwar). 62, 130.11, 370.

KUBJIKĀ: A river flowing into the Narmadā. 130.13.

KURAṄGA: Perhaps = Koringa, near the mouth of the Godāvarī (Dey p. 109). 201.

KURUKṢETRA: The sacred region of Punjab (now in Haryana State) between the rivers Dṛṣadvatī and Sarasvatī. 58.3, 59, 62, 69, 119, 130.11, 226, 277.11, 354.1, 370, 372, 373.

KUŚATARPAṆA: A tīrtha at the confluence of the Godāvarī and Praṇītā Rivers. 130.22.

KUŚĀVARTA: A tīrtha at Tryambaka, near Nasik, Maharashtra (Dey p. 111). 370.

KṚṢṆAVEṆĀ: The modern Krishnavena and Krishna in Karnataka and Andhra Pradesh. 130.25, 130.35, 130.37.

KṚṢṆĀ: The river Krishna, which rises in southern Maharashtra and flows through Karnataka and Andhra Pradesh. 254.

KEDĀRA: Modern Kedarnath tīrtha in Tehri Garhwal, Uttar Pradesh. 61, 130.11, 130.71, 370.

KOKA: A river, perhaps = Kauśikī. 354.

KOKĀMUKHA: A tīrtha in Purnea District, Bihar; or in Nepal (see D. C. Sircar, *Indian Historical Quarterly* XXI, pp. 56-60). 130.11.

KOṆĀDITYA: Konarak in Puri District, Orissa. 265.1.

KAUŚIKĪ: Either the modern Kosi or Kusi River in Rohilkhand (Uttar Pradesh); or the Kosi of Nepal and Tirhut. 130.2.

GAṄGĀ: The Ganges, holiest river of India. 57 (2X), 58, 129.6, 129.9, 130, 130.36, 130.75, 200.1, 218, 228.3, 228.4, 233, 244, 246.1, 254, 256, 256.1, 257, 258, 259 (2X), 259.2, 259.11 (4X), 259.12, 264.3 (2X), 265.3, 278.8, 297.1, 306.1, 307, 353.1, 354, 355, 356, 357, 357.1, 359.1 (2X), 361, 370, 372, 383, 409, 544.4, 545.13 (2X), 625.3, 626, 627, 628, 629, 632, 634, 638, 639.14, 641, 642, 651, 662.2, 664 (2X), 676, 677, 677.3.

GAṄGĀDVĀRA: The famed tīrtha of Haridwar in northwestern Uttar Pradesh, near the source of the Ganges. 62, 129.10, 370, 373.

GAṄGĀSĀGARA (SAṂGAMA): Modern Sagar Island in 24 Parganas, West Bengal, where the Ganges enters the ocean. 122.1, 129.10.

GAṆA: = Gaṇamukteśvara, modern Garhmuktesar in Meerut District, Uttar Pradesh. 130.11.

GAṆḌAKĪ: The modern Gandak River of north Bihar, entering the Ganges near Patna. 130.2, 677.2.

GAṆḌAKĪBĀHU: Probably the Choti Gandak (Little Gandak), a tributary of the Gharghara in eastern Uttar Pradesh. 200.

GAYĀ: Modern Gaya, the great tīrtha of south Bihar. 130.11, 149, 150 (2X), 151, 155, 155.1, (2X), 226, 228.1, 228.2, 228.3, 259.11, 269.1, 274.3, 274.4, 274.6, 274.8, 274.9, 275.3, 277.1, 277.3, 277.10, 342, 370, 372, 373, 442, 554.8, 555, 556, 557, 557.1, 558, 558.1, 558.2, 558.4, 558.6, 576.1, 578.2, 587.4, 599.6, 601, 605.4, 617.9, 617.11, 618, 618.2, 618.4, 618.6, 618.7, 618.9, 618.11, 630, 631.

GAYĀŚĪRṢA: A hill at Gayā. 606.

GOKARṆA: Modern Gokarn, a Śaiva tīrtha on the west coast of India, south of Goa. 130.11.

GODĀVARĪ: The great river of Maharashtra and Andhra Pradesh. 55, 130.18, 130.33, 149, 151, 350, 370.

GOMATĪ: The modern Gumti of Avadh, entering the Ganges near Benares. 130.2, 254, 358.

GAUTAMĪ: =Godāvarī. 355.

GHARGHARA: The modern Ghaggar River in Avadh and north-eastern Uttar Pradesh. 66, 354.

GHṚTAVATĪ: Not identified. 130.1.

CAKRAKOṬA: Not identified. 130.77.

CAKRAPUṢKARIṆĪ: A tank at Benares. 545.

CANDRABHĀGĀ: The modern Chenab, one of the five great rivers of the Punjab. 130.2, 358.

CITRAPATHĀ: The river Chitrarathi or Chitravati, a tributary of the Pennar in southern Andhra Pradesh (Dey p. 50). 384.

JĀHNAVĪ: =Gaṅgā. 130.34, 130.35, 130.70, 130.71, 130.72, 255, 297, 299, 349, 663.

JVĀLĀMUKHĪ: A tīrtha in Kangra District, Himachal Pradesh, located on a volcanic outlet. 130.10.

TĀPĪ: The modern Tapti River in Maharashtra and Gujarat, flowing into the Arabian Sea near Surat. 55, 130.15, 350.

TĀMRAPARṆĪ: The modern Tambravari River in Tirunelveli District, Tamil Nadu (Dey p. 203). 130.47.

TUṄGABHADRĀ: A river of Karnataka and Andhra Pradesh, entering the Krishna near Kurnool. 55, 130.26, 130.36, 130.39, 350.

DṚṢADVATĪ: The ancient river which formed the southern boundary of Kurukṣetra. Its modern identification is problematic. Most scholars identify it with the Chitang. 130.1, 170.

DEVAPRAYĀGA: The confluence of the Bhāgīrathī and Alakanandā Rivers in Tehri District of northern Uttar Pradesh. 231.8, 24.32.

DEVIKĀ: Either the Deva River in Avadh, the lower portion of the Śarayū; or the Deeg in Punjab (see D. C. Sircar, *Studies in the Geography of Ancient and Medieval India*, Delhi 1971, pp. 49-50). 130.2.

DVĀRAVATĪ: Modern Dvarka, at the western tip of the Kathiawar Peninsula. One of the seven holy cities. 129.14, 130.11.

NARMADĀ: The great river of Maharashtra, entering the Arabian Sea at Broach. 55, 57, 130, 130.11, 130.12, 351, 358, 370, 373.

NITYAJALĀ: Not identified. 130.2.

NIVṚTTI: A river in the south, flowing into the Krishna. Not otherwise identified. 130.32, 130.40.

NĪLAPARVATA: A holy hill near Haridwar. 370.

NAIMIṢA, NAIMIṢĀRAṆYA: The forest country around modern Nimsar in Avadh. 58.3, 59, 61, 62, 69, 130.11, 228.1, 370, 372, 373.

PAÑCANADA: (1) The combined stream of the five rivers of the Punjab. 130.11. (2) The (mythical) place where five rivers (Gaṅgā, Yamunā, Sarasvatī, Dhūtapāpā, and Kiraṇā) meet. Usually located at Benares (see Kane p. 636), but here at Prayāga. 238.

PADMANĀBHA: Modern Padmanabhapuram (also called Ananta-padmanabha, Anantpur) near Kanyakumari, Tamil Nadu. 130.11, 130.77.

PAMPĀ: A tributary of the Tuṅgabhadrā in Bellary District, Karnataka (Dey p. 144). 130.27.

PAYASVINĪ: (1) Modern Paisuni, a tributary of the Yamunā in Banda District, Uttar Pradesh. 130.1. (2) Modern Papanasini River in Travancore (Dey p. 156). 130.47.

PAYOṢṆĪ: A tributary of the Tāpī in the western Deccan (see text, 130.17). Not, as some say, = Pen-ganga, as that is not a tributary of the Tāpī, nor = Pūrṇā, as that is enumerated separately in the text (130.24). 55, 130.16, 350.

PĀTĀLAGAṄGĀ: A subterranean river near Śrīśaila. 130.42.

PUṆḌARĪKA: Pandharpur, a tīrtha on the south bank of the Bhīmarathī in Sholapur District, Maharashtra. 171.

PUṆYĀRAṆYA: Not identified. 130.11.

PURĪNDRA: Not identified. 130.11.

PURUṢOTTAMA: Jagannathapuri (Puri), Orissa. 130.11, 130.77.

PUṢKARA: The great tīrtha of Rajasthan, near Ajmer. 54.1, 58.3, 59, 60, 61, 62, 69, 90.4, 97.2, 130.11, 228.1, 228.2, 236 (2X), 368, 370, 371 (2X), 372, 373, 672.2.

PŪRṆAPUṆYĀ: Not identified. 130.2.

PŪRṆĀ: A tributary of the Godāvarī in Parbhani District, Maharashtra. 130.24.

POṢYA: Variant of Koka, q. v. 66.

PAUNAḤPUNYĀ: The modern Punpun River in Bihar, entering the Ganges near Patna. 130.2.

PRAṆĪTĀ: The modern Pranahita River, which forms the border between Chanda District, Madhya Pradesh and Adilabad District, Andhra Pradesh. 130.23.

PRABHĀSA: The great tīrtha of Somnath on the southern coast of the Kathiawar Peninsula. 53, 54.1, 129.14, 130.11, 169, 235.8, 250.1, 264.2, 370.

PRAYĀGA: Modern Allahabad, at the confluence of the Ganges and Yamuna. 9, 62, 63, 64, 110, 118, 118.1 (3X), 118.5, 129.10, 156, 231.1, 231.2, 231.7, 231.8, 233.3, 234, 234.1, 234.2, 235.2, 235.4, 235.5, 235.7, 235.8, 235.11 (2X), 235.19, 238, 238.2, 239.1, 240.2, 244.1, 245, 245.1, 246.1, 246.2, 259.1, 259.11, 260.1, 260.2, 262.12, 262.15, 262.17, 262.23, 262.24, 262.26 (2X), 262.29, 262.31, 262.35, 264.1, 264.3 (2X), 274.7, 275.3, 277.7, 278.3, 278.6, 289.5, 370, 372, 373, 544.1, 544.4, 545.2, 545.14, 628.1, 639.15.

PHALGUTĪRTHA: A tīrtha on the Phalgu River of south Bihar (=Gayā?). 370.

BADARĪ: =Badaryāśrama, q. v. 62.

BADARYĀŚRAMA: Modern Badrinath in Garhwal, Uttar Pradesh. 130.11,

BĀHUDĀ : Modern Dhabala or Burha-rapti River in Avadh (Dey p. 131). 130.2, 373.

BILVAKA : A tīrtha mentioned in the MBh and several Purāṇas, but its location is not known. 370.

BRAHMAYONI : A cave on a hiil at Gayā (according to some, = Gayāśīrṣa). 38.01.

BRAHMEŚVARA : A tīrtha at Śrīśaila on the Krishna. 130.41.

BHADRAKARṆAKA : A tīrtha of Mahādeva on the bank of the western Narmadā River ; modern Karnapur or Karnali (Dey p. 31). 370.

BHĀGĪRATHĪ : = Gaṅgā. 55, 56.4, 129.2, 129.5, 129.8. (Also a tributary of the Gaṅgā in the Himalayas: see under Devaprayāga.)

BHĀSKARAKṢETRA : = Koṇāditya (Konarak). See text, 265.1, 256.1, 257, 259.11, 264.3 (2x).

BHĪMARATHĪ : The modern Bhima River, tributary of the Krishna in southern Maharashtra and northern Karnataka. 55, 130.29, 130.38, 350.

BHĪMEŚVARA : Probably modern Bhimavaram near the mouth of the Godāvarī. 130.21.

BHṚGUTUṄGA : A mountain on the east bank of the Gandak in Nepal. 370, 373.

MAṆIKARṆĪ, MAṆIKARṆIKĀ : A famous ghat at Benares. 207, 220, 544.4, 544.7, 545.1, 545.4, 545.5, 545.6. 545.7, 545.12, 545.15, 545.16, 545.19, 546.2.

MATHURĀ : On the Yamuna in western Uttar Pradesh; one of the seven holy cities. 129.12, 130.11.

MADHUMATĪ : A river in Kashmir, tributary of the Vitastā. 130.1.

MANDĀKINĪ : The modern Mandakin River, a tributary of the Paisuni (Payasvinī) in Bundelkhand. 130.2.

MARUDVṚDHĀ : The modern Marudwardhan or Marubardhan River, a tributary of the Chenab in Kashmir (Dey p.127). 130.1.

MALĀPAHĀRIṆĪ : The modern Malaprabha River, a tributary of the Krishnaveni in Karnataka. 130.31, 130.37.

MALLIKĀRJUNA : A tīrtha at Śrīśaila. 130.42.

MAHĀNADĪ: A great river of Madhya Pradesh and Orissa. 130.11.

MAHĀLAKṢMĪDARŚANASTHĀNA : Not identified. 130.77.

MAHĀLAYA : = Oṃkāranātha or Amareśvara tīrtha at Mandhata on the Narmadā in eastern Madhya Pradesh (Dey pp. 117, 142). 130.11.

MĀTṚTĪRTHA : A tīrtha on the north bank of the Narmadā (KūPu II. 41. 40; Kane p. 781). 247 (2x).

MĀNASA : Lake Manasarovar in western Tibet. 60.

MĀYĀPURĪ : A tīrtha near Haridwar. 217.2.

MĀHĪṢMATĪ : Maheshwar tīrtha on the Narmadā, 40 miles south of Indore, Madhya Pradesh. 130.9.

YAMUNĀ : The sacred river of Uttar Pradesh, modern Jumna. 55, 129.11, 129.15, 130, 170, 351, 354, 355.1, 356.

RUDRAKOṬI : A tīrtha of Kurukṣetra; or (Dey p. 171) "on the Nerbuda [Narmadā] near its source." 130.11.

LIṄGĀLAYA : Not identified. 130.44.

LOṆĀRA : The tīrtha of Lenar in Berar, near Melshar (Dey pp. 115, 39). 130.77, 227.1.

LOHITA : The Brahmaputra River of eastern India. 66, 354.

VAÑJARĀ : The Manjara, a tributary of the Godavari in Nizamabad District, Andhra Pradesh. 130.22.

VARĀHAPARVATA : A mountain at Baramula, Kashmir. 370.

VĀRĀṆASĪ : Benares in eastern Uttar Pradesh, the holiest city of India. 5, 64, 65, 129.10, 234, 370, 373.

VĀRUṆĪ : Probably = Vāraṇā or Vāruṇā, a river at Benares. 130.2.

VIJAYEŚA : A famous tīrtha of Kashmir, near modern Bijnor. 130.11.

VITASTĀ : The modern Jhelum River of Kashmir. 55, 130.1.

VIPĀŚĀ : The modern Beas River in Punjab. 130.1.

VIRAJA : Modern Jajpur tīrtha in Orissa. 226, 226.1, 227, 227.1, 228.

VIŚĀLA : Probably = Ujjāyinī, modern Ujjain in western Madhya Pradesh. 226, 228.2, 259.11.

VIŚOKĀ : A river in Kashmir, the modern Veśan (Kane p. 823). 55, 351.

VIṢṆUPADĪ : = Gaṅgā. 663.

VIHASTĀ : Probably a variant for Vitastā, q. v. 351.

VEṆIKĀ : The Wain-ganga, a tributary of the Godāvarī in Madhya Pradesh. 55, 350.

VEṆĪ : The confluence of the Gaṅgā and Yamunā at Prayāga. 544.4.

VETRAVATĪ : The modern Betwa River, a tributary of the Yamunā in Madhya Pradesh and Uttar Pradesh. 130.2, 370.

ŚAṄKODDHĀRA : An island, now called Baṭi, off Okha at the tip of the Kathiawar Peninsula. 122.1.

ŚATADRU : The modern Sutlej River in Punjab. 66, 354.

ŚAMBHALAGRĀMA : The town of Sambhal in Moradabad District, Uttar Pradesh (Rohilkhand). 130.11.

ŚARAYŪ : The modern Sarju River, a tributary of the Gharghara in Bahraich District, Uttar Pradesh. 130.2, 358.

ŚARĀVATĪ : Probably the modern Rapti River of Avadh. 130.1.

ŚĀLAGRĀMA : A tīrtha at the source of the Gandak River in Nepal. 130.11, 418, 442.14.

ŚUKLATĪRTHA : A tīrtha on the north bank of the Narmadā near Broach. 130.14.

ŚUTUDRĪ : = Śatadru, q.v. 130.1.

ŚUNĪ : (Not a tīrtha !) A cursed river (see text). Not located. 130.62.

ŚOṆA : The modern Son River, a major tributary of the Ganges in Madhya Pradesh and Bihar. 66, 130.7, 354.

ŚRĪRAṄGA : Modern Śrīraṅgam on the Kāverī near Trichonopoly (Tirucchirapalli). 130.11, 130.77.

ŚRĪŚAILA, ŚRĪPARVATA : A holy hill on the Krishna River in Kurnool District, Andhra Pradesh. 130.11, 130.49, 149, 370.

SADĀNĪRĀ : = Karatoyā, q. v.

SAṂNIHITĪ, SAṂNIHATĪ : = The region around Kurukṣetra (? See Kane, p. 801). 130.11, 373.

SAPTAGODĀVARA : The seven mouths of the Godāvarī, i.e. its delta region in Andhra Pradesh. 130.21.

SARASVATĪ : (1) The holy river of the Punjab, which flows through Kurukṣetra (see text, 354.1). 55,57,130, 170, 351,354, 354.1, 355, 356, 370, 372, 668.2 (2x), 669, 670. 1, 671.6. (2) A river in Gujarat (the 'Pratyaksarasvatī'; Dey p. 181). 129.13, 129.15.

SAHASRAVAKTRĀ : Not identified. 130.2.

SINDHU : The Indus River of modern Pakistan. 66, 354, 358.

SINDHUSĀGARA : The confluence of the Indus with the ocean in Sindh. 62.

SETU, SETURĀMEŚVARA : The tīrtha at 'Adam's Bridge' between India and Śrī Laṅkā (Ceylon) in Tamil Nadu. 130.11, 130.68, 130.70, 130.73.

HARIHARA : Modern Harihar tīrtha on the Tuṅgabhadrā near Chitaldrug, Karnataka. 130.28.

HIMĀCALA : The Himalayas. 370,

HIMĀLAYA : = Himācala. 373.

HIRAṆYĀKṢA : A river; not identified. 66.

HIRAṆYĀKHYA : = Hiraṇyākṣa. 354,

APPENDIX B

INDEX OF QUOTATIONS

Numbers given in parentheses appear in the text without identification, but are found in the texts under which they are listed in this index.

अग्निपुराण २४६, (५३५), ५८१

अङ्गिरस् ५३४

अत्रि ३४७, ६००

अपरार्क २८३, २८६

अमरकोश (२२)

आदित्यपुराण १२६, २२८

आश्वलायन गृह्यसूत्र (४२२), (४८०)

आश्वलायन श्रौतसूत्र (४७६), (४९०), (५०५)

उशनस् ५१७, ५९८, ६१७

ऋग्वेद (१७), (४१९), (४२०), (४२८), (४२९), (४४३), (ऋग्वेद खिल), (४४४), (४४५), (४४६), (४४७), (४५१), (४५२), (४५३), (४५४), (४५५), (४५८), (४५९), (४६४), (४७८)

ऐतरेय ब्राह्मण (३९)

कल्पतरु ४९७; also cited in ११८-११८.२, २२४.४-२२५.१, ६५३.२-३.

कातीय (कात्यायन श्रौतसूत्र) (२७२), ४७७

कात्यायन ८९, ३५३, ५०८, ५४३, ५५२, ५५९, ५७६

कार्ष्णाजिनि ३९६, ५७०

कालादर्श ५४७, ५४८; also cited in ५५८.३, ६१५.१, ६१८.४, ६१८.९

काशीखण्ड–see स्कन्दपुराण

कुमारिलभट्ट ('भट्टपाद, भट्टचरण') २३, २४, (१६५), २२२, २२४, (२३५), २६०, (२६६), ४८८

कूर्मपुराण ('कौर्मं, कौर्म्यं') २७, ४५, ८२, ८३, ८६, १०४, ११०, १११, १२१, १७१, १८६, ३०३, ३७०, ३७९, ५७३, ६५३

कोणादित्यमाहात्म्य—see ब्रह्मपुराण

गरुडपुराण (गारुड) ४२, ५१, १९८, १९९, (४४१), ५०७, (६२१), (६२४), ६५७, ६५८, ६५९
गार्ग्य १४४, २९१, ३३९, ३९१, (३९४)
गालव ५८७
गीता (भगवद्गीता) १८०
गोभिल ११७, १२०
गोभिल गृह्यसूत्र (४२१), (४३१)
गौतम ५७५
चतुर्लक्षणी–see वेदान्त सूत्र
चतुर्विंशतिमत ५८०, ५८८, ६०३
चित्रपथामाहात्म्य ३८४
छागलेय ५९६
जातुकर्ण्य ५९१
जाबालि ११५, ३२२, ३९९, ५४२, ५९९
जैमिनि ('इति न्याय, इति सूत्र') १६६, २६४, २७०, २७४, २७९, ४२६, ४६०, ५४६, ६२२, ६७४
तैत्तिरीय ब्राह्मण ('आपस्तम्बानाम्') २९५
तैत्तिरीय संहिता (४५६), (४५७)
दानधर्म–see भारत
दिवोदास, दिवोदासीय ५२३, ६०९; also cited in ५११.१, ६१६.३, ६३९.१७
देवल १२९, २२५, २२६, ३४६, ३५४, ३७२, ४१२, ५२७, ५३०, ५७७, ६२०, ६४०, ६६१, ६६६, ६६८
देवीपुराण ३२४, ३८१, ४०२, ४०६, ५३२, ६४८
धर्मविवृत्ति ६८६
नागरखण्ड–see स्कन्दपुराण
नारद २९६
नारदीय (पुराण) २१४, ६६०, ६७९, ६८०
निगम ३५६, ३५९, ५६०
न्यायसुधा ('भट्टसोमेश्वर') २२३, २६२, ४८९
पद्मपुराण (पाद्म) ३६८, ३६९, ४०३, ५००, ५६७, ६४९, ६५१, ६५४, ६५६

पराशर ३११
पारस्कर गृह्यसूत्र, श्राद्धसूत्र (४२५)
पार्थसारथिमिश्र २६१
'पुराण' ६३३
पुलस्त्य १७३ (शंखपुलस्त्य), ६०१
पैठीनसि १०७, १९६, ३१५, ३१९, ३८५
प्रचेतस् ५४१
प्रदीप ५६३
प्रभासखण्ड–see स्कन्दपुराण
प्रयोगपारिजात ३३१
बृहस्पति १९१, ४००, ४३२, ५०३, (५०४), ५८२
ब्रह्मपुराण (ब्राह्म) ५४, ५५, ६०, ६२, ७७, ८०, ८१, ८५, ९०, १५३, (१८३), १८४, (२४२), २६५, २८२, ३५०, ३७८, ४३४, ६५०, ६६४, ६६५, ६७२, ६७५, ६७८
ब्रह्मवैवर्त (पुराण) २२०, (२३२), २३७, २५१
ब्रह्माण्ड (पुराण) ६२५, ६२६
भट्टचरण, भट्टपाद–see कुमारिलभट्ट
भट्टसोमेश्वर–see न्यायसुधा
भविष्य, भविष्यत् (पुराण) ३६३, ४०९, ५८९, ६१३, ६७७
भविष्योत्तर (पुराण) ३४९
भागवत (पुराण) २५, ३६
भारत (महाभारत, व्यास) १०, १३, १९, २०, २१, (२८), ३०, ३४, ३५, ३७, ३८, ४३, ४६, ४७, ४८, ५२, ५३, ५९, ७२, ७३, ७४, ७५.३, ७६, ९१, ९४, ९८, १०९, १९६, १७०, १७२, १८७, २०१, २०२, २३६, २४५, २६३, २९२, ३००, ३०१, ३६१, ३८३, ३९३, ६५५, ६७३
भाष्यकृत्–see शबर
भाष्यार्थसंग्रह ४९२
मत्स्यपुराण (मात्स्य) ३८, ४६, ७०, ११०, १११, ११८, २३९, २४०, ३५२, ३६०, ३६९, ६५३.१
मदनपारिजात १९२, ३१३; also cited in ३४४.४, ५११.१, ५८५.१, ६१६.२

मनु १६, ३३, ८७, ९२, ९३, (९७), १००, १०२, १५८, १७९, ३९७, (४६६), ५६२, ६११
मरीचि ३४०, ४९८, ५२४, ६०२
महाभारत–see भारत
महार्णवप्रकाश १२३
मार्कण्डेयपुराण ३१६
मेधातिथि ९६
मैत्रायणीय परिशिष्ट ५५४, ५५६, ५५७
यम ३१२, ३७७, ६२७, ६२८
याज्ञवल्क्य ३२, ७८, १०१, १३१, ४३५, ४३६, ४३७, ४६१, (४७०), (४७२), (४७५), (५०६), ५३८, (५६१)
योगयाज्ञवल्क्य ३६४
रत्नमाला १३४, १४७
रामकौतुक ३९५
रामोत्तरतापनीयोपनिषद् (४१७)
लघ्वाश्वलायन स्मृति (१९५)
लल्ल १३८, ६८५
लौगाक्षि ५५५, ५८४
वराहपुराण ४९४, ५०१
वसिष्ठ ३६७, ५६६
वाजसनेयी संहिता (४३०), (४६५), (४७९), (४८१), (४८२), (४८३), (४८४), (४८५)
वामनपुराण ६०७
वायुपुराण (वायवीय) ५०, १५०, १५५, २२७, ३२८, (३३७), ३७४, ३९८, ४४२, ६०६
विष्णु (स्मृति, स्मरण) १५६, १९४, ३७१, ३८८, ४६७, ४८७, ४९५, ६१४
विष्णुधर्मोत्तर (पुराण) ३७६
विष्णुपुराण (वैष्णव) ११३, १५७, ३२७, ३२९, ४३३, ५३१, (५४०), ५५३
वृत्तशत १४८
वृद्धगार्ग्य २९०, ३९२

वृद्धयाज्ञवल्क्य ३१०

वृद्धशातातप ५९०

वृद्धश्लोक ५३७

वेदान्तसूत्र ('व्यासोक्त चतुर्लक्षणी') ५६३

व्याघ्रपाद ३४८, ३६६

व्यास ७१, ५१४, ६३९ (see also भारत)

व्यासोक्तचतुर्लक्षणी–see वेदान्तसूत्र

शंख ४०, ४१, १०६, १७३ (शंखपुलस्त्यौ), २९८ (गद्यशंख), ३२१, ३७३, ३८२, ५८३, ६७१

शतपथ ब्राह्मण (४२७), (४३८), (४४८), (४५०)

शबर ('भाष्यकृत्, इति न्याय') २२१, २७१, ३३८

शांखायन ५७९

शातातप ९५, ३०९, ६१८

शिवपुराण ६४

शूलपाणि (श्राद्धविवेक) ३८७, ४९६, ५०२, ६१५

षट्त्रिंशन्मत १९०, ५२०

संग्रह ६०४

सत्यव्रत ५३३, ५९५

सुमन्तु ३३०, ५०९, ५१०, ५१३, ५२५, ५८६, ५९२, ६१६

स्कन्दपुराण (including प्रभासखण्ड, काशीखण्ड, etc.) १२, १५, ३१, ५७, ६१, ६३, ६५, ६८, ६९, ७५, ८८, ९९, (१०३), १०८, ११४, ११९, १२७, १३०, १५२, १५४, (१७७), १७८, १८१, (१८५), (२०४), (२०६), २०७, २०८, २१२, २१३, २१५, २१६, २१७, २१८, २१९, २२९, २३१, २३८, २४७, २४९, २५०, (२५७), ३२३, ३४४, ३८६, ३९०, ४०४, (५११), ५४५, ५५०, ६३८, (६४२), ६४३, (६५२), ६६३, ६७६, ६८१, ६८२.

'इति स्मृति, स्मरण, स्मर्यंते; स्मृत्यन्तरम्' १८, ७९, ८४, १२५, १८२, २७८, २९५, ३४५, ५१६, ५५८, ५७१, ५८५, ६१२

स्मृतिचन्द्रिका (२७६), (२७७), ४०१

स्मृतिदर्पण १७५, २०३, ३१७, ६०८; also cited in ५५८.३

स्मृतिरत्नावली १६१, ३७५, ४०५, ४११, ५९७; also cited in ४९५.३, ५११.३, ५७६.१, ६१६.३

स्मृतिसंग्रह ३५५, ३६२

स्मृत्यर्थसार ३१८, ३४१, ३४३, ५६८, ५७८; also cited in ५२३.१

हारीत ४६८, ५२८

हिरण्यकेशिन् गृह्यसूत्र ४९१, (४९३)

हेमाद्रि ४९९, ५४९, ५९३; also cited in ५८५.२, ५८७.३, ६०५.३

APPENDIX C

INDEX OF श्लोक-s AND मन्त्र-s

अकल्कलो निरारम्भो १७३
अकालेऽप्यथवा काले ३२३, ३८६
अकुर्वन् वित्तशाठ्यं यः ५३१
अक्रोधनश्च राजेन्द्र १७३
अगाधे विमले शुद्धे ७२
अग्न आ याहि वीतये ४४४
अग्निष्टोमादिभिर्यज्ञैर् ४६
अग्नौ हुतेन देवस्थाः ४३२
अग्रभागं ततस्तेभ्यो ३७८
अग्राह्यास्त्वागता ह्यापो ३०६
अग्रे पृष्ठे वामभागे ६४६
अग्रे मृत्युमवाप्नोति ६४६
अङ्गवङ्गकलिङ्गेषु १२५
अजा गौर्महिषी चैव ३६५
अजिनं कम्बला दर्भा ६३७
अज्ञानेनापि यस्येह ४६
अटव्यः सर्वतः पुण्या ३७६
अतः शास्त्राभियुक्तानाम् २६०
अतस्तीर्थे न गृह्णीयात् ६५३
अतीचारगतो जीवस् १४५
अतीतकुलकोटीनां ३२८, ३३७
अत्र पितरो मादयध्वं ४३०, ४८२
अथ चेत् प्रतिगृह्णाति ६५२
अदृष्यान्यपि दृश्यानि ६८१
अद्धीद् इन्द्र प्रस्थितेम हवींषि ४५१
अधिमासे च जन्मर्क्षे १५१
अध्वनि च क्रोशपूरण १६०

अनुपोष्य त्रिरात्राणि ४६
अनेका मातरो यस्य ५८७
अन्तर् मातामहान् कृत्वा ५९८
अन्ते निवेशयेद् यस्तु ५९९
अन्नहोमे तथा स्पर्शे ४९२
अन्नाभावे द्विजाभावे ५२६
अन्यतीर्थेषु गङ्गायाः ६६४
अन्ये च बहवस्तीर्थाः २४०
अन्येभ्यस्त्वथ देवेभ्यो ६५०
अन्वष्टका तथा मातृ- ५८३
अपवित्रमपि प्राप्य ३६१
अपुत्रा पुत्रवत् पत्नी ५६५
अपूर्वदेवतां दृष्ट्वा १४४
अभावे कूपवापीनाम् ३६६
अभिसंगम्य तीर्थानि १२९
अमीमदन्त पितरः ४८४
अम्बुमध्ये गवां गोष्ठे ६८८
अयनद्वितये श्राद्धं ४१३
अयमेव विधिः प्रोक्तः ४९४, ५०१
अरण्यं देवतास्थानं ६६६
अर्घ्यद्रव्यविशेषेण ६४२
अर्घ्यमावाहनञ्चैव ४०७
अर्थार्थी पुरुषो राजन् २०
अर्धं तीर्थफलं तस्य १०७
अवनेजनं पिण्डदानम् ५३७
अश्रद्दधानः पापात्मा १७७
अष्टकृत्वो मन्त्रजपैः ६४१
अष्टाङ्गोऽर्घोऽयमुद्दिष्टस् ६४३
असमर्थस्तु यानेन १२०
अस्तंगते गुरौ शुक्रे ६२९
अस्थिक्षेपं गयाश्राद्धं ६३०
अस्थिक्षेपं गयाश्राद्धं ६३१
अस्थीनि मातापितृवंशजानि ६३४

अस्पृष्टहीनजातिः स ६३८

अस्वर्ग्यं लोकविद्विष्टं ५६१

अहं दाशुषे वि भजामि भोजनम् ४५८

अहं भुवं वसुनः पूर्व्यस् पतिर् ४५५

आक्रान्तं दैत्यजठरं २२७

आगत्य दृष्ट्वा मणिकर्णिकायाम् २०७

आगत्य मणिकर्ण्यां तु २२०, २५१

आचार्यगुरुशिष्येभ्यः ५८८

आच्या जानु दक्षिणतः ४१९, ४२८

आत्मा नदी संयमतोयपूर्णा ७१

आदौ कृत्वा तु वपनं २१६

आदौ गत्वा गयाशीर्षे ६०६

आदौ तु कर्कटे देवि ३४९

आदौ पिता ततो माता ३३३

आन्वष्टक्यं गयाप्राप्तौ ५५७

आपः क्षीरं कुशाग्राणि ६४३

आपद्यनग्नौ तीर्थे च ५०८

आपद्यनग्नौ तीर्थे च ५०९

आ ब्रह्मणो ये पितृवंशजाता ६२३

आब्रह्मस्तम्बपर्यन्तं ३२८, ३३७

आब्रह्मस्तम्बपर्यन्तं ३३५

आब्रह्मस्तम्बपर्यन्तं ३३६

आमं ददत् तु कौन्तेय ५१४

आमं ददति चेद् राजन्न् ५१६

आमं ददद्धि कौन्तेय ५१५

आमश्राद्धं तु पूर्वाह्णे ५२८

आमश्राद्धं यदा कुर्याद् ५२०

आमश्राद्धं यदा कुर्याद् ५१७

आमश्राद्धं यदा कुर्यात् ५१९

आमेन पिण्डं दद्याच्चेद् ५२१

आयन्तु नः पितरः सोम्यासः ४६५, ४७९

आ याहि पथिभिर् ईकितेभिः ४४३

आयुः प्रजां धनं विद्यां ४३६

आवाहनं न तीर्थे स्यान् ४१०
आवाहनं स्वधाशब्दं ५६६
आवाहने स्वधाकारे ५२४
आवेष्ट्य नेत्रवस्त्रेण ६३८
आसीनासो अरुणीनामुपस्थे ४२०
इन्द्र आगच्छ हरिव आगच्छ ४४८
इन्द्रियाणाञ्च पञ्चानां २१
इन्द्रो दिव इन्द्र ईशे पृथिव्याः ४५३
इमं मन्त्रं समुच्चार्य २०६
इयं राजर्षिभिर्याता ४८
इह चाहं संनिहितस् ४१७
इहैवैधि माप च्योष्ठाः ४४७
ईशानमस्य जगतः स्वर्दृशम् ४५४
उच्चा दिवि दक्षिणावन्तो अस्थुर् १७
उदकं शोणितं दद्यात् २३०, २५३
उदङ्मुखः प्राङ्मुखो वा २८६
उदयति दिशि यस्यां याति यत्र भ्रमाद् वा १४७
उद्धरेत् सप्तगोत्राणि ४४०
उद्यतस्तु गयां गन्तुं १५५
उद्वाहे पुत्रजनने ५५४
उपप्लवे शीतलभानुभान्वोर् ६८५
उपवासं ततः कुर्यात् २१२, २१७
उपवासो व्रतं होमस् ६८६
उपसर्पादिभिर्मन्त्रैः ६३६
उपाकर्मणि चोत्सर्गे ३६७
ऊर्जं वहन्तीर्...तर्पयत पितृन् ४८१
ऊर्ध्वबाहुर्विरौम्येष २८
ऋणानि त्रीण्यपाकृत्य ८६
ऋषिभिः क्रतवः प्रोक्ता ३८
ऋषीणां परमं गुह्यम् ३८
एकचित्यां समारूढौ ५८५
एकभक्तेन नक्तेन १३१
एकां चण्ड्यां रवेः सप्त ६४४

एकया प्रतिधापिबद् ४५२
एकयोजनविस्तीर्णा ६७७
एतच्च पित्रादिपिण्डा- ५७९
एतच्चानुपनीतोऽपि ५६७
एतत् ते कथितं देवि ६९
एतत् ते कथितं देवि ७५
एतद्वः पितरो वास ४८५
एतद् वः पितरो वास ४८६
एता नद्यः पुण्यतमा ५५
एतानि वसुभिः साध्यैर् ४७
एवं शरीरशौचेन ७६
एवं कुरुष्व कौन्तेय २३९, २४०
एवं कुर्वंस्तस्य तीर्थाद् यदुक्त १५३
एवं कृते प्रेतपुरे स्थितस्य ६२५
एवं कृते विधानेऽस्मिन् २२८
एवं गच्छंस्तस्य तीर्थाद् यदुक्त १६३
एवमादिषु चान्येषु ३७०
एवमादिषु तीर्थेषु ३७४
एष ते तत मधुमान् ४९३
एषामभावे कुर्याच्च ५१०
एषु तीर्थेषु यच्छ्राद्धं ३६९
ऐभिर् अग्ने सरथं याहि ४४६
ऐश्वर्यलोभान्मोहाद् वा १११
ओं नमो देवदेवाय २०८
ओं पिता पितामहश्चैव ६२४
कक्षोपस्थशिखावर्जम् २८८
कथयिष्यामि ते वत्स ११०
कपित्थबिल्वमात्रान् वा ५३४
करतोयां कुरङ्गञ्च २०१
करतोयां समासाद्य २०२
करतोये सदानीरे २०३
कर्कटादौ रजोदुष्टा ३५८
कर्मणा मनसा वाचा ३२

कर्मणामल्पमहतां १६५
कर्मनाशाजलस्पर्शात् २००
कर्षूसमन्वितं मुक्त्वा ५७६
कामं क्रोधञ्च लोभञ्च १७२
कामं क्रोधञ्च लोभञ्च ६५५
कामस्य नेन्द्रियप्रीतिर् २५
कामोदकप्रदानं ते ३२९
· · ·काम्ये च घुरिलोचनाव् ५०४
कार्याणि मलमासेऽपि ३१२
कालभेदे न तन्त्रं स्याद् ६०४
काले नमस्यशुद्धं स्यात् ३६२
कियन्ति तानि तीर्थानि ५४
कीर्तनाच्चैव तीर्थस्य ४४
कुम्भे कर्कटके चैव २९३
कुरुक्षेत्रादितीर्थानि ११९
कुरुते तत्र पापञ्चेद् ६५८
कुर्यादहरहः श्राद्धं ६१७
कुशैः सम्मार्जयेदस्थीन्य् ६३७
कुशोऽसि कुशपुत्रोऽसि ३२०
कृतपारणको हृष्टो १५२
केचिदिच्छन्ति नारीणां ५८०
केदारञ्च प्रयागञ्च ६१
केदारे फल्गुतीर्थे च ३७०
केनापि न कृतं यत् तद् ५६
केवलं गुणसम्पन्नः ७४
केशानां यावती संख्या २९७
क्षयाहे केवलाः कार्या ५९६
क्षेत्राग्न्यापः सुरा विप्रा ६७
क्षौरं नैमित्तिकं कार्यं २९५
गङ्गा च यमुना चैव ३५४
गङ्गातोयेषु यस्यास्थि ६२७
गङ्गादितीर्थेषु वसन्ति मत्स्या १८४
गङ्गाद्वारे प्रभासे च ३७०

गङ्गाद्वारे प्रयागे च ३७३
गङ्गा धर्मद्रवः पुण्या ३५६
गङ्गां प्राप्य सरिच्छ्रेष्ठां २५६
गङ्गां प्राप्य सरिच्छ्रेष्ठां २५९
गङ्गां सम्प्राप्य यो धीमान् २५९
गङ्गायां सर्वकालेषु १५०
गङ्गासीमान्न लंघन्ति ६७७
गङ्गेयं सरितां श्रेष्ठा ५८
गच्छ गेहं महाभाग ८५
गच्छेद् देशान्तरं यस्तु १५७
गणेशं ब्राह्मणान् नत्वा १५४
गत्वा स्नानं प्रकुर्वीत २११, २८२
गयां प्रसङ्गतो गत्वा ५५८
गवाश्वादिगतं पूर्वं २६६
गिरिषु ख्याततीर्थेषु ३२६
गुरुं चैवाप्युपासीत ७८
गुर्वादित्ये गुरौ सिंहे १४०
गुर्वादित्ये गुरौ सिंहे १४१
गृहे तु यत्कृतं पापं ६५८
गृहे दशगुणं दानं ६८९
गोत्रादिचरणं सर्वं ५७१
गोदावरी भीमरथी ५५, ३५०
गोदावर्यां गयायाञ्च १४९
गोभिर्युक्तेन यानेन ११७
गोमूत्रं गोमयं क्षीरं ६३७
गोयाने गोवधः प्रोक्तो ११२
ग्रहणोद्वाहसङ्क्रान्ति- ३१०
चतुर्विधानि तीर्थानि ५४
चरन् वै मधु विन्दति ३९
चित्तमन्तर्गतं दुष्टं ६९
चित्तमन्तर्गतं दुष्टं १८३
चित्राविशाखानलसार्पयाम्य- १३४
जगदाप्यायनोद्भूतं ३२९

जनार्दने च विक्रीते ६५१
जन्मप्रभृति यत्पापं ६८
जपस्तपस्तीर्थयात्रा ६२
जलेचरा भूमिलया ३२७
जायन्ते च म्रियन्ते च ६६
जीवनार्थं हतं तीर्थं ६५१
जीवमाने न देयं स्याद् ६१३
ज्ञानं तीर्थं धृतिस्तीर्थं ६६
ततः पिण्डमुपादाय ६२०
ततः प्रभृति वै प्रेतः ४६८
ततः सायाह्नदत्तं हि ३८८
ततो गत्वा सुतीर्थेषु ६३७
ततो ग्रामान्तरं गत्वा १५५
ततो जलाशयं गत्वा ६३७
ततो होमं प्रकुर्वीत ६३७
तत्त्वविस्त्वनहंबुद्धिस् ७३
तत्र न प्रतिगृह्णीयात् ६७२
तत्र यः सवितुः क्षेत्रे २६५
तत्र सर्वाणि तीर्थानि २४७
तत्र स्नानं प्रकुर्वीत २५०
तथा पुण्यानि तीर्थानि ४३
तथैव शूद्रसंस्पृष्टं ६७६
तदहश्चेत् प्रदुष्येत ३८६
तपनस्य सुता गङ्गा ३५५
तया विना यतस्तीर्थे ८५
तर्पणं पितृदेवानां ६४०
तर्पणं प्रत्यहं कार्यं ३४४
तस्मात् सर्वप्रयत्नेन २५०
तस्मादेतैर्विहीनस्तु ११५
तस्माद् भार्यां विना सिद्धिः ८५
तस्माद् भौमेषु तीर्थेषु ७५
तातास्बत्रितयं सपत्नजननी मातामहादित्रयम् ३३४
तारिताः पितरस्तेन ४६

तावदस्य वृथा तीर्थं १७६
तावद्वर्षसहस्राणि २५५
तिथितीर्थविशेषेषु ३४३
तिर्यग्यवोदराण्यष्टाव् १३२
तिर्यग्योनिं न गच्छेच्च ५०
तिलमन्नं च पानीयं ५३६
तिलैर्व्रीहियवैर्माषैर् १५८
तिलैः सप्ताष्टभिर्वापि ५४०
तिलोऽसि···स्वधया पितॄन् ४८०
तीक्ष्णदंष्ट्र महाकाय २०९
तीराद् गव्यूतिमात्रं तु ६७६
तीर्थं चलित्वा यः कोऽपि १९८
तीर्थं प्राप्य प्रसङ्गेन १०६
तीर्थं प्राप्यानुषङ्गेन ३२१
तीर्थमधिगम्य व्रतो— ६६८
तीर्थमासाद्य कुर्वीत २१४
तीर्थयात्राकृता सिद्धिस् ८५
तीर्थयात्रां चिकीर्षुः प्राग् १५२
तीर्थयात्रां प्रकुर्वन्ति १८६
तीर्थश्राद्धेषु वर्जयेद् २६८
तीर्थश्राद्धे सदा पिण्डान् ५३६
तीर्थस्नानं जपो होमो ३१२
तीर्थस्नानं महादानं ६८४
तीर्थानि गच्छता नित्यं १८२
तीर्थानि च यथोक्तेन १७२
तीर्थानुगमनं पद्भ्यां ११४
तीर्थान्यनुसरन् वीरः ५०
तीर्थायतनगोष्ठेषु ३६८
तीर्थे गच्छन् चरेत् सन्ध्यास् १८९
तीर्थे गत्वा तु यच्छ्राद्धं ५०७
तीर्थे तिथिविशेषे च ३४२
तीर्थे द्रव्योपपत्तौ च ३८२
तीर्थे प्रतिग्रहो यस्तु ६५१

तीर्थे विवाहे यात्रायां १९१
तीर्थे श्राद्धं प्रकुर्वीत ५१०
तीर्थेषु चैव सर्वेषु ६०३
तीर्थेषु ब्राह्मणं नैव ४०२
तीर्थै रकुर्वन्नित्यादि— १२६
तीर्थोपवासः कर्तव्यः २१३, २२९, २४९
तीर्थोपवासं कुर्वीत २१२
तीर्थोपवासं कृत्वा स २१८
तृप्तप्रश्नोऽवगाहश्च ५२२
तृप्यन्तु पितरः सर्वे ४७१
ते तृप्तास्तर्पयन्त्येनं ४३५, ४३७
त्रिभिः सारस्वतं तोयं १३०
त्रिभ्यो यदेकं जायेत ५४
त्रिमुहूर्तं तु सायाह्नस् ३९८
त्वया सा वञ्चिता मूढ ८५
दक्षिणं कर्णमारभ्य २८६
दक्षिणाप्रवणें देशे ३७६
दत्तौरसेतरेषां तु ५६९
दद्याद् यच्च द्विजातिभ्यः ५१८
दर्शश्राद्धं गयाश्राद्धं ५५५
दशकोटिसहस्राणि २३६
···दशमांशं लभेत सः ३१७
दशाहाभ्यन्तरे यस्य ६३२
दानमिज्या तपः शौचं ६९
दानं तीर्थं दमस्तीर्थं ६९
दारुणेषु च सर्वेषु ३९३
दारुणेषु तु सर्वेषु २९२
दार्शिकस्य युगादेश्च ५४८
दीर्घकालेन तपसा १५
दुर्जरं पातकं तीर्थे ६५६
देवमाल्यापनयनं ६४८
देवयात्राविवाहेषु १९०
देवानां दर्शनं पुण्यं ६४१

देवान् पितॄन् ब्राह्मणांश्चैव साधून् १५३
देवाश्च पितरो यस्माद् ४०६
देवासुरास्तथा नागा ३२७
देशानां तु विशेषेण ३७०
देहं सुपुष्टं विरजं तु यौवनं ७६
दैवकर्मणि पित्र्ये च १९७
दौहित्रपुत्रदाराश्च ५८६
द्रव्यमन्नं फलं तोयं ६४६
द्रव्याभावे द्विजाभावे ५११
द्रव्यार्थस्पर्शसंयोगे १६
द्वादशैता महानद्यो ३५१
द्विजस्याब्धौ तु नौयातुः १२४
द्विर्भोजनं तृतीयांशं ११५
द्वे बहूनि निमित्तानि ५४३
द्वौ दैवे प्राक् त्रयः पित्र्ये ४७२
द्वौ मासौ मत्स्यमांसेन १५८
धनं च धर्मैकफलम् ३६
धनञ्जयोऽपि धर्मात्मा ६३८
धनुःसहस्राण्यष्टौ तु ३६२
धर्म एव प्लवो नान्यः १३
धर्म एव हतो हन्ति ३३
धर्मञ्चार्थञ्च कामञ्च १०
धर्मं पूर्वं धनं मध्ये ३७
धर्ममूलं जगद् राजन् ३५
धर्मात् संजायते ह्यर्थो २७
धर्मात् सुखञ्च ज्ञानञ्च १२
धर्मादर्थोऽर्थतः कामः २६
धर्माद् राज्यं धनं सौख्यम् ३१
धर्मेण हि सहायेन १६
ध्यानपूते ज्ञानजले ६९
ध्रियमाणे तु पितरि ६११
न काष्ठे विद्यते देवो ६५९
न कुर्यात् सूतकं भिक्षुः ३४५, ५७१

नक्तं हविष्यान्नमनोदनं वा १६२
नक्षत्रे च न कुर्वीत ३९३
नक्षत्रे तु न कुर्वीत २६२
न चात्र श्येनगृध्रादीन् ४१२
न जलप्लुतदेहस्य ६६
न जीवत्पितृकः कुर्याच् ६१६
न तीर्थे पातकं कुर्यात् ६५६
न तीर्थे प्रतिगृह्णीयात् ६५१
···न तु तत्तीरवासिनाम् ३५६
न ते शक्या दरिद्रेण ३८
नदीतटेषु तीर्थेषु ३७२
नदीतीरेषु तीर्थेषु ५७३
नदीसरिद्देवखात– ३०२
न देवः पर्वताग्रेषु ६६१
न नदीषु नदीं ब्रूयात् ६६१
नन्दायां भार्गवदिने ३६१
नन्दाश्वकामरव्यार– ३६५
न परीक्ष्यो द्विजस्तीर्थे ४०४
नमोनमस्ययोर्मध्ये ३४६
नमो वः पितरो रसाय ४८३
'नमोऽस्तु धर्माय' वदन् प्रविश्य ६२५
नरकस्था दिवं यान्ति ४४१
नरके वसते घोरे ११०
नरकेषु समस्तेषु ३२७
नरयानं चाश्वतरी– १२१
नर्मदायां कुशावर्ते ३७०
न वारं न च नक्षत्रं ३६०
न वेदबलमाश्रित्य ६५२
न शरीरमलत्यागान् ६६
न हि कामेन कामोऽन्यः २०
नानृजुर्नाकृतात्मा च ३०१
नान्तरा भोजनं कुर्याद् २७७
नान्दीमुखेऽष्टकाश्राद्धे ६१८

नायं लोकोऽस्ति न परो १८०
नार्पयन्ति हरौ लोके ६६५
नार्वाक् संवत्सरात् प्रोक्त ६८७
नावाहनं न दिग्बन्धो ४०८
नाव्रतो नाकृतात्मा च ३००
नासौ तत्फलमाप्नोति २५०
नास्ति स्त्रीणां पृथग् यज्ञो १०२
निगृहीतेन्द्रियग्रामो ६६
नित्यनैमित्तिके कुर्यात् ४००
नित्यश्राद्धं न कुर्वीत ५५०
नित्यं नैमित्तिकञ्चैव ३९९
निरन्तरं तीर्थसेवा ९५
निवृत्तिसंज्ञके धर्मे २९
निशामय महाप्राज्ञ ५४५
नीचस्थे वक्रसंस्थेऽप्यतिचेरणगते बालवृद्धास्तगे वा १३८
नृणां पापकृतां तीर्थं १०३, १२७, १७८
नृपविप्राज्ञया यज्ञे २९६
नेता च त्वमृषीन् यस्मात् १०९
नेपालकम्बलेनाथ ६३८
नैकश्राद्धद्वयं कुर्यात् ५४१
नैव प्राप्तस्य लोपोऽस्ति ५२७
नो तेषां प्रतिशुक्रयानमशुभं ये वत्सभृग्वाङ्गिरो-- १४८
नोद्धरेत् प्रथमं पात्रं ४२२
नौकायानमयानं स्याद् १२२
पक्षयोरुभयो राजन् ३४०
पक्षश्राद्धे हिरण्ये चाप्य् ३३०
पञ्चगव्येन संस्नाप्य ६३८
पट्टवस्त्रञ्च कौशेयं ६३९
पदे पदेऽश्वमेधस्य १६७
पद्भ्यां कराभ्यां जानुभ्यां २०५
परकीयगृहे यस्तु ३७८
परकीयप्रदेशेषु ३७७
परद्रव्येष्वभिध्यानं १७४

परलोकं नयत्याशु १६
परान्नभोजने देवि २१२
परिग्रहाच्च साधुनां ५२
पशोः पशुपतेरग्रे ६४७
पाकाभावेऽधिकारः स्याद् ५०६
पाखण्डपूजितं लिङ्गं ६७६
पाण्डवै राज्यलाभाय १२६
पात्राभावेऽखिलं कृत्वा ५२७
पापानां पापशमनः २१२
पारणं कृतवांस्ततः २१६
पावमानी 'ममाग्ने' च ६३७
पिण्डदानञ्च तच्छस्तं ३८१
पिण्डदानं तु तच्छस्तं ५२६
पिण्डनिर्वपनं तत्र ६०७
पिण्डमात्रं प्रदातव्यम् ५३०
पिण्डांस्तु गोजविप्रेभ्यो ५३८
पिन्डांस्तेभ्यः सदा दद्यात् ५८८
पितरो यत्र पूज्यन्ते ५७५
पिता यस्य तु वृत्तः स्यात् ४६६
पितुः पुत्रेण कर्तव्या ५५२
पितृपात्रं तदुत्तानम् ४७५
पितृपात्रेषु प्रेतयात्रं प्रसेचयेद् ४७०
पितृभ्यश्च तदा श्राद्धं ४३४
पितृभ्यो रजतं देयं ४७४
पितृमातामहावादौ ५६७
पितृवंशे मृता ये च ६२१
पितृवर्गे मातृवर्गे ६१६
पितृव्यभ्रातृमातृणाम् ५६४
पितृष्वसा मातृष्वसा ३३३
पितृणां प्रथमं दानं ५९५
पितॄनतर्पयित्वा तु ३३२, ६७०
पितॄन् हविषे अत्तवे ४२६, ४६४, ४७८
पित्रादिनवदैवत्यं ५८१

पित्र्यं जीवत्पितुर्नोक्तम् ५६०
पित्र्ये कर्मणि विद्वद्भिर् ४७३
पुण्डरीकं महातीर्थं १७१
पुण्यक्षेत्राभिगमनं ६६०
पुण्याम्भसा समायोगाद् ३६०
पुत्रद्रव्यादि संत्यज्य ४२
पुवं ददाति दाशुषे ४५६
पुत्रः पौत्रः प्रपौत्रो वा ५५३
पुत्रेषु दारान् निक्षिप्य ८७
पुरूरवार्द्रवौ चैव ५०३
पुष्करेष्वक्षयं श्राद्धं ३७१
पूतां पुण्यतमां भार्यां ८५
पूर्वमावाहनं तीर्थे २१०
पूर्वेद्युर्मन्त्रितान् विप्रान् ४२३
पृथिव्यां नैमिषं पुण्यं ५९
पृथिव्यां सर्वतीर्थेषु ३०३
प्रतिकृतिं कुशमयीं ३१६
प्रतिग्रहाद् उपावृत्तः १७३
प्रतिस्रोतो रजोयोगो ३०७
प्रत्यक्षविधिनाभावे ४८६
प्रत्याब्दिकेषु चालभ्य-- ५४७
प्रत्यावृत्तोदके स्नानं ३०५
प्रथमं कर्कटे देवि ३५७
प्रथमं चालभेत् तीर्थं २०६
प्रथमं तीर्थराजं तु ६३
प्रभावादद्भुताद् भूमेः ७५, २६३
प्रयागञ्च कुरुक्षेत्रं ६२
प्रयागं सर्वतीर्थेभ्यो २४५
प्रयागतीर्थयात्रार्थी ११०
प्रयागश्चापि तीर्थेन्द्रः २३८
प्रयागे तीर्थयात्रायां १५६
प्रयागे वपनं कुर्याद् २३४
प्रयान्ति पण्यगन्धाढ्या १७०

प्रवाहमवधिं कृत्वा ६७२
प्रवाहाभिमुखो मज्जेद् ३२२
प्रवृत्तिसंज्ञके धर्मे ११
प्राजापत्ये च पौष्णे च ३९२
प्राप्तैरेव च कर्तव्यं ३२४, ३८१
प्राप्यन्ते पार्थिवैरेते ३८
प्रायश्चित्ती च विबुधस् १०४
प्रायश्चित्ती व्रजेतीर्थं ८४
प्रायश्चित्ती व्रजेत् तीर्थं १०५, १२८
प्रारम्भो वरणं यज्ञे १९५
प्रीत्या श्राद्धं तु कर्तव्यं ५९०
प्रेते पितृत्वमापन्ने ४६७
प्रैषानुप्रैषसंयुक्तं ५२७
प्रोक्षयेत् पञ्चगव्येन ६३५
बदरेण समान् वापि ५३४
बहूनामथ वा द्वाभ्यां ६००
बाले वा यदि वा वृद्धे १४३
बाल्ययौवनवत्या वा १००
ब्रह्माङ्गलग्नं विप्रेभ्यो ६५०
ब्राह्मणः क्षत्रियो वैश्यः ९१
ब्राह्मणं न परीक्षेत ४०३
ब्राह्मणानां भूमिदानं ६४०
ब्राह्मणाय प्रदातव्यं ५१६
ब्राह्मी सरस्वती मूर्तिर् ५७
भगवन् केन विधिना ११८
भर्तुः श्राद्धं तु या नारी ६१०
भागीरथी नर्मदा च ५५
भागीरथी नर्मदा च ३५१
भाद्रशुक्लचतुर्दश्यां ६७३
भानवेऽर्घं प्रदद्यात्तु ६४२
भानौ भौमे त्रयोदश्यां ३३९, ३९४
भार्या पचति चैवान्नं ८५
भार्याविरहितो वापि ५६७

भावं ततो हृत्कमले निधाय १८४
भावितैः करणैः पूर्वम् १८७
भुक्तो वाप्यथवाभुक्तो ३८३
भुक्तो वाप्यथवाभुक्तो ३८४
भोजयन् प्रत्यवायी स्यात् ३८४
भौमानां मानसं तीर्थं ५१३
भ्रातॄणामविभक्तानाम् ६०
मक्षिकापादमात्रं यः ५६२
मनसश्च पृथिव्याश्च ६४१
मनस्विनस्तीर्थयात्रापरायणास् ७९
मन्त्रे तीर्थे द्विजे देवे १६९
मया गयां समासाद्य १८५
महदम्बु समं वापि ४४२
महातीर्थस्य गमनं ३६३
महादानानि ये विप्रा ६८३
महानदीषु सर्वासु ६५२
महानिशा तु विज्ञेया ५५६
महालये गयाश्राद्धे ३११
मांसाशने पञ्चदश्य् ६०१
मातरं पितरं जायां २६९
मातामहस्तत्पिता च ३१६
मातामहानामप्येवं ६२४
मातुः कुलं पितृकुलं ४८७, ६१४
मानसान्यपि तीर्थानि ६३३, ६८
मानसान्यपि तीर्थानि ६९
मानुषाणि च लोकेषु ५४
मार्कण्डेयपुलस्त्याज-- १२६
मार्गेऽन्तरा नदीप्राप्तौ ६६९
माहात्म्यं सर्वतीर्थानां २४६
मित्राणि सख्यः पशवश्च वृक्षास् ६२३
मित्राय गुरवे श्राद्धं ५९२
मुख्यदृष्टार्थतास्वार्थ-- ४८८
मुण्डनञ्चोपवासञ्च २३१

मुण्डनञ्चोपवासञ्च २५४
मुण्डनं चोपवासश्च २२६
मुत् प्रीतिः प्रमदो हर्षः २२
मुमुक्षुभिस्तीर्थगतं द्विजेन्द्रैः ८८
मूर्तयो ब्रह्मविष्णवर्क– ६५
मृताहनि समासेन ५८४
मोक्षो बा परमं श्रेय १०
यज्ञाधिकारेऽप्यथवा निवृत्ते ८१
यतः कुतश्चित् संप्राप्य ५४०
यतिः शूद्रश्च विधवा २८७
यत्किञ्चित् कुरुते पापं २५०
यत्रक्वचन संस्थानां ३२७
यत्र गङ्गा महाराज ६७८
यत्र यत्र दृढा भक्तिर् ६६१
यत्र स्थानेषु यत्तीर्थं ६६२
यत्र स्नानं जयो होमः ४५, ३०४
यथाकथञ्चित् त्रिगुणः १३१
यथा बलं क्रियाहीनं ७६
यथा शरीरस्योद्देशाः ७५
यदन्यत्र कृतं पापं ६५४
यदह्नि तीर्थप्राप्तिः स्यात् २१५
यद् आपिपेष [मातरम्] ४३८
यदा प्रतिष्ठितं लिङ्गं ६८०
यदि सोमं न विन्देत २७३
यदैव दृश्यते तत्र ३८४
यद्येकत्र भवेयाताम् ६०२
यन्मे माता प्रलुलोभ ४६१
यश्चान्यं कारयेच्छक्त्या १०८
यस्तीर्थसम्मुखो भूत्वा १६६
यस्तु तीर्थे नरः स्नात्वा ३२५
यस्तु लौल्याद् द्विजः क्षेत्रे ६५२
यस्मिन्काले नृणामस्थि ६२६
यस्य धर्मध्वजो नित्यं १७६

यस्य हस्तौ च पादौ च १७३
य स्येष्टिधर्मेष्वधिकारितास्ति ८०
यः शूद्रसंस्कृतं लिङ्गं ६८२
यः शूद्रेणार्चितं लिङ्गं ६७६
यः स्वधर्मान् परित्यज्य ८२
यानमर्धफलं हन्ति ११६
यानानि तु परित्यज्य २०४
यानि कानि च पापानि २८०
यानि यानि च तीर्थानि ६६५
यान्यगम्यानि तीर्थानि ४७
या याः काश्चित् तीर्थयात्रा मुनीन्द्रैः ७७
यावत् स पारणं कर्तुम् २१८
यावदस्थि मनुष्याणां ६२८
यावन्ति नखलोमानि २५५
यावन्ति नखलोमानि २५८
यावन्ति नखलोमानि २६६
यावन्नोदेति भगवान् ३५२
याः शोषमुपगच्छन्ति ३५३
येनैकादशसंख्यानि १८१
येऽबान्धवा बान्धवा वा ३२७
ये मे कुले लुप्तपिण्डाः ६२१
येषु तीर्थेषु ये देवा ६९०
यो दरद्रैरपि विधिः ३८
यो यः कश्चित् तीर्थयात्रां तु गच्छेत् १५३
यो यस्य स्त्रियं धनं वा ५७०
योऽशुद्धः पिशुनः क्रूरो ६६
योषिद्भिः पूजितं लिङ्गं ६७९
यौगादिकं मासिकं च ४०१
रक्षेत् कन्यां पिता विन्नां १०१
रजस्तमोविरहितैस्‌ ५१
रजोदुष्टेऽम्भसि स्नानं ३६४
रविक्षेत्रं गते जीवे १३६
रव्यारसौरवारेषु २६०

रात्रौ श्राद्धं न कुर्वीत ३९७
रात्रौ स्नानं न कुर्वीत ३०९
लोकेऽस्मिन् द्विविधं तीर्थं ५३
वनानि गिरयो नद्यस् ३८०
वपनं मैथुनं तीर्थं ६८४
वराहपर्वते चैव ३७०
वर्षातपे सदा छत्री ११३
वसुरुद्रादितिसुताः ४६१
वाक्पाणिपादचापल्यं २७५
वापिकूपतडागयागगमनक्षौरप्रतिष्ठाव्रतं १४२
वायवा याहि दर्शत ४४५
वाराणस्यां कुरुक्षेत्रे ३७३
वाराणस्यां महादेवः ६५
वाराणस्यां महादेवं ६४
विकारेष्वनिषिद्धोहाः ४८८
विद्या वित्तं वपुः शौर्यं ३०
विना तीर्थं विना यज्ञं २८९
विप्रसेवैव शूद्रस्य ९३
विभक्तास्तु पृथक् कुर्युः ५६३
विरूपा आमगर्भाश्च ६२१
विवाहदुर्गयज्ञेषु १९६, ३१५, ३८५
विवाहमौञ्जीचूडासु २९४
विवाहव्रतचूडासु ३९६
विवाहे चोपनयने ३४१
विशिष्टख्यातलिङ्गेषु ६४०
विषयेष्वतिसंरागो ६९
वृद्धिमात्रे तथान्यत्र ३९६
वृद्धौ तीर्थे च संन्यस्ते ६१२
वृद्धौ सत्याञ्च तन्मासि ३४१
वृषे मेषे झषे कुम्भे १४६
व्रतयज्ञविवाहेषु १९४
शङ्करं मनसा ध्यायन् २५०
शमीपत्रप्रमाणेन ५३५

शाकमूलफलान्नैस्तु ५३३
शालग्रामशिलायां तु ४१८
शाल्मलीतिन्तिणीनिम्ब-- ३०८
शिरस्त्वाद्येन पिण्डेन ४३६
शिवं प्रदक्षिणं कुर्वन् ६४५
शुन्धन्तां पितरः ४६०
शुभे तिथौ शुभे वारे १५४
शूद्रस्तु द्विजशुश्रूषा- ९४
शूद्राणां तु सधर्माणः ६७
शूद्रोऽप्यमन्त्रकं कुर्याद् ५००
शूद्रो वानुपनीतो वा ६८२
शृणु तीर्थानि गदतो ६६
शृणु देवि प्रवक्ष्यामि ६१
शृणु देवि विशालाक्षि ६५
शेलुश्च खदिरश्चैषां ३०८
शोणसिन्धुहिरण्याख्याः ३५४
शोणः सिन्धुर्हिरण्याक्षः ६६
शौनकोऽहं प्रवक्ष्यामि ६३५
श्राद्धकृत् सत्यवादी च ४२४
श्राद्धदानं गृहे गत्वा ८५
श्राद्धस्य पूजितो देशो ३७२
श्राद्धं कृत्वा तु तस्यैव ५४२
श्राद्धञ्च तत्र कर्तव्यं ३८१, ४०६
श्राद्धं तत् तैर्थिकं प्रोक्त ३८१
श्राद्धं तत्र तु कर्तव्यं २६७
श्राद्धैस्तु पितरस्तृप्ति ४३३
श्रौतस्मार्तक्रियाः कर्तुं ६६७
श्वःसुत्याम् आगच्छ मघवन् ४४९
षड्भ्यः पितृभ्यस्तदनु ४६६
षष्ठ्यमापूर्णिमापात— २९१
षष्ठ्यष्टमीद्वादशीषु १३३
षोडशांशं स लभते ६०५
संवत्सरं द्विमासोनं ५५१

संवत्सरे द्विमासोने २७८
स काम इति मे बुद्धिः २१
सक्तुभिः पिण्डदानञ्च ५३२
सचैलमादौ स्नात्वा तु ५४५
सत्यं तीर्थं क्षमा तीर्थं ६९
सत्यं तीर्थं दया तीर्थं ७०
सदा चैव तु शूद्राणाम् ५०९
सदा चैव तु शूद्राणाम् ५१३
सदैव हि जलान्तेषु ५१२
संन्यासिनं तीर्थगतं ६५७
सपिण्डीकरणादूर्ध्वं ५७४
सपिण्डीकरणादूर्ध्वं ५९१
सपिण्डीकरणादूर्ध्वं ५९२
सपितुः पितृकृत्येषु ५५९
सपुत्रया न कर्तव्यं ५६४
सप्तम्यां रविवारे च ३४०
सभर्तृकानां तत्रैव २५०
सम्प्रस्थितस्तीर्थयात्रां १८८
सरस्वती च सावित्री २०८
सरस्वतीदृषद्वत्यौ १७०
सर्वतीर्थमयी गङ्गा २३३, २४४
सर्वतीर्थस्थ च स्नानात् २४८
सर्वतीर्थानि देवाश्च २३२, २३७
सर्वतीर्थानि पुण्यानि ४०
सर्वतीर्थेषु यत्पुण्यं २४३
सर्वथा धर्ममूलोऽर्थो ३४
सर्वस्वनाशेऽप्यथवा नृपस्तु ९०
सर्वाणि तीर्थानि वसन्ति तत्र २४१
सर्वाणि तीर्थान्यपि चाग्निहोत्र— ८०, २४२
सर्वाः समुद्रगाः पुण्याः १२९
सर्वेण गाङ्गेन जलेन सम्यङ् १८४
सर्वे प्रस्रवणाः पुण्याः ४१
सर्वेषामेव तीर्थानां २०८

सहाग्निर्वा सपत्नीको ८३
सहाग्निर्वा सपत्नीको ८४
सह्याद्रेः परमं तीर्थं २४७
सागरस्वननिर्घोष २०९
सायं प्रातर् द्विजातीनां २७६
सार्धं हस्तशतं यावद् ६७५
सिंहकर्कटयोर्मध्ये ३४७
सिंहकर्कटयोर्मध्ये ३४८
सिंहस्थितं मघासंस्थं १४२
सिद्धान्ने तु विधिर्यः स्याद् ५१८, ५२५
सुतभ्रातृपितृव्याश्च ३३३
सेवितेऽपि सदा तीर्थे ६५७
सोमसौम्यगुरुशुक्रवासराः १३६
स्त्रीणामनुपनीतानां ६८२
स्त्रीणाममन्त्रकं श्राद्धं ४९८
स्थानं च लभेत् नित्यं ४९
स्थितो वै नृपतेर्द्वारि ६५२
स्नाति यो मानसे तीर्थे ७४
स्नात्वा ततः पञ्चगव्येन सिक्त्वा ६२५
स्नानकालेऽन्यतीर्थेषु ६६३
स्नानजं फलमाप्नोति १६४
स्नानं दानं तीर्थयात्रां ९९
स्नानादिकं विधायादौ २५२
स्पृष्ट्वा स्पृष्ट्वा तथा स्नानं ६३७
स्वकार्येऽप्यन्यकार्ये वा ६५३
स्वभर्तृप्रभृतित्रिभ्यः ६०८
स्वल्पोऽपि नार्थः प्रतिशुक्रयाने १४७
स्वेन भर्त्रा समं श्राद्धं ५८२
हविःशेषात् ततो मुष्टिं ५७७
हविष्यान्नेन वै मासं ५०६
हस्तेन्दुमैत्रश्रवणाश्विपुष्य— १३४
हस्तो वितस्तिद्वितयं १३२
मञ्च मौक्तिकं रूप्यं ६३७
मश्राद्धं ततः कुर्यात् ६३७

APPENDIX D

GLOSSARY OF SANSKRIT TERMS IN THE TRANSLATION

This index defines technical and other terms which cannot be adequately translated and have therefore been left in Sanskrit in the translation. However, not all such terms are included in this glossary, the following categories being omitted :

(1) Basic concepts of Hinduism, such as varṇa, śūdra, etc., it being assumed that the reader will have some familiarity with the essentials of Hindu thought.

(2) Realia such as names of trees, stars, etc.

(3) Names of gods and other deities, which can be easily identified in dictionaries and other standard reference works.

(4) Terms which are adequately explained in the commentatorial sections of the text itself.

In certain cases, however, terms from among these categories *are* included in the glossary, where they have some particular importance in connection with the major subjects of the text.

agniṣṭut : The first day of the agniṣṭoma sacrifice, and of the pañcadaśarātra sattra. In the latter, its details are superseded by those of the dvādaśāha sacrifice (215.4).

agniṣṭoma : An important Vedic soma sacrifice. Its benefits are less than those of pilgrimage (46).

agniṣvātta : A class of secondary ancestral deities (classified as gaṇa-devatā). The word 'pitṛ' can apply to them (466.1).

agnihotra : The fundamental Vedic Agni-sacrifice. All tīrthas cannot equal it (for a householder) (80, 242). May be both optional (kāmya) and occasional (naimittika) (165.5) (and regular, nitya; see 545.15). Option as to offering materials (215.13). Prescribed in various Vedic schools (235.18). Oblation done by adhvaryu priest (281.1). The optional agnihotra can satisfy the requirement of the regular agnihotra (545.15). Miscellaneous (277).

adhvaryu : The Vedic priest of the Yajur Veda. Performs oblation in agnihotra etc. (281.1).

anulomaja : One born of mixed caste but "with the hair," i.e. in the proper way, namely of a higher caste father and lower caste mother. They follow the dharma of the twice-born (96.2). Cf. *pratilomaja.*

anuvacana : A recitation of summoning, pronounced by the Maitrāvaruṇa priest in the jyotiṣṭoma (cf. *puronuvākya*) (412.22, 24).

anvaṣṭakā (*śrāddha*) : The day after an *aṣṭakā* day, i.e. the ninth days of the dark half of the months Āgrahāyaṇa, Pauṣa, Māgha, and Phālguṇa. Śrāddha done separately for women on anvaṣṭakā day (583). Order of offering in anvaṣṭakā-śrāddha (597).

apośāna : A ritual performed in the cooked-food śrāddha. Sense of the term is disputed; probable meaning is 'sipping of water' (see note in translation, 521.2). Also mentioned in 522.

avama (*dina*) : A lunar day which corresponds exactly with a solar day. An inauspicious day (137). One should not travel on an avama day (133).

aveṣṭi : Name of a particular offering which can be a part of the rājasūya sacrifice, or an independent offering (546.2). In the former case, no benefit from it is specified, but in the latter case its benefit is given (545.20, 546.1,7). Subject of a section of the MS (262.10).

aśvamedha : The royal Vedic horse sacrifice. Its benefit is realized at every step of a pilgrimage to Gayā (163.1, 167), or by fasting and bathing at the Karatoyā or Kuraṅga (201, 202). A thousand thousands of aśvamedhas not equal to shaving at Prabhāsa (250).

aṣṭakā-śrāddha : The śrāddha performed on an aṣṭakā day, i.e. the eighth day of the dark half of the months Āgrahāyaṇa, Pauṣa, Māgha, and Phālguṇa. Śrāddha done separately for women on an aṣṭakā day (618).

ānvaṣṭakya : The śrāddha performed on an *anvaṣṭakā* day. Ānvaṣṭakya-śrāddha for mother (557, 558.5). (More usually spelled anvaṣṭakya.)

Ābhīra : An outcaste cowherd. A liṅga worshipped by Ābhīras is polluted (679).

ābhyudayika (*śrāddha*) : A śrāddha performed on an auspicious occasion, such as the birth of a son; but not at the outset of a pilgrimage (159. 3-5). Cf. nāndīmukhaśrāddha.

āhavanīya : One of the three Vedic (śrauta) sacrificial fires, built on a square fireplace (235.3, 281.1, 412.11).

uparava : Name of the four pits for grinding soma which are dug in the jyotiṣṭoma sacrifice (485.7).

uparavamantra : The mantra used in the digging of the uparava pits in the jyotiṣṭoma : 'Rakṣohano valgahano vaiṣṇavān khanāmi' (485.7).

upasad : A sacrificial ceremony taking up three or more days during a complex soma sacrifice. Use of subrahmaṇya offering in (215.4).

Urukramaviṣṇu (*yāga*) : An optional sacrifice to Viṣṇu-Urukrama, made incidentally to an offering to the Viśvedevas. It is not necessary to summon Viṣṇu to this offering(442.12).

ūha : Modification of a mantra. Does not mean 'recital' of the mantra (493.2-3). (See Glossary of Mīmāṃsā Terms.)

ṛc : A verse of the Ṛg Veda. Not normally subject to modification (ūha) (476-476.1), unless specifically prescribed (524.4). Miscellaneous (639.4).

ṛtvij : A sacrificial priest. His aid is necessary for performance of sacrifices (37.1, 38.3), or of śrāddha by those who are not allowed to perform it themselves (568).

ekoddiṣṭa (*śrāddha*) : A śrāddha which is performed for a single ancestor; as opposed to pārvaṇa śrāddha, which is performed for three ancestors. Modification of mantras in ekoddiṣṭa (494.5, 495-496). Ekoddiṣṭa should be done at midday (528). The offering of piṇḍas is principal to ekoddiṣṭa (531.2). Not offered to ancestors after their sapiṇḍīkaraṇa (574). May be offered to female ancestors (583). Certain relatives receive only ekoddiṣṭa śrāddha (590.4-592, 610.15, 615.13, 618.6-7). Optional ekoddiṣṭas (599.5). Combined performance (tantra) of ekoddiṣṭas (599.7, 602.2). Ekoddiṣṭa performed after pārvaṇa (601.1-602). Feeding of brāhmaṇas in ekoddiṣṭa (602.3-603). Performance by widows (610-610.1). Special rules at Gayā (617.9-10, 618.2).

karaṇa : A mixed caste, son of a śūdra woman and a vaiśya man. Must perform śrāddha without mantras (497.1, 499.2, 499.5).

karmadhāraya : A 'co-ordinate' nominal compound; one in which the members have the same case function (262.3). A karmadhāraya is preferable to a bahuvrīhi if there is a question of interpretation of a compound (262.8-12).

kali (*yuga*) : The last and worst of the four eons. A twice-born man forbidden to travel by ship in kali era (123.4). Kṣetrajas (q.v.) and other types of sons forbidden in kali era (569, 569.1).

kālasūtra : Name of a hell. One goes there for offering to his female ancestors last in a śrāddha (599).

kutapa : The eighth muhūrta (q.v.) of the day. This is the best time to perform śrāddha (473).

kulika : An inauspicious muhūrta (q.v.) (137). For method of calculating a kulika, see MuCi I.37 and commentary.

kuśa : The sacred grass Poa cynosuroides, used in various rites; in tarpaṇa (130.22, 337.1, 344); in bathing for another's sake (319-320.1); in the throwing of bones in a tīrtha (637, 639.3-4); and in the water-offering (643).

kṛcchra : A kind of penance (prāyaścitta). Various pilgrimages are equivalent to various numbers of kṛcchras (129.2-130.84 p.p.). Kṛcchra here refers to the specific kṛcchra called Prājāpatya; this described (130.88-131.1).

kṛta (*yuga*) : The first and best of the four eons. In it, dharma is intact (116.10).

krāntisamatva : A quality of certain astronomical passages (sama, as opposed to bṛhat and jaghanya). An inauspicious occasion (137).

krośa : A measure of distance, equal to one-fourth of a yojana (q.v.), and thus about two miles (117.2, 129.5, 132, 544.5, 676.1). One should not travel more than a krośa after performing a śrāddha (159.12-160.1).

kṣāmavatī : A kind of penitential offering, to be offered to Agni when one's house burns. Combined performance of (545.11).

kṣetraja : A son begotten by another person on one's own wife. Not legally recognized in the kali era (568.1).

gajacchāyā : 'The elephant's shadow,' a particular astronomical conjunction at which śrāddha is to be performed (400). Defined by Aparārka (I.218, p. 427) as the 13th day of a fortnight on which the moon is in Maghā and the sun is in Hasta.

gañja : An inauspicious astronomical conjunction; piṇḍas not to be offered then (395, 395.7).

gaṇa (*devatā*) : Various kinds of deities who are worshipped together in groups (gaṇa), such as the Maruts or the Agniṣvātta pitṛs (q.v.) (466.1).

gaṇḍānta : An inauspicious time at the beginning or end of various nakṣatras (137). See MuCi VI. 43.

gavīdhuka : Coix barbata; not a suitable offering material (265.9).

gavyūti : A measure of distance, equal to two krośas (q.v.), and 1/2 yojana (q.v.); approximately four miles (676-676.1).

gṛhamedhīya-ājyabhāga : The two ājyabhāga (clarified butter) offerings to the Gṛhamedhin (household deities) Maruts. They are an original, not a modified, rite (493.5).

gotra : A clan name, especially among brāhmaṇas (440, 460.2, 502.2, 571). In ancestral rites, the recipient's gotra to be mentioned along with his personal name (344, 502.2, 568, 639.11).

caraṇa : Vedic school or branch. Upon renunciation one leaves his caraṇa (571).

cāturmāsya : The sacrifices performed at the beginning of the four-month seasons. Contain an ancestral offering (554.4).

cāndrāyaṇa : A particular penance, in which the daily amount of food taken decreases and increases with the waning and waxing of the moon. The penalty for neglecting one's parents' bones (633).

jaya : A class of 'victory' mantras; see VS III. 4.4.1, III.4.6.1 (412.9).

tatpuruṣa : A nominal compound in which the first member qualifies the second. The first member may fulfil any case function; for instance the genitive (262.8).

tarpaṇa : See Introduction, vi.c. Part of tīrtha ritual (130. 86, 315.2, 375, 380.2, 381, 381.1, 386, 539.2, 540.3-4, 551.3, 640). For benefit of dead relatives (320.4, 432). Forbidden times for tarpaṇa (346, 364, 394, 396, 684). Done only once in a day (541). Not to be done by one whose father is alive (555). Order of offering (597). Part of ritual of throwing bones in tīrtha (637, 639.7). Must be done when one crosses a river during a pilgrimage (670, 670.3, 671.2-3).

Tarpaṇa is discussed in detail in 322.2-345 p.p. See Introduction, vii, xvii for contents of this section.

tīrtha : See Introduction, ii, vi. 9 for definitions etc., and vii for topics.

tīrtha-śrāddha : Śrāddha which is performed at a tīrtha. Discussed in detail in 368-624.1 p.p. (also 268). See Introduction vii. xix-xxv.

tulāpuruṣa : A religious donation of a man's weight in gold (18.1, 449.2).

tridinaspṛś : A solar day which comes into contact with three lunar days. One should not travel on such a day (133).

triṣṭubh : A common Vedic meter of four pādas of eleven syllables each (636.1, 639.2, 639.9).

darśa : The sacrifice offered on the new-moon day (215.25).

darśa-pūrṇamāsa : The sacrifices offered on new and full moon days (118.6). The benefits of their component parts are realized in combination (545.11).

dvandva : A 'copulative' nominal compound, in which the members of the compound are to be understood as connected by the word 'and' (262.10).

dvādaśāha : A twelve days' sacrifice, which is the archetype for the pañcadaśarātra sattra (q.v.) (215.4).

nāndīmukha : A śrāddha offered on an auspicious occasion, such as a wedding (195). Combination with regular śrāddha (549). Offerings to female ancestors in (618). Cf. ābhyudayika-śrāddha.

nigada : A kind of yajur-mantra, which is used to address someone. They are pronounced loudly, although yajus-s in general are pronounced softly (618.14).

Niṣāda : A tribe of hunters. The compound 'Niṣāda-sthapati' means, 'Niṣāda-chief,' not 'chief of the Niṣādas' (262.8).

pañcadaśarātra 'The fifteen nights' sacrifice'; a complex sacrifice; its first day is based on the agniṣṭut sacrifice, and the remaining days on the dvādaśāha (215.4). Agni-mantra not used in the first day (215.4,18).

parighārdha : The first half of the 19th yoga (parigha); an inauspicious time (137).

parvan : The new and full moon days; also the eighth and fourteenth days of each half-month. There are fixed times for the performace of various mandatory (nitya) rites (288. 3-4, 384, 389.7, 390, 567, 688).

pāta : Same as vyatīpāta, q.v. (290.3, 395.8). Shaving and other acts not to be performed on a pāta (290, 291). Piṇḍas not to be offered (395).

pāda-kṛcchra : A penance lasting four days. Three consecutive pādakṛcchras constitute a prājāpatyakṛcchra (q.v.) (131, 131.1).

pāraśava : A mixed caste, son of a brāhmaṇa father and a śūdra mother. They perform śrāddha without mantras (497.1, 499.2,5).

pārvaṇa-śrāddha : The basic śrāddha rite, performed for three ancestors at a time (as opposed to ekoddiṣṭa, q.v.). The archetype of all other śrāddhas, such as tīrtha-śrāddha (159.6. 502.4, 503, 506.2, 556). Mantras modified in pārvaṇa (494.4). To be performed in the afternoon (528). Beneficiaries of pārvaṇa-śrāddha (558.2, 573-619.2 p.p.). Miscellaneous (162.7, 486.7).

pāvamānī : The Vedic hymns addressed to Soma while being purified; especially the hymns of maṇḍala IX of the Ṛg Veda (637, 639.4).

piṇḍa : A ball of rice or other food substance offered to the ancestors in a śrāddha. Offering piṇḍas is a principal part of śrāddha. Forbidden at certain times (339, 393.5), and to certain persons (345, 571). To be given at tīrthas (381). Omitted from śrāddha at certain times (413-414). Offered to pretas (439, 605.4-607). Given in raw-food śrāddha (518, 520, 521). Piṇḍas to be given at a tīrtha even when śraddha not done (528.2-531.2). Materials for piṇḍa (531.3-533.1, 536). Size of piṇḍa (533. 2-535). Functions of piṇḍas in tīrtha-śrāddha (537-539.1). May be omitted from tīrtha-śrāddha (539.2-540.5). Offered in soma sacrifice (554.5). Omitted from 'declared' śrāddha (566-566.1). Number of piṇḍas in śrāddha (576). Offered together for husband and wife (583.3-584.1). Offered for mother's co-wives (586.2-

587.1). Recipients of piṇḍas in tīrtha-śrāddha (588); and in śrāddha by son whose father is alive (614). One piṇḍa offered to all relatives in common (619.3-624). Miscellaneous (230, 526, 579, 639.7).

piṇḍapitṛyajña : The Vedic śrāddha ritual as prescribed in the Gṛhya- and Śrauta-sūtras. Can be performed only by keepers of sacred fire (617.1).

pitṛ : (1) In its technical sense, a deceased ancestor for whom sapiṇḍīkaraṇa (q.v.) has been performed, and who is thus no longer a preta (q.v.) (495.1-11).

(2) In its literal meaning, a person's biological father (and also his antecedents, living or dead). The dual meaning of the word 'pitṛ' must be recognized in connection with the question of modification of mantras in śrāddha (465.2-468.2, 486.9-14, 490.2, 496).

(3) The word 'pitṛ' also applies to the gods who serve along with the human ancestors as deities of a śrāddha (460.2-461).

puṇḍarīka : Name of a sacrifice. Its benefit can be obtained by going to Puṇḍarīka tīrtha (171).

purāṇaikoddiṣṭa : An ekoddiṣṭa śrāddha (q.v.) performed for a deceased ancestor who has become a pitṛ (q.v.). Modification of mantras takes place as in pārvaṇa śrāddha (494.5). Cf. pretaikoddiṣṭa.

puronuvākya : A mantra of invitation to a deity. Serves as both praiṣa- and anuvacana-mantra in the jyotiṣṭoma (412.24).

pratilomaja: One born of mixed caste "against the hair," i.e. in an improper way, of a higher caste mother and a lower caste father. May perform pilgrimages (96.3), but only if it does not interfere with their serving the twice-born (93.1-95.1). cf. anulomaja.

prastha : A measure of volume, attributed various different values. A 'Magadhan' prastha = 12 1/2 palas (642).

prājāpatya (*kṛcchra*) : A particular kind of penance (126.1). (Referred to in the text as simply kṛcchra, q.v.) Consists of three consecutive pāda-kṛcchras (q.v.) (130.88). Lasts for twelve days (131.1).

prāṇabhṛt : Term used to denote a brick used in ritual with a mantra beginning with the word 'prāṇabhṛt.' The term used loosely to include other bricks as well (26.6). Cf. sṛṣṭi.

preta : A deceased ancestor who has not yet become a pitṛ (q.v.) by performance of sapiṇḍīkaraṇa (q.v.) (467, 468). Tarpaṇa for pretas (342, 343). Modification of word 'pitṛ' to 'preta' in preta-śrāddha (495-495.12). Offering of śrāddha to preta by non-relatives (605.4-607). Offerings when father is preta (614). Pretas dwell in the south (625). Liberation of preta by throwing his bones in a tīrtha (625). Cf. preta-śrāddha, pretaikoddiṣṭa.

preta-śrāddha : Śrāddha performed for an ancestor who is a preta (q.v.). Prohibited times for (390.1-393.4). To be performed during intercalary month (400). Provides the preta with a body (439.1). Cf. preta, pretaikoddiṣṭa.

pretaikoddiṣṭa : An ekoddiṣṭa śrāddha (q.v.) performed for an ancestor who is a preta (q.v.). Modification of mantras in (494.5-495.12). Cf. purāṇaikoddiṣṭa.

praiṣa : The summons pronounced by the Maitrāvaruṇa priest to the hotṛ priest (412.22-24).

bahuvrīhi : A nominal compound whose members together denote an object different from that which each of them denotes separately (anyapadārtha) (231.1-2,9, 235.25, 260.2, 262.17). A bahuvrīhi necessarily involves indirect expression (lakṣaṇā), so that other types of compounds are preferred (262.8-9).

manvādi (*śrāddha*) : (The śrāddha performed on) the days on which the fourteen manvantaras (eons of Manu) begin; namely the 9th day of the bright half of Āśvina, the 12th of the bright half of Kārttika, the 3rd of the bright half of Caitra and Bhādrapada, the moonless day of Phālguṇa, the 11th of the bright half of Pauṣa, the 10th of the bright half of Āṣāḍha, the 7th of the bright half of Māgha, the 8th of the dark half of Śrāvaṇa, and the full moon days of Āṣāḍha, Kārttika, Phālguṇa, Caitra, and Jyeṣṭha. These śrāddhas to be performed twice if they fall in an intercalary month (401). Combined performance of (547.3-548.1).

mahālaya (*śrāddha*) : A special śrāddha to be performed during the dark half of the month of Bhādrapada. Not performed in an intercalary month (401.1). Permissible to use only one brāhmaṇa (526). Mother's co-wives receive offerings in (587.4). Combined performance in (601). Offered by widows (608.2). Order of offerings in (333, 334).

māṣa : The bean of the plant Phaseolus radiatus (158). It is not to be offered in sacrifice (265.5-275 p.p.).

mīmāṃsā : The science of interpretation of Vedic text and ritual (more specifically, Pūrva-mīmāṃsā) (220.4, 442.7).

mīmāṃsaka : A scholar of Mīmāṃsā (q.v.) (118.7, 215.23, 272.3).

mudga : The bean of the plant Phaseolus mungo. Used in sacrifice (265.5-275 p.p.).

muhūrta : A measure of time, equal to one thirtieth of one day or 48 minutes (398).

mūrdhāvasikta : A mixed caste, offspring of a brāhmaṇa father and a kṣatriya mother. Follow the dharma of the twice-born (96.2).

maitrāvaruṇa : A priest who serves as assistant to the hotṛ priest in the jyotiṣṭoma sacrifice (412.22).

mauñjī : The girdle of muñja grass worn by a brāhmaṇa. The ceremony of tying on the mauñjī forbidden at certain times (138); and shaving is forbidden for a half year after the ceremony (294).

yajus : A mantra of the Yajur Veda; to be muttered in a low tone, unless it is a nigada (q.v.) (618.14-15).

yugādi (*śrāddha*) : (The śrāddha performed on) the days on which the four eons (yuga) begin; namely the 3rd day of the bright half of Vaiśākha, the 9th of the bright half of Kārttika, the 13th of the dark half of Bhādrapada, and the 15th of the dark half of Māgha. To be performed twice if it falls in an intercalary month (401). Combined performance of (547.3-548).

yojana : A measure of distance, equal to four krośas, or about nine miles (117.2, 125.1 (chapter heading), 129.2-130.83 p.p., 677-678.2). Calculation of its distance (132).

rathantara-sāman : Name of a certain sāman (sung mantra). May be optionally chosen in jyotiṣṭoma sacrifice (220.5).

rājasūya : The sacrifice performed at the coronation of a king. Its benefits compared to that of pilgrimage (163.2). Benefits of its component parts realized in combination (545.11). Contains an aveṣṭi offering (q.v.) (545.20).

raurava : Name of a hell. One goes there for failing to shave at the Gaṅgā (256), or for paying homage to an image worshipped by women (679).

vitasti : A measure of length, equal to twelve fingers' widths (132).

viśvajit : A one-day soma sacrifice. Its benefit, not prescribed, is assumed to be the attainment of heaven (the viśvajinnyāya, 168.1).

viśvedeva : A class of ten gods, a different pair of whom is invoked in different types of śrāddha (503.1, 505.2-3). (See Kane, *History of Dharmaśāstra*, vol. IV p. 457.)

viṣṭikaraṇa : A particular inauspicious karaṇa, or half-part of a lunar day (see Monier-Williams, *Sanskrit-English Dictionary*, p. 254 col.1) (137).

vaidhṛti : An inauspicious astronomical conjunction of the sun and moon (see Monier-Williams, *Sanskrit-English Dictonary* p. 1023 col.1) (137). Piṇḍas not to be offered at a vaidhṛti (395, 395.7).

vyatīpāta : A particular inauspicious astronomical conjunction (137). Defined by Vṛddhamanu quoted in Aparārka (I.218, p. 426) as a new-moon day (amā) which falls on a Tuesday and whose nakṣatra is Śrāvaṇa, Aśvin, Dhaniṣṭhā, Ārdrā, or Āśleṣā. Same as pāta, q.v. (290.3, 395.8). Occasion for śrāddha (547.3).

śrāddha : See Introduction, VI.b. To be performed at tīrthas (45, 252, 304, 315.2, 640, 671.4), and at Gayā especially (150). To be performed before and after a pilgrimage (152.1-162.10). Prohibited elements in (267-268). No shaving on day of śrāddha (290). For benefit of dead relatives (320.4). To be done at a tīrtha at any time (323). Not to be done by mendicants etc. (345). Performed in connection with ceremony of throwing bones in tīrtha (630, 631, 637, 639.5-6). Miscellaneous (330-330.4, 334.3, 684).

These and other topics concerning śrāddha are discussed in detail in 368-624.1 p.p. For details see Introduction, VII. xix-xxv.

Also see listings in this glossary under various types of śrāddha : aṣṭakā-śrāddha, ānvaṣṭakya, ābhyudayika, ekoddiṣṭa, tīrtha-śrāddha, nāndīmukha, pārvaṇa-śrāddha, piṇḍapitṛyajña, purāṇaikoddiṣṭa, preta-śrāddha, pretaikoddiṣṭa, manvādi, mahālaya, yugādi, sapiṇḍana, sapiṇḍīkaraṇa.

sattra : A class of complex soma sacrifices which last for thirteen or more days. Begins at the declaration of intent to perform (195).

sandhyā : The three 'juncture' times in a day; morning, noon, and evening. A ritual (sandhyāvandana, sandhyopāsana, or sandhyopāsti) consisting of water offerings, mantras, etc. must be performed at every sandhyā (189. 189.1, 338.5). This ritual prescribed in various smṛtis (235.18). Not to be done in impure waters (364). Certain acts not to be performed at sandhyā times (308.2, 340, 389.2, 397, 398, 400.1, 400.7); exceptions (389.14).

sapiṇḍana : Same as sapiṇḍīkaraṇa, q.v. (630).

sapaṇḍīkaraṇa : The ceremony whereby a dead ancestor who is a preta becomes a pitṛ (466.1, 467, 495.1). Part of the śrāddha performed one year after the death of the ancestor (the śrāddha itself is also known as sapiṇḍīkaraṇa) (466.1). After sapiṇḍīkaraṇa only pārvaṇa-śrāddha to be offered for some relatives (574), but ekoddiṣṭa to others (591, 592). Miscellaneous (584.2, 639.5).

sāmidhenī : A group of mantras which are recited in connection with kindling the sacrificial fire. Repetition of these verses in the darśa-pūrṇamāsa (118.6).

sāṃnāyya : An offering of fresh hot milk and curds. Combined performance in (545.11).

subrahmaṇyā : Name of a recitation of invitation to the gods. An Indra mantra is used in it in the pañcadaśarātra and dvādaśāha sacrifices, but an Agni mantra in the agniṣṭut sacrifice (215.4).

sṛṣṭi : Term used to denote a brick used in ritual with a mantra beginning with the word 'sṛṣṭi.' The term used loosely to include other bricks as well (26.6). (Cf. prāṇabhṛt.)

somasūtra : The channel that draws off the water with which a liṅga has been bathed. Must not be crossed when circumambulating a Śiva-liṅga (645, 645.1).

sautrāmaṇī : Name of an Indra-sacrifice, one of the haviryajñas. Provides benefits to the ancestors of the performer (438.1).

svadhā : An exclamation spoken at the time of presenting an offering to the ancestors (490.9, 524, 524.2, 566).

svāhā : An exclamation pronounced at the time of presenting an offering to a god (463.6).

sviṣṭakṛt : Name of an offering to Agni in the darśa-pūrṇamāsa etc. The oblations made before it are done with the middle tone (505).

hanta : An exclamation of greeting; a ceremonial reception of a guest with this exclamation (541).

APPENDIX E

GLOSSARY OF MĪMĀṂSĀ AND OTHER TECHNICAL TERMS

Many of the Mīmāṃsā terms below, such as vidhi, arthavāda, anuvāda, etc. apply properly to Vedic texts, but are used in later smṛti literature to apply to Purāṇic and epic texts as well. The term 'authoritative texts' is used in this glossary to cover both of these usages.

Further information concerning some of these terms will be found in the footnotes to the relevant passages in the translation.

aṅga: A subsidiary act or object of a principal (pradhāna) ritual. May be mandatory parts of a required rite (185.2, 215.7, 504.2-4) or elements of an optional act (504.2-4, 506.2). An aṅga is that which makes the principal fruitful (412.10). 162.1,5, 163.2, 164.8, 13,15, 176.2, 215.23-24, 322.2, 330.3-4, 412.12, 504.2.

aṅgin: The recipient or locus of a subsidiary. 412.9.

atideśa: 'Transferral' or 'extension.' Particularly, the transferral of ritual details from the archetypal act (prakṛti) to the modified rite (vikṛti) (215.4, 615.11). 162.8, 475.2, 486.3, 488).

adṛṣṭa: An invisible or transcendental purpose of a ritual act. An act can have no more than one invisible result (215.9,11). No modification of mantras with invisible purpose (414.7-9, 463.3,488). If a visible purpose can be understood, an invisible purpose may not be construed (461.6). Invisible results are generated by acts with visible results (462.3). 278.13, 463.4, 475.4.

anārabhyavidhāna: A generally applicable prescription, one not prescribed in reference to a specific rite. 235.9.

anuvāda, anuvādaka : A supplementary passage or reference in an authoritative text which merely repeats something previously prescribed. A kind of arthavāda, q.v. Anuvāda has no meaning of its own (235.22). Preferable to interpret passages as prescriptions rather than an anuvādas (235.21).

235.18-22. See also kriyamāṇānuvāda, avayutyānuvāda, nityānuvāda.

antaraṅga: That benefit, detail, etc. which is more closely connected with the principal matter, and which should therefore be chosen. Opposite of bahiraṅga, q.v. 168.1, 171.3-4, 605.2. Cf. upasthiti, lāghava.

apakarṣa: Drawing back of ritual details. When a part of an archetypal sacrifice, such as a pre-sacrifice, is performed earlier in a modified sacrifice, then the subsidiary acts that precede that part in the archetype are drawn back with it to an earlier time in the modified rite. 215.23-25.

apūrva : The transcendental result of a ritual act, the force which causes it to yield its prescribed benefit to the performer. This, rather than the deity (devatā), is the main object of the ritual (423.5,7). 488, 545.11.

apūrvavidhi: An absolute prescription, which lays down a new matter not previously treated; the basic type of prescription, as opposed to niyamavidhi and parisaṃkhyā, q. v. 235.8, 15-16.

abhilāpa: The declaration of the object (i.e. the person for whose benefit the rite is done) of a rite. Not a mantra, and ūha does not apply to it (493.8-494.1, 502.1). 495.9.

arthavāda: An explanatory or commendatory passage in an authoritative text. As opposed to a prescription (vidhi) (122.4, 7-8). Used to explain the benefits of acts or details (163.2,164.7). Made for the sake of something else, not for its own sake, and may contradict something stated elsewhere in an authoritative text (442.3-4). 24, 165.2. Cf. hetvarthavāda, anuvāda.

avayutyānuvāda: A kind of supplementary passage (anuvāda) which singles out (avayutya) and restates a particular instance of a more general rule; a partial supplementary passage. Thus for example the rules given in the Matsyapurāṇa as applying to a pilgrimage to Prayāga should be taken as an avayutyānuvāda, repeating in a particular context the general rules for all pilgrimages as given by Jābāli and Gobhila (in 115-118.4). Preferable to interpret a passage as a vidhi than as an avayutyānuvāda (122.11, 235.14-15). 118.5, 122.11.

aveṣṭyadhikaraṇa: Śab. II.3.2.3. In this section it is determined that the word 'rājan' applies to kṣatriyas only, never to brāhmaṇas. 262.10.

ānarthakyapratihatānāṃ viparītaṃ balābalam iti nyāya: The rule that a weaker rule in an authoritative text is not cancelled by a stronger rule or rules which contradict it, on the grounds that every authoritative rule must have a purpose of its own. 215.17.

utpattivākya: Originative sentence (=utpattividhi, originative prescription). A simple prescription of an act alone, as opposed to a viśiṣṭavidhi (q.v.) and a guṇavidhi. 215.14,25.

utpattiśiṣṭaguṇa: A particularity or accessory given in the originative prescription of the act itself, i. e. in a viśiṣṭavidhi. Such an originative particularity cannot be cancelled by a particularity separately applied to a previously prescribed act (utpannaśiṣṭaguṇa, q. v.). 215.12.

utpannaśiṣṭaguṇa: A particularity or accessory separately prescribed for a previously prescribed act. This kind of accessory is weaker than one prescribed in the originative prescription of the act itself (utpattiśiṣṭaguṇa), and cannot overrule it. 215.12-13.

uddeśya: The 'intended aim' of a prescription; that which a sentence is intended to prescribe. The intended aim of a sentence may not be modified in that same sentence, as that produces vākyabheda (q.v.) (116.6, 159.7, 260.6-262.15 p.p., 412.19,21-22). 605.2.

upalakṣaṇa: 'Implication,' mentioning something in connection with a single item with an implied application to other similar items; pars pro toto. 296.1, 548.1, 554.3, 641.1, 671.3, 672.1, 685.2.

upasaṃhāra: A restricting statement on a more general prescription. A general rule which is in some way not clear is subject to an upasaṃhāra (234.5, 235). 234.4-235.1, 412.3.

upasthiti: 'Coming' or 'bringing to mind.' That is referred to in a text which most readily comes to mind from the context (upasthiter lāghavam) (159.4; also cf. 281.8). Avoid interpretations which involve that which less readily comes to mind (upasthiter gauravam) (168.1, 171.5).

ubhayārtyadhikaraṇa: The Section on the Ruining of Both (Offerings); MS VI. 4.6.22-23. Establishes that the modifier of the intended aim (uddeśya) of prescriptions is not intended (avivakṣita). Not a mere restatement of the Grahaikatvanyāya (260.12-262). 412.19. Also known as ārtyadhikaraṇa. Cf. vākyabheda.

ūha: 'Modification' of a mantra of an archetypal rite (prakṛti) when it must be changed to apply to a modified rite (vikṛti). For instance, a mantra may be modified to address a different deity (423.2-5). A ṛc normally does not undergo modification (476). A mantra will not be modified in the vikṛti if it did not have a literally appropriate sense in the prakṛti (485.6-7). Modification only takes place in limited circumstances (463.3-489). 449.3-7; 463.3-495.12 p.p.

kapiñjalanyāya: 'The rule of the partidges'; an unspecified plural is to be taken as prescribing three things. See Śab. XI. 1.8.43. 159.6.

kāmya: An optional act, to be performed whenever one desires to gain some particular benefit. An act may be both optional and occasional (naimittika) (166.1). Optional supersedes regular (nitya) (503.1, 504.2-4). Optional details are not transferred to a modified rite (506. 2-3). 215.9, 225.3, 504, 505.2, 506.1, 599.5.

kriyamāṇānuvāda: 'A supplementary reference to what is being done'; a mantra such as 'Yuvā suvāsā' which merely describes what is already being done, as opposed to a mantra which causes the action by stimulating the priest or sacrificer to act. See Śab. XII.3.16.36-37. 338.6.

guṇa: An accessory to a ritual (506.2). Cf. guṇaphalādhikāra etc.

guṇaphalādhikāra, *guṇaphalavidhi*, *guṇaphalasaṃbandha*, *guṇaphalopabandha*: Prescriptions which authorize the (optional) use of a particular accessory in order to produce a specified benefit; e.g. 'Dadhnendriyakāmasya juhuyāt,' 'He should offer with sour milk for one desirous of power,' wherein the guṇa is dadhi, and the phala is indriya. 506.1, 373.1, 281.9.

godohananyāya: The rule of the cow's-milk vessel; MS III. 6. 3.10. An optional element supersedes a regular element. 503.1.

gaurava: (1) Excess verbiage, unnecessary prescription (545.21); overloading of sense, attributing an excessively complex meaning to a prescription (215.10, 284.1, 373.2). (2) Difficulty or excessive effort (in bringing something to mind); see upasthiti (168.1, 171.5). Cf. lāghava.

grahaikatva (*adhikaraṇa*): The Section on the Singularity of the Cups; MS III.1.7.13-14. In the prescription 'Grahaṃ saṃmārṣṭi' ('He wipes the cup') the singular number is not really intended (avivakṣita), because it modifies the intended aim (uddeśya) of the sentence. Modification of the intended aim causes vākyabheda (q.v.). Cf. ubhayārtyadhikaraṇa. Also called Grahanyāya. 231.3-4, 233.1, 262.6.

codaka: The rule of transfer, whereby details are transferred from archetype to modified rite. Similar to atideśa. 215.18, 24, 505.1.

tantra: Combined performance of several similar acts. The performance of one of them satisfies the requirement of performing all of them. Permissible when the place, time, and performer of the several acts are the same (544.3, 545.1). Principal as well as subsidiary acts may be performed in combination (545.10-11). The apūrva (q.v.) of acts performed in combination arises from them collectively (545.11). 215.4, 545.3,12, 546.6, 599.7, 600, 601, 602.2, 603.4, 604, 604.2, 617.7.

dṛṣṭa(*artha*): A visible, or non-transcendental purpose of a ritual act. Preferable to an invisible (adṛṣṭa) purpose (461.6). 462.3, 463.4, 488.

devatādhikaraṇa (*navame vigrahādinirākaraṇa*: *navame devatāyā vigrahādipañcanirākṛti*): MS IX. 1. 5.6-10. In this section it is established that according to Mīmāṃsā doctrine deities such as the god Indra do not have bodies. 414.5,10, 423.2, 449.3, 462.6-463.1.

doṣatraya: 'The three faults' inherent in a prescription of exclusion (parisaṃkhyā, q.v.) The three faults are śrutahāni, aśrutakalpanā, and prāptabādha, 'departure from what is literally stated, construing what is not literally stated, and superseding what has been already established.' (The three faults are also called svārthaprahāṇa, parārthakalpanā, and prāptabādha.) Because of these inherent faults, one should avoid interpreting a prescription as a parisaṃkhyā whenever possible. (For a fuller explanation of the doṣatraya see Edgerton's MNP Ś 246 and translation.) 235.13, 262.34, 529.2.

dvārabādha: 'Ruling out the reason' for doing something. If the reason (dvāra) for a procedure in the archetype is not present in the modified rite, the procedure is dropped. Cf. svayaṃkṛtedhmavedyoś chedanoddhanana, an example of dvārabādha. 414.1.

nāmadheya: Denomination, one of the five parts of the Veda (vidhi, mantra, arthavāda, nāmadheya, and niṣedha). Nāmadheya comprises the names of rituals prescribed in the Veda, such as 'darśa-pūrṇamāsa.' 281.9.

nitya: A regular, mandatory act to be performed on specified fixed occasions. A nitya rite is mandatory (āvaśyaka) (215.8, 599.4-5). Must be performed even during an impure time such as an intercalary month (399, 400). Optional element supersedes a regular element (503.1, 504.2-4). May be done by one who has committed a minor sin (572.1). Regular act not to be combined with non-regular act (639.18). 506.1, 548.2-550.

nityānuvāda: 'A supplementary reference to a known fact'; a passage which restates something which is already known, in that it prohibits something which is obviously impossible. 276.5-7. Cf. Śab. I. 2.2.18.

nimitta: The special occasion or occasioning factor on which an occasional act (naimittika) must be performed. If one fails to perform the occasioned act when the occasion arises he incurs a sin (166.2, 197.3). An occasion yet to arise may condition an occasioned act (220.3-224.1). When an occasion arises, the occasioned act must be performed immediately if possible (387.4-5); but exceptions permitted (389.7). When different occasions arise together, the occasioned acts are to be performed separately; but exceptions possible (540.5-546.8 p.p.). 260.9-262.2 p.p., 278.6-7, 281.5, 286.2, 288.4, 296.1, 314.2, 387.1,4, 400.2, 412.1-4,17-19,27,413.1-414,414.4, 519.2, 528.1, 550.2, 560.2, 604.5, 639.20.

niyamavidhi: A delimiting prescription; one which completes a previous prescription that failed to apply to all relevant cases. As opposed to apūrvavidhi and parisaṃkhyā. 235.10.

niyamādṛṣṭārtha : An act with an invisible purpose connected with a restriction on the act. Even acts which have a visible purpose may carry an invisible purpose related to restrictions of time, place, etc. placed on the act. This invisible purpose is merely a co-product, not a reason for doing the act itself (462.4). 462.2.

niṣādasthapatiśabda [*nyāya*]:'The word 'Niṣāda-chief'', discussed in Śab. VI. 1.13.51. Such a compound word should be taken as a karmadhāraya rather than a tatpuruṣa. 262.8.

niṣedhānuvāda: A supplementary passage of prohibition. 489.

naimittika: An 'occasional,' or 'specially occasioned' act; one which must be performed whenever the appropriate occasion (nimitta) arises. An act may be both occasional and optional (kāmya) (166.1). Failure to perform the occasioned act when the occasion arises produces a sin (197.3). Occasional act is mandatory (āvaśyaka) (215.7, 503.1). Occasional act may be caused by an occasion which is to arise in the future 220.3-224.1). Occasional act to be performed even during prohibited times (295, 308.2-310, 399, 400). If possible, occasional act to be performed immediately when occasion arises (387.1, 389.4-5). Occasional acts with different occasioning factors must be performed separately; but exceptions possible (540.5-546.8 p.p.). May be done by one who has committed a minor sin (572.1). 278.7, 288.4, 344.2, 389.15, 687.

padavākya: A specific prescription supersedes a more general one, but only when the general prescription retains a function of its own (see bādha). See 235.2-4 and note on translation.

parisaṃkhyā, *parisaṃkhyāna*: A prescription of exclusion, intended to rule out all alternatives but one; a rule of the form "One should do this, and only this." Interpreting a prescription as a parisaṃkhyā always causes the three faults of śrutahāni, aśrutakalpanā, and prāptabādha (see under doṣatraya), and thus should be avoided whenever possible (235.13, 262.34, 529.2). Parisaṃkhyā contrasts with apūrvavidhi and niyamavidhi. 235.11, 262.24-25, 274.3, 276.1, 277.2-3, 288.1, 493.5, 584.4, 585.2.

pāśanyāya: MS IX. 3.5.15-19. A mantra with a grammatical number which does not strictly apply may be used in an archetypal rite, if it applies in other respects. Since the number does not apply in the archetype, it will not be modified to apply in the modified rite (485.7, 486.3).

prakaraṇa: Context. Direct statement (śruti) overrules interpretation based on context, but only if the two conflict (118.3-7). Overruled by definitive precept (paribhāṣā) (502). 171.3, 281.15, 506.3, 609.1.

prakṛti: An archetypal rite, from which other, modified rites (vikṛti) are obtained by transfer (atideśa; cf. also codaka). For instance, among śrāddhas, the pārvaṇa śrāddha is the prakṛti, and all other śrāddhas are modified forms of it. 215.4,24, 423.5-6, 465.1, 477, 485.7, 486.3, 13, 16, 17, 487.3, 488, 489.1, 490.6, 502.4.

pratiprasava: A suspension in a specific case of a general rule. 556.1.

prasaṅga: Incidental achievement or performance of an act by another act. Prasaṅga occurs when an act performed for the sake of one aim (uddeśya) incidentally satisfies the requirement of another aim (unlike tantra where a multitude of acts with the same aim is performed in combination). Like tantra, prasaṅga is not permitted if there is a difference in performer (561.1-2, 617.7) or materials (547.3-4). 545.15-16, 546.6, 548, 549, 550, 610.13.

bahiraṅga: A benefit, detail, etc. which is less closely connecte. with the principal matter, and which thus should be rejected Opposite of antaraṅga, q.v. Cf. upasthiti, gaurava. 168.1.

bādha: Supersession, cancellation, or ruling out of an element An element of an archetype may for various reasons be superseded or cancelled in the modified rite. A single element is superseded by several elements (215.4). Bādha should not be absolute (235.2-4; see padavākya). An optional element supersedes a regular element (503.1; see godohana-nyāya).215.17,235.13,414.1,4,462.1,504.2-4,505.1,560.3. See also dvārabādha.

rāgataḥ prāpti: Establishment by natural inclination; such acts as men tend to do naturally may be prohibited without being otherwise established. Other prohibited acts must first be established by prescription. 262.32.

lakṣaṇā: Indirect expression; reading into a word an implied, rather than explicit meaning. To be avoided whenever possible. A bahuvrīhi compound always involves lakṣaṇā, while a karmadhāraya does not (262.8-9) (cf. niṣādasthapatiśabda). 157.4, 275.2, 615.7.

lāghava: (1) Simplicity or economy of verbiage; making every authoritative text meaningful in itself (546.1). Interpretation of prescriptions in the simplest way (215.11). (2) Readiness or ease in bringing something to mind (see upasthiti) (159.4, 281.8). Cf. gaurava.

vākya: Syntactic connection (samabhivyāhāra); interpretation by reference to an entire sentence. 171.3.

vākyabheda: 'Splitting of the sentence,' a fault which arises from prescribing more than one thing in the same prescription. Thus, except in a viśiṣṭa-vidhi, one may not interpret a rule as prescribing both a rite (the uddeśya) and an accessory or detail of the rite. Thus the grammatical number etc. of the intended aim (uddeśya) of a prescription cannot be taken literally but must be considered to be 'not intended' (avivakṣita), or else vākyabheda results. Cf. grahaikatvādhikaraṇa and ubhayārtyadhikaraṇa. 284.1, 412.19, 21, 25, 449.7.

vikalpa; *vaikalpika*: An optional choice as to procedure in ritual acts; optional. Produced when two or more alternatives are prescribed by equally authoritative words (215.2). 209.1, 215.11, 224.2, 581.1, 639.1.

vikṛti: A modified ritual (or 'ectype') based on the archetypal rite (prakṛti). Similar features are adopted from the archetype by transferral (atideśa). Different features are specifically prescribed for the vikṛti. For example, tīrthaśrāddha is a vikṛti of the archetypal pārvaṇa śrāddha (502.4). 423.5-6, 477, 477.1, 486.1, 3, 8, 13, 16, 487.3, 489.1, 490.4.

vidhi: A prescription in a Vedic or other authoritative text. The principal part of the Veda according to Pūrva-mīmāṃsā, as distinct from arthavāda, mantra, nāmadheya, and niṣedha. For instances in the text, see the various sub-types of vidhi: apūrvavidhi, niyamavidhi, parisaṃkhyā; also see utpattivākya viśiṣṭavidhi, utpattiśiṣṭaguṇa, utpannaśiṣṭaguṇa.

viśiṣṭa-vidhi: A modified prescription, which prescribes both an act and an accessory (guṇa) at once. To be avoided when possible, because it incurs gaurava. 373.2.

viśvajin-nyāya: When the benefit of a prescribed act is not specified, it may be assumed to be heaven. See Śab. IV. 3.7.15. 168.1.

śeṣa: A supplement to a principal rite. Similar to aṅga, and thus used in 412.11-12. That which assists the principal is a śeṣa.

śeṣin: The recipient or locus of a supplement (śeṣa). 412.7.

śruti: A 'direct' or 'literal statement' of an authoritative text. Overrules contextual statement (prakaraṇa), but only when there is a conflict between the two (118.5-6). Must be modified to prevent a meaningless statement (157.2). Overrules interpretation based on order of reading (pāṭhakrama) (215.16). An independent expression, as opposed to a statement dependent on syntactic connection (412.5).

saṃyogapṛthaktva: 'Separateness of connections,' whereby something may have a dual nature in different circumstances. For example, śrāddha may be both optional and occasional (165.5-166.1). Cf. MS IV.3.3.5. 426.3, 503.1, 545.5.

svayaṃkṛtedhmavedyoś chedanoddhanana: 'The cutting and turning up of the natural firewood and altar (is not performed)'; an example of dvārabādha, q. v. Śab. X. 1.1.3 (varṇaka 1). 414.1 (see note on translation there).

hetvarthavāda: 'A commendatory statement of cause,' a particular type of arthavāda in which a ritual element is commended by a statement of the reason for its use. See Śab. I. 2.3.26-30. 414.2.

Appendix F

INDEX OF MĪMĀṂSĀ TEXTS

The sentences listed below are not treated in the text as quotations proper, as they are cited merely for purposes of comparison or in order to suggest the application of the relevant Mīmāṃsā rule about their interpretation. Thus most of these are cited with the phrase 'itivat' ('as in the case of...').

Most of these sentences are cited in the Mīmāṃsā texts as Vedic prescriptions. However, the problem of locating them in extant Vedic texts is very complex; many of them appear in variant forms, or not at all, in the extant Veda. The relevance of these sentences for our present purpose is their appearance and discussion in the Mīmāṃsā, so that the problem of their location in the Veda will not be approached here. Discussions of this problem may be found in Jha's translation of the Śabara Bhāṣya and in Garge's *Citations in Śabara Bhāṣya.* For the location and significance of these texts in the Mīmāṃsā see the footnotes to the appropriate parts of the translation.

Agāre gāvo vāsyantām 412.7
Agniṃ citavān 281.4
Agnyabhāve tu viprasya pāṇāv evopapādayet 412.11
Aditiḥ pāśān pramumoktv etān 262.17, 485.7
Anāhutir vai jartilāś ca gavīdhukāś ca 265.9, 272.2, 274.7, 10
Apaśavo vā anye goaśvebhyaḥ paśavo goaśvāḥ 122.3, 265.11
Ayajñiyā vai māṣāḥ 265.5,11, 270.1, 274.8
Ayajño vā eṣaḥ 265.11
Ava rakṣo divaḥ sapatnaṃ vadhyāsam ity avahanti 338.1
Āgneyaṃ caturdhā karoti 234.5
Ācāryās tu 262.17
Etayānnādyakāmaṃ yājayet 546.1
Kṛte caturguṇo dharmaḥ 116.10
Grahaṃ saṃmārṣṭi 231.4, 260.2

Tatra jayān juhuyāt	412.9
Tapte payasi dadhy ānayati	412.7
Tiṣṭhantaṃ paśuṃ prayajanti	215.23
Tena hy annaṃ kriyate	414.2
Dadhnendriyakāmasya	373.1
Na mātā vardhate na pitā	423.4
Nāntarikṣe na divi cāgniś cetavyaḥ	277.5
Patnīṃ saṃnahya	262.21
Puroḍāśaṃ caturdhā karoti	234.5
Pūrvedyur amāvāsyāyāṃ vediṃ karoti	215.25
Prajākāmo nābhidaghnaṃ cinvīta	281.2
Prayājaśeṣaṃ haviḥṣu kṣārayet	262.1
Prayājaśeṣeṇa havīṃṣy abhighārayati	260.6,14, 262.5
Bhinne juhoti	412.17
Maitrāvaruṇaḥ preṣyati cānu cāha	412.22
Maudgaś carur bhavati	265.5
Ya iṣṭyā	545.5
Yad āhavanīye juhoti	281·1, 412.11
Yasya puroḍāśau kṣāyataḥ	116.6, 260. 6,14, 262.5
Yasya sarvāṇi havīṃṣi naśyeyur vā duṣyeyur vā	260.6,14, 262.5
Rājapurohitau sāyujyakāmau yājeyātām	116.4, 262.10
Vāyavaḥ stha	262.19, 485.7
Vedir asi barhiṣe tveti trir vediṃ prokṣati	338.1
Vaiśvānaraṃ dvādaśakapālaṃ nirvapet putre jāte	389.7
Samudro vā mahāsattvaḥ	386.5
Somena yajeta	373.2

ग्रन्थेऽस्मिन्गुणगणवत्त्वमुच्यते चेत्
स्वं ग्रन्थं गुणगणवन्तमाह को न।
तत्सन्तः शिरसि कृताञ्जलिस्तु याचे
शोध्यं तत्सदसदिहोच्यते मया यत् ॥

…S AND CORRECTIONS*

	For	Read
	यज्ञाधिकारो	यज्ञाधिकारे
…15	यजेयाताम्	याजेयाताम्
	०पूर्णपुन्या०	०पूर्णपुण्या०
	०मुहर्त०	०मुहूर्त०
…0	विशेष;	विशेषः;
…9.14	विराम्भः	निरारम्भः
50.21	ब० प्र०	ब्र० पु०
55.14	०फलाद्युक्तम	फलादियुक्तम्
64.29	बहुचना०	बहुवचना०
74.28	वोरकर्षा०	वोत्कर्षा०
77.11	कुतस्तराम्	कुतस्तमाम्
77.25	वहिते	विहिते
82.22	परिसंख्यानातृतु०	परिसंख्यानादृतु०
95.12	मारीचिः	मरीचिः
95.14	कुर्यंत्	कुर्यात्
97.13	शुद्धाः	शुद्धा (see Critical Apparatus, III. C. 1)
135.4	पितॄणां	पितृणां
137.22	प्राप्तावैव	प्राप्तावेव
149.23	भार्तारं	भर्तारं
160.7	'प्रत्यासन्न०	ऽप्रत्यासन्न०
160.33	P3 Cl Cl K Ll	P3 Ll
164.22	पितॄन्	पितृन्
171.20	उखर०	उत्तर०
174.14	काण्ठ०	कण्ठ०
187.4, 189.3, 189.28, 198.6, 227.6, and 322.9	Places	Cities

*Minor typographical errors are not listed.

Page and line	*For*	*Read*
205.5	first	the first
235.26	Glossarial Index	Glossary
253.1	three	(omit)
287.26	of	on
288.1	Chapter	Section
290.14	head-	chief
300.20	with	within
305.23	(?)	(3)
309.3	on the place	(omit)
343.26	tat	tad
349.11	according	"according
367.27	at	as
395.5	good	food
416.9	going	doing
432.21	Dadhidrāvan	Dadhikrāvan
443.33	yojana	1 yojana
452.21	1197	1897
463.2	38.01	380 1
489.5-25		Omit ३८४ in line 5; read all numbers through line 23 one line up; read ६३३ on line 24 and ६६ on line 25.
501.6	vii,xvii	VII, xvii
501.7	ii, vi. 9	II, VIa
501.8	vii	VII
501.11	vii, xix-xxv	VII. xix-xxv
502.19	159.6	159.5
521.28	grahaikatra	grahaikatva